Māmaka Kaiao

Nā huaʻōlelo i hōʻiliʻili ʻia, haku ʻia, a ʻāpono ʻia e ke Kōmike Huaʻōlelo
mai ka makahiki 1987 a hiki i ka makahiki 1997.

Kōmike Huaʻōlelo:

Larry L. Kimura, Luna Hoʻomalu
Hōkūlani Cleeland, Luna Kāhuakomo
Keao NeSmith
Kalena Silva
William H. Wilson
Laiana Wong

Kuleana Kope © 1998 na ka ʻAha Pūnana Leo
a me ka Hale Kuamoʻo,
Ka Haka ʻUla O Keʻelikōlani, Kulanui o Hawaiʻi ma Hilo

Nōna nā kuleana a pau.

ʻAʻole e hana kope ʻia kēia puke a i ʻole kekahi hapa o kēia puke ma nā ʻano like ʻole a pau me ka ʻae ʻole ma ka palapala o ka mea nōna ke kuleana.

ISBN 1-58191-005-3

Paʻi ʻia a hoʻomalele ʻia e ka ʻAha Pūnana Leo me ka Hale Kuamoʻo
ma o ke Kuʻikahi Kulanui o Hawaiʻi me ke kālā haʻawina
na ka ʻOihana Hoʻonaʻauao Pekelala no ka Hoʻonaʻauao ʻŌiwi Hawaiʻi.

Kōmike Huaʻōlelo
Hale Kuamoʻo–Kikowaena ʻŌlelo Hawaiʻi
Ke Kulanui o Hawaiʻi ma Hilo
200 West Kāwili Street
Hilo, Hawaiʻi 96720-4091
hale_kuamoo@leoki.uhh.hawaii.edu

E nā Pūʻali Mūkīkī Wai Momona o ka ʻŌlelo Hawaiʻi:

ʻO nā hoa hoʻi e ʻapo a e paʻa nei i nā ʻōlelo Hawaiʻi hou e hoʻoneʻe nei iā kākou i loko o kēia au e holo nei, eia ke Kōmike Huaʻōlelo ke paneʻe aku nei i puke i loaʻa nā huaʻōlelo hou i ʻāpono ʻia i nā makahiki 1996 a me ka 1997, me ka manaʻo he wahi kōkua liʻiliʻi wale nō, ʻoiai, ua lehulehu nā huaʻōlelo i koe, a he maʻū nō i ka laua o ka hana a ke Kōmike. Aia nō ke ola o kā kākou ʻōlelo i ka hana, a ʻaʻohe hana nui ke alu ʻia e kākou a pau. E hoʻoikaika kākou iā kākou iho ma o ke ola o kā kākou ʻōlelo. E hoʻomau!

Larry L. Kimura
Luna Hoʻomalu, Kōmike Huaʻōlelo

Māmaka Kaiao
He Puke Hua'ōlelo Hawai'i Hou

E nā mamo o ka 'āina e 'i'ini nei, e ho'oikaika nei, e pa'u nei ho'i i ka ho'omāhuahua a'e i ka 'ōlelo 'ōiwi o Hawai'i 'Imi Loa nei, aloha pumehana kākou a pau loa.

He mau makahiki pōkole wale iho nei nō i hala, aia kā kākou 'ōlelo e kāpekepeke ana ma ka'e o ka lua o ka make loa. Ma muli na'e o ke kū 'ana o ko nā mokupuni me ka 'auamo like i ka ukana nui he aloha i ka 'ōlelo, aia nō ke 'īnana hou maila. Pēlā i kupu mai ai 'o *Māmaka Kaiao* nei he wahi hua o ko kākou māmaka like 'ana i ka 'ōlelo o ka 'āina a puka he kaiao hou o Hawai'i nei.

Ke Kōmike Hua'ōlelo

Ua ho'okumu 'ia ke Kōmike Hua'ōlelo mua loa i ka MH 1987 a me ka 1988 no ka haku 'ana i nā hua'ōlelo no nā mea hou o kēia au i 'ike 'ole 'ia ho'i e nā kūpuna o ka wā ma mua. Aia ma ia kōmike mua loa nā kūpuna a me nā mānaleo Hawai'i i 'ike i ka waiwai nui o ia hana, 'o ia ho'i, 'o Elama Kanahele, Lani Kapuni, Albert Like, Josephine Lindsey, Joseph Maka'ai, Sarah Nākoa a me Helen Wahineokai, me ke kōkua o Kalani Akana, Kana'i Kapeliela, Haunani Makuakāne-Drechsel a me Leinani Raffipiy. Ke moe maila kekahi o ia mau kōmike i ka moe kau a ho'oilo, a 'oiai ua ho'i akula ke kai i waho, aia nō ke koe hūlalilali maila nā momi waiwai i uka. Mahalo a nui loa iā 'oukou e nā kōmike mua loa pākahi a pau.

I kēia manawa, ke hō'ili'ili a haku hua'ōlelo nei ke kōmike e kū nei, 'o ia ho'i, 'o Larry Kimura (Luna Ho'omalu; Kulanui o Hawai'i ma Hilo), Hōkūlani Cleeland (Luna Kāhuakomo; Kula Ni'ihau o Kekaha, Kaua'i), Keao NeSmith (Kulanui o Hawai'i ma Mānoa), Kalena Silva (Kulanui o Hawai'i ma Hilo), William H. Wilson (Kulanui o Hawai'i ma Hilo), Laiana Wong (Kulanui o Hawai'i ma Mānoa) a me nā lālā 'elua i ha'alele iho nei i ke kōmike 'o Kamoa'e Walk (Kulanui 'o Brigham Young ma Lā'ie) lāua 'o No'eau Warner (Kulanui o Hawai'i ma Mānoa).

Nā Hua'ōlelo

E like me ka laha 'ana a'e o ka 'ōlelo ma o nā kula Pūnana Leo, nā kula kaiapuni Hawai'i a me nā papa 'ōlelo Hawai'i o nā kula ki'eki'e, nā kulanui a me ke kaiaulu, pēlā ka nui 'ana a'e o nā hua'ōlelo hou e pono ai kākou me ko kēia mua aku. Aia ma *Māmaka Kaiao* nā hua'ōlelo hou o nā 'ano like 'ole e la'a me *ho'okolohua* (ka 'epekema), *huina peleleu* (ka makemakika), *ka'i* (ka ha'uki), *pāhina* (ka mea'ai), a nui hou aku. Aia ma ka māhele mua nā hua'ōlelo Hawai'i i ho'oka'ina 'ia e like me ka pī'āpā Hawai'i me ka unuhi

Pelekānia ma hope o kēlā me kēia hua'ōlelo. Aia ma ka māhele 'elua nā hua'ōlelo Pelekānia me ka Hawai'i ma hope.

Aia ma lalo iho nei ke kulekele haku hua'ōlelo no nā hua'ōlelo i ho'okomo 'ia i loko o *Māmaka Kaiao* nei:

1. He hua'ōlelo i pa'i 'ia ma ka puke wehewehe 'ōlelo me ka loli iki paha o ka pela 'ana (e la'a me *hua'ōlelo*).
2. He hua'ōlelo i lohe 'ia mai ka mānaleo i pa'a 'ole na'e i loko o ka puke wehewehe 'ōlelo (*kāka'ahi*), a i 'ole, i pa'a 'ole ia mana'o a ka mānaleo ma ka puke wehewehe 'ōlelo (*nemonemo*).
3. Wehewehe 'ia ka mana'o me nā hua'ōlelo Hawai'i (*poho lā'au pōulia*).
4. Ho'ākea 'ia ka mana'o o kekahi hua'ōlelo i loko o ka puke wehewehe 'ōlelo (*kaulua*).
5. He hua'ōlelo a hapa hua'ōlelo Polenekia paha i ho'ohana 'ia me kona mana'o piha (*pounamu*), a i 'ole, me ka ho'ololi iki 'ia (*hua na'ina'i*).
6. He hua'ōlelo lāhui 'ē i ho'ohawai'i 'ia ka pela 'ana (*ponī*).
7. He hua'ōlelo i hana 'ia me ka ho'opili 'ana aku i nā māhele o kekahi mau hua'ōlelo 'ē a'e (*pūnaewele*).
8. He hua'ōlelo i hana 'ia ma ka ho'opōkole 'ia 'ana o kekahi hua'ōlelo a mau hua'ōlelo Hawai'i paha (*pepili*).

'Oiai ua puka mua 'o *Māmaka Kaiao* i mua o ka lehulehu i ka makahiki i kapa 'ia 'o ia ka Makahiki o ka 'Ōlelo Hawai'i, he puke kū makahiki ia e puka ana i kēlā makahiki kēia makahiki me nā hua'ōlelo a pau i 'āpono 'ia e ke kōmike. Inā he hua'ōlelo kāu e ho'okomo 'ia paha i loko o *Māmaka Kaiao*, e ho'ouna mai i:

>Kōmike Hua'ōlelo
>Hale Kuamo'o–Kikowaena 'Ōlelo Hawai'i
>Ke Kulanui o Hawai'i ma Hilo
>200 West Kāwili Street
>Hilo, Hawai'i 96720-4091

No laila, e nā hoa e māmaka like ana i ka 'ōlelo a puka he kaiao hou o Hawai'i nei, e apo mai i kēia wahi puke nei, e ho'opa'a iho i nā hua'ōlelo, a e ho'opuka a ho'olaha aku ma ka hale, ma ke kula, ma ka hana, ma nā wahi kūpono ho'i a pau i ola ka 'ōlelo, 'a'ole e kāpekepeke hou ma ka'e o ka lua o ka make loa, akā, e pa'a a wali maika'i i ka waha o nā kumu, nā haumāna, nā 'ohana, nā hoaaloha a me ka lehulehu ākea o kēia hanauna a i ia hanauna aku, ia hanauna aku a i ka wā pau 'ole.

Kalena Silva
Kōmike Hua'ōlelo

Māmaka Kaiao
A Modern Hawaiian Vocabulary

A warm aloha to all.

Only a few years ago, Hawaiian teetered on the edge of extinction. Through considerable effort, however, the language of this land is now making a remarkable recovery. *Māmaka Kaiao* is the result of many people rallying together to carry forward (*māmaka*) the precious gift of our native language into the dawning (*kaiao*) of a new era.

The Lexicon Committee

The first Lexicon Committee was established in 1987-1988 to create words for concepts and material culture unknown to our ancestors. Committee members were native speakers of Hawaiian, most of them elderly, who saw the value in and the need for creating new Hawaiian words. Elama Kanahele, Lani Kapuni, Albert Like, Josephine Lindsey, Joseph Makaʻai, Sarah Nākoa, and Helen Wahineokai were assisted by recorders Kalani Akana, Kanaʻi Kapeliela, Haunani Makuakāne-Drechsel and Leinani Raffipiy. Although some of these first committee members have passed on, the fruits of their labor form the foundation upon which the present committee's work is based.

Present committee members include Larry Kimura (committee chair; University of Hawaiʻi at Hilo), Hōkūlani Cleeland (editor; Kula Niʻihau o Kekaha on Kauaʻi), Keao NeSmith (University of Hawaiʻi at Mānoa), Kalena Silva (University of Hawaiʻi at Hilo), William H. Wilson (University of Hawaiʻi at Hilo), Laiana Wong (University of Hawaiʻi at Mānoa), and two past members, Kamoaʻe Walk (Brigham Young University at Lāʻie) and Noʻeau Warner (University of Hawaiʻi at Mānoa).

The Words

As Hawaiian gains strength through use in Pūnana Leo and Hawaiian immersion schools, as well as in Hawaiian language classes held at high schools, universities, community colleges, and elsewhere, the need for new words applicable to modern contexts increases. Users of *Māmaka Kaiao* will find that it contains a great variety of words such as *hoʻokolohua* (experiment), *huina peleleu* (obtuse angle), *kaʻi* (coach), *pāhina* (topping, as for ice cream), and many more. The first section of the book contains words listed in Hawaiian alphabetical order with each entry followed by an English translation. The second section contains English entries followed by the Hawaiian.

The words found in *Māmaka Kaiao* were created using the following guidelines:

1. The word is found in the most recent edition of the Hawaiian Dictionary by Mary Kawena Pūkuʻi and Samuel H. Elbert, sometimes with variations in orthography (e.g., *huaʻōlelo*).
2. The word is used by native speakers but is not found in the Hawaiian Dictionary (*kākaʻahi*), or the definition heard from native speakers is not in the Hawaiian Dictionary (*nemonemo*).
3. The word is descriptive of some function or feature (*poho lāʻau pōulia*).
4. The word, found in the Hawaiian Dictionary, has been given an extended meaning (*kaulua*).
5. The word or part of a word from a Polynesian language is used with its full meaning (*pounamu*) or with slight modification (*hua naʻinaʻi*).
6. The word is a Hawaiianized spelling of a word from another language (*ponī*).
7. The word was formed by combining elements from different words (*pūnaewele*).
8. The word was formed by shortening a word and/or combining it with other shortened words (*pepili*).

Although *Māmaka Kaiao* was first made widely available to the public during the Year of the Hawaiian Language, an issue including all new words approved by the Lexicon Committee will be published each year. If you have new Hawaiian words which you would like the committee to review for possible publication in *Māmaka Kaiao*, or if you would like to order the most recent update of new words not included in this edition, write to:

> Kōmike Huaʻōlelo
> Hale Kuamoʻo–Kikowaena ʻŌlelo Hawaiʻi
> Ke Kulanui o Hawaiʻi ma Hilo
> 200 West Kāwili
> Hilo, Hawaiʻi 96720-4091

The root of any culture is its language. For Hawaiian culture to survive, the Hawaiian language must flourish. Use these new words and make them part of your life. Let us continue resolutely to carry forward this precious gift, the native language of Hawaiʻi, into the dawning of a new era.

Kalena Silva
Lexicon Committee

Ka Manaʻo o nā Hua Hōʻailona

abb.	abbreviation
Bib.	Bible
Cant.	Cantonese
cf.	compare
comb.	combined form
dic.	dictionary definition
e.g.	for example
Eng.	English
ext. mng.	extended meaning
Fr.	French
Gr.	Greek
i.e.	that is
inv.	invention
Japn.	Japanese
Lat.	Latin
lit.	literally
mān.	*mānaleo* (native speaker)
new mng.	new meaning
PPN	Proto Polynesian
redup.	reduplication
sh.	shortened form
Sp.	Spanish
Tah.	Tahitian
trad.	traditional literary sources
var.	variation
ham	*hamani* (transitive verb)
heh	*hehele* (intransitive verb)
ʻaʻ	*ʻaʻano* (stative verb)
kik	*kikino* (common noun)
iʻoa	*iʻoa* (proper noun)

Nā Mānaleo i Hōʻike ʻia

E K	Elama Kanahele
H H L H	Helen Haleola Lee Hong
H K M	Harry Kunihi Mitchell
J P M	Joseph Puipui Makaai
K K K	Kaui Keola Keamoai
L K	Louise Keliihoomalu
M M L H	Martha Manoanoa Lum Ho
M W	Minnie Whitford

Nā Palapala i Hōʻike ʻia

Bihopa	Bihopa, E. A. *Haawina Mua o ka Hoailona Helu*
Bounty	*He Moolelo no na Luina Kipi o ka Moku Bounty*
Legendre	Legendre, A. M. *Ke Anahonua*
Judd	Judd et al. *Hawaiian Language Imprints, 1822-1899*
Pakaa	Nakuina, Moses K. *Pakaa a me Ku-a-Pakaa*
Wilcox	Wilcox, Robert

Māhele ʻŌlelo Hawaiʻi

Māmaka Kaiao
Māhele ʻŌlelo Hawaiʻi

A

aeʻo·lele *kik* Pogo stick. *Lit.*, stilt (for) jumping.

ao *kik* Cloud, general term. *Dic.* See entries below and *lālahilewa, loa, ʻōpua. Hōkelo ao.* Cloud chamber, i.e. a scientific device which detects nuclear particles through the formation of cloud tracks.

ao *Ala ao.* Diurnal, i.e. active during the daytime. *Mea ao ʻē.* Extraterrestrial, space alien.

ā·ohi·ohi *ham* Resistance, i.e. opposition to the flow of electricity, or any opposition that slows down or prevents movement of electrons through a conductor. *Sh. kāohiohi. Āohiohi ea.* Air resistance, i.e. the force of air against a moving object. *Lima āohiohi.* Resistance arm, i.e. the distance from the fulcrum to the resistance force in a lever. *Manehu āohiohi.* Resistance force.

ao kū·lohe·lohe *kik* Nature. *Lit.*, natural world. *Puni ao kūlohelohe.* Naturalist. Also *kanaka puni ao kūlohelohe.*

Ao·tea·roa *iʻoa* New Zealand. *I ka hiki ʻana o ke kanaka mua ʻo Kupe i ka ʻāina ʻo Aotearoa, ʻike akula ʻo ia he ao keʻokeʻo lōʻihi ma luna o ia ʻāina.* When the first man, Kupe, arrived at the land of New Zealand he saw a long white cloud over the land. *Māori.* Also *Nukilani.*

au *kik* Mood. *ʻO ka hoʻāeae, he au pilialoha kōna.* The *hoʻāeae* (style of chanting) has a romantic mood. *Naue ka manawa i ke au o ka puolo.* The time moves to the mood of the music. *Dic., ext. mng. Au manaʻo.* Tone, as of a literary work.

au *kik* Current. *Dic.* See entries below. *Au uila.* Electic current.

au·kahi *heh* Direct current (DC). *Dic., ext. mng.* Cf. *au māʻaloʻalo. Uila aukahi.* Direct current electricity. *Mālamalama aukahi.* Coherent light, i.e. light in which all the waves vibrate in a single plane, with the crests and troughs all aligned.

au kā·ʻei pō·ʻai waena honua *kik* Equatorial current, in oceanography. *Lit.*, equator zone current.

au kikī *kik* Stream current, in oceanography. *Lit.*, swiftly flowing current.

au makani kikī *kik* Jet stream. *Lit.*, swift wind current.

au mā·ʻalo·ʻalo *kik* Alternating current (AC). *Lit.*, current passing back and forth. *Cf. aukahi. Uila au māʻaloʻalo.* Alternating current electricity.

Au Palaʻo *kik* Kingdom, in Egyptology. *Lit.*, age (of) Pharoahs. See entries below.

Au Palaʻo Kū·hou *kik* New Kingdom, in Egyptology, 1574-1085 BC. *Ua noho Palaʻo ke keiki ʻo Tutankhamen i ke Au Palaʻo Kūhou o ʻAikupita.* The boy Tutankhamen ruled as Pharoah over Egypt during the New Kingdom.

Au Palaʻo Kū·kahiko *kik* Old Kingdom, in Egyptology, 2780-2280 BC. *Kaulana ke Au Palaʻo Kūkahiko o ʻAikupita i ka mohala hikiwawe ʻana o ka ʻoihana kuhikuhipuʻuone.* The Old Kingdom is marked by rapid mastery of stone architecture.

Au Palaʻo Kū·waena *kik* Middle Kingdom, in Egyptology, 2133-1780 BC. *Ua hoʻokumu ʻia ʻo Tebesa i kikowaena o ka hoʻomana ma ʻAikupita i ke Au Palaʻo Kūwaena.* Thebes became established as the religious center of Egypt during the Middle Kingdom.

au·pana *kik* Rhythm, in linguistics. *Comb. au + pana. Cf. papana.*

au pa‘a·hau *kik* Ice age. *Nui ka nūnē ‘ana a ka po‘e ‘epekema no ke kumu o ke au pa‘ahau, ‘o ia ho‘i ka wā i pa‘a ai ka honua holo‘oko‘a i ka hau.* There is much speculation among scientists as to how the ice age began when the whole world was frozen in ice. *Lit.,* frozen age.

au·puni *kik* Government; national. *Dic.* Cf. *kaumoku‘āina, kau‘āina, māhele ‘āina, moku‘āina, pekelala.* See entries below. *Pāka aupuni.* National park. *‘Oihana Pāka Aupuni.* National Park Service.

au·puni ‘ao·‘ao ‘elua *kik* Two-party system of government. *‘Oiai ua loa‘a he mau ‘ao‘ao kālai‘āina ma ke aupuni o ‘Amelika Hui pū ‘ia, ‘ōlelo wale ‘ia nō he aupuni ‘ao‘ao ‘elua ia no ka nānā nui ‘ia o ‘elua wale nō ‘ao‘ao.* Although there are a number of political parties in the U.S., it is generally said that it is a two-party system since only two parties are considered by most. *Lit.,* two-party government. Cf. *‘elua hale.*

au·puni ‘eme·pela *kik* Empire. *Wahi a ka ‘ōlelo kahiko, " ‘A‘ohe napo‘o ‘ana o ka lā ma luna o ke aupuni ‘emepela Beretānia."* As the old saying goes, "The sun never sets on the British empire." *Lit.,* emperor kingdom.

au ‘ae‘a *kik* Drift current, in oceanography. *Lit.,* wandering current.

ahe·ahe *kik/‘a* Gentle breeze; dust raised and small branches move, in meteorology. *Dic.* See *makani.*

ahi *Pale ahi.* Flame retardant.

ahi·ho‘o·le·a·le‘a *kik* Fireworks. *Lit.,* fire (for) amusement. See *ahikao, ihoihokī, hōkūpa‘alima, lūpahū, pahūpahū.*

ahi·kao *kik* Rocket, as space or fireworks. *Dic., ext. mng.* See *ahiho‘ole‘ale‘a, kelena moku ahikao. Ahikao hā‘awe.* Manned Maneuvering Unit, as for a space flight. *Moku ahikao.* Spaceship, rocket ship.

Ahi·wela *i‘oa* Fomalhaut, a star. *Mān.* (HA).

aho ‘ea *kik* Monofilament. *Mān.* (KKK).

ahu ea *kik* Air mass, as in weather. *Lit.,* mass (of) air.

ahu·oi *kik/ham* Clue; to give a clue about. Comb. *a + huoi.*

ahu ho‘o·koe *kik* Cache, as in computer program. *Lit.,* cache pile. See *ho‘okoe.*

ahu kā·loa‘a *kik* Capital, i.e. anything produced in an economy that is accumulated or used to produce other goods and services. *Ke pi‘i pa‘a mau mai nei ka nui ahu kāloa‘a o ka pā‘oihana a Kale ma ke kumuloa‘a a me ka lako.* Kale's business has been steadily increasing its capital in profits as well as equipment. *Lit.,* business collection. See *paikāloa‘a.*

ahu·papa *kik* Composite, as volcanic cone. *Lit.,* mound (of) strata. *Pu‘u ahupapa.* Composite cone.

ahu·wale See *ho‘oku‘ia ahuwale. Hopena ahuwale.* Predictable, as the ending of a story. *Mo‘olelo hopena ahuwale.* Predictable story.

aka *‘a* Shadowed, as on computer or in typesetting. *Dic., ext. def.* See *ho‘āka.*

aka ani·ani *kik* Reflection, in math. *Lit.,* mirror reflection. See *‘ālikelike aka.*

aka·ki‘i *kik* Photo negative. *Dic.*

ā·kea *‘a* Width or breadth, in math. *Dic.* Also *ana ākea.* See *laulā.* Cf. *loa, lō‘ihi, hohonu, ki‘eki‘e.*

ake·aka·mai *kik* Science. *Dic.* Also *‘epekema.*

akua *Ho‘omana akua kahi.* Monotheism; monotheistic. *Ho‘omana akua lehulehu.* Polytheism; polytheistic.

ala *kik* Aisle, as in a supermarket. *Dic., ext. mng.* Also *alakaha.* See entries below.

ala *kik* Lane, as on a highway or in a bowling alley. *Dic., ext. mng.*

ala ao *'a'* Diurnal, i.e. active during the daytime. *Lawe 'ia mai nei ka manakuke i Hawai'i nei no ke kāohi i ka 'iole, akā, he ala ao ka manakuke a he ala pō ka 'iole, no laila, 'a'ohe i kō ka makemake.* The mongoose was brought to Hawai'i to control the rat population, but the mongoose is diurnal and the rat is nocturnal, so the objective was not achieved. *Lit.,* awake (during) daylight. Cf. *ala pō, ala mōlehu.*

ala hā·nuku *kik* Alley, alleyway. See *hānuku.*

ala hei·hei kī·ke'e·ke'e *kik* Slalom course. *Lit.,* zigzag race path.

ala hekehi *kik* Hiking trail.

ala·hiō *kik* Ramp. *Lit.,* inclined path.

ala·kau *kik* Mode of transportation, as motor vehicle, space vehicle, etc. Comb. *ala + kau.*

ala·kaha *kik* Aisle, as in a supermarket. *Lit.,* way (to) pass by. Also *ala.*

ala·kalaiwa *kik* Driveway.

ala·ka'i *Leo alaka'i.* One who sings the melody of a song. *Puke alaka'i.* Teacher's guide, manual.

ala·kō *ham* To drag, as in computer program. *E alakō i ka 'iole, a kuhikuhi i ke ki'iona.* Drag the mouse, and point at the icon. *Dic., ext. mng.* Also *ki'i a alakō. Alakō ma luna o; alakō a kau ma luna o.* To drag onto.

ala ku'u moku·lele *kik* Runway. See *ku'u, ala lele mokulele.*

ala lele moku·lele *kik* Flight corridor. *Lit.,* path (of) airplane flight.

ala mō·lehu *'a'* Crepuscular, i.e. appearing or flying in the twilight. *He lele kekahi mau 'ano 'ōpe'ape'a i nā hola mōlehulehu o ke ahiahi, no ka mea, he ala mōlehu ia mau 'ano holoholona.* Some kinds of bats fly only in the twilight hours of the evening because they are crepuscular creatures. *Lit.,* awake (during) twilight. Cf. *ala ao, ala pō.*

ala nu'u·kia *kik* Mission, as in the mission statement of an organization. *Lit.,* vision path. See *nu'ukia. 'Ōlelo ala nu'ukia.* Mission statement.

ala pili·pā *kik* Parallel, as of a computer port. *Lit.,* parallel path. *Awa ala pilipā.* Parallel port.

ala·pine *kik* Frequency, in math. *Dic., ext. def.*

ala·pī·pā *kik* Sidewalk. *Lit.,* sidewalk path.

ala·pi'i mele *kik* Musical scale: *pā, kō, lī, hā, nō, lā, mī, pā. Dic.* Also *pākōlī.*

ala pō *'a'* Nocturnal. *Lit.,* awake (at) night. Cf. *ala ao, ala mōlehu.*

ala pū·ka'ina *kik* Serial, as of a computer port. *Lit.,* series path.

alelo *kik* Tongue. *Dic. Kū'au alelo.* Back of tongue. *Lau alelo.* Blade. *Mole alelo.* Root. *Waena alelo.* Central portion. *Wēlau alelo.* Tip.

alelo·mo'o *kik* Party favor. *Lit.,* lizard tongue.

ā·lia·lia *kik* Marsh, with salt or brackish water and no trees. *Dic., ext. mng.* See *nāele, 'olokele. Ālialia wai maoli.* Fresh-water marsh.

alo *kik* Face, as one side of a space figure, in math. *Dic., ext. mng.* See *kā'ei alo, pale alo,* and entries under *'ōpaka.*

alo ua *kik* Rainy side, as of a mountain.

aloha *Kinipōpō aloha.* Aloha ball, in volleyball.

alu *kik/heh* Drive, as for cans; to conduct a drive. *Dic., ext. mng. Alu hō'ili'ili nūpepa.* Newspaper drive. *Alu ho'oma'ema'e pā kula.* School clean-up drive.

a.m. Ante meridium, a.m. (pronounced *'āmū*). *Eng.* See *p.m.*

AM *kik* AM, amplitude modulation (pronounced *'āmū*). *Eng.* Cf. *FM.* See *'anini laulā hawewe.*

ama *kik* Port or left side of a double-hulled canoe or a ship when looking forward. *Lit.*, outrigger float. Cf. *ʻākea, muku.*

amo hao *ham* Weight lifting; to lift weights. *Lit.*, lift iron. Also *hāpai hao.*

ana *kik/ham* Measurement; dimension, in math. *ʻEhia ke ana o kēia lumi?* What are the dimensions of this room? *Dic., ext. mng.* Also *nui.* See entries below. *Ana ākea, ana laulā.* Width. *Ana hohonu, ana kiʻekiʻe.* Height. *Ana loa, ana lōʻihi.* Length.

ana au uila *kik* Ammeter, an instrument used to measure the amount of electric current in a circuit. *Lit.*, electric current gauge.

ana ikehu kā-ʻokoʻa *kik* Calorimeter, an instrument used to measure changes in thermal energy. *Lit.*, thermal energy gauge.

ana ō·laʻi *kik* Seismograph. Also *mīkini ana ōlaʻi.*

ana hele wā·wae *kik* Pedometer. *Lit.*, gauge (for) walking.

ana·honua *kik* Geometry. *Dic.* Also *moleanahonua. Papakui anahonua.* Geoboard.

ana hoʻo·hā·like *kik* Standard, i.e. an established model or example. *Lit.*, standard (for) comparison. *Hoʻopaʻa i ke ana hoʻohālike.* To set the standard.

ana huina *kik* Protractor. *Lit.*, angle measurement. *Ana huina kūpono.* Right angle protractor.

ana kau·maha wai *kik* Hydrometer. *Lit.*, water weight gauge. Cf. *ana kawaūea.*

ana kahe pele *kik* Lava tube. *Lit.*, cave (where) lava flows.

ana·kahi *kik* Unit of measurement. *Dic.* Cf. *kūana helu. Anakahi mekalika.* Metric unit of measure. *Anakahi ʻAmelika.* US standard or customary unit of measurement. *Anakahi nuipaʻa ʻātoma.* Atomic mass unit. See *nuipaʻa ʻātoma. Hakina anakahi.* Unit fraction.

ana·kahi uila *kik* Volt, in electricity. *ʻO ka 7,200 anakahi uila ka ʻawelika o ka nui o ke anakahi uila o nā uea o nā pou kelepona o kaʻe o nā alanui.* 7,200 volts is the average voltage contained in the utility lines along side the roads. *Lit.*, electric unit of measurement. Cf. *ʻome.*

ana kawa·ū·ea *kik* Hygrometer. *Lit.*, humidity gauge. Cf. *ana kaumaha wai. Ana kawaūea ʻōpuʻu pulu a maloʻo.* Wet-and-dry-bulb hygrometer. *Ana kawaūea kūlua.* Psychrometer. *Maʻa ana kawaūea kūlua.* Sling psychrometer.

ana kilo lani *kik* Sextant. *Lit.*, gauge (for) astronomy.

ana kiʻe·kiʻena *kik* Altimeter. *Lit.*, altitude gauge.

ana·konu *kik* Equilibrium. *Ke kaulike ʻelua manehu i ka puhu ʻana o kekahi i kekahi, paʻa maila ke anakonu.* When two opposing forces are equal, equilibrium is achieved. (Sāmoan *agatonu* [equal].) *Mīkā anakonu.* Isostasy, i.e. the equilibrium of the earth's crust, in geology.

ana·kuhi *kik* Template. Comb. *ana + kuhi. Anakuhi mahaka.* Stencil.

ana·lahi *ʻa* Regular, as in shape. Sh. *ana + maʻalahi. Huinalehulehu analahi.* Regular polygon. *Kinona analahi.* Regular shape. Cf. *laukua.*

ana·lula *kik* Pattern, as a word or sentence pattern in Hawaiian grammar. Comb. *ana + lula.* Cf. *lauana. Puke aʻo analula.* Pattern book, as for teaching grammatical patterns in reading.

ana mā·mā makani *kik* Anemometer. *Lit.*, wind speed gauge.

ana·manaʻo *kik/ham* Opinion survey, poll; to conduct an opinion survey or poll. Comb. *ana + manaʻo.* See entry below.

Māmaka Kaiao / 4

ana·mana'o pā·loka *ham* To canvass, i.e. go door to door handing out political information and asking people which candidate they support. *Mana'o aku ka meia he pono ke mālama 'ia he anamana'o pāloka ma ke kaona e 'ike ai i ka papaha o kōna lanakila 'ana ma ka holo moho hou 'ana.* The mayor felt it was necessary to canvass the town to see what his chances would be of winning a re-election bid. *Lit.,* ballot poll.

ana mī·kā ea *kik* Barometer. *Lit.,* air pressure gauge. *Ana mīkā ea kuhikuhi.* Aneroid barometer.

anana 'ē·heu *kik* Wingspan. *Lit.,* distance between wing tips.

ana·paona *kik* Scales, as used for weighing something. *Dic. Anapaona home.* Bathroom scales. *Usu. anapaona. Anapaona kaulike.* Balance scales. *Anapaona pilina.* Spring scales.

ana pi'i wela *ham* Specific heat, in physics. *Lit.,* measurement (of) heat increase.

ana·po'o *heh* To set, as the sun. *Ni'ihau.* Usu. *napo'o.*

ana·puni *kik* Circumference, in math; perimeter. *Dic.*

ana·waena *kik* Diameter, in math. *Dic.*

ana wela *kik/ham* Thermometer; to take the temperature of. *Dic./lit.,* measure heat. See *anu, mahana, mehana, wela, kēkelē.*

ana 'akika *ham* Acid indicator. *Lit.,* measure acid. *Pepa ana 'akika.* Litmus paper.

ana 'ome *kik* Ohmmeter. *Lit.,* Ohm gauge. See *'ome.*

ane ko'e *kik* Mealworm. *Comb. ane + ko'e.* Cf. *ane 'uku.*

ane 'uku *kik* Mealy bug. *Dic., sp. var.*

ani·au *kik* Climate. *Lit.,* air movement (over) time. Cf. *anilā. Aniau hāiki.* Microclimate. *Lit.,* restricted climate.

ani·ani *kik* Mirror. *Dic.* Also *aniani nānā, aniani kilohi, aniani kilo.* See entries below. *Aniani 'e'ele.* Concave mirror. *Aniani 'e'emu.* Convex mirror.

ani·ani awe *kik* Fiberglass. *Lit.,* thread glass. Cf. *aniani 'ea.*

ani·ani ho'o·nui 'ike *kik* Magnifying glass, hand lens. *Dic.* Cf. *aniani kaulona.*

ani·ani kau·lona *kik* Lens, as for a camera or microscope. *Lit.,* glass (for) observing closely. Cf. *aniani ho'onui 'ike. Aniani kaulona 'e'ele.* Concave lens. *Aniani kaulona 'e'emu.* Convex lens.

ani·ani kau·pane'e *kik* Slide, as for a microscope. *Usu. aniani. Lit.,* glass for placing and pushing along. See *paepae aniani kaupane'e.*

ani·ani kilohi ka'a *kik* Rear-view mirror. Also *aniani ka'a.*

ani·ani kilohi pai·kikala *kik* Rear-view mirror for bicycle. Also *aniani kilo paikikala, aniani paikikala.*

ani·ani kū *kik* Full-length mirror. *Dic.*

ani·ani pāiki *kik* Small mirror kept in purse. Also *aniani li'ili'i.*

ani·ani pa'a lima *kik* Hand mirror. *Dic.* Also *aniani lima.*

ani·ani 'ea *kik* Plexiglass. *Lit.,* plastic glass. Cf. *aniani awe.*

ani·lā *kik* Weather. *Lit,* air movement (during the) day. Cf. *aniau.*

anu *'a* Temperature, when weather considered cold. *'Ehia ke anu o kēia lā?* How cold is it today? *Lit.,* cold. Cf. *mahana, mehana, wela.* See *kēkelē.*

Ā·nui *i'oa* Perseus, a constellation. *Māori.*

anp Abbreviation for *anapuni* (perimeter).

anw Abbreviation for *anawaena* (diameter).

apo laho·lio *kik* Rubber band.

apo lohe *kik* Headphone, headset. *Lit,* band (for) hearing. See *pihi lohe.*

apo po'o *kik* Hairband. *Ni'ihau.*

apu·apu *kik* Rasp (tool). *Dic.* Cf. *waiehu.*

awa *kik* Port, as in a computer. *Dic., ext. mng. Awa ala pilipā.* Parallel port. *Awa ala pūkaʻina.* Serial port.

awāwa uma *kik* U-shaped valley. *Lit.,* curve valley.

awāwa kū·hō·hō *kik* Canyon. *Lit.,* deep valley. See *Hakaʻama.*

awāwa mā·wae *kik* Rift valley. *Lit.,* fissure valley. *Pae awāwa māwae.* Series of rift valleys.

awe ō·ewe *kik* Chromosome. *Lit.,* gene thread.

awe uholo uila *kik* Brush, i.e. a contact that supplies electric current to a commutator. *Lit.,* strand (through which) electricity runs. Cf. *mea uholo uila.* See *ʻūkake uila.*

awe pale ahi *kik* Asbestos. *Lit.,* thread (which) resists fire.

aʻa·haʻa·pupū *kik* Arteriolosclerosis, in medicine. *ʻO ke aʻahaʻapupū, ʻo ia ka paʻa ʻana ʻo loko o ka ʻili o ke aʻa koko puʻuwai a hoʻēmi ʻia ke kahe o ke koko.* Arteriosclerosis is the hardening of the inner walls of the arteries slowing blood flow. Comb. *aʻa + haʻapupū.* Cf. *aʻalāʻau.*

aʻa koko kino *kik* Vein. Comb. *aʻa koko + kino.* Also *aʻa kino.* Cf. *aʻa koko puʻuwai.*

aʻa koko puʻu·wai *kik* Artery. Comb. *aʻa koko + puʻuwai.* Also *aʻa puʻuwai.* Cf. *aʻa koko kino.*

aʻa·lā·au *kik* Arteriosclerosis, atherosclerosis, hardening of the arteries, in medicine. Comb. *aʻa + lāʻau.* Cf. *aʻahaʻapupū.*

aʻa·lolo *kik* Nerve. *Dic.*

aʻa·lonoa *kik* Receptor, as of nerve endings in the body, in biology. *ʻO ke aʻalonoa o ke aʻalolo ke ʻike mua i ke kūlale.* The receptors of the nerves are the first to sense stimuli. Comb. *aʻa + lonoa.* *Aʻalonoa mīkā.* Pressure receptor. *Aʻalonoa ʻono.* Taste receptor.

aʻi·aʻi *ʻa* Transparent. *Dic., ext. mng.*

aʻi·aʻi hau·ʻoki *ʻa* Opaque. *Lit.,* frosty clear.

aʻo See *pahu aʻo.*

aʻo hou *ham* To reteach. *Lit.,* teach again. *Puke aʻo hou.* Reteaching book.

E

ea *kik* Fume. *Dic.* Also *ea puka.* *Āohiohi ea.* Air resistance, i.e. the force of air against a moving object. *Ana mīkā ea.* Barometer. *Pōhaku puka ea.* Air stone, i.e. the porous rock in an aquarium that creates tiny bubbles at the surface of the water to facilitate the exchange of gases. *Pūnuku ea make.* Gas mask, as used during World War II.

ea·ea *ʻa* Aerated; aerobic, i.e. living, active, or occurring only in the presence of oxygen. *Dic., ext. mng.* See *hōʻeaea. Ka hoʻohāpopo eaea ʻana.* Aerobic decomposition. *Ka hoʻohāpopo eaea ʻole ʻana.* Anaerobic decomposition.

ea puka *kik* Fume. *Lit.,* emitting fume. Also *ea.*

eo (i/iā) *ʻa* To lose. *Ua eo ʻo Punahou iā Kamehameha.* Punahou lost to Kamehameha. *Ua eo iaʻu kāu mau kinikini.* I won your Pogs. *Ua lilo iaʻu ke eo.* I won. *Dic.* See *hāʻule.*

ē·ulu *kik* Top of a tree or plant. *Dic.*

ehu *kik* Pollen. *Dic.* See entries below and *hoʻehu pua. Ehu pua.* Flower pollen. *Waiū ehu.* Powdered milk. Also *waiū pauka.*

ehu·ō *kik* Inertia. Comb. *ehu + ō.*

ehu·ola *kik* Vigor. *Ke mālama pono ʻia ke olakino, he ehuola ke kino no ka wā lōʻihi o ke ola ʻana.* When you keep your health in good condition, your body will have vigor for a long time in your lifetime. Sh. *ehuehu + ola.* Cf. *hāʻehuola.*

ehu kī·kina *kik* Visible airborne particles, as from a spray can. Comb. *ehu + kīkina.* See *kīkina.*

ehu lepo *kik* Dust. *Dic.* Also *ehu.*

ehu poho *kik* Chalk dust. Cf. *ehu lepo.*

emi See entries below and *woela emi*. *'Ōnaehana mīkā emi.* Low pressure system, in meteorology. Cf. *'ōnaehana mīkā pi'i*.

emi iho *'a'* Less than, in math. Also *'oi aku ke emi*. Cf. *nui a'e*.

emi ha'a·ha'a loa *'a'* Greatest decrease, in math. *Lit.*, lowest decrease. Cf. *pi'i ki'eki'e loa*.

emi ka mā·mā holo *'a'* To decelerate; decelerated. *Lit.*, the running speed decreases. Cf. *emi māmā holo, ho'ēmi i ka māmā holo*. See also *pi'i ka māmā holo, ho'opi'i i ka māmā holo*.

emi mā·mā holo *kik* Deceleration. *Lit.*, decrease (of) progress. Cf. *emi ka māmā holo, pi'i māmā holo*.

I

Iā·maika *i'oa* Jamaica; Jamaican. *Dic., sp. var.* Also *Iāmeka*.

Iā·meka *i'oa* Jamaica; Jamaican. *Dic.* Also *Iāmaika*.

Ian. Abbreviation for *Ianuali* (January).

Ianu·ali *i'oa* January. *Dic., sp. var.* Abb. *Ian*.

Iape·tusa *i'oa* Iapetus, a moon of Saturn. *Eng.*

iā·pona *kik* Jabong, a type of citrus. *Japn.* See *pomelo*.

Ie·mene Hema *i'oa* South Yemen; South Yemenite, South Yemeni. *Comb. Eng.* + *hema*.

Ie·mene 'Ā·kau *i'oa* North Yemen; North Yemenite, North Yemeni. *Comb. Eng.* + *'ākau*.

ioio *kik* Yoyo. *Eng.*

Iowi·ana *i'oa* Jovian, in astronomy. *Eng. Hōkūhele Iowiana*. Jovian planet.

Iore·dāne *i'oa* Jordan; Jordanian. *Trad.*

Iose·mite *i'oa* Yosemite. *Ka Pāka Aupuni 'o Iosemite*. Yosemite National Park.

Iul. Abbreviation for *Iulai* (July).

Iu·lai *i'oa* July. *Dic.* Abb. *Iul*.

Iun. Abbreviation for *Iune* (June).

Iune *i'oa* June. *Dic.* Abb. *Iun*.

iuni·pela *kik* Juniper. *Dic.*

Iugo·sola·wia *i'oa* Yugoslavia; Yugoslavian. *Eng.*

ihi *ham* To peel, as an orange or taro. *Dic.* Cf. *uhole*.

iho *kik* Battery. *Dic.* Also *pakalē*. See *'ōmole iho uila. Iho poke*. Battery for flashlight, radio, etc. *Iho 'eono*. Six-volt battery. *Iho 'umikūmālua*. Twelve-volt battery. *Iho pihi*. Button-shape battery. See *'ōmole iho uila*.

iho *kik* Axle, i.e. a shaft on which a wheel turns. *Dic.* Also *paepae komo huila*.

iho *kik* Axis, in math. *Dic. Nā iho kuhikuhina*. Coordinate axes, i.e. two intersecting perpendicular number lines used for graphing ordered number pairs in math. See *kuhikuhina*.

iho *kik* Nucleus of a syllable, in linguistics. *Dic., ext. mng.*

iho·iho·kī *kik* Roman candle (fireworks). *Lit.*, shooting candle. See *ahiho'ole'ale'a*.

ihu *kik* Bow, of a boat. *Dic.*

ikaika hawewe kani *kik* Amplitude, i.e. the amount of energy in a sound wave. See *hawewe kani*.

ika·kani *kik* Decibel. *Lit.*, sound strength.

ikehu *kik* Energy, power. *Sh. ika* + *ehu*. See entries below. *Pālākiō ikehu ōla'i*. Richter scale.

ikehu uila *kik* Charge, as electric. *Lit.*, electric energy. *Ikehu uila hohoki*. Neutral charge. Also *ikehu hohoki*. See *hohoki, ho'oikehu. Ikehu uila puhi wāwahie*. Thermoelectric power. *Ikehu uila wai kahe*. Hydroelectric power.

ikehu kā·'oko'a *kik* Thermal energy, i.e. the total energy of all the particles in an object. *Lit.*, whole energy. *Ana ikehu kā'oko'a*. Calorimeter, an instrument used to measure changes in thermal energy.

ikehu nuke·lea *kik* Nuclear energy.

ikehu·ʻā *kik* Calorie. *Lit.*, burning energy. *Ikehuʻā pākaukani.* Kilocalorie. Abb. *ikpk*.

iki *ʻa*ʻ Little, small. *Dic. Manamana iki.* Little finger. Also *manamana liʻiliʻi.*

-iku Suffix in chemical compounds and terms: -ic.

ikpk Abbreviation for *ikehuʻā pākaukani* (kilocalorie).

ili *ʻa*ʻ Transplanted. *Dic., ext. mng.* Cf. *hoʻoili. Puʻuwai ili.* Transplanted heart.

ili *heh* Distribution or to be distributed, as data on a graph, in math. Sh. *hoʻoili.* Cf. *kākuhi, waiho, ʻanopili hoʻoili.* See entry below. *Ka ili o ka ua.* Rain distribution. *Ka ili o ka ʻikepili.* Data distribution.

ili pū·ʻuo *heh* Population distribution, in geography. *Ua loli ka ili pūʻuo kanaka i loko o nā makahiki 100 i hala aʻe nei mai ka noho nui ʻana ma kahi kuaʻāina a ka neʻe nui ʻana i kahi o nā kūlanakauhale.* Human population distribution in the last 100 years has changed from people mostly living in rural areas to people moving and mostly inhabiting areas near the cities. Also *ili pūʻuo kanaka.*

ilo *heh* To germinate, sprout; maggot. *Dic.* See *hoʻoilo. Ilo ʻakaʻakai.* Onion maggot.

Ilo·ano *iʻoa* Libra, a constellation. *Mān.* (HA).

inoa *kik* Name, as of file in computer program. *ʻO wai (ka inoa o) ka palapala?* What is the name of the document? *Dic.* See entries below. *Inoa o ke pihi.* Name of key.

inoa *kik* Title, as of a book or story. *Dic.* Also *poʻo inoa.*

inoa *Kālaikapa inoa.* Taxonomy, the science of classifying plants and animals.

ipu *kik* Squash, general term. *Dic., ext mng.* See *palaʻai.*

ipu·hao hana kai *kik* Sauce pan. *Lit.*, pan (for) making sauce.

ipu·leo *kik* Microphone. *Lit.*, voice vessel. Also *mea hoʻolele leo* (dic.). *Mea kīkoʻo ipuleo.* Boom operator, as for movie or video production.

ipu lua *kik* Toilet bowl. Cf. *ipu mimi, noho lua.*

ipu mimi *kik* Urinal, bedpan. Cf. *ipu lua.* See *mīana.*

ipu·ʻala *kik* Cantaloupe. *Dic.* See *meleni.*

iwi *kik* Side of a sporting field or court. *Lit.*, stones or earth ridge marking land boundary. Also *ʻaoʻao.* Cf. *poʻo.* See entries below and *haʻihaʻi iwi, kimeki iwi, palaku iwi. Laina iwi.* Side line. Also *laina ʻaoʻao. Laina iwi kī.* Side line of the key on a basketball court.

iwi kamumu *kik* Cartilage. *Dic.*

iwi·kua·moʻo *kik* Vertebrate. *Lit.*, (with) backbone. See *iwikuamoʻo ʻole. Holoholona iwikuamoʻo.* Vertebrate animal.

iwi·kua·moʻo ʻole *kik* Invertebrate. *Lit.*, without backbone. See *iwikuamoʻo. Holoholona iwikuamoʻo ʻole.* Invertebrate animal.

iwi kū·loko *kik* Endoskeleton. *Lit.*, internal bones. Cf. *iwi kūwaho.*

iwi kū·waho *kik* Exoskeleton. *Lit.*, external bones. Cf. *iwi kūloko.*

iwi pā·ʻani *kik* Domino. *Lit.*, playing bone. See *pāʻani iwi.*

iwi·puhi *kik* Herringbone weave. *Dic.* Also *maka puhi.*

iwi wili·wili *kik* Bonemeal. *Trad.* Cf. *ʻiʻo wiliwili.*

iʻa *kik* Fish or any marine animal. *Dic.* See entries below. *Kini iʻa.* Canned fish. *Mahi iʻa.* Aquaculture. *ʻOihana Iʻa me ka Holoholona Lōhiu o ʻAmelika.* US Fish and Wildlife Service.

iʻa·uli *kik* Bluefish. Comb. *iʻa + uli.*

iʻa kai *kik* Marine animal. *Dic.* + *kai.*

iʻa kapi *kik* Guppy. Comb. *iʻa* + Eng.

iʻa·kea *kik* Whitefish. Comb. *iʻa + kea.*

iʻa makika *kik* Mosquito fish, medaka.

iʻa moli *kik* Molly. Comb. *iʻa* + Eng.

iʻa puna·kea *kik* Trout. *Lit.*, rainbow fish.

O

oe·oe uahi *kik* Smoke alarm. *Lit.*, smoke siren.

ō·ewe *kik* Gene; genetic. Comb. *ō + ēwe*. Cf. *welo*. See *awe ōewe, hoʻoliliuewe, kālaiōewe*.

oho *kik* Capillary, i.e. one of the minute blood vessels between the arteries and the veins. *No ka liʻiliʻi loa o kekahi mau oho, pono e nānā ʻia me ka ʻohe hoʻonui ʻike.* Since some capilaries are so small, they must be observed using a microscope. *Dic., new mng.*

Ohta-san See *ʻukulele Ohta-san.*

oka lā·ʻau *kik* Sawdust. *Dic.*

ola *Pōʻaiapuni ola.* Life cycle.

ola·kino *kik* Health. *Dic. Kūlana olakino.* Health status. *Kākoʻo ʻoihana olakino.* Allied health professional. *ʻInikua olakino.* Medical insurance. *Helu ʻinikua olakino.* Medical coverage number.

ola mehana *heh* Mesophilic, i.e. midtemperature-loving. *Lit.*, live (in) warmth. Cf. *ola wela. Koʻohune ola mehana.* Mesophilic bacteria.

ola wela *heh* Thermophilic, i.e. heat-loving. *Lit.*, live (in) heat. Cf. *ola mehana. Koʻohune ola wela.* Thermophilic bacteria.

ō·la·ʻi *kik* Earthquake. *Dic. Kiko ōlaʻi.* Epicenter. *Pālākiō ikehu ōlaʻi.* Richter scale.

olo·pī *kik* Bead. Comb. *olo + Eng.*

omo *ham* To absorb. *Dic.* See *ʻuomo*. Cf. *omowaho*. See *kaupokupoku omo*.

omo·ā·ea *heh* To evaporate. *Lit.*, evaporate into air.

omo·ola *kik/heh* Parasite; to live as a parasite. Comb. *omo + ola*. See *kauomolia, koʻe omoola.*

omo hoʻo·kulu *kik* Dropper (eyedropper, etc.). *Lit.*, suction tube (for) dropping liquid.

omo·waho *ham* To adsorb. Comb. *omo + waho*. Cf. *omo. ʻAe omowaho.* Solvent front, i.e. the leading edge of a moving solvent as in a developing chromatogram.

omo wela *ham* Endothermic., i.e. absorbs heat. Cf. *kuʻu wela*.

one *Lalo one.* Subsand.

one ʻā *kik* Cinder (volcanic). *Dic.* See *ʻākeke*.

ono See *pihi wili ono*.

ō·puhe *kik* Finch, general term. *Kaulana ka pae moku ʻo Galapagosa no ka nui a me ka laulā o nā ʻano manu ōpuhe o ia wahi.* The Galapagos Islands are famous for the many and varied types of finches that are found there. Metathesis of *hōpue* See English entries under finch. *Ōpuhe pao lāʻau.* Woodpecker finch.

ō·puna *kik* Calcite. *Sh. one + puna.*

oʻi·oʻina lewa lipo *kik* Space station. *Lit.*, resting place for travelers (in) space.

U

ua *kik* Rainfall. *Lit.*, rain. *Alo ua.* Rainy side, as of a mountain. *Ua pili pali.* Orographic rainfall. *Ka ili o ka ua.* Rain distribution. *Palapala ʻāina ua.* Rainfall map. *Wai ua.* Rain water.

uai *heh* To slide, as a door. *Dic. Laka uai.* Sliding latch. *Puka uai.* Sliding door. Also *ʻīpuka uai*.

ua oki Cut! i.e. a command to stop the filming of a movie or video scene (pronounced *uoki*). *Dic., ext. mng.*

uahi See *puka uahi*.

ua·ke·ʻe *kik* Curve or turn, as in a road or on a trail. *Dic. Uakeʻe hiō.* Banked curve, as on a race track.

uaki *ham* To time. *Dic., ext. mng.* Also *uāki*. Cf. *helu manawa*. See *uaki helu manawa. Helu uaki.* To tell time. Also *helu uāki*.

uaki helu manawa *kik* Stopwatch. *Lit.*, watch (to) compute time. Also *uāki helu manawa*. See *helu manawa*.

Māmaka Kaiao / 9

uaki hoʻāla *kik* Alarm clock. *Lit.*, clock (for) waking. Also *uāki hoʻāla*.

uaki kiko·hoʻe *kik* Digital watch or clock. *Lit.*, watch (with) digits. Also *uāki kikohoʻe*. Cf. *uaki lima kuhikuhi*.

uaki lima kuhi·kuhi *kik* Analog watch or clock, i.e. a watch or clock with hands. Also *uāki lima kuhikuhi*. Cf. *uaki kikohoʻe*.

uate *kik* Watt. *Eng. Abb. uat.* See *kilouate*.

uea Wire. *Dic.* See entries below and *kaula uea*. *Uea nikoroma*. Nichrome wire.

uea kau lole *kik* Hanger. *Lit.*, wire (for) placing clothes. See *lāʻau kau lole*, *mea kau lole*, *ʻea kau lole*.

uea makika *kik* Screen, as for windows. *Lit.*, mosquito wire. Also *makaʻaha*.

uea nā·kiʻi *kik* Twist tie, as used with plastic bags. *Lit.*, tying wire.

uea peleki *kik* Brake cable, as on bicycle. *Niʻihau*.

Uēki ʻAi·lana *iʻoa* Wake Island. *Eng.*

uepa *kik* Wax. *Dic., ext. mng.* Also *pīlali*. Cf. *uepa ihoiho*, *ʻōihoiho*.

uepa iho·iho *kik* Paraffin. *Lit.*, candle wax seal.

uila *kik* Electricity. *Dic.* See entries below and *ana au uila, anakahi uila, awe uholo uila, lapaʻau hoʻomiki uila, luna uila, mea uholo uila, puka uila, puni uila, ʻōmole iho uila, ʻuiki uila, ʻūkake uila, ʻūʻōki puni uila*.

uila au·kahi *kik* Direct current (DC) electricity. Cf. *uila au māʻaloʻalo*.

uila au mā·ʻalo·ʻalo *kik* Alternating current (AC) electricity. *Lit.*, electricity (with) current passing back and forth. Cf. *uila aukahi*.

uila huila makani *kik* Wind-generated electricity. *Lit.*, electricity (from) windmill. See *uila māhu pele, uila puhi wāwahie, uila wai kahe*.

uila māhu pele *kik* Geothermal electricity. *Lit.*, electricity (from) volcanic steam. See *uila huila makani, uila puhi wāwahie, uila wai kahe*.

uila puhi wā·wahie *kik* Thermoelectricity; thermoelectric. *Lit.*, electricity (from) burning fuel. See *uila huila makani, uila māhu pele, uila wai kahe. Ikehu uila puhi wāwahie.* Thermoelectric power.

uila wai kahe *kik* Hydroelectricity; hydroelectric. *Lit.*, electricity (from) flowing water. See *uila huila makani, uila māhu pele, uila puhi wāwahie. Ikehu uila wai kahe.* Hydroelectric power.

uini·hapa ʻako·pie *kik* Adobe block. *Lit.*, adobe brick.

uipo·uila *kik* Whippoorwill. *Eng.* Also *manu uipouila*.

uhi *Lepo uhi.* Topsoil. Cf. *lalo lepo*.

uhi·moe *kik* Bedspread. *Dic.*

uhole *ham.* To peel or strip, as a banana. *Dic.* Cf. *ihi*.

uholo uila See *awe uholo uila, mea uholo uila*.

ukali *kik* Satellite. *Dic., ext. mng.* Also *poelele*. Cf. *hōkū ukali*.

Ukali·aliʻi *iʻoa* Mercury (the planet). *Dic.*

uku hoʻo·mau *kik* Pension. *Ua lawe au i ka uku hoʻomau i loko o Iune.* I drew my pension in June. *Dic.*

uku leka *kik* Postage. *Lit.*, letter fee.

uku paneʻe *kik* Interest, as on principal when borrowing money. *Dic.* See *kumupaʻa. Pākēneka uku paneʻe.* Rate of interest.

uku·wai *kik* Portion of a canoe between forward and aft outrigger booms. *Dic.*

uku ʻē·kena *kik* Commission, i.e. a fee paid to an agent for transacting business or performing a service. *Lit.*, agent pay. Also *uku ʻākena*. See *komikina*.

uku ʻini·kua *kik* Insurance premium. *Dic.*

ulahi *kik* Flake. Sh. *unahi* + *lahi*. *Ulahi i'a*. Fish flake. *Ulahi mea'ai i'a*. Fish food flake. *Ulahi hau*. Snowflake. *Ulahi 'okamila*. Oatmeal flake.

ula kahi See *kapuahi ula kahi*.

ula pā·papa *kik* Slipper lobster. *Dic.*, new mng. Also *ula 'āpapapa*. Cf. *'ōmā*.

ula 'ā·papapa *kik* Slipper lobster. Ni'ihau. Also *ula pāpapa*. Cf. *'ōmā*.

ulele *heh* To take off, as a bird or plane taking flight. *Trad.* See *kīloi ulele, pa'i ulele*.

ulele hua *ham* To set type, as for video captions. Comb. *ulele* + *hua*. *Mea ulele hua*. Character operator.

ulele kikī *heh* Fast break, as in basketball; to make a fast break. *'Āha'i akula ka ho'okūkū iā Lāhainā Luna no kō lākou ma'alea aku i kō lākou hoa paio i ka ulele kikī*. Lāhainā Luna really took the game due to their outwitting their opponent in the fast break. *Lit.*, leap swiftly into action. Cf. *kīloi ulele kikī*. See *kuemi*.

ule'o *kik* Pendulum. Sh. *uleule* + *'olo*. See *'ukē*.

ulia *kik* Accident. *Dic. Ulia ka'a*. Car accident, automobile accident.

ulu *heh* To grow. *Dic.* See entries below. *Ulu papakū*. To grow vertically. *Ulu papamoe*. To grow horizontally. *Palena ulu*. Grow limit.

ulu *kik* Compression, i.e. the most dense concentration of wave particles in a compressional wave. *Dic.*, new mng. Cf. *wele*. See *hawewe papamoe*.

ulu·ā·hewa *'a'* To grow wild and lush. *Dic.* Cf. *ulu wale*.

ulu·lā·'au See *ho'oneo 'āina ululā'au*.

ulūlu *heh* Strong, as wind; large branches in motion and whistling heard in wires between utility poles, in meteorology. *Dic.*, ext. mng. See *makani*.

uluna *kik* Pillow. *Dic. Pale uluna*. Pillowcase.

ulu wale *heh* To grow wild, as weeds. *Dic.* Cf. *uluāhewa*.

uma *kik* Curve, as on a graph or as a geometric curve. *Dic.*, ext. mng. See *awāwa uma, uma kī*.

umauma *'Au umauma*. Breast stroke; to swim the breast stroke. See *kīloi umauma*.

umauma moa *kik* Chicken breast.

uma kī *kik* Top of the key on a basketball court. *Lit.*, key curve. Also *uma, pōheo*. See *pukakī*.

uma pala·pola *kik* Parabolic curve. Comb. *uma* + Eng.

umu·ko'a *kik* Artificial reef. Comb. *umu* + *ko'a*.

una honua *kik* Plate, as in geology. *Lit.*, earth shell. *Ka Una Honua Kokosa*. Cocos Plate. *Ka Una Honua Naseka*. Nazca Plate. *Ka Una Honua 'Eulāsia*. Eurasian Plate. *Ka Una Honua 'Īnionūhōlani*. Indo-Australian Plate. *Ku'ina una honua*. Plate techtonics.

une kini *kik* Tab, as on soda cans. *Lit.*, can lever. *Une kini koloaka*. Soda can tab.

une kukui *kik* Light controls, as for stage productions. *Lit.*, lever (for) lights.

unuhi kū·ana *ham* Expanded form, in math; to expand. *E unuhi kūana i ka helu 395*. Expand the number 395 [395 = 300 + 90 + 5]. *Lit.*, interrupt place value. *Helu unuhi kūana*. Expanded numeral.

unu·kā *kik* Asphalt. Sh. *unu* + *kā*. See *ho'ūnukā*.

H

hā *kik* Fa, the fourth note on the musical scale. *Dic.* See *pākōlī*.

haia·hū *kik* Deviation, in math. Comb. *haia* + *hū*. Cf. *haiakonu*. *Haiahū kūmau*. Standard deviation.

haia·konu *'a'* Normal, in math. Sh. *haia* + *waenakonu*. Cf. *haiahū*.

haia·mui *kik* Caucus, a meeting of political party leaders to determine policy, choose candidates, etc. *Hālāwai nā ʻaoʻao kālaiʻāina ma kahi kaʻawale ma ka haiamui no ka hoʻoholo ʻana ʻo wai ana lā nā luna o ia mau ʻaoʻao no kēia makahiki.* Political parties meet separately in caucus to decide who will be their party leaders for the year. *Comb. hai- + a + mui.*

hāiki *Pahuhopu hāiki.* Objective.

haiko·kene *kik* Hydrogen. *Eng. Haikokene lua ʻokikene lua.* Hydrogen peroxide (H_2O_2).

hai·lawe *ham* To barter. *Ma mua o ka hoʻopaʻa ʻana i ka ʻōnaehana kālā, ʻo ka hailawe ʻana ka hana maʻamau a ka poʻe o Hawaiʻi nei.* Before establishing the cash system, the barter system was prevalent among those living here in Hawaiʻi. *Dic. Ka hailawe ʻana.* Barter system.

haina·kā *kik* Handkerchief. *Dic.* Also *hinakā*.

Hai·peli·ona *iʻoa* Hyperion, a moon of Saturn. *Eng.*

hai·pili·kia *kik* Pest, as any plant or animal detrimental to humans or their interests. *Sh. hailepo + pilikia.*

hai·doro·kolo·riku Hydrochloric. *Eng. ʻAkika haidorokoloriku.* Hydrochloric acid.

hao *kik* Rim of basket, in basketball. *E ʻahaʻi a ka hao.* Take it to the rim. *Dic., ext. mng.* Also *kuku*. See entries below and *hīnaʻi, hupa*.

hao hoʻo·kani *kik* Tuning fork. *Niʻihau.* Also *ʻō hoʻokani* (preceded by *ke*).

hao kau lole *kik* Clothes rack, as on wheels in a clothing store. *Niʻihau.* Also *haka lole*.

hao keko *kik* Monkey bars, a kind of playground equipment. *Lit.*, monkey iron. Cf. *hao pīnana*.

hao kope *kik* Garden rake. See *kope*.

hao pela *kik* Bedframe. *Lit.*, mattress iron. See *kūmoe*.

hao pī·nana *kik* Jungle gym, a kind of playground equipment. *Lit.*, iron for climbing. Cf. *hao keko*.

hā·oʻo *ʻa*ʻ Cured, i.e. prepared by chemical or physical processing for keeping or use. *Comb. hā- + oʻo.* See *hoʻohāoʻo*.

Hau·hoa *iʻoa* Zuben Elgenubi, a star. *Mān. (HA).*

hau·kōhi *kik* Shave ice, snow cone. *Mān.*

hau·kona *kik* Hawthorne. *Eng. Pīʻai haukona.* Hawthorne berry.

hau·lāpa *kik* Balsa. *Lit.*, raft hau.

hau·mia *kik* Pollution. *Dic., ext. mng. Haumia ea.* Air pollution.

hau·naele kū·loko *kik* Civil unrest. *Hoʻāla ʻia aʻela he haunaele kūloko ma ke kūlanakauhale no ka nui loa o nā hihia ma waena o ka poʻe e noho ana ma ia wahi.* Civil unrest was created in the city due to the tremendous amount of tension between the people who live in the area. *Trad.*

hau·naku *kik* Defensive middle guard, nose guard, nose tackle, in football. *Dic., new mng.*

hau·neneʻe *kik* Glacier. *Lit.*, creeping ice. *Ka hauneneʻe ʻana.* Glaciation. *I ka hauneneʻe ʻana, paʻapū nā kuahiwi a me ka ʻāina i ka hau no nā makahiki he nui ka lōʻihi.* In glaciation, the mountains and land become covered with ice for a period of many years. *Ka Pāka Aupuni ʻo Hauneneʻe.* Glacier National Park.

hau·waiū·tepe *kik* Frozen yogurt. *Lit.*, ice yogurt. Cf. *haukalima* (dic.). See *waiūtepe*.

haha *heh* To pant, as a dog. *Dic.*

hā hā *kik* Four-by-four. *Papa hā hā.* Four-by-four board or lumber. See *lua hā*.

hahai holo·holona *Hoʻomalu lawaiʻa a me ka hahai holoholona.* Fish and game management; to manage fish and game.

hahaina *kik* Function, in math. Comb. *hahai* + *-na*. Cf. *hana, lawelawe hana*. *Hahaina lālani*. Linear function.

hahai ʻō·kuhi *ham* To follow directions. See *ʻōkuhi*.

hahī *kik* Fricative, in lingustics. *Onomatopoeia*.

hahili poloka *kik* Antennariv Commersonil, a kind of fish. *Lit.,* frog fish.

haka *kik* Heart (shape). *Dic., ext. mng*.

haka ihu *kik* Nasal cavity. *Lit.,* nose open space.

haka·haka See *kaʻele, pani hakahaka, paʻi hakahaka*.

haka·haka pā *kik* Disk space, as on computer hard drive or floppy disk. *Ua lawa kūpono ka hakahaka pā o kēia pā malule*. There is just enough disk space on this floppy disk. *Lit.,* disk vacant space.

haka kau *kik* Shelf. *Dic. Haka kau puke*. Bookshelf.

haka kau·laʻi pā *kik* Dish rack. *Lit.,* rack (for) drying dishes.

haka·kino *kik* Structure, as of a molecule. Comb. *haka + kino*.

haka·lama *kik* Syllabary. Comb. *hā + kā + lā + mā*. See *huahakalama*.

haka lole *kik* Clothes rack, as on wheels in a clothing store. Also *hao kau lole*.

haka moni *kik* Pharynx, in anatomy. *Lit.,* open space (for) swallowing. *Haka moni o lalo*. Laryngopharynx, i.e. the lower part of the pharynx adjacent to the larynx. *Haka moni o luna*. Nasopharynx, i.e. the portion of the pharynx behind the nasal cavity and above the soft palate. *Haka moni o waena*. Oropharynx, i.e. the lower part of the pharynx contiguous to the mouth.

haka moʻoni *kik* Cochlea, i.e. inner ear cavity. *Lit.,* spiral open space.

haka pā·ʻā·lua *kik* Code style, as in computer program. *Lit.,* code rack.

haka waha *kik* Oral cavity. *Lit.,* mouth open space. Cf. *puka niho*.

Haka·ʻama *iʻoa* Grand Canyon. (Hualapai elder river.) Also *ke awāwa kūhōhō nui ʻo Haka'ama*. *Ka muliwai ʻo Haka'ama*. Colorado River. See *Kololako*.

haki *kik* Crease, as on a pair of pants. *Niʻihau*. Also *ʻopi*.

hakina *kik* Fraction, in math. *Dic. Hakina anakahi*. Unit fraction. *Hakina heluna like*. Equivalent fraction. *Hakina lapa*. Improper fraction. *Hakina palena haʻahaʻa loa*. Lowest-terms fraction.

hakina·heʻe *kik* Geologic fault, as San Andreas Fault. *Lit.,* slipping break.

haki wale *heh* Fragile, easily broken. *Dic*. Cf. *nahā wale, pāloli*.

haku *kik* Sponge-like material in sprouting coconut. *Dic*. Cf. *niu haku*. See entries below and *lumi moe haku, pepeke haku*.

haku·ahua *ham/ʻaʻ* To synthesize, as compounds; synthetic. *Dic., ext. mng*. *Nā pūhui i hakuahua ʻia*. Synthesized compounds.

haku·ika *kik* Mollusk. Sh. *pōhaku + kuita* (Proto Eastern Oceanic, squid).

haku·hia *ʻaʻ* Invented. *Ua hakuhia iā ia kekahi mīkini hou*. A new machine was invented by him/her. Comb. *haku + -hia*. Cf. *hoʻohakuhia*.

haku·hune *kik* Tuff, i.e. a rock composed of finer kinds of detritus, usually more or less stratified and in various states of consolidation, in geology. Sh. *pōhaku + hune*. *Puʻu hakuhune*. Tuff cone.

haku·kuleke *kik* Turquoise (the mineral). Comb. *haku + Kuleke*.

haku·lau *ham* To design. *Lit.,* arrange (a) design.

haku·lau kahua *ham* To design sets, as for movie or video production. *Mea hakulau kahua*. Set designer.

haku·leʻi *ʻaʻ* Nonfiction. Sh. *haku + poloreʻi*. Cf. *hakupuni*. *Puke hakuleʻi*. Nonfiction book.

haku·loli *ham* To adapt, as a written document by shortening or lengthening, or by changing the form or style. Comb. *haku* + *loli*. See *hōʻano hou*.

haku mele *ham* Composer; to compose songs or chants. *Dic.*

haku·puni *ʻa* Fiction; fictitious. Comb. *haku* + *puni*. Cf. *hakuleʻi*. See *mōhihiʻo*. *Hakupuni kohu ʻoiaʻiʻo*. Realistic fiction. *Hakupuni mōʻaukala*. Historical fiction. *Puke hakupuni*. Fiction book.

haku·ʻala *kik* Kidney. *Niʻihau*.

haku·ʻili *kik* Gravel. Sh. *pōhaku* + *ʻiliʻili*.

hala akula i waho Out, in volleyball. *Niʻihau*. See *ʻauka*.

hala kahiki *kik* Pineapple. *Dic.* Also *painaʻāpala*.

hala ka pā·lulu *ʻa* To pass through the block, in volleyball. *Niʻihau*.

hā·lana See *wai hālana*.

hala·pohe *ʻa* Extinct. Comb. *hala* + *pohe* (Tah., dead). Also *make loa, nalowale loa*. *ʻAne halapohe*. Endangered. See *Kānāwai Lāhulu ʻAne Halapohe*.

hā·lā·wai hoʻo·lohe *kik* Hearing, i.e. a time for presenting official testimony or argument. *Lit.*, meeting (for) listening. Also *ʻaha hoʻolohe*.

hā·lā·wai hoʻo·na·au·ao *kik* Workshop. *Lit.*, meeting (for) educating.

hā·lā·wai malū *kik* Subconference, in telecommunications. *Lit.*, secret meeting.

hale See entries below and *lāʻau hoʻomaʻemaʻe hale, ʻelua hale*.

hale aʻo kilo hō·kū *kik* Planetarium. *Lit.*, building (for) teaching astronomy. Cf. *hale kilo hōkū*.

hale hana kiʻi·ʻoni·ʻoni *kik* Movie studio, i.e. the building itself. *Lit.*, building (for) making movies. Cf. *keʻena hana kiʻiʻoniʻoni*.

hale haʻuki *kik* Gymnasium. *Lit.*, sports building. Cf. *hale hoʻoikaika kino*.

hale hoʻo·ikaika kino *kik* Athletic club, fitness center. *Lit.*, building (for) strengthening (the) body. Cf. *hale haʻuki*.

hale hoʻo·ulu mea·kanu *kik* Greenhouse. *Dic.*

hale hoʻo·malu maʻi *kik* Quarantine station. Comb. dic. + *maʻi*.

hale kau lā·ʻau *kik* Treehouse. *Trad.*

hale kā·piʻo *kik* Lean-to shelter. *Dic.*

hale kiaʻi ulu·lā·ʻau *kik* Ranger watchtower, esp. one used for watching for forest fires. *Lit.*, building (for) guarding forests. See *lanakia*.

hale kilo hō·kū *kik* Observatory. *Lit.*, astronomy building. Cf. *hale aʻo kilo hōkū*.

hale kū·ʻai *kik* Store. *Dic.* *Hale kūʻai mahi māla*. Garden store, gardening store.

hale lio *kik* Stable. *Dic.*

hale mā·lama ʻī·lio *kik* Kennel, an establishment for boarding or breeding dogs. *Lit.*, building (for) taking care of dogs. Cf. *pene halihali, pene ʻīlio*.

hale moe *kik* Dormitory. *Dic.* Cf. *hale noho haumāna*.

hale noho *kik* Residence. *Dic.* Also *wahi noho*.

hale noho hau·māna *kik* Residence hall, dormitory, as at a school. *Lit.*, house where students live. Cf. *hale moe*.

hale·peʻa *kik* Tent. *Dic., sp. var.* *Pine halepeʻa*. Tent stake.

hale ʻaina *kik* Restaurant. *Dic.* *Hale ʻaina meaʻai hikiwawe*. Fast-food restaurant. *ʻO ka maʻalahi o ka hale ʻaina meaʻai hikiwawe, ʻo ia hoʻi ka loaʻa koke, akā, ʻaʻole ia ka meaʻai paiola loa o ke ʻano*. The convenience of fast food restaurants is that they are easy to find, however, the food there is not the most nutritious.

hale ʻī·lio *kik* Doghouse. See *hale mālama ʻīlio*.

hali·lele *ham* Airmail; to send by airmail. Comb. *hali* + *lele*. *Leka halilele*. Airmail letter. *Poʻoleka halilele*. Airmail stamp.

hā·lino *ʻaʻ* Fluorescent, as colors. Sh. *hāweo* + *lino*. Cf. *hāweo*. *ʻĀkala hālino*. Fluorescent pink.

hā·liʻi moe *kik* Bedsheet. *Dic.* Also *hāliʻi pela*.

hā·liʻi papa·hele *kik* Rug, as for living room or any large room. Also *moena*. See *moena weleweka, pale papahele*.

hā·liʻi ʻea *kik* Plastic sheeting, general term. *Lit.*, plastic spread. See *ʻea painaʻāpala*.

hā·loko·loko *kik* Puddle. *Dic.*

halo ʻā·pika·pika *kik* Suction cup fin, as beneath the stomach of an *ʻoʻopu*. *Lit.*, fin (with) suction cups.

hā·mau *ʻaʻ* Silence; silent. *Dic.* E *hāmau (kō ke kahua)!* Quiet (on the set)!

hā·mama *ʻaʻ* Wide open. See *hemo*.

hā·me·ʻa *kik* Device, doohickey, gadget, gizmo, thingamajig, i.e. something made or used for a particular purpose. *Loaʻa kekahi hāmeʻa no ka hoʻāwīwī ʻana i ke paʻi ʻana*. There's a device for speeding up the printing. Comb. *hā-* + *meʻa* (Tongan for *mea*). See entries below and *maomeka, mauhaʻa, mea hana*. *Hāmeʻa huakomo*. Input device, as on a computer. *Hāmeʻa huapuka*. Output device.

hā·me·ʻa hana kino·ea *kik* Gas generator, i.e. a device used for producing gases as in a chemistry lab. *Lit.*, device (for) making gas.

hā·me·ʻa poka·kaʻa *kik* Block and tackle, an arrangement of pulleys and rope or cable used to lift or haul. *Lit.*, pulley device.

hā·me·ʻe *kik* Character, as in a story; role, as in a play or movie. Comb. *hā-* + *meʻe*.

hā·me·ʻa hoʻāʻo *kik* Tester, as a battery tester. *Lit.*, device (for) testing. Cf. *mīkini hoʻāʻo*. *Hāmeʻa hoʻāʻo iho*. Battery tester (not a machine).

hamu·iʻa *ham* Carnivore; carnivorous. Comb. *hamu* + *iʻa*. See entries below. *ʻEnuhe hamuiʻa*. Carnivorous caterpillar (Eupithecia spp).

hamu·hika *ham* Cannibal, among animals, insects, etc. *Nui nā ʻano holoholona ʻāhiu, he hamuhika ke ʻano a hoʻēmi ʻia ka nui o kā lākou mau keiki ponoʻī e ola a hiki i ka piha ʻana o ke ola ʻana*. Many types of animals in the wild are cannibalistic by nature and the number of their own young who achieve a full life is diminished in this way. Comb. *hamu* + *hika-*. Cf. *ʻai kanaka* (dic.).

hamu·lau *ham* Herbivore; herbivorous. Comb. *hamu* + *lau*. *Hamulau lāʻau*. Browser, i.e. an animal that eats twigs and leaves. *Hamulau mauʻu*. Grazer, i.e. an animal that eats grass.

hamu·pela *ham* Scavenger; to scavenge. Comb. *hamu* + *pela*.

hamu·ʻakoʻa *ham* Omnivore; omnivorous. Comb. *hamu* + *ʻakoʻa* (var. of *ʻokoʻa*).

hamu·ʻelala *ham* Insectivore, insectivorous. Comb. *hamu* + *ʻelala*.

hana *kik* Errand. *Dic.* *Nui kaʻu mau hana e hana ai i ke kaona i kēia lā*. I have a lot of errands to do/run in town today.

hana *kik* Function, as on a calculator or computer keyboard. Cf. *hahaina, lawelawe hana*. See *hana hoʻomākalakala*. *Pihi hana* (preceded by *ke*). Function key.

hā·nā *kik* Wood shavings. *Dic.*

hana a loaʻa ka hāʻina To solve. *E hana a loaʻa ka hāʻina o ka polopolema helu ʻekolu*. Solve problem three. *Lit.*, do until gotten. Also *hoʻomākalakala*.

hā·nai *ham* To feed, as paper into a printer or copy machine. *Dic., ext. mng.* *Hānai kaʻe*. To edge feed. *Hānai waena*. To center feed. *Hānai ʻakomi*. To auto feed. *Ua hoʻopaʻa ʻia ka mīkini paʻi ma ka hānai ʻakomi*. The printer has been set to auto feed.

hā·nai *ham* To feed, assist, as in basketball and most team sports except baseball. *Iā Magic Johnson ka nui loa o nā hānai o ka NBA holoʻokoʻa.* Magic Johnson has the most assists in the entire NBA. *Dic., ext.mng.* See entries below and *hāʻawi.* To serve, in volleyball; to set or set up (the ball), as from number 2 to number 3. *Niʻihau.* Cf. *hānai puʻupuʻu, paʻi ulele. Mea hānai, hānai.* Setter.

hānai·ahuhu *kik* Pet. *Dic. Hale kūʻai hānaiahuhu.* Pet shop.

hā·nai i hope To make a back set, in volleyball. *Lit.*, set back Also *hānai kīkala.*

hā·nai kī·kala *ham* To make a back set, in volleyball. *Niʻihau.* Also *hānai i hope.*

hā·nai lō·ʻihi *ham* To make an outside set, in volleyball. *Niʻihau.*

hā·nai pō·kole *ham* To make a short set, in volleyball. *Niʻihau.*

Hā·nai·pono *iʻoa* Mirphack, a star. *Mān. (HA).*

hā·nai puʻu·puʻu *ham* To serve underhand, in volleyball. *Niʻihau.* Cf. *kuʻi puʻupuʻu.*

hana hoʻo·mā·kala·kala *kik* Operation, in math. *Lit.*, solving activity. *Hana hoʻomākalakala huli hope.* Inverse operation.

hana hoʻo·nanea *ʻOihana o nā Pāka a me nā Hana Hoʻonanea.* Department of Parks and Recreation.

hana keaka *ham* To act, as in a play, movie or video production. *Dic., ext. mng.* See *ʻōhua, hāmeʻe. Mea hana keaka.* Actor. *Moʻolelo hana keaka.* Script.

hana keaka *ham* To act out, as a math problem. *Dic., ext. def.*

hana kolohe *heh* To fake or hit, in volleyball. *Niʻihau.* Also *mīʻoi wale.*

hana komo pae *kik* Rite of passage, initiation. See *komo pae, hoʻokomo pae.*

hana kope *ham* To copy, make a copy.

hana maʻa·lahi *ham* User friendly, as a computer program. *Ua lohe aku nei wau he hana maʻalahi ka Macintosh.* I've heard that the Macintosh is user friendly. *Lit.*, do easily.

hanana *kik* Event, as in math; also as a happening in a story. *Dic., ext. mng.*

hana ʻia ma kau·hale Homemade. *Lit.*, made at home.

haneli Hundred. *Mān.* See *hapa haneli.*

hano *kik* Cylinder; thermos. *Dic., ext. mng.* See *hano hoʻokolohua, paukū ʻolokaʻa. Hano ana.* Graduated cylinder.

hano·hano *ʻa*ʻ Distinction. *Dic.* Cf. *hoʻomaikaʻi. Me ka hanohano.* With distinction, as when graduating from a college or university.

hano hoʻo·kolo·hua *kik* Test tube. *Lit.*, experiment container. *Kū hano hoʻokolohua.* Ring stand.

hano kā·nuku *kik* Beaker. *Lit.*, beaker container.

hano kui *kik* Syringe. *Lit.*, needle syringe.

hano ʻohi *kik* Collection tube, e.g. a test tube used to collect gas generated in an experiment.

hanu *heh* Respiration; respiratory. *Dic., ext. mng.* See *lāʻau make hanu, paipu hanu. ʻŌnaehana hanu.* Respiratory system.

hā·nuku *kik* Narrow passageway, as in a canyon. Comb. *hā + nuku.* Cf. *ala hānuku.*

hanuʻu *heh* To fluctuate, as the tide. *Dic.*

hāpa *kik* Harp, the musical instrument. *Dic.* See *nīʻaukani. Pila hāpa, hāpa paʻa lima.* Autoharp.

hā·pai *ham* To lift, make a double hit, in volleyball. *Niʻihau.* See *ʻaʻena paʻi lua. ʻAʻena hāpai.* Carrying violation.

hā·pai hao *ham* Weight lifting; to lift weights. *Lit.*, lift iron. Also *amo hao.*

hapa·hā *kik* Quarter (the coin). *Dic. ʻĀpana hapahā.* Quadrant.

hapa haneli *kik* Hundreths; centi-, a prefix meaning one hundredth (c). *Dic., ext. mng., sp. var.* Abb. hhn. Also *keni-*.

hapa kau·kani *kik* Milli-, a prefix meaning one thousandth (m). Comb. *hapa + kaukani.* Abb. hkk. *Hapa kaukani kekona.* Millisecond, in math.

hapa kili·ona *kik* Pico-, a prefix meaning one trillionth (p). Comb. *hapa + kiliona.* Abb. hkl.

hapa kolona *kik* Semicolon. *Lit.*, half colon. See *kolona*.

hā·pale *kik* Trowel, as used for digging. *Dic.*

hapa·lua kā·lā *kik* Half dollar. *Dic.* Also *hapalua*.

hapa·lua kā·lani *kik* Half gallon.

hapa·malu See *papa hapamalu*.

hapa mili·ona *kik* Micro-, a prefix meaning one millionth (u). Comb. *hapa + miliona.* Abb. hml. *Hapa miliona kekona.* Microsecond, in math.

hapa mo'a *'a'* Medium rare, as meat. *Makemake wau i ka'u pipi kō'ala he hapa mo'a.* I like my grilled steak medium rare. *Lit.*, partial cooked. Also *mo'a hapa*.

hapa mua *kik* Front-end, in math. *Lit.*, front part. *Kikoho'e hapa mua.* Front-end digit. *Koho hapa mua.* Front-end estimation.

hā·pana *kik* Sample, as a small part of a larger whole. Sh., *hapa + 'āpana.* Cf. *la'ana. Hāpana pono koho.* Random sample. *Nā ki'ina 'ohi hāpana.* Sampling methods.

hā·pane *kik* Response, as to a stimulus. Comb. *hā- + pane.*

hapa pili·ona *kik* Nano-, a prefix meaning one billionth (n). Comb. *hapa + piliona.* Abb. hpl.

hapa 'umi Deci-, a prefix meaning one tenth (d). *Dic., ext. mng., sp. var.* Abb. h'm.

hapa 'umi *kik* Tenths; deci- a prefix meaning one tenth (d). *Dic., ext. mng., sp. var.* Abb. h'm. Also *keki-*. Cf. *hapa'umi*.

hapa·'umi *kik* Nickel (five cents). *Dic.* Cf. *nikala*.

hā·pa'u·pa'u *'a'* Dull (not shiny). *Dic., ext. mng.*

Hā·pela *i'oa* Hubble. *Eng. Ka 'ohenānā lewa lipo 'o Hāpela.* Hubble space telescope.

hā·popopo *'a'* Decomposed, putrefied. Comb. *hā- + popopo.* See *ho'ohāpopopo*.

hapū *kik* Clan, subtribe. *Māori.* Cf. *'alaea, nāki*.

Hawai'i *i'oa* Hawai'i; Hawaiian. *Dic.*

hā·weo *'a'* Glowing, as in the dark; phosphorescent. *Dic., ext. mng.* Cf. *hālino. Kukui hāweo.* Fluorescent light.

hawewe Wave, in scientific usage. *Dic., ext. mng.* See entries below and *ho'olaulā hawewe, laulā hawewe, 'anini laulā hawewe.*

hawewe kani *kik* Sound waves, as used in measuring ocean depths. *Lit.*, sound vibration. See *ho'opapā hohonu. Ikaika hawewe kani.* Amplitude, i.e. the amount of energy in a sound wave. *Koā hawewe kani.* Sound wavelength.

hawewe papa·moe *kik* Compressional wave, i.e. a wave in which matter vibrates in the same direction as the wave moves. *Lit.*, horizontal wave. Cf. *hawewe 'ale'ale.* See *ulu, wele.*

hawewe 'ale·'ale *kik* Transverse wave, i.e. a wave in which matter vibrates at right angles to the direction in which the wave moves. *Lit.*, undulating wave. Cf. *hawewe papamoe*.

ha'a·'a·e Sideward Comb. *ha'a- + a'e.* See *ha'alalo, ha'aluna. 'Ehia 'ao'ao ha'aa'e?* Pages across, as in computer program.

hā·'ae *kik* Saliva; salivary. *Dic. Lōku'u hā'ae.* Salivary gland.

ha'a·ha'a See *woela ha'aha'a*.

haʻa·kipu *ham* To breed animals or propagate plants. (Māori *whakatipu*.) Cf. *hoʻēhu pua, hoʻopiʻi* (dic.).

haʻa·kupu ʻaila·kele *kik/ʻa* Adipogenesis, i.e. the formation of fat or fatty tissue in a body; adipogenetic. Comb. *haʻa-* + *kupu* + *ʻailakele*. See *ʻailakele, ʻaʻaʻa hunaola ʻailakele*.

haʻa·lalo Downward. Comb. *haʻa-* + *lalo*. Cf. *haʻaaʻe, haʻaluna*. See *kolikoli*. *Ehia ʻaoʻao haʻalalo?* Pages down, as in computer program.

haʻa·lele *ham* To evacuate, as a building. *Dic*. Cf. *hoʻohaʻalele*.

haʻa·lele *ham* To quit, as a computer program. *Dic., ext. mng.*

haʻa·liu *ham* To process. *ʻO ka nui o nā meaʻai i kūʻai ʻia ma loko o ke kini, he meaʻai ia i haʻaliu ʻia.* Most foods sold in cans is processed food. Comb. *haʻa-* + *liu* (Sāmoan, alter, change). *Waiūpaʻa i haʻaliu ʻia*. Process(ed) cheese.

haʻa·loko Inward. Comb. *haʻa-* + *loko*. Cf. *haʻawaho*.

haʻa·luna Upward. Comb. *haʻa-* + *luna*. Cf. *haʻaaʻe, haʻalalo*. See *kolikoli*.

Haʻa·moa *iʻoa* Sāmoa; Sāmoan. *Dic.* Also *Kāmoa*. *Haʻamoa ʻAmelika*. American Sāmoa; American Sāmoan. Also *Kāmoa ʻAmelika*.

haʻa·pupū See *aʻahaʻapupū*. *Puʻu haʻapupū*. Speed bump, as on a road or in a parking lot.

haʻa·waho Outward. Comb. *haʻa-* + *waho*. Cf. *haʻaloko*.

hā·ʻawi *ham* To set or set up (the ball), in volleyball. *Niʻihau*. Also *hānai*. *Hāʻawi i ke kinipōpō i kekahi ʻaoʻao*. Side out, in volleyball. Also *kaʻa paʻi ulele, kaʻa*. *ʻAi hāʻawi wale*. Ace, in volleyball. Also *ʻeki*.

hā·ʻawi·aholo *ham* To give and go, in basketball. *Ma ka hāʻawiaholo ʻia aku o ke kinipōpō iā ia i ʻāhaʻi ai ʻo Limanui a hiki loa i ka hīnaʻi.* Limanui took off with the ball on the give and go all the way to the basket. *Lit.,* give and run.

haʻa·wina kā·lā hele kula *kik* Scholarship. *Lit.,* monetary grant (for) going to school. Also *haʻawina kālā*. *Haʻawina kālā ʻālapa*. Athletic scholarship.

haʻa·wina ʻai *kik* Serving of food. *Lit.,* food portion.

hā·ʻaʻa ʻai *kik* Fiber, as referring to diet. *He mea nui ka hāʻaʻa ʻai ma ka papaʻai, no ka mea, he kōkua ma ka wāwahi ʻai ʻana.* Fiber is an important part of the diet since it helps in the digestion of food. *Lit.,* edible fibrous.

hā·ʻehu·ola *kik* Healthful, healthy, wholesome, i.e. promoting physical health. Comb. *hā-* + *ehuola*. See *ehuola*. *Meaʻai hāʻehuola*. Health food.

haʻi *kik* Expression, in math. *Dic., ext. mng.* See entries below and *haʻihelu, haʻilula*. *Haʻi hōʻailona helu*. Algebraic expression.

haʻi·haʻi iwi *ham* Osteopathy; to practice osteopathy. *Dic., ext. mng. Kauka haʻihaʻi iwi.* Osteopath.

haʻi·haʻi kā·nā·wai *ham* To break the law. *Dic*. Also *ʻaʻe kānāwai*. Cf. *pale kānāwai*.

haʻi·helu *kik* Numerical problem (as 2+3); equation (as 2+3=5). Comb. *haʻi* + *helu*. See *haʻi, haʻilula*. *Haʻihelu kemikala*. Chemical equation. *Haʻihelu kemikala kaulike*. Balanced chemical equation. *Haʻihelu lālani*. Linear equation.

haʻi heluna like *kik* Equivalent expression, in math. *Lit.,* equal amount expression.

haʻi hou ma kekahi ʻano *ham* To paraphrase orally. *E Manai, e haʻi hou mai i ka moʻolelo i haʻi ʻia aʻe nei ma kekahi ʻano ʻokoʻa.* Manai, retell the story that was just told another way. *Lit.,* retell in another way. See *kākau hou ma kekahi ʻano*.

haʻi·lono *ʻOihana haʻilono*. Journalism.

ha'i·lula *kik* Formula, in math and science. Comb. *ha'i + lula*. See *ha'i, ha'ihelu*. *Ha'ilula kemikala*. Chemical formula.

ha'i mua *'Ōlelo ha'i mua*. Foreword, preface, as in a book. Also *'ōlelo mua*. Cf. *'ōlelo ho'ākāka*.

hā·'ina *kik* Solution, answer to a problem. *Dic., sp. var.* See *'imi hā'ina*. *Hana a loa'a ka hā'ina*. To solve.

ha'i·nole *ham* To stimulate, as with a drug. *Dic., ext. mng.* Cf. *kūlale*. *Lā'au ha'inole*. Stimulant.

ha'i waha *ham* Oral. *Dic.* Cf. *palapala*. See *mo'olelo ha'i waha*. *Hō'ike ha'i waha*. Oral report. *Ka'a'ike ha'i waha*. Oral communication. *Mo'okalaleo ha'i waha*. Oral literature.

ha'i·'ō·lelo *kik* Speech. *Dic.* See *hō'ike ha'i waha, mikolololehua*. *Ha'i'ōlelo hō'ike*. Oral report, presented as a speech. *Ha'i'ōlelo ho'ohuli mana'o*. Persuasive speech. *Ha'i'ōlelo kūhaha'i*. Narrative speech. *Ha'i'ōlelo mikolololehua*. Expressive speech, speech to entertain.

hā·'oi *kik* Baritone. Sh. *'ehā + 'oi*. *'Ukulele hā'oi*. Baritone 'ukulele.

ha'uki *kik* Sport. (Tah. *ha'uti*.) See *'uao ha'uki*. *Hale ha'uki*. Gymnasium.

ha'uki Helene *kik* Track and field. *Lit.*, Greek sport. *Nā ha'uki Helene*. Track and field events.

hā·'ule *heh* To lose, as in sports. *Dic.* Cf. *eo*. *Māhele hā'ule*. Consolation bracket, as in a sports tournament.

hā·'ule·ā·pa'a *kik* Deadfall, a kind of animal trap. *Lit.*, fall until secure.

hā·'ule·lau *kik* Autumn, fall. *Dic., sp. var.* See *māuiili*.

ha'u·poho *kik* Parachute. Sh. *puha'u + poho*.

-hate Suffix in chemical compounds and terms: -ate.

hei *'a* Addiction; addicted. *Ua hei 'o ia i ka paka*. S/he was addicted to cigarettes. *Dic., ext. mng.*

hei·hei ho'o·ili *kik* Relay race. Also *kūkini ho'oili*. See *maile ho'oili*.

Heiti *i'oa* Haiti; Haitian. *Eng.*

heona *'a* Artistic, i.e. esthetically appealing or having artistic talent. *Ua heona kāu mau ki'i; he kanaka heona maoli 'oe*. Your pictures are esthetically pleasing; you're really an artistic person. *Lit.*, an attraction. Cf. *ho'oheona, pāheona*.

hehelo pā·pā·lina *kik* Rouge, blush, as makeup. *Lit.*, cheek reddishness.

hehena *Ma'i hehena*. Maniacal delirium.

hehe'e *heh* To melt. *Dic.* *Kēkelē hehe'e*. Melting point.

hehu *kik* Seedling, as of *'ilima* plants. *Dic.* See *kauwowo*.

hekehi *heh* Hike; to go on a hike. Sh. *hele + ke'ehi*/metathesis of *ke'ehi*. Cf. *holoholo wāwae*. *Ala hekehi*. Hiking trail. *Kāma'a hekehi*. Hiking shoe. *Mea hekehi*. Hiker.

heke·kale *kik* Hectare, a metric unit of land measurement. *Eng.* Also *heketare*. Abb. *ht*.

hē·kī *kik* Jet. Sh. *hele + kikī*. *Mokulele hēkī*. Jet airplane.

hekili See *manu hekili*.

heko- Hecto-, i.e. a prefix meaning hundred. *Eng.* Also *pāhaneli*. See entries below.

heko·kalame *kik* Hectogram. *Eng.* Abb. *hkkal*.

heko·lika *kik* Hectoliter. *Eng.* Abb. *hkl*.

heko·mika *kik* Hectometer. *Eng.* Abb. *hkm*.

hele·uī *kik* Halloween. *Eng.* Also *lā ho'omāka'uka'u*. *Pū heleuī*. Jack-o'-lantern. Also *pala'ai heleuī*.

hele·kona *kik* Walkathon. Comb. *hele* + Eng.

hele·kopa *kik* Helicopter. *Ni'ihau*. Also *mokulele helekopa*.

hele lana·kila *heh* To go freely, i.e. to have freedom to go wherever one pleases, to "have the run of the place." *He hele lanakila wale nō mākou i kō mākou noho ʻana i ke kākela o ke keiki aliʻi.* We were given the run of the house while we stayed at the castle of the prince. *Trad.* (20,000 Lekue ma Lalo o ke Kai). Cf. *noa* (dic.).

hele lewa lipo *heh* Spacewalk. *Lit.*, walk (in) space.

Helene *iʻoa* Greece; Greek, Grecian. *Dic.*

hele wale *Kinipōpō hele wale.* Kill, in volleyball.

Hele·ʻekela *iʻoa* Uranus. *Dic., sp. var.*

Hēli *iʻoa* Halley. *Eng. Ka hōkū puhipaka ʻo Hēli.* Halley's comet.

helu *kik* Amount. *Dic., ext. mng. Eia ʻelua pūʻulu helu ʻelua.* Here are two groups of twos. *Dic., ext. mng.* Also *heluna.* See entries below and *mīkini helu.*

helu *kik* Size, as of clothes. *Mān.*

helu uaki *ham* To tell time. Also *helu uāki.* Cf. *helu manawa.*

helu heluna *kik* Cardinal number. *Lit.*, amount number. Cf. *helu kaʻina.*

helu·helu pā See *mīkini heluhelu pā.*

helu·helu pā·kā·kā *ham* To skim read. *Comb. heluhelu* + redup. of *pākā. Ka heluhelu pākākā ʻana.* Skim reading.

helu hoʻo·hana *kik* Constant, in math. *Lit.*, number (for) use.

helu hoʻo·hui *kik* Addend, in math. *Lit.*, number (for) adding.

helu hoʻo·nui *kik* Factor, in math. *Lit.*, number (for) multiplying. See *helu hoʻonui kemikala. Helu hoʻonui like.* Common factor. *Helu hoʻonui like kiʻekiʻe loa.* Greatest common factor. *Papa helu hoʻonui kumu.* Factor tree.

helu hoʻo·nui kemi·kala *kik* Coefficient, i.e. a number placed in front of a chemical symbol or formula in order to balance the chemical equation. *Lit.*, number (to) add to (a) chemical.

helu kau·like *kik* Even number. *Dic.* See *helu kauʻewa.*

helu kau·ʻewa *kik* Odd number. *Lit.*, number placed unevenly. See *helu kaulike.*

helu kaha *ham* Tally; to tally. *Lit.*, count (with) marks.

helu kanaka *ham* Census, a periodic official enumeration of a population and its characteristics. *Ma ʻAmelika Hui Pū ʻia, mālama ʻia ka helu kanaka i kēlā me kēia ʻumi makahiki.* In the United States the census is conducted every ten years. *Dic.*

helu kaʻina *kik* Ordinal number. *Lit.*, number (that shows) sequence. Cf. *helu heluna.*

helu komo *kik* Divisor, in math. *Dic.*

helu kū·ana *ham* Counting on, a strategy used in mental math. E.g., 83 + 30 = 113: add 3 tens; think 83, 93, 103, 113. *Lit.*, place value counting.

helu kuhi *kik* Zip code. *Lit.*, pointing number. See entry below.

helu kuhi puke *kik* Call number, as for a library book. *Lit.*, number pointing (to) book. *Kāleka helu kuhi puke.* Catalog card, as in a library. See *pahu kāleka kuhi puke.*

helu kumu *kik* Prime number, in math. *Lit.*, base number. *Helu kumu kūlua.* Twin primes.

helu laka *kik* Combination, as for a lock. *Lit.*, lock number. Cf. *laka helu.*

helu lele *ham* To skip count, in math. *Lit.*, jump count.

helu Loma *kik* Roman numeral.

helu maoli *kik* Real number, in math.

helu mā·hoe *kik* Double number, same number used twice, in math. *Lit.*, twin number. Cf. *kaulua.*

helu mā·hua *kik* Multiple, in math. *Lit.,* multiplied number. Also *māhua. Helu māhua like.* Common multiple. *Helu māhua like haʻahaʻa loa.* Least common multiple.

helu maka·hiki kala·pona *kik* Carbon dating, radiocarbon date. *Ma ka helu makahiki kalapona ʻana, hiki ke ʻike ʻia ka wā i paʻa mai ai kekahi pōhaku a i ʻole ka wā i hana ʻia ai kekahi mea koehana.* By carbon dating, the time a rock was formed or the time an artifact was made can be determined. *Lit.,* number (of) carbon years.

helu manawa *kik/ham* Time, recorded duration; to time, as speed, duration, etc. *He aha kou helu manawa ma ka holo kikī haneli ʻīā?* What was your time on the hundred-yard dash? *Lit.,* to count time. Cf. *helu uaki.* See *uaki.*

heluna *kik* Amount. *Dic.* Also *helu.* See *helu heluna.*

heluna huna ʻāne *kik* Atomic number. *Lit.,* proton amount. See *huna ʻāne.*

helu naʻau *ham* Mental math. *Lit.,* mind counting. Also *makemakika naʻau.*

helu pana puʻu·wai *kik* Heart rate, pulse rate. *Lit.,* heart pulse count.

helu piha *kik* Whole number or integer, in math. *Lit.,* complete number. *Helu piha ʻiʻo.* Positive integer. *Helu piha ʻiʻo ʻole.* Negative integer.

helu puka *kik* Quotient. *Dic.*

helu puʻu·naue koena *kik* Irrational number, in math. *Lit.,* indivisible number. *Helu puʻunaue koena ʻole.* Rational number.

helu puʻu·naue lua *kik* Composite number.

helu·wawe *ham* To speed read. *Sh. heluhelu + wawe.* Cf. *kāwawe. Ka heluwawe ʻana.* Speed reading.

heluʻai *kik* Score, as in sports or games. *Dic., ext. mng.* See *ʻai. Papa heluʻai.* Scoreboard.

helu ʻini·kua ola·kino *kik* Medical coverage number. *Lit.,* health insurance number. See *ʻinikua olakino.*

helu ʻiʻo *kik* Positive number. *Lit.,* number (with) substance. Cf. *helu ʻiʻo ʻole.*

helu ʻiʻo ʻole *kik* Negative number. *Lit.,* number without substance. Cf. *helu ʻiʻo. ʻEkolu ʻiʻo ʻole.* Negative three (-3).

helu ʻō·lapa *ham* To count down, as in launching a rocket; countdown. *Lit.,* lift-off count.

helu ʻō·ʻā *kik* Mixed number, in math, as 3 3/4. *Lit.,* mixed number.

hema *kik* South. *Dic.* Abb. *Hm. Kōʻai hema.* Counterclockwise. *Poepoe hapa hema.* Southern hemisphere.

hema·laka *kik* Hemlock. *Eng.*

hemo *ʻaʻ* Open, as for business; unlocked; ajar. See entry below and *hāmama.*

hemo *ʻaʻ* To be open, as for a play in basketball. *ʻOiai ua hemo kekahi hoa kime ma lalo pono o ka hīnaʻi, kī paʻewa wale akula ʻo Mānea.* Even though one of his teammates was open right under the basket, Mānea went ahead and made a bad shot. *Dic., ext. mng.* See *hoʻohemo.*

hene moku·honua *kik* Continental slope. *Lit.,* continent slope. Cf. *holopapa mokuhonua.*

henua *Pilina henua.* Relative location, in geography. Cf. *kuhikuhina.*

hewa See *kaha pela hewa, keʻehi hewa, palena ʻāluna o ka hewa.*

hewa kū·pili *kik* Logic error, as message on calculator display that shows an operation is not logical.

heʻe *kik* Squid (local definition); octopus (Haole definition). *Dic.* Cf. *mūheʻe.*

heʻe *ham* To skim, as milk. *Dic. Waiū heʻe.* Skim milk.

heʻe·aholo *heh* To leach, i.e. the action of liquid percolating through layers of soil thus removing nutrients from the soil. Comb. *heʻe + a + holo.* Cf. *hoʻoheʻeaholo.*

heʻe hau *heh* To ski, in snow. *Lit.,* slide (on) snow. See *heʻe wai. Heʻe hau peʻa ʻāina.* To cross-country ski.

heʻena *kik* Ramp, as for skateboarding. Comb. *heʻe + -na.* Cf. *alahiō. Heʻena papa huila.* Skateboard ramp.

heʻe wai *heh* To water ski. *Lit.,* slide (on) water. See *heʻe hau.*

hero·ina *kik* Heroin. *Ua waiho aku ʻo Marvin i loko o ka haukapila no ka lapaʻau ʻana i kōna hei i ka heroina.* Marvin was laid up in the hospital for treatment for his heroin addiction. *Eng.*

hese *kik* Witch. *German. Nananana hese ʻeleʻele.* Black widow, a kind of spider. Also *nanana hese ʻeleʻele.*

hia·moe pono *heh* To sleep well. *E hiamoe pono ʻoe.* Good night; sleep well. Also *e hiamoe maikaʻi ʻoe; a hui hou i kakahiaka.*

Hiapo *iʻoa* Equatorial Countercurrent, in oceanography. *Mān.* (HA).

hia·ʻume *ʻa*ʻ To have an affinity for (something). Comb. *hia-* (to be disposed to) *+ ʻume.*

hiō *ʻa*ʻ Italic. *Lit.,* slanting. Also *hua hiō.* See *uakeʻe hiō, hoʻohiō.*

hiu *kik* Chip, as used in poker, checkers, counting, etc. *Dic. ext. mng.*

hihi *Pāma hihi.* Rattan.

hihia *kik* Problem or difficulty, as in the plot of a story. *Dic.* See *hopena holo.*

hika- A prefix meaning self- or auto-. *PPN kita* (one, the indefinite pronoun). See entries below.

hika·pili·olana Comb. *hika-* + *piliolana.* Autobiography; autobiographical. *Moʻolelo hikapiliolana.* Autobiography, autobiographical story.

hiki·ā·loa *ʻa*ʻ Long-range, long-term. Comb. *hiki + ā + loa. Papa hoʻolālā hikiāloa.* Long-range plan, long-term plan. See *papa hoʻolālā.*

hiki·ā·lō·pū *ʻa*ʻ Medium-range, medium-term. Comb. *hiki + ā + lōpū. Papa hoʻolālā hikiālōpū.* Medium-range plan, medium-term plan. See *papa hoʻolālā.*

hiki·ā·poko *ʻa*ʻ Short-range, short-term. Comb. *hiki + ā + poko. Papa hoʻolālā hikiāpoko.* Short-range plan, short-term plan. See *papa hoʻolālā.*

hiki hope *heh* Late, as registration for a conference. *Lit.,* arriving after. See *hiki mua. Kāinoa hiki hope.* Late registration.

hiki mua *heh* Pre-, early, beforehand, as registration for a conference. *Dic., ext. def.* See *hiki hope. Kāinoa hiki mua.* Preregistration.

hikina *kik* East. *Dic.* Abb. *Hk. Poepoe hapa hikina.* Eastern hemisphere.

Hikina Waena *iʻoa* Middle East; Middle Eastern.

hiki·wawe *Meaʻai hikiwawe.* Fast food. *Hale ʻaina meaʻai hikiwawe.* Fast-food restaurant.

Hiki·wawe *iʻoa* Sadr, a star. *Mān.* (HA).

hiku *ham* To pick, as an ʻukulele or guitar. *Mān.* Also *panapana.*

hili *ham* To spike (the ball), in volleyball. *Niʻihau.* Also *pākī.* See *kuʻi puʻupuʻu, pākī, paʻi pālahalaha, ʻai hele wale. Hili laina.* Line spike. *Hili ʻaoʻao.* Angle spike. *Manawa hili.* At bat, up (to bat), in baseball.

hili·uma *kik* Helium. *Eng.*

hī·meni kū·launa like *ham* To sing in harmony.

hī·nā·lea nā·ʻuke *kik* Cleaner wrasse (labroides Phthirophegus), a kind of fish. *Lit.,* wrasse (which) searches for lice.

Hina·lua *i'oa* Achernar, a star. *Mān.* (HA).

hī·na'i *kik* Basket, in basketball; basketball net. *Komo mau kāna mau kī 'ana i ka hīha'i.* His shots always make it into the basket. *Dic., ext. mng.* See *hao, hupa, kuku, pōhīna'i. Papa hīna'i.* Backboard. *'Ai hīna'i.* Basket (score). *'Ai hīna'i kolu.* Three pointer.

hinu·kele *kik* Grease, as used in machines or for tools with moving parts. Comb. *hinu + kele.*

hipo·pō·kamu *kik* Hippopotamus. *Dic., sp. var.*

hī·pu'u *kik* Knot. *Dic.* See entry below.

hī·pu'u pewa *kik* Bow, as ribbon or string. *Lit.,* fishtail knot. Cf. *lei 'ā'ī pewa.*

hi'o·hia *'a'* Discovered, existence revealed. *Ua hi'ohia 'o Hawai'i nei no ko nā 'āina 'ē iā Kāpena Kuke.* Hawai'i was discovered for foreigners by Captain Cook. Comb. *hi'o* (Tah., look) + *-hia.* Cf. *kaunānā. Mea hi'ohia.* Find, as an archeological find.

hi'o·hi'ona *kik* Effects, as in special effects. *Dic., ext. mng. Hi'ohi'ona na'iau.* Special effects. See *kani keaka. Luna hi'ohi'ona na'iau.* Special effects coordinator, as for movie or video production. *Hi'ohi'ona pa'i.* Printer effects, as on a computer printer. *Ho'ona'iau (i ka hi'ohi'ona).* To add special effects.

hi'ona *kik* General appearance, impression; feature. *Dic.* Cf. *hi'onaina.* See entries below and *hi'ona 'āina. Hi'ona na ke kanaka.* Man-made topographical feature.

hi'o·naina *kik* Landscape. Sh. *hi'ona'ona + 'āina.* Cf. *hi'ona.* See *kāhi'onaina.*

hi'ona kaha *kik* Cross section, in math. *Lit.,* appearance (when) cut open.

hi'ona·pā·'ili *kik* Texture. *Lit.,* features (when) touched.

hi'ona wai *kik* Body of water; water form or feature, as a lake, pond, river, etc., in geography. *'O ka hi'ona wai, he muliwai, he loko wai, he kahawai, he wailele, a pēlā aku nō.* A water feature can be a river, lake, stream, waterfall, and the like. *Lit.,* water feature. Cf. *hi'ona 'āina.*

hi'ona 'āina *kik* Contour, as the elevations of a particular place; land feature, as a mountain, valley, etc.; topography. *Palapala hi'ona 'āina.* Topographic map.

hi'u *kik* Tails, as in coin toss. *Dic., ext. mng.* Also *'ao'ao hi'u.* See entry below and *po'o.*

hi'u *kik* Tip of leaf, as hala. *Mān.* (MW). Also *welelau. Mān.* Cf. *po'o.*

-hite Suffix in chemical compounds and terms: -ite.

hoa helu ho'o·nui like kahi *kik* Relatively prime numbers, in math, i.e. numbers which share one factor between them, and that factor is 1. *Lit.,* companion common factor (of) one.

hoaka See entries below. *Pae moku hoaka.* Island arc.

hoa kaia·home *kik* Neighbor, not necessarily next door. See *kaiahome.*

hoaka kī·kolu *kik* Three-point arc, in basketball. *Lit.,* three-shot arch.

hoaka kū *kik* Arch, as the Arch of Triumph in Paris. *Lit.,* standing arch.

hoa mā·hu'i *kik* Emulation, as in a computer printer. *Lit.,* imitating companion.

hoa paio *kik* Opponent, as in a sporting event. *'O Punahou ka hoa paio o Kamehameha i kēia ho'okūkū nei.* Punahou is the opponent of Kamehameha in this game. *Dic.*

hoe·hoena o ke kai *kik* Tide. *Lit.,* breathing of the sea.

hou See *puka kikī hou.*

hou loa *'a'* Brand new. *Lit.,* very new.

houpo *kik* Diaphragm. *Dic.*

Māmaka Kaiao / 23

hohoki *'a'* Neutral, as particles in an atom. Redup. of *hoki*. See *ikehu uila hohoki*. See also *'āne, 'ine. Huna hohoki*. Neutron.

hohonu *'a'* Height or depth, in math. *Dic., ext. mng. 'Ehia 'īniha ka loa, ka laulā a me ka hohonu o kēnā pahu?* How many inches is the length, width and height of that box? Also *ana hohonu*. Cf. *ākea, laulā, loa, lō'ihi*. See *ki'eki'e*.

hō·kē *kik* Hockey. *Fr. Hōkē alanui*. Street hockey.

hō·keo *kik* Kit, as of equipment needed for a particular activity. *Dic., ext. mng.* Cf. *kini lapa'au, kini poho ea, poho lā'au pōulia*. See entries below. *Hōkeo kūmau ho'ā'o lepo*. Standard soil-testing kit.

hō·keo 'ike·pili *kik* Database, as in computer program; data bank, an organized collection of information, in math. *Lit.*, data container. See *'ikepili. Polokalamu hōkeo 'ikepili*. Database program.

hō·kelo *kik* Container, general term. *Dic., ext. mng.* See entries below.

hō·kelo ao *kik* Cloud chamber, i.e. a scientific device which detects nuclear particles through the formation of cloud tracks. *Lit.*, cloud container.

hō·kelo hu'a *kik* Bubble chamber, in chemistry. *Lit.*, bubble container.

hokona *ham* To market (something), i.e. to make available and promote the sale of a product. Comb. *hoko* (*Māori*, buy, sell) + -*na*.

hō·kū *Hua hōkū.* Starfruit.

hokua *kik* Crest of a wave. *Dic.* Also *hokua o ka nalu, hokua o ka 'ale*. Cf. *honua*.

hō·kū ukali *kik* Satellite star. *Dic.* Cf. *ukali, poelele*.

hō·kū·hele *kik* Planet. *Dic., sp. var. Hōkūhele Iowiana*. Jovian planet. *Hōkūhele o waho loa*. Outer planet.

hō·kū kai *kik* Starfish. *Dic.*

hō·kū·kimo *kik* Jack, as used in the game of jacks. See *kimo*.

Hō·kū·loa *i'oa* Venus. *Dic.*

hō·kū·na'i *kik* Asteroid. Sh. *hōkū* + *na'ina'i* (*Tah.*, small). *Kā'ei hōkūna'i*. Asteroid belt.

hō·kū·pa'a·lima *kik* Sparkler (fireworks). *Lit.*, hand-held star. See *ahiho'ole'ale'a*.

hō·kū puhi·paka *kik* Comet. *Dic.* Cf. *hōkū welowelo. Ka hōkū puhipaka 'o Hēli*. Halley's comet.

hō·kū welo·welo *kik* Shooting star. *Dic.* Cf. *hōkū puhipaka*.

Hō·kū·'ula *i'oa* Mars. *Dic.* Also *Hōkū'ulapīna'au*.

Hō·kū·'ula·pī·na'au *i'oa* Mars. Sh. *Hōkū'ula* + *Holoholopīna'au* (to differentiate from other stars called *Hōkū'ula*). Also *Hōkū'ula*.

hola *kik* Hour. *Dic.* Abb. *hl.*

hola kū·pono On time. *'A'ole 'o ia i hō'ea mai i ka hola kūpono; ua lohi 'o ia*. S/he didn't arrive on time; s/he was late.

hō·lapu See *mū hōlapu pale 'ea pau*.

holo *kik/heh* Run. See *holoē, 'ai holo. Holo 'ekolu haneli 'iā*. Three hundred-yard run.

holo a lele loloa *kik/heh* Running long jump.

holo·ē *kik* Hallway. *Eng.* Also *holo*.

holoi *ham* To delete or clear, as in computer program. *E holoi i ka 'ikepili e kū nei*. Clear the existing data. *Dic., ext. mng. Holoi i hope*. To backspace, as on an IBM computer; to delete, as with delete key on a Macintosh computer.

Holo·ika·uaua *i'oa* Pearl and Hermes Reef. *Lit.*, (Hawaiian monk seal that) swims in the rough.

holo hau *heh* To ice skate. *Lit.*, run (on) ice. See *kāma'a holo hau*.

holo·holo *heh* Traveling, in basketball; to travel. *Ua lilo ke kinipōpō iā Waiākea no ka holoholo ʻana a ke kūkahi o Hilo.* The ball was turned over to Waiākea after the point guard for Hilo traveled. *Dic., ext. mng.*

holo·holona See entries below and *hoʻomalu lawaiʻa a me ka hahai holoholona. Loea holoholona lōhiu.* Wildlife expert. *ʻAhahui Makaʻala Holoholona.* Humane Society. *ʻOihana Iʻa me ka Holoholona Lōhiu o ʻAmelika.* US Fish and Wildlife Service.

holo·holona iwi·kua·moʻo *kik* Vertebrate animal. *Lit.*, animal (with) backbone. See *holoholona iwikuamoʻo ʻole*.

holo·holona iwi·kua·moʻo ʻole *kik* Invertebrate animal. *Lit.*, animal without backbone. See *holoholona iwikuamoʻo*.

holo·holona lō·hiu *kik* Wildlife. *Lit.*, naturally wild animals.

holo·holona ʻai waiū *kik* Mammal. *Lit.*, animal (which) suckles. Also *māmela*.

holo·holo wā·wae *heh* Stroll; to go for a stroll. *Lit.*, stroll (by) foot. Cf. *hekehi*.

holo hoʻo·ili *kik/heh* Shuttle run. *Lit.*, transfer run. Cf. *kūkini hoʻoili*.

holo·kahi *heh* One way, as a street or trip. *E makaʻala i nā alanui holokahi o ke kaona ke kalaiwa ʻoe ma ia wahi.* Be careful of the one way streets in town when driving through there. *Lit.*, one ride. Cf. *holopuni*.

holo kā·maʻa huila *heh* To roller skate. *Lit.*, run (on) wheeled shoes. See *kāmaʻa huila*.

holo kele wai *kik* Runoff, as water running from the land into the sea. *Lit.*, muddy flow.

holo kikī *kik./heh* Dash, sprint. *Lit.*, swift run. *Holo kikī haneli mika.* Hundred-meter dash.

holo lapa huila *heh* To skate with rollerblades. *Lit.*, run (on) wheeled ridges. See *kāmaʻa lapa huila*.

holo·leʻa *kik* A ride, as at a carnival or amusement park. Sh. *holo + leʻaleʻa*.

holo lola *kik* Film movement, as in a movie or video camera. *Lit.*, cassette running.

holo·mua *heh* To improve. *Dic. He mau manaʻo e holomua ai ka hana.* Suggested improvements. *ʻAukā holomua.* Fill bar, in computer program.

holona kaʻa *kik* Drive-through, as at a restaurant or bank. Cf. *holona makani*.

holona makani *kik* Breezeway, as an open area between buildings. Comb. *holo + -na + makani*. Cf. *holona kaʻa*.

holo·papa moku·honua *kik* Continental shelf. *Lit.*, continent ledge. Cf. *hene mokuhonua*.

holo papa peʻa *heh* To windsurf. See *papa peʻa*.

holo peki *kik/heh* Jogging; to jog. *Lit.*, jog running.

holo puni *heh* To run a lap, take a lap. *Dic., ext. mng.*

holo·puni *heh* Round trip. *Lit.*, complete circuit ride.

hō·loʻa *ham* To dispense, provide in measured quantities. Sh. *hō + loaʻa*, also Tah. *hōroʻa* [to give]. See *ʻūhōloʻa*.

hō·lua hau *kik* Sled, for snow. *Lit.*, snow sled.

homeka *kik* Land snail. *Dic.*

hō·mona *kik* Hormone. *Eng. Hōmona hoʻāʻa, hōmona hoʻoaʻa.* Rooting hormone. *ʻŌnaehana hōmona.* Endocrine system, in biology.

hona *kik* Grosbeak finch (chloridops kona). *Lit.*, name of a tree frequented by this finch. Cf. *hōpue* (dic.). See *nuku ʻekue, ʻainohu Kauō, ʻainohu Nīhoa*.

hone *kik* Syrup. *Niʻihau.* Also *malakeke*.

Hono·durasa *iʻoa* Honduras; Honduran. *Eng.*

Honua *iʻoa* Earth (the planet). *Ua haʻalele ka moku ahiao iā Honua i nehinei.* The rocket ship left Earth yesterday. *Dic.* See *pāpaʻa honua, ʻīkoi honua*.

honua *kik* Trough of a wave. *Dic.* Also *honua o ka nalu, honua o ka ʻale.* Cf. *hokua.* See *mekala honua ʻākilikai.*

Honua·iā·kea *iʻoa* Palmyra island. *Lit.,* name of Pele's canoe when travelling to Hawaiʻi.

honu pahu *kik* Box turtle.

hope hō·ʻulu·ʻulu palapala *kik* Subsummary, as in computer program. *Lit.,* behind document summary.

hope kahua *kik* Subfield, as in computer program. *Lit.,* behind field. See *kahua.*

hopena *kik* Conclusion; effect. *Dic.* See entries below and *kumu. Hoʻoholo i hopena.* To draw a conclusion. *Palapala Hōʻike Hopena Kaiapuni.* Environmental Impact Statement (EIS).

hopena *kik* Outcome; a possible result in a probability experiment, in math. *Dic., ext. mng.* See *ʻōpaʻa hopena.*

hopena ahu·wale *ham* Predictable, as the ending of a story. *Lit.,* obvious ending. *Moʻolelo hopena ahuwale.* Predictable story.

hopena holo *kik* Resolution or solution, as of a problem in a story. *Lit.,* determined solution. See *hihia.*

hope wai·hona ʻike *kik* Virtual memory, as in computer program. *Lit.,* substitute memory.

hopo hala·pohe *ʻa*̄ Threatened, as rare plants or animals. *Lit.,* anxious (lest) extinct. Also *hopo make loa, hopo nalowale loa.* Cf. *ʻane halapohe.*

hopu See *ʻai hopu. Kaha hopu.* A line written from the end of one paragraph to the beginning of the next paragraph to indicate that the two paragraphs should be combined, in proofreading.

Hopu·hopu *iʻoa* Rasalhague, a star. *Mān.* (HA).

hopuna·helu *kik* Math sentence, number sentence. Comb. *hopuna + helu.* Cf. *hopunaʻōlelo.*

hopuna·ʻō·lelo *kik* Sentence, as a grammatical unit. *Mān. Hopunaʻōlelo wehe kumuhana.* Topic sentence, as of a paragraph. Cf. *hoʻomaka.*

hoʻā *ham* To turn on, as a light, radio, TV, etc. *Mān.* Cf. *hoʻopio.*

hō·ʻae *heh* To yield, as in traffic. *Dic., ext. mng. Hōʻailona hōʻae.* Yield sign.

hō·ʻai·lona *kik* Sign, as traffic signs. *Dic., ext. mng.* Cf. *papa hoʻolaha.* See entries below. *Hōʻailona hōʻae.* Yield sign. *Hōʻailona hoʻokū.* Stop sign.

hō·ʻai·lona *kik/ham* Symbol, sign, as in math. *Dic.* To symbolize, stand for. *"Inā hoʻi he huahelu ʻokoʻa ka mea i hōʻailona ʻia e ka A, e like nō hoʻi ka hana ʻana."* Even if A symbolizes a different number, the process is the same. (Bihopa) See entry below and *pihi hōʻailona.*

hō·ʻai·lona helu *kik* Algebra. *Dic. Haʻi hōʻailona helu.* Algebraic expression.

hō·ʻai·lona mele *kik* Clef, in music. *Lit.,* song sign. *Hōʻailona mele leo kāne.* Bass clef. Also *leo kāne. Hōʻailona mele leo wahine.* Treble clef. Also *leo wahine.*

hōʻaiʻē *Kumu hōʻaiʻē.* Credit, as at a bank or store.

hō·ʻaui·kala *kik* Chromatography. *Lit.,* deviate color. See *palaholo silaka g. Hōʻauikala papa lahilahi.* Thin-layer chromatography. *Hōʻauikala pepa.* Paper chromatography. *Kiʻi hōʻauikala.* Chromatograph. *Pepa hōʻauikala.* Chromatographic paper.

hō·ʻauka *ham* To tag or strike out, in baseball. Comb. *hō- + ʻauka.* Cf. *ʻauka.*

hoʻā·hewa *ham* To impeach, i.e. formally accuse (a public official) of misconduct in office. *He mea koʻikoʻi maoli ka hana hewa a ka pelekikena e pono ai ke kū ʻo ia i ka mea i hoʻāhewa ʻia ai.* The misdeeds of the president must have been very serious if he was found guilty of the things he is being impeached for. *Trad.*

hoʻāhu *ham* To lay away, store away, accumulate. *Dic. Waihona hoʻāhu kālā.* Savings account, as in bank. See *lumi hoʻāhu, waihona hoʻāhu, waihona kālā.*

hoʻā·hua kua·hene *ham* Shield building; to build a shield (volcano). *Lit.*, pile up shields.

hoʻāka *ham* To shadow, as on computer or in typesetting. Comb. *hoʻ-* + *aka.* See *aka.*

hoʻā·kāka See *ʻaoʻao hoʻākāka.* *ʻŌlelo hoʻākāka.* Introduction, as in a book. Cf. *ʻōlelo haʻi mua.*

hoʻā·kea *ham* To extend, as text in computer word processing. *Dic., ext. mng.* Cf. *hoʻohāiki.*

hoʻāla *ham* To format, initialize, as a computer disk. *Dic., ext. mng.* Cf. *hoʻonohonoho. Hoʻāla hou.* To reformat.

hō·ʻalo *ham* To alternate, as in computer program. *Dic., ext. mng. Pihi hōʻalo* (preceded by *ke*). Alternate key.

hoʻā·mana *ham* To let, as in math problems; to assign a value or power. *E hoʻāmana ʻia ke K he 15 kōna waiwai.* Let K equal 15. *Dic., ext. mng.*

hoʻāna·kahi *ham* To unitize, in math. Comb. *hoʻ-* + *anakahi.*

hoʻāni *ham* To wave something. *Dic., ext. mng.*

hō·ʻano hou *ham* To modernize a written document using modern spelling and punctuation standards. *Lit.*, cause new style. See *hakuloli.*

hō·ʻano hou *ham* To update, as a computer program. Cf. *hoʻopuka hou loa.*

hō·ʻanuʻu *ham* To dump, in volleyball. *Niʻihau.*

hoʻā·a *ham* To enable to develop roots. Comb. *hoʻ-* + *aʻa.* Also *hoʻoaʻa. Hōmona hoʻāʻa.* Rooting hormone.

hoʻāʻo *ham* To test (for something), as in a scientific experiment. *Dic.* Cf. *hoʻāʻoamaka.* See *hāmeʻa hoʻāʻo, mīkini hoʻāʻo.*

hoʻā·o·amaka *kik* Trial, as a test in a probability experiment, in math. Comb. *hoʻāʻo* + *a* + *maka.* Cf. *hoʻāʻo.*

hoʻāʻo mua See *hōʻike hoʻāʻo mua.*

hō·ʻea·ea *ham* To aerate. Comb. *hoʻ-* + *eaea.* See *eaea.*

hoʻēhu pua *ham* To pollinate. *Lit.*, cause flower pollen. Cf. *hoʻopiʻi kaʻakepa.* See *ehu. Hōʻehu pua kaʻakepa.* To cross-pollinate.

hō·ʻeleu mō·ʻaui *ham* Catalyst, i.e. a substance which increases the rate of a chemical reaction without being permanently changed itself. *Lit.*, animate reaction. Also *ʻūmōʻauiwawe.*

hoʻēmi *kik/ham* Discount; to discount. *ʻEhia ka hoʻēmi o kēia uaki?* Whatʻs the discount on this watch? *Dic.*

hoʻēmi *ham* Discount; to discount, as a price for merchandise. *Ke loaʻa kēia kūpona iā ʻoe, he loaʻa mai ka hoʻēmi iā ʻoe ma ka hale kūʻai.* If you have this coupon you can get a discount at the store. *Dic.*

hoʻēmi i ka mā·mā holo *ham* To decelerate. *Lit.*, cause to decelerate. Cf. *emi ka māmā holo.* See also *piʻi ka māmā holo, hoʻopiʻi i ka māmā holo.*

hoʻēmi kino *ham* To diet, reduce. *Dic.* See *papaʻai.*

hoʻēmi woela *kik* Vowel reduction, in linguistics. *Lit.*, reduce vowels. See *pua woela* and entries under *woela.*

hoʻi *heh* To revert, as in computer program. *Dic., ext. mng. Hoʻi i ka mālama.* To revert to previous save.

hō·ʻio·kine *ham* To iodize. Comb. *hō-* + Eng. See *ʻiokine.*

hoʻi·hoʻi *ham* To save, in volleyball. *Niʻihau.* Also *lou.*

hoʻi·hoʻi mai *ham* To undo, as in computer program. *Lit.*, return. Cf. *hoʻokaʻawale, hoʻōki.*

hō·ʻike *kik* Display, as on computer screen. *Dic., ext. mng.* See entries below.

Māmaka Kaiao / 27

hō·‘ike *ham* To report. *Dic.* Cf. *hō‘ike ha‘i waha, hō‘ike palapala.* See entries below. *Ha‘i‘ōlelo hō‘ike.* Oral report, presented as a speech.

hō·‘ike ha‘i waha *kik* Oral report. Also *‘ōlelo hō‘ike.* Cf. *hō‘ike palapala.*

hō·‘ike honua *kik* Geography. *Dic. Nā kuhikuhina hō‘ike honua.* Geographical coordinates.

hō·‘ike hua pihi *kik* Key caps, on computer program. *Lit.,* show key letters.

hō·‘ike mana‘o *ham* To prewrite, as part of the writing process, i.e. introducing the topic through brainstorming, discussion, presentations, etc. *Lit.,* show ideas. See *kūkā ma ka pū‘ulu.*

hō·‘ike mua a‘o *kik* Pretest. *Lit.,* first-try test. Cf. *hō‘ike muli a‘o.*

hō·‘ike muli a‘o *kik* Posttest. *Lit.,* after-teaching test. Cf. *hō‘ike mua a‘o.*

hō·‘ike pala·pala *kik* Written report. *Lit.,* report (by) writing. Cf. *hō‘ike ha‘i waha.*

hō·‘ike ‘ia Given, as in a math problem.

hō·‘ike·‘ike *kik* Fair. *Dic.* Also *fea.* See entry below and *papa hō‘ike‘ike. Hō‘ike‘ike ‘epekema.* Science fair. *Hō‘ike‘ike kalana.* County Fair. *Hō‘ike‘ike moku‘āina.* State fair.

hō·‘ike·‘ike *ham* To show and tell, as in a preschool or elementary school class. *Dic., ext. mng.*

hō·‘ili·‘ili *ham* To collect. *Dic.* See *hō‘ili‘ilina.*

hō·‘ili·‘ilina *kik* Collection. Comb. *hō‘ili‘ili + -na. Hō‘ili‘ilina po‘oleka.* Stamp collection.

hō·‘ī·pale *ham* To insulate. Comb. *hō- + ‘īpale.* See *‘īpale.*

ho‘o·a‘a *ham* To enable to develop roots. *Dic.* Also *ho‘ā‘a. Hōmona ho‘oa‘a.* Rooting hormone.

hō·oia *ham* To verify, check, give proof, as for a math problem. *Dic., ext. mng.*

ho‘o·ikaika pu‘u·wai *ham* Aerobic. *Lit.,* strengthen heart. Cf. *eaea.* See *‘onilele. Hana ho‘oikaika pu‘uwai.* Aerobic activity. *‘Ai ho‘oikaika pu‘uwai.* Aerobic point.

ho‘o·ikehu *ham* To charge, as a battery. Comb. *ho‘o- + ikehu.*

ho‘o·ili *ham* To transfer, as funds in a bank account. *Dic.* See entries below.

ho‘o·ili *ham* To transplant. *Dic., ext. mng.* Cf. *ili.* See *‘anopili ho‘oili. Ho‘oili pu‘uwai.* To transplant a heart.

ho‘o·ili *ham* To download, as in computer program. *Dic., ext. mng.* Cf. *ho‘ouka.* See *mīkini ho‘oili ki‘i.*

ho‘o·ili *ham* To hand off (the ball), in football. *Ua ho‘oili aku nei ‘o ia i ke kinipōpō i ka helu 42.* He handed off the ball to number 42. *Dic., ext. mng.*

ho‘o·ilo *kik* Winter. *Dic.* See entry below and *māuiki‘iki‘i.*

ho‘o·ilo *ham* To cause to germinate, sprout. *Dic.* See *ilo, pī‘ai ho‘oilo.*

hō·‘oi·‘ene·hana *ham* To industrialize; developing, as a Third World Country. *I ka wā hō‘oi‘enehana o nā ‘āina o ‘Eulopa, kūkulu nui ‘ia nā hale wili like ‘ole he nui.* In the industrialization period of the European nations, many factories of various types were built. Comb. *hō- + ‘oi‘enehana.* Cf. *‘oi‘enehana. ‘Āina hō‘oi‘enehana.* Developing country; Third World Country.

ho‘o·uahi *ham* To smoke, as meat or fish. *Dic.*

ho‘o·uka *ham* To load, as a computer program; to install, as software. *E ho‘ouka ana wau i ka waihona ma ka PLH i hiki iā ‘oe ke ho‘oili ma kāu kamepiula.* I'm going to load the file on the BBS so that you can download it onto your computer. *Dic., ext. mng.* Cf. *ho‘oili.* See entry below.

ho‘o·uka *kik/ham* Attack, raid. *Dic. Ho‘ouka pāna‘i.* Counterattack. *Pū‘ali ho‘ouka kaua.* Marine corps.

ho‘o·ulu See entry below and *kāmāhuaola, pahu ho‘oulu meakanu.*

hoʻo·ulu pā·kuʻi *ham* To grow by grafting. *Nui nā kala like ʻole o nā pua mēlia e pua nei ma ke kumu mēlia hoʻokahi a koʻu hoa noho ma muli o kāna hoʻoulu pākuʻi ʻana mai nā kumulāʻau like ʻole mai.* Many different colored plumeria flowers are blooming one plumeria tree that belongs to my neighbor; he accomplished this by grafting from different trees. See *pākuʻi*.

hoʻo·una *ham/iʻoa* To enter, as in computer program; enter, as the enter key by the number pad on an extended computer keyboard. *E kōmi iā hoʻouna.* Press enter. See *kāhoʻi, kāhuakomo*. Lit., send. *Pihi hoʻouna* (preceded by *ke*). Enter key.

hoʻo·uʻi·uʻi *ham* To put on makeup. *Niʻihau. Aia ʻo Tita ke noho nei i mua o ke aniani me ka hoʻouʻiuʻi pū.* Tita's sitting in front of the mirror putting on makeup. Also *hoʻonaninani*.

hoʻo·hāiki *ham* To condense, as text in computer document. *Dic., ext. mng.* Cf. *hoʻākea*.

hoʻo·hā·oʻo *ham* To cure, i.e. to prepare by chemical or physical processing for keeping or use. Comb. *hoʻo- + hāoʻo.* See *hāoʻo*.

hoʻo·hau·mia See *kumu hoʻohaumia*.

hoʻo·haku·hia *ham* To invent. See *hakuhia*.

hoʻo·haliʻa maka·hiki See *puke hoʻohaliʻa makahiki*.

hoʻo·hana See entry below and *helu hoʻohana, wā hoʻohana*.

hoʻo·hana ʻāina *ham* Land use, in geography. Lit., use land. *Komikina Hoʻohana ʻĀina o ka Mokuʻāina.* State Land Use Commission.

hoʻo·hani *ham* To hint at, give a hint. *Dic. ʻŌlelo hoʻohani.* Hint.

hoʻo·hanini *ham* To dump. *Dic., ext. mng. Kalaka hoʻohanini.* Dump truck.

hoʻo·hā·popopo *ham* To decompose, putrefy. Comb. *hoʻo- + hāpopopo.* See *hāpopopo. Ka hoʻohāpopo eaea ʻana.* Aerobic decomposition/putrefaction. *Ka hoʻohāpopo eaea ʻole ʻana.* Anaerobic decomposition/putrefaction.

hoʻo·haʻa·lele *ham* To evacuate, as people from a building. Comb. *hoʻo- + haʻalele.* Cf. *haʻalele*.

hoʻo·heona *ham* To make artistic, decorate artistically. See *heona*.

hoʻo·heheʻe *ham* To dissolve (something). *Dic.*

hoʻo·heheʻe meaʻai *ham* To digest food. *Trad.* See *hoʻowali ʻai, hoʻonapele* (dic.). *ʻŌnaehana hoʻoheheʻe meaʻai.* Digestive system.

hoʻo·hele moe·ā *ham* To utilize guided imagery. Lit., cause to imagine.

hoʻo·hemo *ham* To disconnect, as in computer program. *Dic., ext. mng.* Cf. *hoʻokuʻi.* See entry below.

hoʻo·hemo *ham* To get oneself open, as for a play in basketball. *Kīloi mau ʻia ke kinipōpō iā Kaina, no ka mea, ʻeleu ʻo ia i ka hoʻohemo.* The ball always gets passed to Kaina since he's so quick to make himself open. *Dic., ext. mng.* See *hemo*.

hoʻo·heʻe·aholo *ham* To leach, i.e. subject to the action of percolating liquid. Comb. *hoʻo- + heʻeaholo.* See *heʻeaholo*.

hoʻo·hiō *ham* To tip or tilt, as a glass containing water. *Dic., ext. mng.* See entry below.

hoʻo·hiō *ham* To italicize. *E aho nō kēia huaʻōlelo ke hoʻohiō ʻia.* It would be better if this word were italicized. Lit., cause to slant. See *hiō*.

hoʻo·hiki See *palapala hoʻohiki*.

hoʻo·hilu·hilu *ham* Fancy, elegant. *Dic., ext. mng.*

hoʻo·hina *ham* To tackle (someone), in football. *Dic., ext. mng.* Also *kulaʻi.* Cf. *kūlua*.

hoʻo·hinu·hinu *ʻAila hoʻohinuhinu.* Wax, as for polishing a car.

ho‘ōho *ham* To exclaim. *Dic.* ‘*Ōlelo ho‘ōho.* Exclamatory statement; to make such a statement.

Ho‘o·hoku·ika·lani *i‘oa* Daughter of Wākea and Papa. *Dic.*

ho‘o·holo *ham* To start, as a machine; to play, as a film or tape. *Dic., ext. def.*

ho‘o·holo *ham* To control, as in computer program. *Dic., ext. mng. Ho‘oholo laulā.* General controls, as in computer program. *Papa ho‘oholo.* Control panel. *Pihi ho‘oholo* (preceded by *ke*). Control key.

ho‘o·holo i hopena *ham* To draw a conclusion. *Lit.,* determine a conclusion.

ho‘o·holo pili la‘ana *kik/ham* Inductive reasoning, i.e. generalizing from examples, in math. *Lit.,* decide concerning examples.

ho‘o·holu·nape *ham* Blowing of the wind; palm fronds and tree branches sway, and whitecaps form on the ocean, in meteorology. Comb. *ho‘o-* + *holu nape.* See *makani.*

ho‘o·hua ‘*Ōnaehana ho‘ohua.* Reproductive system, in biology.

ho‘o·hui *ham* To add, in math; to connect, as dots, etc. *Dic.* Cf. *hō‘ulu-‘ulu. Helu ho‘ohui.* Addend.

ho‘o·huli *ham* To flip, as to turn a figure to its reverse side, in math. *Dic., ext. mng.* Cf. *ho‘one‘e.*

ho‘o·huli mana‘o *ham* To induce change of opinion, persuade. *Dic., ext. mng. Ha‘i‘ōlelo ho‘ohuli mana‘o.* Persuasive speech. See *ha‘i‘ōlelo.*

ho‘o·hūpō *heh* To feign ignorance, "act dumb." *Mān.* Also *ho‘opalō.*

ho‘o·hu‘u *ham* To imply. *Ke ho‘ohu‘u mai nei ‘oe na‘u i hana?* Are you implying that I did it? (Tongan *fakahu‘u.*) See *hu‘u.*

ho‘o·kae See entries below.

ho‘o·kae kanaka *ham* Misanthropy, hatred of mankind. ‘*O ke kanaka ho‘okae kanaka, ‘a‘ohe ōna hilina‘i a he inaina ho‘i i nā kānaka.* Someone who is misanthropic is distrustful and has malice toward mankind. *Lit.,* despise mankind.

ho‘o·kae kāne *ham* Misandry, hatred of males. *Lit.,* despise men.

ho‘o·kae keka *ham* Sexism. ‘*Ike ‘ia ka ho‘okae keka ma waena o nā keka ‘elua i kekahi manawa; aia nō i ka pā‘ewa‘ewa o ka mana‘o o kekahi pū‘ulu keka i kekahi.* Sexism exists among both sexes at times; it all depends on the bias a group of one sex has toward the other sex. *Lit.,* despise (because of) gender.

ho‘o·kae wahine *ham* Misogyny, hatred of women. *Lit.,* despise women.

ho‘o·kai·aka *ham* To dilute. Comb. *ho‘o-* + *kaiaka.* Cf. *pa‘ipa‘i.*

ho‘o·kau·alewa *ham* To balance something. *Hiki iā ‘oe ke ho‘okaualewa i kēnā peni ma kou manamana lima?* Can you balance this pen on your finger? Comb. *ho‘o-* + *kaualewa.* Cf. *kaualewa.*

ho‘o·kau·apono *heh* To compensate. Comb. *ho‘o-* + *kauapono.* See *kauapono.* ‘*Ōnaehana ho‘okauapono.* Balancing mechanism, in biology.

ho‘o·kau·lihi *ham* To justify, as type in printing. Comb. *ho‘okau* + *lihi.* See *kaulihi, kauwaena. Ho‘okaulihi hema.* To justify left. *Ho‘okaulihi ‘ākau.* To justify right. *Ho‘okaulihi like.* To justify full. *Kaha ho‘okaulihi.* Two vertical lines written to the left of lines of print to indicate that the left margin should be justified, in proofreading.

ho‘o·kau·waena *ham* To center justify. *Ua ho‘okauwaena ‘ia ka ‘ao‘ao mua o kēia palapala.* The first page of this document is center justified. Comb. *ho‘o-* + *kauwaena.* Cf. *ho‘okaulihi, kauwaena.*

ho‘o·kau·weli *ham* Horror, as stories or movies. Comb. *ho‘okau* + *weli. Ki‘i‘oni‘oni ho‘okauweli.* Horror movie.

ho‘o·kahe wai *ham* To irrigate. *Lit.,* to irrigate (with) water.

ho‘o·kahua *Lauana ho‘okahua.* Settlement pattern, in geography.

ho‘o·kahuli au·puni *ham* Revolution, as against a government. *Dic. Kaua ho‘okahuli aupuni.* Revolutionary war.

ho‘o·kake ka‘ina *ham* To mix up the order, jumble. *Lit.,* to disturb (the) order.

ho‘o·kala·kala *ham* To unsmooth, as in computer program. *Lit.,* cause (to be) rough. Cf. *ho‘olaumania.*

ho‘o·kala·kupua *ham* Magic, as supernatural or enchanted. *Dic.* Cf. *pāha‘ohuna.*

ho‘okani See *hao ho‘okani, mīkini ho‘okani pāleo, mīkini lola.*

ho‘o·kā·wai·hia *ham* To hydrolyze. Comb. *ho‘-* + *kā* + *wai* + *-hia. Ka ho‘okāwaihia ‘ana.* Hydrolysis.

ho‘o·kā·wā·holo *ham* To tab, as on computer or typewriter. Comb. *ho‘o-* + *kāwāholo.* Cf. *kīpo‘o.* See *kāwāholo.*

ho‘o·ka‘a·hua *Kaha ho‘oka‘ahua.* A "straight" Z-shaped line written to indicate where two words written as one should be separated, in proofreading. Also *kaha ho‘okōā.* Cf. *kaha ka‘ahua.*

ho‘o·ka‘a·wale *ham* To separate. *Dic. Pale ho‘oka‘awale.* Buffer.

ho‘o·ka‘a·wale *ham* To put away, as in computer program. *Dic., ext. mng.* Cf. *ho‘iho‘i mai, ho‘ōki.*

ho‘o·ka‘a·wale ‘ao·‘ao *ham* Page break, as in computer program. *E ho‘oka‘awale i ka ‘ao‘ao ma hope o kēia paukū.* Insert a page break after this paragraph. *Lit.,* cause a page division.

ho‘o·ka‘a·‘ike *ham* To communicate. Comb. *ho‘o-* + *ka‘a‘ike.* See *ka‘a‘ike.*

ho‘o·kā·‘ele *ham* To bold, set in boldface type. Comb. *ho‘o-* + *kā‘ele.* See *kā‘ele.*

ho‘o·ka‘ina *ham* To put in order, sequence. Comb. *ho‘o-* + *ka‘ina.* Cf. *ho‘olauka‘i.* See entries below. *Ho‘o·ka‘ina pī‘āpā.* To alphabetize, put in alphabetical order.

ho‘o·ka‘ina maka·koho *ham* To prioritize, set priorities. Cf. *ho‘omakakoho.* See *makakoho.*

ho‘o·ka‘ina mana‘o *ham* To sequence ideas, as in a composition.

ho‘o·ka‘ina pae *ham* To rank, as from small to large. *Lit.,* put ranks in sequence. See *pae.*

ho‘o·ka‘o·hau *ham* To freeze dry. Comb. *ho‘o-* + *ka‘ohau.* See *ka‘ohau.*

ho‘o·kē See *hūkē.*

ho‘o·kele See entry below and *luna ho‘okele, pahu ho‘okele.*

ho‘o·kele wa‘a *ham* Wayfinding; to wayfind. *Lit.,* sail (a) canoe. Also *kele moana.*

ho‘o·kemua *ham* To assimilate. *He ho‘okemua ka nui o ka po‘e komone‘e o kekahi ‘āina iā lākou iho i ka noho ‘ana o kō ia ‘āina.* Most immigrants to a country assimilate themselves into the lifestyle of that counrty. Comb. *ho‘o-* + *kemua.* See *kemua.*

ho‘ōki *ham* To cancel, as in computer function. *E ho‘ōki i ke pa‘i ‘ana.* Cancel the print job. *Dic., ext. mng.* Cf. *ho‘iho‘i mai, ho‘oka‘awale. ‘Aelike ho‘ōki.* Cloture, i.e. a method of ending debate and causing an immediate vote to be taken. *Ma hope o ka paio kālaimana‘o ‘ana ‘elua lā, ‘akahi nō a kāhea ka luna o ka ‘aha kenekoa no ka ho‘ōki ‘ana.* After two days of debate the senate leader finally called for cloture.

ho‘o·kī·ki‘i *ham* To cause to tilt, as the camera when filming a movie or video production. *Dic., ext. mng.*

ho‘o·kipa See *lumi ho‘okipa.*

ho‘o·kiwi·kā *ham* To urbanize. See *kiwikā.*

ho‘o·kō See *palapala ho‘okō. Māhele mana ho‘okō.* Executive branch (of a government).

ho‘o·kō·ā *Kaha ho‘okōā*. Same as *kaha ho‘oka‘ahua*. *Pihi ho‘okōā*. Space bar, on typewriter or computer keyboard, variant term (preceded by *ke*). Also *pihi ka‘ahua*.

ho‘o·koana *ham* To set spacing, as single- or double-space on a typewriter. Comb. *ho‘o-* + *koana*. See *koana, ka‘ahua*.

ho‘o·koe *ham* To cache, as in computer function. *Ua ho‘okoe ‘ia kēia pā*. This disk has been cached. *Eng., ext. mng*. See *ahu ho‘okoe*. *Ho‘okoe pā*. To cache disks.

ho‘o·kokoke *ham* To cluster, i.e. find addends or factors that are nearly alike, in math. *Dic., ext. mng*. See entry below.

ho‘o·kokoke *ham* To zoom in, as with a movie or video camera. *Dic., ext. mng*. Cf. *ho‘olaulā*.

ho‘o·kolamu *ham* To line up vertically, place in columns. *E ho‘okolamu i kēia palapala no ka nūpepa e puka ana*. Make this document into column format for the newspaper that's coming out. Comb. *ho‘o-* + *kolamu*.

ho‘o·kolo·hua *kik/ham* Experiment; to experiment, as in a laboratory. Comb. *ho‘okolo* + *hua*. See *pahiki ho‘okolohua*. *Ho‘okolohua no*. To experiment on. *Ho‘okolohua me*. To experiment with.

ho‘o·kolo·kolo *Māhele ‘aha ho‘okolokolo*. Judicial branch (of a government). *Mana ho‘okolokolo*. Appellate jurisdiction, i.e. a court's authority to hear an appeal of a decision made by another court.

ho‘o·kolo·naio *ham* To colonize, particularly from the perspective of a people who have been colonized by a dominant culture or political entity. Comb. *ho‘o-* + *kolonaio*. Cf. *ho‘opanalā‘au*. See *kolonaio*.

ho‘o·komo *ham* To file, as files in a file cabinet. *Ho‘okomo ‘ia aku nei kōna waihona ma kōna inoa hope*. His file was filed under his last name. *Dic., ext. mng*. Also *waiho*. See entries below.

ho‘o·komo *ham* To insert, put in, as disk into computer. *Dic*. *Kaha ho‘okomo*. Caret (^, ˇ), a mark used to show where something is to be inserted, in proofreading. *Lina ho‘okomo*. A circle around a period, colon, or semicolon to show that it has been inserted.

ho‘okomo i ke kinipōpō *ham* To sink (make) a basket, in basketball. *Dic., ext. mng*.

ho‘o·komo pae *ham* To initiate. Comb. *ho‘o-* + *komo pae*. See *komo pae, hana komo pae*.

ho‘o·konu·konu *ham* To regulate, i.e. to fix the time, amount, degree or rate of something by making adjustments. (Tongan *fakatonutonu*.) *Lōku‘u ho‘okonukonu pūnao*. Thyroid gland.

ho‘o·kuene *kik/ham* Setup; to setup, as in computer program. Lit., lay out, arrange. *Ho‘okuene ‘ao‘ao*. Page setup.

ho‘o·kū·o‘o *heh* To act serious, "get serious." Comb. *ho‘o-* + *kūo‘o*.

ho‘o·kū·kohu·kohu *ham* To simulate. Comb. *ho‘o-* + *kū* + *kohukohu*. Cf. *ho‘omeamea*.

ho‘o·kū·kū *ham* To compare. *E ho‘okūkū ‘oe i kēia mau pū‘olo manakō*. *‘O ka pū‘olo hea ka mea i ‘oi aku kona kaumaha?* Compare these bags of mango. Which bag is heavier? *Dic*.

ho‘o·kū·kū *kik/heh* Tournament, in sports. *Ni‘ihau*. Also *ho‘okūkū moho*. See entries below. *Ho‘okūkū pōpa‘ipa‘i*. Volleyball tournament.

ho‘o·kū·kū hana pani·olo *kik* Rodeo. Lit., contest (of) cowboy activities.

ho‘o·kū·kū kahu·lui *kik* Championship, in sports. Lit., championship match. See *ho‘okūkū kio, ho‘okūkū moho*.

ho‘o·kū·kū kio *kik* Scrimmage, as for sports. Lit., mock warfare match. See *ho‘okūkū kahului, ho‘okūkū moho*.

hoʻo·kū·kū moho *kik* Tournament, as for sports; playoff or finals, as in sporting events. *Lit.*, champion match. Also *hoʻokūkū*. See *hoʻokūkū kio, hoʻokūkū kahului.*

ho'o·kū·launa *ham* To harmonize. *E hoʻokūlauna kākou i kēia hīmeni.* Let's harmonize this song. Comb. *hoʻo-* + *kūlauna.* See *kūlauna.*

ho'o·kulu *ham* To dink, i.e. to mishit or clip (the ball), in volleyball. *Niʻihau.* Also *paʻi lihi.* See *ʻai hele wale.*

ho'o·kū·lua *ham* To pair off. Comb. *hoʻo-* + *kūlua.* Cf. *kūlua (dic.).*

ho'o·kumu *Palapala hoʻokumu.* Charter, a document defining the organization of a city, colony, or corporate body.

ho'o·kū·pa'i *ham* To stack, as windows in computer program. Comb. *hoʻo-* + *kūpaʻi. Hoʻokūpaʻi pukaaniani.* To stack windows.

ho'o·kū·pī *ham* To reflect, as light, heat or sound. *Hoʻokūpī ʻia ka mālamalama ma ke aniani.* Light is reflected in the mirror. Comb. *hoʻo-* + *kūpī.* See *kūpī.*

ho'o·ku'e·maka *heh* To frown. *Dic.* Cf. *pūtē.*

ho'o·ku'i *ham* To crash, as cars; to bump or bang into. *Dic.* See entries below.

ho'o·ku'i *ham* To open or complete, as an electric circuit. *Dic., ext. mng.* See *ʻoki.*

ho'o·ku'i *ham* To connect, as in computer program. *E ʻoluʻolu e hoʻo-kuʻi i ka mōkema me ke kamepiula.* Please connect the modem to the computer. *Dic., ext. mng.* Cf. *hoʻohemo.* See *kuʻina.*

ho'o·ku'i *Kaha hoʻokuʻi.* A curved line (or lines) linking two letters or words to indicate that the letters or words should be joined, in proofreading.

ho'o·ku'ia *ham* To foul deliberately, in team sports such as basketball. *ʻAʻole ʻo ia i ʻūpoʻi i ke kinipōpō; hoʻokuʻia ahuwale ʻē ʻia ʻo ia e ke kūpale.* He didn't get a chance to dunk the ball; he was intentionally fouled by the defender. *Dic., ext. mng.* Cf. *kuʻia.* See entry below. *Hoʻokuʻia ahuwale.* To commit an intentional foul. *Hoʻokuʻia kīpaku.* To commit a flagrant foul.

ho'o·ku'ia *ham* Checks and balances, as in government. *Hoʻokumu ʻia ka hoʻokuʻia ma waena o nā māhele nui ʻekolu o ke aupuni pekelala o ʻAmelika i mea e makaʻala ai i ka hoʻokō ʻia o ka mana o kēlā me kēia māhele.* The system of checks and balances between the three divisions of the federal government of the U.S. was set up so that the exercise of power among each division could be checked. *Dic.*

ho'o·ku'i helu wahi *kik/ham* Mail merge, as in computer program. *Lit.*, splice addresses. Cf. *hoʻokuʻi pū.*

ho'o·ku'i·ku'i *ham* To splice, as film or video segments for movie or video production. *Dic., ext. mng. Luna hoʻokuʻikuʻi.* Assemble editor.

ho'o·ku'i pū *ham* To merge, as in computer program. *Lit.*, join together. Cf. *hoʻokuʻi helu wahi.*

ho'o·ku'u *Hoʻokuʻu i ka wai o ka lua.* To flush a toilet. *Niʻihau.* Also *hoʻo-holo i ka wai. Dic. ʻAu hoʻokuʻu wai o ka lua.* Toilet handle (preceded by *ke*).

ho'o·ku'u hua·'ine *ham* To ovulate. *Lit.*, release ovum. See *huaʻine.*

ho'o·lau·ka'i *ham* To coordinate, put in order. Comb. *hoʻo-* + *laukaʻi.* See *hoʻokaʻina, laukaʻi.*

ho'o·lau·lā *ham* To generalize; to zoom out, as with a movie or video camera. *Dic., ext. mng.* Cf. *hoʻokokoke.* See *hoʻolaulā hawewe.*

ho'o·lau·laha *ham* To publicize. *Dic. Mea hoʻolaulaha.* Publicist.

hoʻo·lau·lā hawewe *ham* To amplify, i.e. to increase the amplitude of a wave. *Lit.*, widen waves. See *laulā hawewe*.

hoʻo·lau·mania *ham* To smooth, as in computer program. *Dic., ext. mng.* Cf. *hoʻokalakala*.

hoʻo·laha See *papa hoʻolaha, Papa Lawelawe Hoʻolaha*.

hoʻo·lako ʻai·ʻē *ham* To lend, as money lent at interest. Comb. *hoʻo- + lako ʻaiʻē*. Cf. *lawe ʻaiʻē, ʻae*. See *lako ʻaiʻē*.

hoʻo·lālā See *papa hoʻolālā. Keʻena Hoʻolālā o ke Kalana*. County Planning Department. *ʻOihana Hoʻolālā a me ka Hoʻomohala Waiwai o ka Mokuʻāina ʻo Hawaiʻi*. Hawaiʻi State Department of Planning and Economic Development.

hō·ʻola·lau manaʻo *ham* To cause hallucination. Comb. *hō- + ʻolalau + manaʻo*. Cf. *manaʻo ʻolalau* (dic.). *Mea hōʻolalau manaʻo*. Hallucinogen.

hoʻo·lā·lani *ham* To align, as type in computer program. *E hoʻolālani i nā kinona ma ʻekolu kolamu a me ʻekolu lālani*. Align the shapes in three columns and three rows. *Dic., ext. mng. Kaha hoʻolālani*. Horizontal lines written above and below a word or words to indicate that they should be written or printed straight, in proofreading.

hoʻo·lana *Manehu hoʻolana*. Buoyant force, i.e. the upward force of a fluid on an object in it.

hoʻō·lapa *ham* To cause to blast off, as a rocket; to launch, as a spaceship. Comb. *ho- + ʻōlapa*. Cf. *ʻōlapa. Kahua hoʻōlapa*. Launch pad.

hoʻo·lawe *ham* Subtraction; to subtract, in math. *Dic.* Cf. *lawe*.

hō·ʻole *Laʻana hōʻole*. Counterexample.

hoʻo·lei See *pana hoʻolei*.

hoʻo·lei·alewa *ham* To juggle. *Lit.*, toss as floating.

hoʻo·lele See *mīkini hoʻolele kiʻiaka, mīkini hoʻolele kiʻiʻoniʻoni, pākū hoʻolele kiʻi, pahu hoʻolele leo*.

hoʻo·like *ham* Associative, in math. *Dic., ext. mng. ʻAnopili hoʻolike*. Associative property.

hoʻo·like·like *ham* To match, as in game of concentration. *Dic., ext. mng.*

hoʻo·liliu·ewe *ham* To engineer genetically. Comb. *hoʻo- + liliuewe*. See *liliuewe. Ka hoʻoliliuewe ʻana*. Genetic engineering.

hoʻo·liliu·welo *heh* To adapt biologically. Comb. *hoʻo- + liliuwelo. Malele hoʻoliliuwelo*. Adaptive radiation.

hoʻo·lilo *ham* To change something into a different form or product. *Ua hoʻolilo ke keiki i ka ʻili lāʻau i pepa*. The child changed the bark into paper. *Dic., ext. mng.*

hoʻo·lohe *Hālāwai hoʻolohe*. Hearing, i.e. a time for presenting official testimony or argument. Also *ʻaha hoʻolohe*.

hō·ʻolo·keʻa *ham* To outline, as a summary of topics and subtopics using letters and numbers in headings. Comb. *hō- + ʻolokeʻa*. See *ʻolokeʻa*.

hoʻo·loli *ham* To edit, as on a computer. *Dic., ext. mng.* See *pākuʻi hoʻololi* and entries under *hoʻoponopono*.

hō·ʻolu ea See *mīkini hōʻolu ea*.

hoʻo·lulu See *lumi hoʻolulu*.

hoʻo·lū·maua *ham* To fertilize, as an egg. *Hoʻolūmaua ʻia nā kowaū a ka ʻoʻopu wahine e ke kāne*. The female ʻoʻopu's eggs are fertilized by a male. Comb. *hoʻo- + lūmaua*. See *lūmaua*.

hoʻo·luʻu *Palai hoʻoluʻu*. To deep-fry.

hoʻo·mai·kaʻi *ham* To praise. *Dic.* Cf. *hanohano. Me ka hoʻomaikaʻi*. With honors, as when graduating from a college or university. *Me ka hoʻomaikaʻi nui*. With high honors.

hoʻo·mau·lia *ham* To calculate. Comb. *hoʻomau* (to make secure) + *-lia*. Also *huli a loaʻa, huli*.

ho‘o·maha *kik* Intermission. *Dic., ext. mng. Ho‘omaha hapalua.* Halftime, as in sports or games. *Manawa ho‘omaha.* Time out, in team sports such as volleyball.

ho‘o·mahaka *ham* To trace, as a picture. *Ni‘ihau,* from *māka.*

ho‘o·mā·hele *ham* To build, in math. *E ho‘omāhele i kēia ha‘i hō‘ailona helu.* Build this algebraic expression (i.e. by showing its separate steps). *Dic., ext. mng.* Cf. *ho‘omakala.*

ho‘o·mahola *ham* To expand or explode, as a file in computer program. *E ho‘omahola i kēia waihona.* Expand this file. To extend, as a math problem which can be extended into other similar problems or situations. *E ho‘omahola a‘e i kēia polopolema ma ka haku ‘ana i kekahi mau polopolema ‘ano like.* Extend this problem by making up some similar problems. Comb. *ho‘o- + mahola.* See *mahola, ‘opi, ‘opihia.*

ho‘o·maka *ham* To begin, start, as a computer program. *Dic.* See *ha‘alele; hopuna‘ōlelo wehe kumuhana, kino, pau. Ka ho‘omaka ‘ana.* Opening, as of a story.

ho‘o·maka·koho *ham* To make something a priority. Comb. *ho‘o- + makakoho.* Cf. *ho‘oka‘ina makakoho.* See *makakoho.*

ho‘o·makala *ham* To undo, in math. *Ho‘omakala nā hana ho‘omākalakala huli hope kekahi i kekahi.* Inverse operations undo each other. *Dic.* Cf. *ho‘omāhele.*

ho‘o·mā·kala·kala *ham* To solve; to decode. *Dic., new mng.* Also *hana a loa‘a ka hā‘ina.* Cf. *ho‘oponopono pilikia.* See *mākalakala. Ho‘omākalakala i ka polopolema.* To solve a problem. *Hana ho‘omākalakala.* Operation. *Hana ho‘omākalakala huli hope.* Inverse operation. *Ka‘ina ho‘omākalakala.* Order of operations.

ho‘o·make·‘aka Humorous. *Dic., ext. mng., sp. var. Puke ho‘omake‘aka.* Humorous book, in literature.

ho‘o·mā·lama·lama *ham* To light, as a set for a movie or video production. *Luna ho‘omālamalama.* Lighting director.

ho‘o·malele *ham* To distribute, as in delivering or making publications available to the public. *Dic., ext. mng.* Cf. *kāka‘ahi.*

ho‘o·mā·lō *ham* To stretch, as for warming up before exercise. *E aho ‘oe e ho‘omālō ma mua o ka ho‘okūkū i ‘ole ai e huki ke a‘a.* You'd better stretch before the game so that you don't pull a muscle. *Dic., ext. mng. Ho‘omālō ‘ā‘ī.* Neck stretches, i.e. a warm-up exercise for sports such as volleyball; also to do this exercise.

ho‘o·malu See entries below and *‘āina ho‘omalu. ‘Ōnaehana Ho‘omalu ‘Āina Kūlohelohe.* Natural Areas Reserves System (NARS).

ho‘o·mālū *Lā‘au ho‘omālū.* Barbiturate.

ho‘o·malu lawai‘a a me ka hahai holo·holona *ham* Fish and game management; to manage fish and game. *Lit.,* protect fishing and animal hunting.

ho‘o·malule *heh* To molt, as a crab its shell. *Dic.* Cf. *māunu.*

ho‘o·malu ma‘i *ham* Quarantine. *Ho‘omalu ma‘i ‘ia nā holoholona i lawe ‘ia mai i Hawai‘i nei mai nā ‘āina ‘ē mai no kekahi kōā o ka manawa.* Animals brought to Hawai‘i from other lands are put in quarantine for a period of time. *Dic. Hale ho‘omalu ma‘i.* Quarantine station.

ho‘o·mana akua kahi *kik* Monotheism; monotheistic. *Ho‘okumu ‘ia nā ho‘omana Mohameka, Iudaio, a me ke Kalikiano ma luna o ke kumu a‘o o ka ho‘omana akua kahi.* The Muslim, Jewish, and Christian religions are based upon the principle of monotheism. *Lit.,* religion (with) only one god. Cf. *ho‘omana akua lehulehu.*

hoʻo·mana akua lehu·lehu *kik* Polytheism; polytheistic. *Ma ka hoʻomana akua lehulehu o ka nui o nā lāhui Polenekia, mālama nui ʻia kekahi akua ma mua o kekahi.* In the polytheistic religions among most Polynesian people, some gods are venerated more so than other gods. *Lit.,* religion (with) numerous gods. Cf. *hoʻomana akua kahi.*

hoʻo·mā·nalo wai kai *kik* To desalinate, desalinize salty water. *Lit.,* remove saltiness (of) sea water.

hoʻo·mā·neʻo·neʻo *ham* To tickle. *Dic.*

hoʻo·maʻa *ham* To adapt to. *Dic.* See *maʻa.*

hoʻo·maʻaka *ham* To capitalize (a letter of the alphabet). Comb. *hoʻo-* + *maʻaka.* See *hoʻonaʻinaʻi. Kaha hoʻomaʻaka.* Three lines drawn under a letter to indicate that the letter is to be capitalized, in proofreading.

hoʻo·maʻa·lahi *ham* To simplify, as in a math problem. Comb. *hoʻo-* + *maʻalahi.*

hoʻo·maʻa·ma·ʻa *ham* To practice. *Dic. Puke hoʻomaʻamaʻa haʻawina, puke hoʻomaʻamaʻa.* Practice book.

hoʻo·maʻe·maʻe hale See *lāʻau hoʻomaʻemaʻe hale.*

hoʻo·mā·ʻe·ele *ham* To anesthetize. Redup. of *hoʻomāʻele. Lāʻau hoʻomāʻeʻele.* Anesthetic.

hoʻo·mea·mea *kik/ham* Simulation, in math. *Dic., ext. mng.* Cf. *hoʻokūkohukohu.*

hoʻo·mehana Honua *ham* Global warming, greenhouse effect. *Lit.,* warm Earth.

hoʻo·meheu *ham* To outline, as type on computer or in typesetting. Comb. *hoʻo-* + *meheu.* Cf. *mahaka.* See *meheu.*

hoʻo·mī·kā *ham* To pressurize. Comb. *hoʻo-* + *mīkā. Hoʻomīkā ʻia.* Pressurized.

hoʻo·miki uila *Lapaʻau hoʻomiki uila.* Shock therapy.

hoʻo·moana *heh* To camp. *Dic.* Cf. *ʻāpoʻe. Kahua hoʻomoana.* Campground. *Kaʻa hoʻomoana.* Camper; camping vehicle.

hoʻo·moe *ham* To incubate, hatch (eggs). *Niʻihau. Mīkini hoʻomoe hua.* Incubator (for eggs). See *kanaka hoʻomoe paipu.*

hoʻo·moe·ā *ham* To imagine deliberately. *E hoʻāʻo ʻoe e hoʻomoeā he ʻelepani ʻoe.* Try to imagine that you're an elephant. Cf. *moeā.*

hoʻo·mohala wai·wai *ham* Economic development. *I ka wā o ka pupū o ka mohala ʻana o ka hoʻokele waiwai o ka Mokuʻāina, pono e ʻimi i nā ʻano like ʻole o ka hoʻomohala waiwai ʻana.* Whenever the State economic growth is weak, other types of economic development must be sought. *Lit.,* develop wealth. *ʻOihana Hoʻolālā a me ka Hoʻomohala Waiwai o ka Mokuʻāina ʻo Hawaiʻi.* Hawaiʻi State Department of Planning and Economic Development.

hoʻo·momona *ham* To fertilize. *Dic.* Cf. *kīpulu. Mea hoʻomomona lepo.* Fertilizer. *Mea hoʻomomona lepo kāʻokoʻa.* Complete fertilizer, i.e. fertilizer which contains the six necessary elements for plant growth.

hō·ʻomo·ʻomo *ham* To model, mold or shape, as clay. *Dic., ext. def.*

hoʻo·nā *ham* To settle, as a claim. *Dic. ʻAha hoʻonā ʻāina.* Land court. *ʻŌnaehana hoʻonā ʻāina.* Land registration system.

hoʻo·nalo·peʻe *ham* To camouflage. Comb. *hoʻo-* + *nalo* + *peʻe.* See *nalopeʻe.*

hoʻo·nanā *Lele hoʻonanā.* Aggression, as a threat of attack by one country upon another. Cf. *lele kaua.*

hoʻo·nanea *ʻOihana o nā Pāka a me nā Hana Hoʻonanea.* Department of Parks and Recreation.

hoʻo·nani·nani *ham* To put on makeup. *Niʻihau.* Also *hoʻouʻiuʻi.*

hoʻo·naʻi·au *ham* To add special effects. Comb. *hoʻo-* + *naʻiau.* Usu. *hoʻonaʻiau i ka hiʻohiʻona.* See *naʻiau, hiʻohiʻona naʻiau.*

hoʻo·naʻi·naʻi *ham* To change (a letter of the alphabet) from capital to lower case. Comb. *hoʻo-* + *naʻinaʻi.* See *hoʻomaʻaka. Kaha hoʻonaʻinaʻi.* A line drawn diagonally through a capital letter to indicate that the letter is to be written in lower case, in proofreading.

hoʻo·nco ʻāina ulu·lāʻau *ham* Deforestation; to deforest.

hoʻo·neʻe *ham* To move, as files in computer program. *Dic.* See entry below. *Kaha hoʻoneʻe.* A circle around a word or words with an arrow going from the words to the place where they are to be moved, in proofreading.

hoʻo·neʻe *ham* To slide, without flipping or turning, as a geometric figure, in math. *Dic., ext. mng.* Cf. *hoʻohuli.*

hoʻo·noho *ham* To set up, as printer specifications for computer. *Dic., ext. mng.*

hoʻo·noho kū·ana helu *ham* To rename, in math. *Lit.,* arrange place value.

hoʻo·noho·noho *ham* To format, as a document in a computer program. *Dic., ext. mng.* Cf. *hoʻonohonohona, hoʻāla.*

hoʻo·noho·nohona *kik* Format, as in computer program. Comb. *hoʻonohonoho* + *-na.* Cf. *hoʻonohonoho. Hoʻonohonohona pilikino.* Custom format.

hoʻo·nonia·kahi *ham* To integrate, i.e. incorporate (parts) into a whole. *He noniakahi kekahi mau polokalama kamepiula ma ka hoʻononiakahi pū ʻana i nā hana kikokiko palapala me ka hōkeo ʻikepili, a me kekahi mau ʻano o ka lako polokalamu pū kekahi.* Some computer programs are integrated by integrating word processing functions together with database and other software functions. Comb. *hoʻo-* + *noniakahi.* See *noniakahi.*

hō·ʻono·ʻono *ham* To make tasty. *Dic. Mea hōʻonoʻono.* Flavoring.

hoʻo·nui *ham* Multiplication; to multiply. *Dic.* See entries below and *helu hoʻonui kemikala. Kaha hoʻonui.* Multiplication sign. *ʻAnopili ʻole o ka hoʻonui.* Zero property of multiplication (preceded by *ke*).

hoʻo·nui leo See *pahu hoʻonui leo.*

hoʻo·nui pā·anuʻu *ham* Factorial, in math. Comb. *hoʻonui* + *pā* + *ʻanuʻu. ʻEono hoʻonui pāʻanuʻu.* Six factorial (6!).

hoʻo·nui ʻike *ham* Enrichment; to enrich, i.e. to increase knowledge. *Lit.,* increase knowledge. *Puke hoʻonui ʻike.* Enrichment book, challenge book.

hoʻo·pai·ola *ham* To enrich, i.e. to improve the nutritive value of something. Comb. *hoʻo-* + *paiola. Hoʻopaiola ʻia.* Enriched.

hoʻo·pā uila *ham* To utilize the process of electrolysis. See *pā uila.*

hoʻo·pau·pili·kia See *lumi hoʻopaupilikia.*

hoʻo·pahemo *ham* To take off line, as a computer system. *Na ka luna pūnaewele i hoʻopahemo i ka ʻōnaehana i hiki iā ia ke hoʻouka i kekahi mau lako polokalamu hou ma luna o ka pūnaewele.* The system was taken off-line so that the network supervisor could install some new software onto the network. Comb. *hoʻo-* + *pahemo.* Cf. *hoʻopaʻeʻe.* See *pahemo.*

hoʻo·paheʻe See *kele hoʻopaheʻe.*

hoʻo·pā·hiʻa *ham* Touch pass, in basketball; to make such a pass. *Hoʻopāhiʻa ʻia aku nei ke kinipōpō e Nalu iā Piko, a laila, iā Kekua.* The ball was touch passed by Nalu to Piko, and then to Kekua. Comb. *hoʻo-* + *pāhiʻa.*

hoʻo·palai See *kīloi hoʻopalai.*

hoʻo·pale kā·kau *ham* To write protect, as a computer file or disk. *Ua hoʻopale kākau ʻia kēia pā e aʻu.* This disk has been write protected by me. *Lit.,* ward off writing. *Hoʻopale kākau ʻia.* Write protected.

hoʻo·palō *heh* To feign ignorance, "act dumb." *Dic.* Also *hoʻohūpō.*

hoʻo·pana·lā·ʻau *ham* To colonize, as a land by either people, animals or plants. Comb. *hoʻo-* + *panalāʻau.* Cf. *hoʻokolonaio.*

hoʻo·panoa *heh* Desertification, i.e. the processes by which an area becomes a desert, in geography. *Dic., ext. mng.*

hoʻo·papā hohonu *ham* To measure depth, as in the ocean. *Lit.,* to cause echoes in depths. See *hawewe kani.*

hoʻo·papa·kū *ham* To make vertical. Comb. *hoʻo-* + *papakū.* See *papakū.*

hoʻo·papaʻa *ham* To backup, as a file in computer program. *E hoʻopapaʻa i kēia waihona.* Backup this file. Comb. *hoʻo-* + *papaʻa.*

hoʻo·paʻa *ham* To set, as margins or tabs on computer file or typewriter. *E hoʻopaʻa i nā kāwāholo ma kēlā me kēia ʻumi kaʻahua.* Set the tabs every ten spaces. *Dic., ext. mng.* See entries below. *Hoʻopaʻa i nā lihi.* To set the margins. *Hoʻopaʻa i nā kāwāholo.* To set the tabs.

hoʻo·paʻa *ham* To record, as on a cassette. *Dic.* Also *ʻoki. Mīkini hoʻopaʻa leo.* Tape recorder.

hoʻo·paʻa *ham* To turn off, as water. *Mān. Hoʻopaʻa i ke kī wai.* To turn off the water.

hoʻo·paʻa·hau *ham* To freeze (something). Sh. *hoʻopaʻa i ka hau.* Cf. *paʻahau.*

hoʻo·paʻa moʻo·helu kā·lā To make a budget. *E hoʻopaʻa kākou i moʻohelu kālā no ka pāʻina Kalikimaka.* Let's make a budget for the Christmas party. *Lit.,* fix (a) budget.

hoʻo·paʻa·pū·hia *ham* To concentrate, i.e. make less dilute. Cf. *hoʻokaiaka.* See *paʻapūhia.*

hoʻo·paʻeʻe To bring on line, as a computer system. *Ua hoʻopaʻeʻe ʻia maila ka ʻōnaehna ma hope o ka hoʻoponopono ʻia e ka luna pūnaewele.* The system was brought on-line after the network supervisor fixed the problem. Comb. *hoʻo-* + *paʻeʻe.* Cf. *hoʻopahemo.* See *paʻeʻe.*

hoʻo·pio *ham* To turn off, as a light, radio, TV, etc. *Mān.* Cf. *hoʻā.*

hoʻo·piha *kik* Washer, as used in plumbing. *Niʻihau.* Also *pihi hoʻopiha.* See entries below.

hoʻo·piha kaha *ham* To supplement, as angles, in math. *Lit.,* fill (a) line. Cf. *hoʻopiha kūpono. Nā huina hoʻopiha kaha.* Supplementary angles, i.e. two angles whose measures have a sum of 180°.

hoʻo·piha kū·pono *ham* To complement, as angles, in math. *Lit.,* fill right (angle). Cf. *hoʻopiha kaha. Nā huina hoʻopiha kūpono.* Complementary angles, i.e. two angles whose measures have a sum of 90°.

hoʻo·pī·ka·ʻo *ham* To dehydrate (something). *Hoʻopīkaʻo ʻia nā ʻāpana maiʻa ma loko o ka mīkini hoʻopīkaʻo.* Banana pieces are dehydrated in the dehydrating machine. Comb. *hoʻo-* + *pīkaʻo.* See *pīkaʻo.*

hoʻo·pili *ham* To match, as one thing to its counterpart by drawing a line. *Dic., ext. mng.*

hoʻo·pili·pili *ham* Imitation. *Waiū hoʻopilipili.* Imitation milk.

hoʻo·pili pū *ham* To aggregate, i.e. bind together *Lit.,* cause to unite.

hoʻo·piʻi *ham* To breed, impregnate. *Dic.* Cf. *haʻakipu.* See entries below and *pākēneka hoʻopiʻi.*

ho‘o·pi‘i *'Aha pane ho'opi'i.* Arraignment, i.e. a court hearing in which a defendant is formally charged with a crime and enters a plea of guilty or not guilty. *I kēia lā, ho'opi'i 'ia aku nei ke kanaka i hopu 'ia e pōā ana i ka panakō.* The man who was caught robbing the bank was arraigned today. See *ho'opi'i kū'ē.*

ho‘o·pi‘i i ka māmā holo *ham* To accelerate. *Lit.*, cause to accelerate. Cf. *pi'i ka māmā holo.* See also *emi ka māmā holo, ho'ēmi i ka māmā holo.*

ho‘o·pi‘i i ke koi pohō *ham* To make a claim for damages, as to an insurance company. See *koi pohō.*

ho‘o·pi‘i kaha *ham* Bonus, extra credit, as a class assignment or question on a quiz. *Lit.*, raise grade. Also *'ai keu. Nīnau ho'opi'i kaha.* Bonus question, extra credit question.

ho‘o·pi‘i ka‘a·kepa *ham* To crossbreed. *Lit.*, breed diagonally. Cf. *ho'ēhu pua ka'akepa.*

ho‘o·pi‘i kū·‘ē *ham* To appeal, i.e. ask a higher court to review a decision made by a lower court. *Ua ho'opane'e 'ia ka mana'o ho'oholo a ka luna ho'okolokolo ma kahi o ka ho'opi'i kū'ē 'ia mai o kōna mana'o e ka mea i ho'āhewa 'ia.* The judge's decision is suspended pending an appeal of his decision by the accused. *Lit.*, appeal (in) opposition. See *'aha pane ho'opi'i.*

ho‘o·pono·pono See entries below. *Pukaaniani ho'oponopono.* Edit screen, in computer program.

ho‘o·pono·pono kahua *ham* To decorate sets, as for a movie or video production. *Mea ho'oponopono kahua.* Set decorator.

ho‘o·pono·pono kani *ham* To edit sound, as for a movie or video production. Cf. *kani keaka. Luna ho'oponopono kani.* Sound editor.

ho‘o·pono·pono ki‘i·‘oni·‘oni *ham* To edit, as movies or movie productions. *Lit.*, edit movies. See *ho'oponopono kani, ho'oponopono wikiō. Hale ho'oponopono ki'i'oni'oni.* Editing facility (for movies).

ho‘o·pono·pono lau·oho *ham* To style hair, as for a play, movie or video production. *Mea ho'oponopono lauoho.* Hair stylist.

ho‘o·pono·pono pili·kia *ham* To solve a problem, i.e. resolve a difficulty. Cf. *huli hā'ina, 'imi hā'ina.* See *ho'omākalakala.*

ho‘o·pono·pono wiki·ō *ham* To edit, as videos or video productions. *Lit.*, edit videos. See *ho'oponopono kani, ho'oponopono ki'i'oni'oni. Hale ho'oponopono wikiō.* Editing facility (for videos).

ho‘o·pō·‘ai·apuni *ham* To recycle. Comb. *ho'o-* + *pō'aiapuni.* See *pō'aiapuni.*

ho‘o·pū·hala·lū *ham* To inflate, fill with air. *Dic.* Also *puhi a piha.* See *'ananu'u.*

ho‘o·puka *ham* To produce, as a movie or video production. *Dic., ext. mng.* See *kuhikuhi, manakia ho'opuka, luna 'enehana. Luna ho'opuka.* Producer. *Luna ho'opuka papahana.* Project producer.

ho‘o·puka *ham* To publish. *Dic., ext. mng.* See *ho'opuka hou loa, ho'opuka ho'oponopono 'ia.*

ho‘o·puka hou loa *kik/ham* An update, as of a computer program. *Lit.*, newest issue. Cf. *ho'opuka ho'oponopono 'ia, hō'ano hou.*

ho‘o·puka ho‘o·pono·pono ‘ia *kik/ham* Interim or maintenance release, as of a computer program. *Lit.*, cause regulated emergence.

ho‘o·puka·puka *ham* To invest. *Dic. Kea ho'opukapuka.* Stock, as in the stock market. *Mea ho'opukapuka kālā.* Investment. Also *ho'opukapuka.*

ho‘o·pū·nana *heh* To nest. *Dic. Kau ho'opūnana.* Nesting season.

ho·o·pū·ʻulu *ham* To group, in math; to form or break into groups. *Dic., ext. mng.* See *pūʻulu*. *ʻAnopili hoʻopūʻulu*. Grouping property.

ho·o·wela wai See *pahu hoʻowela wai*.

hō·ʻulu·ʻulu *kik/ham* Addition, in math. *Dic.* Cf. *hoʻohui*.

hō·ʻulu·ʻulu manaʻo *kik/ham* Summary; to summarize. *Dic.*

hō·ʻulu·ʻulu pala·pala *kik* Document summary, as in computer program. *E hōʻike ʻia ka mea nānā i kikokiko ma ka hōʻuluʻulu palapala.* The typist will be shown in the document summary. See *hope hōʻuluʻulu palapala*.

hoʻūnu·kā *ham* To pave with asphalt. See *unukā, kīpapa* (dic.).

hū *kik* Yeast, baking powder. *Dic., mān.* See *pauka koka*.

hū *kik* Overflow error, as on a calculator display. *Lit.*, overflow.

hū See *manu hū*.

hua *kik* Corm, as of taro. *Trad.* See entries below and *ʻauhua*.

hua *kik* Sound segment, in linguistics. *Dic., ext. mng.*

hua·aka *kik* Palindrome, a word or sentence that reads the same backward as forward. *Lit.*, reflection word.

hua·aʻa *kik* Tuber. Comb. *hua + aʻa*.

hua inoa *kik* Initial. *Lit.*, name letter. Cf. *hua hōʻailona*. See *pūlima hua*.

hua·haka·lama *kik* Syllabary symbol, in linguistics. Comb. *hua + hakalama*. See *hakalama*.

hua·hana *kik* Product, i.e. something that has been produced or manufactured. *Lit.*, fruit (of) labor. *Luna huahana.* Product manager.

hua·helu *kik* Figure or number (the character), numeral. *Dic.* See *helu Loma*.

hua hō·kū *kik* Starfruit.

hua hope hā·ʻule *kik* Apocope, in linguistics. *Lit.*, drop word ending.

hua hō·ʻai·lona *kik* Abbreviation. *Dic.* Cf. *hua inoa*.

hua·kani *kik* Tone, in music. *Dic., sp. var.*

hua kanu *kik* Bulb, as of a lily or tulip. *Dic. ʻŌmaka hua kanu.* Bulb tip.

hua·kaʻi maka·hiʻo *kik/heh* Excursion, field trip. *Lit.*, trip for exploring. Also *huakaʻi*.

hua·kō *kik* Fructose. *He mea hoʻomomona ka huakō ma loko o ka wai meli a me nā ʻano huaʻai he nui nō.* Fructose is a sweetener found in honey and many kinds of fruits. Comb. *hua + kō*. Cf. *monakō*.

hua komo *kik* Epenthetic sound, in linguistics. *Lit.*, sound (which) enters.

hua·komo *kik* Input, as in computer program. Comb. *hua + komo*. Cf. *huapuka*. See *kāhuakomo*. *Hāmeʻa huakomo.* Input device, as on a computer.

hua kumu ʻoka *kik* Acorn. *Lit.*, oak tree seed. Also *ʻēkona*.

hua·lau *kik* Variable, a symbol that can stand for any quantitative value, in math. *Lit.*, many numbers.

hua·leo *kik* Phoneme, in linguistics. *Lit.*, language segment. See *puana hualeo, puanaleo*.

hua·loaʻa *kik* Product, in multiplication. *Dic. Hualoaʻa kaupeʻa.* Cross product.

hua maʻaka *kik* Upper case (capital) letter. Comb. *hua + maʻaka* (*Rarotongan*, big). Cf. *hua naʻinaʻi*.

hua·mele *kik* Note, on music staff. *Dic., sp. var.* See *kī, kōkua huamele*. *Huamele laina.* Line note.

hua naʻi·naʻi *kik* Lower case (small) letter. Comb. *hua + naʻinaʻi* (*Tah.*, small). Cf. *hua maʻaka*.

hua·neʻe *kik* Anagram. Comb. *hua + neʻe*.

hua·pala·pala *kik* Letter (of the alphabet). *Dic., sp. var.*

hua pa‘i *kik* Character, as of type in computer program. Usu. *hua*. *‘A‘ole pa‘i kēia mīkini pa‘i i kekahi mau hua pa‘i*. This printer doesn't print certain characters. *Lit.*, print letter.

hua·puka *kik* Output, as in computer program. Comb. *hua* + *puka*. Cf. *huakomo*. See *kāhuapuka*.

hua waina malo‘o *kik* Raisin. *Lit.*, dry grape.

hua·‘ai kiwi *kik* Kiwi fruit. Also *lahomāpū*.

hua·‘āne *kik* Spermatozoon, sperm. Comb. *hua* + *-‘āne*. Cf. *hua‘ine*. See *keakea* (dic.).

hua‘i *ham* To open, as an imu. *Hua‘i i ka imu*. To open an imu. *Dic.* Cf. *ku‘i i ka imu*.

hua·‘ine *kik* Ovum, in biology. Comb. *hua* + *-‘ine*. Cf. *hua‘āne*. *Ho‘oku‘u hua‘ine*. To ovulate. *Lōkino hua‘ine*. Ovary.

hua·‘ōlelo *kik* Word. *Dic., sp. var.* See entries below. *Mākau hua‘ōlelo*. Word skill.

hua·‘ōlelo mana‘o like *kik* Synonym. *Lit.*, word (with) same meaning.

hua·‘ōlelo mana‘o ‘ē·ko‘a *kik* Antonym. *Lit.*, word (with) opposite meaning.

hua·‘ōlelo puana like *kik* Homonym. *Lit.*, word (with) same pronunciation.

huelo·pō·poki *kik* Cattail.

huē·woela *kik* Diphthong. Comb. *hue* + *woela*.

hui *heh* To intersect, as lines on a grid, in math. *Dic., ext. mng.* See entries below and *kaha huina*.

hui *kik* Conference, in sports. *Dic., ext. mng.* Cf. *‘aha kūkā*. See *Hui Pōpeku Aupuni, Hui Pōpeku ‘Amelika, ku‘ikahi*.

hui *Nā Hui Nui ‘Elima*. The Big Five, i.e. the five corporations that controlled most of the sugar industry in Hawai‘i.

hui·hui hō·kū *kik* Constellation. *Lit.*, star constellation.

hui·huina *kik* Combination, mixture; composite. *‘Ehia huihuina o kēia mau waiho‘olu‘u i hiki ai ke loa‘a?* How many possible combinations do these colors have? Comb. *huihui* + *-na*. *Hāpana huihuina*. Composite sample.

huika *kik* Wheat. *Dic.* See entries under *palaoa*. *Huika piha*. Whole wheat. *Pua huika*. Straw.

huika See entries under *palaoa*.

hui·kaina *kik* Set, i.e. a collection of like items or elements. Comb. *hui* + *kaina*, kind. Cf. *‘ōpa‘a*.

hui kau·pe‘a *kik/heh* The intersection of two or more lines, all of which go through the intersection point, in math; to intersect thus. *Lit.*, crossed meeting. Cf. *hui po‘o*.

hui kea See *waiho‘olu‘u hui kea*.

hui·ku‘i *‘a‘* Integrated, as computer software. Comb. *hui* + *ku‘i*.

hui ku‘i·kahi *kik/heh* Alliance, i.e. a group of nations that have agreed to help or protect each other; to form such an alliance. *Ke komo nei nā aupuni o Palani a me ‘Enelani i ka hui ku‘ikahi e ho‘opau ai i ke kaua ma ka Hikina Waena*. France and England are joining the alliance to end the war in the Middle East. *Lit.*, alliance (formed by) treaty.

huila *kik* Wheel. *Dic.* See entry below and *paepae komo huila*. *Huila paiki·kala*. Bicycle wheel.

huila makani *kik* Windmill. *Ni‘ihau. Uila huila makani*. Wind-generated electricity.

huina *kik* Angle, in math. *Dic.* See entries below and *ho‘opiha kaha, ho‘opiha kūpono, kaha huina*. *Huina peleleu*. Obtuse angle. *Huina ‘oi*. Acute angle.

huina·iwa *kik* Nonagon, i.e. a nine-sided polygon. Comb. *huina* + *iwa*.

huina·ono *kik* Hexagon. *Dic.*

Māmaka Kaiao / 41

huina·hā *kik* Quadrilateral. *Dic.* See entries below.

huina·hā hiō like *kik* Rhombus. *Dic.* + *like.*

huina·hā like *kik* Square (geometric shape). *Dic.*

huina·hā lō·'ihi *kik* Rectangle. *Lit.,* long quadrilateral. *Huinahā lō'ihi kula.* Golden rectangle, i.e. a rectangle in which the ratio of the width to the length is the same as that of the length to the sum of the width plus the length. *'Ōpaka huinahā lō'ihi.* Rectangular prism.

huina·hā pa'a pili·pā *kik* Trapezoid. *Lit.,* quadrilateral (with one) pair (of) parallel (sides). Cf. *huinahā pilipā.*

huina·hā pili·pā *kik* Parallelogram. *Lit.,* parallel quadrilateral. Cf. *huinahā pa'a pilipā.*

huina·hiku *kik* Heptagon, i.e. a seven-sided polygon. *Dic.*

huina kaha *kik* Straight angle, i.e. an angle that has a measure of 180°, in math. *Lit.,* line angle.

huina ke'a *kik* Intersection of two lines on a grid. *Lit.,* cross junction. Also *huina.* Cf. *kiko huina. Nā kaha huina.* Intersecting lines.

huina kiko·waena *kik* Central angle, an angle that has its vertex at the center of a circle, in math. *Lit.,* center angle.

huina·kolu *kik* Triangle. *Dic. Huinakolu like.* Equilateral triangle. *Huinakolu peleleu.* Obtuse triangle. *Huinakolu 'elua 'ao'ao like.* Isosceles triangle. *Huinakolu 'ao'ao like 'ole.* Scalene triangle. *Huinakolu 'oi.* Acute triangle.

huina kū·pī *kik* Angle of reflection, i.e. the angle between a reflected wave and the normal to the barrier from which it is reflected. *Lit.,* reflecting angle. Cf. *huina papā.*

huina kū·pono *kik* Right angle. *Lit.,* perpendicular angle. *Ana huina kūpono.* Right angle protractor.

huina kū·waho *kik* Exterior angle, in math. *Lit.,* external angle.

huina·lehu·lehu *kik* Polygon. *Lit.,* many angles. *Huinalehulehu analahi.* Regular polygon.

huina·lima *kik* Pentagon. *Dic.*

huina·nui *kik* Sum, total. *Lit.,* grand total. See entries below.

huina·nui hapa *kik* Subtotal. *Lit.,* partial total. See *huinanui pau loa.*

huina·nui pau loa *kik* Grand total. See *huinanui hapa.*

huina papā *kik* Angle of incidence, i.e. the angle made between a wave striking a barrier and the normal to the surface. *Lit.,* echo angle. Cf. *huina kūpī.*

huina·walu *kik* Octagon. *Dic.*

huina 'oi *kik* Acute angle.

huina 'umi *kik* Decagon, i.e. a ten-sided polygon, in math. *Comb. huina + 'umi.*

Hui Pō·peku Au·puni *kik* National Football Conference (NFC).

Hui Pō·peku 'Ame·lika *kik* American Football Conference. (AFC).

hui po'o *kik/heh* The intersection of two lines wherein one or both lines do not continue beyond the point of intersection, in math; to intersect thus. *Lit.,* end meeting. Cf. *hui kaupe'a.*

hui 'āina *kik* Union, as of states or countries into one political entity. *Lit.,* union (of) lands.

huo·huoi *Ma'i huohuoi.* Schizophrenia. *Ma'i huki huohuoi.* Schizophrenic convulsion.

huhu·pao *kik* Borer, a kind of insect. *Comb. huhu + pao.*

huka *kik* Zipper. *Ni'ihau.*

hū·ka'a *kik* Resin, for musical instrument strings. *Dic., ext. mng. Hūka'a 'ea.* Acrylic.

hū·kē *ham* To blow one's nose. *Dic.* Also *ho'okē.*

huki *Ma'i huki.* Convulsion. *Ma'i huki huohuoi.* Schizophrenic convulsion.

huki·alewa *heh* Chin-up, pull-up. *Lit.*, pull when hanging. See *pohoalo, pohokua*. *Hukialewa pohoalo*. Pull-up. *Hukialewa pohokua*. Chin-up.

huki pō·pō *kik/ham* Center, in football; to hike (the ball). *Lit.*, pull (the) ball. Also *huki i ka pōpō, huki i ke kinipōpō (ham.)*. Cf. *kūlima*.

huku ʻou pele *kik* Dike (geological formation). *Lit.*, projection (of) protruding lava.

hula·hula·kona *kik* Dance-a-thon. Comb. *hulahula* + Eng.

hule·hulei *heh* To seesaw, teetertotter. *Dic.* See *papa hulei*.

huli- Scientific study of, -ology, with no specific intent to influence change. *Dic., ext. mng.* Cf. *kālai-, kilo*.

huli *kik* Direction. *Ua loli ka huli o ka makani i ka pō.* The direction of the wind changed during the night. *Dic., new mng.* See entries below.

huli *ham* To find, search for, as in computer program. *Dic. Huli a kuapo.* To find and change, search and replace, in computer program.

huli *ham* To evaluate, i.e. to find the number that an algebraic expression names, in math. *Dic., ext. mng.* See *huli a loaʻa*.

huli a loaʻa *ham* To find, calculate, in math. Also *huli*. *Dic.* Cf. *hoʻomaulia*.

huli hā·ʻina, huli i ka hā·ʻina *ham* To solve a problem, i.e. look for a solution. Cf. *hoʻoponopono pilikia, ʻimi hāʻina*.

huli helu hoʻo·nui kumu *ham* Prime factorization, in math. *Lit.*, search for base multiplication number. See *helu kumu*.

huli·hia *ʻa* Upside down. *Dic.* See *lolea*.

huli·honua *kik* Geology. *Dic., sp. var. Kahua hulihonua*. Geological site.

huli hope *ʻa* Inverse, in math. *Dic. Hana hoʻomākalakala huli hope*. Inverse operation.

huli·kanaka *kik* Anthropology. *Dic., sp. var.*

huli·koe·hana *kik* Archaeology. Comb. *huli-* + *koehana*. See *koehana*. *Kahua hulikoehana*. Archaeological site. *Kanaka hulikoehana*. Archaeologist. Also *mea hulikoehana*.

huli kumu·kū·ʻai *ham* Cost analysis. *Ma ka huli kumukūʻai ʻana, huli ʻia ke kumukūʻai e pono ai kekahi huahana e kūʻai ʻia ana ma ka mākeke.* In cost analysis, an appropriate price is sought for certain products to be sold at the market. *Lit.*, study price.

hū·lili *kik* Railing support, balluster. *Mān*. Also *ʻūlili*. Cf. *paehumu*. *Kahena hulili*. Riffle, as in a stream.

huli lole·lole *ham* To scan search, as with audio or video equipment. *Lit.*, search (by) skimming through.

huli·mō·ʻali·haku *kik* Paleontology. Comb. *huli-* + *mōʻalihaku*. *Kanaka hulimōʻalihaku*. Paleontologist. Also *mea hulimōʻalihaku*.

hulu *kik* Wool. *Dic.* See entries below. *Hulu aniani*. Glass wool.

hulu *kik* Format, as of a computer file. *Dic., new mng. Hulu waihona*. File format.

hulu·heu *kik* Cilium, cilia. Comb. *hulu* + *heu*.

hulu·hulu aʻa *kik* Root hairs. *Lit.*, rootlet fur.

hulu koko *kik* Blood type. *Ke huli ʻia nei ka poʻe i like ka hulu koko me ke keiki i loaʻa i ka maʻi no ka hāʻawi mai i ke koko nōna.* Blood donors are being sought who have the same blood type as the child who is inflicted with the disease. *Lit.*, blood kind.

hulu māpa *kik* Mop head. *Lit.*, mop plumage.

hulu pena *kik* Paint brush. *Lit.*, paint plumage. Cf. *lola pena, pena lola*.

hulu·pō·ʻē·ʻē *kik* Sphagnum. Comb. *hulu* + *poʻēʻē*. Also *mākōpiʻi hulupōʻēʻē*. See *mākōpiʻi*.

huna *kik* Ceiling. *Niʻihau.* Also *kilina.* See entries below and *lumi huna.*

huna *kik* Particle, as in an atom. *Dic., ext. mng.* See *huna hohoki, huna ʻālepa, huna ʻāne, huna ʻine, huna beta.*

huna *kik* Bit, i.e. a computer unit of information. *ʻEwalu huna o ka ʻai.* There are eight bits to a byte. *Dic., ext. mng.* See *ʻai.*

huna·ola *kik* Biological cell. Comb. *huna + ola.* *ʻAʻaʻa hunaola.* Tissue, as structural material of a plant or animal. *ʻAʻaʻa hunaola ʻailakele.* Adipose tissue, i.e. animal tissue in which fat is stored.

huna·ola koko *kik* Blood cell. *Hunaola koko keʻokeʻo.* White blood cell. *Hunaola koko ʻulaʻula.* Red blood cell.

huna hohoki *kik* Neutron. *Lit.,* neutral particle. See *huna ʻāne, huna ʻine.*

huna·huna See entries below and *puke hunahuna, ʻōmole ʻapo hunahuna.*

huna·huna palaoa *kik* Bread crumbs.

huna·huna ʻike *kik* Trivia. *Lit.,* bits (of) information.

huna kau·kala *kik* Pigment grain, in biology.

Huna·kalia *iʻoa* Hungary; Hungarian. *Dic.* Also *Hunagaria.*

huna ʻā·lepa *kik* Alpha particle, i.e. a positively charged particle made up of two protons and two neutrons. See *huna beta.*

huna ʻāne *kik* Proton. *Lit.,* positive particle. See *huna ʻine, huna hohoki.*

huna ʻine *kik* Electron. *Lit.,* negative particle. See *huna ʻāne, huna hohoki.*

huna beta *kik* Beta particle, i.e. a negatively charged electron moving at high speed. See *huna ʻālepa.*

Huna·garia *iʻoa* Hungary; Hungarian. *Dic.* Also *Hunakalia.*

hune hulili *kik* Glitter. *Lit.,* tiny sparkles.

hune·hune ʻū·pī *kik* Vermiculite. *Lit.,* very fine sponge.

hupa *kik* Basket, in basketball. *Dic., ext. mng.* Also *hīnaʻi.* Cf. *ʻai hīnaʻi.* See *hao, kuku. Papa hupa.* Backboard. Also *papa hīnaʻi.*

huʻa *Hōkelo huʻa.* Bubble chamber, in chemistry.

huʻa·kai *kik* Sponge, the aquatic animal. *Dic.* Cf. *ʻūpī* (dic.).

huʻi·huʻi *ʻa* Cold. *Dic.* See *kuʻina. Kuʻina huʻihuʻi.* Cold front, as of weather.

huʻu *ham* To infer. Sh. *hoʻohuʻu.* See *hoʻohuʻu.*

hhn Abbreviation for *hapa haneli* (centi-).

Hk Abbreviation for *hikina* (east).

hkk Abbreviation for *hapa kaukani* (milli-).

hkkal Abbreviation for *hekokalame* (hectogram).

hkl Abbreviation for *hapa kiliona* (pico-) and *hekolika* (hectoliter).

hkm Abbreviation for *hekomika* (hectometer).

hl Abbreviation for *hola* (hour).

Hm Abbreviation for *hema* (south).

hml Abbreviation for *hapa miliona* (micro-).

hpl Abbreviation for *hapa piliona* (nano-).

hʻm Abbreviation for *hapa ʻumi* (deci-).

ht Abbreviation for *hekekale, heketare* (hectare).

K

k Abbreviation for *kana* (ton).

K Abbreviation for *koena* (difference, remainder).

kā- A prefix indicating a process. *Dic., ext. mng.* See entries below.

kā *kik* Tar. *Dic.* Also *tā.* See *kēpau kā.*

kaea *kik* Tire. *Eng.* Also *taea. Kaea paikikala.* Bicycle tire.

Māmaka Kaiao / 44

kā·ehu·ehu *ham* To dust, i.e. to brush or apply lightly a thin coat, such as sulphur to a plant. Comb. *kā-* + *'ehuehu*.

kae·kene *kik* Sewage sludge. Sh. *kae* + *kukene* (Ni'ihau). See *kāemikala*. *Kaekene maka*. Raw sewage.

kā·emi·kala *ham* To treat chemically, as sewage. Sh. *kā-* + *emi* + *kemikala*. *Ke kaekene i kāemikala 'ia*. Treated sewage. See *kaekene*.

kaia- A prefix which indicates a clustering together. See entries below.

kaia·ola *kik* Ecosystem. Comb. *kaia-* + *ola*. See *kālaikaiaola*.

kaia·ulu *kik* Community. *Dic.*, *sp. var*. Cf. *kaiahale, kaiahome*. See *'ōnaehana olakino kaiaulu*.

kaia·ulu 'ā·ha'i *kik* Climax community, in biology. *Lit.*, winning community.

kaia·hale *kik* Housing development, subdivision. Comb. *kaia-* + *hale*. Cf. *kaiaulu, kaiahome*.

kaia·home *kik* Neighborhood. Comb. *kaia-* + *home*. Cf. *kaiaulu, kaiahale*.

kai·aka 'a' Diluted. *Dic.* See *ho'okaiaka*.

kai·aka See *wa'a kaiaka*.

kaia·mea·ola *kik* Biological community, as in science. Comb. *kaia-* + *meaola*. *Kaiameaola kūlohelohe*. Natural biological community.

kai·ana·side *kik* Cyanide. *Eng*. *Potasiuma kaianaside*. Potassium cyanide.

kaia·noho *kik* Habitat. Comb. *kaia-* + *noho*.

kaia·pili *kik* Society, i.e. an enduring social group. Comb. *kaia-* + *pili*.

kaia·puni *kik* Environment; medium. Comb. *kaia-* + *puni*. See entry below. *Kaiapuni a'o*. Learning environment. *Kula kaiapuni Hawai'i*. Hawaiian medium school. *Papa kaiapuni Hawai'i*. Hawaiian medium class. *Palapala Hō'ike Hopena Kaiapuni*. Environmental Impact Statement (EIS).

kaia·puni ho'ōla piha *kik* Total healing environment. *Lit.*, complete healing environment.

kaia·wao *kik* Biome. Comb. *kaia-* + *wao*.

Kai·kana *i'oa* Titan, a moon of Saturn. *Eng*.

kai·kona *kik* Daikon. *Japn*.

kaila hou *kik* Modern. *Lit.*, new style.

kaila hua *kik* Print style or attribute, as italic or bold in printing or computer program. *Lit.*, letter style.

kai·mana pō·hili *kik* Baseball diamond, infield. *Lit.*, baseball diamond. Cf. *kahua pōhili*.

kai·mine *kik* Saimin. *Japn*.

kā·inoa *kik/ham* Registration; to register, as for a class; to borrow or check out something by signing for it. *Ua kāinoa 'oe i kēnā puke?* Did you check out that book? Comb. *kā* + *inoa*. See entries below and *palapala kāinoa*.

kā·inoa hiki hope *kik* Late registration. *Lit.*, registration arriving after. Cf. *kāinoa hiki mua*.

kā·inoa hiki mua *kik* Preregistration, early registration. *Lit.*, registration beforehand. Cf. *kāinoa hiki hope*.

kā·inoa komo *ham* To register or check in, as at a conference or hotel. Also *kāinoa*. Cf. *kāinoa puka*. *Palapala kāinoa*. Registration form.

kā·inoa puka *ham* To check out, as of a hotel. Cf. *kāinoa komo*.

kāohi *ham* To control. *Kāohi 'ia ka ma'i ma ka 'ai 'ana i ka lā'au*. Sickness is controlled by taking medication. *Dic.* See entries below.

kāohi mea·ola *ham* Biological control. *'O ke kāohi meaola kekahi mea e no'ono'o 'ia nei no ke kāohi 'ana i nā lā'au a me nā holoholona malihini e ho'opilikia nei i nā kaiapuni 'ōiwi o Hawai'i.* Biological control is one method being considered to control introduced plants and animals that are damaging native environments in Hawai'i. *Lit.,* control living things.

kāohi wai hā·lana *ham* Flood control. *Lit.,* control floods.

kaola kā·wele *kik* Towel rack. *Lit.,* towel bar.

kao lele *kik* Missile. *Dic., ext. mng. Kao lele pahū.* Missile bomb.

kaomi *kik/ham* Click; to click, press or depress, as in computer program. *Dic., ext. mng.* Also *kōmi.* See *pa'ina.*

kaona *kik* Downtown. *Dic., ext. mng.* Cf. *kiwikā, kūlanakauhale, 'āpana pā'oihana kauwaena. Kaona ukali.* Suburb.

kao wā·wahie kino·pa'a *kik* Solid rocket booster. *Lit.,* solid fuel rocket. Also *kao wāwahie pa'a.*

kau- A prefix meaning complex, as referring to vitamins. *Dic., ext. mng. Kauwikamina B.* B-complex vitamin.

kau *kik* Season. *Dic. Kau ho'opūnana.* Nesting season.

kau *'Ālikelike kau.* Translation symmetry, in math. See *kaha kau, 'ālikelike.*

kaua See entry below and *pale kaua. Lele kaua.* Aggression, as an attack by one country upon another. Cf. *lele ho'onanā. Pū'ali kaua lewa.* Air force. *Pū'ali kaua moana.* Navy. Also *'au moku kaua, 'oihana moku. Kahua pū'ali kaua moana.* Navy base. *Pū'ali ho'ouka kaua.* Marine corps.

kaua ko'e·ko'e *kik* Cold war, i.e. intense rivalry between nations but without military combat. *He kanahā makahiki i pa'a ai ke kaua ko'eko'e ma waena o Wakinekona a me Mokekao.* The cold war between Washington and Moscow lasted for forty years. *Lit.,* chilled war.

kau·alewa *'a'* Balanced, as equal distribution of weight. Comb. *kau + a + lewa.* Cf. *ho'okaualewa, kaulike.*

kau·ana·kahi *kik/ham* Calibration; to calibrate. Comb. *kau + anakahi.*

Kau·ano *i'oa* Alnilam, a star. *Inv.*

kau·apono *kik* Compensation. Sh. *kaualewa + ho'oponopono.* See *ho'okauapono.*

kau·ō *ham* To tow. *Dic.* See entries below. *Kalaka kauō.* Tow truck.

kau·ō *kik* Egg white or yolk. *Dic. Kauō ke'oke'o.* Egg white. *Kauō melemele.* Egg yolk.

Kau·ō *i'oa* Laysan island. *Lit.,* yolk or white of an egg. *'Ainohu Kauō.* Laysan finch (telespiza cantanc).

kau·omo·lia *kik* Host, as of a parasite. Comb. *kau + omo + -lia.* See *omoola.*

kau·ha'a *kik/ham* Subscript, as in computer program or printing. Comb. *kau + ha'a.* Cf. *kaupi'i.*

kau·helu *kik* Notation, in math. Comb. *kau + helu. Kauhelu pāho'onui.* Exponential notation. *Kauhelu 'epekema.* Scientific notation.

kau·hope See *woela kauhope.*

Kauka *kik* Doctor, for use as a title before a person's name. See entries below. *'O Kauka Halenui ke kauka nāna i lapa'au mai ia'u.* Doctor Halenui is the doctor who treated me. *Dic.* Abb. *Kk.*

kauka ha'i·ha'i iwi *kik* Osteopath. *Lit.,* osteopathy doctor. See *ha'iha'i iwi.*

kauka ho'o·polo·lei niho *kik* Orthodontist. *Lit.,* doctor (who) straightens teeth.

Māmaka Kaiao / 46

kau·kala *kik* Pigment. Comb. *kau* + *kala*. *Huna kaukala*. Pigment grain, in biology.

kaukani See *hapa kaukani*.

kauka pālomi *kik* Chiropractor. *Lit.*, chiropractic doctor.

kau·kaʻi *Kumuloli kaukaʻi*. Dependent variable.

kau·koma *kik* Glaucoma. *Ke hāpōpō mālie mai nei ka ʻike ʻana o koʻu kupuna kāne no kōna loaʻa i ke kaukoma*. My grandfather's vision is gradually getting cloudy because he has glaucoma. *Eng.*

kaula *kik* String, as on an ʻukulele or guitar. *Mān.* See entries below and *ʻukulele*, *ʻukulele ʻewalu kaula*. Names of strings on an ʻukulele: *ke kaula o luna loa* (G), *ke kaula ʻelua*, (C), *ke kaula ʻekolu* (E), *ke kaula ʻehā* (A).

kaula uea *kik* Cable. *Dic.* Also *uea*.

kaula·hao *kik* Chain. *Dic. Kaulahao paikikala*. Bicycle chain.

kaula hō·ʻike piʻo *kik* Chord, of an arc, in math. *Legendre*.

kaula kau·laʻi lole *kik* Clothesline. *Dic.*

kaula kaʻi *kik* Leash. *Lit.*, rope (for) leading.

kaula lele *kik* Jump rope. *Cf. lele kaula*.

kau lalo *kik* Footer, as in computer documents. *Lit.*, placed below. *Cf. kau luna*.

kaula piko *kik* Safety line, as in a spacecraft. *Lit.*, navel string.

kau lā·ʻau *ʻa* Arborial. *Lit.*, set (on a) tree. *Hale kau lāʻau*. Treehouse. *Poloka kau lāʻau ʻalani*. Orange tree frog.

kau·lele *ʻa* Overtime. *Dic. Uku kaulele*. Overtime pay. *Hana kaulele*. Overtime (work). *Hola kaulele*. Overtime (hours).

kau·lihi *ʻa* Justified, as type in printing. Comb. *kau* + *lihi*. See *hoʻokaulihi*, *hoʻokauwaena*, *kauwaena*. *Kaulihi hema*. Left justified. *Kaulihi ʻākau*. Right justified. *Kaulihi like*. Full justified.

kau·like *ʻa* Balanced, evenly balanced, in science; even, in math; fair, just, equitable. *Dic., ext. mng. Cf. kaualewa*. See *kauʻewa*. *Haʻihelu kemikala kaulike*. Balanced chemical equation. *Helu kaulike*. Even number. *Manehu kaulike*. Balanced force. *Pāʻani kaulike*. A fair game, as one in which each player has the same chance of winning.

kau·like ʻole *ʻa* Inequality, in math. *Lit.*, not equal. *ʻŌlelo no ke kaulike ʻole*. Inequality statement.

kau lole See *uea kau lole*.

kau·lona See *aniani kaulona*.

kau·lua *kik* Double, in math. *ʻO ka 8 ke kaulua o ka 4*. Eight is the double of four. *Dic., ext. mng. Cf. helu māhoe*.

kau luna *kik* Header, as in computer documents. *Lit.*, placed above. *Cf. kau lalo*.

kau·maha *ʻa* Weight, in math. *Dic. Ana kaumaha wai*. Hydrometer.

kau·mī·kini *kik* Compound machine. Comb. *kau* + *mīkini* (cf. *kauhale*/dic.).

kau·moku·ʻāina *kik* Country, nation-state; national. Comb. *kau* (plural marker) + *mokuʻāina*. *Cf. aupuni, kauʻāina, māhele ʻāina, mokuʻāina, pekelala*. See entry below. *Kupa kaumokuʻāina pālua, makaʻāinana kaumokuʻāina pālua*. Dual citizen. *ʻAhahui kaumokuʻāina*. National organization.

kau·moku·ʻāina muli pana·lā·ʻau *kik* Postcolonial country. *Lit.*, after colony country. Also *ʻāina muli panalāʻau*.

kau·mua See *woela kaumua*.

kau·nā·nā *ham* To discover. *Dic. Cf. hiʻohia*.

kauna palaki niho *kik* Toothbrush holder. *Lit.*, toothbrush placement.

Māmaka Kaiao / 47

kau·no'o *kik* Learning center. Sh. *kau + no'ono'o.*

kau·paku See *lumi kaupaku.*

kau·pale *ham* To defend against, as an opponent in sports. *Me he nalo mumulu 'o Ewing ma ke kaupale 'ana iā Olajuwon.* Ewing was like a fly all over Olajuwon while defending him. *Lit.*, thrust aside. Cf. *kūpale, pale.*

kau·palena *ham* To set a deadline. *Dic.* See *palena pau.*

kau·pe'a See *hui kaupe'a.*

kau pipi *'Aleku'u kau pipi.* Cattle egret.

kau·pi'i *kik/ham* Superscript, as in computer program or printing. Comb. *kau + pi'i.* Cf. *kauha'a.*

kau·poku See *papa kaupoku. 'Iole kaupoku.* Roof rat.

kau·poku·lani *kik* Outdoor. Comb. *kaupoku + lani.* See *maluhale. Ha'uki kaupokulani.* Outdoor sport. *Mākeke kaupokulani.* Outdoor market. *'Aha mele kaupokulani.* Outdoor concert.

kau·poku·poku omo *kik* Hood, as an exhaust hood above a stove. Redup. of *kaupoku + omo.* Also *kaupokupoku.*

kau·waena *ham* To center, as type on printed page. Comb. *kau + waena.* See *ho'okauwaena, ho'okaulihi, kaulihi, woela kauwaena. 'Āpana pā'oihana kauwaena.* Central business district. Cf. *kaona.*

kau·wela *kik* Summer. *Dic., sp. var.* See *māuiki'iki'i.*

kau·wika·mina B *kik* B-complex vitamin. Comb. *kau- + wikamina + B.*

kau·wowo *kik* Shoot from root of a plant. *Dic.* Also *kawowo, kā, 'elia (mān., J. Nākoa), ilo (mān., Kawa'a, Kapuni).* See *hehu, kawowo.*

kau·'āina *kik* International. Comb. *kau + 'āina.* See *kaumoku'āina.*

kau·'ewa *Helu kau'ewa.* Odd number. See *helu kaulike.*

kaha *heh* To drive, in basketball. *Ua kaha palamimo 'o Ioredāne ma waena o nā kūpale 'ehā.* Jordan slyly cut right through the four defenders. *Dic., ext. mng. Kīloi kaha.* Lead pass; to throw such a pass.

kaha *kik* Line. *Dic.* Also *kaha laina.* See entries below and *huina kaha. 'Āpana kaha.* Line segment. *Helu kaha.* To tally.

kaha ana *kik* Benchmark, in math. *Lit.*, mark (for) measuring.

kaha·apo *kik* Parenthesis. *Dic.* See *kahaapo kihikihi. Kahaapo wehe.* Open parenthesis. *Kahaapo pani.* Close parenthesis.

kaha·apo kihi·kihi *kik* Bracket, in punctuation. *Lit.*, angular parenthesis. *Kahaapo kihikihi wehe.* Open bracket. *Kahaapo kihikihi pani.* Close bracket.

kā·hā·inu *kik* Water dispenser, as in a bird cage. Comb. *kā- + hāinu.* Cf. *kāhānai.*

kaha·hā·nai *kik* Radius of a circle. *Dic.*

kaha hiō *kik* Slash, in printing (/). *Lit.*, mark (that) leans up. Also *kaha hiō pi'i. Kaha hiō iho.* Backslash (\).

kaha hopu *kik* A line written from the end of one paragraph to the beginning of the next paragraph to indicate that the two paragraphs should be combined, in proofreading. *Lit.*, mark (for) grasping.

kaha ho'o·kau·lihi *kik* Two vertical lines written to the left of lines of print to indicate that the left margin should be justified, in proofreading. *Lit.*, mark (for) justifying.

kaha ho'o·ka'a·hua *kik* A "straight" Z-shaped line written to indicate where two words written as one should be separated, in proofreading. Comb. *kaha + ho'o- + ka'ahua.* Also *kaha ho'okōā.* Cf. *kaha ka'ahua.*

kaha hoʻo·kō·ā *kik* A "straight" Z-shaped line written to indicate where two words written as one should be separated, in proofreading. *Lit.*, mark (for) separating by a space. Also *kaha hoʻokaʻahua.* Cf. *kaha kaʻahua.*

kaha hoʻo·komo *kik* Caret (^, ˇ), a mark used to show where something is to be inserted, in proofreading. *Lit.*, mark (for) inserting. Cf. *lina hoʻokomo.*

kaha hoʻo·kuʻi *kik* A curved line (or lines) linking two letters or words to indicate that the letters or words should be joined, in proofreading. *Lit.*, mark (for) connecting.

kaha hoʻo·lā·lani *kik* Horizontal lines written above and below a word or words to indicate that they should be written or printed straight, in proofreading. *Lit.*, mark (for) placing in rows.

kaha hoʻo·lawe *kik* Minus sign. *Dic.*

kaha hoʻo·maʻaka *kik* Three lines drawn under a letter to indicate that the letter is to be capitalized, in proofreading. *Lit.*, mark (for) capitalizing. Cf. *kaha hoʻonaʻinaʻi.*

kaha hoʻo·naʻi·naʻi *kik* A line drawn diagonally through a capital letter to indicate that the letter is not to be capitalized, in proofreading. *Lit.*, mark (for) writing in lower case. Cf. *kaha hoʻomaʻaka.*

kaha hoʻo·neʻe *kik* A circle around a word or words with an arrow going from the words to the place where they are to be moved, in proofreading. *Lit.*, mark (for) moving.

kaha hoʻo·nui *kik* Multiplication sign. *Dic.*

kaha hui *kik* Plus sign. *Dic.*

kaha huina *kik* Intersecting line.

kaha kau *kik* Directrix, in math. *Lit.*, placed line.

kaha·kaha kolohe *kik* Graffiti. *ʻO ka hōʻea maila nō ia o nā mākaʻi i ka manawa kūpono no ka hopu ʻana i ka poʻe keiki ma ke kahakaha kolohe ʻana.* The police arrived just in time to catch the kids in the act of graffiti. *Lit.*, destructive markings.

kaha kā·lā *kik* Dollar sign ($). Cf. *kaha kēneka.*

kaha kā·pae *kik* A line used to indicate that something is to be deleted, in proofreading. *Lit.*, mark (for) deleting.

kaha kaʻa·hua *kik* A pound sign (#) used to indicate that a space should be inserted, in proofreading; a superscript number written next to the symbol indicates the number of spaces if more than one (#²). *Lit.*, space mark. Cf. *kaha hoʻokaʻahua.*

kaha kē·neka *kik* Cent sign (¢). Cf. *kaha kālā.*

kaha kiko *kik/ham* Punctuation mark; to punctuate. Comb. *kaha + kiko.*

kaha kinona *ham* To complete, as a geometric figure, in math. *E kaha kinona iā DXCH no ka hana ʻana i ka huinakolu DXC.* Complete DXCH to form triangle DXC. *Lit.*, draw (a) geometric figure.

kaha kiʻi kū·kulu *ham* To draft, as blueprints; draftsman, drafter. *Lit.*, draw blueprints.

kaha koe *ham* To etch. *Lit.*, draw (by) scratching. *Kiʻi kaha koe.* Etching.

kaha kuapo *kik* A curved line written over a word or letter and then under the adjoining word or letter to indicate that the order of the words or letters should be reversed, in proofreading. *Lit.*, mark (for) exchanging.

kaha laina *kik* Line, in math. Also *kaha.*

kaha lala *kik* Diagonal, a segment other than a side connecting two vertices of a polygon, in math. *Lit.*, diagonal line.

kaha·lalo *ham* To underline. *E kahalalo i kēia lālani kikokikona.* Underline this line of text. Comb. *kaha + lalo*. Cf. *kahalina, kahape'a, kahawaena*.

kaha like *kik* Equal sign.

kaha·lina *ham* To circle, draw a circle around. *Lit.*, draw (a) ring. Cf. *kahalalo, kahape'a, kahawaena*.

kaha maha *kik* Dash, in punctuation. *Dic.* Cf. *kaha moe*.

kaha·makau *kik* Check mark. *Lit.*, fishhook mark.

kaha moe *kik/ham* Hyphen; to hyphenate. *E kaha moe i ka hua'ōlelo i loa'a ai ke kaha moe ma hope o ka huapalapala a.* Hyphenate the word so that the hyphen appears after the letter a. *Dic., ext. mng.* Cf. *kaha maha*.

kaha mo'o·lelo See *mo'olelo kaha*.

kā·hā·nai *kik* Feeder, as for birds. Comb. *kā- + hānai*. Cf. *kāhāinu*.

kahana lonoa *ham* Lateral line, i.e. a linear series of sensory pores and tubes along the side of a fish, in biology. *Lit.*, drawing (a) line (of) senses.

kaha nuku muli·wai *kik* Delta (of a river). *Ma ke kaha nuku muliwai o ka muliwai 'o Nile ma 'Aikupita kahi o nā kahua kauhale kanaka kahiko loa a puni ka honua.* The delta of the Nile river in Egypt is where some of the most ancient human settlements are found. *Lit.*, place (of the) river mouth.

kaha pala·pala 'āina *ham* To field map a site. *Lit.*, draw (a) map.

kaha pā lihi *kik* Tangent, i.e. a line which touches a circle at one point, in math. *Lit.*, line barely touching (a circle).

kaha pela hewa *kik* A circle around a misspelled word with the letters *ph* (*pela hewa*) written above the word, in proofreading. *Lit.*, spelling error mark.

kaha·pe'a *ham* To cross out. Comb. *kaha + pe'a*. Cf. *kahalina, kahalalo, kahawaena*.

kaha puana·'ī *kik* Quotation mark. See *puana'ī*. *Kaha puana'ī pākahi wehe.* Single open quote; printer's symbol for *'okina*. *Kaha puana'ī pālua pani.* Double close quote.

kaha pu'u·naue *kik* Division sign. *Dic.*

kaha·waena *ham* To strike through or line out, as on a typewriter or computer; also used to indicate that the letters or words lined out are to be deleted and replaced by those written above, in proofreading. Cf. *kahalalo, kahaluna, kahape'a*.

kaha·wai *Ko'ana kahawai.* Stream sediment. *'Aumana kahawai.* Stream tributary.

kaha waiho *kik* A series of dots written under a word or words which have been lined out to show that no change should be made from the original, in proofreading; stet. *Lit.*, mark (for) leaving (as is).

kaha·'imo *kik* Cursor, I-bar, or insertion point in computer program. *Lit.*, blinking mark. Cf. *nahau 'iole*.

kaha 'oki hapa·lua *kik* Bisector, in math. *Lit.*, line (for) bisecting. See *'oki hapalua*. *Kaha 'oki hapalua kūpono.* Perpendicular bisector.

kaha 'oki pō·'ai *kik* Secant, i.e. a line which intersects a circle at two points, in math. *Lit.*, line (which) cuts (a) circle.

kaha 'oki·'oki *kik* Transversal, i.e. a line that intersects two given lines, in math. *Lit.*, cutting line.

kahe See *uila wai kahe*.

kā·hea See *pahu kāhea*.

kahe·aholo *kik* Traffic, especially the movement of. *Pa'apū ke kaheaholo ka'a i kēia lā.* Traffic is congested today. Comb./sh. *kaheāwai + holo*. *Kaheaholo ka'a*. Highway traffic. *Kaheaholo mokulele*. Air traffic.

kā·hela See *pa'i kāhela*.

kahena hulili *kik* Riffle, as in a stream. *Lit.*, undulating flowing.

kahena koko *kik* Bloodstream. Comb. *kahena* + *koko*.

kahena wai *kik* Stream bed. *Dic.* Also *papakū kahawai, papakū.*

kahi See *hoʻomana akua kahi, ʻūlau kahi.*

kahi·ā·uli *ham* To shade, as with a pencil; to block or highlight text, as in computer program. Comb. *kahi* + *a* + *uli.*

kahiko *Puka kahiko.* Anus, i.e. the posterior opening of the alimentary canal. Also *puka ʻamo.*

kā·hili·hili *ham* To dust, as with a duster. *Dic., ext. mng. Mea kāhilihili.* Duster.

kā·hiʻo·naina *ham* To landscape, as a yard. Comb. *kā* + *hiʻonaina.* See *hiʻonaina.*

kahi ʻū·miʻi lau·oho *kik* Folding hairclip with teeth. *Niʻihau.*

kā·hoʻi *ham/iʻoa* To use the enter or return key on a computer or typewriter keyboard in order to return the cursor or carriage to the left margin on a new line; enter or return, as the key just above the shift key on a computer keyboard. *E kōmi iā kāhoʻi.* Press enter or return. Comb. *kā* + *hoʻi.* See *hoʻouna, kāhuakomo. Pihi kāhoʻi.* Return key (preceded by *ke*).

kahu *kik* Controller, administrator, as for computer network. *E hōʻike i ka pilikia i ke kahu pūnaewele.* Report the problem to the network administrator. *Dic., ext. mng. Kahu pūnaewele.* Network controller, network administrator.

kahua *kik* Site. *Dic.* See entries below. *Kahua hulihonua.* Geological site. *Kahua hulikoehana.* Archaelogical site.

kahua *kik* Base. *Dic.* See entries below. *Kahua pūʻali koa.* Military base. *Kahua pūʻali kaua moana.* Navy base.

kahua *kik* Court, as for basketball; field, as for football. *E hoʻoholo ʻia nō ia ma ke kāhua pōhīnaʻi.* Let's settle this on the basketball court. *Dic., ext. mng. Kahua pōhīnaʻi.* Basketball court. *Kahua pōpeku.* Football field. Also *kahua.*

kahua *kik* Field, as in a database. *Dic., ext. mng. Hope kahua.* Subfield.

kahua *kik* Set, as for movie or video production. *Dic., ext. mng.* See *pono kahua. Mea kūkulu kahua.* Stagehand, grip. *Luna kūkulu kahua.* Stage manager, key grip. *Mea hakulau kahua.* Set designer. *Mea hoʻoponopono kahua.* Set decorator.

kahua hamo·hamo holo·holona *kik* Petting zoo. *Lit.,* site (for) petting animals.

kahua hana *kik* Principle, as an accepted rule of action. *Dic.* Also *kulehana.* See *kulehana.*

kahua hoʻo·moana *kik* Campground. *Dic.* See *ʻāpoʻe.*

kā·hua·komo *ham* To enter or input, as typing data into a computer database or a calculator. Comb. *kā* + *huakomo.* Cf. *kāhuapuka.* See *hoʻouna, huakomo, kāhoʻi. Kāhuakomo ʻikepili.* To input data.

kahua paʻa *kik* Home screen, in computer program. *Dic., ext. mng.* See *papa kuhikuhi kahua paʻa.*

kahua pō·hili *kik* Baseball field. Cf. *kaimana pōhili.*

kahua pō·paʻi·paʻi *kik* Volleyball court. Also *pahu.*

kā·hua·puka *ham* To output, as data in computer program. Comb. *kā* + *huapuka.* Cf. *kāhuakomo.* See *huapuka. Kāhuapuka ʻikepili.* To output data.

kahu·lui *Hoʻokūkū kahului.* Championship, in sports. See *hoʻokūkū kio, hoʻokūkū moho.*

kahu pāka *kik* Park keeper.

kā·kai *kik* Handle for lifting, as of bucket or suitcase. *Dic.* Cf. *pōheo, ʻau. Kākai pahu ʻukulele.* ʻUkulele case handle.

kā·kau hou ma kekahi ʻano *ham* To paraphrase, in writing. *E kākau i nā ʻōlelo a ka mea haʻiʻōlelo ma kekahi ʻano.* Paraphrase on paper what the speaker said. *Lit.,* rewrite in another way. See *haʻi hou ma kekahi ʻano.*

kā·kau maoli *ham* Script; to write in script. *Ni'ihau.* Cf. *kākau pākahikahi.* See *limahiō.*

kā·kau maka·kū *ham* Creative writing. *Lit.,* write (with) creative imagination.

kā·kau mo'o·lelo ki'i·'oni·'oni *ham* To write a screenplay. Also *kākau mo'olelo. Mea kākau mo'olelo ki'i'oni'oni.* Screenwriter. Also *mea kākau ki'i'oni'oni.*

kā·kau pā·kahi·kahi *ham* Print; to print, as in handwriting. *Ni'ihau.* Cf. *kākau maoli.* See *limahakahaka.*

kā·kau 'ō·lelo *kik* Secretary; scribe. *Na ke kākau 'ōlelo e ho'onohonoho pono i nā hana o ke ke'ena me ka maiau.* The secretary will keep the office organized and operating efficiently. *Dic.*

kakaha *kik/ham* Notes, as taken during a lecture, etc.; to take such notes. *'A'ole wau i kakaha i ka ha'i'ōlelo o nehinei.* I didn't take notes on yesterday's lecture. *Dic., ext. mng.* Cf. *memo.*

kaka·lina *'Ūhōlo'a kakalina.* Carburetor, as in an internal combustion engine.

kakani *'a'* Crunchy, as fresh potato chips. *Dic., ext. mng.* Also *nakeke.* See *kamumu, nakekeke.*

kā·ka'ahi *ham* To dole out or deal, as cards; to distribute or pass out, as papers in a class. *Ni'ihau.* Cf. *ho'omalele.* See *kakekake.*

kā·ka'i·kahi *'a'* Few, sparse. *U a kāka'ikahi wale nō ka hua 'ulu o kā mākou kumu 'ulu i kēia kau.* There were only a few 'ulu fruits on our 'ulu tree this season. *Dic., sp. var.* See *kaka'ikahi* (dic.).

kake *ham* To shift, as on computer or typewriter keyboard. *Dic., ext. mng. Pihi kake* (preceded by *ke*). Shift key.

kake·kake *ham* To shuffle, as cards. *Dic.* See *kāka'ahi.*

kake·ka'i *ham* To collate. *Lit.* mix (into) order.

kake ka'ina *kik/ham* Permutation, i.e. a selection of objects from a set in a particular order, in math; to permute. *Lit.,* mixing (in) order.

kā·kele *heh* Transform, i.e. sliding in plate techtonics, in geology. *Dic., ext. mng.* Cf. *ku'i, ne'e 'oā. Palena kākele.* Transform boundary.

kakena *kik* Disk drive, as on a computer. Comb. *kake* + *-na. Kakena pa'aloko.* Hard drive. *Kakena kūloko.* Internal drive. *Kakena kūwaho.* External drive.

kāki *ham* To charge. *Dic.* See entries below and *mo'okāki, waihona. Waihona kāki.* Charge account, credit account, as in a bank.

kā·kiko *ham* To bitmap, a style of printing a graphic image as on a computer printer. Comb. *kā* + *kiko.* Cf. *ki'i kiko. Kākiko miomio.* Precision bitmapping.

kāki koho *kik* Estimated cost or charge, as for services. Cf. *kumukū'ai koho.* See *koho.*

kāki kū·'ai·emi *kik* Sale price. *Lit.,* sale charge. Cf. *kāki koho.*

kā·kino·ea *ham* Gasification; also to gasify, i.e. convert into gas. Comb. *kā-* + *kinoea. Kākinoea lānahu.* Coal gasification, i.e. the process in which steam and hot coal produce hydrocarbons.

kāki 'ole *'a'* Toll free. *Lit.,* no charge. *Helu kelepona kāki 'ole.* Toll-free number.

Kakoka Hema *i'oa* South Dakota; South Dakotan. *Dic.* Also *Dakota Hema.*

Kakoka 'Ā·kau *i'oa* North Dakota; North Dakotan. *Dic.* Also *Dakota 'Ākau.*

kā·komo *ham* To import; also as in a computer program. *Hiki ke kākomo 'ia ka 'ikepili mai kekahi hōkeo 'ikepili a i kekahi.* Data can be imported from one database to another. Comb. *kā-* + *komo.* Cf. *kāpuka.*

kako·pone *kik* Saxophone. *Eng.* Also *pū kakopone.*

kā·ko·ʻo *Manaʻo kākoʻo.* Supporting idea, as in a composition.

kā·ko·ʻo ho·ʻo·na·au·ao *kik* Education support staff. *Lit.,* support (for) educating.

kā·ko·ʻo ʻoi·hana ola·kino *kik* Allied health professional. *Lit.,* health occupation support.

kaku·ana *kik* Takuwan. *Japn.*

kā·kuhi *ham* To chart, make a chart, graph. *E kākuhi ʻoe i ka nui o ka ua o Waiʻaleʻale no hoʻokahi makahiki.* Chart the rainfall on Waiʻaleʻale for one year. To distribute data, as on a graph. Also *kākuhi i ka ʻikepili.* Sh. *kākau + kuhikuhi.* Cf. *ili, waiho.* See *pakuhi kaʻina. Kākuhi kaʻina.* To make a flow chart. *Kākuhi i ke kiko.* To graph the point. *Mīkini kākuhi.* Graphing calculator.

kā·kuna *kik* Cartoon. *Eng.* Also *kātuna, kākuni.*

kā·kuni See *kākuna.*

kal Abbreviation for *kalame* (gram).

kala *kik* Crayon. *Eng.* Also *peni kala. Niʻihau. Kala meaʻai.* Food coloring.

kala *kik* Collar. *Dic.* Also *ʻāʻī, ʻāʻī lole, ʻāʻī kala.*

kala ʻa Into the net, in volleyball. *Niʻihau (from the name of the fish).*

kā·lā *kik* Cash, currency, dollar, money. *Dic.* See *kumupaʻa, mīkini ʻohi kālā, manu kālā. Kālā heleleʻi.* Loose change. *Niʻihau.* Cf. *kenikeni. Kālā keʻokeʻo.* Silver dollar. *Dic. Kālā kini.* Petty cash. *Niʻihau.* Cf. *kini kālā. Kālā kūʻike.* Cash. *Kālā mālama.* Savings, as money saved on a sale item. *Kaha kālā.* Dollar sign. *ʻOihana Kālā o ka Mokuʻāina ʻo Hawaiʻi.* Hawaiʻi State Department of Finance.

kā·lai- Scientific study of, -ology (with potential intent to influence change). *Dic., ext. mng.* Cf. *huli-, kilo.* See entries below.

kā·lai *ham* To hoe. *Dic.* Also *hō.* See *koʻi kālai.*

kā·lai·ao·paku *kik* Physical science. Comb./sh. *kālai- + ao + pōhaku.*

kā·lai·ani·au *kik* Climatology. *Hoʻāʻo ka poʻe kālaianiau e koho i ke kumu o kekahi mau mea i hana ʻia ma ke aniau.* Climatologists try to determine the source of certain climactic phenomena. Comb. *kālai- + aniau.* Cf. *kālaianilā. Kanaka kālaianiau.* Climatologist. Also *mea kālaianiau.*

kā·lai·ani·lā *kik* Meteorology. Comb. *kālai- + anilā.* Cf. *kālaianiau.*

kā·lai·ō·ewe *kik* Genetics. Comb. *kālai- + ōewe.* See *ōewe.*

kā·lai·honua *kik* Geophysics. Comb. *kālai- + honua.* Cf. *hulihonua.*

kā·lai·hoʻo·kele wai·wai *kik* Economics. *Ma kā mākou papa kālaihoʻokele waiwai, aʻo mākou i nā ʻōnaehana hoʻokele waiwai like ʻole o nā ʻāina like ʻole.* In our economics class, we learn about the different economic systems of different countries. Sh. *kālai- + noʻeau hoʻokele waiwai* (dic.).

kā·lai·kaia·ola *kik* Ecology. *Lit.,* scientific study of (the) ecosystem. See *kaiaola.*

kā·lai·kalaima *kik* Criminology, i.e. the study of crime and criminals. Comb. *kālai- + kalaima.* Cf. *kālaimeheu kalaima. Kanaka kālaikalaima.* Criminologist. Also *mea kālaikalaima.*

kā·lai·kani *kik* Science of acoustics. *Lit.,* scientific study of sound.

kā·lai·kanu *kik* Horticulture. Comb. *kālai- + kanu. Mea kālaikanu.* Horticulturist.

kā·lai·kapa inoa *kik* Taxonomy, the science of classifying plants and animals. *Lit.,* scientific study of giving names.

kalaiki·kala *kik* Tricycle. *Eng.* Cf. *paikikala.*

kalaiki·kala lawe ʻō·hua *kik* Pedicab. *Lit.,* tricycle (for) taking passengers.

Kalai·kona *iʻoa* Triton, a moon of Neptune. *Eng.*

kā·lai·kū·lohea *kik* Physics. Comb./sh. *kālai- + ao kūlohelohe + -a*.

kā·lai·lai *ham* To analyze. Redup. of *kālai-*. See *kālai-*.

kā·lai·lau nahele *kik* Botany. Comb. *kālai- + lau nahele*.

kā·lai·launa kanaka *kik* Sociology. Comb. *kālai- + launa + kanaka*.

kā·lai·leo *kik* Phonology, in linguistics. *Lit.*, scientific study of voice.

kalaima See *kālaimeheu kalaima, meheu kalaima*.

kā·lai·mana'o *kik* Philosophy. Comb. *kālai- + mana'o*.

kā·lai·mea·ola *kik* Biology. *Lit.*, scientific study of living things. *Kanaka kālaimeaola, mea kālaimeaola*. Biologist. *Kālaimeaolahune*. Microbiology.

kā·lai·mea·ola *'Ohana kālaimeaola*. Biological family.

kā·lai·meheu kalaima *kik* Criminalistics, i.e. the scientific study of physical evidence in the commission of crimes. Comb. *kālai- + meheu kalaima*. Cf. *kālaikalaima*. *Kanaka kālaimeheu kalaima*. Criminalist. Also *mea kālaimeheu kalaima*.

kā·lai·puolo *kik* Musicology. Comb. *kālai- + puolo*. *Kālaipuolo lāhui*. Ethnomusicology. *Mea kālaipuolo, kanaka kālaipuolo*. Musicologist.

kā·lai·wai *kik* Hydrology. *Ma ke kālaiwai, nānā 'ia ke 'ano a me ka pō'aiapuni 'ana o ka wai ma luna a ma lalo ho'i o ka 'ili o ka honua.* In hydrology the nature and cycles of water are examined both above and below the earth's surface. Comb. *kālai- + wai*. *Kanaka kālaiwai*. Hydrologist. Also *mea kālaiwai*.

kalaiwa paiki·kala *kik* Handlebars. Ni'ihau. Also *'au paikikala* (preceded by *ke*).

kā·lai·'ō·lelo *kik* Linguistics. Comb. *kālai- + 'ōlelo*.

kalaona *kik* Clown. *Eng*.

kala·kala *'a'* Low-quality print resolution, as on a computer printer. *Dic., ext. mng.* Cf. *miomio*.

kala·kuhi *kik/ham* Color code; to color code (something). Comb. *kala + kuhi*.

kalame *kik* Gram. *Eng.* Abb. *kal*. See *māikikalame*.

kala·mela *kik* Caramel. *Eng.* *Kanakē kalamela*. Caramel candy.

kala·mena *kik* Salamander. *Eng.* Also *salamena*. *Kalamena kua'ula*. Red-backed salamander.

kalana *kik* County. *Dic. Hō'ike'ike kalana*. County fair. See *fea*.

kā·lana kā·kau *kik* Notebook, tablet. *Dic.* Cf. *puke lina kui*.

kala·nakula *kik* Tarantula. *Eng.* Also *nananana kalanakula, nanana kalanakula*.

kā·lani *kik* Gallon. *Dic.* Abb. *kln*. *Hapalua kālani*. Half gallon. *'Ōmole kālani*. Gallon jar, gallon jug.

kala·paike *kik* Graphite. *Eng.*

kala·pepelo *kik* Propaganda. *I ka wā kaua, nui ke kalapepelo e ho'opuka 'ia e ke aupuni.* In time of war, a lot of propaganda is put out by the government. Comb. *kala + pepelo*.

kala·pona *kik* Carbon. *Eng.* Also *karabona*. Cf. *'ōpa'u*. See entry below. *Helu makahiki kalapona*. Carbon dating, radiocarbon date. *'Akika kalapona*. Carbonic acid. *'Akika pūhui kalapona*. Carboxylic acid.

kala·pona 'oki·kene lua *kik* Carbon dioxide. *Lit.*, two-oxygen carbon. Also *karabona diokesaside*. *Pō'aiapuni 'okikene kalapona 'okikene lua*. Oxygen-carbon dioxide cycle.

kalapu See *'ili kalapu wāwae*.

kala·puna *kik* Seagull. (Maori *tarāpunga*.)

kala·wake *kik* Cravat. *Eng. Lei 'ā'ī kalawake*. Necktie. Also *lei kalawake*.

Kale *i'oa* Charles. *Eng. Ke kānāwai a Kale.* Charles' law, in science, i.e. the volume of a gas increases as its temperature increases if the pressure remains constant.

kalē *kik* Modeling clay. *Eng.* Cf. *palēkō, pālolo.*

kaleila *kik* Trailer. *Eng.* Cf. *pākihuila.*

Kaleiwa·hana *kik* A nickname for ClarisWorks, the computer program. *Ni'ihau.*

kā·leka *kik* Card. *Eng.* See entries below. *Kāleka aloha.* Greeting card. *Kāleka lā hānau.* Birthday card. *Kāleka piha makahiki.* Birthday or anniversary card. *Kāleka puka kula, kāleka hemo kula.* Graduation card.

kā·leka a'o *kik* Flash card. *Lit.,* teaching card.

kā·leka ola·kino *kik* Fitness card, as for sports or physical education. *He hō'ike kāna kāleka olakino he ahuahu wale nō kōna olakino.* Her fitness card showed that she was in good health. *Lit.,* health card.

kā·leka helu kuhi puke *kik* Catalog card, as in a library. *Lit.,* call-number card. See *helu kuhi puke.*

kā·leka kāki *kik* Charge card. Also *'ea kāki.*

Kale·kale *i'oa* Southern Equatorial Current, in oceanography. *Mān. (HA).*

kā·leka pahu *kik* Index card. *Lit.,* box card.

kā·leka po'o·leka *kik* Postcard. *Lit.,* postage stamp card.

kale·kona *kik* Dragon, as in fairy tales. *Dic.* Also *kelekona.*

kā·lele *kik/ham* Accent or stress, in linguistics. *Dic., ext. mng.*

kale palaoa *kik* Batter, as when making pancakes. *Mān.*

Kale·piana *i'oa* Caribbean. *Dic.* Also *Karebiana.*

Kale·poni *i'oa* California; Californian. *Dic. Mau'u Kaleponi.* California grass.

kale 'ai *kik* Residue of poi after pounding, or of milk after beating. *Dic., dic. ext. mng.*

kā·liki *kik* Brace, as for body parts. *Dic., ext. mng. Kāliki pūlima.* Wrist brace.

Kali·leo *i'oa* Galileo, Galilean. *Eng. Nā mahina 'o Kalileo.* Galilean moons.

kalina *kik* Fungus, general term. PPN *taringa* (ear).

kalina pa'u *kik* Smut, a kind of plant disease or the fungus which causes it. *Lit.,* soot fungus. *Kalina pa'u kūlina.* Corn smut.

kā·lino *ham* To weave, as on a loom. Sh. *kāmola + lino.*

kā·lī pahū·pahū *kik* String of firecrackers. See *ahiho'ole'ale'a.*

kali·palaoa *kik* Cauliflower. *Dic.*

kali·puna *kik* Calcium Sh. Eng. + *puna.*

Kalito *i'oa* Callisto, a moon of Jupiter. *Eng.*

kalo *Kipi kalo.* Taro chip.

kā·loa'a *kik* Business, i.e. purchase and sale of goods and services. Comb. *kā- + loa'a.* Cf. *'oihana, pā'oihana.*

kā·loa'a See *ahu kāloa'a, paikāloa'a. Pō'aiapuni kāloa'a.* Business cycle, i.e. a repeated series of economic growth and recession.

kalo kala·koa *kik* Caladium. *Dic.*

Kalo·laina *i'oa* Carolina; Caroline. *Dic. Kalolaina Hema.* South Carolina; South Carolinean. *Kalolaina 'Ākau.* North Carolina; North Carolinean. *Pae Moku Kalolaina.* Caroline Isles. Also *Pae Moku Karolaina.*

Kā·lona *i'oa* Charon, a moon of Pluto. *Eng.*

kalo Pā·kē *kik* Lotus. *Lit.,* Chinese taro. Also *līkao.*

Kalua·koke *i'oa* Bellatrix, a star. *Mān. (HA).*

kalu·hā *kik* Papyrus. *Dic.*

kaluli *kik* Slurry, a viscous solution of liquid and a solid. *Eng.*

kā·lu'u See *palekona kālu'u.*

kā·mahaka *ham* To make a rubbing, as of petroglyphs. Comb. *kā-* + *mahaka (māka).* See *mahaka.*

kā·mā·hua·ola *kik* Hydroponics, i.e. the growing of plants in a nutrient solution. Comb. *kā-* + *māhuaola. Hoʻoulu kāmāhuaola wai.* To grow hydroponically in water. *Hoʻoulu kāmāhuaola one.* To grow hydroponically in sand. *Hoʻoulu kāmāhuaola hunehune ʻūpī.* To grow hydroponically in vermiculite. *Māʻōʻāna kāmāhuaola.* Hydroponic solution.

kā maka·wela *ham* To slash and burn, a method of land cultivation. *Lit.,* turn the soil (of) land cleared by burning.

kama·kū·aka *kik* Kumquat. *Eng.*

kā·mala *kik* Booth, as at a carnival. *Dic.*

kama·loli *kik* Slug, a gastropod closely related to land snails. *Dic.*

kama·poko *kik* Fish cake, kamaboko. *Japn.*

kā·maʻa hekehi *kik* Hiking shoe.

kā·maʻa hele hau *kik* Snow shoe. *Lit.,* shoe (for) walking (on) snow.

kā·maʻa holo hau *kik* Ice skate. See *holo hau.*

kā·maʻa huila *kik* Roller skate. See *holo kāmaʻa huila.*

kā·maʻa lapa huila *kik* Rollerblade. See *holo lapa huila.*

kā·maʻa lole *kik* Sneaker, tennis shoe. *Lit.,* cloth shoe.

kā·maʻa poho·pū *kik* Loafer, slip-on style shoe. *Lit.,* pouch together shoe.

kā·maʻa puki heʻe hau *kik* Ski boot. See *heʻe hau.*

kā·maʻa ʻili helei *kik* Oxford, saddle shoe. *Lit.,* shoe (with) straddling strap.

Kama·bodia *iʻoa* Cambodia; Cambodian. *Eng.*

Kameha·meha *Pulelehua Kamehameha.* Kamehameha butterfly.

kame·piula *kik* Computer. *Eng.* Also *lolouila, mīkini hoʻonohonoho ʻikena. Kamepiula lawelima.* Laptop computer. Also *lolouila lawelima.*

Kame·runa *iʻoa* Cameroon, Cameroun; Cameroonian, Camerounian. *Eng.*

Kā·moa *iʻoa* Sāmoa; Sāmoan. *Dic.* Also *Haʻamoa. Kāmoa ʻAmelika.* American Sāmoa; American Sāmoan. Also *Haʻamoa ʻAmelika.*

kā·mua *kik/ham* Draft, i.e. a preliminary version; to prepare a draft. Sh. *kākau/kaha* + *mua. Kāmua ʻekahi.* First draft. *Kāmua ʻelua.* Second draft.

kamumu *ʻa* Crunchy, general term, but especially for *loli, ʻopihi,* etc. *Dic.* See *kakani, nakeke, nakekeke.*

kana *kik* Ton. *Dic.* Abb. *k.*

kana·uika *kik* Sandwich. *Eng.*

Kana Helena *Mauna Kana Helena.* Mount Saint Helens. Also *Mauna Sana Helena.*

kanaka See entries below. *Hoʻokae kanaka.* Misanthropy, hatred of mankind. See *hoʻokae.*

Kana·kā *iʻoa* Canada; Canadian. *Dic., sp. var.*

kanaka iwi *kik* Skeleton, as for Halloween. *Lit.,* bone man. Also *kelekona.* Cf. *kinanahiwi.*

kanaka hau *kik* Snowman.

kanaka hana uila *kik* Electrician. *Niʻihau.*

kanaka hoʻo·moe paipu *kik* Plumber. *Niʻihau.* Also *wilipaipu.*

kanaka huli·honua *kik* Geologist. See *hulihonua.*

kanaka luʻu kai *kik* Scuba diver. *Lit.,* person (who) dives (in the) sea.

kanaka maka·ʻala ʻupena *kik* Referee, in volleyball. *Niʻihau.* See *ʻuao.*

kanaka puni ao kū·lohe·lohe *kik* Naturalist. *Lit.,* person (who is) fond (of) nature. Also *puni ao kūlohelohe.*

Kana·kawia *iʻoa* Scandanavia; Scandanavian. *Eng.*

kanaka ʻea *kik* Mannequin. *Kāhiko ʻia ke kanaka ʻea no ka hōʻikeʻike ʻana i ke ʻano o nā paikini hou o ka hale kūʻai.* The mannequins are dressed up to display the new fashions that the store has to offer. *Niʻihau.*

kanaka ʻepe·kema *kik* Scientist. Also *kanaka akeakamai.*

kana·kē *kik* Candy. *Dic. Kanakē kalamela.* Caramel candy. *Kanakē koʻokoʻo.* Candy cane. *Kanakē ʻau.* Lollipop, sucker. Also *kō omōmo.*

kā·nā·wai *kik* Act, as a law, decree or edict, in government. *Ua kākoʻo ʻia ka Papahana Kula Kaiapuni Hawaiʻi ma o ke Kānāwai Hoʻonaʻauao ʻŌiwi Hawaiʻi o ʻAmelika Hui Pū ʻia.* The Hawaiian Language Immersion Program has been supported through the United States Native Hawaiian Education Act. *Dic.* See entries below and *haʻihaʻi kānāwai, pale kānāwai, ʻaʻe kānāwai.* See also *Kale, Poila. Kānāwai Lāhulu ʻAne Halapohe.* Endangered Species Act. *Mana kaukānāwai.* Legislative powers. *Pae kānāwai.* Legal alien; to arrive as a legal alien. Cf. *pae malū. Papa kānāwai.* Code, i.e. a systematic collection of existing laws. *Papa kānāwai wai o ka mokuʻāina.* State water code. *ʻAʻa kānāwai.* Civil disobedience, i.e. breaking a law because it goes against personal morals.

kā·nā·wai kī·wila *kik* Civil law. *Pili ke kānāwai kīwila i nā pono o ke kanaka, ʻaʻole naʻe ka hana kalaima ʻana.* Civil law has to do with the rights of individuals, not necessarily the committing of crimes. *Dic.* Also *kānāwai sīwila.*

kā·nā·wai kumu *kik* Common law. *Trad.* See other entries in dictionary.

kāne *Hoʻokae kāne.* Misandry, hatred of males. See *hoʻokae.*

kā·nela *kik* Channel, station, as on radio or television. *Eng.*

Kāne·milo·haʻi *iʻoa* Kure island. *Lit.*, name of Pele's brother left as outguard on northwestern shoal as they travelled from Tahiti to Hawaiʻi.

Kane·sasa *iʻoa* Kansas; Kansan. *Dic.*

kani *kik* Sound effects, as on computer. *Dic., ext. mng.* See *kani keaka, pīpa.*

kani See *māmā kani, palena holo kani.*

kani·olo See *pū kaniolo.*

kani keaka *kik* Sound effects, as for a play, movie or video production. *Lit.*, theater sounds. *Luna kani keaka.* Sound effects coordinator. Cf. *luna hoʻoponopono kani, mea ʻenehana kani.*

kani·kela *kik* Consul. *Hoʻokohu ʻia ke kanikela e ke aupuni e noho ʻelele ma kekahi ʻāina no ka mālama ʻana i nā hana pāʻoihana a me nā hana ʻē aʻe o kōna aupuni ma ia ʻāina e noho ʻelele nei ʻo ia.* The consul is appointed by the government to live in another country as a representative of the government to protect the economic and other interests of his government in the country he is appointed to reside in. *Dic. Kanikela nui.* Ambassador, i.e. an official representative to a foreign country.

kani koʻele *kik/heh* To tick, as a clock. *Koʻele maila ke kani a ka uaki.* The clock ticked. *Lit.*, ticking sound.

Kani·meki *iʻoa* Ganymede, a moon of Jupiter. *Eng.*

kāni·wala See *pāka kāniwala.*

kani ʻā *kik* Dial tone, on a telephone. *Lit.*, turned-on sound.

kani·ʻā·ʻī *kik* Larynx. *Dic.* Also *paipu hanu o luna.*

kā·nono *heh* To infiltrate, i.e. to pass through by filtering or permeating, in science. Comb. *kā- + nono.*

kanu *kik/ham* Crop or planting, i.e. the number of plantings of a particular plant. *ʻEkolu kanu laiki ʻana o kēia loʻi o ka makahiki.* This paddy produces three crops of rice per year. Cf. *meaulu.*

Māmaka Kaiao / 57

kā·nuku *kik* Funnel; hopper. *Dic.; dic., ext. mng. Ka'a kānuku.* Hopper car, as on a train.

kapa *kik* Blanket. *Dic.* Also *kapa moe. Kapa uila.* Electric blanket. *Kapa huluhulu.* Heavy or woolen blanket. Also *huluhulu. Kapa kuiki.* Quilt.

kā pā·ani·ani *ham* To knit. *Lit.,* knit yarn. See *pāaniani.*

kā·pae *Kaha kāpae.* A line used to indicate that something is to be deleted, in proofreading.

kapa·uli *kik* Ground cover. *Comb. kapa + uli.*

kapa kai *Pū'ali pale kapa kai.* Coast guard. See entry below.

Kapa Kai Palaoa *i'oa* Ivory Coast; Ivorian.

kā·pala *ham* To print, i.e. to impress or stamp something in or on something else. *Dic.* See entry below. *Lau kāpala.* A print.

kā·pala *ham* To fingerprint, i.e. take the fingerprints of (someone). *Dic., ext. mng.* Also *kāpala i ka meheu manamana lima (māka manamana lima, ki'i manamana lima).* Cf. *'ohi.*

kā·pala·pala *ham* To draft or draw up documents. *Kanaka kāpalapala.* A person who draws up documents.

kā·pana *kik* Syllable. *Sh. kālele + pana.*

Kapa·nui *i'oa* Dipha, a star. *Mān.* (HA).

Kapela *i'oa* Ankaa, a star. *Mān.* (HA).

kapi *kik* Cubby hole. *Eng.*

kā·piki meo·neki *kik* Cole slaw. *Lit.,* mayonnaise cabbage.

kā·piki ponī *kik* Skunk cabbage.

Kapiko·owā·kea *i'oa* Equator. *Ua 'a'e wale 'ia akula 'o Kapikoowākea e Hōkūle'a i kōna holo 'ana mai Hawai'i a Tahiti.* The equator was crossed by the Hōkūle'a as it sailed from Hawai'i to Tahiti. *Dic., sp. var.* Also *pō'ai waena honua.*

kā·pili *ham* To build, put together. *Dic. Kāpili kūkohu mokulele.* To build a model airplane. *Hana kāpili.* To manufacture. *Hui hana kāpili, kanaka hana kāpili.* Manufacturer. *'Oihana kāpili, 'oi'enehana kāpili.* Manufacturing industry.

kā·pi'o *Hale kāpi'o.* Lean-to shelter. *Dic.*

kā·pi'o·kaha *kik/ham* Construction; to construct, as in making a surveying figure with the use of only a compass and a straightedge in geometry. *Comb. kā + pi'o + kaha.*

Kapona *i'oa* Gabon; Gabonese. *Eng.* Also *Gabona.*

kā·pō·ai See *'ūpā kāpō'ai.*

Kapo'e *i'oa* Alpha Tuscanae, a star. *Mān.* (HA).

kapu·ahi See entries below. *Pā kapuahi.* Burner, as on a stove.

kapu·ahi ula kahi *kik* Bunsen burner. *Lit.,* burner (with) single flame.

kapu·ahi ho'o·pume·hana *kik* Fireplace. *Lit.,* stove (for) warming.

kapu·ahi Mika *kik* Meeker burner. *Comb. kapuahi + Eng.*

kapu·ahi papa·kau *kik* Hot plate. *Lit.,* counter stove. Cf. *pā kapuahi.*

kapu·ahi puka·puka *kik* Fisher burner. *Lit.,* burner (with) many holes.

kapu·a'i *kik* Foot (unit of measurement). *Dic.* Abb. *kp.*

kapu·a'i kuea *kik* Square foot, lay term. Cf. *kapua'i pāho'onui lua.*

kapu·a'i pā·ho'o·nui lua *kik* Square foot, in math. Abb. $kp\ ph^2$. Cf. *kapua'i kuea.*

kapu·hau See *pāpale kapuhau.*

kā·puka *ham* To export. *Comb. kā- + puka.* See *kākomo.*

kā·puka 'ai *kik/ham* Producer, i.e. an organism that can make its own food, such as green plants. *Lit.,* export food.

kapu 'au·'au *kik* Bathtub. *Dic.*

kā·wā *kik* Discrepancy. *'Ehia ke kāwā o ke koho?* How much is the discrepancy of the estimate? *Dic., ext. mng.*

kā·wā *kik* Space, as in tab settings on computer or typewriter. *Dic., ext. mng.* See *kāwāholo, ka'ahua, koana.*

kā·wā ola *kik* Life span. *Lit.,* life's length of time.

kawa·ū *'a'* Damp or moist with fog or dew, wet from cold. *Dic.*

kawa·ū·ea *kik* Humidity. Comb. *kawaū + ea. Pā kawaūea.* Relative humidity. *Ana kawaūea.* Hygrometer.

kā·wā·holo *kik* Tab, as on computer or typewriter. Comb. *kāwā + holo.* See *ho'okāwāholo, kāwā, kake. Pihi kāwāholo* (preceded by *ke*). Tab key.

kā·wawe *kik/ham* Any document which has been written using speed writing; to speed write. Comb. *kā- + wawe.* Cf. *heluwawe.*

kā·wele *ham* To dust or wipe with a cloth. *Dic. Kāwele malo'o.* To dust with a dry cloth. *Kāwele ma'ū.* To dust with a damp cloth.

kā·wī *ham* To extract. *Dic., ext. mng.* See *kāwina.*

kawia See *'iole kawia.*

kā·wina *kik* Extract. Comb. *kāwī + -na.* See *kāwī. Kāwina wanila.* Vanilla extract.

kawowo *kik* Sprout. See *hehu, kauwowo. Dic., ext. mng. Kawowo pāpapa.* Bean sprout. *Kawowo 'alapapa.* Alfalfa sprout.

ka'a *kik* Ground vehicle with wheels or runners. *Dic.* See entries below.

ka'a·ahi kau lewa *kik* Elevated train, as Japan monorail. *Lit.,* suspended train.

ka'ao *kik* A traditional tale, especially one relating to a particular culture; folktale. *Dic.* Also *mo'oka'ao.* See entries below.

ka'ao kele moana *kik* A traditional tale describing ocean travels, such as those of Kila, Mō'īkeha or Pā'ao.

ka'ao kupua *kik* A traditional tale whose primary character is a demigod, such as Kamapua'a, Māui, Pele or 'Aukelenuia'īkū. *Lit.,* demigod tale.

ka'ao me'e *kik* A traditional tale which describes the adventures of a particular character, such as Kawelo or Punia. *Lit.,* hero tale.

ka'a hau *kik* Snowmobile.

ka'a hali·hali *kik* Shuttle. *Lit.,* vehicle (for) transporting.

ka'ahi hewa *heh* Over the line, in volleyball. *Ni'ihau.* Also *ke'ehi hewa.*

ka'a holo one *kik* Dune buggy. *Lit.,* vehicle (for) traveling (on) sand.

ka'a holo mahina *kik* Lunar rover. *Lit.,* vehicle (for) traveling (on the) moon.

ka'a·hope *'a'* Elapsed, as of time. *Dic., ext. mng. Hola ka'ahope.* Elapsed time.

ka'a ho'o·moana *kik* Camper; camping vehicle. *Lit.,* camping car.

ka'a·hua *kik* Space, as between words when typing on computer or typewriter. Sh. *ka'awale + hua'ōlelo.* Cf. *kāwā, koana. Kaha ka'ahua.* A pound sign (#) used to indicate that a space should be inserted, in proofreading; a superscript number written next to the symbol indicates the number of spaces if more than one (#²). *Pihi ka'ahua.* Space bar (preceded by *ke*).

ka'a huki palau *kik* Tractor. *Lit.,* vehicle (for) pulling (a) plow. Also *ka'a palau.*

ka'a kau·paku pelu *kik* Convertible (car). *Lit.,* car (with) folding roof. Also *ka'a kaupoku pelu, ka'a kaupuku pelu.*

ka'a·kā·lai *kik* Strategy or approach, as in solving a math problem. *E koho 'oe i ke ka'akālai kūpono no keia polopolema.* Choose the appropriate strategy for this problem. Cf. *ka'a kaua, kālaimana'o* (dic.).

ka'a·ka'a *'a'* Open, as a frame in a computer program. *Dic., ext. mng.* Cf. *pa'a. Mōlina ka'aka'a.* Open frame.

ka'a·kepa *heh* To warp, as in Nintendo games (not as wood). *Dic., ext. mng.* See *pihi pīna'i, ho'opi'i ka'akepa. Kā'ei ka'akepa.* Warp zone.

ka'a·konelo *kik* Subway (train). *Lit.*, tunnel vehicle. *Ala ka'akonelo.* Subway (tunnel). *Kahua ka'akonelo.* Subway station.

ka'a·kuene *ham* To map, as a computer keyboard. Comb. *ka'a* + *kuene.* Cf. *'ōkuene. Ka'akuene papa pihi.* Keyboard mapping.

ka'a·lehia *kik* Gymnastics; gymnast. *Lit.*, skilled twisting and turning.

ka'a limo *kik* Limousine. Comb. *ka'a* + Eng.

ka'a lola *kik* Roller coaster. *Lit.*, roller vehicle.

ka'a mā·keke *kik* Shopping cart. *Lit.*, market cart.

kā·'ama·wāhi·wai *kik* Photolysis. Comb. *kā* + *'ama* + *wāhi* + *wai.* Cf. *kā'ama'ai.*

kā·'ama·'ai *kik* Photosynthesis. Comb. *kā* + *'ama* + *'ai* (create edible light).

ka'a mio *kik* Sports car. *Lit.*, streamlined car.

ka'a·ne'e *ham* Play, as a particular maneuver in a sporting event; to execute a play. *Ua lapuwale kēlā ka'ane'e; ua lilo ho'i ke kinipōpō i kekahi 'ao'ao.* That was a pretty dumb play; they lost the ball to the other side. Sh. *ka'akālai* + *ne'e.*

ka'a pahu *kik* Pushcart.

ka'a·pahu *kik* Boxcar, as of train.

ka'a pa'i ulele *kik/'a'* Side out, in volleyball. *Ka'a koke ke pa'i ulele iā lākou.* They are good at siding out. *Lit.*, transferred service. Also *ka'a, hā'awi i ke kinipōpō i kekahi 'ao'ao.*

ka'a·pē·pē *kik* Baby carriage.

ka'a·wale *Pūhui naikokene ka'awale.* Free nitrogen compund.

kā·'awe *kik* Strap. *Mān.* See *lole wāwae kā'awe, pala'ili kā'awe, pale'ili kā'awe. Kā'awe kalipa.* Slipper strap.

Ka'ā·wela *i'oa* Jupiter. *Dic.*

Ka'a·wili *i'oa* Mintaka, a star. *Mān.* (HA).

ka'a·wili·wili See *makani ka'awiliwili.*

ka'a·'au·huki *kik* Child's wagon. *Lit.*, wagon (with) handle (for) pulling.

ka'a·'ike *kik* Communication. *'A'ohe ka'a'ike ma waena o ke kamepiula a me ka mīkini pa'i.* There's no communication between the computer and the printer. *Lit.*, transferred knowledge. See *ho'oka'a'ike, keleka'a'ike. Ka'a'ike ha'i waha, ka'a'ike waha.* Oral communication. *Ka'a'ike pāna'i.* Intercommunication, two-way communication.

ka'a·'ike ha'i waha *kik* Oral communication. Also *ka'a'ike waha.*

ka'e *kik* Edge, as of a three-dimensional geometric figure. *Dic., ext. mng.* See *ka'e pololei.*

kā·'ei *kik* Zone. *Dic.* See entries below and *ka'akepa, pale kā'ei. Kā'ei kopikala.* The tropics. *Lit.*, tropical zone. *Kā'ei hola.* Time zone, as Pacific or Rocky Mountain. *Kā'ei manehu uila.* Electrical force field. *Kā'ei māwae.* Rift zone. *Palapala kā'ei meakanu.* Vegetation zonation sheet.

kā·'ei alo *kik* Foreground, as in a photo or movie/video scene. Cf. *kā'ei kua.*

kā·'ei iki *kik* Subzone. *'O kahi o ka 'o'ole'a loa o ka mālama 'ia, 'o ia ke kā'ei iki mālama.* The preservation subzone within the conservation district is the most restrictive. *Lit.*, small zone.

kā·'ei hō·kū·na'i *kik* Asteroid belt.

kā·'ei kau lā *kik* Solar constant. *Lit.*, zone (where) sun shines.

kā·'ei ki'i kā·lai *kik* Frieze. *Lit.*, sash of carved images.

kā·'ei kua *kik* Background, as in a photo or movie/video scene, or on a computer screen. *E holo ana kekahi polokalamu ma ke kā'ei kua.* The other program is running in the background. Cf. *kā'ei alo.*

kā·'ei ku'ina kopi·kala *kik* Intertropical convergent zone (ITCZ). *Lit.*, tropical junction zone. *Abb.* KKK.

kā·'ei 'ā·'ī *kik* Scarf. *Lit.*, neck sash.

ka'ele *'a'* Empty, as a bowl. Usu. *hakahaka. Dic.*

kā·'ele *'a'* Bold, on computer or in typesetting; boldface. *Dic., ext. mng.* See *ho'okā'ele.*

ka'e polo·lei *kik* Straightedge.

ka'i *kik/ham* Coach; to train (someone), as for sports. *Dic., ext. mng. Ka'i hana keaka.* Drama coach. *Ka'i ha'uki.* Sports trainer. *Ka'i pu'ukani.* Vocal coach. *Ka'i 'ālapa.* Coach for sports or physical education.

ka'i *kik* Onset of a syllable, in linguistics. *Lit.*, lead.

ka'ina *kik* Order, sequence. *Dic.* See entries below and *ho'oka'ina, pakuhi ka'ina.*

ka'ina hana *kik* Procedure, process to follow. *Lit.*, sequence (of) tasks.

ka'ina ho'i hope See *'anopili ka'ina ho'i hope.*

ka'ina ho'o·mā·kala·kala *kik* Order of operations, in math problems. *Lit.*, solving order.

ka'ina pī·'ā·pā *kik* Alphabetical order. *Lit.*, alphabet order. See *ho'oka'ina pī'āpā.*

ka'ina wā·wae *kik* Steps, as in a dance or routine. *Lit.*, foot sequence.

ka'ina 'ē·ko'a *kik* Vice versa. *Lit.*, opposite order. Also *ka'ina 'oko'a.*

ka'i wā·wae *kik/heh* Stride; to stride. *'Ehia 'īniha ka lō'ihi o kōna ka'i wāwae?* How many inches is the length of his stride? *Lit.*, step (by) foot.

ka'o·hau *'a'* Freeze-dried. *Comb. ka'o + hau.* See *ho'oka'ohau.*

kā·'oki·kene *'a'* To oxidize; oxidized. *Comb. kā + 'okikene.*

ka'oko *'a'* Dormant. (Tah., *sleep.*)

kā·'oko'a *'a'* Complete. *Dic., ext. mng. Mea ho'omomona lepo kā'oko'a.* Complete fertilizer, i.e. fertilizer which contains the six necessary elements for plant growth. *Ikehu kā'oko'a.* Thermal energy. See *ana ikehu kā'oko'a.*

ka'u·ka'u *kik* Delay, as in computer program. *Nui ke ka'uka'u ma waena o ke kōmi 'ana i ke pihi a me ka hana.* There is a long delay between pressing the key and the action. *Dic., ext. mng.*

ka'ū·mana *Pua ka'ūmana.* Azalea.

Kada *i'oa* Chad; Chadian. *Eng.*

kara·bona·hate *kik* Carbonate. *Eng. Kupuriku karabonahate.* Cupric carbonate. *Ferousa karabonahate.* Ferrous carbonate.

kara·bona mono·kesa·side *kik* Carbon monoxide. *Eng.*

kara·bona dio·kesa·side *kik* Carbon dioxide. *Eng.* Also *kalapona 'okikene lua.*

kara·bona disuli·faside *kik* Carbon disulfide. *Eng.*

Kare·biana *i'oa* Caribbean. *Dic.* Also *Kalepiana.*

Karo·laina See *Kaloloaina.*

Kata·kila *i'oa* Catskills, a mountain range. *Eng.*

kā·tuna *kik* Cartoon. *Eng.* Also *kākuna, kākuni. Puke kātuna.* Comic book.

kea See *kea ho'opukapuka.*

Keao·pō *i'oa* Alphekka, a star in the constellation Corona Borealis. *Mān.* (HA).

kea ho'o·puka·puka *kik* Stock, as in the stock market. *Lit.*, stock (for) speculating. Also *kea.*

keaka·ika·'ā·wai *kik* Jack-in-the-pulpit, a kind of flower.

keaka·pahu *kik* Jack-in-the-box. *Lit.*, jack box.

Kei·moka *i'oa* Deimos, a moon of Mars. *Eng.*

Keo·kia *i'oa* Georgia; Georgian. *Dic.*

Keola *kik* Name of Hawaiian language version of Bingo.

keu *'a'* Extended, as of computer memory; enhanced or expanded, as a computer keyboard. *'Oi aku ka nui o nā pihi ma ka papa pihi keu.* There are more keys on the expanded keyboard. *Dic., ext. mng.* Cf. *māhuahua. Waihona 'ike keu.* Extended memory. *Papa pihi keu.* Enhanced keyboard, expanded keyboard.

keu See *'ai keu.*

kē·uli *kik* Blue jay. Usu. *manu kēuli.* Comb. Eng. + *uli.*

keu pono *kik* Advantage. *Ua maopopo le'a ke keu pono o Ku'ulei ma mua o Ku'uhoni.* The advantage of Ku'ulei over Ku'uhoni was obvious. *Lit.,* extra benefit.

Keho'o·ea *i'oa* Lyra, a constellation. *Dic.*

kek Abbreviation for *kekamika* (decameter).

Kek. Abbreviation for *Kekemapa* (December). Also *Dek.*

keka- Deca-, i.e. a prefix meaning ten. *Eng.* Also *pā'umi.* See entries below.

keka *kik* Cheddar. *Eng.* See entry below. *Waiūpa'a keka.* Cheddar cheese.

keka *Ho'okae keka.* Sexism. See *ho'okae.*

keka·kalame *kik* Decagram. *Eng.* Abb. *kekal.*

kekal Abbreviation for *kekakalame* (decagram).

keka·lika *kik* Decaliter. *Eng.* Abb. *kel.*

keka·mika *kik* Decameter. *Eng.* Abb. *kek.*

Kekeka *i'oa* Texas; Texan. *Dic.* Also *Tekasa, Teseta.*

kekeke *kik* Decade. *Eng.*

kē·kelē *kik* Degree. *Dic., sp. var. He 'umi kēkelē Kelekia.* Ten degrees Celsius. *'Elima kēkelē Palanaheika.* Five degrees Fahrenheit. *'Ehia kēkelē PH ke anu [ka mahana, ka mehana, ka wela] o ka Po'ahā?* How many degrees Fahrenheit was the temperature on Thursday? *Lit.,* freezing degree. See entries below.

kē·kelē hehe'e *kik* Melting point. *Lit.,* degree (for) melting.

kē·kelē paila *kik* Boiling point. *Lit.,* degree (for) boiling.

kē·kelē pa'a·hau *kik* Freezing point. *Lit.,* degree (for) freezing.

Keke·mapa *i'oa* December. *Dic.,* sp. var. Abb. *Kek.* Also *Dekemapa.*

keki- Deci-, i.e. a prefix meaning one tenth. *Eng.* Also *hapa 'umi.* See entries below.

keki·kalame *kik* Decigram. *Eng.* Abb. *kkkal.*

keki·lika *kik* Deciliter. *Eng.* Abb. *kkl.*

keki·mala *kik* Decimal. *Dic. Kiko kekimala.* Decimal point. *Kekimala pani.* Terminating decimal. *Kekimala pīna'i.* Repeating decimal. *Kekimala 'ō'ā.* Mixed decimal. *Kuana kekimala.* Decimal place. *'Ōnaehana kekimala.* Decimal system.

keki·mika *kik* Decimeter. *Eng.* Abb. *kkm.*

keko See *palaoa keko.*

keko·hala *kik/ham* Sexual harassment; to subject to sexual harassment. *Japn.*

Keko·kia *i'oa* Scotland; Scot, Scots, Scottish. *Dic.* Also *Sekotia.*

keko lekuka *kik* Rhesus monkey. Comb. *keko* + Eng.

kekona *kik* Second. *Dic.* Abb. *kkn.*

keko pueo *kik* Owl monkey.

Keko·solo·wakia *i'oa* Czechoslovakia; Czech. *Eng.*

kel Abbreviation for *kekalika* (decaliter).

Kela·uea *i'oa* Delaware; Delawarean. *Dic., sp. var.* Also *Delauea.*

kelaka See *manu kelaka.*

kela·lani *kik* Astronaut. *Lit.,* sky sailor.

kela·wini *kik* Gale. *Dic.* Also *makani kelawini.*

kele ama kā·moe *heh* Beam reach on the port side, i.e. sailing at a 90° angle from the direction of the wind, with the port side windward. *Lit.*, sail straight port. *Cf. kele ʻākea kāmoe.*

kele ama kaʻa·kepa *heh* Broad reach on the port side, i.e. sailing downwind at an angle between 90° and directly downwind, with the port side windward. *Lit.*, sail diagonal port. *Cf. kele ʻākea kaʻakepa.*

kele ama kū·nihi *heh* Close hauled on the port side, i.e. sailing into the wind at the closest angle possible, generally 67°, with the port side windward. *Lit.*, sail sideways port. *Cf. kele ʻākea kūnihi.*

kele·awe *kik* Brass. *Dic. Cf. kele-awekini, keleaweʻula.*

kele·awe·kini *kik* Bronze. *Lit.*, tin brass.

kele·aweˈula *kik* Copper. *Comb. keleawe + ʻula.*

kele hoʻo·paheʻe *kik* Vaseline, petrolatum. *Lit.*, lubricating jelly.

kele kaʻa·lalo *heh* To sail directly downwind. *Lit.*, sail to leeward.

kele·kaʻa·ʻike *kik* Telecommunication. *Comb. kele-* [Eng.] + *kaʻaʻike.*

Keleke *iʻoa* Crete; Cretan. *Dic.* Also *Kerete.*

Kele·kia *kik* Celsius. *Eng. Abb. Klk.* See *kēkelē.*

kele·kona *kik* Skeleton, as for Halloween. *Eng.* Also *kanaka iwi. Cf. kinanahiwi.*

kele·kona *kik* Dragon, as in fairy tales. *Dic.* Also *kalekona.* See entry below.

keleku *kik* Circus. *Eng.*

Kele·mā·nia *iʻoa* Germany; German. *Dic.*

kele moana *heh* Wayfinding; to wayfind. *Lit.*, sail (the) ocean. Also *hoʻokele waʻa.* See *kaʻao kele moana.*

kelena moku ahi·kao *kik* Space capsule. *Comb. kele + -na + moku ahikao.*

kele pahē *kik* Jam. *Lit.*, pulp jelly.

kele·paʻi *ham* To fax. *Sh. kelepona + paʻi. Mīkini kelepaʻi.* Fax machine.

kele·pona See *ʻapo kelepona.*

kele·wī *kik* Abbreviation for *kelewikiona* (television). *Dic.* Also *kīwī.*

kele·wiki·ona *kik* Television. *Dic. Abb. kelewī, kīwī.*

Kele·wine *iʻoa* Kelvin. *Eng. ʻOle Kelewine.* Zero degrees K (Kelvin); absolute zero, i.e. a hypothetical temperature characterized by complete absence of heat.

kele ʻā·kea kā·moe *heh* Beam reach on the starboard side, i.e. sailing at a 90° angle from the direction of the wind, with the starboard side windward. *Lit.*, sail straight starboard. *Cf. kele ama kāmoe.*

kele ʻā·kea kaʻa·kepa *heh* Broad reach on the starboard side, i.e. sailing downwind at an angle between 90° and directly downwind, with the starboard side windward. *Lit.*, sail diagonal starboard. *Cf. kele ama kaʻakepa.*

kele ʻā·kea kū·nihi *heh* Close hauled on the starboard side, i.e. sailing into the wind at the closest angle possible, generally 67°, with the starboard side windward. *Lit.*, sail sideways starboard. *Cf. kele ama kūnihi.*

keli *kik* Cherry. *Eng.*

kē·lia *kik* Terrier. (Lat. *terrarius.*) Also *ʻīlio kēlia.*

keluka *kik* Thrush. *Dic.* Also *manu keluka. Manu keluka ululāʻau.* Wood thrush.

kelu·lose *kik* Cellulose. *Eng.*

keme·pale *ʻa* Temperate, in science. *Eng. Cf. kopikala. Nahele kemepale.* Temperate forest.

kemika *kik* Chemistry. *Eng. Kemika meaola.* Biochemistry.

kemi·kala Chemical. *Eng.* See *kāemikala*. *Ha'ihelu kemikala.* Chemical equation. *Ha'ihelu kemikala kaulike.* Balanced chemical equation. *Ha'ilula kemikala.* Chemical formula. *Helu ho'onui kemikala.* Coefficient. *Loli kemikala.* Chemical change. *Mā'ō'āna kemikala.* Chemical solution. *Mō'aui kemikala.* Chemical activity. *'Anopili kemikala.* Chemical property (preceded by *ke*). *'Ō'ā kemikala 'ia.* Chemically combined.

kemo·kalaka *Lepupalika Kemokalaka 'o Konokō.* Democratic Republic of the Congo.

kēmu *kik* Board game, as checkers. *Eng. Papa kēmu.* Game board.

kemua *'a'* To be assimilated. *Ua kemua maoli ka po'e komone'e o nā 'āina 'Eulopa i ka noho 'ana o kō 'Amelika ma hope o ke komone'e 'ana i 'Amelika.* European immigrants assimilated well into the lifestyle of Americans after immigrating to the US Comb. *kemu + -a.* See *ho'okemua*.

kena·kena *'a'* To experience a suffocating sensation. *Dic., ext. mng.*

kē·neka *kik* Cent. *Dic. Kaha kēneka.* Cent sign.

Kene·kī *i'oa* Tennessee; Tennessean. *Dic.* Also *Tenesī*.

Kene·kuke *i'oa* Kentucky; Kentuckian. *Dic.* Also *Kenetuke*.

Kenele *Pae Moku Kenele.* Canary Isles.

Kene·maka *i'oa* Denmark; Dane; Danish. *Dic.* Also *Denemaka*.

Kene·tuke *i'oa* Kentucky; Kentuckian. *Dic.* Also *Kenekuke*.

keni- Centi-, i.e. a prefix meaning one hundredth. *Eng.* Also *hapa haneli*. See entries below.

Kenia *i'oa* Kenya; Kenyan. *Eng.*

keni·kalame *kik* Centigram. *Eng.* Abb. *kkal*.

kenika manu *kik* Badminton. *Lit.,* bird tennis.

kenika pā·kau·kau *kik* Ping-pong, table tennis.

keni·keni *kik* Dime, loose change. *Dic.* Cf. *kālā helele'i*.

keni·lika *kik* Centiliter. *Eng.* Abb. *kl*.

keni·mika *kik* Centimeter. *Eng.* Abb. *knm*.

Kep. Abbreviation for *Kepakemapa* (September).

kepa *kik/ham* Spur; to spur; to gore with a tusk. Var. of *kēpā*. See *palaka kepa*. *Niho kepa*. Boar's tusk. *Ni'ihau*.

kepa *ham* To contract labor. *Dic.*

kē·pau *kik* Lead; leaden. *Dic.*

kē·pau kā *kik* Asphalt compound, i.e. a brown or black tar-like substance, a variety of distilled tar (bitumen) found in a natural state or obtained by evaporating petroleum; pitch. *Lit.,* tar pitch. See *kā*.

Kepa·kemapa *i'oa* September. *Dic.* Abb. *Kep*.

Kepa·nia *i'oa* Spain. *Dic.* Also *Sepania*.

kepela *kik* Zebrina, a kind of flower. Usu. *pua kepela*. *Lit.,* zebra.

kepila See *'iole kepila*.

kē·puka *kik/ham* Trick, prank; to play such tricks, usually with malicious intent. *Dic., ext. mng.* Cf. *nalea, pāha'ohuna*.

kewe *'a'* Wraparound, as a window or eyeglasses. *Dic., ext. mng. Pukaaniani kewe.* Wraparound window.

kewe kopa·lā *kik* Steam shovel. *Lit.,* crane shovel.

ke'ehi hewa *heh* Over the line, in volleyball. *Ni'ihau*. Also *ka'ahi hewa*.

ke'e·lelena *kik* Trampoline. Sh. *ke'ehi + lele + -na*.

ke'ena hana ki'i·'oni·'oni *kik* Movie studio, i.e. the company responsible for making movies. *Lit.,* studio (for) making movies. Cf. *hale hana ki'i'oni'oni*. *Kumu ke'ena hana ki'i'oni'oni*. Studio teacher.

ke'ena ho'o·kolo·hua *kik* Laboratory. *Lit.,* room (for) experiments.

Ke'ena Ho'o·lā·lā o ke Kalana *kik* County Planning Department.

Ke‘ena Ho‘o·noho·noho Ha‘a·wina *kik* Office of Instructional Services (OIS). *Lit.*, office (for) organizing lessons.

ke‘ena kili·lau *kik* Shower stall. See *kililau*.

ke‘ena mā·lama pō·ulia *kik* Emergency facility, emergency room. *Lit.*, room (to) take care of emergencies.

ke‘ena pū·lumi *kik* Broom closet.

ke‘o·ke‘o *Palaoa ke‘oke‘o.* White bread. See entries under *palaoa*.

Kerete *i‘oa* Crete; Cretan. *Dic.* Also *Keleke*.

kesa·‘ō *kik* Tic-tac-toe. Comb. *kesa* + *‘ō (XO)*.

kī *kik/ham* Shot; to shoot, as in basketball. *Dic., ext. mng.* See entries below and *komohia, kuhō, pākī*.

kī *kik/ham* Key, in music; peg, as for tuning stringed instruments; to tune, as a stringed instrument. *Dic.; Ni‘ihau.* See *huamele, ki‘eleo*.

kī *ham* To tune up, as an engine. *Ua kī ‘o ia i ka ‘enekini o kōna ka‘a.* He tuned up his car's engine. *Dic., ext. mng.*

kī See *puna kī*.

kia *kik* Gear, as in machinery. *Eng.* See *kia pihi*.

kia·ho‘o·mana‘o *kik* Monument. *Dic.* See *Kūkā‘oko‘a Kiaho‘omana‘o. Pāka kiaho‘omana‘o aupuni.* National monument (park administered by the government).

kiaka *kik* Teak, a kind of wood. *Eng.*

kia lō *kik* Roe deer. Comb. *kia* + *Eng.*

kia pihi *ham* Remote control; to control by remote control. *Lit.*, button steering. See *lima kia pihi*.

kia‘i *kik* Security guard. Also *kia‘i pō; māka‘i kia‘i (pō). Ni‘ihau.*

kio *Ho‘okūkū kio.* Scrimmage, as for sports. See *ho‘okūkū kahului, ho‘okūkū moho*.

kioia See *pānini kioia*.

kiola *ham* To throw underhand. *Dic., ext. mng.* Cf. *nou*.

Kione *i‘oa* Dione, a moon of Saturn. *Eng.*

kiu *kik* Cue, as in the game of pool. *Eng. Kiu pahupahu.* Pool cue.

kiu·lela *kik* Squirrel. *Dic. Kiulela ‘Ālika.* Arctic ground squirrel. *Kiulela ‘akuiki.* Chipmonk. Also *‘akuiki*.

kiuna *kik* Oriental-style scroll, usually decorative. (Cant. *gyun*.)

kiupe *kik* Tube. *Eng.*

kiupe ho‘o·lohe *kik* Stethoscope. *Lit.*, tube (for) listening. Also *‘ili ho‘olohe pu‘uwai*.

kīhei *kik* Light blanket, shawl. *Dic.* Also *kīhei pili*.

kihi *kik* Corner, particularly an outside corner. *Dic.* Cf. *kū‘ono, po‘opo‘o*.

kihi·kihi *kik* Brim, of a hat. *Mān. (MW).* Also *pekekeu.* Cf. *laulau*.

kihi·‘aki *kik* Vertex, in math. *Legendre.*

kī·hoe *kik* Nomad. *‘A‘ohe noho pa‘a ka po‘e kīhoe ma kahi ho‘okahi no ka wā lō‘ihi, no ka mea, pono lākou e huli mau i kahi kūpono e lako ai ka noho ‘ana.* Nomads do not stay very long in one place since they must constantly search for places with enough to sustain themselves. *Dic., ext. mng.*

kī·kā *kik* Guitar; cigar. *Dic.* For guitar parts, see *‘ukulele.* See also *‘ukulele pahu kīkā*.

kika·kī See *manu kikakī*.

kī·kala *Hānai kīkala.* To make a back set, in volleyball. Also *hānai i hope*.

kī·kē·kē *‘Elelū kīkēkē.* American cockroach (Periplaneta americana).

kī·kē·koa *kik* Maui parrotbill (pseudonestor xanthophrys). Comb. *kīkē* + *koa*.

kikī See *puka kikī hou*.

kī·kī *ham* To spray. *Dic., ext. mng.* Cf. *kīkina*.

kikihi *kik* Doorframe. *Dic.*

kikiki *ham* To cheat. *Dic.*

kī kī·ko‘o *ham* Lay-up, in basketball; to make such a shot. *Lit.*, extending shot. Also *kī pai*.

kī·kina *kik* Substance, as sprayed from an aerosol can. Comb. *kīkī* + *-na*. See *ehu kīkina, pena kīkina.*

kiki'u·wai *kik* Xylem. Redup. of *ki'u* [rootlet] + *wai.* Cf. *kiki'u'ai.*

kiki'u·'ai *kik* Phloem. Redup. of *ki'u* [rootlet] + *'ai.* Cf. *kiki'uwai.*

kiko *kik* Point, in math. *Dic., ext. mng.* See entries below. *Kiko kekimala.* Decimal point.

kiko *kik* Point, a unit of measurement for type size. *He 'umikūmālua ka nui ma'amau o kēlā kinona hua.* Twelve point is the standard size for that font. *Dic., ext. mng.* No abbreviation.

kiko ō·la'i *kik* Epicenter. *Lit.,* earthquake point.

kiko·ho'e *kik* Digit, in math. *'Ehia kikoho'e o ka helu 327? 'Ekolu ona kikoho'e.* How many digits are in the number 327? It has three digits. Comb. *kiko* + *ho'e (Tah.,* one). *Kikoho'e hapa mua.* Front-end digit.

kiko ho'o·maha *kik* Comma. *Dic.* Also *kiko koma.*

kiko huina *kik* Dot on a grid. *Lit.,* point (on a) junction. Cf. *huina ke'a.*

kiko kau *kik* Focus point. *Lit.,* placed dot.

kiko kau·waena *kik* Midpoint, in math. *Lit.,* centered point.

kiko·kiko *ham* To type. *Dic.* Also *pa'i hakahaka.* See *pakuhi kikokiko.*

kiko·kikona *kik* Text of a document, as in computer program. Comb. *kikokiko* + *-na.*

kiko kolu *kik* Ellipsis, in punctuation. *Lit.,* three punctuation marks.

kiko koma *kik* Comma. *Dic., new mng.* Also *kiko ho'omaha.*

kiko kuhia *kik* Reference point, in math; reference object, as in science. See *kuhia.*

kiko lā *kik* Sunspot. Cf. *lapa ahi lā, puapua'i lā, 'ale ahi lā.*

kī·kolu *Hoaka kīkolu.* Three-point arc, in basketball.

kiko nī·nau *kik* Question mark. *Dic.*

kiko pau *kik* Period, in punctuation. *Lit.,* ending punctuation mark.

kiko pū·'iwa *kik* Exclamation point. *Dic.*

kiko·wā *'a'* Synchronic, in linguistics. Comb. *kiko* + *wā.* Cf. *kōāwā. Lula kikowā.* Synchronic rule.

kiko·waena *kik* Center of a circle. *Dic.* See entries below and *huina kikowaena.*

kiko·waena kahi *kik* Concentric. *Lit.,* one center. *Nā pō'ai kikowaena kahi.* Concentric circles.

kiko·waena kilo ani·lā *kik* Weather station. *Lit.,* center (for) forecasting weather.

kiko·waena kū·'ai *kik* Shopping center, mall.

kiko·waena pā·nā·nā *kik* Field station, as used when mapping a certain area. *Lit.,* compass center.

kiko·waena pū·nae·wele *kik* Network server, as for computer network. *Lit.,* network central.

kiko·waena wili *kik* Turn center, in math.

kiko·'ī *'a'* Specific. Sh. *ke kiko o ka 'ī. Mea kiko'ī, mea li'ili'i kiko'ī, mea li'ili'i.* Detail.

kī·ko'o *ham* To draw or withdraw money from the bank. *Dic.* See *pila kīko'o, waihona kālā; kī kīko'o. Waihona kīko'o.* Checking account, as in bank.

kī·ko'o ipu·leo *ham* To operate a boom, as for movie or video production. *Lit.,* extend microphone. *Mea kīko'o ipuleo.* Boom operator.

kī·ko'u *ham* Cultivator; to cultivate. *Dic., ext. mng. Kīko'u pa'a lima.* Hand cultivator.

kī kū *ham* Set shot, in basketball; to make such a shot. *Holo akula 'o ia, a laila, kū ihola, a kī kū 'o ia.* He ran and then stopped, and made a set shot. *Lit.,* standing shot.

kila·okolo·mona *kik* Seal-of-Solomon, a kind of flower. *Eng.*

kī·lau·ea See *lua kīlauea*. *Pāka Aupuni 'o Kīlauea.* Hawai'i Volcanoes National Park.

kila pao *kik* Chisel. *Dic.*

kile *kik* Tile. *Eng. Kile lāmeka.* Ceramic tile. *Kile papahele.* Floor tile. Also *kile 'ili, moena 'ili 'āpanapana.* See *moena 'ili.*

Kile *i'oa* Chile; Chilean. *Dic.* Also *Kili.*

kī·leo See *palaku kīleo.*

kī lele *ham* Jump shot, in basketball; to make such a shot. *'Eleu wale nō 'o Muggsy Bogues ma ke kī lele.* Muggsy Bogues is a great jump shooter.

kī·lepa·lepa *kik* Pompom. *Dic., ext. mng.* Also *pōpō kīlepalepa.*

kili *kik* Chili. *Eng.*

Kili *i'oa* Chile; Chilean. *Dic.* Also *Kile.*

kili·ala *kik* Cereal. *Eng.* Also *siriala.*

kili·ona See *hapa kiliona.*

kī·like·like *kik* Assimilation, in linguistics. *Comb. kī* + redup. of *like.*

kiliki o lapu Trick or treat. *Lit.*, treat or else (be) haunted.

kili·lau *kik* Shower, for bathing. *Lit.*, many raindrops. *Kililau lima.* Hand-held shower. See *ke'ena kililau, pale kililau, pāpale kililau, po'o kililau, 'au'au kililau.*

kilina *kik* Ceiling. *Dic.* Also *huna.*

kilo- Kilo-, i.e. a prefix meaning thousand. *Eng.* Also *pākaukani.* See entries below.

kilo *kik* Kilo. *Dic. Abb. kl.*

kilo *ham* To study (i.e. examine, observe) something. *Dic., ext. mng.* Cf. *huli, kālai-.*

kī·loi *ham* To empty trash, as in computer program. *Dic., sp. var., ext. mng.*

kī·loi *ham* To pass, in basketball. *E maka'ala mau i ke kanaka hemo e kīloi ai ke kinipōpō.* Always keep an eye out for the open man to pass the ball to. *Dic., ext. mng.* See entries below.

kī·loi ulele *ham* Inbound pass, in basketball; to throw such a pass. *Kīloi ulele akula 'o Shawn Kemp iā Gary Payton ma lalo o ka hīna'i, a komo ihola ka 'ai lua.* Shawn Kemp made an inbound pass to Gary Payton under the basket, and he made it in for two. *Lit.*, pass into action.

kī·loi ulele kikī *ham* Lead pass, in basketball; to throw such a pass. *He kīloi ulele kikī ke kīloi 'ana i ke kinipōpō i mua o ka hou kime e holo ala i ka hīna'i.* A lead pass is when the ball is passed ahead of a teammate as he makes a run for the basket. *Lit.*, swift inbound pass. Also *kīloi kaha.* Cf. *ulele kikī.*

kī·loi umauma *ham* Chest pass, in basketball; to throw such a pass. *Inā makemake 'oe e kīloi 'āwīwī i ke kinipōpō, e kīloi umauma 'oe.* If you want to make a quick pass, you make it a chest pass.

kī·loi ho'o·palai *ham* Blind pass, no-look pass, in basketball; to throw such a pass. *He kīloi ma'alea ke kīloi ho'opalai.* The blind pass is meant to be sneaky. *Lit.*, pass (with) face turned away.

kī·loi kaha *ham* Lead pass, in basketball; to throw such a pass. *Lit.*, drive pass. Also *kīloi ulele kikī.*

kī·loi kua *ham* Behind-the-back pass, in basketball; to throw such a pass. *Inā ke hiki mai nei ke kūpale mai mua mai ou, e kīloi kua i kou hoa kime ma ka 'ao'ao ou.* If the defender is coming at you from ahead, you can make a behind-the-back pass to your teammate on the side of you. *Lit.*, back pass.

kī·loi palemo *ham* Back-door pass, in basketball; to throw such a pass. *He ka'ane'e kūlele 'e'epa maika'i ke kīloi palemo e lanakila ai.* The back-door pass is a clever offensive play for scoring. *Lit.*, slip-away pass.

kī·loi papa·hele *ham* Bounce pass, in basketball; to throw such a pass. *Kīloi papahele 'o Moano ma waena o nā wāwae o Kahu a hiki iā Pono.* Moano made a bounce pass between the legs of Kahu and over to Pono. *Lit.,* floor pass.

kī·loi papa'i *ham* Tip pass, in basketball; to throw such a pass. *Kīko'o akula 'o Kā'eo i kōna lima e kīloi papa'i i ke kinipōpō iā Lā'au.* Kā'eo reached out his hand to tip pass the ball to Lā'au. slapping pass. Cf. *kī papa'i.*

kī·loi pa'ewa *ham* To throw away (the ball), in basketball. *Eo ihola mākou iā Leilehua ma muli o ke kīloi pa'ewa 'ana o Nānuha i ke kinipōpō i waho.* We lost the game to Leilehua because Nānuha threw the ball away. *Lit.,* throw wrong.

kī·loi pi'o *ham* Lob pass, in basketball; to throw such a pass. *He ki'eki'e ke kīloi pi'o i 'ole e 'apo 'ia ke kinipōpō e ka hoa paio.* A lob pass is high so that the ball doesn't get caught by the opponents. *Lit.,* arched pass. Cf. *kī pi'o.*

kī·loi 'ao·'ao *ham* Hook pass, in basketball; to throw such a pass. *'O ke kīloi 'ao'ao wale akula nō ia o ka helu 4 ma luna o ka mea e kaupale ana iā ia.* Number 4 made a hook pass right over the one who was defending him. *Lit.,* side pass.

kilo·uate *kik* Kilowatt. *Eng. Abb.* klt. See *uate.*

kilo·kalame *kik* Kilogram. *Eng. Abb.* klkal.

kilo lani *Ana kilo lani.* Sextant.

kilo·lika *kik* Kiloliter. *Eng. Abb.* kll.

kilo·mika *kik* Kilometer. *Eng. Abb.* klm.

kimeki iwi *kik* Cast, as for a broken arm. Comb. Ni'ihau + *iwi.* Also *puna.*

kimo *kik* Jacks (the game). *Dic.* See *hōkūkimo.*

kimu *kik* Precipitation. Samoan *timu* (rain).

Kina *i'oa* China; Chinese. *Dic.* See *Pākē, 'Āina Pākē.*

kina·mona *kik* Cinnamon. *Dic.*

kinamu *kik* Gingham. *Dic.*

kinana·hiwi *kik* Skeleton. Comb. *tinana* [Maori: body] + *hiwi.* Cf. *kanaka iwi, kelekona.*

Kī·na'u *i'oa* Avior, a star. *Mān.* (HA).

kini See entries below. *Une kini.* Tab, as on soda cans. *Une kini koloaka.* Soda can tab.

kini ea lu'u kai *kik* Scuba tank. Usu. *kini ea. Lit.,* air can (for) diving (in the) sea. Cf. *lu'u kini ea.*

kini i'a *kik* Canned fish.

kini ho'o·pio ahi *kik* Fire extinguisher. Also *kini kinai ahi.*

kini ho'o·pulu mea·kanu *kik* Watering can.

kini hue·wai *kik* Canteen. *Lit.,* water gourd can.

kinika *kik* Sink, as in kitchen or bathroom. *Eng.*

kini kā·lā *kik* Cashbox. *Lit.,* money can. Cf. *kālā kini.*

kiniki *kik* Zinc. *Eng.*

kini kī·kī *kik* Aerosol can. *Lit.,* can (which) sprays.

kini·kila See *lāpaki kinikila.*

kini kinai ahi *kik* Fire extinguisher. Also *kini ho'opio ahi.*

kini·kona *kik* Quinine. *Eng. (from cinchona, the tree from which quinine is made).*

kini lapa·'au *kik* First aid kit. *Lit.,* medical can. Also *poho lā'au pōulia.*

kini·pai *kik* Pot pie. Comb. *kini + pai.*

kini paipu ahi *kik* Muffler, as on a car. Ni'ihau. Cf. *paipu ahi.*

kini pipi *kik* Can of corned beef; canned corned beef. *Mān.* Cf. *pipi kini.*

kini poho ea *kik* Repair kit, for tires. Ni'ihau.

kini·pō·pō *kik* Ball. *Dic.* See entries below.

kini·pō·pō aloha *kik* Aloha ball, in volleyball. Ni'ihau.

Māmaka Kaiao / 68

kini·pō·pō hele wale *kik* Kill, in volleyball. *Niʻihau.*

kini·pō·pō pō·hili *kik* Baseball (ball). See *pōhili.*

kini·pō·pō pō·hī·naʻi *kik* Basketball (ball). See *pōhīnaʻi.*

kini·pō·pō pō·peku *kik* Football (ball). See *pōpeku.*

kini·pō·pō pō·wā·wae *kik* Soccer ball. See *pōwāwae.*

kini ʻai·ō *kik* Lunch pail. *Niʻihau.* Also *kini ʻai.*

kini ʻoki·kene *kik* Oxygen tank.

kini tuna *kik* Can of tuna.

kino *kik* Body, as of a composition or text. *Dic., ext. mng.* See *hoʻomaka, pau.*

kī noa *ham* Free throw, in basketball; to make such a shot. *He 65% ʻo John Stockton ma ka laina kī noa.* John Stockton is 65% at the free-throw line. See *laina kī noa. Kī noa pākahi.* Single free throw. *Kī noa kī hou.* One-and-one free throw. *Kī noa pālua.* Two-shot free throw.

kino·ea *kik* Gas, gaseous, as opposed to solid or liquid. Comb. *kino + ea.* Cf. *kinopaʻa, kinowai.* See *hāmeʻa hana kinoea.*

kino·hapa *kik* Numerator, in math. *Lit.*, partial body. Cf. *kinopiha.*

kino hua·helu *kik* Standard form, as for numbers. *ʻO ke kino huahelu o ke kanakolu, penei nō ia: 30.* This is the standard form of thirty: 30. *Lit.*, number form.

kino lā·toma *kik* Allotrope, i.e. a different molecular form of an element, in science. *Lit.*, molecule body.

kinona *kik* Shape; geometric figure. Comb. *kino + -na.* See entries below. *Kinona analahi.* Regular shape.

kinona hua *kik* Font, typeface, as in printing or computer program. *E hoʻololi i ke kinona hua.* Change the font. *Lit.*, letter shape. *Pāpahu kinona hua.* Font cartridge.

kinona like *kik* Image, in math. *Lit.*, same shape. *Kinona aka like o kekahi ʻaoʻao.* Reflection image. *Kinona like o kekahi ʻaoʻao.* Rotation image. *Kinona like kau.* Translation image. *Kinona like wili.* Turn image. *Kinona like wili hapalua.* Half-turn image. *Kinona like wili hapahā.* Quarter-turn image. Also *kinona like wili 1/4.*

kinona papa *kik* Plane figure, a figure that lies on a flat surface, in math. *Lit.*, flat-surface shape.

kinona paʻa *kik* Solid figure, in math. *Lit.*, solid shape.

kinona pihana·haka *kik* Space figure, in math. *Lit.*, volume figure.

kinona ʻano like *kik* Similar figure, in math.

kino·paʻa *kik* Solid, as opposed to liquid or gas. Comb. *kino + paʻa.* Also *paʻa.* Cf. *kinoea, kinowai. Kao wāwahie kinopaʻa.* Sold rocket booster.

kino·piha *kik* Denominator, in math. *Lit.*, complete body. Cf. *kinohapa. Kinopiha haʻahaʻa loa.* Least common denominator.

kino·wai *kik* Liquid. Comb. *kino + wai.* Cf. *kinoea, kinopaʻa.*

kī pai *ham* Lay-up, in basketball; to make such a shot. *Kupanaha maoli ka lele ʻana o Koʻi ma luna o ka pūʻulu kūpale no ke kī pai ʻana a komo.* That was an amazing leap Koʻi made over the herd of defenders to make the layup shot. *Lit.*, raising shot. Also *kī kīkoʻo.*

kī·paku See *hoʻokuʻia kīpaku.*

kī papa *ham* Bank shot, in basketball; to make such a shot. *He ʻupena wale nō ke kī mua, a laila, he kī papa ka lua.* The first shot was all net, then the second one was a bank shot. *Lit.*, backboard shot.

kī·pā·pali *kik* Small cliffs; hilly. *Dic.*

kī·papa puka·ani·ani *kik* Tile windows, as in computer program. *Lit.*, window pavement.

kī papaʻi *ham* Tip-in, as a basket in basketball; to make such a shot. *ʻEono āna ʻai ma ke kī papaʻi ʻana.* He has six points by tip-ins. Lit., slapping shot. Cf. *kīloi papaʻi.*

kī·pehi *ham* To hit, as with a racket. *Dic., ext. mng. Kīpehi pohoalo.* To hit forehand. *Kīpehi pohokua.* To hit backhand.

kī·peku *ham* To eject, as disk from computer or video cassette from a VCR. *E kīpeku i ke pā mai ke kakena.* Eject the disk from the drive. *Niʻihau, ext. mng.*

kipi *kik* Chip, as potato chip. *Eng. Kipi ʻuala kahiki.* Potato chip. *Kipi kalo.* Taro chip.

kī piʻo *ham* Hook shot, in basketball; to make such a shot. *He kīloi piʻo nui ʻo Kareem Abdul Jabar, no ka mea, mio wale nō ʻo ia ma ia hana.* Kareem Abdul Jabar does a lot of hook shots because he is so good at it. Lit., arched shot. Cf. *kīloi piʻo.*

kī·poka *kik* Porcupine. *Dic.*

kipola *kik* Tiple, a musical instrument with ten strings. *Eng.*

kī·poʻo *ham* To indent, as the first line of a paragraph on a typewriter or computer. *E kīpoʻo i ka laina mua ʻelima kaʻahua mai ka lihi hema mai.* Indent the first line five spaces from the left margin. Sh. *kīpoʻopoʻo + poʻo hou.* Cf. *hoʻokawāholo.*

kī·poʻo·poʻo See *palaoa kīpoʻopoʻo.*

kī·pulu *kik/ham* Compost; to compost. *Dic., ext. mng.* Cf. *hoʻomomona. Hana kīpulu.* To make compost.

kī·puni *ʻa* Hygroscopic. *Dic., ext. mng. Wai kīpuni.* Hygroscopic water.

kī wai *kik* Faucet. *Mān. ʻAu kī wai* (preceded by *ke*). Faucet handle.

kī·wī *kik* Abbreviation for *kelewikiona* (television); TV. *Dic.* Also *kelewī.* See *ʻohe kīwī. Papakaumaka kīwī.* TV screen. *Pahu papakaumaka kīwī.* TV monitor.

kiwi·kā *kik* City, urban area; municipal (note that in Hawaiʻi most things are county rather than municipal). (Lat. *civicus.*) See *hoʻokiwikā.* Cf. *kaona, kūlanakauhale. Kahua pāʻani kolepa kiwikā.* Municipal golf course. *ʻĀina kumu wai kiwikā.* Municipal watershed.

kī·wī·kona *kik* Telethon. Comb. *kīwī* + Eng.

kī·wila *Kānāwai kīwila.* Civil law. Also *kānāwai sīwila.*

kī ʻai kolu *ham* Three-point shot, in basketball; to attempt such a shot. *He kī ʻai kolu kekahi hapalua o kāna mau ʻai.* Half of his points are three-pointers. Cf. *ʻai kolu.*

kī·ʻaha *kik* Cup, as a unit of measurement. *Dic., ext. mng.* Abb. kh. *Kīʻaha ana.* Measuring cup.

kiʻe Abbreviation for *kiʻekiʻe* (height).

kiʻei *ham* To peer. *Dic.* Also *ʻōwī.*

kiʻe·kiʻe *ʻa* Height. *Dic.* Abb. *kiʻe.* Also *ana kiʻekiʻe.* See *hohonu, kiʻekiʻena.* Cf. *ākea, laulā, loa, lōʻihi.* See also *woela kiʻekiʻe.*

kiʻe·kiʻena *kik* Altitude, elevation. *Dic.* See *kiʻekiʻe. Ana kiʻekiʻena.* Altimeter. *Kiʻekiʻena nalu, kiʻekiʻena ʻale, kiʻekiʻena.* Height, as of a wave. See *koā.*

kiʻe·leo *kik* Pitch, in linguistics and music. Sh. *kiʻekiʻe o ka leo. Kiʻeleo haʻahaʻa.* Low pitch. *Kiʻeleo kiʻekiʻe.* High pitch.

kiʻena·o·a *kik* Skyscraper. Sh. *kiʻikiʻena + oʻa.* Cf. *nuʻuoʻa.*

kiʻi *kik* Figure, as illustration in a textbook; graphics. *Ua komolike ʻo kiʻi A a me kiʻi E.* Figures A and E are congruent. *Dic., ext. mng.* See entries below and *pakuhi kiʻi. Mea ʻenehana kiʻi.* Graphics technician, as for movie or video production.

kiʻi *ham* To receive a serve, in volleyball; also first pass. *Niʻihau.*

ki'i a ala·kō *ham* To drag, as in computer program. *Lit.*, fetch and drag. Also *alakō*. *Alakō ma luna o; alakō a kau ma luna o.* To drag onto.

ki'i·aka *kik* Slide (photographic transparency). Comb. *ki'i + aka.* See *pākū ho'olele ki'i. Mīkini ho'olele ki'iaka.* Slide projector. *Mōlina ki'iaka.* Slide mount.

ki'i·ona *kik* Icon, as in computer program. Sh. *ki'i + Eng.*

ki'i hō·'aui·kala *kik* Chromatograph. *Lit.*, chromatography diagram. See *hō'auikala.*

ki'i ho'o·maka'u manu *kik* Scarecrow. *Lit.*, image (for) frightening birds.

ki'i kaha koe *kik* Etching. *Lit.*, etched picture. Cf. *ki'i māio.* See *kaha koe.*

ki'i kiko *kik* Bitmap; a bitmapped graphic image. *Ua kākiko 'ia kēia ki'i kiko ma kēnā mīkini pa'i.* This bitmapped graphic image was bitmapped on that printer. *Lit.*, dot picture. Cf. *kākiko.*

ki'i·kuhi *kik* Diagram, schematic drawing. Sh. *ki'i + kuhikuhi. Ki'ikuhi pahiki.* Tree diagram, in math. *Ki'ikuhi Wene.* Venn diagram, i.e. a diagram using overlapping circles to show relationship of data.

ki'i kū·kulu *kik* Blueprint. *Lit.*, diagram (for) building. Also *ki'i kūkulu hale.*

ki'i ku'i·kepa *kik* Sculpture. *Dic.*

ki'i lima *kik* Puppet. *Lit.*, hand doll. Also *pāpeka, pāpeta.* See *pāpeka kaula.*

ki'i·lou *ham* To save, in basketball. *Lele po'o wale 'o Kekoa ma waena o ke anaina nānā iā ia e ki'ilou ana i ke kinipōpō.* Kekoa just dove headlong right into the crowd when he went to save the ball. Comb. *ki'i + lou.*

ki'i māio *kik* Lithograph. *Lit.*, grooved picture. Cf. *ki'i kaha koe.*

ki'i mana·mana lima *kik* Fingerprint. *Lit.*, finger picture. Also *māka manamana lima, meheu manamana lima.* See *kāpala, māioio manamana lima. 'Ohi i ke ki'i manamana lima.* To collect fingerprints.

ki'ina *kik* Movements, as in dancing. *Dic., ext. mng.* See entries below. *Ki'ina lima.* Hand movements. *Ki'ina wāwae.* Foot movements.

ki'ina hana *kik* Method, technique. Comb. *ki'ina + hana.* Also *ki'ina. Nā ki'ina 'ohi hāpana.* Sampling methods.

ki'ina leo *kik* Intonation. *Dic.*

ki'i·pā *heh* To vamp, as in hula or singing. *Dic.*

ki'i pā·lā·kiō *kik* Scale drawing, in math.

ki'i pa'i *kik* Photograph, shot. Cf. *pa'i ki'i.*

ki'i·'oni·'oni See *mīkini ho'olele ki'i'oni'oni, mo'olelo ki'i'oni'oni, pākū ho'olele ki'i.*

kī·'ō·ko'a·ko'a *kik* Dissimilation, in linguistics. Comb. *kī* + redup. of *'oko'a.*

ki'o wai *kik* Pool of water, as in a stream. *Dic.*

kī·'o'e *ham* To skim; to ladle, scoop. *Dic.* Also *'o'e.* See *puna kī'o'e.*

kita·rahate *kik* Citrate. *Eng. Sodiuma kitarahate.* Sodium citrate.

ki'o wai wai·lele *kik* Plunge pool. *Lit.*, waterfall pool.

kō *kik* Re, the second note on the musical scale. *Dic.* See *pākōlī.*

kō *Mimi kō.* Diabetes. Also *ma'i kōpa'a.*

koa *Kahua pū'ali koa.* Military base. *Pū'ali koa.* Army; military service. *Pū'ali koa kūikawā* Militia.

kō·ā *kik* Crack or space, as between fence boards. *Dic., ext. mng.* Cf. *'oā.*

kō·ā *kik* Length, as of a wave; wavelength. *Dic., ext. mng., sp. var.* Also *kōā nalu, kōā 'ale.* See *ki'eki'ena. Kōā hawewe kani.* Sound wavelength.

koali lele·pinao *kik* Trapeze. *Dic., ext. mng.* See *lelepinao.*

koana *kik* Spacing, as lines in a printed document. *Dic., ext. mng.* Cf. *kaʻahua.* See *hoʻokoana. Koana pākahi.* Single space, single-line spacing. *Koana pākahi me ka hapalua.* One and one-half space, One and one-half line spacing. *Koana pālua.* Double space, double-line spacing.

kō·ā·wā *ʻa* Diachronic, in linguistics. Comb. *kōā + wā.* Cf. *kikowā. Lula kōāwā.* Diachronic rule.

koe *ham* To strike, as a match. *Dic.* Cf. *koekoe.* See *kaha koe.*

koea a mania *ʻa* Eroded smooth. *Dic.*

koe·hana *kik* Artifact. Comb. *koe + hana.* See *hulikoehana.*

koe·koe *ham* To strum, as an ʻukulele or guitar. *Dic.* Cf. *koe.*

koena *kik* Remainder, difference, in math. *Dic.* Abb. *K.* Change, as from a purchase. Cf. *kālā heleleʻi.*

kō·ī *Wai kōī.* Cataract, i.e. steep rapids in a large river.

koi·ū *kik* Shoyu, soy sauce. *Dic. Pāpapa koiū.* Soybean.

koi·hā *kik* Weight, as for scales, etc. *Tah.*

koina *kik* Requirement. Comb. *koi + -na.*

koi pohō *kik* Claim for damages, as to an insurance company. *Dic. Hoʻopiʻi i ke koi pohō.* To make a claim for damages.

kō omōmo *kik* Lollipop, sucker. *Dic., ext. mng.* Also *kanakē ʻau.*

koho *ham* To choose, as in computer program; choice; option, as on computer keyboard. *Dic., ext. mng.* See entries below. *Pihi koho.* Option key (preceded by *ke*). *Papa koho.* Menu bar.

koho *kik/ham* Guess, estimate; to guess, estimate. *Dic.* See *kohoemi, kohoʻoi. Koho hapa mua.* Front-end estimation, in math. *Koho pāloka wae moho, wae moho.* Primary election. *ʻĀmana koho.* Dichotomous key.

koho·emi *ham* To underestimate. Comb. *koho + emi.* See *kohoʻoi.*

koho·koho *kik* Multiple-choice. *Dic., ext. mng.* Also *pane kohokoho. Nīnau kohokoho.* Multiple-choice question.

koho·lā kua·piʻo *kik* Humpback whale. *Lit.,* arched-back whale.

koho pā·lā·kiō *kik* Scale selection, as in computer program.

koho·ʻoi *ham* To overestimate. Comb. *koho + ʻoi.* See *kohoemi.*

kohu *kik* Sap. *Dic.*

kō hua·mele *kik* Duration, in music. *Lit.,* hold a note in music.

kohu ʻoia·ʻi·ʻo *ʻa* Realistic. *Lit.,* resembling truth. *Hakupuni kohu ʻoiaʻiʻo.* Realistic fiction.

koka *kik* Cord, a unit for measuring firewood. *Dic.*

kō·kaha *kik/heh* Condensation; to condense, as gas to liquid. (Māori *tōtā.*)

Koka Rika *iʻoa* Costa Rica; Costa Rican. *Eng.*

kō·keina *kik* Cocaine. *Eng.*

kokeiʻa *kik* Prairie dog. (Ute *toceyʻa.*)

koke·kau *kik/ʻa* Approximation; approximate. *He kokekau wale nō kēia hāʻina ma muli o ka loaʻa ʻole mai o ka ʻikepili ʻauiliʻi.* This answer is only an approxi- mation because of a lack of precise data. *E koho i ka huapalapala nona ka ʻili kokekau o kēia huinakolu.* Choose the letter with the approximate area of this triangle.

koki·kone *kik* Cortisone, a hormone used in the treatment of arthritis. *Eng.* See entry below. *Kokikone wai.* Hydrocortisone.

koko *kik* Blood. *Dic. Hulu koko.* Blood type. *Hunaola koko.* Blood cell. *Hunaola koko keʻokeʻo.* White blood cell. *Hunaola koko ʻulaʻula.* Red blood cell. *Kahena koko.* Bloodstream. *Koko huʻihuʻi.* Cold-blooded, as an animal. *Koko mehana.* Warm-blooded. *Monakō koko.* Blood glucose. *Pākela koko piʻi.* Hypertension, i.e. abnormally high arterial blood pressure.

koko *kik* Rare, as meat. *Dic., ext. mng.* Also *kokoko.*

kokoke *'a'* Close, near. *Dic.* See *laulā, lōpū. Pa'i kokoke.* Close-up, as of a photograph or in movie or video production (preceded by *ke*). *Pa'i a kokoke.* To take a close-up. *Pa'i kokoke loa.* Extreme close-up. *Pa'i a kokoke loa.* To take an extreme close-up.

kokoko *'a'* Rare, as meat. *Dic.* Also *koko.*

ko·ko·leka pā·hoe·hoe *kik* Fudge. Lit., *pāhoehoe*-like chocolate.

Kō·ko'o·lua *i'oa* Mirach, a star. *Mān. (HA).*

Kokosa *i'oa* Cocos. *Eng. Ka Una Honua Kokosa.* Cocos Plate.

kō·kua See entries below and *mea kōkua helu. Lawelawe kōkua.* Social services.

kō·kua huamele *kik* Musical staff. *Makua Laiana.* Also *ko'oko'o, kumu 'ākōlī.*

kō·kua nele *kik/ham* Welfare, i.e. public financial assistance for needy persons. *Kūkulu 'ia nā papahana kōkua nele na ke aupuni no ke kōkua i ka lehulehu ma nā pono ma kahi o ka loa'a 'ole o ka hana, ka lawa 'ole o ke kālā, a me ka uku ho'omau no ka wā rītaia.* Government welfare programs were set up to provide public aid for those who are in need of unemployment benefits, financial assistance, and pensions. Lit., help needy (persons).

kolamu *kik* Column. *Dic.* See *ho'okolamu. Pukaaniani kolamu 'ikepili.* List editor screen, in computer program.

Kō·lea Hema *i'oa* South Korea; South Korean. *Dic.* Also *Kōrea Hema.*

Kō·lea 'Ā·kau *i'oa* North Korea; North Korean. *Dic.* Also *Kōrea 'Ākau.*

koleke *kik* College, as a division or department within a university. *Eng. Koleke mahi'ai.* College of agriculture. *Koleke pāheona me ka 'epekema.* College of arts and sciences.

kolepa *kik* Golf. *Dic. Kahua pā'ani kolepa kiwikā.* Municipal golf course. *'Ūhili kolepa.* Golf club.

koli *kik* Meteor. *Dic.*

koli·koli *ham* To round off, in math. *Dic., new mng.* See *'uala kahiki kolikoli. Kolikoli ha'alalo.* To round down. *Kolikoli ha'aluna.* To round up.

kolo *'Au kolo.* Free-style or crawl, in swimming; to swim using this style. *Dic.*

kolohe *Hana kolohe.* To fake or hit, in volleyball. *Kahakaha kolohe.* Graffiti.

Kolo·lako *i'oa* Colorado; Coloradan. *Dic.* Also *Kolorado.* See *Haka'ama. Ka muliwai 'o Kololako.* Colorado River.

Kolome·pia *i'oa* Colombia; Colombian. *Eng.* Also *Kolomebia.*

Kolome·bia *i'oa* Colombia; Colombian. *Eng.* Also *Kolomepia.*

kolona *kik* Colon, in punctuation. *Dic.* See *hapa kolona.*

kolo·naio *'a'* Colonized, particularly from the perspective of a people who have been colonized by a dominant culture or political entity. *Eng.* See *ho'okolonaio, ho'opanalā'au.*

kolo·nahe *heh* Blowing softly, as a gentle breeze; leaves in constant motion in meteorology. *Dic.* See *makani.*

kolo·palake *kik* Chloroplast. *Eng.*

kolo·pila *kik* Chlorophyll. *Eng.* See *palasika.*

kolo·poma *kik* Chloroform. *Eng.*

Kolo·rado *i'oa* Colorado; Coloradan. *Dic.* Also *Kololako.*

kolo·rine *kik* Chlorine. *Eng.*

kolori·side *kik* Chloride. *Eng. Kobalata koloriside.* Cobalt chloride. *Satanousa koloriside.* Stannous chloride.

koloro·dane *kik* Chlorodane. *Eng.*

koloro·foloro·kala·pona *kik* Chlorofluorocarbon. *Ho'ohewa nui 'ia ke kolorofolorokalapona no ka ho'opilikia 'ana i ke kā'ei 'okikene kolu o ka lewapuni.* Chlorofluorocarbons are often blamed for damaging the ozone layer of our atmosphere. *Eng.*

kolū·kalaiwa *kik* Screwdriver. *Mān.* See *kui nao.*

koma *Kiko koma.* Comma. *Dic.* Also *kiko hoʻomaha.*

koma luna *kik* Apostrophe. *Dic.*

kōmi *ham* Click; to click, press or depress, as in computer program. *E kōmi pālua i ka ʻiole ma luna o ke kiʻiona.* Double click the mouse on the icon. *Niʻihau; dic., ext. mng.* Also *kaomi.* See *kōmi ʻōkuhi, paʻina.*

komi·kina *kik* Commission. *Dic.* See *uku ʻēkena. Komikina Hoʻohana ʻĀina o ka Mokuʻāina.* State Land Use Commission. *Komikina wai.* Water commission.

Komi·nika *iʻoa* Dominican. *Dic. Lepupalika Kominika.* Dominican Republic.

kōmi ʻō·kuhi *kik* Macro, as in computer program. *Lit.,* press directions.

komo *kik* Ring. *Dic.* See *helu komo. Manamana komo.* Ring finger. Also *manamana pili.*

komo (i loko o) *heh* To access, as in computer program. *E komo i loko o ka polokalamu ma ke kōmi ʻana iā ʻOia.* Access the program by clicking on OK. *Dic., ext. mng.*

komo·hana *kik* West. *Dic. Abb. Km. Poepoe hapa komohana.* Western hemisphere.

komo·hia *ʻa* Made a basket, in basketball. *Komohia (ka hīnaʻi) iā ʻoe!* You made a basket! *Dic., ext. mng.* Also *hoʻokomo i ke kinipōpō* (to make a basket). See *kī.*

komo·like *heh* Congruent. Comb. *komo + like. Huinakolu komolike.* Congruent triangle. *Kinona komolike.* Congruent figure.

komo·neʻe *heh* To immigrate. *Ua komoneʻe lākou i loko o Hawaiʻi nei.* They immigrated to Hawaiʻi. Comb. *komo + neʻe.* Cf. *pukaneʻe.*

komo pae *heh* Passage, initiation, as into a group. *Lit.,* enter (a) group. See *hoʻokomo pae. Hana komo pae.* Rite of passage, initiation.

komo pū *heh* Included. *Lit.,* include together with. *ʻAuhau komo pū.* Tax included. *He ʻeono kālā ʻauhau komo pū o kēia palaʻili.* This T-shirt is six dollars, tax included.

komosa *kik* Cosmos, a kind of flower. *Eng.*

-kona -thon. *Eng.* See *helekona, hulahulakona, kīwīkona,* etc.

kone ala·nui *kik* Cone used as traffic marker. *Lit.,* street cone. See *papale kone.*

koneka *kik* Consonant. *Eng.*

Kone·kikuka *iʻoa* Connecticut. *Dic.* Also *Konetikuta.*

kō·nelo *kik* Tunnel. *Niʻihau (Eng.).*

kone ʻai·kalima *kik* Ice cream cone.

Kone·tikuta *iʻoa* Connecticut. *Dic.* Also *Konekikuka.*

Kono·kō *iʻoa* Congo; Congolese. *Eng. Lepupalika Kemokalaka ʻo Konokō.* Democratic Republic of the Congo.

kopa *kik* Soap. *Dic. Kopa kahi ʻumiʻumi.* Shaving soap. Usu. *kopa ʻumiʻumi. Kopa lauoho.* Shampoo. *Pā kopa* (preceded by *ke*). Soap dish.

kopa·laka *kik* Cobalt. *Eng.* Also *kobalata.*

kopa·lā lima *kik* Garden trowel. *Lit.,* hand shovel.

kopa·lā liʻiliʻi *kik* Small spade, as a garden tool. *Lit.,* small shovel.

kō·paʻa *Maʻi kōpaʻa.* Diabetes. Also *mimi kō.*

kope *kik* Copy, as of a document. *Dic.* See *papaʻa. Hana kope.* To copy, make a copy. *Kope kumu.* Original or master copy, i.e. a master used for making additional copies.

kope *ham* To rake. *Dic.* Also *kope-kope, pūlumi. Kope ʻōpala.* Rake, as for leaves. *Hao kope.* Garden rake.

kō·pia *kik* Carbohydrate. Comb. *kō + pia.*

kopi·ana *kik* Scorpion. *Dic.* See other entries in dictionary.

kō·pia·ā *kik/heh* Respiration; to respire. *Lit.,* burning carbohydrates.

Māmaka Kaiao / 74

kopi·kala *'a'* Tropic; tropical. *'A'ohe ona wahi ulu, koe wale nō ma nā 'āina kopikala.* It only grows in tropic lands. Eng. *Kā'ei kopikala.* The tropics. *Kā'ei ku'ina kopikala.* Intertropical convergent zone (ITCZ). *Lalo kopikala.* Subtropical. *'Ino kopikala.* Tropical storm. Cf. *kemepale.*

kō·pū mea·ola *kik* Biomass. Comb. *kōpū* (sh. *tōpūtanga* [*Māori*, mass]) + *meaola.*

kō·'ai hema *ham* Counterclockwise. *E kīloi i ke kinipōpō ma ke kō'ai hema.* Throw the ball counterclockwise. Lit., stir (to the) left. Cf. *kō'ai 'ākau.*

kō·'ai 'ā·kau *ham* Clockwise. *E holo a puni ka hale ma ke kō'ai 'ākau.* Run around the house clockwise. Lit., stir (to the) right. Cf. *kō'ai hema.*

ko·'a·ko'ana *kik* Precipitate, i.e. a substance separated from a solution or suspension by chemical or physical change. Redup. of *ko'ana.*

kō·'ala See *'oma kō'ala.*

ko'ana kai *kik* Marine sediment. Lit., sea sediment.

ko'ana kaha·wai *kik* Stream sediment.

Ko'ana·ko'a *i'oa* Kingman Reef. Lit., settling (of) coral.

ko'e *kik* Worm. Dic. See entries below.

ko'e omo·ola *kik* Parasitic worm, e.g. heartworm, nematode, roundworm, tapeworm, etc. Lit., parasite worm.

ko'e honua *kik* Earthworm.

ko'e·ko'e *Kaua ko'eko'e.* Cold war, i.e. intense rivalry between nations but without military combat.

ko'e·lau *kik* Fluke. Comb. *ko'e + lau. Ko'elau ake.* Liver fluke.

ko'e moe·'alā *kik* Polychaete worm, a kind of worm found underneath stream rocks. Also *moe'alā.*

ko'e pā·ki'i *kik* Planaria. Lit., flat worm.

ko'e pā·laha·laha *kik* Flatworm. Cf. *ko'e poepoe.*

ko'e poe·poe *kik* Roundworm. Cf. *ko'e pālahalaha.*

ko'e pu'u·wai *kik* Heartworm.

ko'e 'ele·muku *kik* Nematode. Comb. *ko'e + elemutu* (*Tokelau*, worm).

ko'e 'ula *kik* Tubifex. Lit., red worm.

ko'i *kik* Axe. Dic. Also *ko'i lipi. Mān.* See *ko'i kālai.*

kō·'ie·'ie *Wai kō'ie'ie.* Run, as in a stream.

ko'i kā·lai *kik* Hoe. Lit, adze (for) hoeing. Also *hō, 'ō'ō kālai.* See *kālai.*

ko'o·hune *kik* Bacteria. Lit., small staff (from Greek). *Ko'ohune ola mehana.* Mesophilic bacteria. *Ko'ohune ola wela.* Thermophilic bacteria. *Ko'ohune naikokene.* Azobacter, a type of bacteria containing nitrogen.

ko'o·ko'o See *kōkua huamele.*

ko'o lele *kik* Pole vault. Lit., pole (for) jumping. See *lele ko'o.*

ko'o lima *kik/heh* Pushup; to do pushups. Dic.

ko'o puka *kik* Doorstop. Lit., door prop. Also *ko'o 'īpuka.*

ko'u *ham* To jab with fingertips, in volleyball. Ni'ihau.

koba·lata kolori·side *kik* Cobalt chloride. Eng.

Kō·rea Hema *i'oa* South Korea; South Korean. Dic., sp. var. Also *Kōlea Hema.*

Kō·rea 'Ā·kau *i'oa* North Korea; North Korean. Dic., sp. var. Also *Kōlea 'Ākau.*

kū *kik* Stand. Ni'ihau (Eng. calque). See *kī kū. Kū ko'okolu.* Tripod. *Kū pena ki'i.* Easel.

kua *'Au kua.* Back stroke, in swimming; to swim the back stroke. Lit., swim (on the) back. See *kā'ei kua, kīloi kua.*

kua uma *kik* Beam, of a boat. Lit., stern beam.

kua hao paiki·kala *kik* Crossbar (on a bicycle). Ni'ihau.

kua·hene *kik* Shield, as in volcanoes. Comb. *kua-* + *hene.* Cf. *pale kaua. Hoʻāhua kuahene.* Shield building; to build a shield (volcano). *Lua pele kuahene.* Shield volcano. *Lua pele kuahene kuamua.* Primary shield volcano.

kua·hope Final or terminal, as last in time, order or importance. Comb. *kua* + *hope.* See *kuamua, kualua, kuakolu. ʻĀmanapuʻu kuahope.* Terminal bronchiole, in anatomy.

kuaka *kik* Quart. *Dic.* Abb. *kk.*

kū·ā·kea *ʻa*ʻ Open, as a primary election. *Dic., ext. mng., sp. var.* Cf. *kūloko. Wae moho kūākea.* Open primary.

Kuake·mala *iʻoa* Guatemala; Guatemalan. *Dic.*

kua·kolu Tertiary, as third in time, order or importance. *Dic., ext. def.* See *kuamua, kualua, kuahope. ʻĀmanapuʻu kuakolu.* Tertiary bronchus, segmental bronchus, in anatomy.

kua·lā *kik* Dorsal fin, of a fish, nonscientific term. *Dic.* See entry below. *Kualā laukua.* Dorsal fin, of a fish, scientific term. *Kualā laumua.* Anterior dorsal fin. *Kualā lauhope.* Posterior dorsal fin.

kua·lā *kik* Rain in small area while sun is shining, sometimes considered an omen of misfortune. *Mān. (HHLH).* Also *ua kualā.*

kua·lapa waena moana *kik* Mid-ocean ridge. *Lit.,* ocean middle ridge.

kū·aloli *ʻa*ʻ Metamorphosis. *He kūaloli ka ʻenuhe ke puka ʻo ia mai loko mai o kōna wiliʻōkaʻi ma ke ʻano he pulelehua.* The catepillar experiences a metamorphosis when it emerges from the cocoon as a butterfly. Comb. *kū* + *a* + *loli. Kūaloli kino.* Morphological metamorphosis.

kua·lua Secondary, as second in time, order or importance. *Dic., ext. def.* See *kuamua, kuakolu, kuahope. ʻĀ kualua.* Secondary activity, of a volano. *ʻĀmanapuʻu kualua.* Secondary bronchus, lobar bronchus, in anatomy.

kua·manawa *kik* Prehistoric. *Lit.,* back (of) time.

Kua·manō *iʻoa* La Pérouse Rock. *Lit.,* shark's back.

kua·mua Primary, as first in time, order or importance. Comb. *kua* + *mua.* See *kualua, kuakolu, kuahope. Hū pele kuamua.* Primary volcanic activity. *Lua pele kuahene kuamua.* Primary shield volcano. *ʻĀmanapuʻu kuamua.* Primary bronchus, in anatomy.

kū·ana *kik* Place value (usually in compound terms). Comb. *kū* + *ana.* See entries below and *unuhi kūana, helu kūana.*

kū·ana haneli *kik* Hundreds, as place value, in math.

kū·ana helu *kik* Unit of counting; place value of a number. *Lit.,* number place value. Cf. *anakahi.* See *helu kūana.*

kū·ana kā·lā *kik* Monetary denomination.

kū·ana keki·mala *kik* Decimal place. See *kiko kekimala.*

kua·naki *kik* Quota. (Māori *kua nawhi.*)

kuana pepa *kik* Orientation, as of page in computer program. *Lit.,* paper position. *Kuana kū.* Portrait orientation. *Kuana moe.* Landscape orientation.

kū·ana ʻekahi *kik* Ones, as place value, in math.

kuana·ʻike *kik* Perspective. *Lit.,* position (of) sight or knowledge.

kū·ana ʻumi *kik* Tens, as place value, in math.

kua noho *kik* Seat back.

kua·papa *kik* -base. *He kinowai kuapapa wai i kapa 'ia he koko.* A water-base fluid called blood. (Māori *tūāpapa* [foundation].) *Pena kuapapa wai.* Water-base paint. *'Anahaidaraside kuapapa.* Basic anhydride, a metallic oxide that forms a base when added to water.

kua·pele *kik* Volcanic mountain. Comb. *kua-* + *pele*.

kua·pi'o *Koholā kuapi'o.* Humpback whale.

kuapo *ham* To trade, in math; to change or replace, as in a search-and-replace feature in computer program. *Dic., ext. mng. Huli a kuapo.* To find and change, search and replace.

kuapo *heh* To rotate, in volleyball; also to switch sides. *Ni'ihau. Kaha kuapo.* A curved line written over a word or letter and then under the adjoining word or letter to indicate that the order of the words or letters should be reversed, in proofreading.

kuapo hao *kik* Rim of a wheel. *Ni'ihau.*

kū·awa *kik* Guava. *Mān./dic., sp. var.*

kua·wehi *'a'* Ultraviolet. *Dic., ext. mng. Kukuna kuawehi.* Ultraviolet ray.

kua'i *ham* To remove, as an opihi from its shell. *Dic.* Also *poke, po'e*.

kuea *kik* Frame, as in bowling; space, as on a game board such as Monopoly. *Dic., ext. mng.* See *kapua'i kuea. Kuea maika.* Bowling frame. *Kuea huki pepa.* Chance space, in Monopoly.

kueka ha'uki *kik* Sweatshirt. *Lit.*, sports sweater. *Lole kueka ha'uki.* Warm-up suit.

Kue·kene *i'oa* Sweden; Swede; Swedish. *Eng.*

kue·kueni *heh* To vibrate. *Ke ho'okani 'ia ka mīkini pāleo a nui ka leo, hiki ke ho'opā i ke kuekueni o ka pahu leo me ka lima.* If you play the stereo loudly you can feel the vibration of the speaker with your hand. *Dic.*

kuemi *heh* To bring back out, in basketball; also to slow down, as in a fast break. *Kuemi iki akula 'o Mina ma ke po'o o ka pukakī i hiki i nā hoa kime ke ho'onohonoho iā lākou iho.* Mina brought out the ball a little outside the top of the key so that his teammates could position themselves. *Lit.*, step back. Also *kuemi iki*.

kuene moku·lele *kik* Flight attendant. *Lit.*, airplane steward.

Kuete *i'oa* Kuwait; Kuwaiti. *Eng.*

kui See entries below and *pulu kui.*

kū·ika·wā *Kumu kūikawā.* Extenuating circumstances. *Pū'ali koa kūikawā.* Militia.

kū i ke au *'a'* Trend. *Lit.*, existing in the era. See *mea kū i ke au.*

kuiki kukui *kik* Light switch. *Mān.* Also *pana kukui.*

Kuiki·lana *i'oa* Switzerland; Swiss. *Dic.* Also *Kuikilani.*

Kuiki·lani See *waiūpa'a Kuikilani.*

Kuiki·lani *i'oa* Switzerland; Swiss. *Eng.* Also *Kuikilana.*

kui·kina *kik* Narcissus. (Cant. suisin.) *Kuikina haole.* Daffodil.

kui kolū *kik* Bolt, as in nuts and bolts. *Ni'ihau.* See *pihi wili.*

kui·kui *kik* Candlenut; light (var. of *kukui*). *Ni'ihau.*

kui lā·'au *kik* Wooden peg. *Dic.*

kui mō·pina *kik* Hypodermic needle. *Ni'ihau.*

kui nao *kik* Screw. *Dic.* See *kolūkalaiwa.*

kui pahu *kik* Thumbtack. *Dic.*

kui 'ū·mi'i pepa *kik* Staple, for paper. *Ni'ihau.* See *mea 'ūmi'i pepa, mea wehe 'ūmi'i.*

kū·olo·kū See *manu kūolokū.*

kū·ono *kik* First off the bench or six man, i.e. first alternate or substitute player, in basketball. *'O Kimo ke kūono; 'o ia ka mea e pani ana no Palani.* Kimo is the six man; he's the one taking Palani's place. Sh. *kūlana* + *'eono*.

kū·hā *kik* Power forward or four man, in basketball. *'O Larry Johnson ke kūhā po'okela o ka NBA no kōna lō'ihi a māmā.* Larry Johnson is the best power forward in the NBA because he is so tall and quick. Sh. *kūlana + 'ehā.*

kū·haha'i *heh* To narrate orally, as in a speech. Comb. *kū* + redup. of *ha'i. Ha'i'ōlelo kūhaha'i.* Narrative speech.

kū hano ho'o·kolo·hua *kik* Ring stand, as for a test tube. See *hano ho'okolohua.*

kū·helu *'a'* Official, as representative or language. Sh. *kū i ka helu* (can be counted). Cf. *pōnolu. Kūhelu 'ole.* Unofficial; non-standard, as in units of measurement.

kuhi See *mana'o kuhi.*

kuhia *kik* Referent, in math (O class). Sh. *kuhi + 'ia.*

kuhia *kik* Note, as in a book or research paper. *Dic., ext. mng. Kuhia o hope.* Endnote. *Kuhia o lalo.* Footnote.

kuhi·akau *kik* Hypothesis. Comb. *kuhi + a + kau.*

kuhi hewa o ka maka Optical illusion. *Lit.,* illusion of the eyes.

kuhi·kuhi *ham* To point, as a mouse arrow in computer program. *Dic., ext. mng.* See entries below and *papa kuhikuhi. Manamana kuhikuhi.* Index finger. Also *manamana miki.*

kuhi·kuhi *ham* To show, demonstrate, as how a math problem is solved. *E kuhikuhi mai 'oe i kāu polopolema.* Show me how you did your problem. *Dic.*

kuhi·kuhi *ham* To direct, as a movie or video production. *Dic., ext. mng.* See *ho'omālamalama, ho'opuka, pāheona. Luna kuhikuhi.* Director. *Hope luna kuhikuhi.* Assistant director. *Po'o kuhikuhi.* Executive director.

kuhi·kuhi *kik/ham* Indicator; to indicate. *Dic., ext. mng. Ninahaidirina kuhikuhi.* Ninhydrin indicator.

kuhi·kuhi lā·'au *kik/ham* Prescription for drug or medication; to prescribe (a medication). *Dic. + lā'au.* Cf. *kū'ai wale. Lā'au kuhikuhi.* Prescription drug or medication.

kuhi·kuhina *kik* Reference; coordinate, in math or science; absolute location, in geography. *Dic., ext. mng.* Cf. *pilina henua. Nā kuhikuhina hō'ike honua.* Geographical coordinates. *Papa kuhikuhina.* Coordinate plane. *Pa'a helu kuhikuhina.* Ordered pair, in math.

kuhi lihi *kik* Page guide, as in a computer document or dictionary. *Lit.,* margin pointing.

kuhi lima *kik/ham* Hand gesture; to gesture with the hands; to use sign language. *'Ōlelo kuhi lima.* Sign language. *'Ōlelo kuhi lima 'Amelika.* American Sign Language (ASL).

kuhi·makani *kik* Weather vane, wind vane. Comb. *kuhi + makani.*

kuhina *'Aha kuhina.* Cabinet, a council that advises a president, sovereign, etc.

kuhi puke See *helu kuhi puke.*

kuhi·'ī *kik/ham* Specifications, specs; to specify. Sh. *kuhikuhi + kiko'ī.*

kuhō *ham* Swish, rimless, i.e. to make a basket without touching the rim in basketball. *Dic., ext. mng.* See *kī.*

kū·hou *'a'* New, used only in special terminology. Comb. *kū + hou. Au Pala'o Kūhou.* New Kingdom, in Egyptology.

kū·hō·hō See *awāwa kūhōhō.*

kū honua See *papa kū honua.*

kū·hō·'ai·lona *ham* To stand for, as in a math problem. *Kūhō'ailona ke X no ka nui o nā 'ikamu i hō'ike 'ia.* X stands for the number of objects given. Comb. *kū + hō'ailona.*

kū·ho'e *kik* Record, greatest achievement or performance to date. *E ho'ā'o ana 'o ia e mākia i ke kūho'e.* S/he's going to try to set the record. Comb. *kū + ho'e* (Tah., one). Cf. *mākia.*

Māmaka Kaiao / 78

kū·kā *heh* To confer. *Dic. Kūkā ma ka pūʻulu.* To conference, as part of the writing process. See *hōʻike manaʻo.*

kū·kae·pele ʻoki·kene lua *kik* Sulfur dioxide. *Lit.,* sulfur double oxygen. Also *sulufura diokesaside.*

kū kau *ʻa*ʻ Seasonal. *Lit.,* exist (in the) season. Also *kū i ke kau.*

kū·kau·kaʻi *ʻaʻ* Interdependence; interdependent. Comb. *kū + kaukaʻi.*

kū·kahi *kik* Point guard or one man, in basketball; guard, in football. *ʻO ke kūkahi ka mea holo kikī nui a hiki i kekahi poʻo o ke kahua.* The point guard is the one who sprints all the way to the other end of the court. Sh. *kūlana + ʻekahi. Kūkahi hema.* Left guard. *Kūkahi ʻākau.* Right guard.

Kū·kahi·kahi *iʻoa* Northern Equatorial Current, in oceanography. *Mān.* (HA).

kū·kahiko *ʻaʻ* Old, olden, used only in special terminology. Comb. *kū + kahiko. Au Palaʻo Kūkahiko.* Old Kingdom, in Egyptology.

kū kāki *kik* Metered parking or any parking for which there is a charge. *Lit.,* parking (with a) charge. See *mīka kāki.*

kū·kala maka·ʻala *kik/ham* Watch, as in weather report. *Lit.,* proclaim vigilance. Cf. *kūkala pōʻino. Kūkala makaʻala makani pāhili.* Hurricane watch. *Kūkala makaʻala wai hālana.* Flood watch.

kū·kala pō·ʻino *kik/ham* Warning, as in weather report. *Lit.,* proclaim danger. Cf. *kūkala makaʻala. Kūkala pōʻino makani pāhili.* Hurricane warning. *Kūkala pōʻino wai hālana.* Flood warning.

kū kā·nā·wai *ʻaʻ* Legal. *Dic.* (*kū i ke kānāwai*).

kū·kaʻi leka *kik/ham* Written correspondence; to correspond by letter. *Dic. Papa kūkaʻi leka.* Correspondence course.

kū·kaʻi·pā *kik* Interactive, as computer programs. Comb. *kūkaʻi + pā.*

kū·kaʻi ʻae·like ʻuni·ona *h a m* Collective bargaining. *ʻOiai ʻaʻole i hiki i ka ʻuniona a me ka hui ke hoʻopaʻa i ka ʻaelike, ua kauoha ʻia ia mau ʻaoʻao e komo pū i ke kūkaʻi ʻaelike ʻuniona e ka luna hoʻokolokolo i mea e hōʻalo ai i ka ʻolohani.* Since the union and the company could not settle the contract, both sides were ordered by the judge to enter into collective bargaining to avert a strike. *Lit.,* union contract exchange.

kū·kā·ʻokoʻa *kik* Freedom, liberty. *ʻIvanahō.* Also *kūnoa.* See entry below.

Kū·kā·ʻokoʻa Kia·ho·ʻo·manaʻo *iʻoa* Statue of Liberty. *Lit.,* freedom monument. Also *Kūkāʻokoʻa, ke kiahoʻomanaʻo ʻo Kūkāʻokoʻa.*

kuke See *lumi kuke. Kumu paina Kuke.* Cook pine. Also *paina Kuke.*

kū·kini hoʻo·ili *kik* Relay race. *Lit.,* transfer race. Also *heihei hoʻoili.* Cf. *holo hoʻoili.* See *maile hoʻoili.*

kū·kohu *kik* Model, usually miniature. Comb. *kū + kohu.* See *kāpili. Kūkohu moku.* Model boat.

kū·kolu *kik* Swing man, shooting forward or three man, in basketball. *E makaʻala ʻoe i ke kūkolu; he loea ʻo ia i ke kī ʻai kolu.* Make sure you keep an eye out for the swing man; he's really good at the triple shot. Sh. *kūlana + ʻekolu.*

kuku *kik* Rim of basket, in basketball. *Lewa liʻiliʻi akula ʻo David Robinson ma ke kuku ma hope o kāna ʻūpoʻi ʻana.* David Johnson hung onto the rim a little while after dunking the ball. *Dic., ext. mng.* Also *hao.* See *hīnaʻi, hupa.*

kukui hā·weo *kik* Fluorescent light. See *hāweo.*

kukui hoʻo·kū *kik* Stoplight, traffic light.

kukui hoʻo·mehana *kik* Heating lamp. *Lit.,* light (for) warming.

kukui kū *kik* Lamp (standing). *Niʻihau.* Also *kukui kū hale. Kukui kū pākaukau.* Table lamp

kukui lā·kene *kik* Hanging lantern, as Japanese type. Comb. *kukui +* Eng.

kukui·po‘o *kik* Headlight. *Ni‘ihau.* Also *kukuipo‘o o mua.*

kukui ‘oaka *kik* Flash, as for a camera. Also *‘oaka. Dic.*

kukui ‘owaka·waka *kik* Reflector. Also *‘owakawaka.*

kū·kulu *Nā kūkulu ‘ehā.* The four cardinal points, or four primary directions of the compass, in geography. *Nā kūkulu o waena.* Intermediate directions. *‘Oi‘enehana kūkulu.* Construction industry.

kū·kulu·ae‘o *kik* Stilt, either bird or toy. *Dic.*

kū·kulu hale *ham* To develop land, as the work of a developer. *Ua kū‘ai aku nei lākou i kēlā ‘āina no ke kūkulu hale ‘ana.* They bought that land in order to develop it. *Lit.,* build houses. Also *kūkulu hale ma luna o ka ‘āina.*

kū·kulu hula·hula *ham* Choreographer; to choreograph. *Lit.,* arrange dances.

kū·kulu kahua *Mea kūkulu kahua.* Stagehand, grip. *Luna kūkulu kahua.* Stage manager, key grip, as for movie or video production.

kū·kulu mā·mala *ham* To phrase, as in written compositions. *‘Ano hemahema ke kūkulu māmala ‘ana i nā hopuna‘ōlelo i loko o kēia paukū.* The phrasing of the sentences in this paragraph is rather awkward. *Lit.,* arrange (sentence) fragments. *Cf. puana māmala.* See *paukūkū.*

kū·kulu puolo *ham* Music arranger; to arrange music. *Lit.,* arrange music.

kukuna *kik* Spoke, as on a bicycle wheel; antenna, as of a lobster, insect, television, etc. *Dic.* See entries below. *Kukuna huila paikikala.* Bicycle wheel spoke.

kukuna·oka·lā *kik* Mangrove. *Dic., sp. var.*

kukuna kua·wehi *kik* Ultraviolet ray. *Dic., ext. mng.*

kukuna lewa lipo *kik* Cosmic ray. *Lit.,* outer space ray.

kukuna pō·pa‘i·pa‘i *kik* Volleyball antenna. Also *kukuna. ‘A‘ena kukuna.* Antenna violation.

kukuna wana·‘ā *kik* Laser beam.

kū·launa *‘a* In harmony, in music. *Kūlauna ka hīmeni ‘ana o lākou.* Their singing is in harmony. *E ho‘olohe kākou i nā leo kūlauna.* Let's listen to the harmonizing parts. Comb. *kū + launa.* See *ho‘okūlauna. Hīmeni kūlauna like.* To sing in harmony.

kula ho‘o·wela wai *kik* Water heater. *Mān.* Also *pahu ho‘owela wai.*

kula kama·li‘i *kik* Preschool. *Lit.,* school (for) children.

kula lau·laha *kik* Plain, expanse of flat land. *Lit.,* widespread plain. Also *‘āina kula laulaha. Cf. nu‘u laulaha.*

kū·lale *kik/ham* Stimulus; to stimulate. *Sh. kumu + ho‘olalelale. Cf. ha‘inole.*

kulali *kik* Curare, a poison for South American Indians' arrows; also a muscle relaxant in modern medicine. *Carib.*

kulalo *kik* Stalagmite. *Sh. kulu + lalo. Cf. kuluna.*

kula mau‘u *kik* Meadow, grassy field. *Dic.*

kū·lana *kik* Status, rank, as position or social standing. *Dic., ext. mng. Cf. pae.* See *kūlana pale, moho. Kūlana olakino.* Health status. *Kūlana ‘elua.* Runner-up, second place. *Ua puka wau i ke kūlana ‘elua.* I took second place.

kū·lana·kau·hale *kik* Town, city (general term). *Dic. Cf. kaona, kiwikā.*

kū·lana pale *kik* Defensive stance, as in basketball. *Mākaukau ‘o Pa‘a ma ke kūlana pale e kali ala i ka mea kūlele e holo mai.* Pa‘a is set in the defensive stance waiting for the offender to come at him. *Lit.,* defense stance.

kula·nui kaia·ulu *kik* Community college.

kulaʻi *kik/ham* Tackle, i.e. the act of seizing and throwing down an opposing player with the ball, in football; to tackle (someone). *Dic., ext. mng.* Also *hoʻohina.* Cf. *kūlua.*

kulaʻi hā·puʻu *heh* To be sleeping or snoring, as a response when asked where someone is. *Aia ʻo ia ke kulaʻi hāpuʻu ala ma ka hale.* S/he's sleeping in the house. *Mān. (MMLH).*

kule *kik* Joule, a unit of energy. *Eng. Kule pāpiliona.* Gigajoule.

kule·ana *kik* Privilege or rights, as in a computer network. *Dic., ext. mng.*

kule·hana *kik* Principle, as an accepted rule of action. *Sh. kuleana + hana.* Also *kahua hana.* Cf. *kulekele. Ke kulehana a ʻAkimika.* Archimedes' principle, i.e. the buoyant force on an object submerged in a fluid is equal to the weight of the fluid displaced by that object, in science. *Ke kulehana a Penuli.* Bernoulli's principle. *Kulehana huinahā lōʻihi hapalua.* Half-rectangle principle. *Kulehana no ka helu ʻana.* Basic counting principle.

Kuleke *iʻoa* Turkey; Turk; Turkish. *Dic.* Also *Tureke.*

kule·kele *kik* Policy. *Sh. kuleana + hoʻokele.*

kū·lele *heh* Offense, as in sporting events; to play offense. *Dic., ext. mng.* Cf. *kūpale, pale.* See entries below.

kū·lele alo *kik* Man offense, i.e. offense for attacking face defense, in basketball. *Kū koke ihola ka ʻaoʻao kūlele ma ke kūlele alo.* The offense quickly set themselves up in the man offense. *Lit.,* face offense.

kū·lele kā·ʻei *kik* Zone offense, in basketball. *Ua kū nā mea kūlele ma waho o ke kī ma ke kūlele kāʻei.* The offense stood outside the key in zone offense.

kū·liu·kolu *heh* Triple-threat position, in basketball; to execute such a position. *ʻAʻohe kūliukolu ke ʻole ka paʻa o ke kinipōpō i ka lima.* In order to be in a triple-threat position, one must be in possession of the ball. *Sh. kū + liuliu + ʻekolu.*

kū·liu loko *kik* Low post, in basketball. *Sh. kūliukolu + loko.* Cf. *kūliu waho.*

kū·liu waho *kik* High post, in basketball. *Sh. kūliukolu + waho.* Cf. *kūliu loko.*

kū lima *kik/heh* Handstand; to do a handstand. Cf. *kū poʻo.*

kū·lima *kik* Center or five man, in basketball. *He būtalo ʻo Shaq ma ke kūlana kūlima.* Shaq is the bull in the center position. *Sh. kūlana + ʻelima.* Cf. *huki pōpō.*

kulo *kik* Judo. *Niʻihau (Eng.).* See *paʻi kulo.*

kū·lohe·lohe *ʻa* Natural, lacking human intervention or contamination; raw, unprocessed, as raw materials. *Comb. kū- + lohelohe* (bare, uninterfered with). See *puni ao kūlohelohe, ʻakika ʻūpalu kūlohelohe. Ao kūlohelohe.* Nature. *Kaiameaola kūlohelohe.* Natural biological community. *Manehu kūlohelohe.* Natural force. *Makelia kūlohelohe, memea kūlohelohe.* Raw material. *Meaʻai kūlohelohe.* Natural food. *ʻŌnaehana Hoʻomalu ʻĀina Kūlohelohe.* Natural Areas Reserves System (NARS).

kū·loko *ʻa* Internal; closed, as a primary election. *Dic., ext. mng.* Cf. *kūākea, kūwaho, paʻaloko. Haunaele kūloko.* Civil unrest. *Kakena kūloko.* Internal drive, on a computer. *Memo kūloko.* Internal memo, as in telecommunication. *Wae moho kūloko.* Closed primary. *ʻIli kūloko.* Subcutus, in biology.

kū·lua *kik* Twin, in math. *Dic., ext. mng. Helu kumu kūlua.* Twin primes.

kū·lua *kik* Shooting guard or two man, in basketball; tackle, either an offensive or defensive player, in football. Sh. *kulana* + *'elua*. Cf. *kula'i*. *Kūlua hema*. Left tackle. *Kūlua 'ākau*. Right tackle.

kuluna *kik* Stalactite. Sh. *kulu* + *luna*. Cf. *kulalo*.

kuluna hau *kik* Icicle. Lit., ice stalactite. *Dic.* Also *kulu hau pa'a*.

kū·mau *'a'* Standard, as in deviation, in math. *Dic., ext. mng.* Cf. *ma'amau*. See *papa hua'ōlelo kūmau*. *Haiahū kūmau*. Standard deviation.

kū·maka *'a'* Visible. *Dic.* See *kūnalohia*.

kū·mī·kini *'a'* Mechanical, mechanics. *He mau 'āpana 'oni kō ka hāme'a kūmīkini*. Mechanical devices have moving parts in them. Comb. *kū* + *mīkini*.

kū·moe *kik* Headboard of bed. *Dic., ext. mng.* See *hao pela*.

kū·mole *kik* Reference, source, as a dictionary or other reference material. Sh. *kumu* + *mole*. Cf. *molekumu*, *puke noi'i*.

kumu *kik* Cause. *Dic.* See entries below and *hopena*. *Kānāwai kumu*. Common law.

kumu *kik* End of a sporting field or court. *Dic., ext. mng.* Also *po'o*. Cf. *iwi*. *Laina kumu*. End line. Also *laina po'o*.

kumu i'a *kik* Large school of fish, such as *akule* or *aku*. *Mān.* Cf. *naho i'a*.

kumu·hana *kik* General subject or topic, as in literature. *Dic.* *Hopuna'ōlelo wehe kumuhana*. Topic sentence, as of a paragraph. *Palapala 'āina kumuhana*. Thematic map. *Puke kumuhana*. Information book.

kumu honua *kik* Creation, origin of the world. *Dic.* *Mo'okalaleo kumu honua*. Creation literature, i.e. literature which describes the origin of the world.

kumu hō·'ai·'ē *kik* Credit, as at a bank or store. *'Ehia ka palena kumu hō'ai'ē ma kāu 'ea kāki?* What's the credit limit on your credit card? *Lit.*, credit base.

kumu ho·o·hau·mia *kik* Source pollution. *'O ke kumu kahi e ho'ohaumia 'ia nei ka 'āina, kapa 'ia ia 'ano haumia 'ana he kumu ho'ohaumia*. The source of pollution of the land is referred to as source pollution. *Lit.*, source causing pollution. *Kumu ho'ohaumia 'ike 'ia*. Point source pollution. *Kumu ho'ohaumia 'ike 'ole 'ia*. Non-point source pollution.

kumu ho·'o·hā·like *kik* Example, model, as of behavior. *Ua lilo ke kumu kula i kumu ho'ohālike no kāna mau haumāna*. The schoolteacher became a model for his students. *Mān.* Cf. *la'ana*.

kumu ho·'o·hā·like·like *kik* Control or control group, as in an experiment. *Lit.*, basis (for) comparison.

kumu ho·'o·hui *kik* Base, in math. *Lit.*, base (for) joining. *Kumu ho'ohui 'elima*. Base five.

kumu ho·'o·hui 'elua *kik* Binary, i.e. a base-two system of numeration, in math. *Lit.*, base two.

kumu kū·ika·wā *kik* Extenuating circumstances. *Lit.*, special reason.

kumu·kū·'ai *kik* Quote, i.e. a stated price, as for merchandise. *Dic., ext. mng.* Cf. *kumukū'ai koho*. See entries below. *Huli kumukū'ai*. Cost analysis.

kumu·kū·'ai ana·kahi *kik* Unit price, in math. *Lit.*, price (per) unit of measurement.

kumu·kū·'ai hale kū·'ai *kik* Retail price. *Lit.*, store price. Cf. *kumukū'ai kālepa*.

kumu·kū·'ai kā·lepa *kik* Wholesale price. *Lit.*, merchant price. Cf. *kumukū'ai hale kū'ai*.

kumu·kū·'ai koho *kik* Estimated price, as for goods. Cf. *kāki koho*. See *koho*.

kumu·lā·'au 'ō·pio·pio *kik* Sapling. *Lit.*, young tree.

kumu·lilo *kik* Loss. *Dic.* Cf. *kumuloaʻa.*

kumu·loaʻa *kik* Profit. *Dic.* Cf. *kumulilo* and dictionary entries.

kumu·loli *kik* Variable, as in a scientific experiment. *Lit.,* changing base. Cf. *hualau. Kumuloli kaukaʻi.* Dependent variable. *Kumuloli kūʻokoʻa.* Independent variable.

kumu loni·kū *kik* Prime meridian, in geography. *Lit.,* longitude base. Also *kumu lonitū.*

kumu·manaʻo *Papa kumumanaʻo.* Agenda, as for a meeting.

kumu·mea *kik* Element. *ʻO nā kumumea ʻehā o ke ao nei, ʻo ia nō ka honua, ka wai, ke ea a me ke ahi.* The four basic elements of the earth are earth, water, air and fire. Comb. *kumu + mea.* See *pūhui kumumea lua.*

kumu paina Kuke *kik* Cook pine. *Lit.,* Cook pine tree. Also *paina Kuke.*

kumu pā·hoʻo·nui *kik* Base, in exponential notation, in math. *Lit.,* exponent base. See entry below.

kumu pā·hoʻo·nui lua *kik* Square root, in math. *Lit.,* square base.

kumu·paʻa *kik* Principal, i.e. money loaned, usually at a given interest rate and for a specified time. *Dic.* Also *kālā kumupaʻa.* See *uku paneʻe.*

kumu puʻu·naue *kik* Dividend, in math. *Dic., sp. var.*

kumu wai *ʻĀina kumu wai.* Watershed, i.e. an area from which water drains. *ʻĀina kumu wai kiwikā.* Municipal water shed.

kumu waina *kik* Grapevine. *Dic.*

kumu·wai·wai *kik* Resource, i.e. a source of supply. *Dic., sp. var. Kumuwaiwai kūlohelohe.* Natural resource. *ʻOihana Kumuwaiwai ʻĀina.* Department of Land and Natural Resources (DLNR).

kumu welo *kik* Heredity. *Lit.,* basis (of) hereditary traits. See *welo.*

kumu ʻā·kō·lī See *kōkua huamele.*

kumu·ʻiʻo *kik* Protein. Comb. *kumu + ʻiʻo.* Also *polokina.*

kūna kaʻa ʻō·hua *kik* Bus stop. *Lit.,* bus stopping place.

kū·nalo·hia *ʻa* Invisible. *Lit.,* (in a) state of disappearance. See *kūmaka.*

kū·nā·nahu *kik* Black, porous, light rock used to scrape interior of gourds. *Niʻihau (KKK).*

kuni See *peni kuni.*

kuni·kia *kik* Trademark. Comb. *kuni + kia.*

kuni·pona *kik* Abacus. (Cant. *shun-pon.*)

kū·noa *ʻa* Freedom; free, exempt from external restrictions. Sh. *kū i ka noa.* Cf. *kaʻawale,* not in use; *kūʻokoʻa,* independent; *manuahi,* no charge.

kunuko *kik* Junco, a kind of bird. *Eng.* Also *manu kunuko.*

kupa *kik* Citizen. *Hoʻomalu ʻia nā pono o nā kupa o ka ʻāina e ke kānāwai.* The rights of the citizens of the country are protected by law. *Dic.* Also *makaʻāinana. Kupa kaumokuʻāina pālua.* Dual citizen. Also *makaʻāinana kaumokuʻāina pālua.*

Kupa *iʻoa* Cuba; Cuban. *Dic.* Also *Kuba.*

kū·pale *ham* To defend, as your basket in basketball. *Hoʻi hikiwawe akula ka ʻaoʻao kūpale e kūpale aku i ka hīnaʻi.* The defense quickly returned to defend their basket. *Dic.* Cf. *kaupale, pale.*

kū·papa *ʻa* Neutral, as neither base nor acid on a pH scale. *Māori.*

kū·papa·kū *kik* Bedrock. *Dic.*

kupe·kio *kik* Edible oyster. Comb. *kupe + kio.* Cf. *pipi.*

Kupelo *iʻoa* Cyprus; Cypriot. *Dic.* Also *Kupero.*

Kupero *iʻoa* Cyprus; Cypriot. *Dic.* Also *Kupelo.*

kū·pī *heh* To reflect, as light, heat or sound. *Ke kūpī nei ka mālamalama mai ke aniani mai.* Light is reflecting off the mirror. Sh. *kūpinaʻi.* See *hoʻokūpī, huina kūpī.*

kū·pili ʻaʻ Logic; logical. *Lit.*, (in a) state of close association. See *hewa kūpili. Noʻonoʻo kūpili.* Logical thinking.

kū·pita *kik* Cubit, an ancient unit of measurement used in Bible times. *Dic., sp. var.*

kū·pona *kik* Coupon. *Eng.*

kū·pono ʻaʻ Reasonable. *Dic., ext. mng. Kumukūʻai kūpono.* Reasonable price.

kū·pono ʻaʻ Perpendicular, in math. *Dic.* See *hoʻopiha kūpono. Kaha ʻoki hapalua kūpono.* Perpendicular bisector. *Nā kaha kūpono.* Perpendicular lines.

kū poʻo *kik/heh* Headstand; to do a headstand. Cf. *kū lima.*

kupua See *kaʻao kupua.*

kupu·lau *kik* Spring. *Dic.* See *māuiili.*

kupu·riku ʻaʻ Cupric. *Kupuriku karabonahate.* Cupric carbonate. *Kupuriku ʻokesaside.* Cupric oxide. *Kupuriku sulafahate.* Cupric sulfate. *Kupuriku sulafaside.* Cupric sulfide.

kū·waena ʻaʻ Median middle, used only in special terminology. *Lit.*, exist (in the) middle. See *laina kūwaena. Au Palaʻo Kūwaena.* Middle Kingdom, in Egyptology. *Helu kūwaena.* Median (number), in math. *ʻIli kūwaena.* Dermis, in biology.

kū·waho ʻaʻ External. Comb. *kū + waho.* Cf. *kūloko, paʻaloko. Huina kūwaho.* Exterior angle, in math. *Kakena kūwaho.* External drive, on a computer. *ʻIli kūwaho.* Epidermis, in biology.

kū·ʻai·emi *kik/ham* Sale; to be or put on sale. Comb. *kūʻai + emi. Nā kīwī kūʻaiemi.* TVs on sale. *Kūʻaiemi ʻia nā kīwī.* The TVs are on sale.

kū·ʻai wale *ham* Over-the-counter. Cf. *kuhikuhi lāʻau. Lāʻau kūʻai wale.* Over-the-counter drug or medication.

kū·ʻau alelo *kik* Back of tongue. *Lit.*, tongue stem. See *lau alelo, mole alelo, waena alelo, wēlau alelo.*

kū·ʻē *Hoʻopiʻi kūʻē.* To appeal, i.e. ask a higher court to review a decision made by a lower court.

kū·ʻē lula *ham* Exception to a rule. *Lit.*, contrary (to) rules.

kuʻe·maka See *pena kuʻemaka.*

kū·ʻē·ʻē See *paʻa manehu kūʻēʻē.*

kuʻi *ham* To set, as an imu. *Niʻihau.* Cf. *huaʻi.* See entries below. *Kuʻi i ka imu.* To set an imu.

kuʻi *ham* Convergent, i.e. meeting in plate techtonics, in geology. *Dic., ext. mng.* Cf. *kākele, neʻe ʻoā. Palena kuʻi.* Convergent boundary.

kuʻia *kik* Error, as in computer program. *Ua loaʻa kekahi kuʻia ma ke paʻi ʻana.* An error occurred while printing. *Dic. ext. mng.*

kuʻia ʻaʻ Foul, in team sports such as basketball. *Ua kuʻia iā Keoni ʻo Kekoa, a kipaku ʻia ʻo Keoni, no ka mea, ʻelima āna kuʻia.* Keoni fouled Kekoa, and Keoni was ejected because he had committed five fouls. *Dic., ext. mng.* Cf. *hoʻokuʻia.* See entries below.

kuʻia kime ʻaʻ Team foul, in team sports such as basketball. *Na ʻŌlani ke kuʻia kime mua; ua paʻi hewa ʻo ia i ka lima o kōna hoa paio iā ia e kī ana.* ʻŌlani committed the first team foul; he accidentally hit his opponent's arm as he was shooting.

kuʻia kū·helu ʻaʻ Technical foul, in team sports such as basketball. *Ua kū ʻia ka naʻau o ke kime i ke kuʻia kūhelu i kā lākou kaʻi.* The team felt bad about the technical foul that their coach had committed. *Lit.*, official foul.

kuʻia kū·lele ʻaʻ Offensive foul, in team sports such as basketball. *Na ka mea kūlele ke kuʻia kūlele inā nāna e kulaʻi ʻino i kōna mea kūpale.* The offender commits the offensive foul if he was the one to knock down his defender. *Lit.*, offense foul.

ku'ia pili·kino *'a'* Personal foul, in team sports such as basketball. *Ke ho'ā'o nei 'o Moe e akahele i kōna pā'ani 'ana, no ka mea, 'ehā āna ku'ia pilikino; ho'okahi koe a e kipaku 'ia 'o ia.* Moe is trying to be careful while playing, since he already has four personal fouls; one more and he'll be ejected.

ku'ia 'ā·ke'a *'a'* Blocking foul, in basketball. *Ua ku'ia 'āke'a iā Hāloa 'o Nani Boy, 'oiai ua ne'e mai 'o Hāloa i mua pono o Nani Boy iā ia ala e kaha mai ana i ka hupa.* Hāloa committed a blocking foul against Nani Boy, since Hāloa moved directly in front of Nani Boy as he was driving towards the basket. *Lit.*, block out foul.

ku'i·hao *ham* To weld. *Ni'ihau.*

ku'i·kahi *kik* Consortium. *Ua komo nā 'ahahui pā'oihana a me kekahi 'oihana o ke aupuni i ke ku'ikahi no ka ho'okō 'ana i ka papahana.* Commercial enterprises and a government agency entered into a consortium to implement the program. *Dic., ext. mng.* See entries below. *Hui ku'ikahi.* Alliance, i.e. a group of nations that have agreed to help or protect each other; to form such an alliance.

ku'i·kahi *kik* League, in sports. *Dic.* See entries below and *hui*.

Ku'i·kahi Pō·hili Au·puni *kik* National Baseball League.

Ku'i·kahi Pō·hili 'Ame·lika *kik* American Baseball League.

Ku'i·kahi Pō·peku Au·puni *kik* National Football League (NFL).

kū·'ike See *kālā kū'ike, waiwai kū'ike.*

kū·'ikena *kik* Fact. Comb. *kū* + *'ikena. Puke noi'i kū'ikena.* Encyclopedia.

ku'i·koli *ham* To compromise. Comb. *ku'i* + *koli.*

ku'ina *kik* Connection, as in computer program. *Dic., ext. mng.* See *ho'oku'i.*

ku'ina *kik* Front, as of weather. *Lit.*, junction. *Ku'ina hu'ihu'i.* Cold front. *Ku'ina mehana.* Warm front. *Ku'ina pa'a.* Stationary front.

ku'ina una honua *kik* Plate techtonics, in geology. See *kākele, ku'i, ne'e 'oā, palena.*

ku'ina mea·'ai *kik* Food chain. *Lit.*, food joining. Cf. *'upena mea'ai.*

ku'i nuke·liu *kik* Nuclear fusion. *Lit.*, joining (of) nuclei.

ku'i pā·na'i *ham* Counterpunch. Cf. *ho'ouka pāna'i.*

ku'i·pē *ham* To cancel, i.e. the compression of one wave at the same time as the rarefaction of another wave, in science. *Dic., ext. mng., sp. var.* See *ku'ipēhia.*

ku'i·pē·hia *'a'* To be cancelled (out), in science or argumentation; cancellation. Comb. *ku'ipē* + *-hia.* See *ku'ipē.*

ku'i pu'u·pu'u *ham* To spike with closed fist, in volleyball. *Ni'ihau.* Cf. *hānai pu'upu'u.* See *hili, pa'i pālahalaha.*

ku'i 'ā·mana *ham* To bump (the ball), in volleyball. *Lit.*, Y-shaped strike.

kū·'oko'a *Kumuloli kū'oko'a.* Independent variable.

kū·'ono *kik* Inside corner, nook. *Dic.* Also *po'opo'o.* Cf. *kihi.*

kū·'ono *kik* Cell, as in databases or tables. *Ua piha nā kū'ono o ka pakuhi maka'aha.* The cells of the spreadsheet are full. *Dic., ext. mng.*

ku'u *heh* To land, as an airplane or bird. *Ni'ihau.*

ku'u·loko *Lōku'u ku'uloko.* Endocrine gland. Cf. *lōku'u kūwaho.*

ku'una *kik* Traditional. *Dic. Mo'okalaleo ku'una.* Traditional literature.

kū 'ū·niu *kik* Pivot, as a position in basketball; pivot point. *Lit.*, pivot stand. See *'ūniu.*

ku'u·waho *Lōku'u kū'uwaho.* Exocrine gland. Cf. *lōku'u kūloko.*

Māmaka Kaiao / 85

ku'u wela *ham* Exothermic, i.e. giving off heat. Cf. *omo wela*.

Kuba *i'oa* Cuba; Cuban. *Dic.* Also *Kupa*.

kh Abbreviation for *kī'aha* (cup).

khh Abbreviation for *kahahānai* (radius).

kk Abbreviation for *kuaka* (quart).

Kk. Abbreviation for *Kauka* (Doctor), for use as a title before a person's name. *Kk. Halenui (Kauka Halenui).* Dr. Halenui.

kkal Abbreviation for *kenikalame* (centigram).

KKK Abbreviation for *kā'ei ku'ina kopikala* (intertropical convergent zone; ITCZ).

kkkal Abbreviation for *kekikalame* (decigram).

kkl Abbreviation for *kekilika* (deciliter).

kkm Abbreviation for *kekimika* (decimeter).

kkn Abbreviation for *kekona* (second).

kl Abbreviation for *kilo* (kilo), *kenilika* (centiliter).

Klk Abbreviation for *Kelekia* (Celsius).

klkal Abbreviation for *kilokalame* (kilogram).

kll Abbreviation for *kilolika* (kiloliter).

klm Abbreviation for *kilomika* (kilometer).

kln Abbreviation for *kālani* (gallon).

klt Abbreviation for *kilouate* (kilowatt).

Km Abbreviation for *komohana* (west).

knm Abbreviation for *kenimika* (centimeter).

kp Abbreviation for *kapua'i* (foot).

kp ph^2 Abbreviation for *kapua'i pāho'onui lua* (square foot).

L

l Abbreviation for *lika* (liter).

lā *kik* Day, date. *Dic.* No abbreviation. Date. Format for date in Hawaiian: Day/month/year: *10 Iune 1993*. June 10, 1993. Abbreviations use Roman numerals for month to avoid confusion: *10/VI/93*. 6/10/93.

lā *kik* Fin, as of a fish, general term. *Dic. Nā lā o ka i'a.* The fins of a fish. *Nī'au lā.* Ray, i.e. one of the bony spines supporting the membrane of a fish's fin.

lā *kik* La, the sixth note on the musical scale. *Dic.* See *pākōlī*.

lae·kahi *kik* Specialist. Comb. *lae* + *kahi.* Cf. *lae'ula* (dic.).

laiki *kik* Rice. *Dic.* Also *lāisi. Laiki ke'oke'o.* White rice. Also *lāisi ke'oke'o. Laiki māku'e.* Brown rice. Also *lāisi māku'e. Laiki mōchī.* Mochi rice. Also *lāisi mōchī. Pōpō laiki.* Rice ball, musubi. Also *pōpō lāisi, musubī*.

lai·kī *kik* Lychee, litchi. *Dic.*

laimi *kik* Lime. *Eng.*

laina *kik* Line, as on basketball court. *Dic., ext. mng.* See entries below. *Laina iwi kī.* Side line of the key on a basketball court. *Laina kumu.* Base or end line. *Laina 'ao'ao.* Side line.

laina helu *kik* Number line, in math.

laina helu lā *kik* International date line. *Lit.*, line (for) counting days.

laina hī·na'i *kik* End line, on basketball court. *Nou wale akula 'o Barkley i ke kinipōpō mai ka laina hīna'i a hiki i ka hoa kime ma kekahi po'o o ke kahua.* Barkley whipped the ball from the base line to his teammate at the other end of the court. *Lit.*, basket line. Also *laina hupa, laina kumu, laina po'o*.

laina ho'o·uka *kik* Scrimmage line, in football. *Lit.*, attack line.

laina hupa *kik* End line, on basketball court. *Ho'omaka ka 'ao'ao kūlele mai ka laina hupa a holo i kekahi 'ao'ao.* The offense starts from the end line and goes all the way to the other end. *Lit.*, basket line. Also *laina hīna'i, laina kumu, laina po'o*.

laina kā·lai·lai *kik* Transect, i.e. a sample area, as of vegetation, usually in the form of a long strip. *Lit.*, line (to) analyze.

laina kī noa *kik* Free throw line, in basketball. *Inā hoʻokuʻia ʻia ʻoe iā ʻoe e kaha ana i ka hīnaʻi ma loko o ka puka kī, e hele ʻoe i ka laina kī noa.* If you are fouled while driving to the basket within the key, you will go to the free throw line.

laina kū·lele *kik* Offensive line, in football. *Lit.*, offense line.

laina kū·pale *kik* Defensive line, in football. *Lit.*, defending line. Also *laina pale*.

laina kū·waena *kik* Half-court line, on basketball court. *Kī ʻia ke kinipōpō mai ka laina kūwaena mai, a ʻuāʻuā aʻela ke anaina i ke komo ʻana i loko o ka hīnaʻi.* The ball was shot rom the halfcourt line, and the crowd screamed when the ball went in the basket. *Lit.*, median line.

laina laki·kū *kik* Parallel, i.e. an imaginary circle on the earth's surface parallel to the equator and designated in degrees of latitude. *Lit.*, latitude line. Also *laina latitū*.

laina lena *kik* Line of sight, sight line. Also *laina ʻike*.

laina manawa *kik* Time line.

laina pale *kik* Defensive line, in football. *Lit.*, defense line. Also *laina kūpale*.

laina pā·weo *kik* Skew line, in math. See *pāweo*.

laina ʻekolu mika *kik* Three-meter line, in volleyball. See *laina ʻumi kapuaʻi, ʻaʻena ʻekolu mika*.

laina ʻike *kik* Line of sight, sight line. *Lit.*, line (to) see. Also *laina lena*.

laina ʻike·pili *kik* Data stream, as in computer program. *Lit.*, data line.

laina ʻumi kapu·aʻi *kik* Ten-foot line, in volleyball. *Niʻihau*. See *laina ʻekolu mika, ʻaʻena ʻumi kapuaʻi*.

lāisi *kik* Rice. *Niʻihau*. See *laiki*.

laoa See *lāʻau make laoa*.

Laosa *iʻoa* Laos; Laotian. *Eng.*

lau- A prefix meaning multi- or many. *Dic., ext. def. Nā moku ahikao lauʻenekini.* Multiengined spaceships.

lau alelo *kik* Blade of tongue. *Lit.*, tongue blade. See *kūʻau alelo, mole alelo, waena alelo, wēlau alelo*.

lau·alo *kik* Ventral, in biology. Comb. *lau + alo*. Cf. *lauhope, laukua, laumua*.

lau·ana *kik* Pattern, repeating series. Comb. *lau + ana*. See entry below. *Lauana helu.* Number pattern. *Lauana hoʻokahua.* Settlement pattern, in geography.

lau·ana wā *kik* Meter, in music. *Lit.*, time pattern.

lau·ele *heh* To daydream. *Dic., ext. mng.*

lau·ika *kik* Mode, as the number(s) that occur most often in a set, in math. Comb. *lau + ika* (strong pattern).

lau hihi pā *kik* Ivy. *Lit.*, leaf (which) creeps (on) walls. Also *ʻaiwi*.

lau·hope *kik* Posterior, in biology. Comb. *lau + hope*. Cf. *laualo, laukua, laumua*. *Kualā lauhope.* Posterior dorsal fin, of a fish.

lau kala·koa *kik* Croton. *Lit.*, variegated leaves. Cf. *lau noʻe*.

lau kā·pala *kik* Print, as something impressed or stamped with a print. *Lit.*, printed design. See *kāpala*.

lau·kaʻi *ʻaʻ* Coordinated, put in order. Comb. *lau + kaʻi*. See *hoʻolaukaʻi*.

lau·kaʻina *kik* Sequence, in math. Comb. *lau + kaʻina*.

lau·kua *ʻaʻ* Irregular, as in shape; amorphous, i.e. having no regular crystalline form. *Dic., ext. mng.* Cf. *analahi*. *Kinona laukua.* Irregular shape. *ʻAkano laukua.* Amorphous substance.

lau·kua *kik* Dorsal, in biology. Comb. *lau + kua*. Cf. *laualo, lauhope, laumua*. *Kualā laukua.* Dorsal fin, of a fish.

lau·lā *'a'* Wide. *Dic.* See entries below and *kokoke, lōpū.* See also *pahuhopu laulā. Pa'i laulā.* Wide shot, as of a photograph or in movie or video production (preceded by *ke*). *Pa'i a laulā.* To take a wide shot. *Pa'i laulā loa.* Extreme wide shot. *Pa'i a laulā loa.* To take an extreme wide shot.

lau·lā *'a'* Width or breadth, in math. *Dic.* Abb. *ll.* Also *ana laulā, ākea.* Cf. *loa, lō'ihi, hohonu, ki'eki'e.* See *laulā loli.* Range, i.e. the difference between the largest and smallest number or value. *Dic., ext. mng.* Also *laulā loa.*

lau·lau *kik* Brim, as of a floppy hat. *Mān.* (MW). Cf. *kihikihi, pekekeu.*

lau·laha See *kula laulaha.*

lau·lā hawewe *kik* Amplitude, i.e. the greatest distance the particles in a wave rise or fall from their rest position, in science. *Lit.,* vibration width. See *ho'olaulā hawewe, 'anini laulā hawewe.*

lau·lahi *kik* Sheet, as of stamps. Comb. *lau + lahi. Laulahi po'oleka.* Sheet of stamps.

lau·lā loli *kik* Variable width, as in computer program.

lau·like See *mana'o laulike.*

lau li'i *'A'apehihi lau li'i.* Philodendron.

lau loa *'a'* Lengthwise. *Dic.*

lau·mua *kik* Anterior, in biology. Comb. *lau + mua.* Cf. *laualo, lauhope, laukua. Kualā laumua.* Anterior dorsal fin, of a fish.

launa *'a'* Compatible, as of computer programs; corresponding, in math. *Ua launa kēia lako polokalamu hou me kāu kamepiula.* This new software is compatible with your computer. *Dic., ext. mng.* Cf. *launa 'ole.* See *'a'ohe launa. Hulu waihona launa.* Compatible file format. *'Ao'ao launa.* Corresponding side, in math.

lau nahele 'ō·iwi *kik* Natural vegetation. *Lit.,* native plants.

launa 'ole *'a'* Incompatible, as of computer programs. *He hulu waihona launa 'ole kēia.* This is an incompatible file format. *Lit.,* not compatible. Cf. *launa.*

lau·nea *'a'* Bare, as a tree without leaves. *Dic.*

lau no'e *kik* Coleus. *Lit.,* colored leaf. Cf. *lau kalakoa.*

lau·pa'a·hapa *'Ailakele laupa'ahapa.* Polyunsaturated fat.

lau po'o kuni *kik* Letterhead design. See *po'o kuni.*

lau·'ai *kik* Vegetable. *Maika'i ka lau'ai no ke olakino.* Vegetables are good for you. *Dic., ext. mng., sp. var.* See *'aila meakanu.*

lau·'ala *kik* Herb, as basil, thyme, etc. *'O ke kōko'olau, he lau'ala lapa'au ia i kī maika'i no ka lapa'au 'ana i kekahi mau 'ano ma'i.* Kōko'olau is a kind of herb with medical properties which makes a good tea for treating some kinds of sickness. Comb. *lau + 'ala.*

lau 'ī·nana *kik* Cotyledon. *Lit.,* leaf (from) stirring of life. *Lau 'īnana kahi.* Monocotyledon. *Lau 'īnana lua.* Dicotyledon.

lahi See *pūaina lahi.*

laho·mā·pū *kik* Kiwi fruit. Comb. *laho + māpū.* Also *hua'ai kiwi.*

lā·hui *kik* Species, in biology. *Dic.* See *kālaipuolo lāhui.*

lā·hulu *kik* Species, in biology. Sh. *lāhui + hulu.* Also *lāhui. Kānāwai Lāhulu 'Ane Halapohe.* Endangered Species Act. *Pili lāhulu.* Related species.

laka *kik/ham* Lock; to lock. *E laka 'oe i ka 'īpuka a pa'a.* Lock the door. *Dic.* See *pahu laka.*

lakau·ā *'a'* Domesticated, as a pet or for work. Sh. *laka + kauā.* Cf. *'āhiu, lōhiu.*

laka uai *kik* Sliding latch. *Lit.,* sliding lock.

laka helu *kik* Combination lock. *Lit.,* lock (with) numbers. Cf. *helu laka.*

laka maʻaka *kik* Caps lock, as on computer or typewriter keyboard. *Pihi laka maʻaka.* Caps lock key (preceded by *ke*). Also *pihi laka.*

lāke See *manu lāke.*

lakeke *kik* Blouse. *Dic./Niʻihau.* Also *palauki.* Cf. *lākeke.*

lā·keke *kik* Jacket. *Eng.* Cf. *lakeke.*

laki *Pili helu laki.* Lottery.

lā·kiō *kik* Ratio; rate, i.e. a ratio that compares different kinds of units, in math; quantity, amount or degree of something measured per unit of something else, as of time. *Eng.* See entries below and *pakuhi lākiō. Ma ka lākiō he 60 mil/hl.* At the rate of 60 mph.

lā·kiō like *kik* Proportion, in math; equal ratio. *Lit.*, same ratio.

lā·kiō paʻa·pū wai *kik* Specific gravity, relative gravity. *Lit.*, water density ratio.

lakika *kik* Radish. *Eng.*

laki·kū *kik* Latitude. *Dic.* Also *latitū.* Cf. *lonikū. Laina lakikū.* Parallel, i.e. an imaginary circle on the earth's surface parallel to the equator and designated in degrees of latitude. Also *laina latitū.*

lako hao *kik* Hardware, such as tools made of metal. *Lit.*, supply (of) metal tools. Cf. *lako paʻa. Hale kūʻai lako hao.* Hardware store.

lako hanu *kik* Breathing equipment, as for use in space exploration.

lako hoʻo·nani *kik* Jewelry. Also *lako kāhiko.* Cf. *lako kula* (dic.).

lako kā·hiko *kik* Jewelry. Also *lako hoʻonani.* Cf. *lako kula* (dic.).

lako·lako *kik* Accessories, peripherals, as for a computer. *Dic., ext. mng.*

lako paʻa *kik* Hardware, as for a computer. *Lit.*, solid gear. Cf. *lako polokalamu, lako hao.*

lako polo·kalamu *kik* Software, as for a computer. *Lit.*, program gear. Cf. *lako paʻa.*

lako ʻai·ʻē *kik/ʻa* Loan, i.e. money lent at interest; to have a loan. *Lit.*, provision (through) debt. Also *ʻaiʻē.* Cf. *hoʻolako ʻaiʻē, lawe ʻaiʻē.*

lakuna *kik* Raccoon. *Dic.*

lala *kik* Diagonal. *E kau i kēia mau kikohoʻe i like ka huinanui ma nā lala pākahi me ka -3.* Arrange these digits so that their total will be -3 on each diagonal. *Dic.* See *lala kūpono, kaha lala.*

lala *kik* Split end, in football. *Dic., new mng.* Cf. *muku.* See *ʻāwaʻa lala.*

lā·lā *kik* Member, as of an organization. *Dic. Nā lālā o ka papa.* Board members.

lā·lā *kik* Phrase, in grammar. *Dic., ext. mng.* Cf. *māmalaʻōlelo.*

lā·lahi·lewa *Ao lālahilewa.* Cirrus cloud. *Sh./comb. lahilahi + lewa.*

lala kū·pono *kik* Hypotenuse. *Lit.*, perpendicular diagonal.

lā·lani *Haʻihelu lālani.* Linear equation. *Pālākiō lālani.* Linear scale, in geography.

lala·ʻē *ʻa* Eccentric. *Comb. lala + ʻē.* See *ʻūlala* (dic.).

lā·lelo *kik* Lateral, in linguistics. *Sh. lā + alelo.*

lali·noka *kik* Hieroglyph, hieroglyphics. *ʻAʻole i maopopo ʻia ka lalinoka a ka poʻe ʻAikupita a hiki i ka hoʻomaopopo ʻia ʻana ma ka hoʻohālike ʻana i ka lalinoka o ka pōhaku Roseta me kekahi mau ʻōlelo i kākau pū ʻia ma luna o ia pōhaku.* Egyptian hieroglyphics was not understood until it was figured out by comparing hieroglyphs found on the Rosetta stone with other languages which were also enscribed on that stone. (Assyrian *rahleenos.*)

lā·liʻi *ʻa* Detailed, intricate, as a design. *He lau lāliʻi maoli kēia lau kapa kuiki.* This is a very intricate quilt design. *Dic.*

lalo Sub-, under-. *Dic., ext. mng.* See entries below and *papa o lalo.*

lalo one *kik* Subsand.

lalo honua *kik* Underground. *Lit.*, beneath (the) land.

lalo kai *kik* Submarine, submerged, undersea. *Lit.*, beneath (the) sea. *Lua pele lalo kai.* Submerged volcano. *Papa ʻanuʻu lalo kai.* Underwater terrace.

lalo kopi·kala *kik* Subtropical.

lalo lepo *kik* Subsoil. Cf. *lepo uhi.*

lalo ʻala·paina *kik* Subalpine. *Lit.*, below alpine. See *ʻalapaina. Ululāʻau lalo ʻalapaina.* Subalpine forest.

lā·meka *kik* Ceramic. *Eng. Kile lāmeka.* Ceramic tile.

lā·mia *kik* Lemur. *He pili lāhui ka lāmia no ke keko ma kekahi ʻano, akā, no ka nui kūpono o ka ʻokoʻa mai ke keko, ua manaʻo ʻia he lāhui ʻokoʻa aʻe nō.* The lemur is a related species to the monkey, but because of some marked differences, it is considered a different species altogether. *Gr.*

lami·neka *ham* To laminate. *Eng.*

lā·nahu *kik* Coal. *Dic.* Cf. *nānahu. Kākinoea lānahu.* Coal gasification.

lana·kia *kik* Ranger. *Eng.* See *hale kiaʻi ululāʻau.*

lana·kila *Hele lanakila.* To go freely, i.e. to have freedom to go wherever one pleases, to "have the run of the place." *Māhele lanakila.* Winner's bracket, as in a sports tournament.

lani·uma *kik* Geranium. *Dic.*

Lani·haʻi *iʻoa* Al Nair-Alpha Gruis, a star. *Mān. (HA).*

Lani·hou *iʻoa* Mira, a star. *Mān. (HA).*

Lani·holo·ʻokoʻa *iʻoa* Segin, a star. *Mān. (HA).*

lapa *ʻa*̒ Wild or roughhousing, as an overactive or unruly child. *Dic.* Cf. *ʻāhiu.*

lapa *ʻa*̒ Improper, in math. *Dic., ext. def. Hakina lapa.* Improper fraction.

lāpa *kik* Raft. *Bounty. Lāpa laholio.* Rubber raft. *Lāpa lāʻau.* Wooden raft.

lapa ahi lā *kik* Solar flare. *Lit.*, flash (of) solar fire. Cf. *kiko lā, puapuaʻi lā, ʻale ahi lā.*

lā·paki *kik* Rabbit. *Dic.* Also *lāpiki, ʻiole lāpiki.* See entries below.

lā·paki huelo pulu·pulu *kik* Cottontail rabbit. Also *lāpiki huelo pulupulu, ʻiole lāpiki huelo pulupulu,*

lā·paki kini·kila *kik* Chinchilla rabbit. Comb. *lāpaki* + Eng. Also *lāpiki kinikila, ʻiole lāpiki kinikila.*

lapa niho *kik* Alveolar, in linguistics. *Lit.*, tooth ridge.

lapa puki *kik* Rubber boot. *Eng.* Also *laba puki, puki lapa.*

lapa·ʻau hoʻo·miki uila *kik* Shock therapy. *Hana ʻia ka lapaʻau hoʻomiki uila no ka lapaʻau ʻana i kekahi mau ʻano maʻi o ka lolo.* Shock treatment is used for some kinds of mental disorders. *Lit.*, treat (by) causing alertness (with) electricity.

lā·piki *kik* Rabbit. Usu. *ʻiole lāpiki.* Niʻihau. Also *lāpaki.* See entries under *lāpaki.*

lapu *ʻa*̒ Haunted. *Dic. Hale lapu.* Haunted house (not Halloween variety). *Kiliki o lapu.* Trick or treat.

Lā·pule *kik* Sunday. *Dic.* Abb. *Lp.*

lawaiʻa *Hoʻomalu lawaiʻa a me ka hahai holoholona.* Fish and game management; to manage fish and game.

lawe *ham* Minus. *Dic.* Cf. *hoʻolawe.*

lawe·kahiki *ham* To introduce, as plants and animals to a particular place; to borrow, as a word from another language. *Lit.*, bring (from) a foreign land. See *malihini. Nā lāʻau a me nā holoholona i lawekahiki ʻia mai.* Introduced plants and animals. *He huaʻōlelo i lawekahiki ʻia.* A borrowed word.

lawe·lawe *kik* Service. *Dic.* See entry below and *Papa Lawelawe Hoʻolaha. Lawelawe kōkua.* Social services. *Lawelawe poʻokela.* High-quality service. *ʻOihana lawelawe.* Service industry.

lawe·lawe hana *kik* Function, as on a calculator. *Dic., ext. mng.* Cf. *hana, hahaina.*

lawe·lawe kō·kua *ham* Social services. *Lit.*, serve (by) helping.

lawe·lima *ham* Portable; laptop, as a computer. *Lit.*, (can be) taken (by) hand. *Kamepiula lawelima, lolouila lawelima.* Laptop computer.

lawe mā·lama *ham* To adopt, as a highway or other public area for environmental cleanup or maintenance. *Ma ka papahana lawe mālama alaloa na ke aupuni, hiki ke lawe mālama kekahi 'ahahui i kekahi māhele o ke alaloa, a hō'ike'ike 'ia ka inoa o ka hui nāna e mālama.* In the highway adoption program of the government, an organization can adopt a section of highway to take care of, and the name of the organization that cares for that section is displayed. *Lit.*, take (to) care for. Cf. *lawe hānai* (dic.).

lawena *kik* Behavior, as the way animals act. *Dic., ext. mng. Lawena 'ike hānau.* Instinctive behavior. *Lawena 'apo.* Learned behavior.

lawe 'ai·'ē *ham* To borrow, take on credit. *Dic.* Cf. *ho'olako 'ai'ē, lako 'ai'ē, 'ae.*

lā·'au *kik* Medicine, medicinal drug, medication; wood. *Dic., ext. mng.* See entries below and *papa pānela. Lā'au kuhikuhi.* Prescription drug or medication. *Lā'au kū'ai wale.* Over-the-counter drug or medication.

lā·'au ana ki·e·ki·ena *kik* Elevation pole, as for surveying. *Lit.*, elevation surveying rod. See *lā'au ana 'āina, lena māka.*

lā·'au ana 'āina *kik* Range pole, surveying rod. *Dic.* + *'āina.* See *lā'au ana ki'ekiena, lena māka.*

lā·'au ha'i·nole *kik* Stimulant. *Lit.*, drug (for) stimulating.

lā·'au ho'o·loha *kik* Depressant. *Lit.*, drug which causes depression.

lā·'au ho'o·mā·lū *kik* Barbiturate. *He lā'au ka lā'au ho'omālū no ka hana 'ana a mālie ke kino me ka ho'omaka hiamoe nō ho'i.* Barbiturates are used to calm the body down and make one drowsy. Comb. *lā'au* + *ho'o-* + *mālū* (*Tokelau,* calm).

lā·'au ho'o·ma'e·ma'e hale *kik* Household product, i.e. any of a variety of products used for cleaning floors, sinks, etc. *Ni'ihau.*

lā·'au ho'o·mā·'e·'ele *kik* Anesthetic. *Lit.*, medicine (to) anesthetize. See *ho'omā'e'ele.*

lā·'au kau·kahi *kik* Balance beam. *Lit.*, solitary rod. Cf. *lā'au kaulua.*

lā·'au kau lole *kik* Hanger (made of wood). *Lit.*, wood (for) placing clothes. See *uea kau lole, mea kau lole, 'ea kau lole.*

lā·'au kau·lua *kik* Parallel bars. *Lit.*, double rods. Cf. *lā'au kaukahi. Lā'au kaulua kaulike.* Even parallel bars. *Lā'au kaulua kaulike 'ole.* Uneven parallel bars.

lā·'au ko'o·ko'o *kik* Vaccine. *Lit.*, support medicine.

lā·'au kuhi·kuhi *kik* Pointer, as used in a classroom. *Dic.*

lā·'au make *kik* Poison. *Dic.* See *'alidirina, dielidirina. Lā'au make hanu.* Fumigant. *Lā'au make laoa.* Systemic insecticide. *Lā'au make pā 'ili.* Contact poison. *Lā'au make 'ai.* Stomach poison.

lā·'au make hai·pili·kia *kik* Pesticide. *Lit.*, poison (for) pests. Also *lā'au haipilikia.*

lā·'au make nā·hele·hele *kik* Herbicide. *Lit.*, poison (for) weeds.

lā·'au pulu·pulu *kik* Cotton swab, Q-tip. *Lit.*, cotton stick.

lā·'au 'ai *kik* Chopstick. *Dic*

lā·'au 'ona *kik* Narcotic drug. *Lit.*, intoxicating drug.

la'a·lā·'au *kik* Bush, shrub. *Dic. Wao la'alā'au.* Alpine shrubland.

la'a·loa *'Elelū la'aloa.* German cockroach (Blattella germanica).

la'ana *kik* Example; specimen. *E ha'i mai i la'ana o ka i'a ke'oke'o.* Give me an example of a white fish. Comb. *la'a* + *-na.* Cf. *kumu ho'ohālike, hāpana. La'ana hō'ole.* Counterexample.

lā-'ape *kik* Monstera. Comb. *lau* + *'ape.*

lati·tū See *lakikū.*

lā·toma *kik* Molecule. Sh. *lā-* [as in *lāhui, lālei*] + *'ātoma. Kino lātoma.* Allotrope, i.e. a different molecular form of an element, in science.

lei o Pele *kik* Ring of fire, in geology. *Lit.,* Pele's lei.

lei 'ā·'ī *kik* Necktie. *Dic.* Also *lei 'ā'ī kalawake, lei kalawake.* Cf. *hīpu'u pewa. Lei 'ā'ī pewa.* Bow tie.

leo *kik* Melody, tune. *Dic.* Also *'ea.* See entries below and *hō'ailona mele, pahu leo, pahu ho'onui leo.*

leo *kik* Voice, as in linguistics. *Dic.* See *palapala leo.*

leo ala·ka'i *kik* One who sings the melody of a song. *Ni'ihau.*

leo·paki kikī *kik* Cheetah. *Lit.,* swift leopard.

leo 'ekahi *kik* Soprano. *Lit.,* first voice. *'Ukulele leo 'ekahi.* Soprano 'ukulele.

leo 'ekolu *kik* Tenor. *Lit.,* third voice. *'Ukulele leo 'ekolu.* Tenor 'ukulele.

lehe·lehe *kik* Labial, in linguistics. *Lit.,* lips. See *pena lehelehe, 'umi'umi lehelehe.*

lehi·lehia 'a' Coordinated, having physical dexterity. Redup. of *lehia,* deft.

lehu·lehu See *ho'omana akua lehulehu. 'Āina no ka lehulehu.* Public land.

leka *kik* Slat. *Ua ho'ololi 'ia nā leka o ka pukaaniani 'ōlepe i nehinei.* The jalousie slats were changed yesterday. Mān. (HHLH, MMLH). See *pepa leka.*

leka uila *kik* Electronic mail, E-mail, as in telecommunication. *Lit.,* electric letter.

leka·pī *kik* Recipe. *Eng.*

leka wehe·wehe *kik* Cover letter. *Lit.,* letter (of) explanation.

leke·uma *kik* Legume. *Eng.*

lekesa *kik* Latex. *Eng.*

leki *kik* Tape. *Dic.* See entries below.

leki a'a *kik* Strapping tape, filament tape. *Lit.,* rootlet tape.

lē·kiō *kik* Radio. *Dic.* Also *pahu ho'olele leo.*

leki uea *kik* Cloth duct tape, electrician's tape. *Lit.,* tape (for) wires.

leki pahu *kik* Masking tape, freezer tape. *Lit.,* tape (for) boxes.

leki pepa *kik* Paper tape, as for packages. *Lit.,* tape (made of) paper.

leki 'ea *kik* Transparent tape, Scotch tape. *Lit.,* plastic tape.

lele *heh* To log off, log out, as of a network or other computer system. *Dic.,* new mng. See *kī lele.* Cf. *'e'e. E lele i.* "Goto," as in computer program. *Helu lele.* To skip count, in math.

lele ha'a·luna *heh* Vertical jump. *Lit.,* upward jump.

lele ho'o·nanā *ham* Aggression, as a threat of attack by one country upon another. *Mana'o 'ia he lele ho'onanā ka holo 'ana o nā pū'ali koa o 'Iraka ma waho o ka palena i ho'opa'a 'ia e kō ka hui ku'ikahi.* The crossing over of Iraqi troops outside the borders set by the alliance was considered an act of aggression (not an attack). *Lit.,* rush out aggressively (as to provoke a fight). Cf. *lele kaua.*

lele kaua *ham* Aggression, as an attack by one country upon another. *Ua lele kaua 'o Kihaapi'ilani me kōna 'au moku i kō Maui hikina i mea e ho'opau ai i ka noho ali'i 'ana o Pi'ilani.* In an act of aggression, Kihaapi'ilani and his fleet attacked east Maui in order to topple the reign of Pi'ilani. *Lit.,* rush out to make war. Cf. *lele ho'onanā.*

lele kaula *heh* To jump rope. Cf. *kaula lele. Hō'ike lele kaula kanakolu kekona.* Thirty-second jump rope test.

lele·kē Palaunu *heh* Brownian motion, in chemistry. *Lit.*, Brown leaping here and there.
lele·kī·kē *heh* To volley, as a volleyball. *Lit.*, fly back and forth. Cf. *paʻi manamana, pohu.*
lele kiʻe·kiʻe *heh* High jump.
lele koali *kik* Free swing, as a single rope hanging from a tree branch. *Dic.* Cf. *paiō.*
lele koʻo *heh* To pole vault. See *koʻo lele.*
lele lewa lipo kanaka *heh* Manned space flight. *Lit.*, human space flight.
lele loloa *heh* Standing long jump. *Lit.*, long jump.
lele·neo *heh* To bounce, as a check. Usu. *ua hoʻihoʻi ʻia (ka pila kīkoʻo) no ka lawa ʻole o ke kālā ma ka waihona panakō.* Comb. *lele + neo.*
lele niniu *heh* Centrifugal, i.e. acting in a direction away from a center. *Lit.*, spinning flying. Cf. *ʻume niniu. Manehu lele niniu.* Centrifugal force.
lele paʻi *heh* Jump ball, in basketball. *Lilo ihola ke kinipōpō iā Waimea ma ka lele paʻi ʻana ma ka hoʻomaka ʻana o ka hoʻokūkū.* The ball went to Waimea on the jump ball at the start of the game. *Lit.*, jump (and) slap.
lele·pinao *heh* To use a trapeze. *Dic., ext. mng.* See *koali lelepinao.*
lele ʻē *heh* Encroachment, in football. *Lit.*, premature jump. Cf. *mīʻoi. Lele ʻē na ke kūpale.* Defensive encroachment.
lele ʻole *Moho lele ʻole.* Flightless rail.
lele ʻō·pū *heh* To dive, in volleyball. *Lit.*, stomach jump. Also *luʻu, moe pālahalaha.*
lemi See *wai lemi.*
lena *Laina lena.* Line of sight, sight line. Also *laina ʻike.* See entry below.
lena māka *kik* Sighter, as for surveying. *Lit.*, sight (a) target. *Lima lena māka.* Sighter arm.
lene·kila *kik* Lentil. *Dic.*
Lepa·nona *iʻoa* Lebanon; Lebanese. *Dic.* Also *Lebanona.*

lepe *kik* Tab, as the tab on an audio cassette which can be removed to prevent erasing of what has been recorded, or an index tab on a notebook divider page. *Dic., ext. mng.* See entries below.
lepe unuhi *kik* Subtitle. *Lit.*, translation hem.
lepe kiʻi *kik/ham* Caption, as for a picture; to caption. *Lit.*, picture hem.
lepe·pepei·ao *kik* Ear lobe. Comb. *lepe + pepeiao.*
lepe puke *kik* Bookmark. *Lit.*, book attachment.
lepili *kik* Label, tag; to label. *Eng. Lepili māhuaola.* Food label, as for giving product information on a package of food.
lepo *kik* Soil. *Dic.* See entries below. *Hōkeo kūmau hoʻāʻo lepo.* Standard soil-testing kit. *Lalo lepo.* Subsoil. *Lepo uhi.* Topsoil. *Lepo makaili.* Alluvial soil.
lepo kanu mea·kanu *kik* Potting soil. *Lit.*, dirt (for) planting plants. Cf. *ʻelekanu.*
lepo·piloki *kik* Leptospirosis. *Eng.*
lepo pohō *kik* Mud. *Niʻihau.* Also *ʻūkele.*
Lepupa·lika Kemo·kalaka ʻo Kono·kō *iʻoa* Democratic Republic of the Congo.
Lepupa·lika Komi·nika *iʻoa* Dominican Republic. *Dic.* See *Kominika.*
Lepupa·lika ʻApe·lika Waena *iʻoa* Central African Republic.
lewa *kik* Space. *Dic.* See *lewapuni. Lewa lipo.* Outer space. *Kukuna lewa lipo.* Cosmic ray. *Palapala lewa lipo.* Space map. *Paʻalole hele lewa.* Space suit. *Pūʻali kaua lewa.* Air force.
lewa·lana *ʻa* Weightless, as when in outer space. Comb. *lewa + lana.* Cf. *ʻumekaumaha ʻole.*
lewa·lani·haʻa *kik* Troposphere. Comb. *lewa + lani + haʻa.*

lewa·puni *kik* Atmosphere, as around planets. *Lit.*, surrounding atmosphere. See *lewa*.

Leba·nona *i'oa* Lebanon; Lebanese. *Dic.* Also *Lepanona*.

lī *kik* Mi, the third note on the musical scale. *Dic.* See *pākōlī*.

lī·oho *kik* Algae, general term. *Sh. limu + oho*.

liona kai *kik* Sea lion.

lio pai·pai *kik* Rocking horse.

lio pone *kik* Pony. *Comb. lio* + Eng.

lihi *kik* Margin, as on printed page. *Dic., ext. mng.* See *pili lihi. Lihi hema.* Left margin. *Lihi 'ākau.* Right margin. *Lihi o luna.* Top margin. *Lihi o lalo.* Bottom margin. *Ho'opa'a i nā lihi.* To set the margins.

lihi·lihi maka ku'i *kik* False eyelashes. *Ni'ihau.* See *pena lihilihi maka. Kau i ka lihilihi maka ku'i.* To put on false eyelashes. Also *komo i ka lihilihi maka ku'i* (Ni'ihau).

lika *kik* Liter. *Dic. Abb. l.*

lī·kaia *heh* To retire. *Eng.* Also *ho'omaha loa, rītaia*.

lī·kao *kik* Lotus. (Chinese *lingao*.) Also *kalo Pākē*.

like *'a'* Common, as in math terms; equal or equality, as a mathematical relation of being exactly the same. *Dic., ext. mng.* See *huinakolu like. Helu ho'onui like.* Common factor. *Helu māhua like.* Common multiple. *Lākiō like.* Equal ratio. *Like ka papaha o nā mea e loa'a ana.* Equally likely outcomes.

like·like See *pa'a likelike*.

liko *kik* Newly opened leaf. *Dic.* Cf. *mu'o*. See *piko*.

lī·lia 'Aiku·pika *kik* Agapanthus. *Lit.*, Egyptian lily. Also *līlia 'Aigupita*.

lī·lia 'Ape·lika *kik* Amaryllis. *Lit.*, African lily.

liliu·ewe *heh* To evolve. *Sh. liliu* (Tongan, to adapt) + *ōewe*. Cf. *ho'oliliuewe. Ka liliuewe 'ana.* Evolution.

liliu·welo *'a'* To be biologically adapted to. *Ua liliuwelo ka 'i'iwi i ka ulu 'ōhi'a.* The *'i'iwi* is biologically adapted to the *'ōhi'a* forest. *Comb. liliu* [Tongan, to adapt] + *welo*. See *ho'oliliuwelo*.

Lili'u See *'ukulele Lili'u*.

lilo *'a'* Turnover, in basketball. *Ua lilo ke kinipōpō iā Georgetown 'umi manawa i ka hapa mua wale nō o ka ho'okūkū.* The ball was turned over to Georgetown ten times in only the first half of the game. *Dic., ext. mng.* See entry below.

lilo ka 'ai iā Mea Point for Mea. *Ni'ihau*.

lima ā·ohi·ohi *kik* Resistance arm, i.e. the distance from the fulcrum to the resistance force in a lever.

lima·haka·haka *kik* Print, as in handwriting. *E kākau limahakahaka 'oe i kēia mau hua'ōlelo.* Print these words. *Lit.*, space hand. Cf. *limahiō*. See *kākau pākahikahi*.

lima·hana *kik* Member of a work crew. *Dic., ext. mng. Nā limahana pa'i wikiō.* Video production crew.

lima·hiō *kik* Script, as in handwriting. *E kākau limahiō i kou inoa.* Write your name in script. *Lit.*, slant hand. Cf. *limahakahaka*. See *kākau maoli*.

lima·hilu *kik* Calligraphy. *Comb. lima + hilu*.

lima kia pihi *kik* Remote manipulator arm, space crane. *Lit.*, remote control crab claw. See *kia pihi*.

lima kuhi·kuhi *kik* Hand, as of an analog clock or watch. *Lima kuhikuhi minuke.* Minute hand. *Lima kuhikuhi hola.* Hour hand.

lina *kik* Green onion (white bulb with purple inside). *Mān. (RNM).* Cf. *'o'a*.

lina ho'o·komo *kik* A circle around a period, colon, or semicolon to show that it has been inserted, in proofreading. *Lit.*, ring (for) inserting. Cf. *kaha ho'okomo*.

lina hoʻolana *kik* Swimming tube. *Lit.*, ring (for) floating. Cf. *pela hoʻolana*.

lina kui *kik* Ring, as in a ring binder. *Lit.*, ring to string (paper). *Puke lina kui.* Ring binder.

lina·lina *Palaoa linalina.* Unleavened pancake. *Dic.*

lina poe·poe *kik* Circular shape; circle, as in preschool programs; to sit in a circle. *E noho lina poepoe kākou.* Let's sit in a circle. *Lit.*, round ring.

lina poe·poe holo wā·wae *kik* Track, course for running events in track and field. *Lit.*, round track (for) running.

lina puhi huʻa·huʻa *kik* Bubble wand, for blowing bubbles. *Lit.*, ring (for) blowing bubbles.

lina ʻulī·keke *kik* Tambourine. *Lit.*, baby rattle ring.

lino·hau See *lumi linohau*.

linole·uma *kik* Linoleum, linoleum flooring. *Dic.* Also *moena ʻili*.

Lipe·lia *iʻoa* Liberia; Liberian. *Dic.* Also *Liberia*.

lī·pine *kik* Film, as for a movie or video; footage, as of video tape; recording tape. *Dic., ext. mng., sp. var.* Cf. *minuke līpine*. See entries below and *līpine pōkaʻa. Līpine maʻemaʻe.* Blank footage. *Līpine paʻi maka.* Raw footage.

lī·pine ana *kik* Tape measure, as tailor's or for track events, etc. *Lit.*, measuring ribbon. Cf. *lula poho*.

lī·pine pō·kaʻa *kik* Reel-to-reel tape. *Lit.*, reel tape. Cf. *pōkaʻa līpine*.

liʻi Abbreviation for *liʻiliʻi* (small).

liʻi·liʻi *ʻa*ʻ Little, small. *Dic.* See entry below. *Manamana liʻiliʻi.* Little finger. Also *manamana iki. Mea liʻiliʻi.* Detail. Also *mea liʻiliʻi kikoʻī, mea kikoʻī*.

liʻi·liʻi *ʻa*ʻ Small, as drink size. *Dic.* Abb. *liʻi.* See *lōpū, nui, nui keu. Koloaka liʻiliʻi.* Small soda.

Libe·ria *iʻoa* Liberia; Liberian. *Eng.* Also *Lipelia*.

Libia *iʻoa* Libya; Libyan. *Eng.*

liti·uma *kik* Lithium. *Eng.*

lō Abbreviation for *lōpū* (medium), *lōʻihi* (length).

loa *ʻa*ʻ Length, in math. *Dic.* No abbreviation. Also *ana loa*. See *lōʻihi*. Cf. *ākea, laulā, hohonu, kiʻekiʻe*.

loa *ʻa*ʻ Long. *Dic. Manamana loa.* Middle finger. Also *manamana waena*.

loa Extra, i.e. beyond the usual size, extent or degree. *Dic., ext. mng. Pākā loa.* Extra lean, as meat.

loa *Ao loa.* Stratus cloud. *Dic.*

loaʻa paʻa mau *kik* Sustained yield, as in crop production. *Ma ka mahi ʻai ʻana, kanu hou ʻia ka meaulu i ʻohi ʻia i mea e mālama ai i ka loaʻa paʻa mau.* In farming, crops are replanted after harvesting to ensure sustained yield. *Lit.*, constant harvest.

loea holo·holona lō·hiu *kik* Wildlife expert.

loi *ham* To look over critically; to scrutinize. *Dic. Noʻonoʻo loi.* Critical thinking.

loio See *pepa loio*.

loi·hape *ham* To proofread. *Lit.*, scrutinize (for) inaccuracies.

loi·pā·lā·kiō *ham* To rate, as on a scale. *Lit.*, scrutinize (on a) scale.

loi·pela *kik/ham* Spell checker; to spell check, as of a computer document. *Lit.*, scrutinize spelling.

lou *kik* Hook, as for hanging things. *Dic.* See entries below. *Lou kau lole.* Clothes hook.

lou *kik* Bond. *Dic., ext. mng.* See *ʻūlou. Lou ʻātoma.* Bond between atoms or ions as a result of gaining, losing or sharing electrons.

lou *ham* To save, in volleyball. *Niʻihau.* Also *hoʻihoʻi*.

lou·lou *ham* To link, as in computer program. *Dic., ext. mng. Loulou waihona.* File link. *Loulou ʻikepili.* Data link.

lou·pili *kik* Velcro. Comb. *lou + pili. Mea hoʻopaʻa loupili.* Velcro fastener.

loha·loha *kik* Larva of damselfly and other dragonflies. *Dic.* Also *lohelohe*.

lohe·lohe *kik* Larva of damselfly and other dragonflies. *Dic.* Also *lohaloha*.

lō·hiu *'a'* Naturally wild, as tiger, *'i'iwi, 'a'ali'i*, etc. Sh. *loko + 'āhiu*. See *'āhiu, lākauā, 'ōhuka. Holoholona lōhiu.* Wildlife. *Pōpoki lōhiu.* Wildcat. *'Oihana I'a me ka Holoholona Lōhiu o 'Amelika.* US Fish and Wildlife Service.

loke lā·'au *kik* Wood rose.

lokeni *kik* Rotenone, a chemical compound. (Japn. *roten*.)

Loke 'Ai·lana *i'oa* Rhode Island; Rhode Islander. *Dic.* Also *Rode 'Ailana*.

lō·kino *kik* Organ, as of an animal. Sh. *loko + kino.* See entry below. *'Ōnaehana lōkino.* Organ system, in biology.

lō·kino hua·'ine *kik* Ovary. *Lit.*, ovum organ. See *hua'ine*.

lō·kō *kik* Logo. *Eng.*

lō·ku'u *kik* Gland. Sh. *loko + ho'oku'u.* See entries below.

lō·ku'u hā·'ae *kik* Salivary gland. *Lit.*, saliva organ.

lō·ku'u ho'o·konu·konu pū·nao *kik* Thyroid gland. *Lit.*, gland (which) regulates metabolism.

lō·ku'u ku'u·loko *kik* Endocrine gland. Comb. *lōku'u + ku'u + loko.* Cf. *lōku'u ku'uwaho.* See *'ōnaehana hōmona*.

lō·ku'u ku'u·waho *kik* Exocrine gland. Comb. *lōku'u + ku'u + waho.* Cf. *lōku'u ku'uloko*.

lō·ku'u 'ana·pu'u *kik* Lymph gland, lymph node.

lola *kik* Cassette, as for music tapes or videos. *Ni'ihau.* See *mīkini lola. Lola wikiō.* Video cassette.

lola *kik* Roller; to roll. *Kimalola.* Steamroller. *Dic. Lola pena.* Paint roller. *Pena lola.* To paint with a roller.

lola palaoa *kik* Rolling pin. *Lit.*, bread rolling pin.

lole See entries below and *hao kau lole, pepa lole pipi, 'āpā lole*.

lolea *'a'* Inside out. *Dic.* See *hulihia*.

lole ana kino·ea *kik* Gas fading control fabric, as in meteorology.

lole ana 'oki·kene kolu *kik* Ozone-sensitive fabric. *Lit.*, cloth (that) measures ozone.

lole o lalo *kik* Bottom (clothing). Cf. *lole o luna; pale'ili o lalo* (dic.).

lole o luna *kik* Top (clothing). Cf. *lole o lalo; pale'ili o luna* (dic.).

lole kueka ha'uki *kik* Warm-up suit, as for sports. *Lit.*, sweatshirt clothes. See *kueka ha'uki*.

lole·lole *ham* To thumb through, as a magazine. *Ni'ihau.* To scroll or scan, as in a computer program. *Lolelole i mua.* To scan forward. *Lolelole i hope.* To scan backward.

lole moe pō *kik* Pajamas, nightgown. *Dic.*

lole pipi See *mea lole pipi*.

lole wā·wae kā·'awe *kik* Coveralls, overalls. *Ni'ihau.* Also *lole wāwae 'epane*.

lole wā·wae pala·'ili *kik* Underpants. *Ni'ihau.* Also *palema'i.* See *palema'i*.

lole wā·wae 'epane *kik* Coveralls, overalls. *Dic.* Also *lole wāwae kā'awe*.

loli honua *kik* Geologic change. *Lit.*, earth change.

loli kemi·kala *kik/'a'* Chemical change.

lolo·uila *kik* Computer. Comb. *lolo + uila.* Also *kamepiula, mīkini ho'onohonoho 'ikena. Lolouila lawelima.* Laptop computer. Also *kamepiula lawelima*.

lolo·kū *'Ōnaehana lolokū.* Nervous system.

Loma *Helu Loma.* Roman numeral.

lona hulei *kik* Fulcrum. *Lit.*, seesaw block.

loni·kū *kik* Longitude. *Dic.* Also *lonitū.* Cf. *lakikū. Kumu lonikū.* Prime Meridian. Also *kumu lonitū*.

loni·tū See *lonikū*.

lonoa *kik* Sense, as of taste, smell, etc. (PPN *rongo* + *-a*). *Kahana lonoa.* Lateral line, i.e. a linear series of sensory pores and tubes along the side of a fish, in biology. *Lonoa alelo.* Sense of taste. *Lonoa ihu.* Sense of smell. *Lonoa maka.* Sense of sight. *Lonoa pepeiao.* Sense of hearing. *Lonoa ʻili.* Sense of touch.

lopako *kik* Robot. *Eng.*

lopi niho *kik/ham* Dental floss; to floss (one's teeth). *E lopi ʻoe i nā niho ou me kēia lopi niho.* Floss your teeth with this dental floss. *Lit.,* thread (for) teeth.

lō·pū *ʻaʻ* Medium, as drink size or as of a photograph or in movie or video production. *Sh. roto* [Tah., *waena*] + *pū.* Abb. *lō.* See *liʻiliʻi, nui, nui keu; kokoke, laulā. Koloaka lōpū.* Medium soda. *Paʻi lōpū.* Medium shot (preceded by *ke*). *Paʻi a lōpū.* To take a medium shot (preceded by *ke*). *Wela lōpū.* Medium heat.

lō·ʻihi *ʻaʻ* Length, in math. *Dic.* Abb. *lō.* Also *ana lōʻihi, loa.* Cf. *ākea, laulā, hohonu, kiʻekiʻe.* See *hānai lōʻihi.*

lū See *pakuhi lū.*

lua *kik* Bathroom; toilet. *Dic.* See *lumi ʻauʻau, lumi hoʻopaupilikia.*

lua hā *kik* Two-by-four. *Papa lua hā.* Two-by-four board or lumber. *Dic.*

lua kī·lau·ea *kik* Caldera. *Lit.,* kīlauea crater (named for the caldera on Hawaiʻi).

lua like *kik* Duplicate, as in computer program. *Dic.*

lua pele *kik* Volcano. *Dic.* See *kuahene, pele. Lua pele kuahene.* Shield volcano. *Lua pele kuahene kuamua.* Primary shield volcano. *Lua pele lalo kai.* Submerged volcano. *Lua pele ʻā.* Active volcano.

lua·poʻi *kik* Prey. *He luapoʻi ka ʻiole na ka ʻio.* Mice are a prey of the hawk. *Sh. luaahi* + *poʻi.* Cf. *poʻiiʻa.*

Luiki·ana *iʻoa* Louisiana; Louisianan, Louisianian. *Dic.* Also *Luisiana.*

Luisi·ana *iʻoa* Louisiana; Louisianan, Louisianian. *Dic.* Also *Luikiana.*

Lū·kia *iʻoa* Russia; Russian. *Dic., sp. var.* Also *Rūsia.*

lū·kī·mia *kik* Leukemia. *Eng.*

lū·kini pō·ʻae·ʻae *kik* Deodorant. *Lit.,* underarm perfume.

Luku·ʻāina *iʻoa* Komephoros, a star. *Mān.* (HA).

lula *kik* Ruler (measuring device). *Dic.* See *lula poho. Lula lāʻau.* Wooden ruler.

lula hahaina *kik* Function rule, in math.

lula poho *kik* Tape measure (carpenter's). *Lit.,* ruler (in a) pouch. Cf. *līpine ana.*

luli·luli See *waiū luliluli.*

lulumi *ham* To press, in basketball. *Lulumi nui akula nā kūpale iā Pila i ka pau ʻana o nā kekona hope loa o ka hoʻokūkū.* The defense pressed hard on Pila in the last few seconds of the game. *Dic., ext. mng. Lulumi hapa.* Half-court press. *Lulumi ʻekolu hapahā.* Three-quarter-court press. *Lulumi piha.* Full-court press. *Pale lulumi.* Press defense.

lulu ʻala·neo *kik* Rain shadow. *Aia ka ʻaoʻao Kona ma ka ʻaoʻao lulu ʻalaneo o nā kuahiwi Koʻolau.* The leeward side is found on the rain shadow side of the windward mountains. *Lit.,* unclouded shelter.

lū·maua *ʻaʻ* Fertilized, as an egg. Comb. *lū* + *mau* + *-a.* See *hoʻolūmaua.*

lumi hoʻāhu *kik* Storeroom. *Dic.* Cf. *waihona hōʻahu.*

lumi hoʻo·kipa *kik* Living room. *Dic.*

lumi hoʻo·lulu *kik* Waiting room.

lumi hoʻo·pau·pili·kia *kik* Bathroom. *Lit.,* room (for) going to the bathroom. Also *lua, lumi ʻauʻau.*

lumi huna *kik* Attic. *Lit.,* ceiling room. See also *lumi kaupaku.*

lumi kau·paku *kik* Attic. *Lit.*, room (under the) roof. Also *lumi kaupoku, lumi kaupuku, lumi huna.*

lumi kuke *kik* Kitchen. *Dic.*

lumi lino·hau *kik* Deluxe room, as in a hotel. *Lit.*, ornamented room. Cf. *lumi maʻamau.*

lumi maʻa·mau *kik* Standard room, as in a hotel. *Lit.*, ordinary room. Cf. *lumi linohau.*

lumi moe *kik* Bedroom. *Dic. Lumi moe haku.* Master bedroom. *Lumi moe malihini.* Guest room.

lumi ʻaina *kik* Dining room. *Dic.*

lumi ʻau·ʻau *kik* Bathroom. *Dic.* Also *lua, lumi hoʻopaupilikia.*

lumi ʻohana *kik* Family room.

luna *kik* One in charge of a particular activity, such as a coordinator, editor, manager, etc. *Dic., ext. def.* See entries below and other entries under *hiʻo-hiʻona naʻiau, hoʻokuʻikuʻi, hoʻopono-pono kani, hoʻopuka, huahana, kūkulu kahua, pāhaʻoweli, ʻenehana,* etc.

luna *kik* Dean, as in a college or university. *Dic., ext. mng.* See *luna kulanui. Luna koleke pāheona me ka ʻepekema.* Dean of the college of arts and sciences.

luna uila *kik* Gaffer, as for movie or video production. *Lit.*, electrical supervisor. *Hope luna uila.* Best boy, i.e. an assistant gaffer.

luna hō·ʻoia *kik* Auditor. *Dic.*

luna hoʻo·kele *kik* Director, i.e. one who serves as a leader in conducting any kind of business. *Lit.*, leader (who) conducts business. *Papa luna hoʻokele.* Administration, i.e. a team of executive branch officials appointed by the President, in government.

luna hoʻo·mā·lama·lama *kik* Lighting director, as for movie or video production. *Lit.*, supervisor (for) illuminating.

luna hoʻo·malu *kik* Moderator, as of a panel. *Dic., ext. mng.*

luna kula·nui *kik* Provost, as of a college or university. *Lit.*, college supervisor. Cf. *pelekikena, poʻo kulanui.*

luna pā·heona *kik* Art director, as for movie or video production. *Lit.*, art supervisor.

luna·ʻike·hala *kik* Conscience. *Dic. Noho ka hewa i ka lunaʻikehala.* To have a guilty conscience.

lū·pahū *kik* "Pop-pop" fireworks that explode on impact. Comb. *lū + pahū.* See *ahihoʻoleʻaleʻa.*

lupe·kau *kik* Hang glider. *Lit.*, kite (for) riding.

lū·ʻau Haole *kik* Spinach. *Lit.*, foreign taro tops.

luʻu *heh* To dive, in volleyball. *Niʻihau.* Also *lele ʻōpū, moe pālahalaha.*

luʻu kini ea *heh* Scuba diving; to scuba dive. *Lit.*, dive (with a) scuba tank. See *kanaka luʻu kai, kini ea luʻu kai.*

luʻu lewa *heh* To sky dive. *Mea luʻu lewa.* Sky diver.

luʻu nalu poʻi *heh* Running under the jump rope. *Mān.* See *ʻoni a ka moku.*

ll Abbreviation for *laulā* (width).

Lp Abbreviation for *Lāpule* (Sunday).

M

m Abbreviation for *mika* (meter).

māio *ʻa* Calm, cool-headed, even-tempered. *Mān.* See *kiʻi māio.*

mā·ioio mana·mana lima *kik* Groove on finger as appears in finger-print. See *meheu manamana lima.*

maika *kik/ham* Bowling. *Dic. Kuea maika.* Bowling frame. *Pine maika.* Bowling pin.

mai·keni *kik* Maytansine, a chemical compound once investigated for therapeutic uses but later found to be too toxic for human use. (Sp. *maiten.*)

māiki 'a' Microscopic; micro-. *Kiko nā hua he piohē māiki.* Eggs hatch into microscopic larvae. *Dic., ext. mng.* Cf. *mānui.* '*Umekaumaha māiki.* Microgravity. *Meaola māiki.* Microorganism.

māiki·kalame *kik* Microgram. Comb. *māiki + kalame.*

maiko·lona *kik* Micron (0.0001 cm). *Eng.*

maile hoʻo·ili *kik* Baton used in relay race. See *holo hoʻoili, kūkini hoʻoili, heihei hoʻoili.*

maile pana *kik* Bandmaster's baton. *Lit.,* wand (for) beating time. Cf. *'aukaʻi pāna, 'aukaʻi wili.*

māina *kik* Minor, as a minor academic field of study. *Eng.* Cf. *mēkia.*

Maine *iʻoa* Maine. *Dic.* Also *Meine.*

maiʻao *kik* Hoof. *Dic.*

maiʻuʻu *kik* Claw. *Dic.*

maoli See *kākau maoli.*

mao·meka *kik* Apparatus, device, mechanism, ordinarily including some mechanical part or parts. Sh. *ma o + mekanika.* See *hāmeʻa, mauhaʻa, mea hana.*

Maui *iʻoa* Maui, the island. Cf. *Māui.*

Māui *iʻoa* Māui, the demigod. Cf. *Maui.*

māui·ili *kik* Equinox. Comb. *māui + ili.* Cf. *māuikiʻikiʻi. Ka māuiili o ka hāʻulelau.* Autumnal equinox. *Ka māuiili o ke kupulau.* Vernal equinox.

māui·kiʻi·kiʻi *kik* Solstice. Comb. *māui + kiʻikiʻi.* Cf. *māuiili. Ka māuikiʻikiʻi o ke kauwela.* Summer solstice. *Ka māuikiʻikiʻi o ka hoʻoilo.* Winter solstice.

mau·haʻa *kik* Instrument, as a specialized tool for a particular occupation. Tah. See *hāmeʻa, maomeka, mea hana.*

mauna *kik* Mount. *Dic., ext. mng. Mauna 'Eweleka.* Mount Everest. *Mauna 'Olumepika.* Mount Olympus; Olympus Mons, a volcano on Mars.

mauna kai *kik* Seamount. *Mauna kai pālahalaha.* Guyot. *Pae Mauna Kai ʻEmepela.* Emperor Seamounts. Also *Pae Mauna Kai ʻo ʻEmepela.*

Mauna Kana Helena *iʻoa* Mount Saint Helens. *Eng.* Also *Mauna Sana Helena.*

Mauna Pō·haku *iʻoa* Utah; Utahan, Utahn. *Dic.* Also *ʻŪtā.*

māunu *heh* To molt, as a snake its skin. *Dic.* Cf. *hoʻomalule.*

mau·paʻa 'a' To consist of, be composed of, be made up of. Comb. *mau + paʻa.* See *ʻūmaupaʻa.*

mau·ʻa·e *ham* To override, as in computer program. *Dic., ext. mng.*

mauʻu *kik* Grass (general term), lawn. *Dic.* Also *mahiki.* See entries below. *ʻOki i ka mauʻu.* To mow the lawn.

mauʻu Kale·poni *kik* California grass. *He lāʻau malihini ka mauʻu Kaleponi e laha ʻino nei ma ka ʻāina o nā mokupuni nui a pau o Hawaiʻi.* California grass is an introduced plant that is overrunning the land on all the major islands of Hawaiʻi.

mauʻu pī·neki *kik* Nutgrass.

mauʻu ʻohe *kik* Reed. *Lit.* bamboo grass.

Mau·ri·ta·nia *iʻoa* Mauritania; Mauritanian. *Eng.*

mahaka *kik* Outline, as a line marking the outer limits of an object or figure. Niʻihau (from *māka*). Cf. *meheu. Anakuhi mahaka.* Stencil.

mahaka maka *kik* Eye liner. *Lit.,* eye tracing.

maha·kea *Mahi ʻai mahakea.* Shifting cultivation, in geography.

mahako·nia *kik* Mahogany, the wood. *Eng.*

maha·melo *kik* Marshmallow. *Eng.* Also *masamelo.*

mahana 'a' Temperature, when weather considered warm. *ʻEhia ka mahana o kēia lā? Lit.,* warm. Also *mehana.* Cf. *anu, wela.* See *kēkelē* and entries under *mehana.*

mā·hele *kik* Branch, as of a government. *Dic., ext. mng., sp. var.* See entries below. *Māhele mana hoʻokō.* Executive branch. *Māhele ʻaha hoʻokolokolo.* Judicial branch. *Māhele ʻahaʻōlelo.* Legislative branch.

mā·hele *kik* Bracket, as in a sports tournament. *Dic., ext. mng., sp. var. Māhele hāʻule.* Consolation bracket. *Māhele lanakila.* Winner's bracket.

mā·hele hana *Nā māhele hana.* Jobs, as for movie or video production. *Lit.,* work categories. *Papa māhele hana.* Call sheet, i.e. a list of jobs.

mā·hele hapa *kik* Fractional part. *Māhele hapalua.* One-half (part).

mā·hele manawa *ham* To take turns. *Lit.,* apportion turns.

mā·hele pā *kik* Disk partitioning, in computer hard drive. *Lit.,* disk division.

mā·hele ʻāina *kik* Geographic region; regional. Cf. *aupuni. ʻAhahui māhele ʻāina.* Regional organization.

mahi iʻa *ham* Aquaculture. *He hiki ke lilo ka ʻoihana mahi iʻa i ʻoihana puka maoli o ke kālā ke hana laulā ʻia.* The aquaculture industry can become a very lucrative one if done widely. *Lit.,* cultivate marine animals or plants.

mahiki *kik* Grass (general term), lawn. *Niʻihau.* Also *mauʻu. ʻOki i ka mahiki.* To mow the lawn.

mahi·kua *kik* Defensive linebacker, in football. *Sh. mahimahi + kua.*

mahi māla *ham* To garden; gardening. *Lit.,* cultivate (a) garden. *Hale kūʻai mahi māla.* Garden store, gardening store. *Puke mahi māla.* Gardening book.

mahina *kik* Month. *Dic.* Abb. *mhn.* Also *māhina.*

mahi ʻai See entry below. *ʻOihana Mahi ʻAi o ka Mokuʻāina.* State Department of Agriculture.

mahi ʻai maha·kea *ham* Shifting cultivation, in geography. *Lit.,* fallow land cultivation.

mā·hoe *kik* Double, as when throwing dice. *Dic., ext. mng. Helu māhoe.* Double number, i.e. the same number used twice, in math.

mahola *ʻa* Expanded or exploded, as a file in computer program. *Ua mahola ka waihona ʻopihia.* The compressed file has been expanded. *Dic., ext. mng.* Cf. *māhuahua, ʻopi.* See *hoʻomahola. Waihona mahola.* Expanded file.

mahola·hune *ʻa* Diffusion; to be diffused. *Ua maholahune ke kinoea i loko o ke ea, a ʻaʻohe pilikia i kēia manawa.* The gas has diffused into the air and now there is no danger. Comb. *mahola + hune.*

mā·hua *kik* Multiple, in math. *Dic., ext. mng.* Also *helu māhua.*

mā·hua·ola *kik* Nutrient. *Lit.,* to increase life. *Lepili māhuaola.* Food label, as for giving product information on a package of food. *Māhuaola māiki.* Micronutrient. *Māhuaola mānui.* Macronutrient. *ʻOulu māhuaola.* Nutrient culture.

mā·hua·hua *ʻa* Expanded, as of computer memory. *Dic., ext. mng.* Cf. *keu, mahola. Waihona ʻike māhuahua.* Expanded memory.

māhu·ea *kik* Vapor. *Dic., ext. mng.*

māhu pele See *uila māhu pele.*

maka *Palaoa maka.* Flour. *Palaoa maka huika piha.* Whole wheat flour. See entries under *palaoa.*

māka *kik* Target. *Dic.*

mā·kā *kik* Obsidian. *Dic., ext. mng.*

maka·ani·ani kau·pale *kik* Safety glasses, protective glasses or goggles. *Lit.,* glasses placed (to) protect.

maka·ani·ani kala *kik* Sun glasses. *Niʻihau.* Also *makaaniani lā.*

maka·ani·ani lā *kik* Sun glasses. Also *makaaniani kala.*

maka·ani·ani luʻu kai *kik* Diving goggles or mask. *Lit.,* glasses (for) diving (in the) sea. Also *makaaniani luʻu.*

maka·ili *kik* Alluvial. *Loaʻa ka lepo makaili ma kahi e kahe ai nā kahawai.* Alluvial soil is found in areas where streams flow. *Dic., ext. mng. Lepo makaili.* Alluvial soil.

mā·kau *kik* Skill. *Sh. mākaukau.* See entries below.

mā·kau ola *kik* Practical life skill.

mā·kau hoʻo·pakele ola *kik* Life-saving skill.

mā·kau hua·ʻō·lelo *kik* Word skill.

mā·kau kino *kik* Physical education. *Lit.*, physical skill.

makau·nalo *kik* Fly, fishhook with feathers. *Lit.*, fly fishhook.

mā·kau noʻo·noʻo *kik* Thinking skills. *Puke mākau noʻonoʻo.* Building thinking skills book.

mā·kau pilina·ʻō·lelo *kik* Grammar or sentence structure skill.

mā·kau ʻō·lelo *kik* Language arts.

Mā·kahi *iʻoa* Scheat, a star. *Mān. (HA).*

maka·hiki *kik* Year. *Dic. Abb. MH. Makahiki holo kukuna lā.* Light year. See *māmā kukuna lā.*

maka·hiʻo *ham* To explore. *E hele kākou i ka makahiʻo ʻana.* Let's go exploring. *Comb. maka + hiʻo (Tah., look). Huakaʻi makahiʻo.* Excursion, field trip.

maka·kina *kik* Magazine. *Eng.* Also *makasina.*

maka·kiʻi See *nananana makakiʻi.*

maka·koho *kik* Priority. *Comb. maka + koho.* See *hoʻomakakoho. Hoʻokaʻina makakoho.* To prioritize, set priorities

maka·kū *kik/heh* Creative imagination; to use one's imagination. *Dic.* Cf. *moeā. Kākau makakū.* Creative writing.

maka·kui *kik* Fine point, fine line, as of a pen point. *Dic., ext. mng., sp. var. Peni makakui.* Fine-point pen.

Maka·kukeka *iʻoa* Massachusetts. *Dic.* Also *Masakuseta.*

maka·kumu *ʻa* Primitive. *Comb. maka + kumu.*

mā·kala *kik* Muscle. *Niʻihau (Eng.). Mākala ʻōpū.* Abdominal muscle. *ʻŌnaehana mākala.* Muscular system, in biology.

Mā·kala *iʻoa* Marshall Islands; Marshallese. *Dic.* Also *Mākala ʻAilana, Pae Moku Mākala.*

maka·lau *kik* Tesselation, in math. *Comb. maka + lau.*

maka·launa *ʻa* Compatible, as numbers, in math. *Dic., ext. mng. Helu makalauna.* Compatible number.

mā·kala·kala *ʻa* Decoded, solved. *Dic., new mng.* See *hoʻomākalakala.*

mā·kala ʻamo *kik* Sphincter, i.e. an annular muscle surrounding and able to contract or close a bodily opening or channel. *Lit.*, anal muscle. See *puka ʻamo.*

Mā·kala ʻAi·lana *iʻoa* Marshall Islands; Marshallese. *Dic.* Also *Mākala, Pae Moku Mākala.*

maka·like *kik* Daisy, marguerite. *Dic.*

maka·lina *kik* Margarine, oleomargarine. *Eng.*

maka·liʻi See *pākū makaliʻi, waiehu makaliʻi.*

maka·loni *kik* Macaroni. *Eng.*

māka mana·mana lima *kik* Fingerprint. *Niʻihau.* Also *kiʻi manamana lima, meheu manamana lima.* See *māioio manamana lima.*

māka mana·mana lima See *kāpala. ʻOhi i ka māka manamana lima.* To collect fingerprints.

makana *Palapala makana.* Gift certificate.

maka·neki·uma *kik* Magnesium. *Eng.*

makani *kik* Wind. *Dic.* See *pohu, kolonahe, aheahe, hoʻoholunape, ulūlu, ʻena makani.* See also *holona makani, huila makani.*

makani kaʻa·wili·wili *kik* Tornado. *Dic., sp. var.*

makani pā·hili *kik* Hurricane. *Dic.* *Kūkala maka'ala makani pāhili.* Hurricane watch. *Kūkala pō'ino makani pāhili.* Hurricane warning.

maka pū·alu *kik* Twill plaiting. *Mān. (MW).* Also *'o'eno.*

maka puhi *kik* Herringbone weave. *Mān. (MW).* Also *iwipuhi.*

maka·wela *Kā makawela.* To slash and burn, a method of land cultivation.

Maka·wela *i'oa* Miaplacidus, a star in the constellation Carina. *Mān. (HA).*

maka·'āi·nana *kik* Citizen. *Dic.* Also *kupa. Maka'āinana kaumoku'āina pālua.* Dual citizen. Also *kupa kaumoku'āina pālua.*

maka·'aha *kik* Grid. *Dic., ext. mng., sp. var.* See *pakuhi maka'aha.* *Pepa maka'aha.* Graph paper.

maka·'aha *kik* Screen, as for windows. *Ni'ihau.* Also *uea makika.* See *pani puka uea makika.*

maka·'ala ma'aka *ham* Case sensitive, as in computer program. *Lit.,* alert (for) capitals.

maka·'ala 'upena *Kanaka maka'ala 'upena.* Referee, in volleyball. See *'uao.*

mā·ka'i *Manu māka'i.* Cardinal. *Mān.* Also *manu 'ula'ula.*

Mā·ka'i *i'oa* Enif, a star. *Mān. (HA).*

ma ka 'ikamu À la carte, as on a menu. Also *'oka pākahikahi.*

mā·ka'i kia'i *kik* Security guard. Also *kia'i, kia'i pō, māka'i kia'i pō.*

maka 'ole See *nananana maka 'ole.*

make *Pūnuku ea make.* Gas mask, as used during World War II.

make·hana *'a'* Useful. Cf. *make-pono* (dic.).

make hopena *'a'* To die a bad death, as in punishment for evil deeds. *Mān. (JPM).*

make·kana *kik* Mustang. *Eng.* Also *masetana.*

make·lia *kik* Material, a general term but not relating to cloth. *Dic.* Also *memea. Makelia kūlohelohe.* Raw material.

make loa *'a'* Extinct. *Dic., ext. mng.* Also *halapohe, nalowale loa. 'Ane make loa.* Endangered.

make·make *kik* Preference. *Dic., ext. mng. Nā makemake.* Preferences, as in computer program.

make·makika na'au *kik* Mental math. Also *helu na'au.*

make·naiko·kene *'a'* Chlorosis, i.e. a condition in plants as a result of deficient nitrogen. *Comb. make + naikokene.* Cf. *make wai, make 'ai* (dic.).

mā·kē·neki *kik* Magnet. *Dic.*

mā·kia *ham* To set, as a record. *Na wai i mākia i ke kūho'e o ka lele loloa i ka makahiki 1988?* Who is it that set the record for the standing long jump in 1988? *Dic., ext. mng.* Cf. *kūho'e.*

Mā·koi *i'oa* The star in the center of the constellation Carina. *Mān. (HA).*

mā·kole *Manu wiliō mākole.* Red-eyed vireo.

mā·kō·pi'i *kik* Moss, general term. *Dic., ext. mng.* See *hulupō'ē'ē. Mākōpi'i 'elenahu.* Peat moss.

mā·kua·kua *heh/'a'* To age, as a person; aged. *Dic., ext. mng. Ka mākuakua 'ana.* Aging.

Makulu *i'oa* Saturn. *Dic.*

mā·ku'e *Palaoa māku'e.* Brown bread, a layman's term for any bread made with dark flour. See entries under *palaoa.*

Mal. Abbreviation for *Malaki* (March).

māla *Mahi māla.* To garden; gardening. See *mahi māla.*

Malai·sia *i'oa* Malaysia; Malaysian. *Eng.*

Malaui *i'oa* Malawi; Malawian. *Eng.*

māla hō·'ike·'ike mea·kanu *kik* Botannical garden. *Lit.,* garden for displaying plants.

mala·keke *kik* Syrup. *Dic., ext. mng.* Also *hone.*

Malaki *i'oa* March. *Dic.* Abb. *Mal.*

mala·kona *kik* Marathon. *Eng.*

mā·lalai·oa *kik* Artisan, craftsman. *'O ke kanaka mālalaioa, he mākaukau loa i kekahi hana no'eau e hō'ike'ike 'ia ai, a i 'ole, e ho'ohana maoli 'ia ai ma ka noho 'ana.* An artisan is someone who is skilled at a particular trade or art to be displayed or for practical everyday use. *Dic., ext. mng.*

mā·lama *ham* To save, as in computer program. *Dic., ext. mng.* See entry below. *Mālama ma ka inoa 'o.* To save as. *Ho'i i ka mālama.* To revert to previous save.

mā·lama *Lawe mālama.* To adopt, as a highway or other public area for environmental cleanup or maintenance.

mā·lama·lama au·kahi *kik* Coherent light, i.e. light in which all the waves vibrate in a single plane, with the crests and troughs all aligned. *Lit.,* flowing together light.

mala·ria *kik* Malaria. *Eng. Malaria manu.* Avian malaria.

mala·tiona *kik* Malathion. *Eng.*

malele *heh* Radiation; to radiate. *Dic., ext. mng.* Cf. *pāhawewe. Malele ho'oliliuwelo.* Adaptive radiation, in biology.

Māli *i'oa* Mali; Malian. *Eng.*

mā·lī *kik* Mallee bird, of Australia. *Eng.* Also *manu mālī.*

mali·hini *'a'* Introduced, as plants and animals to a particular place. *Dic.* See *lawekahiki, lumi moe malihini.*

mā·liko *kik* Transparency, as for an overhead projector. *Dic., ext. mng.*

Māli·neli *i'oa* Marineris. *Eng. Ke awāwa 'o Malineli.* Valles Marineris, a valley on Mars.

mā·lō *'a'* Tense, as articulation in linguistics. *Dic., ext. mng.* Cf. *'alu. Woela mālō.* Tense vowel.

mā·lolo *'Au mālolo.* Butterfly stroke, in swimming; to swim the butterfly stroke. *Lit.,* swim (like) *mālolo* fish.

malū *Hālāwai malū.* Subconference, in telecommunications. *Pae malū.* Illegal alien; to arrive as an illegal alien. Cf. *pae kānāwai.*

mā·lua·wai *kik* Large pond, lake. *Ni'ihau.*

malu·hale *kik* Indoor. Comb. *malu + hale.* Cf. *kaupokulani. Ha'uki maluhale.* Indoor sport. *Mākeke maluhale.* Indoor market. *'Aha mele maluhale.* Indoor concert.

malule *'a'* Floppy, as computer disk. *Dic., ext. mng. Pā malule.* Floppy disk (preceded by *ke*). Cf. *pā pa'aloko.*

mā·mā *kik* Tempo, in music. *Dic., ext. mng.* See entries below.

mā·mā holo *'a'* Speed. *Lit.,* going speed. See *pi'i ka māmā holo, ho'opi'i i ka māmā holo, emi ka māmā holo, ho'ēmi i ka māmā holo. 'Awelike māmā holo.* Average speed.

mā·mā kani *kik* Speed of sound. Also *māmā holo o ke kani.* Cf. *māmā kukuna lā.* See *palena holo kani.*

mā·mā kukuna lā *kik* Speed of light. *Lit.,* speed (of) sun's ray. Also *māmā holo o ke kukuna lā.* Cf. *māmā kani.* See *makahiki holo kukuna lā.*

mā·mala·mala *kik* Sliver, splinter. Redup. of *māmala.*

mā·mala·'ō·lelo *kik* Phrase, in literary or general use. *Dic.* Cf. *lālā.*

mā·mela *kik* Mammal. *Eng.* Also *holoholona 'ai waiū.*

mā·mota *kik* Groundhog, marmot. *Eng.*

mana *kik* Version, as of computer program, network, etc. *Dic., ext. mng.*

manā *'a'* Nasal, in linguistics. *Onomatopoeia.*

mana ho'o·kō *Māhele mana ho'okō.* Executive branch (of a government).

mana hoʻo·kolo·kolo *kik* Appellate jurisdiction, i.e. a court's authority to hear an appeal of a decision made by another court. *Ke hoʻokō nei ka ʻAha Hoʻokolokolo Kiʻekiʻe i kōna mana hoʻokolokolo ma ke kauoha ʻana e hoʻokolokolo ʻia ka mea i hoʻāhewa ʻia ma ka ʻAha Hoʻokolokolo Kiʻekiʻe.* The Supreme Court is exercising it's appellate jurisdiction in ordering that it try the case of the accused in Supreme Court. *Lit.*, authority (to) try in court.

mana kau kā·nā·wai *kik* Legislative powers. *Trad.*

mana·kanika *kik* Manganese. *Eng.*

mana·kia *kik* Manager. *Eng.* See *hoʻopuka*. *Manakia ʻenehana.* Production manager, as for a movie or video production.

mana·koho *ʻElele manakoho.* Elector, as in the US Electoral College.

mana·mana *kik* Finger. *Dic.* Also *manamana lima.* See entries below and *paʻi manamana.*

mana·mana iki *kik* Little finger. *Dic.* Also *manamana liʻiliʻi.*

mana·mana komo *kik* Ring finger. *Niʻihau.* Also *manamana pili.*

mana·mana kuhi·kuhi *kik* Index finger. *Niʻihau.* Also *manamana miki.*

mana·mana li·i·li·i *kik* Little finger. *Dic.*

mana·mana loa *kik* Middle finger. *Dic.* Also *manamana waena.*

mana·mana miki *kik* Index finger. *Dic.* Also *manamana kuhikuhi.*

mana·mana nui *kik* Thumb. *Dic.*

mana·mana pili *kik* Ring finger. *Dic.* Also *manamana komo.*

mana·mana waena *kik* Middle finger. *Niʻihau.* Also *manamana loa.*

manawa *kik* Time. *Dic.* See entries below and *uaki*. *Helu manawa.* Time, as recorded duration; to time, as speed, duration, etc. *Laina manawa.* Time line. *Ma mua o ka manawa, ma mua o ka hola.* Early. *No ka manawa.* Pro tem, pro tempore. *Pelekikena no ka manawa.* President pro tem.

manawa hili *kik* At bat, up (to bat), in baseball. *Lit.*, time (to) bat.

manawa hoʻo·maha *kik* Time out, in team sports such as volleyball. *Niʻihau.*

manawa ʻā·nō *kik* Real time, as in computer program. *Hiki ke kolekole i ka manawa ʻānō ma ka Leokī.* You can chat in real time in Leokī. *Lit.*, present time.

manaʻo *kik* Concept. *Dic., ext. mng. Au manaʻo.* Tone, as of a literary work. *Hoʻokaʻina manaʻo.* To sequence ideas, as in a composition. *Puaʻi manaʻo.* To brainstorm.

manaʻo·haʻi *kik* Theorem, in math. *Dic. Manaʻohaʻi o Paekakoleo.* Pythagorean theorum.

manaʻo kā·koʻo *kik* Supporting idea, as in a composition.

manaʻo kuhi *kik/ham* Assumption; to assume. *Lit.*, assuming thought.

manaʻo lau·like *kik* Thesaurus entry. *Comb. manaʻo + lau + like. Puke manaʻo laulike.* Thesaurus. *Puke manaʻo laulike.* Thesaurus, as in computer program.

manaʻo nui *kik* Main idea or thought, as of a paragraph or story. *Dic., ext. mng.*

manehu *kik* Force, power to affect physical relations or conditions. *Sh. mana + ehu.* See *paʻa manehu kūʻēʻē. Kāʻei manehu uila.* Electrical force field. *Manehu āohiohi.* Resistance force. *Manehu hoʻolana.* Buoyant force, i.e. the upward force of a fluid on an object in it. *Manehu kūlohelohe.* Natural force. *Manehu lā.* Solar power. *Manehu lele niniu.* Centrifugal force. *Manehu kaulike.* Balanced force. *Manehu ʻume niniu.* Centripetal force.

Māmaka Kaiao / 104

manehu ʻā·nai *kik* Friction, as when one thing rubs against another. *Lit.*, friction force. Also *ʻānai*.
mania *Pena paʻa mania.* Enamel.
mā·noa·noa *ʻaʻ* Coarse, as sand. *Niʻihau/dic.* Cf. *ʻaeʻae.*
manono *ham* To percolate, as water passing through a porous substance. *Dic., ext. mng.*
māno·wai *ʻŌnaehana mānowai.* Circulatory system.
mā·no·ʻa·no·ʻa *ʻaʻ* Thick (var. of *mānoanoa*). *Dic.*
manu *kik* Bird. *Dic.* See entries below.
mā·nui *ʻaʻ* Macro-. *ʻO ka māhuaola mānui, he kumumea kemikala ia i pono e loaʻa nui i ka lāʻau no ka ulu maikaʻi ʻana o ka lāʻau.* A macronutrient is a chemical element that plants need in large amounts for the good growth of plants. Sh. *māiki + nui.* Cf. *māiki.*
manu hekili *kik* Thunderbird.
manu hū *kik* Hummingbird. *Lit.*, bird (that) hums.
manu kā·lā *kik* Sparrow. *Niʻihau.*
manu kelaka *kik* Thrasher, a bird related to the thrush. Comb. *manu* + Eng.
manu keluka *kik* Thrush. *Lit.*, thrush bird. *Manu keluka ululāʻau.* Wood thrush.
manu kika·kī *kik* Chickadee. Comb. *manu* + Eng.
manu kū·olo·kū *kik* Warbler. *Lit.*, warbling bird.
manu lāke *kik* Lark. Comb. *manu* + Eng.
manu mā·kaʻi *kik* Cardinal. *Mān.* Also *manu ʻulaʻula.*
manu mū·kī·kī *kik* Honeycreeper (general term). *Lit.*, bird (that) sucks.
manunu *kik/heh* Tremor, as of an earthquake; to tremor. *Dic.*
manu nū·hata *kik* Nuthatch, a kind of bird. Comb. *manu* + Eng.
manu pao lā·ʻau *kik* Woodpecker. *Lit.*, bird (that) pecks wood.

manu pala·miko *kik* Flamingo. *Lit.*, flamingo bird. Also *palamiko.*
manu pale·kaiko *kik* Bird of paradise, the bird. Cf. *pua manu.*
manu peleita *kik* Mejiro. *Niʻihau.*
manu pī·uī·lā·ʻau *kik* Wood peewee, a kind of bird. Comb. *manu* + Eng. + *lāʻau.*
manu pō·poki *kik* Catbird.
manu pupē *kik* Puffin. Comb. *manu* + Eng. Also *pupē.*
manu wili·ō *kik* Vireo, a kind of bird. Comb. *manu* + Eng. *Manu wiliō mākole.* Red-eyed vireo.
manu ʻini·kō *kik* Indigo bunting. *Lit.*, indigo bird.
manu ʻī·piki *kik* Ibis, a flightless bird in prehistoric Hawaiʻi. Comb. *manu* + Eng.
manu ʻoli·ō *kik* Oriole. Comb. *manu* + Eng.
manu ʻula·ʻula *kik* Cardinal. *Dic.* Also *manu mākaʻi.*
māpa *kik/ham* Mop; to mop. *Mān. Hulu māpa.* Mop head.
mā·pina *kik* Muffin. Eng. *Māpina pelene.* Bran muffin.
Mā·pono *iʻoa* Alpheratz, a star. *Mān. (HA).*
mā·pū·naka *kik* Primate, an order of animals including man, apes and monkeys. *kik.* Sh. *māpū + kanaka.*
mā·puna ʻō·lelo *kik* Expression, in grammar, i.e. a term of more than one word which has one meaning, e.g. *a laila. Dic.*
mā·wae See *awāwa māwae.*
maʻa *ʻaʻ* To become adapted to. *Dic.* See *hoʻomaʻa.*
maʻa ana kawa·ū·ea kū·lua *kik* Sling psychrometer. *Lit.*, psychrometer sling. See *ana kawaūea.*
maʻaka *ʻaʻ* Upper case, capital. (Rarotongan, big.) Cf. *naʻinaʻi.* See *hua maʻaka. Makaʻala maʻaka.* Case sensitive, as in computer program.
mā·ʻalo·ʻalo See *uila au māʻaloʻalo.*

Māmaka Kaiao / 105

ma'a·mau See *lumi ma'amau.*

mā·'ele·nono *'a'* Tilth, i.e. the nature of soil with porous texture and well-aggregated crumb structure. Comb. *mā- + 'ele* (sh. *kelekele*, PPN *lepo*) + *nono*. See *pūhuna.*

ma'i See entries below and *ho'omalu ma'i.*

ma'i hehena *kik* Maniacal delirium. *Lit.*, maniac illness.

ma'i huo·huoi *kik* Schizophrenia. Comb. *ma'i* + redup. of *huoi. Ma'i huki huohuoi.* Schizophrenic convulsion.

ma'i huki *kik* Convulsion. *Dic. Ma'i huki huohuoi.* Schizophrenic convulsion.

ma'i kō·pa'a *kik* Diabetes. *Ni'ihau.* Also *mimi kō.*

ma'i pale 'ea pau *kik* AIDS (acquired immune deficiency syndrome). *Lit.*, disease (of) finished resistance (against) infectious diseases. Also *pale 'ea pau.* See *mū hōlapu pale 'ea pau.*

ma'i 'a'ai 'ana·pu'u *kik* Lymphoma. *Lit.*, lymph cancer.

ma'ono *kik* Flavor. Comb. *ma- + 'ono.* Cf. *mea hō'ono'ono.*

mā·'ō·'ā *'a'* To be in solution, a scientific term. Comb. *mea + 'ō'ā.* See *mā'ō'āna, pēmā'ō'ā.*

mā·'ō·'āna *kik* Solution, i.e. a homogeneous mixture. Comb. *mā'ō'ā + -na.* Cf. *pūaina.* See *mā'ō'ā, pēmā'ō'ā. Mā'ō'āna kāmāhuaola.* Hydroponic solution. See *kāmāhuaola. Mā'ō'āna kemikala.* Chemical solution. *Mā'ō'āna 'ūhehe'e wai.* Aqueous solution. See *'ūhehehe'e wai. 'Ūhōlo'a mā'ō'āna.* Buret, i.e. a precision-made piece of glassware used to measure and deliver accurate volumes of solutions.

ma'u·kele *Nahele ma'ukele.* Rain forest. Comb. *nahele + ma'ukele.*

mā·'umi *kik* Denier, i.e. a unit of fineness for nylon, etc. Comb. *mā- + 'umi.*

Mada·gaseka *i'oa* Madagascar; Madagascan. *Dic.*

maria *kik* Maria, a crater-free plain on the surface of the moon. *Eng.*

masa·keke *kik* Mustard. *Eng.*

Masa·kuseta *i'oa* Massachusetts. *Dic.* Also *Makakukeka.*

masa·melo *kik* Marshmallow. *Eng.* Also *mahamelo.*

mea ao 'ē *kik* Extraterrestrial, space alien. *Loa'a maoli anei nā mea ao 'ē ma nā ao 'ē a'e?* Are there actually space aliens on other worlds? *Lit.*, one (from a) different world.

mea ana *kik* Gauge, a measuring instrument. *Lit.*, thing (for) measuring.

mea·ola *kik* Organism. *Lit.*, living thing. See *kōpū meaola. Kāohi meaola.* Biological control. *Kemika meaola.* Biochemistry. *Meaola māiki.* Microorganism.

mea·omōmo *kik* Drinking straw. *Lit.*, object (for) sucking.

mea omo 'elala *kik* Insect sucker, an instrument for drawing an insect into a tube by suction. *Lit.*, thing (that) sucks insects.

mea uholo uila *kik* Conductor, of electricity. *Lit.*, thing (through which) electricity runs. Cf. *awe uholo uila.*

mea·ulu *kik* Crop, i.e. a plant that is grown and harvested, usually for profit. *Dic., ext. mng.* Cf. *kanu.*

mea hana *kik* Tool, as a shovel, crowbar, etc. *Dic.* See *hāme'a, maomeka, mauha'a.*

mea hehe'e *kik* Solute. *Lit.*, melted thing. See *'ūhehe'e.*

mea hehi wā·wae *kik* Pedal. *Lit.*, thing (to) pedal (by) foot.

mea hi'o·hia *kik* Find, as an archeological find. *Lit.*, discovered thing.

mea holo *kik* Running back (general term), in football. *Lit.*, one (who) runs.

mea holoi *kik* Eraser. *Dic.* Also *'ileika.*

mea ho'o·hana *kik* End user, as of computer programs. *Lit.*, one (who) uses.

mea ho'o·kani pila *kik* Musician, particularly one who plays Hawaiian music. *Lit.,* one (who) plays instruments.

mea ho'o·momona lepo *kik* Fertilizer. Comb. *mea* + dic. *Mea ho'omomona lepo kā'oko'a.* Complete fertilizer, i.e. fertilizer which contains the six necessary elements for plant growth.

mea hō·'ono·'ono *kik* Flavoring. *Lit.,* thing to make tasty. Cf. *ma'ono.*

mea ho'o·puka·puka kā·lā *kik* Investment. See *ho'opukapuka.*

mea kau lole *kik* Hanger. *Lit.,* thing (for) placing clothes. Also *uea kau lole, lā'au kau lole, 'ea kau lole.*

mea kā·lai·kanu *kik* Horticulturist. *Lit.,* horticulture person.

mea·kanu *kik* Plant. *Dic., sp. var.* See *pahu ho'oulu meakanu. Meakanu pua.* Flowering plant. *'Aila meakanu.* Vegetable oil.

mea ka'a launa *kik* Contact, a person to whom certain information is communicated. *Lit.,* one in charge of associating.

mea kiko·'ī *kik* Detail. *Lit.,* specific thing. Also *mea li'ili'i, mea li'ili'i kiko'ī.*

mea·kino *kik* Matter, i.e. physical substance. Comb. *mea* + *kino.*

mea kō·kua helu *kik* Counter, as beans or bottle caps to help with math problem. *Lit.,* thing (which) helps count.

mea kū i ke au *kik* Trend. *Lit.,* thing existing in the era. See *kū i ke au.*

mea kū·'ai *kik* Merchandise.

mea li'i·li'i *kik* Detail. *'O ka mea wale nō i koe, 'o ia ka ho'oponopono 'ana i nā mea li'ili'i o ka huaka'i ma mua o ka hele 'ana.* The only thing left to do is to take care of some details for the trip before leaving. *Lit.,* small thing. Also *mea kiko'ī, mea li'ili'i kiko'ī.*

mea lole pipi *kik* Butcher. *Dic.* Also *kanaka lole pipi.*

mea pā·'ani See *pahu mea pā'ani, waihona mea pā'ani.*

mea puolo *kik* Musician (general term). *Lit.,* one (who does) music. Cf. *mea ho'okani pila.*

mea puka *kik* Winner, as in the consolation bracket of a sports tournament. *'O mākou ka mea puka o ka māhele hā'ule.* We were the winners of the consolation bracket. *Lit.,* one (who) emerges (victorious).

mea wehe kini *kik* Can opener. *Dic.*

mea wehe 'ū·mi'i *kik* Staple remover. *Ni'ihau.* Cf. *kui 'ūmi'i pepa, mea 'ūmi'i pepa.*

mea·'ai *kik* Food. *Dic., sp. var.* See entry below and *pū'ulu mea'ai, 'ailakele. Mea'ai waiū.* Dairy product. *Ku'ina mea'ai.* Food chain. *Pūnaewele mea'ai.* Food web.

mea·'ai hiki·wawe *kik* Fast food. *'O ka mea ma'amau, nui ka 'ailakele o ka mea'ai hikiwawe.* Fast foods usually contain a lot of fat. *Lit.,* quickly done food. *Hale 'aina mea'ai hikiwawe.* Fast-food restaurant.

mea 'apo *kik* Receiver, in football. *Lit.,* one (who) catches. See *'apo.*

mea 'ene·hana *kik* Technician. *Lit.,* technology person. *Mea 'enehana kani.* Sound technician, as for movie or video production. *Mea 'enehana ki'i.* Graphics technician.

mea·'ono palauni *kik* Brownie, the dessert. Comb. *mea'ono* + Eng. Also *palauni.*

mea 'ū·mi'i pepa *kik* Stapler (for paper). *Ni'ihau.* See *kui 'ūmi'i pepa, mea wehe 'ūmi'i.*

Mei *i'oa* May. *Dic.* No abbreviation.

Meine *i'oa* Maine. *Eng.* Also *Maine.*

meiwi *kik* Traditional elements of Hawaiian poetry, story telling, oratory and narration. *Sh. mele* + *iwi.*

meo·neki *kik* Mayonnaise. *Eng. Kāpiki meoneki.* Cole slaw.

mehana ʻaʻ Warm; temperature, when weather considered warm. ʻEhia ka mehana o kēia lā? What's the temperature today? Dic. Also mahana. Cf. anu, wela. See kēkelē. Mehana ea, mehana lumi. Room temperature. Kuʻina mehana. Warm front, as of weather.

meheu ʻaʻ Outlined, as on computer or in typesetting. Lit., trace. Cf. mahaka. See entries below and hoʻomeheu.

mē·heu·heu kik Custom, i.e. a learned cultural value or behavior. Dic., ext. mng. Cf. moʻomeheu.

meheu kalaima kik Evidence, as in the commission of a crime. Lit., crime clue. See kālaimeheu kalaima.

meheu mana·mana lima kik Fingerprint. Lit., finger trace. Also māka manamana lima, kiʻi manamana lima. See kāpala, māioio manamana lima. ʻOhi i ka meheu manamana lima. To collect fingerprints.

mekala kik Metal. Dic. Also metala. See entries below. Mekala ʻōʻā. Alloy. Also metala ʻōʻā.

mekala honua ʻā·kili·kai kik Alkaline earth metal, i.e. one of the family of elements in Group 2 of the periodic table. Cf. mekala ʻākilikai.

mekala ʻā·kili·kai kik Alkali metal, i.e. one of the family of elements in Group 1 of the periodic table. Cf. mekala honua ʻākilikai.

meka·lika kik Metric. Eng. Anakahi mekalika. Metric unit of measure. ʻŌnaehana mekalika. Metric system.

mē·kene kik Methane. Eng. Also mētene.

meki kik Iron, the element. Dic.

mē·kia kik Major, as an academic field of specialization. ʻO ka ʻōlelo Hawaiʻi kaʻu mēkia. My major is Hawaiian language. Eng. Cf. māina.

Mekiko iʻoa Mexico; Mexican. Dic.

mela·lemu kik Sloth, the animal. Sh. māmela + lemu. Melalemu pilikua. Giant sloth.

mele kik Poem, poetry (general term; preceded by ke). Dic.

mele·hune kik Mushroom. Niʻihau. Also kūkaelio. Melehune pōpōehu. Puffball, a kind of mushroom.

mele·kulia kik Mercury, the metallic element in chemistry. Eng.

Mele·lana iʻoa Maryland; Marylander. Dic. Also Merelana.

meleni kik Melon. Tah. Also ipu. See ipuʻala.

meli ʻele·ao kik Honeydew, i.e. a sweet juice secreted by aphids. Lit., aphid honey.

melo·kiana kik Melodeon. Dic.

memea kik Material, a general term but not relating to cloth. Redup. of mea. Also makelia. Memea kūlohelohe. Raw material.

memo kik Memo, memorandum; a memo or note for conveying a message to someone; message. Eng. Cf. kakaha. Memo kūloko. Internal memorandum, as in telecommunication.

mē·pala kik Maple. Eng.

meʻe See kaʻao meʻe.

Mere·lana iʻoa Maryland; Marylander. Dic. Also Melelana.

meta·nola kik Methanol. Eng.

meto kik Methyl. Eng.

mī kik Ti, the seventh note on the musical scale. Dic. See pākōlī.

mī·ana kik Urinal. Dic. Cf. ipu mimi.

mio ʻaʻ Streamlined, sleek. Niʻihau. Kaʻa mio. Sports car.

mio·mio ʻaʻ Precision, as high-quality print resolution on a computer printer. Dic., ext. mng. Cf. kalakala. Kākiko miomio. Precision bitmapping.

mio·ʻawi kik Mole, the animal. Comb. miyo + ciʻavi (Ute).

mika kik Meter, the unit of measurement. Dic. Abb. m.

Mika See kapuahi Mika.

mīka *kik* Meter, an instrument that automatically measures and registers quantity. *Eng.* See *mīka kāki, pahu mīka. Mīka kāki.* Parking meter. See *kū kāki.*

mī·kā *kik* Pressure. *Dic., ext. mng. Ana mīkā ea.* Barometer. *A'alonoa mīkā.* Pressure receptor. *Mīkā anakonu.* Isostasy, i.e. the equilibrium of the earth's crust, in geology. *Mīkā ea.* Air pressure, as in a tire. *Mīkā koko.* Blood pressure. *'Ōnaehana mīkā emi.* Low pressure system, in meteorology. *'Ōnaehana mīkā pi'i.* High pressure system.

mika·ō *kik* Utilities, as electricity, gas, etc. Comb. *mīka + ō.*

miki *ham* To take up with the fingers, as poi. *Manamana miki.* Index finger. Also *manamana kuhikuhi.*

Miki·kana *i'oa* Michigan; Michigander, Michiganite. *Dic.*

Miki·kipi *i'oa* Mississippi; Mississippian. *Dic.* Also *Misisipi.*

miki·lima pō·hili *kik* Baseball glove, mitt.

mī·kini *kik* Appliance. *Dic., ext. mng.* See entries below. *Hale kū'ai mīkini.* Appliance store. *Mīkini home.* Home appliance. *Mīkini ke'ena.* Office appliance.

mī·kini ana ō·la'i *kik* Seismograph. *Dic.* Also *ana ōla'i.*

mī·kini helu *kik* Calculator. *Dic., ext. mng. Papakaumaka mīkini helu.* Calculator display screen.

mī·kini helu·helu pā *kik* Co-processor unit (CPU), as for a computer. *He holo lohi wale nō kēia MHP kahiko.* This old CPU runs so slow. *Lit.,* machine (for) reading disks. *Abb. MHP.*

mī·kini ho'ā'o *kik* Tester, as a battery tester, when the tester is a machine. *Lit.,* machine (for) testing. Cf. *hāme'a ho'ā'o. Mīkini ho'ā'o iho.* Battery tester (a machine).

mī·kini ho'o·ili ki'i *kik* Scanner, as for computer program. *Lit.,* machine (to) transfer pictures.

mī·kini ho'o·kani pā·leo *kik* Record player. Also *mīkini pāleo.*

mī·kini ho'o·lele ki'i·aka *kik* Slide projector. *Lit.,* machine (for) projecting slides. Also *mīkini ki'iaka.* See *pākū ho'olele ki'i.*

mī·kini ho'o·lele ki'i·'oni·'oni *kik* Movie projector. *Lit.,* machine (for) projecting movies. Also *mīkini ki'i'oni'oni.* See *pākū ho'olele ki'i.*

mī·kini hō·'olu ea *kik* Air conditioner. *Lit.,* machine (which) cools air. Also *hō'olu ea.*

mī·kini ho'o·moe hua *kik* Incubator (for eggs). *Lit.,* machine (for) hatching eggs.

mī·kini ho'o·pau 'ume·kau·maha *kik* Antigravity machine. *Lit.,* machine (that) cancels gravity. See *'umekaumaha.*

mī·kini ho'o·pa'a leo *kik* Tape recorder. *Lit.,* machine (for) recording voices. See *mīkini lola, mīkini pōka'a leo.*

mī·kini kā·kuhi *kik* Graphing calculator. *Lit.,* machine (for) graphing.

mī·kini kipi·kipi lepo *kik* Rotary tiller, rotary cultivator, Rototiller. *Lit.,* machine (that) digs dirt.

mī·kini lola *kik* Cassette recorder/player. *Lit.,* cassette machine. *Mīkini ho'okani lola.* Cassette player. *Mīkini ho'opa'a lola.* Cassette recorder.

mī·kini pana·kō *kik* Automated-teller machine (ATM). *Lit.,* bank machine.

mī·kini pa'i *kik* Printer, as for a computer. *Lit.,* machine (for) printing.

mī·kini pō·ka'a leo *kik* Reel-to-reel tape recorder/player. *Lit.,* sound reel machine. See *mīkini lola. Mīkini ho'okani pōka'a.* Reel-to-reel tape player. *Mīkini ho'opa'a pōka'a.* Reel-to-reel tape recorder.

mī·kini 'ohi kā·lā *kik* Cash register. *Lit.,* machine (for) collecting money. See *'ohi kālā.*

Miko·uli *i'oa* Missouri; Missourian. *Dic.* Also *Misouri.*

miko·kene *kik* Mitogen, i.e. any substance or agent that stimulates mitotic cell division. *Eng.*

miko·lolo·lehua *ham* To entertain, as in a speech. *Kawelo.* See dic. for other variations of *mikololoehua.* *Ha'i'ōlelo mikololoehua.* Expressive speech, a speech to entertain.

mil Abbreviation for *mile* (mile).

mile *kik* Mile. *Dic.* Abb. *mil. Mile o ka hola.* Miles per hour. Abb. *mil/hl.*

mili- Milli-, i.e. a prefix meaning one thousandth. *Eng.* Also *hapa kaukani.* See entries below.

mili·ona See *hapa miliona.*

mili·kalame *kik* Milligram. *Eng.* Abb. *mkal.*

mili·lika *kik* Milliliter. *Eng.* Abb. *ml.*

mili·mika *kik* Millimeter. *Eng.* Abb. *mm.*

Mima *i'oa* Mimas, a moon very near to Saturn. *Eng.*

mimi kō *kik* Diabetes. *Dic.* Also *ma'i kōpa'a.*

min Abbreviation for *minuke* (minute).

Mine·koka *i'oa* Minnesota; Minnesotan. *Dic.*

mine·lala *kik* Mineral. *Eng.* Also *minerala.*

minuke *kik* Minute (time). *Dic.* Abb. *min.*

minuke lī·pine *kik* Footage, as the number of minutes of video tape shot. *Lit.,* footage minutes. Cf. *līpine.*

mī·'oi *heh* Offsides, in football. *Dic., ext. mng.* Cf. *lele 'ē.* See entry below. *Mī'oi na ke kūlele.* Offsides on the offense.

mī·'oi wale *heh* To fake or hit, in volleyball. *Ni'ihau.* Also *hana kolohe.*

Misi·sipi *i'oa* Mississippi; Mississippian. *Dic.* Also *Mikikipi.*

Miso·uri *i'oa* Missouri; Missourian. *Dic.* Also *Mikouli.*

moa *Pu'upu'u moa.* Chicken pox.

moana *kik* Oceanic. *'O ka Polenekia, he po'e moana lākou.* Polynesians are an oceanic people. *Dic., ext. mng.* See entry below and *waena moana. Pāpa'a moana.* Ocean crust. *Pū'ali kaua moana.* Navy. Also *'au moku kaua, 'oihana moku. Kahua pū'ali kaua moana.* Navy base.

Moana Pā·kī·pika *i'oa* Pacific Ocean. *Dic.*

moe See entries below and *lumi moe.*

moe·ā *heh* To imagine oneself to be something or someone; imaginary. *Sh. moemoeā.* Cf. *ho'omoeā, makakū. Ho'ohele moeā.* To utilize guided imagery. *Laina moeā.* Imaginary line.

moe·apupa *heh* To pupate. Comb. *moe + a + pupa.* See *pupa.*

moe·kau *heh* Hibernation; to hibernate. Comb. *moe + kau.*

moe·kahi *'a'* Consecutive, in sequence. *Pā'ina aku nei wau ma laila 'ekolu ahiahi moekahi i kēlā pule aku nei.* I had dinner there three consecutive evenings last week. *Dic.*

moe·moeā *kik* Fantasy. *Dic.*

moena *kik* Rug, as for living room or any large room. *Dic., ext. mng.* Also *hāli'i papahele.* See *pale papahele. Moena weleweka.* Carpet.

moena 'ili *kik* Linoleum, linoleum flooring. *Ni'ihau.* Also *linoleuma. Moena 'ili 'āpanapana.* Floor tile. Also *kile papahele, kile 'ili.*

moe pā·laha·laha *heh* To dive, in volleyball. *Ni'ihau.* Also *lele 'ōpū, lu'u.*

moe pē·pē *kik* Crib, as for babies. *Lit.,* baby bed.

moe·'alā *kik* Polychaete worm, a kind of worm found underneath stream rocks. Comb. *moe + 'alā.* Also *ko'e moe'alā.* Cf. *moeone* (dic.).

mō·hihi'o *kik* Science fiction. *Sh. mō'ike + hihi'o. Ki'i'oni'oni mōhihi'o.* Science fiction movie.

moho *kik* Candidate, as in politics. *Nui maoli nō ka ʻeu o ka paio kālaimanaʻo o nā moho nui ʻehā i hōʻikeʻike ʻia ma ke kelewikiona i ka pō nei.* The debate between the four main candidates that was broadcast on television last night was very lively. *Dic.* See *wae moho.* Champion, champions. *ʻO mākou ka moho.* We're the champions. *Dic.* See *kūlana ʻelua. Hoʻokūkū moho.* Tournament, as for sports. Also *hoʻokūkū.* See *hoʻokūkū kio, hoʻokūkū kahului.*

moho lele ʻole *kik* Flightless rail. *Lit.*, nonflying rail.

moka *kik* Waste, as of plants and animals. *Dic.*

mō·kema *kik* Modem. *Eng.*

mō·kio *ʻa*ʻ Rounded, in linguistics. *Dic., ext. mng. Woela mōkio.* Rounded vowel.

moko·huila·hā *kik* All-terrain vehicle (ATV). *Sh. mokokaikala + huila + ʻehā.*

moko·kai·kala holo lepo *kik* Dirt bike. *Lit.*, motorcycle (for) riding (on) dirt.

moku *ʻAu moku kaua.* Navy. Also *pūʻali kaua moana, ʻoihana moku.*

moku ahi·kao *kik* Spacecraft, spaceship, rocket ship. *Comb. moku + ahikao.* See *ahikao. Kelena moku ahikao.* Space capsule.

moku·hau·lana *kik* Iceberg. *Lit.*, island (of) floating ice.

moku·hali lewa lipo *kik* Space shuttle. *Sh. mokulele halihali lewa lipo.*

moku·honua *kik* Continent; continental. *Lit.*, earth island. Also *ʻāinapuniʻole. Hene mokuhonua.* Continental slope. *Holopapa mokuhonua.* Continental shelf. *Pāpaʻa mokuhonua.* Continental crust.

moku kau·lua *kik* Catamaran. *Lit.*, double boat.

moku kua·ʻau *kik* Atoll. *Lit.*, lagoon island.

moku·lele hali koa *kik* Military transport aircraft. *Lit.*, military carrying airplane.

moku·lele hele·kopa *kik* Helicopter. *Ua kuʻu ka mokulele helekopa ma luna o ke kahua kū kaʻa no ke kiʻi ʻana i ke kanaka i loaʻa i ka pōulia.* The helicopter landed on the parking lot to pick up the man who was having an emergency. *Niʻihau.* Also *helekopa.*

Moku·mana·mana *iʻoa* Necker Island. *Comb. moku + manamana.*

moku·moku See *palaoa mokumoku.*

Moku·pā·papa *iʻoa* French Frigate Shoals. *Lit.*, low, flat islet.

moku·peʻa holo mā·mā *kik* Clipper, a kind of ship. *Lit.*, sailing ship (that) travels fast.

moku·ʻāina *kik* State, as one of the United States. *Dic. Cf. aupuni, kaumokuʻāina, kauʻāina, māhele ʻāina, pekelala. Hōʻikeʻike mokuʻāina.* State fair. *Pāka mokuʻāina.* State park.

molai·bada·hate *kik* Molybdate. *ʻAmoniuma molaibadahate.* Ammonium molybdate.

molai·bede·numa *kik* Molybdenum. *Eng.*

mole alelo *kik* Root of tongue. *Lit.*, tongue root. See *kūʻau alelo, lau alelo, waena alelo, wēlau alelo.*

mole·ana·honua *kik* Geometry. *Dic.* Also *anahonua.*

mō·lehu *Ala mōlehu.* Crepuscular, i.e. appearing or flying in the twilight. *Cf. ala ao, ala pō.*

mō·lehu·lehu *ʻa*ʻ Dusk, twilight. *Ua hoʻi wau i ka hale i ka mōlehulehu ʻana o ka lā.* I returned home at dusk. *Dic.* Also *hola mōlehulehu.*

mole·kumu *kik* Root, source, derivation or origin, as the etymology of a word. *Comb. mole + kumu. Cf. kūmole.*

mō·lina *kik* Molding, as around windows or doors; frame or mount, as for pictures. *Dic. Mōlina pukaaniani.* Window frame. *Mōlina kiʻi.* Picture frame. *Mōlina kiʻiaka.* Slide mount.

mō·lina *kik* Frame, as in computer program. *Dic., ext. mng. Mōlina kaʻakaʻa.* Open frame. *Mōlina paʻa.* Closed frame.

mō·lina *kik/ham* A single frame of a movie or video film; to frame, as to arrange the content of a photograph, movie or video picture within certain borders. *Dic., ext. mng.*

Moloko *iʻoa* Morocco; Moroccan. *Dic.* Also *Moroko*.

Mona·kana *iʻoa* Montana; Montanan. *Dic.* Also *Monekana*.

mona·kō *kik* Glucose. *Loaʻa nui ka monakō ma loko o kekahi mau ʻano huaʻai a me nā ʻaʻaʻa holoholona kekahi, a he hapa mai kōna momona i ke kōpaʻa maʻamau.* Glucose is usually found in some fruits and animal tissues and is about half as sweet as regular sugar. Sh. *momona + kō*. Cf. *huakō. Monakō koko.* Blood glucose.

mona·mona *kik* Dessert. Sh./redup. *momona*.

mō·neka·kai *kik* Monkfish. Comb. *mōneka + kai*.

Mone·kana *iʻoa* Montana; Montanan. *Dic.* Also *Monakana*.

moni See *haka moni, paipu moni*.

mono·kesa·side *kik* Monoxide. *Eng. Karabona monokesaside.* Carbon monoxide.

Mono·kolia *iʻoa* Mongolia; Mongolian. *Dic.* Also *Monogolia*.

Mono·golia *iʻoa* Mongolia; Mongolian. *Dic.* Also *Monokolia*.

mō·pina *Kui mōpina.* Hypodermic needle.

mō·pine *kik* Morphine. *Eng.*

mō·ʻaui *kik/heh* Reaction; to react, as chemical compounds. Sh. *moʻo- + ʻaui*. Cf. *ʻūmōʻaui. Hōʻeleu mōʻaui, ʻūmōʻauiwawe.* Catalyst. *Mea mōʻaui.* Reactor. *Mōʻaui kemikala.* Chemical activity.

mō·ʻau·kala *kik* History. Sh. *moʻo + au + kala*.

moʻa hapa *ʻa* Medium rare, as meat. *Lit.,* partial cooked. Also *hapa moʻa*.

mō·ʻali·haku *kik* Fossil. Sh. *mōʻali + pōhaku*. Also *wīhaku*.

moʻa loa *ʻa* Well done, as meat. *Lit.,* very cooked.

moʻo·hana *kik* Reptile. Sh. *moʻo + ʻohana*.

moʻo·haʻa·wina *kik* A catalog listing of lessons; a sequence of lessons of a curriculum. *Lit.,* sequence (of) lessons. Cf. *ʻolokeʻa koina papa*.

moʻo·helu *kik* Budget, i.e. a listing of expenditures and receipts. *Trad.* Also *moʻohelu kālā. Hoʻopaʻa moʻohelu kālā.* To make a budget. *Mālama moʻohelu kālā.* Accounting.

moʻo·kāki *kik* Account, as in computer program or any listing of charges. Comb. *moʻo + kāki*.

moʻo·kala·leo *kik* Literature (general term). Comb. *moʻo + kala + leo. Moʻokalaleo haʻi waha.* Oral literature. *Moʻokalaleo kumu honua.* Creation literature. *Moʻokalaleo kuʻuna.* Traditional literature. *Moʻokalaleo palapala.* Written literature.

moʻo·kaʻao *kik* A traditional tale, especially one relating to a particular culture; folktale. *Dic., sp. var.* Also *kaʻao*. See entries below *kaʻao*.

moʻo·kiʻina *kik* Routine. *Lit.,* sequence (of) movements.

moʻo·kū·lana wai·wai *kik* Balance sheet, i.e. a listing of assets, liabilities and owner's equity. Comb. *moʻo + kūlana + waiwai*.

moʻo·kū·ʻau·hau *kik* Genealogy. *Dic., sp. var. Moʻolelo moʻokūʻauhau.* Genealogical story.

moʻo·kū·ʻikena *kik* Record, i.e. a quantity of facts treated as a unit. *Lit.*, fact unit.

moʻo·lako *kik* Inventory. *Sh. moʻolelo + lako.*

moʻo·lelo hana keaka *kik* Script, as for a play or movie. Usu. *moʻolelo. Dic., ext. mng.* Cf. *moʻolelo kiʻiʻoniʻoni. Mea kākau moʻolelo.* Scriptwriter. *Luna kākau moʻolelo.* Script supervisor.

moʻo·lelo haʻi waha *kik* Narration, as in a movie or video production. *Lit.*, story (for) narrating verbally.

moʻo·lelo kaha *kik* Storyboard, as in movie or video production. *Dic., ext. mng. Lima kaha moʻolelo.* Storyboard artist. *Huaʻōlelo kaha moʻolelo.* Storyboard terms.

moʻo·lelo kiʻi·ʻoni·ʻoni *kik* Screenplay. *Lit.*, movie story. See *kākau moʻolelo kiʻiʻoniʻoni. Mea kākau moʻolelo kiʻiʻoniʻoni.* Screenwriter. Also *mea kākau kiʻiʻoniʻoni.*

moʻo·lio *kik* Sea horse. *Dic.*

moʻo·manaʻo See *puke moʻomanaʻo.*

moʻo·meheu *kik* Culture; cultural. Comb. *moʻo + meheu.* Cf. *mēheuheu.*

moʻo·mō·ʻali *kik* Record, as a list of facts about achievements or tasks accomplished; résumé, vita, curriculum vitae. Comb. *moʻo + mōʻali.*

moʻona *kik* Succession. Comb. *moʻo + -na.*

moʻo pila kī·koʻo *kik* Check register. *E hoʻopaʻa i kēia mau pila kīkoʻo i loko o ka moʻo pila kīkoʻo.* Record these cheks in the register. *Lit.*, succession of bank checks.

moʻo pō·haku pele *kik* Lava lizard. *Lit.*, lava rock lizard.

mō·chī *kik* Mochi. *Japn. Laiki mōchī.* Mochi rice. Also *lāisi mōchī.*

Moroko *iʻoa* Morocco; Moroccan. *Eng.* Also *Moloko.*

Mozama·bika *iʻoa* Mozambique; Mozambican. *Eng.*

mū *kik* Checkers. *Dic. Mū Pākē.* Chinese checkers. *Mū kākela.* Chess.

mua See *ʻōlelo mua. Ma mua o ka manawa, ma mua o ka hola.* Early.

mū·heʻe *kik* Cuttlefish (local definition); squid (Haole definition). *Dic.* Cf. *heʻe. Mūheʻe iwi.* Cuttlebone.

mū hōlapu *kik* Virus, as in computer program. *Lit.*, spreading bug. See entry below.

mū hō·lapu pale ʻea pau *kik* HIV (human immunodeficiency virus). *Lit.*, virus (for) finished resistance (against) infectious diseases. See *pale ʻea pau.*

mū·hune *kik* Germ. Comb. *mū + hune. Mūhune ʻino.* Pathogen, a disease-producing agent. See *pale mūhune ʻino.*

mū·kī·kī *Manu mūkīkī.* Honey-creeper, general term. *Lit.*, bird (that) sucks.

muku *kik* Starboard or right side of a single-hulled canoe when looking forward. *Dic., ext. mng.* Cf. *ʻākea, ama.* See entry below.

muku *kik* Tight end, in football. *Dic.*, new mng. Cf. *lala.* See *ʻāwaʻa muku.*

muli After-, post-. *Dic., ext. mng.* See *hōʻike muli aʻo, kaumokuʻāina muli panalāʻau. Haʻuki muli kula.* After-school sports.

muli *kik* Coda of a syllable, in linguistics. *Lit.*, last.

muli·wai *Kaha nuku muliwai.* Delta (of a river). *Nuku muliwai.* Estuary. *ʻAumana muliwai.* River tributary.

munu·kō *kik* Mung. (Ilocano *monggo.*) *Pāpapa munukō.* Mung bean.

mū pao lau *kik* Leaf miner. *Lit.*, insect (that) bores leaves.

muʻo *kik* Bud of a leaf. *Dic.* Cf. *liko.*

musu·bī *kik* Rice ball, musubi. *Japn.* Also *pōpō laiki, pōpō lāisi.*

MH Abbreviation for *makahiki* (year). *Dic.*

mhn Abbreviation for *mahina* (month).

MHP Abbreviation for *mīkini heluhelu pā* (co-processor unit).

mkal Abbreviation for *milikalame* (milligram).

Māmaka Kaiao / 113

ml Abbreviation for *mililika* (milliliter).
mm Abbreviation for *milimika* (millimeter).

N

nāele *kik* Bog, with no trees and soft ground. *Dic.* See *ālialia, ʻolokele.*

nae·lona *kik* Nylon. *Eng.*

naiko·kene *kik* Nitrogen; nitric. *Eng. Koʻohune naikokene.* Azobacter, a type of bacteria containing nitrogen. *Naikokene diokesaside.* Nitrogen dioxide. Also *naikokene ʻokikene lua. Pōʻaiapuni naikokene.* Nitrogen cycle. *Pūhui naikokene kaʻawale.* Free nitrogen compound. *ʻAkika naikokene.* Nitric acid. Also *ʻakika nikiriku.*

Nai·gera *iʻoa* Niger; Nigerien. *Eng.*

Nai·geria *iʻoa* Nigeria; Nigerian. *Eng.*

nau kuai *ham* To grind, as one's teeth. *E nau kuai ana ʻo ia i kōna niho i ka pō nei.* He was grinding his teeth last night. Comb. *nau + kuai.*

naha iʻa *kik* Small school of reef fish, such as *manini. Mān.* Also *naho iʻa.* Cf. *kumu iʻa.*

nahau *kik* Arrow, an indicator. (PPN *ngāsau.*) *Nahau ʻiole.* Mouse arrow, pointer or cursor, as in computer program. Usu. *nahau.* Cf. *kahaʻimo.* See *pihi nahau.*

nā·hā·hā *ʻa* Crumbled. *Dic., ext. mng.*

nahā wale *ʻa* Fragile, as glass. *Lit.,* easily broken. Cf. *haki wale, pāloli.*

nā·hele·hele *kik* Weed. *Dic.* Also *nāʻeleʻele.* See *lāʻau make nāhelehele.*

nā·hele·hesa *kik* Snakeweed. Sh. *nāhelehele + nāhesa.*

nahele maʻu·kele *kik* Rain forest. *Lit.,* rain-forest area forest.

nā·hesa pulu *kik* Bullsnake. Comb. *nāhesa* + Eng.

nahi *kik* Lichen, general term. Sh. *unahi.*

Nā·hiku *iʻoa* Big Dipper. *Dic.*

naho iʻa *kik* Small school of reef fish, such as *manini. Mān.* Also *naha iʻa.* Cf. *kumu iʻa.*

Nā Hui Nui ʻElima *kik* The Big Five, i.e. the five corporations that controlled most of the sugar industry in Hawaiʻi. *Lit.,* the five big corporations.

nakeke *ʻa* Crunchy, as fresh potato chips. *Niʻihau.* Also *nakekeke, kakani.* See *kamumu.*

nake·keke *ʻa* Crunchy, as an apple. Redup. of *nakeke.* Also *nakeke, kakani.* See *kamumu.*

nāki *kik* Tribe of people, outside of Hawaiʻi. *He hoʻokahi ka lāhui Māori o Aotearoa, akā, hoʻomāhelehele ʻia ka poʻe ma nā nāki like ʻole.* The Māori race of New Zealand are one race, but they are distinguished by various tribes. (Māori *ngāti.*) See *hapū, ʻalaea.*

nakili·naka *kik* Tundra. (Inuit *natirnaq.*)

Nā·ki·ʻi·ki·ʻi *iʻoa* Zuben Elschamali, a star. *Mān.* (HA).

nalala *kik* Dinosaur. (PPN *ngarara.*)

nalea *kik* Trick, as a dog's. Sh. *nanea + maʻalea.* Cf. *kēpuka, pāhaʻohuna.*

nalo·peʻe *ʻa* Camouflaged. Comb. *nalo + peʻe.* See *hoʻonalopeʻe.*

nalo·wale loa *ʻa* Extinct. Also *halapohe, make loa. ʻAne nalowale loa.* Endangered.

nalo wiʻu *kik* Midge fly. *Lit.,* fly (whose bite) smarts with pain.

nalo ʻui·ʻuiki *kik* Firefly. *Lit.,* glimmering fly.

nalu *kik* Wave, as surf near the land. *Dic.* Cf. *ʻale.* See *hokua, honua, kiʻekiʻena, kōā. Poʻina nalu.* Where a wave breaks; surf break (preceded by *ke*).

Nalu·kā·kala *iʻoa* Maro Reef. *Lit.,* surf that arrives in combers.

Nami·bia *iʻoa* Namibia; Namibian. *Eng.*

nā·mua *kik* Preview. Sh. *nānā + mua.* See *nānaina. Nāmua paʻi.* Print preview, as in computer program.

Māmaka Kaiao / 114

nā·naina *kik* View, as in computer program; scene or scenery, as for a stage production. *Dic., ext. def.* See *nāmua*. *Nānaina ululāʻau*. Forest scene.

nā·nahu *kik* Charcoal. *Dic.* Cf. *lānahu*.

nana·nana *kik* Spider. *Dic.* Also *nanana*. See entries below and *kalanakula*.

nana·nana hese ʻele·ʻele *kik* Black widow (spider). *Lit.*, black witch spider. Also *nanana hese ʻeleʻele*.

nana·nana maka·kiʻi *kik* Happy face spider. *Lit.*, mask spider. Also *nanana makakiʻi*.

nana·nana maka ʻole *kik* No-eyed big-eyed hunting spider, from Kauaʻi. *Lit.*, no-eyed spider. Also *nanana maka ʻole*.

nane *kik* Puzzle. *Dic. Nane ʻāpana.* Jigsaw puzzle. *Nane huahelu.* Number puzzle. *Nane huaʻōlelo.* Crossword puzzle.

nani·kupu·lau *kik* Spring beauty, a kind of flower. *Comb. nani + kupulau.*

napoe *kik* Grain. (*Filipino*, rice.)

Nawa·hō *iʻoa* Navaho, Navajo. *Mai kumupaʻa mai nei nō nā hana a me ka moʻomeheu o ka Lāhui Nawahō.* The traditions and culture of the Navajo Nation stem from very ancient times. *Eng.*

naʻau *Helu naʻau.* Mental math. Also *makemakika naʻau.*

naʻau·kake ʻAme·lika *kik* Hot dog. *Lit.*, American sausage.

nā·ʻana *kik* Review, checkpoint. *Sh. nānā + ʻana.*

nā·ʻele·ʻele *kik* Weed. *Maui.* See *nāhelehele*.

naʻi·au *ʻa* To have special effects, be enhanced. *Dic., ext. mng.* See *hiʻohiʻona naʻiau.*

nā·ʻī·ā·ʻumi *ham* To boycott, i.e. abstain from buying from or dealing with (a company) as a means of coercion. *Ke hōʻeuʻeu mai nei nā ʻahahui he nui e nāʻīāʻumi i nā huahana o Palani no ka hoʻāʻo hoʻopahū nukelea ma ka Pākīpika.* Many organizations are encouraging that French products be boycotted due to nuclear bomb testing in the Pacific. *Sh. nāʻīʻike + a + ʻumi.*

naʻi·naʻi *ʻa* Lower case, small. *Tah.*, small. Cf. *maʻaka*. See *hua naʻinaʻi*.

naʻo·koko *kik* Cholesterol. *Nui ʻino nā meaʻai maʻamau o kēia wā, ua nui ka naʻokoko o loko, a hiki ke pilikia ke kino i ke aʻahaʻapupū inā ʻaʻole mālama pono ʻia ke ʻano o ka ʻai ʻana.* Many kinds of typical foods these days contain a lot of cholesterol and can result in arteriosclerosis if diet is not checked. (*Māori ngakototo.*)

Naseka *iʻoa* Nazca. *Eng. Ka Una Honua Naseka.* Nazca Plate.

nehe *heh* To rustle, as leaves or the sea. *Dic.*

Neke·lana *iʻoa* The Netherlands; Netherlander; Netherlandian. *Eng.*

nele *Kōkua nele.* Welfare, i.e. public financial assistance for needy persons.

nele wai *ʻa* Anhydrous, i.e. without water. *Lit.*, lack water. Cf. *ʻanahaidaraside.*

nemo·nemo *ʻa* Bald, "balahead/bolohead," as a tire. *Ua ʻai ʻia ka nihoniho o ka taea a nemonemo.* The tread of the tire was worn bald. *Niʻihau.*

nenelu *ʻa* Marshy. *Dic., ext. mng.*

Nepala *iʻoa* Nepal; Nepalese. *Eng.*

Nepa·laka *iʻoa* Nebraska; Nebraskan. *Dic.* Also *Nebaraka.*

Nepe·kune *iʻoa* Neptune. *Eng.*

Newaka *iʻoa* Nevada; Nevadan. *Dic.* Also *Newada.*

Newada *iʻoa* Nevada; Nevadan. *Dic.* Also *Newaka.*

neʻe·kau *heh* Migration; to migrate; migratory. *Lit.*, move (with the) seasons.

Māmaka Kaiao / 115

neʻena *kik* Movement. *Dic.* See *holo lola, puʻu neʻena hau. Neʻena pahu paʻi wikiō.* Video camera movement.

neʻe ʻoa *heh* Divergent, i.e. spreading in plate techtonics, in geology. *Dic., ext. mng.* Cf. *kākele, kuʻi. Palena neʻe ʻoā.* Divergent boundary.

Neba·raka *iʻoa* Nebraska; Nebraskan. *Dic.* Also *Nepalaka.*

nī·ane *kik* Neon. *Eng.*

nī·ele *ʻa*ʻ Curious. *Dic.* Also *pena.*

nioe *kik* Tone, in linguistics, as relating to Chinese or Navaho languages. *Sh. pūpū kani oe.*

niu haku *kik* Sprouting coconut or one with eye emerging. *Dic.* Cf. *haku.*

niho *kik* Tooth. *Dic.* See entries below and *kauka hoʻopololei niho, wili niho, ʻōhiki kauka niho. Nau kuai i ka niho.* To grind the teeth. *Puka niho.* Cavity in a tooth, caries. Cf. *haka waha.*

niho *kik* Dental, in linguistics. *Dic., ext. mng.*

niho ʻaʻ To have whitecaps. *Ua niho ke kai i nehinei.* The sea had whitecaps yesterday. *Mān. (Daisy Pai).* See *ʻale kuakea.*

Nī·hoa Nīhoa, the island. *Niʻihau. ʻAinohu Nīhoa.* Nīhoa finch (telespiza ultima).

niho·niho *kik* Tread, as on a tire. *Niʻihau.* See *nemonemo.*

niho palaka *kik* Prong of electrical plug. *Lit.*, plug tooth. See *palaka, puka uila. Palaka niho lua.* Two-pronged plug. *Palaka niho kolu.* Three-pronged plug.

nikala *kik* Nickel, the metallic element. *Eng.* Cf. *hapaʻumi.*

Nikala·kua *iʻoa* Nicaragua; Nicaraguan. *Dic.* Also *Nikarakua.*

Nikara·kua *iʻoa* Nicaragua; Nicaraguan. *Eng.* Also *Nikalakua.*

niki·riku Nitric. *Eng.* ʻ*Akika nikiriku.* Nitric acid. Also *ʻakika naikokene.*

niko·roma *kik* Nichrome. *Eng. Uea nikoroma.* Nichrome wire.

niko·tina *kik* Nicotine. *Eng.*

nī·nau·ele *ham* To interview. *Dic., ext. mng.* Cf. *ninaninau.*

nī·nau koho·koho *kik* Multiple-choice question. *Lit.*, question (to) select (answers).

nī·nau pā·kā·kā *kik* Leading question. *Dic.*

nina·hai·dirina kuhi·kuhi *kik* Ninhydrin indicator.

nina·nina *kik* Scar. *Niʻihau.* Also *ʻālina* (preceded by *ke*).

nina·ninau *ham* To interrogate. *Dic.* Cf. *nīnauele. Palapala ninaninau.* Questionnaire.

niniu See *ʻume niniu.*

niniki *kik* Membrane. *Sh. nikiniki/* ext. mng.

nī·ʻau *kik* Nut, as on an ʻukulele or guitar. *Niʻihau.* See *ʻukulele. Nī*ʻ*au liʻiliʻi.* Head nut. *Nīʻau nui.* Bridge.

nī·ʻau·kani *kik* Jew's harp. *Dic., sp. var.*

nī·ʻau lā *kik* Ray, i.e. one of the bony spines supporting the membrane of a fish's fin. *Lit.*, fin midrib.

nitara·hate *kik* Nitrate. *Eng.*

nitara·hite *kik* Nitrite. *Eng.*

nō *kik* So, the fifth note on the musical scale. *Dic.* See *pākōlī.*

noa See *kī noa.*

nō·iki *kik* Alveolus, i.e. an air sac of the lungs, in anatomy. (Māori *ngōiti.*) *Pūʻali nōiki.* Alveolar duct.

noiʻi *ham* Investigation; to investigate; to research. *Ke noiʻi nei wau e pili ana i nā lāʻau lapaʻu like ʻole o nā kūpuna Hawaiʻi.* I am doing research on the medicinal practices of the Hawaiian people of old. *Dic. Kanaka noiʻi.* Researcher. *Kanaka noiʻi ʻepekema.* Scientific researcher. *Puke noiʻi.* Reference or resource book, as an encyclopedia. Cf. *kūmole. Puke noiʻi kūʻikena.* Encyclopedia.

nou *ham* To throw overhand; baseball pass, in basketball; to throw such a pass. *Nou 'ia ke kinipōpō ma luna o ka po'ohiwi.* A baseball pass is thrown over the shoulder. *Dic., ext. mng.* Cf. *kiola.*

nō·hie *'a'* Simple, basic, uncomplicated. *PPN.* Cf. *nōhihi.*

nō·hihi *'a'* Complex. Comb. *nō-* [from *nōhie*] + *hihi.* Cf. *nōhie.*

noho kū *kik* Stool without a back. *Lit.,* standing chair.

noho lua *kik* Toilet seat. Cf. *ipu lua.*

noho paiki·kala *kik* Bicycle seat.

noho pi'i mauna *kik* Lift, as a ski lift. *Lit.,* chair (for) climbing mountains.

noho 'ā·mana *kik* Pack saddle. *Dic.*

nō·kahea *'a'* Drainage; to have good drainage. Comb. *nō + kahe + -a.*

no ka manawa *kik* Pro tem, pro tempore. *Trad. Pelekikena no ka manawa.* President pro tem.

Nole·wai *i'oa* Norway; Norwegian, Norse. *Dic.*

nonia·kahi *'a'* Integrated, i.e. incorporated into a whole. *He noniakahi nā kula o waenakonu o nā kūlanakauhale nui me nā 'ano lāhui a me nā kūlana noho kū'ono'ono like 'ole mai 'ō a 'ō.* The schools in the inner cities are integrated with all types of races and economic backgrounds from all around. Comb. *noni + -a + kahi.* See *ho'ononiakahi.*

nono *'a'* Permeability, permeable. *Dic., ext. def.*

Now. Abbreviation for *Nowemapa* (November).

nō·wela *kik* Novel, as a work of literature. *Eng. Nōwela pōkole.* Novelette.

Nowe·mapa *i'oa* November. *Dic.* Abb. *Now.*

no'o·no'o kū·pili *ham* Logical thinking. See *kūpili.*

no'o·no'o loi *ham* Critical thinking. *Lit.,* thought (which) scrutinizes.

nui *'a'* Large, as drink or shirt size. *Dic.* See *li'ili'i, lōpū, nui keu. Koloaka nui.* Large soda. *Manamana nui.* Thumb.

nui kik/'a' Dimension, in math. *Dic.* Also *ana.*

nui a'e *'a'* Greater than, in math. Also *'oi aku ka nui.* Cf. *emi iho.*

Nū·ie·rese *i'oa* New Jersey; New Jerseyite. *Dic., sp. var.* Also *Nūkelese.*

Nū·ioka *i'oa* New York; New Yorker. *Dic., sp. var.*

nui keu *'a'* Extra large (XL), as shirt size. *Lit.,* extra big. *Nui keu pālua.* Double-extra large (XXL). *Nui keu pākolu.* Triple-extra large (XXXL).

nui·pa'a *kik* Mass, bulk. *Lit.,* solid bulk. See entry below.

nui·pa'a 'ā·toma *kik* Atomic mass. *Anakahi nuipa'a 'ātoma.* Atomic mass unit. *'Awelike nuipa'a 'ātoma.* Average atomic mass.

Nū·hame·kia *i'oa* New Hampshire; New Hampshirite, New Hampshireman. *Dic., sp. var.* Also *Nūhamesia.*

Nū·hame·sia *i'oa* New Hampshire; New Hampshirite, New Hampshireman. *Dic., sp. var.* Also *Nūhamekia.*

nū·hata See *manu nūhata.*

Nū·hō·lani *i'oa* Australia; Australian. *Dic.* See *'Inionūhōlani.* *'Elelū Nūhōlani.* Australian cockroach (*Periplaneta australasiae*).

nuka·haku *kik* Boulder, generic term, particularly outside of Hawai'i. *'O ka nukahaku kū ka'awale nunui loa i loa'a ma luna o ka 'ili o ka honua, aia ma Nūhōlani.* The largest free standing boulder that can be found on the surface of the earth is located in Australia. Comb. *nuka + haku.* Cf. *pōhaku 'alā.*

nuke·lea *kik* Nuclear. *Eng. Ikehu nukelea.* Nuclear energy.

Nū·kelese *i'oa* New Jersey; New Jerseyite. *Eng.* Also *Nūierese.*

nuke·liu *kik* Nucleus, as in an atom. *Eng.*

nū·kihu *kik* Proboscis, as of a butterfly. Sh. *nuku + ihu.*

Nuki·lani *i'oa* New Zealand; New Zealander. *Dic., sp. var.* See *Aotearoa.*

Nū·kini *i'oa* New Guinea; New Guinean. *Dic., sp. var.* See *Pāpua Nūkini.*

nuku *kik* Head or foot of trail; pass, in mountains; mouth, as of a river; nozzle. *Dic., ext. mng.* See *hānuku. Kaha nuku muliwai.* Delta (of a river). *Nuku muliwai.* Estuary. *Nuku 'ūpā makani.* Bellows nozzle.

nuku·kikiwi *kik* Jade plant. Comb. *nuku + kikiwi.*

nuku 'ekue *kik* King Kong finch (chloridops regiskongi). Sh. *nuku + pepe'ekue.* See *hona, 'ainohu Kauō, 'ainohu Nīhoa.*

nulu *kik* Noodle. Eng. *Nulu 'Īkālia.* Pasta.

Nū·mekiko *i'oa* New Mexico; New Mexican. *Dic., sp. var.*

nū·mō·nia *kik* Pneumonia. *Mān./dic., sp. var.*

nū·nū *ham* To hum, as a tune. *Ni'ihau.*

nupa pele·maka *kik* Magma chamber. *Lit.,* magma cave.

nu'u·o'a *kik* Highrise, as a building. *Lit.,* protruding blunt height. Cf. *ki'enao'a, nu'uha'a.*

nu'u·ha'a *kik* Lowrise, as a building. Sh. *nu'u + ha'aha'a.* Cf. *nu'uo'a.*

nu'u·kia *kik* Vision, as in the vision statement of an organization. Comb. *nu'u + kia.* See *ala nu'ukia. 'Ōlelo nu'ukia.* Vision statement.

nu'u lau·laha *kik* Plateau, high level land. *Lit.,* spread-out heights. Cf. *kula laulaha.*

P

P1 Abbreviation for *Po'akahi* (Monday).
P2 Abbreviation for *Po'alua* (Tuesday).
P3 Abbreviation for *Po'akolu* (Wednesday).
P4 Abbreviation for *Po'ahā* (Thursday).
P5 Abbreviation for *Po'alima* (Friday).
P6 Abbreviation for *Po'aono* (Saturday).

pā *kik* Disk (preceded by *ke*). *Dic., ext. mng. Pā kamepiula.* Computer disk. *Pā malule.* Floppy disk. *Pā ma'ema'e.* Blank disk. *Pā ho'omaka.* Startup disk. *Pā polokalamu.* Program disk. *Pā pa'aloko.* Hard disk. *Pā pa'aloko wehe.* Removable hard disk.

pā *kik* Do, the first note on the musical scale. *Dic.* See *pākōlī.*

pā ana *kik* Balancing tray for scales (preceded by *ke*). *Lit.,* measuring plate.

pā·ani·ani *kik* Yarn. *Dic., sp. var.* See *kā pāaniani.*

pae *kik* Stage, level of development; level of difficulty, as intermediate or advanced; rank, as in an orderly arrangement. *Ni'ihau; dic., ext. mng.* Cf. *kūlana.* See entries below and *ho'oka'ina pae.*

pae *kik* Chain, range, series of geographical features. *Dic., ext. mng.*

pae *kik* Platform, as DOS, UNIX, Macintosh, etc., for computer program. *Dic., ext. mng. Pae 'ōnaehana.* Operating system.

pae awāwa *kik* Series of valleys.

pae holo·mua *kik* Advanced level.

pae ho'o·maka *kik* Beginning or introductory level.

pā ehu lepo *kik* Dustpan (preceded by *ke*).

pae·humu *kik* Railing, ballustrade. *Dic.* Cf. *'ūlili, hūlili.*

Pae·kako·leo *i'oa* Pythagoras, Pythagorean. *Gr. Mana'oha'i o Paekakoleo.* Pythagorean theorum.

pae kā·nā·wai *heh* Legal alien; to arrive as a legal alien. *'O ka po'e pae kānāwai, he mālama 'ia kō lākou mau pono ma lalo o ke kānāwai o ka 'āina.* Legal aliens have rights that are protected under the laws of the land. *Lit.,* come ashore legally. Cf. *pae malū.*

pae kua·hiwi *kik* Mountain range.

pae lua pele *kik* Chain of craters.

Māmaka Kaiao / 118

Pae Mauna Kai ʻEme·pela *iʻoa* Emperor Seamounts. Also *Pae Mauna Kai ʻo ʻEmepela*.

pae malū *heh* Illegal alien; to arrive as an illegal alien. *Hiki mai ka poʻe pae malū ma nā ʻano like ʻole: ma luna o ka ʻāina, ka moku, a me ka mokulele kekahi.* Illegal aliens arrive by different means: by land, on ship, and by air as well. *Lit.*, come ashore illegally. Cf. *pae kānāwai*.

pae moku hoaka *kik* Island arc. *ʻO nā pae moku ʻo Hawaiʻi a me ʻAleuta he mau laʻana o ia mea he pae moku hoaka.* The Hawaiian and Aleutian archipelagos are examples of island arcs. *Lit.*, arch archipelago.

Pae Moku Kalo·laina *iʻoa* Caroline Isles. *Lit.*, Caroline archipelago. Also *Pae Moku Karolaina*.

Pae Moku Karo·laina *iʻoa* Caroline Isles. *Lit.*, Caroline archipelago. Also *Pae Moku Kalolaina*.

Pae Moku Kenele *iʻoa* Canary Isles. *Lit.*, Canary archipelago.

Pae Moku Mā·kala *iʻoa* Marshall Islands; Marshallese. *Lit.*, Marshall archipelago. Also *Mākala, Mākala ʻAilana*.

Pae Moku Faka·lana *iʻoa* Falkland Islands, Falklands. *Lit.*, Falkland archipelago.

pae·pae ala·piʻi *kik* Staircase landing. *Lit.*, stairs platform.

pae·pae ani·ani kau·pane·ʻe *kik* Stage, as of a microscope. *Lit.*, platform (for) slides. Usu. *paepae*. See *aniani kaupaneʻe*.

pae·pae komo huila *kik* Axle, i.e. a shaft on which a wheel turns. *Dic.* Also *iho*.

pae·pae poho *kik* Chalk tray.

pae·pae puka *kik* Threshold, of a door. *Dic.*

pae·pae puka·ani·ani *kik* Window sill. *Dic.*

pae pū·ʻulu mea·ʻai See *pūʻulu meaʻai*.

pae waena *kik* Intermediate level.

pae·ʻāina *Ka Paeʻāina ʻo ʻAleuta.* Aleutian Islands.

pae ʻakahi akahi *kik* Novice level.

pai- *ham* A prefix meaning to laud, encourage; -ism, a suffix in English meaning devotion or adherence to something. *Dic., ext. mng.* See *paikāloaʻa*.

pai *kik* Pi (π), in math. *Eng.* See *kī pai*.

pai·alewa *ham* Convectional, i.e. to circulate, as air or liquid, between a lower and higher stratum due to variations in density, heat and gravity; convection, convective. *No ka paialewa, ʻike ʻia nā ao ʻōpua nui ma luna o ka mokupuni a me ka ua nui ma uka o nā pali.* Because of convection, large clouds form over the island and rain falls over the interior mountainous sections. *Comb. pai + a + lewa*.

pai·alou *ham* To make a pitch, as a sales pitch, or to "sell" an idea. *Comb. pai + a + lou*.

pai·ō *kik* Fixed swing, as with two or more ropes or chains. *Niʻihau.* Cf. *lele koali*.

paio kā·lai·manaʻo *ham* Debate; to debate. *Dic. Hui paio kālaimanaʻo.* Debate club.

pai·ola *ʻa* Nutritious. *Comb. pai + ola.* Cf. *ʻaiaola*.

pai·ho·ʻāhu kā·loa·ʻa See *paikāloaʻa*.

pai·kā·loa·ʻa *ham* Capitalism. *Ua hoʻohiki maila ke aupuni o Kina e hoʻomau ʻia ana ka ʻōnaehana paikāloaʻa ma Honokaona ma hope o ka hoʻihoʻi ʻia ʻana o ia panalāʻau Beretānia o ka wā ma mua iā Kina.* The Chinese government has promised that it would maintain a capitalistic system in Hong Kong after the former British colony reverts back to China. *Comb. pai- + kāloaʻa.* Also *paihoʻāhu kāloaʻa*. See *ahu kāloaʻa*.

pāiki *kik* Suitcase, purse. *Dic.* Also *pāisi*.

pāiki hā·'awe *kik* Backpack, knapsack. *Lit.,* backpack bag. Also *pāisi hā'awe, 'awe.*

paiki·kala *kik* Bicycle. *Dic.* Cf. *kalaikikala. Kaea paikikala, taea paikikala.* Bicycle tire. *Kaulahao paikikala.* Bicycle chain. *Kalaiwa paikikala, 'au paikikala* (preceded by *ke*). Bicycle handlebars. *Kua hao paikikala.* Bicycle crossbar. *Noho paikikala.* Bicycle seat. *Paikikala holo kuahiwi.* Mountain bike.

pāiki lola *kik* Tape case, cassette holder. Cf. *poho lola.*

paila *heh* To boil. *Dic. Kēkelē paila.* Boiling point. See *kēkelē.*

pai·laha *kik* Credit, as the name of a person who has contributed to a performance. Comb. *hāpai + ho'olaha.*

pai·leki *kik* Pyrex. *Eng. Hano ho'okolohua paileki.* Pyrex test tube.

pai·lola *kik* Wintergreen. *Eng.* (scientific name: *pyrola*).

paina *kik* Pint. *Dic.* Abb. *pin.*

paina *kik* Pine, conifer, or any tree which resembles a pine. Also *paina lau kukuna, paina tidara* (Bib.). See entries below.

paina Kuke *kik* Cook pine. Also *kumu paina Kuke.*

paina luhe *kik* Ironwood. *Lit.,* drooping pine. Also *paina.*

paina Puki·kī *kik* Portuguese cypress. Also *paina tireza* (Bib.).

paina·'ā·pala *kik* Pineapple. *Mān.* Also *hala kahiki. 'Ea paina'āpala.* Polyethylene.

pai pika *kik* Pizza. *Eng.* Also *pika.*

paipu See entries below and *kanaka ho'omoe paipu, wai paipu.*

paipu ahi *kik* Exhaust pipe, as on a car. *Ni'ihau.* Cf. *kini paipu ahi.*

paipu omo wai *kik* Drain. *Ni'ihau.*

paipu hanu *kik* Windpipe, trachea, in anatomy. *Lit.,* pipe (for) breathing. Also *paipu hanu o lalo.* Cf. *paipu moni.* See entry below and *kani'ā'ī. Paipu hanu o luna.* Larynx. *Pani paipu hanu* (preceded by *ke*). Epiglottis.

paipu hanu *kik* Snorkel. *Lit.,* pipe (for) breathing. *'Au'au paipu hanu.* To snorkel.

paipu kinai ahi *kik* Fire hydrant. *Lit.,* pipe (for) extinguishing fire. Also *piula wai*

paipu lawe 'ino *kik* Sewer (pipe). *Dic. Pani paipu lawe 'ino.* Manhole cover, as for a sewer.

paipu·li'i *kik* Pipette. Comb. *paipu + li'i. Paipuli'i 'umelauoho.* Capillary pipette.

paipu moni *kik* Esophagus. *Lit.,* pipe (for) swallowing. Cf. *paipu hanu.*

paiwa *kik* Drama; dramatic. (Tongan *faiva* [entertainment].) *Hana keaka paiwa.* Dramatic play.

pai·roga·lola *kik* Pyrogallol. *Eng.*

pao See *kila pao, manu pao lā'au, mū pao lau. Ōpuhe pao lā'au.* Woodpecker finch.

pao·meki *kik* Hollow tile. Sh. *pao + kimeki.*

paona *kik* Pound (unit of weight). *Dic.* Abb. *pon.*

pau *Ka pau 'ana.* Closing, as of a composition or story. See *ho'omaka, kino.*

pāua *kik* Abalone. *Māori.*

pā uila *kik/'a'* Electrolysis; to be affected by electrolysis. *Lit.,* touched (by) electricity. See *ho'opā uila.*

pauka *Waiū pauka.* Powdered milk. Also *waiū ehu.*

pauka hele·helena *kik* Face powder. *Ni'ihau. Hana i ka pauka helehelena.* To put on face powder. Also *kau i ka pauka helehelena.*

pauka koka *kik* Baking soda. *Lit.,* soda powder. See *hū.*

pauka maka *kik* Eye shadow. *Ni'ihau. Hana i ka pauka maka.* To put on eye shadow.

pauka niho *kik* Toothpaste. *Mān.* See *pani, poho pauka niho.*

pauka 'ī·nika *kik* Toner, as for a computer printer. *Lit.,* ink powder.

Māmaka Kaiao / 120

pau·kū *kik* Paragraph. *Dic.* See *paukūkū.*

pau·kū kā·lele *kik* Accent unit or measure, in linguistics. *Lit.,* stress section.

pau·kū kino *kik* Thorax. *Lit.,* body section. Also *paukū.*

pau·kū·kū *ham* To paragraph, as in written compositions. Redup. of *paukū.* See *kūkulu māmala.*

pau·kū ʻolo·kaʻa *kik* Cylinder, i.e. the shape. *Dic.* See *hano.*

pāuma *kik/ham* Pump; to pump, as air or water. *Dic.* See *peni pāuma. Pāuma ea.* Air pump, as for tires. Also *pāuma paikikala. Pihi pāuma ea* (preceded by *ke*). Air valve, as on a tire.

pāuma lua *kik* Plunger, as for cleaning clogged drains. *Niʻihau.*

pāumu *kik* Farm. *Māori.*

pau ʻole *ʻa* Infinity, in math. *Dic., ext. mng.*

pā hali·hali *kik* Tray (preceded by *ke*). *Dic.*

Pahama *iʻoa* Bahamas; Bahamian. *Dic.* Also *Bahama.*

pā·hana *kik* Project, as for a class. Sh. *papahana.*

pā·haneli Hecto-, a prefix meaning hundred (h). *Dic., ext. mng.* Abb. *ph.*

pā·hawewe *heh* Radiation; to radiate, as in the form of waves. Comb. *pā + hawewe.* Cf. *malele. Pāhawewe ikehu.* Radioactivity. *Pāhawewe lā.* Solar radiation. *Pāhawewe nukelea.* Nuclear radiation. *Pāhawewe ʻātoma.* Atomic radiation.

pā·haʻo·huna *kik/ham* Magic trick, illusion, sleight of hand; to perform a magic trick. *Ua pāhaʻohuna ʻo ia i ke ale pahi kaua.* He performed the sword-swallowing trick. *Lit.,* secretly mysterious. Cf. *hoʻokalakupua.* See *kēpuka.*

pā·haʻo·weli *kik/ham* Stunt, a feat which requires unusual daring or skill, as in a movie or video production; to do or perform a stunt. *E pāhaʻoweli au i ka ulia kaʻa ma ka wikiō.* I'll perform the car accident stunt in the video. Sh. *pāhaʻohuna + weliweli.* Kanaka *pāhaʻoweli.* Stuntperson. *Luna pāhaʻoweli.* Stunt coordinator

pā·heona *kik* Art, artwork; fine arts. *Nui koʻu hoihoi i ka pāheona Pākē.* I'm very interested in Chinese art. Comb. *pā + heona.* See *heona. Luna pāheona.* Art director, as for a movie or video production.

pā·helene *kik* Discus. *Lit.,* Greek disk. *Kīloi pāhelene.* To throw a discus.

pahemo *ʻaʻ* Off-line, i.e. describing the state of an electronic device not ready to receive data, or not connected to a computer or computer network. *Ke ʻā maila kaʻu kamepiula, akā, ʻaʻole pahemo, no ka mea, ʻaʻole i hoʻokuʻi ʻia me ka pūnaewele.* My computer is on, but it is not on-line because it is not connected to the network. *Dic., ext. mng.* Cf. *paʻeʻe.* See *hoʻopahemo.*

paheʻe wai *heh* Water slide; to go on a water slide (Slip 'n' Slide). *Moena paheʻe wai.* Water slide mat.

pā·hia How many to each, to a group? *Pāhia nā ʻōhiʻa a kekahi?* How many *ʻōhiʻa* for each one? *E pāhia ia na kekahi keiki?* How many was it for each child? *Dic.*

pā·hia·hia *kik* Performing art. Sh. *papahana + redup. of hia.*

pahiki *kik* Probability, in math. Sh. *paha + hiki.* Cf. *papaha. Pahiki liʻiliʻi.* Low probability. *Pahiki nui.* High probability. *Pahiki hoʻokolohua.* Experimental probability. *Pahiki makemakika.* Mathematical probability.

pā·hili hau *kik* Blizzard. *Lit.,* strong, snowy wind. Also *makani pāhili hau.* See *makani pāhili.*

pā·hina *kik* Topping, as for ice cream. Sh. *pāpahi + -na.*

pā·hiʻa See *ʻoki pāhiʻa.*

pā·hi‘u *kik* Dart, as for dart game. *Sh. pāhi‘uhi‘u.*

pā·ho‘o·nui *kik* Exponent, in math; power, i.e. a product in which each factor is the same. Comb. *pā- + ho‘onui*. See *kapua‘i pāho‘onui lua, kumu pāho‘onui lua. Pāho‘onui lua.* Square. *Ka pāho‘onui lua o ka helu.* The square of the number. *Pāho‘onui kolu.* Cubed, as in exponential counting.

pahu *kik* Case. *Dic.* Cf. *‘ope.* See *pū‘olo, ‘eke‘eke. Pahu koloaka.* Case of soda. *Pahu pia.* Case of beer.

pahu *kik* Base or plate, as on a baseball diamond. *Mān. Pahu eo.* Home plate. *Pahu ‘ekahi.* First base. *Pahu ‘elua.* Second base. *Pahu ‘ekolu.* Third base.

pahu *kik* Court, as for volleyball. *Ni‘ihau.* Also *kahua pōpa‘ipa‘i.*

pahu *ham* To push. *Dic.* Also *pohu.*

pahu a‘o *kik* Dialog box, in computer program. *Ua ‘ō‘ili ‘emo ‘ole mai nei kekahi pahu a‘o.* A dialog box suddenly appeared. *Lit.,* teaching box.

pahu·honua·ea *kik* Terrarium. *Lit.,* aerated box (of) earth. Cf. *pahumeaolaea, pahuwaiea.*

pahu·hope *kik* Finish point, as in a race. Comb. *pahu + hope.* Cf. *pahukū. Laina pahuhope.* Finish line.

pahu·hopu *kik* Goal. *Dic., sp. var.* Also *pahuhopu laulā. Pahuhopu hāiki.* Objective.

pahu ho‘o·ulu mea·kanu *kik* Planter, as for growing plants. *Lit.,* box (for) growing plants.

pahu ho‘o·kele *kik* Controller, as in Nintendo games. *Lit.,* box (to) steer.

pahu ho‘o·lele leo *kik* Radio. *Ni‘ihau.* Also *lēkiō.*

pahu ho‘o·nui leo *kik* Amplifier. *Lit.,* box (for) increasing sound. Cf. *pahu leo.*

pahu ho‘o·wela wai *kik* Water heater. *Lit.,* tank (for) heating water. Also *kula ho‘owela wai.*

pahu kā·hea *kik* Walkie-talkie. *Ni‘ihau.*

pahu kā·leka kuhi puke *kik* Card catalog, as in a library. *Sh. pahu + kāleka helu kuhi puke.* See *kāleka helu kuhi puke.*

pahu kī·kā See *‘ukulele pahu kīkā.*

pahu·kū *kik* Starting point, as in a race. Comb. *pahu + kū.* Cf. *pahuhope. Laina pahukū.* Starting line.

pahu laka *kik* Locker. Comb. *pahu +* Eng. Also *waihona pāiki.*

pahu leo *kik* Speaker, as for a stereo. *Lit.,* sound box. Cf. *pahu ho‘onui leo.*

pahu·mea·ola·ea *kik* Vivarium. *Lit.,* aerated box (of) living things. Cf. *pahuhonuaea, pahuwaiea.*

pahu mea pā·‘ani *kik* Toy chest, toy box. Also *waihona mea pā‘ani.*

pahu mīka *kik* Meter box.

pā·hune *kik* Platelet (preceded by *ke*). *Lit.,* tiny disk.

pahū·pahū *kik* Firecracker (preceded by *ke*). *Dic.* See *ahiho‘ole‘ale‘a. Kālī pahūpahū.* String of firecrackers.

pahu papa·kau·maka *kik* Monitor, as for a computer or in movie or video production. *Lit.,* screen box. See *papakaumaka. Pahu papakaumaka kamepiula.* Computer monitor. *Pahu papakaumaka kīwī.* TV monitor.

pahu pa‘a·hau *kik* Freezer. See *pa‘ahau.*

pahu pa‘i wiki·ō *kik* Camcorder, video camera. *Lit.,* video camera. See *pa‘i. Ne‘ena pahu pa‘i wikiō.* Video camera movement.

pahu pepa *kik* Cardboard box. *Lit.,* paper box. Cf. *pepa pahu.*

pahu pono ha‘a·wina *kik* Schoolbox. *Lit.,* box (for) lesson supplies.

pahu·wai·ea *kik* Aquarium. *Lit.,* aerated box (of) water. Cf. *pahuhonuaea, pahumeaolaea.*

pahu wai·ū *kik* Milk carton.

pahu wai·hona pepa *kik* File cabinet. *Lit.,* cabinet (for) storing paper.

pahu wai·hona wai·wai *kik* Treasure chest. *Lit.,* chest (for) storing valuables.

pahu wā·wahie kū·waho *kik* External fuel tank, as on a spaceship.

pā·hu'a *kik* Open dirt area in pasture, clearing in range land. *Dic.*

pahu 'ai holo *kik* End zone, on football field. *Lit.,* touchdown box.

pahu 'uiki uila *kik* Fuse box.

pahu 'ume *kik* Bureau, dresser. *Dic.* See *'ume.*

pakā *ham* To dunk (the ball), in basketball. *Ua ka'a ke eo o ka ho'okūkū pakā iā Spud Web.* Spud Web took the slam dunk contest. *Onomatopoeia.* Also *'ūpo'i.* Cf. *pākī.*

paka See entries below. *'Oihana o nā Pāka a me nā Hana Ho'onanea.* Department of Parks and Recreation.

pā·kā *'a'* Lean, as meat. *Dic. Pākā loa.* Extra lean.

pā·kā *ham* To skin, as a pig or sheep. *Ni'ihau. Pākā hapahā.* To quarter, as an animal.

paka au·puni *kik* National park. *Pāka Aupuni 'o Iosemite.* Yosemite National Park. *Pāka Aupuni 'o Haunene'e.* Glacier National Park. *Pāka Aupuni 'o Kīlauea.* Hawai'i Volcanoes National Park. *'Oihana Pāka Aupuni.* National Park Service.

pā·kau *kik* Podium. Also *pākau ha'i'ōlelo. Dic., ext. mng.*

pā·kau·kau See *puna pākaukau.*

pā·kau·kau moe *kik* Bedside table, nightstand (preceded by *ke*). *Lit.,* bed table.

pā·kau·kau wai *kik* Water table, as used in preschools. Cf. *papa wai.*

pā·kau·kani Kilo-, a prefix meaning thousand (k). *Dic., ext. mng.* Abb. *pk.* See *'ai pākaukani. Ikehu'ā pākaukani.* Kilocalorie.

pā·kahi·kahi See *kākau pākahikahi, 'oka pākahikahi.*

pā·kā·kā *Heluhelu pākākā.* To skim read. *Ka heluhelu pākākā 'ana.* Skim reading.

pāka kāni·wala *kik* Amusement park. *Lit.,* carnival park.

paka·lī *kik* Parsley. *Eng.*

pā kapu·ahi *kik* Burner, as on a stove. *Lit.,* stove plate. Cf. *kapuahi papakau.*

pā kawa·ū·ea *kik* Relative humidity. Sh. *pākēneka kawaūea.*

pā·ka'a·pohe *kik* Rosette. Comb. *pāka'a + pohe.*

pake *kik* Putty. *Dic. Pahi pake.* Putty knife.

Pā·kē *i'oa* Chinese. *Dic.* See *kalo Pākē, 'ōpae Pākē. 'Āina Pākē.* China. Also *Kina.*

pā·keke li'i·li'i *kik* Pail. *Lit.,* small bucket.

pakeki *kik* Spaghetti. *Eng.*

pā·kela koko pi'i *kik* Hypertension, i.e. abnormally high arterial blood pressure. *Hiki ke pilikia i ka pākela koko pi'i ke nui loa ka 'alo'ahia.* Extremely high stress can lead to hypertension. *Lit.,* excessive high blood pressure.

pā·kela 'ai lā·'au *'a'* To overdose on drugs. *Lit.,* take drugs to excess.

pake·leke *Pea pakeleke.* Pear, usually Bartlett.

pā·kē·neka *kik* Percent, percentage. *Mān./Eng.* Rate. *Dic., ext. mng.* See entries below. *Pākēneka uku pane'e.* Rate of interest. *Pākēneka 'auhau.* Tax rate.

pā·kē·neka o ka papa·'ai *kik* Percent Daily Value, formerly known as percentage of US Recommended Daily Allowances (USRDA). *Lit.,* percent of diet.

pā·kē·neka ho'o·pi'i *kik* Markup, as in the price of an article. *Lit.,* percentage (of) raising.

pakē pī·neki *kik* Peanut brittle.

pā·kī *ham* To slam dunk, in basketball. *Dic., ext. mng.* See entry below and *kī.*

pā·kī *ham* To spike (the ball), in volleyball. *Dic., ext. mng.* Also *hili.* See *hili, 'ai hele wale. Mea pākī, pākī.* Hitter. *Pākī 'epa.* An off-speed shot, i.e. to make a fake spike.

pāki·huila *kik* Flatbed trailer. *Lit.*, barge (with) wheels. Cf. *kaleila*.

pakika *heh* To skid, as a car; to slip, as on a wet sidewalk. *Dic.*

pā·kili·ona Tera-, a prefix meaning trillion (T). Comb. *pā-* + *kiliona*. Abb. *pkl.*

pā·kimo·kimo *ham* To dribble, as a basketball. Comb. *pā-* + *kimokimo*. Also *pāloiloi, paʻipaʻi*. *Pākimokimo pālua*. To double dribble.

Pakipi *iʻoa* Poughkeepsie. *Eng.*

Pā·kī·pika *Moana Pākīpika*. Pacific Ocean.

pakiʻi *ʻa* Flat, as a tire. *Niʻihau*. Cf. *ʻananuʻu*.

Paki·tana *iʻoa* Pakistan; Pakistani. *Eng.*

pā·kō·lea *ham* To provide physical therapy. *Ma hope o koʻu ulia kaʻa, ua pono wau e hele pinepine i ka pākōlea ʻia ma ke kikowaena pākōlea*. After my car accident I had to go often for physical therapy at the physical therapy center. *Dic., ext. mng. Mea pākōlea*. Physical therapist. Also *kanaka pākōlea*.

pā·kō·lī *kik* Musical scale: *pā, kō, lī, hā, nō, lā, mī, pā*. *Dic.* Also *alapiʻi mele*.

pā kopa *kik* Soap dish (preceded by *ke*).

paku *ham* To block (a shot), in basketball. *Dic., ext. mng.* See entries below. *Paku ʻino*. To roof. *Ua paku ʻino ʻia kā ia nei e ia ala*. He was roofed by that guy.

paku *ham* To block (the ball), in volleyball. *Dic., ext. mng.* Also *pālulu*. See *ʻai hele wale*. *Mea paku, paku*. Blocker.

paku *ʻa* Physical, as a scientific term relating to physical matter. Sh. *pōhaku*. Cf. *kālaiaopaku*. *Nā ʻanopili paku*. Physical properties.

pakuhi *kik* Chart, graph, plot. Sh. *papa* + *kuhikuhi*. See entries below. *Piko pakuhi*. Origin of a graph. Also *piko*.

pakuhi hoʻo·loli *kik* Conversion chart. *Lit.*, chart (for) changing. *Pakuhi hoʻololi mekalika*. Metric conversion chart.

pakuhi kaʻina *kik* Flow chart. See *kākuhi kaʻina*.

pakuhi kiko·kiko *kik* Scattergram, in math. *Lit.*, graph (of) points.

pakuhi kiʻi *kik* Pictograph.

pakuhi lā·kiō *kik* Line graph. *Lit.*, ratio chart.

pakuhi lū *kik* Scattergraph, in math.

pakuhi maka·ʻaha *kik* Spreadsheet, as in computer program. *Lit.*, grid chart. *Polokalamu pakuhi makaʻaha*. Spreadsheet program.

pakuhi pahu me ka ʻumi·ʻumi *kik* Box and whiskers graph, in math.

pakuhi papa *kik* Table, as of statistics, etc. *Lit.*, list chart.

pakuhi paʻa ʻau·kā *kik* Double bar graph, in math. *Lit.*, pair (of) bars graph. Cf. *pakuhi ʻaukā*.

pakuhi pō·ʻai *kik* Circle graph, in math.

pakuhi ʻau·kā *kik* Bar graph. Cf. *pakuhi paʻa ʻaukā*. *Pakuhi ʻaukā alapine*. Histogram, i.e. a bar graph showing frequencies, in math.

pakuhi ʻau me ka lau *kik* Stem and leaf plot, in math.

pā·kū hoʻo·lele kiʻi *kik* Screen for projecting slides or movies. *Lit.*, screen (for) projecting pictures.

pakū·kaʻā *kik* Kingfisher. (Ute *pagūcaʻā*.)

pā·kule·kele *kik* Bureaucracy; bureaucratic. *No ka nui pupū o ka holo o ka pākulekele, ʻaʻohe puka o kaʻu noi i nā luna*. Because of bureaucratic stalling, my request to the administration was not approved. Comb. *pā-* + *kulekele*. *Kanaka pākulekele*. Bureaucrat.

pā·kū maka·liʻi *kik* Marquisette, a kind of curtain. *Lit.*, small-meshed curtain.

pā·kū makika *kik* Mosquito netting. *Dic.*

pakū·pakū See *palaoa pakūpakū*.

pā·kuʻi *ham* To graft. *Dic.* See entries below. *Hoʻoulu pākuʻi.* To grow by grafting. *Pīlali pākuʻi.* Grafting wax.

pā·kuʻi *ham* To annex, in math, as in annexing a zero to show both decimal parts as a hundreth: 6.10 - 3.25 = . *Dic., ext. def.* See *papa huaʻōlelo pākuʻi.*

pā·kuʻi ho·ʻo·loli *kik/ham* Amendment, i.e. an addition or change to a bill, constitution, etc.; to amend. *Nui nā pākuʻi hoʻololi i pākuʻi ʻia i ke kumukānāwai o ka Mokuʻāina.* There have been many amendments added to the State constitution. *Lit.*, addendum (to) amend.

pā·kuʻina *kik* Affix; appendix, as in a book. Comb. *pākuʻi* + *-na*. *Pākuʻina kau hope.* Suffix. *Pākuʻina kau mua.* Prefix. *Pākuʻina kau loko.* Infix.

palaea *kik* Pliers. *Niʻihau.* Also *palaea huki.*

palai hoʻo·luʻu *ham* To deep-fry. *Ma ka palai hoʻoluʻu ʻana, hoʻowela nui ʻia ka ʻaila ma loko o ka ipu hao, a hoʻoluʻu maoli ʻia ka meaʻai ma ke kuke ʻana.* In deep-frying, the oil is made very hot in a pot and the food is actually dipped into it to cook. *Lit.*, fry (by) immersing.

palaina hele·helena *kik* Foundation, for makeup. *Lit.*, smooth face.

palaoa *kik* Bread *Dic.* See entries below. *Hunahuna palaoa.* Bread crumbs.

palaoa huika *kik* Wheat bread. Cf. *palaoa huika piha.* See *palaoa mākuʻe.*

palaoa huika piha *kik* Whole wheat bread. Cf. *palaoa huika.* See *palaoa mākuʻe.*

palaoa keko *kik* Dumplings. *Mān.* Also *palaoa mokumoku, palaoa pakūpakū.*

palaoa keʻo·keʻo *kik* White bread.

palaoa kī·poʻo·poʻo *kik* Waffle. *Lit.*, pitted bread.

palaoa lina·lina *kik* Unleavened pancake. *Dic.*

palaoa lū·lū *kik* Hawaiian-style mush, made of flour and water. *Dic.*

palaoa maka *kik* Flour. *Dic. Palaoa maka huika piha.* Whole wheat flour.

palaoa mā·kuʻe *kik* Brown bread, a layman's term for any bread made with dark flour. See *palaoa hapa huika, palaoa huika.*

palaoa moku·moku *kik* Dumplings. *Dic.* Also *palaoa pakūpakū, palaoa keko.*

palaoa pakū·pakū *kik* Dumplings. *Mān.* Also *palaoa keko, palaoa mokumoku.*

palaoa pikeke *kik* Biscuit. *Lit.*, biscuit (Eng.) bread. Also *pikeke.*

palaoa pū·haʻu·haʻu *kik* Popover. *Lit.*, puffed-out bread.

palaua·lea *kik* Slang. Sh. *pālau* + *walea.*

palauki *kik* Blouse. *Dic.* Also *lakeke.*

pā·lau·moa *kik* Drumstick, as of a chicken. Comb. *pālau* + *moa*. See *ʻūhā moa.*

palauni *kik* Brownie, i.e. the dessert. Usu. *meaʻono palauni. Eng.*

Palaunu *iʻoa* Brown, Brownian. *Eng. Lelekē Palaunu.* Brownian motion, i.e. the random motion of colloidal particles due to their bombardment by molecules of the solvent, in chemistry.

pā·laha·laha See *moe pālahalaha, paʻi pālahalaha.*

pala·hē *ʻaʻ* Mushy, as rice cooked with too much water. *Niʻihau.*

pala·hē·hē *ʻaʻ* Infection; infected. *Dic., ext. mng.*

pala·hō *Pale palahō.* Antiseptic.

pala·holo *kik* Gel. *Dic., new mng.* Cf. *ʻūnina. Palaholo lauoho.* Hair gel, Dep. *Palaholo silaka g.* Silica gel g, i.e. a powder used as the sorbent layer in thin-layer chromatography (pronounced *palaholo silaka gā*).

palaka *kik* Shirt, with short or long sleeves. *Mān.* See entries below. *Palaka aloha.* Aloha shirt.

palaka *kik* Plug. *Ni'ihau (Eng.).* See *niho palaka, puka uila. Palaka uila.* Electrical plug. *Palaka niho lua.* Two-pronged plug. *Palaka niho kolu.* Three-pronged plug.

palaka *kik* Block, i.e. the child's toy. *Dic., ext. mng.* See *pōlaka.*

palaka kepa *kik* Snap cube. *Lit.,* snap block.

palaka kimeki *kik* Pier block, in construction. *Lit.,* cement block. Cf. *paomeki. Palaka kimeki pale mū.* Termite block.

palaka·lī *kik* Broccoli. *Eng.*

pā·lā·kiō *kik* Scale, in math. Comb. *pā + lākiō.* See entries below. *Ki'i pālākiō.* Scale drawing. *Pane pālākiō.* Rating response. *Papa pālākiō.* Conversion scale.

pā·lā·kiō ikehu ōla'i *kik* Richter scale. *Lit.,* earthquake power scale.

pā·lā·kiō lā·lani *kik* Linear scale, in geography. *Lit.,* line scale.

Pala·kila *i'oa* Brazil; Brazilian. *Dic.* Also *Barazila.*

palaki·niuma *kik* Platinum. *Eng.*

palaki 'au·'au *kik* Brush for bathing.

palaku *kik* Palate, in linguistics. *Eng. Palaku iwi.* Hard palate. *Palaku kīleo.* Soft palate.

Pala·kuae *i'oa* Paraguay; Paraguayan. *Dic.* Also *Paraguae.*

palala See *pānini palala.*

palami *kik* Brumby, a wild Australian horse. *Eng.*

pala·miko *kik* Flamingo. *Eng.* Also *manu palamiko.*

Palana·heika *kik* Fahrenheit. *Dic. Abb. Ph.* See *kēkelē.*

Palani *i'oa* France; French. *Dic.* Also *Farani.*

pala·pala *kik/ham* Document, as in computer program; to transcribe; written. *Dic., ext. mng.* Cf. *ha'i waha, palapala leo.* See entries below. *Hō'ike palapala.* Written report. *Mo'okalaleo palapala.* Written literature.

pala·pala hi'ona 'āina *kik* Topographic map. See *hi'ona 'āina.*

pala·pala holo 'āina 'ē *kik* Passport. *Lit.,* document (for) traveling abroad.

Pala·pala Hō·'ike Hopena Kaia·puni *kik* Environmental Impact Statement. *Lit.,* document showing environmental consequences.

pala·pala ho'o·hiki *kik* Guarantee, an assurance of quality or length of use with promise of reimbursement. *Lit.,* promising document. Cf. *palapala ho'okō.*

pala·pala ho'o·kō *kik* Certificate of achievement. *Lit.,* accomplishing certificate.

pala·pala ho'o·kō *kik* Warranty, a written guarantee of integrity of a product with promise to repair or replace. *Lit.,* confirming document. Cf. *palapala ho'ohiki.*

pala·pala ho'o·kumu *kik* Charter, a document defining the organization of a city, colony, or corporate body. *Ma ka hālāwai o kēlā makahiki aku nei i 'āpono 'ia ai ka palapala ho'okumu o ka 'ahahui 'o Nā Pua a Hāloa, a mai ia manawa mai, ua ulu a he mau kaukani ka nui o nā lālā.* At last year's meeting the charter for the association called Nā Pua a Hāloa was approved, and since that time membership has grown into the thousands. *Dic.*

pala·pala kā·inoa *kik* Registration form.

pala·pala kā·'ei mea·kanu *kik* Vegetation zonation sheet.

pala·pala leo *kik* Transcription. *Lit.,* voice document. See *palapala.*

pala·pala lewa lipo *kik* Space map. *Lit.,* outer space document.

pala·pala makana *kik* Gift certificate.

pala·pala nina·ninau *kik* Questionnaire. *Dic.*

pala·pala pono kanaka *kik* Bill of rights. *Sh. palapala o nā pono pilikino o ke kanaka* (dic.).

pala·pala 'āina ua *kik* Rainfall map.

pala·pala ʻāina kahua *kik* Site map.
pala·pala ʻāina kumu·hana *kik* Thematic map. *Lit.*, topic map.
pala·pala ʻoi·hana aʻo *kik* Professional diploma for teaching. *Lit.*, diploma (for) teaching career.
pala·pala ʻoka *kik* Order form. *Lit.*, document for ordering. See *palapala ʻoka kūʻai*.
pala·pala ʻoka kū·ʻai *kik* Purchase order (PO). *Lit.*, order form (for) buying.
pala·pola *kik* Parabola, parabolic. *Eng. Uma palapola.* Parabolic curve.
pala·ʻai *kik* Pumpkin. *Dic.* See *ipu*.
pala·ʻai hele·uī *kik* Jack-oʻ-lantern. *Lit.*, Halloween pumpkin. Also *pū heleuī*.
pala·ʻili *kik* T-shirt; any pullover-style shirt. *Niʻihau.* Cf. *paleʻili*.
pala·ʻili kā·ʻawe *kik* Tank top. *Lit.*, T-shirt (with) strap. Also *paleʻili kāʻawe*. Cf. *palaʻili, paleʻili*.
palaʻo *kik* Walrus. *Dic.* Also *ʻelepani o ke kai*.
Palaʻo *iʻoa* Pharaoh. *Dic.* See *Au Palaʻo Kūhou, Au Palaʻo Kūkahiko, Au Palaʻo Kūwaena*.
pala·sema *kik* Plasma. *Eng.* Also *wai koko*.
pala·sika *kik* Plastid, i.e. tiny structures inside plant cells that contain pigment as well as chlorophyll. *Eng.*
pale *ham* To cover or shield, as one's mouth. *Ke kunu ʻoe, e pale i kou waha me ka lima.* When you cough, cover your mouth with your hand. *Dic.* See entries below and *pūʻali pale kapa kai*.
pale *kik* Inning. *Dic., ext. mng. Pale pōhili.* Baseball inning.
pale *ham* To defend, in sports; defense. *E ka hoa, nāu e pale ka mea lōʻihi, a naʻu e pale kēia mea poupou.* Eh, you defend the tall guy, and I'll watch this short, stubby one. Cf. *kaupale, kūpale; kūlele.* See entries below.
pā·lē *kik* Ballet. *Eng.* Also *hulahula pālē, bālē*.

pale ahi *ham* Flame retardant. *Ninini nui ʻia ka lāʻau pale ahi ma luna o ke ahi hōlapu o ka nahele i mea e hoʻēmi ai i ka laha ʻana.* Large amounts of flame retardent chemicals were dumped onto the raging forest fire to slow its spread. *Lit.*, protect (against) fire. See *awe pale ahi*.
pale alo *ham* Man-to-man defense, as in basketball; to execute such a play. *Ke pale alo kākou, iā ʻoe ʻo Noʻeau.* When we do a man-to-man defense, you take Noʻeau. *Lit.*, face defense.
pā·leo *kik* Record, as for a record player. *Comb. pā + leo.* Also *pāʻōlelo. Mīkini hoʻokani pāleo.* Record player. Also *mīkini pāleo*.
pā·leo·leo *kik/ham* Rap music; to rap. *Dic., ext. mng.*
pale uluna *kik* Pillowcase. *Dic.*
pale·upoʻo *kik* Helmet. *Comb. pale + u (Tah.,* head) *+ poʻo*.
pale hoʻo·kaʻa·wale *kik* Buffer. *Lit.*, shield (for) separating.
pale·kaiko *Manu palekaiko.* Bird of paradise, the bird.
pale kaua *kik* Shield, as for battle. *Dic.* Cf. *kuahene*.
pale kā·nā·wai *ham* To break laws, act as an outlaw. Cf. *haʻihaʻi kānāwai, ʻaʻe kānāwai. Mea pale kānāwai.* Outlaw.
pale kā·ʻei *ham* Zone defense, as in basketball to execute such a play. *Mai hahai wale iā ia; e hoʻi kākou i ka pale kāʻei.* Don't just follow him all over; let's go back to a zone defense.
pale kili·lau *kik* Shower curtain. Cf. *pale pukaaniani.* See *kililau*.
palē·kō *kik* Play-Doh. *Eng.*
pale·kona kā·luʻu *kik* Peregrine falcon. *Lit.*, falcon (that) sweeps and swerves.
pale kuene *kik* Apron. *Niʻihau.* Also *ʻepane*.
pale kukui *kik* Lampshade. *Trad.*
pale lā See *ʻaila pale lā*.
palela *kik* Barrel, a unit of measurement. *Dic. Abb. pll.*

pā·lele *kik* Flying saucer. Comb. *pā + lele.*

pale lepo *kik* Mud guard. *Pale lepo paikikala.* Bicycle mud guard.

pale lulumi *ham* Press defense, as in basketball; to execute such a play. *I loko o nā minuke hope ʻelima, e pale lulumi nui kākou.* In the last five minutes of the game, let's concentrate on the press defense. *Lit.,* defense (by) crowding uncomfortably.

pale·maʻi *kik* Underpants. *Dic.* Also *lole wāwae palaʻili.* Sanitary pad. *Niʻihau usage.*

palemo See *kīloi palemo.*

pale mū·hune ʻino *kik* Antibiotic. *Lit.,* ward off pathogens.

palena *kik* Boundary. *Dic.* See entries below. *Palena kākele.* Transform boundary, in plate techtonics, in geology. *Palena kuʻi.* Convergent boundary. *Palena neʻe ʻoā.* Divergent boundary. *Palena piʻi.* Amplitude, as of a pendulum.

palena *kik* Terms of a fraction, in math. *Dic. Palena haʻahaʻa loa.* Lowest terms.

palena iki *kik* Minimum. *Lit.,* small limit. *Cf. palena nui. Ka palena iki o ke kaumaha.* The minimum weight.

palena ulu *kik* Grow limit, as in a computer program.

palena ū wai *kik* Field capacity, for holding water. *Lit.,* water-soaked limit.

palena holo kani *kik* Sound barrier. *Lit.,* limit (of) flowing sound. *Cf. māmā kani.*

palena nui *kik* Maximum. *Lit.,* large limit. *Cf. palena iki. Ka palena nui o ke kaumaha.* The maximum weight.

palena pau *kik* Deadline. *Lit.,* final limit. See *kaupalena. Hola palena pau.* Deadline (hour). *Lā palena pau.* Deadline (day).

palena papaha *kik* Potential. *Lit.,* limit (of) possibility.

palena ʻā·luna o ka hewa *kik* Greatest possible error, in math. *Lit.,* loosening boundary of error. Abb. *PʻĀH.*

pale pala·hō *ham* Antiseptic. *Hoʻohana ʻia ka lāʻau pale palahō no ka hoʻomaʻemaʻe ʻana i ka lumi hoʻopau pilikia a maʻemaʻe loa.* Antiseptics are used to clean the bathroom so that it is thoroughly clean. *Lit.,* protect (against) rot.

pale papa·hele *kik* Small rug, as in bathroom or beside bed. *Lit.,* floor protection. Also *pale wāwae.* See *hāliʻi papahele, moena, moena weleweka.*

pale peleki *kik* Brake pad.

pale puka·ani·ani *kik* Window curtain. *Dic. Cf. pale kililau, pale pukaaniani ʻōlepelepe.*

pale puka·ani·ani ʻō·lepe·lepe *kik* Venetian blinds. *Lit.,* Venetian blinds window curtain.

pale ʻea See entry below. *ʻŌnaehana pale ʻea.* Immune system, as in mammals.

pale ʻea pau *kik* AIDS (acquired immune deficiency syndrome). *Lit.,* finished resistance (against) infectious diseases. Also *maʻi pale ʻea pau.* See *mū hōlapu pale ʻea pau.*

pale·ʻili *kik* T-shirt. *Dic.,* ext. mng. Also *palaʻili.*

pale·ʻili kā·ʻawe *kik* Tank top. *Lit.,* T-shirt (with) strap. Also *palaʻili kāʻawe. Cf. palaʻili, paleʻili.*

pali See *pili pali.*

pā·like *kik* Reciprocal, in math. Sh. *pānaʻi + like.*

pā·loi·loi *ham* To dribble, as a basketball. Sh. *pā + redup. of kīloi.* Also *pākimokimo, paʻipaʻi. Pāloiloi pālua.* To double dribble.

pā·loka *Anamanaʻo pāloka.* To canvass, i.e. go door to door handing out political information and asking people which candidate they support. *Koho pāloka wae moho.* Primary election. Also *wae moho.*

pā·loke *kik* Parrot. *Eng.* Also *manu pāloke.*

pā·loke·ʻiʻi *kik* Parakeet. *Lit.*, undersized parrot.

pā·loli *ʻa*ʻ Fragile, susceptible to change. *Ua kū ke kaiaola i ka pāloli.* The ecosystem was fragile. Comb. *pā + loli.* Cf. *haki wale, nahā wale.*

pā·lolo *kik* Clay, as for ceramics; clay dirt. *Dic., ext. mng.* Cf. *kalē.*

pā·lomi *ham* Chiropractic; to practice chiropractic. Comb. *pā- + lomi.* *Kauka pālomi.* Chiropractor.

pā·lua See *kupa kaumokuʻāina pālua.*

palu·hē See *pepa paluhē.*

pā·lule *kik* Shirt, with short or long sleeves. *Dic.* Also *palaka.*

pā·lulu *ham* To block (the ball), in volleyball. *Niʻihau.* Also *paku.* See *paku, ʻai hele wale. Hala ka pālulu.* To pass through the block.

pāma *Pāʻā pāma.* Raffia, the fiber of the raffia palm of Madagascar.

pāma hihi *kik* Rattan. *Lit.*, creeping palm.

pā·make *ʻa*ʻ Fatal. *Make aku nei ʻelua keiki ma ka ulia kaʻa pāmake ma ke alaloa o Pāhoa i ka pō nei.* Two boys were killed in a fatal car crash on the Pāhoa highway last night. *Dic.*

pā·malae *kik* Courtyard. Comb. *pā + malae* (Māori *marae*).

pā·maʻi *ʻa*ʻ To be susceptible or vulnerable to disease. *Ua kū ke keiki i ka pāmaʻi.* The child was susceptible to disease. *Dic.* Cf. *pā wale.*

pame·sana *kik* Parmesan. *Eng. Waiūpaʻa pamesana.* Parmesan cheese.

pā·mia *ʻa*ʻ Used, second-hand. Comb. *pā + -mia. Kaʻa pāmia.* Used car.

pā·mili·ona Mega-, a prefix meaning million (M). Comb. *pā- + miliona.* Abb. *pm.* See *ʻai pāmiliona.*

pana *kik* Beat, as in music or linguistics; pulse. *Dic. Puʻuwai pana ʻewaʻewa.* Cardiac arrythmia.

pā·nai·nai *ʻa*ʻ Shallow, as a dish. *Dic.*

pana hoʻo·lei *ham* To flip, as a coin. Comb. *pana + hoʻolei.*

pana·kiō *kik* Banjo. *Eng.*

pana·kiō·lele *kik* Banjolele. *Eng.*

pana·kō hale *kik* Piggy bank. *Lit.*, house bank. See *mīkini panakō.*

pana kukui *kik* Light switch. *Dic., ext. mng.* Also *kuiki kukui.*

pana·lā·ʻau *kik* Colony, as a territory ruled by a more powerful nation. *He panalāʻau ke kūlanakauhale ʻo Makao no Pokukala, aia ma kahi kokoke i Honokaona.* The city of Macao is a colony of Portugal located near Hong Kong. *Dic.* See *kaumokuʻāina muli panalāʻau.*

Pana·mā *iʻoa* Panama; Panamanian. *Dic.*

pā·nā·nā *kik* Compass, as for navigation (preceded by *ke*). *Dic.* Cf. *ʻūpā kāpōʻai.* See *kikowaena pānānā. Pānānā paʻa lima.* Pocket compass.

pana·pana *ham* To pick, as an ʻukulele or guitar. *Mān.* Also *hiku.*

pane hoʻo·piʻi *ʻAha pane hoʻopiʻi.* Arraignment, i.e. a court hearing in which a defendant is formally charged with a crime and enters a plea of guilty or not guilty. See *hoʻopiʻi kūʻē.*

pane koho·koho *kik* Multiple-choice. *Lit.*, multiple-choice reply. Also *kohokoho.*

pā·nela *kik* Panel. *Eng.* Cf. *papa pānela.*

pane pā·lā·kiō *kik* Rating response, in math. *Lit.*, scale response.

pani *kik* Cap, as for toothpaste tube; lid, as for jar (preceded by *ke*). *Dic., ext. mng.* Cf. *poʻi peni.* See *kekimala, paipu lawe ʻino.*

pani *ham* To close, as in computer program. *Dic., ext. mng.* See *wehe.*

pani *ham* Substitute, as in sports; also to substitute (preceded by *ke*). *Auē! Ua ʻunu ke kuʻekuʻe wāwae o Lopaka; ʻo wai ana lā kōna pani?* Shucks! Lopaka's ankle is sprained; who's going to substitute for him? *Dic.* Also *pani hakahaka.*

Māmaka Kaiao / 129

pani haka·haka *kik* Stand-in, as for an actor in a movie or video production. *Dic., ext. mng.* Also *pani*.

pā·niho·niho *kik* Cog. *Niʻihau*. *Pānihoniho o ke kaulahao paikikala*. Bicycle chain cog.

pā·niki pepa *kik* Hole punch, for paper. *Dic*.

pā·nini *kik* Prickly pear cactus; cactus, general term. *Dic., ext. mng.* Also *pānini maoli, pāpipi*. See entries below.

pā·niniu *kik* Spinner, as in board games (preceded by *ke*). Comb. *pā + niniu*.

pā·nini kioia *kik* Cholla, a kind of cactus. Comb. *pānini* + Sp.

pā·nini palala *kik* Barrell cactus. Comb. *pānini* + Eng.

pā·nini ʻokana *kik* Organ pipe cactus. Comb. *pānini* + Eng.

pā·nini ʻoko·tio *kik* Ocotillo, a kind of cactus. Comb. *pānini* + Sp.

pani paipu hanu *kik* Epiglottis, in anatomy (preceded by *ke*). *Lit.,* windpipe stopper. See *paipu hanu*.

pani poʻo *kik* Capping, as the last stage of volcano formation (preceded by *ke*). *Dic., ext. def.* Cf. *panepoʻo* (dic.).

pani puka *kik* Door, as opposed to doorway (preceded by *ke*). *Ua kau ʻo ia i ka wehi Kalikimaka ma ke pani puka*. She placed the Christmas ornament on the door. *Dic.* See *pani puka uea makika*.

pani puka uea makika *kik* Screen door (preceded by *ke*). Also *pani puka makaʻaha*. See *uea makika, makaʻaha*.

pani wai ʻula *kik* Tampon (preceded by *ke*). *Lit.,* menstrual flow stopper.

pani ʻene·kini *kik* Hood, as of a car or truck (preceded by *ke*). *Lit.,* engine cover.

panoa *kik* Desert. *Dic*.

panoko *kik* Metathesis, i.e. transposition of letters, syllables or sounds in a word: e.g., *hāʻukeʻuke/hākuʻekuʻe*. *Rapanui*.

papa *kik* List. *Mān. Papa helu wahi*. Mailing list. *Papa kauoha kamepiula*. List of computer commands.

papa *kik* Board, lumber. *Dic.* See *kī papa*. *Papa lua hā*. Two-by-four board or lumber. *Papa hā hā*. Four-by-four board or lumber.

papa *kik* Two-dimensional, in math. *Dic., ext. mng.* Cf. *paʻa*. *Kinona papa*. Two-dimensional figure.

papa *kik* Layer, as of skin or tissue beneath the skin. *Dic*.

Papa See *Hoʻohokuikalani*.

papā See *huina papā*.

papaina *kik* Papain, an enzyme found in papayas and used as a meat tenderizer. *Eng*.

papa o lalo *kik* Substrate, as in a stream. *Lit.,* bottom stratum.

papaha *kik* Chance, possibility of an indicated outcome, in math. Redup. of *paha*. Cf. *pahiki*. *Like ka papaha o nā mea e loaʻa ana*. Equally likely outcomes. *Palena papaha*. Potential.

papa hana *kik* Informal plan. *Dic., ext. mng.* Cf. *papa hoʻolālā*.

papa hapa·malu *kik* Understory layer of vegetation, as low trees and shrubs. *Lit.,* partially shaded layer. See *papa kū honua, papa kaupoku, papa ʻoiʻoi*.

papa haʻa·wina *kik* Curriculum. *Lit.,* list (of) lessons.

papa·hele *kik* Story, floor, as in a building. *Dic.* See *hāliʻi papahele, kīloi papahele, pale papahele*.

papa helu·ʻai *kik* Scoreboard, as for sports. *He papakaumaka nunui kō ka papa heluʻai o ka hale haʻuki hou o ke Kulanui o Hawaiʻi*. The scoreboard at UH's new special events arena has a huge monitor.

papa hī·naʻi *kik* Backboard, in basketball. *Nāhāhā a okaoka ka papa hīnaʻi ma muli o ka pākī nui a Shaq*. The backboard completely shattered on Shaq's massive slam dunk. *Lit.,* basket board. Also *papa hupa, papa*. See *hīnaʻi, hupa*.

pā·paho *kik* Media, as radio, TV, etc. (Māori *pāpāho*.)

papa·honua *kik* Ground zero, as in field mapping. Comb. *papa + honua*.

papa hō·'ike·'ike *kik* Bulletin board. *Lit.*, board (for) displaying.

papa ho'o·holo *kik* Control panel, on computer. *Lit.*, board to cause to run.

papa ho'o·laha *kik* Sign, as political or business, etc. *Ni'ihau*. Also *hō'ailona*.

papa ho'o·lā·lā *kik* Plan, particularly one which involves thought and decision-making. *Sh. papa hana ho'olālā*. Cf. *papa hana*. See *hikiāpoko, hikiālōpū, hikiāloa*.

pā·pahu *kik* Cartridge, as for a computer printer. Comb. *pā + pahu*. *Pāpahu kinona hua*. Font cartridge. *E ho'okomo i ka pāpahu kinona hua ma loko o ka mīkini pa'i, a pa'i hou*. Insert the font cartridge into the printer and print again.

papa hua·'ōlelo *kik* Dictionary, as in computer program. *Lit.*, list (of) words. Cf. *papa wehewehe 'ōlelo*. *Papa hua'ōlelo kūmau*. Main dictionary. *Papa hua'ōlelo pāku'i*. User dictionary.

papa huila *kik* Skateboard. *Lit.*, wheel board. *He'ena papa huila*. Skateboard ramp.

papa hulei *kik* Seesaw, teetertotter. *Dic.* See *hulehulei*.

papa hupa *kik* Backboard, in basketball. *Lit.*, basket board. Also *papa hīna'i, papa*. See *hīna'i, hupa*.

pā·paka *kik* Crustacean. PPN *pāpaka* (crab). *Pāpaka 'āina*. Land crustacean.

papa·kau *kik* Counter, as in a kitchen. *Mān. Kapuahi papakau*. Hot plate.

papa·kau·maka *kik* Screen, as on a TV or computer monitor. *Lit.*, flat surface (for) fixing eyes (upon). See *pahu papakaumaka*. *Papakaumaka kamepiula*. Computer monitor screen. *Papakaumaka kīwī*. TV screen. *Papakaumaka mīkini helu*. Calculator display screen.

papa kau·poku *kik* Canopy layer of vegetation between *papa hapamalu* and *papa 'oi'oi*. *Lit.*, ceiling layer. See *papa kū honua, papa hapamalu, papa 'oi'oi*.

papa kā·nā·wai *kik* Code, i.e. a systematic collection of existing laws. *Lit.*, list (of) laws. *Papa kānāwai wai o ka moku'āina*. State water code.

pā·pā kā·nā·wai *ham* To outlaw, i.e. make something illegal. *Lit.*, prohibit (by) law.

papa kēmu *kik* Game board. See *kēmu*.

papa kī *kik* Head, as of an 'ukulele or guitar. *Ni'ihau*. See *'ukulele*.

papa koho *kik* Menu bar, on computer screen. *Lit.*, selection list. Cf. *papa kuhikuhi, papa 'ō'ili*.

papa·kū *kik* Riverbed; streambed. *Dic.* Also *papakū muliwai; papakū kahawai, kahena wai*.

papa·kū 'a' Vertical. *Dic., ext. mng.* Cf. *ho'opapakū, papamoe*. *Ulu papakū*. To grow vertically.

papa·kui ana·honua *kik* Geoboard, in math. *Lit.*, geometry nail board.

papa kuhi·kuhi *kik* Table of contents. *Dic. Papa kuhikuhi kiko'ī*. Index. See entry below.

papa kuhi·kuhi *kik* Menu, as in computer program. *Dic., ext. mng.* Cf. *papa koho, papa 'ō'ili*. *Papa kuhikuhi kahua pa'a*. Main menu.

papa kuhi·kuhina *kik* Coordinate plane, in math.

papa kuhi wai·hona *kik* Directory, of computer files. *Lit.*, list pointing out files.

papa kū honua *kik* Ground layer of vegetation. *Lit.*, layer reaching earth. See *papa hapamalu, papa kaupoku, papa 'oi'oi*.

papa kumu·mana'o *kik* Agenda, as for a meeting. *Ho'omakakoho 'ia ka mo'ohelu he makakoho ko'iko'i ma ka papa kumumana'o o ka hālāwai*. The budget was made an important priority at the meeting. *Lit.*, list (of) topics.

pā palai *kik* Frying pan (preceded by *ke*). *Dic.* *'Au pā palai.* Frying pan handle (preceded by *ke*).

papa·lala *'a'* Diagonally. Comb. *papa + lala.* Cf. *papakū, papamoe.* See *lala.*

Papa Lawe·lawe Ho'o·laha *kik* Bulletin Board Service (BBS), on computer programs. *Ua ho'olaha 'ia ka 'aha hālāwai o kēia pule a'e ma ke PLH.* Next week's conference was posted on the BBS. *Lit.,* billboard service. Abb. PLH.

pā·pale *kik* Cap, hat. *Dic. Pāpale kapuhau.* Ski cap, stocking cap. *Pāpale kililau.* Shower cap. *Pāpale kone.* Dunce cap, clown hat. *Pāpale 'au.* Swim cap.

pā·pale·kimo *kik* Condom, for men. Comb. *pāpale + kimo.*

papa luna ho'o·kele *kik* Administration, i.e. a team of executive branch officials appointed by the President, in government. *Ua mana'o mai ka papa luna ho'okele e uku manawale'a aku i nā po'e limahana no ka maika'i loa o kā lākou hana i kēia makahiki.* The administration thought to reward the employees for their excellent work done this year. *Lit.,* board (of) directors. See *luna ho'okele.*

papa mā·hele hana *kik* Call sheet, as a list of jobs for movie or video production. *Lit.,* list (of) job categories.

papa mana'o lau·like *kik* Thesaurus, as in computer program. *Lit.,* list (of words with) similar meanings. See *mana'o laulike, puke mana'o laulike.*

papa mea·kanu *kik* Vegetation layer. *Lit.,* plant layer. See *papa hapamalu, papa kaupoku, papa 'oi'oi.*

papa·moe *'a'* Horizontal. *Dic., ext. mng.* Cf. *papakū.* See *hawewe papamoe. Ulu papamoe.* To grow horizontally.

papana *kik* Rhythm, in music. Redup. of *pana.* Cf. *aupana.*

pā·papa *kik* Bean. *Dic., sp. var.* See *ula pāpapa. Pāpapa ha'a.* Bush bean. *Pāpapa hihi.* String bean. *Pāpapa kele.* Jelly bean. *Pāpapa koiū.* Soybean, soya bean. *Pāpapa laima.* Lima bean. *Pāpapa loloa.* Long bean, a common Filipino dish. *Pāpapa munukō.* Mung bean. *Pāpapa poepoe.* Pea. *Pāpapa 'ūhinihone.* Honey locust bean.

papa pā·lā·kiō *kik* Conversion scale. *Lit.,* scale list.

papa pā·nela *kik* Paneling. Comb. *papa + Eng. Papa pānela lā'au.* Wood paneling.

papa pena *kik* Palette, as in computer program. *Lit.,* paint board.

papa pe'a *kik* Board for windsurfing. *Lit.,* sail board. *Holo papa pe'a.* To windsurf.

papa pihi *kik* Keyboard, as on a computer or typewriter. Comb. *papa + pihi. Papa pihi kamepiula.* Computer keyboard. *Papa pihi keu.* Enhanced keyboard, expanded keyboard.

papa wai *kik* Water table, in geology. *Lit.,* water stratum. Cf. *pākaukau wai.*

papa wai kau luna *kik* Water lens, in geology. *Lit.,* water layer placed on top.

papa wehe·wehe 'ō·lelo *kik* Glossary. *Lit.,* list (to) explain words. Cf. *papa hua'ōlelo.*

papa'a *kik* Archive, backup, as in computer program. *Dic., ext. mng.* See *ho'opapa'a. Kope papa'a.* Backup copy. *Waihona papa'a.* Backup file.

pā·pa'a *kik* Crust, in geology. *Dic., ext. mng. Pāpa'a honua.* Earth's crust. *Pāpa'a moana.* Ocean crust. *Pāpa'a mokuhonua.* Continental crust.

papa·'ai *kik* Diet, i.e. the food that is eaten. *Lit.,* list of food. See *ho'ēmi kino, paiola, 'aiaola. Pākēneka o ka papa'ai.* Percent Daily Value, formerly known as percentage of US Recommended Daily Allowances (USRDA).

papa 'ā·lua·lua *kik* Multiplication tables. Cf. *'ālualua (dic.).*

papa ʻanuʻu lalo kai *kik* Underwater terrace. *Lit.*, undersea terrace layer.

Papa·ʻā·poho *iʻoa* Lisianski island. *Lit.*, flat (with a) depression.

papaʻi See *kīloi papaʻi, kī papaʻi*.

pā·paʻi *heh* To execute a defensive slide, in basketball. *Ke hiki mai ke kūkahi ma ʻaneʻi, e pāpaʻi ʻoe me ia*. When the point guard comes here, slide over to him. *Lit.*, crab.

papa ʻoi·ʻoi *kik* Emergent layer of vegetation, as trees sticking out at top. *Lit.*, layer above. See *papa kū honua, papa hapamalu, papa kaupoku*.

pā·pā·ʻō·lelo *kik* Dialogue, as in a play, movie or video production. *Dic., ext. mng.*

papa ʻō·ili *kik* Pop-up menu, as in computer program. *Lit.*, appearing list.

papa ʻū·miʻi *kik* Clipboard, as in computer program. *Hōʻike papa ʻūmiʻi*. To show clipboard.

pā·peka *kik* Puppet. *Usu. pāpeta. Eng.* Also *kiʻi lima. Pāpeka kaula, pāpeta kaula*. Marionette.

pā peleki *kik* Brake disk (preceded by *ke*).

papi *kik* California poppy. *Eng. Pua papi*. Poppy flower.

pā piki *kik* Petri dish (preceded by *ke*). *Comb. pā* + *Eng.*

pā·pili·ona Giga-, a prefix meaning billion (G). *Comb. pā-* + *piliona*. *Abb. pp*. See *ʻai pāpiliona. Kule pāpiliona*. Gigajoule.

pā·pipi *kik* Prickly pear cactus. *Dic.* Also *pānini, pānini maoli*.

Pā·pua Nū·kini *iʻoa* Papua New Guinea; Papua New Guinean. *Comb. Eng. + dic., sp. var.*

pā wai *kik* Water dish (preceded by *ke*).

pā wale *ʻa* Susceptible, vulnerable. *He pā wale nā manu ʻōiwi o Hawaiʻi i nā maʻi a me nā poʻiiʻa malihini*. Native birds are susceptible to introduced diseases and predators. *Comb. pā* + *wale*. Cf. *pāmaʻi*.

pā·weo *heh* To skew, as a deviation from a straight line, in math. *Dic., ext. mng. Laina pāweo*. Skew line.

pā wili *kik* Dial (preceded by *ke*). *Lit.*, circular object (for) twisting.

paʻa *ʻa* Three-dimensional, in math. *Dic., ext. mng.* Cf. *papa*. See entries below. *Kinona paʻa*. Three-dimensional figure.

paʻa *kik* Geometric solid. *Dic.* See entry below and *kuʻina paʻa, pena paʻa mania*.

paʻa *ʻa* Closed, as a frame in a computer program. *Dic., ext. mng.* Cf. *kaʻakaʻa*. *Mōlina paʻa*. Closed frame.

paʻa·alewa *heh* Flexed-arm hang. *Lit.*, hanging fixed.

paʻa ea *ʻa* Airtight. *Lit.*, hold air. *He hōkelo paʻa ea*. An airtight container.

paʻa·hau *ʻa* Frozen. *Paʻahau ka wai i ke kēkelē ʻole o ke Kelekia*. Water freezes at zero degrees Celsius. *Sh. paʻa i ka hau*. Cf. *hoʻopaʻahau*. See *kēkelē. Au paʻahau*. Ice age. *Pahu paʻahau*. Freezer. *ʻAila ʻaʻalo paʻahau*. Antifreeze.

paʻa·hapa *ʻAilakele paʻahapa*. Unsaturated fat.

paʻa helu *kik* Number pair. *Paʻa helu kuhikuhina*. Coordinates; ordered pair, i.e. two numbers used to give location of a point on a graph, in math.

paʻa·kai ʻepe·soma *kik* Epsom salt.

paʻa like·like *kik* Suit, as in a deck of playing cards. *Niʻihau*.

paʻa lima *ʻa* Held in the hand, hand-held. *Dic. Aniani paʻa lima*. Hand mirror. *Pānānā paʻa lima*. Pocket compass.

paʻa·loko *ʻa* Built-in. *He mōkema paʻaloko kō kēia kamepiula*. This computer has a built-in modem. *Comb. paʻa* + *loko*. Cf. *kūloko*. See *kakena paʻaloko, pā paʻaloko. Waihona ʻike paʻaloko*. Built-in memory, in a computer.

paʻa·lole hele lewa *kik* Space suit. *Lit.*, suit (for) walking (in) space.

pā·ʻā·lua *kik* Code. Sh. *pāpālua* + *ʻalualua*. *Pāʻālua kaʻina hana*. Key code, as for the order to press keys on a calculator to find an answer. *Lit.*, code (showing) order (of) procedure. See *poʻo pāʻālua*.

paʻa mau *ʻa* Sustained. *Dic., ext. mng. Loaʻa paʻa mau*. Sustained yield, as in crop production.

paʻa·mau *kik* Default, as in computer program. *Ua hoʻopaʻa ʻia ke kinona hua paʻamau ma ka Times*. The default font is set at Times. Comb. *paʻa* + *mau*.

paʻa·mā·hua·ola *kik* Nutrient salts, i.e. the deposits that remain after a liquid has been removed. Sh. *paʻakai* + *māhuaola*.

paʻa manehu kū·ʻē·ʻē *kik* Action-reaction pair, i.e. two forces having equal strength but opposite directions, in science. *Lit.*, opposing force pair.

pā·ani iwi *ham* To play dominoes. *Lit.*, play bones. See *iwi pāʻani*.

pā·ʻā pāma *kik* Raffia, the fiber of the raffia palm of Madagascar. *Lit.*, palm fiber.

paʻa·paʻa·ʻina *ʻa* Crisp or brittle, as dry *hala* leaves. *Dic.*

paʻa·poe·poe *kik* Sphere, in math. Comb. *paʻa* + *poepoe*.

paʻa pō·haku *ʻa* Lithified. *He pōhaku ke kumuone i paʻa pōhaku maila i ke au o nā makahiki he nui loa*. Sandstone is a rock which has gone through lithification over a period of many years. *Lit.*, solidified (into) rock.

paʻa·pū *kik* Density, as of a computer disk. *Dic., ext. mng.* See entry below. *Paʻapū emi*. Low density. *Paʻapū ʻoi*. High density. *Paʻapū pūʻuo kanaka*. Population density, for humans only.

paʻapū *Lākiō paʻapū wai*. Specific gravity, relative gravity. *ʻAilakele paʻapū*. Saturated fat.

paʻa·pū·hia *ʻa* Concentrated. Comb. *paʻapū* + *-hia*. Cf. *kaiaka*. See *hoʻopaʻapūhia*. *Wai paʻakai paʻapūhia*. Brine, a concentrated solution of salt or ocean water. Also *wai paʻakai*. See *wai kai*.

paʻa·puna *kik* Calcareous. Comb. *paʻa* + *puna*. *Pōhaku paʻapuna*. Calcareous rock, calcium carbonate.

paʻa·ʻili See entries below.

paʻa·ʻili iwa·kā·lua *kik* Icosahedron, a space figure with twenty faces, in math. Comb. *paʻaʻili* + *iwakālua*.

paʻa·ʻili·ono *kik* Hexahedron, a space figure with six faces, in math; cube, cubic. *Dic., ext mng.* See *paʻaʻiliono analahi*. *ʻIā paʻaʻiliono*. Cubic yard.

paʻa·ʻili·ono ana·lahi *kik* Cube, in math. Comb. *paʻaʻiliono* + *analahi*. Also *paʻaʻiliono*. See *paʻaʻiliono*.

paʻa·ʻili·hā *kik* Tetrahedron, a space figure with four faces, in math. Comb. *paʻaʻili* + *hā*.

paʻa·ʻili lehu·lehu *kik* Polyhedron, a space figure with many faces, in math. Comb. *paʻaʻili* + *lehulehu*. Also *paʻaʻili*.

paʻa·ʻili·walu *kik* Octahedron, a space figure with eight faces, in math. Comb. *paʻaʻili* + *walu*.

paʻa·ʻili ʻumi·kū·mā·lua *kik* Dodecahedron, a space figure with twelve faces, in math. Comb. *paʻaʻili* + *ʻumikūmālua*.

paʻa ʻohe·nā·nā *kik* Binoculars. *Lit.*, pair (of) telescopes.

paʻa·ʻolo·laha *kik* Ovoid. Comb. *paʻa* + *ʻololaha*.

pā·ʻeke *kik* Corral. *Dic.*

paʻewa *kik* Bias, i.e. systematic error in gathering data, in math. Sh. *pāʻewaʻewa*. See *kīloi paʻewa*.

Māmaka Kaiao / 134

pā·ʻewa·ʻewa *kik/ʻaʻ* Bias; biased. *He hoʻāʻo ka puʻe haʻilono e haʻi aku i ka nū hou me ka pāʻewaʻewa ʻole i ʻole e manaʻo ʻia ua ʻume ʻia ka mea haʻilono e kekahi ʻaoʻao.* Journalists attempt to report the news without bias so as not to appear that they are influenced by one side or another. *Dic.*

paʻeʻe *ʻaʻ* On-line, i.e. describing the state of an electronic device ready to receive data, connected to a computer network, or accessible by means of a computer or computer network. *Ke paʻeʻe hou mai nei nā kamepiula ma hope o ka hoʻā hou ʻia ʻana o ka pūnaewele e ka luna pūnaewele.* The computers are coming on-line again after the network supervisor restarted the network. Comb. *pa-* + *ʻeʻe*. Cf. *pahemo.* See *hoʻopaʻeʻe.*

paʻi *ham* To print, as on a computer (preceded by *ke*). *Dic.* See entries below. *Mīkini paʻi.* Printer.

paʻi *kik* Shot, as of a photograph or in movie or video production (preceded by *ke*). *Dic., ext. mng.* See *kokoke, laulā, lōpū, paʻi kiʻi. Nā ʻano paʻi.* Types of shots. *Paʻi laulā.* Wide shot. *Paʻi laulā loa.* Extreme wide shot. *Paʻi lōpū.* Medium shot. *Paʻi kokoke.* Close-up. *Paʻi kokoke loa.* Extreme close-up.

paʻi *ham* To take, shoot or snap, as a photograph (preceded by *ke*). *Dic.* Cf. *ʻāpona.* See entries below and *pahu paʻi wikiō. Mea paʻi kiʻi.* Photographer, cameraperson. *Paʻi kiʻiʻoniʻoni.* To shoot a movie film. *Paʻi wikiō.* To shoot a video.

paʻi ulele *ham* Service, in volleyball; to serve (the ball). *Lit.,* hit (to) get into action. Cf. *hānai, hānai puʻupuʻu. Kaʻa paʻi ulele.* Side out. *ʻAʻena paʻi ulele.* Service violation.

paʻi haka·haka *ham* To type. *Niʻihau.* Also *kikokiko.*

paʻi kā·hela *ham* To pan, as with a movie or video camera (preceded by *ke*). *Lit.,* take (a picture) sweeping backward and forward

paʻi kiʻi *ham* To photograph or take a picture, either still or motion. *Dic.* See *kiʻi paʻi, paʻi.*

paʻi kulo *ham* To make a sidewinder serve, in volleyball. *Niʻihau.*

pā ʻili See *lāʻau make pā ʻili.*

paʻi lihi *ham* To dink, i.e. to mishit or clip (the ball), in volleyball. *Lit.,* slight hit. Also *hoʻokulu.* See *ʻai hele wale.*

paʻi lua *ʻAʻena paʻi lua.* Double-hit violation, in volleyball.

paʻi mana·mana *ham* To volley, i.e. keep the ball in play, in volleyball. *Lit.,* hit (with) fingers. Also *pohu.* Cf. *lelekīkē.*

paʻina *kik* Click, as the sound produced when clicking a computer mouse. *He kuli nui ka paʻina o kēia ʻiole.* This mouse has a loud click to it. *Dic.* See *kōmi, kaomi.*

paʻi·palaoa *kik* Dough. *Lit.,* mix flour.

paʻi pā·laha·laha *ham* To spike with open hand, in volleyball. *Niʻihau.* See *hili, kuʻi puʻupuʻu.*

paʻi·paʻi *ham* To dilute or mix, as a drink. *Dic.* Cf. *hoʻokaiaka. Ua paʻipaʻi ʻia ka lama i ka wai.* The alcoholic beverage was diluted with water.

paʻi·paʻi *ham* To dribble, as a basketball. *Niʻihau.* Also *pākimokimo, pāloiloi.* Cf. *pekupeku.*

paʻi·paʻi pā·lua *ham* To double dribble, in basketball. Also *pākimokimo pālua, pāloiloi pālua.*

pā·ʻoi·hana *kik* Business, i.e. a person or company engaged in business; commercial, i.e. relating to commerce or business. *Nui nā pāʻoihana o ke kaona ʻo Honolulu, ʻo ka hale ʻaina ʻoe, ʻo ka panakō ʻoe, a pēlā aku.* There are many businesses in the city of Honolulu: restaurants, banks, etc. Comb. *pā* + *ʻoihana.* Cf. *kaona, ʻoihana. Pāʻoihana hoʻoulu meakanu.* Commercial growers. *ʻĀpana pāʻoihana kauwaena.* Central business district.

pā·ō·lelo *kik* Record, as for a record player. *Niʻihau.* Also *pāleo.*

pā ʻoma *kik* Baking pan (preceded by *ke*).

paʻu See *kalina paʻu*.

pā·ʻumi Deka-, a prefix meaning ten (da). *Dic., ext. mng.* Abb. *pʻm.*

paʻū·paʻū *kik* Tapa, bark cloth. *Dic.*

paʻu·popo *ʻa* Organic, i.e. relating to the branch of chemistry concerning the carbon compounds of living things. Comb. *paʻu + popo.*

pā CD, pā sēdē See *CD*.

Para·guae *iʻoa* Paraguay; Paraguayan. *Dic.* Also *Palakuae*.

pē- A prefix used for certain scientific terms with the meaning able to, -able, -ability, -ibility, etc. NOTE: pē- + *ʻaʻano*; pē- + *hamani/hehele* + -hia. Var. of *pae*. See entries below.

pea *kik* Avocado. *Dic.* Also *pea Hawaiʻi*. *Pea pakeleke*. Pear, usually Bartlett.

pea Kina *kik* Panda. *Lit.,* Chinese bear.

pea kiʻi *kik* Teddy bear. Also *pea pāʻani*. Cf. *pēpē kiʻi*.

pea pā·ʻani *kik* Teddy bear. *Lit.,* bear (for) playing. Also *pea kiʻi*. Cf. *pēpē kiʻi*.

peawa *kik* Beaver. *Eng. Peawa kuahiwi.* Mountain beaver.

pea ʻĀ·lika *kik* Polar bear. *Lit.,* Arctic bear.

pē·hā·popopo *ʻa* Biodegradable. *ʻO nā huahana kūpono no ke kaiapuni, he pēhāpopopo ke ʻano o ka pūʻolo i wahī ʻia ai.* Products which are environmentally sound are packaged with biodegradable packaging. Comb. *pē- + hāpopopo.*

pē·heu *kik* Mumps. *Niʻihau*.

peka *kik* Peck, a unit of measurment. *Eng.*

peke *kik* Child's scooter. *Inv.* Also *kaʻa peke*. See *pueo peke*.

peke·keu *kik* Brim, of a hat. *Mān.* (MW). Also *kihikihi*. Cf. *laulau*.

peke·lala *ʻa* Federal. *Dic.* Cf. *aupuni*. *ʻAhahui pekelala*. Federal organization.

pēki *heh* To back up. *E pēki ʻoe i hope!* Back up! *Mān.*

pēki *heh* To escape, as in computer program. *Mān., ext. mng. Pihi pēki.* Escape key (preceded by *ke*). *E kōmi i ke pihi pēki a hiki loa i ka papa kuhikuhi kahua paʻa.* Press the escape key all the way back to the main menu.

peki·kulali *kik* Lousewort. *Lat.,* pedicularis.

pekona *kik* Bacon. *Eng.*

peku·nia *kik* Petunia. *Dic.*

peku·peku *ham* To dribble, as with kicks in soccer. *Dic., ext. mng.* Cf. *paʻipaʻi*.

pela *kik* Mattress. *Dic.* Bed. *Niʻihau.* Also *pela moe. Hao pela.* Bedframe. *Pela hoʻolana.* Air mattress.

pēla *kik* Bail, i.e. money a defendant gives a court as a promise to return for trial. *E hoʻopaʻa ana ka luna hoʻokolokolo i ka pēla he ʻumi kaukani kālā no ka hopohopo e mahuka ka mea i hoʻāhewa ʻia i kahi ʻāina ʻē.* Bail has been set by the judge at ten thousand dollars for fear the accused may flee the country. *Dic., sp. var.*

pelaha *kik* Poster. *Sh. pepa + hoʻolaha*. *Pena pelaha*. Tempera paint.

pela hewa *Kaha pela hewa.* A circle around a misspelled word with the letters *ph* (*pela hewa*) written above the word, in proofreading.

pela·hū *kik* Pinwheel, the toy. *Sh. pelamakani + hū.*

pela·makani *kik* Electric fan. *Niʻihau.*

pela·mika *kik* Pyramid shape. *Dic. Pelamika ikehu.* Energy pyramid. *Puʻu pelamika.* Pyramid, as in Egypt.

pele *kik* Volcano; volcanic; bell. *Dic.* See *uila māhu pele, lua pele, ʻūhini nēnē pele. Moʻo pōhaku pele.* Lava lizard. *Piko pele.* Hot spot, in geology. *Puʻu pele.* Volcanic cone.

peleita See *manu peleita*.

peleka *kik* Felt, a type of fabric. *Eng.*

Pele·kāne *i'oa* Britain, England; British, English person; English (of England). *Mān./dic., sp. var.* Cf. *Pelekānia.* See '*Enelani.*

Pele·kā·nia *i'oa* Britain, British; English. *Mān./dic., sp. var.* Cf. *Pelekāne.* '*Ōlelo Pelekānia.* English (language).

peleki *kik* Brake. *Dic. Peleki pā.* Disk brake. *Pā peleki.* Brake disk (preceded by *ke*). *Pale peleki.* Brake pad.

Pele·kiuma *i'oa* Belgium; Belgian. *Dic.* Also *Belegiuma.*

pele·kikena *kik* President, as of a college or university. *Dic.* Cf. *luna kulanui, po'o kulanui.*

pele·leu '*a*' Obtuse. *Dic. Huina peleleu.* Obtuse angle. *Huinakolu peleleu.* Obtuse triangle.

pele·leu *kik* Extension, as of a computer file. *Dic., ext. mng. Peleleu waihona.* File extension.

pele·maka *kik* Magma. *Lit.*, raw lava. *Nupa pelemaka.* Magma chamber. *Pōhaku pelemaka.* Igneous rock, i.e. rock formed by the solidifica- tion of molten magma.

pelena pe'a *kik* Pretzel. *Lit.*, crossed cracker.

pelene *kik* Bran. *Eng. Māpina pelene.* Bran muffin.

pelu *kik* Hem, as of a dress. *Dic. Pelu 'upena.* Hem of a net.

Pelū *i'oa* Peru; Peruvian. *Dic.* Also *Perū.*

pelu 'ō·pū *kik/ham* Situp; to do sit-ups. *Lit.*, bend stomach.

pē·mā·'ō·'ā '*a*' Solubility; soluble. Comb. *pē- + mā'ō'ā.* Cf. *mā'ō'ā, mā'ō'āna. Pēmā'ō'ā wae 'ano.* Selective solubility.

pena '*a*' Curious, *nīele. Maui.* See entries below and *papa pena.*

pena *kik* Paint, i.e. the area within the key below the free throw line on a basketball court. *Kīhele wale ho'i hā 'o Kaunu ma 'ō, ma 'ane'i ma ka pena.* Kaunu was all over the paint. *Dic.*

pena kī·kina *kik/ham* Spray paint; to spray paint.

pena kua·papa wai *kik* Water-base paint. Cf. *pena wai.*

pena ku'e·maka *kik* Eyebrow pencil. *Ni'ihau. Hana i ka pena ku'emaka.* To "put on" or "do" one's eyebrows.

pena lehe·lehe *kik/ham* Lipstick. *Lit.*, lip paint. Also *pena waha.*

pena lihi·lihi maka *kik* Mascara. *Ni'ihau. Hana i ka pena lihilihi maka.* To put on mascara.

pena lola *ham* To paint with a roller. Cf. *lola pena.*

pena maka *kik/ham* Makeup; to put on makeup. *Lit.*, paint (the) face. *Mea pena maka.* Makeup artist, as for a play, movie or video production.

pena pa'a mania *kik* Enamel. *Lit.*, paint (that) hardens smooth.

pena pelaha *kik* Tempera paint. *Lit.*, poster paint.

pena wai *kik* Watercolor. *Lit.*, water paint. Cf. *pena kuapapa wai.*

pena waha *kik/ham* Lipstick. *Ni'ihau.* Also *pena lehelehe.* Cf. *peni pena waha. Hana i ka pena waha.* To put on lipstick.

pena·tomino *kik* Pentomino, in math. *Eng.*

pene *kik* Cage. (*Eng.* pen.) Cf. *hale mālama 'īlio. Pene halihali.* Kennel or crate for transporting animals. *Pene 'īlio.* Kennel, as a shelter for a dog.

Pene·kele·winia *i'oa* Pennsylvania; Pennsylvanian. *Dic.* Also *Peneselevinia.*

pene·kui *kik* Benzoin, a resin used in perfume and cosmetics. (Old Catalan *benjui.*)

pē·ne'e *kik* Mobility, in geography. Comb. *pē- + ne'e.*

pene 'io·'io *kik* Brooder. *Lit.*, cheeping pen.

Pene·sele·vinia *i'oa* Pennsylvania; Pennsylvanian. *Dic.* Also *Penekelewinia.*

peni *kik* Pen. *Dic.* Also *peni ʻīnika.* Niʻihau. See *peni kuni, poʻi peni.*

peni·aliʻi *kik* Pennyroyal, a kind of flower. Comb. Eng. + *aliʻi.*

peni·kala kala *kik* Colored pencil.

peni kuni *kik* Marsh pen, felt pen. Sh. *peni kuni pahu,* pen (for) etching (on) boxes. Niʻihau.

peni pāuma *kik* Fountain pen. *Lit.,* pen (that) pumps.

peni pena waha *kik* Lipliner. Niʻihau. Also *peni pena lehelehe.* Cf. *pena waha.*

Penuli *iʻoa* Bernoulli. *Eng. Ke kulehana a Penuli.* Bernoulli's principle, in science.

Pep. Abbreviation for *Pepeluali* (February).

pepa ana ʻakika *kik* Litmus paper, for measuring pH. *Lit.,* paper (for) measuring acid.

pepa·ā·nue *kik* Construction paper. Sh. *pepa* + *ānuenue.*

pepa hō·ʻaui·kala *kik* Chromatographic paper. *Lit.,* chromatography paper. See *hōʻauikala.*

pepa kā·lā *kik* Bill, i.e. a piece of paper money. *Lit.,* money paper. See *pepa pākahi, ʻōkeni.*

pepa kini *kik* Aluminum foil, tin foil. *Lit.,* tin paper.

pepa leka *kik* Letter-size paper (8-1/2 X 11). *Lit.,* letter paper. See *pepa 11" X 17", pepa loio.*

pepa loio *kik* Legal-size paper (8-1/2 x 14). *Lit.,* lawyer paper. See *pepa 11" X 17", pepa leka.*

pepa lole pipi *kik* Butcher paper. Comb. *pepa* + *mea lole pipi.*

pepa·loni *kik* Pepperoni. *Eng.*

pepa mā·noa·noa *kik* Posterboard. *Lit.,* thick paper.

pepa paia *kik* Wallpaper.

pepa pahu *kik* Cardboard, corrugated paper. *Lit.,* box paper. Cf. *pahu pepa.*

pepa pā·kahi *kik* One dollar bill. *Pepa pālima.* Five dollar bill. *Pepa pāʻumi.* Ten dollar bill.

pepa palu·hē *kik* Papier mâché. *Lit.,* paper reduced to pulp.

pepa papa ʻoka *kik* Oaktag, a strong cardboard used for posters; also called tagboard. *Lit.,* oak board paper.

pepa pī·lali *kik* Wax paper. Also *pepa ʻaila.*

pepa ʻaila *kik* Wax paper. Niʻihau. Also *pepa pīlali.*

pepa 11" X 17" *kik* Tabloid paper (pronounced *pepa ʻumikūmākahi ʻīniha i ka ʻumikūmāhiku ʻīniha*). See *pepa leka, pepa loio.*

pepei·ao *ʻUala kahiki pepeiao.* Scalloped potatoes. *Lit.,* potatoes (like) scallops. Also *ʻuala pepeiao.*

pepeke *kik* Grammatical sentence or clause. Redup. of *feke* (PPN *heʻe*). See entries below.

pepeke haku *kik* Main clause, in grammar. *Lit.,* master *pepeke.*

pepeke ʻō·hua *kik* Dependent clause, in grammar. *Lit.,* dependent *pepeke.*

pē·pē kiʻi *kik* Doll, a child's plaything. Niʻihau. Cf. *pea kiʻi.*

pepelu *kik* Flyer, pamphlet. Sh. *pepa* + *pelu.*

Pepe·luali *iʻoa* February. *Dic.* Abb. *Pep.*

pepewa *ʻa* Webbed, as a duck's feet. Redup of *pewa.*

pepeʻe·kua *kik* Amphibian. (Māori, *pepeketua* [frog].)

pepili *kik* Sticker. Sh. *pepa* + *pipili.*

peʻa See *papa peʻa. Pelena peʻa.* Pretzel.

pē·ʻā·hia *ʻa* Flammable, flammability; also inflammable, inflammability. Comb. *pē-* + *ʻā* + *-hia.*

peʻahi lima *kik* Hand, as opposed to arm. *Dic.*

pē·ano *kik* Mode, as in computer program. Comb. *pē-* + *ʻano.*

pē·ʻume·lau·oho *ʻa* Capillarity. Comb. *pē-* + dic., sp. var. Cf. *ohowele.*

pero·kesa·side *kik* Peroxide. *Eng.* See *haikokene lua ʻokikene lua.*

Perū *i'oa* Peru; Peruvian. *Eng.* Also *Pelū.*

pia·'ai *kik* Starch, a white, tasteless, solid carbohydrate found in plants. *He mea'ai nui ka pia'ai ma ka papa'ai o kānaka.* Starch is a staple in the diet of humans. *Lit.,* edible starch.

pio·hē *kik* Larva. Sh. *'ōpiopio + hē* (caterpillar).

pio·pio *kik* Young chick; sound used to call chickens by imitating a young chick. *Dic.*

pī·uī·lā·'au See *manu pīuīlā'au.*

piula wai *kik* Fire hydrant. *Dic.* Also *paipu kinai ahi.*

piha See *helu piha, waiū piha.*

pihana·haka *kik* Volume. Comb. *pihana + haka.* Cf. *pihana'ū.* Abb. *phk. Kinona pihanahaka.* Space figure, in math.

pihana·'ū *kik* Capacity. Comb. *pihana + -'ū.* Cf. *pihanahaka.*

piha·piha *kik* Gills, of a fish. *Dic.*

Pihe·manu *i'oa* Midway island. *Lit.,* loud din (of) birds.

pihi *kik/ham* Button; to button (preceded by *ke*). *Dic.* Also *pihi lole.*

pihi *kik* Switch, as on radio, TV set, etc. (preceded by *ke*). *Dic., ext. mng.*

pihi *kik* Key, as on typewriter or computer keyboard (preceded by *ke*). *Dic., ext. mng.* See entries below. *Inoa o ke pihi.* Name of key. *Papa pihi.* Keyboard.

pihi hō·'ai·lona *kik* Badge (preceded by *ke*). *Lit.,* symbol button. *Pihi māka'i.* Police badge.

pihi ho'o·holo *kik* Control key, as on computer keyboard (preceded by *ke*). See *ho'oholo.*

pihi ho'o·kō·ā *kik* Space bar, on typewriter or computer keyboard, variant term (preceded by *ke*). *Ni'ihau.* Also *pihi ka'ahua.*

pihi ho'o·mana'o *kik* Memory key, as on calculator keyboard (preceded by *ke*).

pihi ho'o·nui lohe *kik* Hearing aid (preceded by *ke*). *Lit.,* button (to) increase hearing.

pihi ho'o·piha *kik* Washer, as used in plumbing. *Lit.,* button (for) filling. Also *ho'opiha.*

pihi kā·ho'i *kik* Return key, as on typewriter or computer keyboard (preceded by *ke*). See *kāho'i.*

pihi kake *kik* Shift key, as on typewriter or computer keyboard (preceded by *ke*). *Lit.,* key (for) slipping back and forth. See *kake.*

pihi kā·wā·holo *kik* Tab key, as on typewriter or computer keyboard (preceded by *ke*). See *kāwāholo.*

pihi ka'a·hua *kik* Space bar, on typewriter or computer keyboard (preceded by *ke*). See *ka'ahua.*

pihi laka ma'aka *kik* Caps lock key, on typewriter or computer keyboard (preceded by *ke*). *Ua pa'a ke pihi laka ma'aka.* The caps lock key is stuck. Also *pihi laka.*

pihi lohe *kik* Earphone (preceded by *ke*). *Lit.,* hearing button. See *apo lohe.*

pihi nahau *kik* Arrow key, as on computer keyboard (preceded by *ke*). *Pihi nahau holo 'ākau (hema, i luna, i lalo).* Arrow key for moving right (left, up, down).

pihi pāuma ea *kik* Air valve, as on a tire (preceded by *ke*). *Ni'ihau.* See *pāuma.*

pihi·pihi *kik* Washer, as used in plumbing (preceded by *ke*). *Dic.*

pihi pī·na'i *kik* Turbo button, as in Nintendo games (preceded by *ke*). *Lit.,* repeat button. See *ka'akepa.*

pihi·poho *kik* Locket (preceded by *ke*). Comb. *pihi + poho.*

pihi wiki *kik* Hot key, as on computer keyboard (preceded by *ke*). *Lit.,* fast key. *Nā pihi wiki.* Hot keys.

pihi wili *kik* Nut, as in nuts and bolts. *Lit.,* screw nut. Also *pihi.* See *kui kolū. Pihi wili ono.* Hex nut. *Pihi wili 'ēheu.* Wing nut.

pihi ʻū·mi·ʻi *kik* Snap, fastener (preceded by *ke*). *Dic., ext. mng.* Also *ʻūmiʻi*.

pika *kik* Pizza. *Eng.* Also *pai pika*.

pika pua *kik* Flower vase. *Dic.*

pī·kaʻo *ʻa*ʻ Dehydrated. *Hoʻāhu nui ʻia ka meaʻai pīkaʻo i lako ai i ka wā pōpilikia.* Dehydrated food is stored up in order to be well supplied during times of disaster. *Dic.* See *hoʻopīkaʻo*.

pike *kik* Beet. *Eng.*

pikeke *kik* Biscuit. *Eng.* Also *palaoa pikeke*.

piki See *pā piki*.

piko *kik* Node, where a leaf is connected to the stem. *Dic.* See entries below.

piko·lō *kik* Piccolo. *Eng.*

pī·kō·nia *kik* Begonia. *Dic., sp. var.*

piko pakuhi *kik* Origin of a graph. *Lit.*, graph center. Also *piko*.

piko pele *kik* Hot spot, in geology. *Lit.*, volcanic center.

piko ʻume·kau·maha *kik* Center of gravity. See *ʻumekaumaha*.

pila *kik* Any musical instrument, but esp. string instruments. *Dic., ext. mng.* See entries below.

pila *kik* Bill, a draft of a law presented to a legislature. *Dic.*

pila hāpa *kik* Autoharp. *Dic.* Also *hāpa paʻa lima*.

pila kī·koʻo *kik* Bank Check. *Dic.* See entries below.

pila kī·koʻo hua·kaʻi *kik* Traveler's check. *Lit.*, travel check.

pila kī·koʻo pana·kō *kik* Bank draft, cashier's check, certified check. *Lit.*, bank check.

pila kū nui *kik* Bass viol, string bass. *Lit.*, large standing fiddle. Also *pila nui*.

pī·lali *kik* Wax. *Dic.* Also *uepa. Pepa pīlali.* Wax paper. Also *pepa ʻaila. Pīlali pākuʻi.* Grafting wax. See *pākuʻi*.

pī·lali pā·ku·ʻi *kik* Grafting wax. See *pākuʻi*.

pila nui See *pila kū nui*.

pila puhi·puhi *kik* Harmonica. *Dic., sp. var.*

pila ʻoka kā·lā *kik* Money order. *Lit.*, bill (to) order money.

pila ʻu·poho *kik* Bagpipe. *Lit.*, bagpipe fiddle. Also *ʻūpoho*.

pī·leka·leka *kik/ʻa*ʻ Adhesion; adhesive. *Dic., ext. mng.* Cf. *pūʻuoʻuo*.

pili See *manamana pili*.

pili·olana *kik* Biography; biographical. Comb. *pili + ola + ana.* Cf. *hikapiliolana. Nōwela piliolana.* Biographical novel.

pili·ona See *hapa piliona*.

pili helu laki *kik* Lottery. *Lit.*, lucky number betting.

pili hoʻo·kahi pala·pala *ʻa*ʻ Document specific, as in computer program. *He pilikia pili hoʻokahi palapala nō ia.* That problem is definitely document specific. *Lit.*, relative to one document.

pili·kanaka *kik* Social studies. *Lit.*, concerning man.

pili·kino *ʻa*ʻ Custom, custom-made, i.e. made to individual specifications. *Penei ka hana a kaʻu papa pihi pilikino.* This is how my custom-made keyboard works. *Dic., ext. mng. Hoʻonoho-nohona pilikino.* Custom format.

pili lihi *ʻa*ʻ Contiguous. *Lit.*, edges touching.

pilina henua *kik* Relative location, in geography. Comb. *pilina + fenua* (Tah., earth). Cf. *kuhikuhina*.

pilina moe *kik* Bedsprings. *Dic.*

pilina·ʻō·lelo *kik* Grammar. Comb. *pilina + ʻōlelo. Haʻawina pilinaʻōlelo.* Grammar lesson, a lesson related to sentence structure. *Mākau pilinaʻōlelo.* Grammar or sentence structure skill.

pili·pā *ʻa*ʻ Parallel. *Dic., ext. mng.* See *ala pilipā. Nā kaha pilipā.* Parallel lines.

pili pali *kik* Orographic, i.e. dealing with mountains. *Lit.*, associated with cliffs. *Ua pili pali.* Orographic rainfall.

Pilipino *iʻoa* Filipino. *Dic.* Also *Pinopino. ʻĀina Pilipino.* Philippines.

pimeka *kik* Allspice. (Lat. *pimenta dioica*.)

pin Abbreviation for *paina* (pint).

pī·naki *kik* Var. of *pīneki* (peanut). *Mān.*

pī·nalo·nalo *kik* Thrips, a kind of insect. Comb. *pī-* + *nalonalo*.

pina·pinao *kik* Damselfly (Megalagrion spp). Redup. of *pinao*.

pī·na'i *heh* To repeat, as the action of a computer key when held down. *Dic.*, ext. mng. See *kekimala*. *Māmā pīna'i*. Repeat rate. *Pihi pīna'i*. Turbo button, as in Nintendo games (preceded by *ke*).

pine *kik/ham* Clip; to clip together. *Ni'ihau*. *Pine pepa*. Paper clip.

pine hale·pe'a *kik* Tent stake. *Ni'ihau*.

pine kai·apa *kik* Safety pin. *Dic.*

pī·neki *kik* Peanut, groundnut. *Dic.*, sp. var. Any edible nut. *Ni'ihau*. Also *pīnaki, pineki*. *Mau'u pīneki*. Nutgrass.

pī·neki·paka *kik* Peanut butter. *Eng.*

pine lau·oho *kik* Hairclip, barrette. *Ni'ihau*.

pine maika *kik* Bowling pin.

pine 'elala *ham* Insect mounting; to mount insects. *Lit.*, pin insects.

pini·aka *kik* Piñata. *Sp.* Also *piniata*.

Pino·pino *i'oa* Filipino. *Ni'ihau*. Also *Pilipino*. *'Āina Pinopino*. Philippines.

pīpa *kik* Beep, as sound effect on computer. *Eng.*

pipi *kik* Pearl oyster. *Dic.* Cf. *kupekio*. *Pepa lole pipi*. Butcher paper. *'Aleku'u kau pipi*. Cattle egret.

pipi Kele·mā·nia *kik* Fresh corned beef (as opposed to canned). *Lit.*, German beef. Cf. *pipi kini*.

pipi kini *kik* Canned corned beef. *Lit.*, can beef. See *kini pipi, pipi Kelemānia*.

pipi·nola *kik* An edible variety of squash. *Dic.*

pipi 'Ā·lika *kik* Musk-ox. *Lit.*, Arctic ox.

pī·'ai *kik* Berry. *Dic.* See entries below.

pī·'ai ho'o·ilo *kik* Winterberry. Comb. *pī'ai* + *ho'oilo*.

pī·'ai kī *kik* Teaberry. Comb. *pī'ai* + Eng.

pī·'ai poku *kik* Pokeweed. Comb. *pī'ai* + Eng.

pī·'ai 'ele·peli *kik* Elderberry. Comb. *pī'ai* + Eng.

pī·'ā·pā *kik* Alphabet. *Dic.* *Ho'oka'ina pī'āpā*. To alphabetize, put in alphabetical order.

pi'i *'Ōnaehana mīkā pi'i*. High pressure system, in meteorology. Cf. *'ōnaehana mīkā emi*.

pi'i ka māmā holo *heh* To accelerate. *Lit.*, the running speed advances. Cf. *ho'opi'i i ka māmā holo, pi'i māmā holo*. See also *emi ka māmā holo, ho'ēmi i ka māmā holo*.

pi'i ki'e·ki'e loa *kik* Greatest increase, in math. *Lit.*, ascend (to the) highest. Cf. *emi ha'aha'a loa*.

pi'i·komo·ā·ea *kik* Evapotranspiration. Sh. *pi'ikū* + *omoāea*. See *pi'ikū*.

pi'i·kū *kik* Transpiration; to transpire. *Dic.* See *pi'ikomoāea*.

pi'i mā·mā holo *kik* Acceleration. *He aha ka 'oko'a ma waena o ka māmā me ka pi'i māmā holo?* What's the difference between speed and acceleration? *Lit.*, increase (of) progress. Cf. *pi'i ka māmā holo, emi māmā holo*.

pi'i·pi'i See *wai pi'ipi'i*.

pi'o *kik* Arc, in math. *Dic.* See *kaula hō'ike pi'o, kī pi'o, kīloi pi'o*.

pi'ū Abbreviation for *pihana'ū* (capacity).

pō·aka *kik* Crystal. Sh. *pōhaku* + *'oaka*.

poe lā *kik* Solar system. *Judd.*

poe·lele *kik* Satellite. *Lit.*, flying buoy. Also *ukali*. Cf. *hōkū ukali*.

poe·lele ho'o·kolo·hua wā loa *kik* Long Duration Exposure Facility (LDEF), a kind of experimentation satellite placed in orbit by a space shuttle. *Lit.*, long-time experiment satellite.

Poepe *i'oa* Phoebe, the most distant moon of Saturn. *Eng.*

poe·poe *kik* Sphere, globe. *Dic.* Cf. *poepoe hapa.* *Poepoe Honua.* Globe of Earth.

poe·poe hapa *kik* Hemisphere. *Lit.*, half sphere. See *poepoe. Poepoe hapa hema.* Southern hemisphere. *Poepoe hapa hikina.* Eastern hemisphere. *Poepoe hapa komohana.* Western hemisphere. *Poepoe hapa 'ākau.* Northern hemisphere.

poe·poe hapa hema *kik* Southern hemisphere.

poe·poe hapa hikina *kik* Eastern hemisphere.

poe·poe hapa komo·hana *kik* Western hemisphere.

Poila *i'oa* Boyle. *Eng. Ke kānāwai a Poila.* Boyle's law, i.e. decreasing the volume of a gas will increase the pressure the gas exerts if the temperature remains constant, in science.

pō·ulia *kik* Emergency. *Sh. pō'ino* + *ulia. Ke'ena mālama pōulia.* Emergency facility, emergency room.

pou moe *kik* Bedpost.

pou·namu *kik* Jade, jadeite. *Māori.*

pou 'au·makua 'Ili·kini *kik* Totem pole. *Lit.*, pole (of) Indian personal gods.

pohā *kik* Stop, in linguistics. *Dic.*, *ext. mng.*

pō·hā·one *kik* Sandstone. *Comb. pōhā + one.*

pō·hā·hā *kik* Volcanic ejecta. *Ua lele ka pōhāhā ma loko o ke kai.* The volcanic ejecta flew into the sea. *Dic. Pu'u pōhāhā.* Spatter cone.

pō·hahī *kik* Affricate, in linguistics. *Onomatopoeia.*

pō·haku See entries below. *Pa'a pōhaku.* Lithified. *Pōhaku pa'apuna.* Calcareous rock, calcium carbonate.

pō·haku ho'o·pa'a wai *kik* Caprock, in geology. *Lit.*, rock (which) plugs water.

pō·haku·kū·kahi *kik* Monolith. *Comb. pōhaku + kū + kahi.*

pō·haku makua *kik* Parent rock, i.e. rocks in upper surface of the earth which break down to form rocks, sand, dirt, etc.

pō·haku pele *Mo'o pōhaku pele.* Lava lizard.

pō·haku pele·maka *kik* Igneous rock, i.e. rock formed by the solidification of molten magma. *Lit.*, magma rock.

pō·haku puka ea *kik* Air stone, i.e. the porous rock in an aquarium that creates tiny bubbles at the surface of the water to facilitate the exchange of gases. *Lit.*, stone (from which) air emerges.

pō·haku 'alā *kik* Boulder, in Hawai'i, referring to poi pounder-size stones and larger. *Lit.*, *'alā* stone. Cf. *nukahaku.*

pō·heo *kik* Slang term for top of the key on a basketball court. *Usu. uma kī. Dic., ext. mng.* See entries below.

pō·heo *kik* Knob, handle (knob-style only). Also *pōheoheo. Dic.* Cf. *kākai, 'au.*

pō·heo puka *kik* Doorknob. Also *pōheoheo puka. Ni'ihau.*

pō·heo 'ume *kik* Drawer knob. Cf. *'au 'ume.*

pō·hili *kik* Baseball, the sport. *Sh. kinipōpō + hili. Kaimana pōhili.* Baseball diamond, infield. *Kahua pōhili.* Baseball field. *Kinipōpō pōhili.* Baseball, the ball. *Mikilima pōhili.* Baseball glove, mitt. *Pale pōhili.* Baseball inning. *Ku'ikahi Pōhili Aupuni.* National Baseball League. *Ku'ikahi Pōhili 'Amelika.* American Baseball League.

pō·hī·na'i *kik* Basketball, the sport. *Sh. kinipōpō + hīna'i. Kinipōpō pōhīna'i.* Basketball, the ball.

poho *kik* Chalk (preceded by *ke*). *Dic. Poho kala.* Colored chalk. *Ehu poho.* Chalk dust. *Paepae poho.* Chalk tray.

pohō *'a'* Vain attempt, "missed out." *kik.* Pond mud. *Dic. Lepo pohō.* Mud. *Niʻihau.* Cf. *ʻūkele.*

poho·alo *'a'* Forehand, i.e. with palms facing forward. Comb. *poho + alo.* Cf. *pohokua.* See *hukialewa, kīpehi.*

poho·kua *'a'* Backhand, i.e. with palms facing back. Comb. *poho + kua.* Cf. *pohoalo.* See *hukialewa, kīpehi.*

poho·kuiki·lani *kik* Music box. Lit., Switzerland container.

poho lā·ʻau pō·ulia *kik* First aid kit. Lit., emergency medical pouch. Also *kini lapaʻau.*

pohole *'a'* Easy to peel, as small corms of cooked taro. *Mān.*

poho lola *kik* Cassette case, usually made of plastic. Lit., container (for) cassettes. Cf. *pāiki lola.*

poho·luna *ham* To carry or palm (the ball), in basketball. *Ua puhi ka ʻuao i ka ʻūlili iā Ūlei no kāna poholuna ʻana i ke kinipōpō.* The official blew the whistle on Ūlei for palming the ball. Lit., (with) palm (facing) up.

poho mea·kanu *kik* Flower pot. *Dic.*

poho pauka niho *kik* Toothpaste tube. *Niʻihau.* See *pauka niho, pani.*

poho pā·kuʻi *kik* Additional sheet feeder, as for a computer printer. Lit., additional receptacle. Cf. *poho pepa.*

poho palaki niho *kik* Toothbrush container, usually made of plastic.

poho pepa *kik* Sheet feeder, paper tray or cassette, as for a computer printer. Lit., paper container. Cf. *poho pākuʻi.* See *pākuʻina, ʻapoʻo poho pepa.*

pohu *'a'* Calm, as the wind; smoke rises vertically, and direction of wind shown by smoke drift rather than wind vanes, in meteorology. *Dic.* See *makani.*

pohu *ham* To push. *Niʻihau.* Also *pahu.*

pohu *ham* To volley, i.e. keep the ball in play, in volleyball. *Niʻihau.* Also *paʻi manamana.* Cf. *lelekīkē.*

pohu·pani *ham* Displacement; also to displace. Comb. *pohu* (Niʻihau var. of *pahu* [push]) + *pani. Pohupani ea.* Air displacement. *Pohupani wai.* Water displacement.

poka·kaʻa *Hāmeʻa pokakaʻa.* Block and tackle, an arrangement of pulleys and rope or cable used to lift or haul.

pokala *kik* Potash, i.e. potassium carbonate or potassium insoluble compounds. Sh. *potasiuma + kalapona.*

poka maiʻa *kik* Banana poka.

pō·kaʻa lī·pine *kik* Reel for recording tape. Cf. *līpine pōkaʻa.* See *mīkini pōkaʻa leo.*

poke *ham* To remove, as an *ʻopihi* from its shell. *Dic.* Also *kuaʻi, poʻe.*

poke *kik* Period, as each set of three numerals, in math. *Dic., ext. mng.*

poke kaola *kik* Dowel. Lit., bar section.

poki·poki *kik* Sow bug. *Dic.*

poki·poki ā·lia *kik* Brine shrimp, artemia (genus). Lit., brackish *pokipoki.*

poko *kik* Cutworm. *Dic.* Also *ʻenuhe hele pō.*

pō·kole *Hānai pōkole.* To make a short set, in volleyball.

Poko·liko *iʻoa* Puerto Rico; Puerto Rican. *Dic.*

poku See *pīʻai poku.*

Poku·kala *iʻoa* Portugal. *Dic.* Also *Potugala.*

polai- Poly-, a prefix for chemical terms. *Eng. Polaiposapahate.* Polyphosphate.

polai·posa·pahate *kik* Polyphosphate. *Eng.*

pō·laka *kik* City block. *Trad.* Cf. *palaka.*

pola·lau·ahi *kik* Vog. *Dic., ext. mng.*

Pō·lani *iʻoa* Poland; Pole; Polish. *Dic.*

Pola·pola *ʻŌpae Polapola.* Tahitian prawn.

pole·wao *kik* Tadpole, polliwog. *Mān.* (HKM).

poli·ō *kik* Polio. *Eng.*

pō·liu *kik* Mystery, as stories or movies. *Dic., ext. mng. Nōwela pōliu.* Mystery novel.

poloka *kik* Frog. *Dic. Poloka kau lāʻau.* Tree frog. *Poloka kau lāʻau ʻālani.* Orange tree frog. *Poloka mimino.* Wrinkled frog. *Poloka pulu.* Bullfrog.

polo·kalamu *kik* Program, as on TV. *Eng. Poʻo inoa polokalamu* (preceded by *ke*). Program title, as for a TV program.

polo·kalamu *kik* Program, as for computer; application, as in computer program. *Eng.* See *pakuhi makaʻaha, polokalamu kikokiko palapala. Pā polokalamu.* Program disk. *Polokalamu hōkeo ʻikepili.* Database program. *Polokalamu kikokiko palapala.* Word processor.

polo·kalamu lewa lipo *kik* Space program.

polo·kina *kik* Protein. *Eng.* Also *kumuʻiʻo.*

polo·lei *kik* Precision, as in math. *Dic., ext. mng.* See *kaʻe pololei.*

polo·lei aʻe *ʻa*ʻ Across, as in a crossword puzzle.

polo·lia *kik* Jellyfish. *Dic.*

Polo·lika *iʻoa* Florida; Floridan, Floridian. *Dic.* Also *Folorida.*

polo·mine *kik* Bromine. *Eng. Kinoea polomine.* Bromine gas.

polo·polema *kik* Problem, as in math. *Eng.*

poma·lina *kik* Formalin. *Eng.*

pomelo *kik* Pomelo. *Eng.* See *iāpona. ʻĀlani pomelo.* Grapefruit.

pon Abbreviation for *paona* (pound).

pona *kik* Bond, a certificate bought from a government or corporation which agrees to pay back the cost of the bond plus interest after a set period of time. *Dic.*

pō·nalo *kik* Pomace fly, genus Drosophilidae. *Dic., ext. mng. Pōnalo huaʻai.* Fruit fly.

ponī *kik* Skunk. (Ute *poniyi.*)

poni·ʻala *kik* Lavender, both the flower and plant. *Lit.*, fragrant purple.

pono *kik* Equipment. *Dic.* See entries below. *Pono hana wikiō.* Video equipment.

pono haʻa·wina *kik* School supplies. *Lit.*, lesson supplies. *Pahu pono haʻawina.* School box.

pono kahua *kik* Props, as for a play, movie or video production. *Lit.*, stage accessories. See *kahua. Nā pono kahua e pono ai.* Props needed. *Luna pono kahua.* Prop master.

pono kanaka *Palapala pono kanaka.* Bill of rights.

pono koho *ʻaʻ* Random. *Lit.*, select any old way. *Hāpana pono koho.* Random sample.

pono lako *kik* Facility, i.e. something that is built, installed or established to serve a particular purpose. *Ua kūpono loa nā pono lako o kēia kulanui.* The facilities at this university are entirely adequate. *A pehea nā pono lako ma ka hale hoʻoikaika kino?* And how are the facilities at the fitness center? *Lit.*, well-equipped resources.

pō·nolu *ʻaʻ* Informal. *Dic., ext. mng.* Cf. *kūhelu.*

ponu *kik* Beetle. (PPN *fonu.*)

ponu·momi *kik* Ladybug. *Lit.*, jeweled beetle.

ponu ʻili *kik* Dermestid, larder beetle. *Lit.*, skin beetle.

pō·paʻi·paʻi *kik* Volleyball, the sport. Sh. *kinipōpō + paʻipaʻi. Hoʻokūkū pōpaʻipaʻi.* Volleyball tournament. *Kahua pōpaʻipaʻi.* Volleyball court. *Kinipōpō pōpaʻipaʻi.* Volleyball, the ball. *Kukuna pōpaʻipaʻi.* Volleyball antenna. *ʻUpena pōpaʻipaʻi.* Volleyball net.

pō·peku *kik* Football, the sport. Sh. *kinipōpō + peku. Kinipōpō pōpeku.* Football, the ball.

pō·pene *kik* Propane. *Eng.*

pō·pō ani·ani *kik* Glass ball, i.e. a Japanese fishing float.

pō·pō·ehu *Melehune pōpōehu.* Puffball, a kind of mushroom. *Lit.*, pollen ball mushroom.

Popoka *i'oa* Phobos, a moon of Mars. Eng.

pō·poki See *manu pōpoki*.

pō·pō kī·lepa·lepa *kik* Pompom. *Dic., ext. mng.* Also *kīlepalepa*.

pō·poki lō·hiu *kik* Wildcat. *Lit.*, naturally wild cat.

pō·pō laiki *kik* Rice ball, musubi. Also *musubī, pōpō lāisi*.

pō·pō pale mū *kik* Mothball. *Lit.*, ball (to) ward off moths.

pō·pō wehi lā·'au Kaliki·maka *kik* Christmas ball, the tree ornament.

pō·wā·wae *kik* Soccer. Sh. *kinipōpō + wāwae*. *Kinipōpō pōwāwae*. Soccer ball.

Pō·'ā *i'oa* Algol, a star. *Mān. (HA)*.

pō·'ai *kik* Circle, i.e. the geometric shape. *Dic.* Cf. *lina poepoe*. See *pakuhi pō'ai*.

pō·'ai *heh* To orbit. *Ala pō'ai*. Orbit. *Dic.*

pō·'ai·apili *kik* Context. Comb. *pō'ai + a + pili*.

pō·'ai·apuni *kik* Cycle. Comb. *pō'ai + a + puni*. See entry below and *ho'opō'aiapuni*. *Pō'aiapuni ola*. Life cycle.

pō·'ai·apuni kā·loa'a *kik* Business cycle, i.e. a repeated series of economic growth and recession. *Ma ke au o ka pō'aiapuni kāloa'a o kēia manawa, ke puka mai nei ke kūlana ho'okele wai-wai mai kōna wā nāwali*. According to the current business cycle, the economy is coming out of its weak period.

pō·'ai hapa·lua *kik* Semicircle. *Dic.*

pō·'ai lō·'ihi *kik* Oval. *Dic.* Also *'ololaha*. *Pō'ai lō'ihi analahi*. Ellipse.

pō·'ai waena *kik* Center circle, on basketball court.

pō·'ai waena honua *kik* Equator. *Dic.* Also *Kapikoowākea*. Cf. *pō'ai waena lani*.

pō·'ai waena lani *kik* Celestial equator. Sh. *pō'ai waena honua + lani*. Cf. *pō'ai waena honua*.

pō·'ai·wai·akai *'a'* Amphidromous, i.e. migrating from fresh to salt water, or from salt to fresh water, at some stage of the life cycle other than the breeding period. *He pō'aiwaiakai ka noho 'ana o ka 'o'opu nākea, no ka mea, hānau 'ia ia i'a ma uka o ke kahawai ma ke 'ano he piohē, a huki 'ia i kai, a ulu he pua, a laila, ho'i hou i uka o ke kahawai, a ulu he makua*. The life of the 'o'opu nākea fish is amphidromous since it is born upland in the stream as larvae and taken out to sea where it grows into its post-larvae stage of development, then returns upstream where it becomes an adult. Comb. *pō'ai + wai + a + kai*.

Po'a·ono *kik* Saturday. *Dic., sp. var.* Abb. *P6*.

Po'a·hā *kik* Thursday. *Dic., sp. var.* Abb. *P4*.

Po'a·kahi *kik* Monday. *Dic., sp.var.* Abb. *P1*.

Po'a·kolu *kik* Wednesday. *Dic., sp. var.* Abb. *P3*.

Po'a·lima *kik* Friday. *Dic., sp. var.* Abb. *P5*.

Po'a·lua *kik* Tuesday. *Dic., sp. var.* Abb. *P2*.

po'e *ham* To remove, as an *'opihi* from its shell. Var. of *poke*. Also *kua'i*.

po'i·i·'a *kik/ham* Predator; to prey; predatory. *He po'ii'a ka 'io i ka 'iole*. A hawk is a predator of mice. Comb. *po'i + i'a*. Cf. *luapo'i*.

po'ina nalu *kik* Where a wave breaks; surf break (preceded by *ka*). *Dic.*

po'i peni *kik* Pen cap (preceded by *ke*). Ni'ihau. Cf. *pani*.

po'o *kik* Heads, as in coin toss (preceded by *ke*). *Dic., ext. mng.* Also *'ao'ao po'o*. See *hi'u*. See also *hui po'o, pani po'o*.

po'o *kik* End of a sporting field or court (preceded by *ke*). *Dic., ext. mng.* Also *kumu*. Cf. *iwi*. *Laina po'o*. End line.

po'o *kik* Base of leaf, as *hala* (preceded by *ke*). *Dic.* Cf. *hi'u*.

poʻo inoa *kik* Title, as of a book or story, or at the beginning of a movie or video production (preceded by *ke*). *Lit.*, title heading. Also *inoa*. *Poʻo inoa polokalamu.* Program title, as for a TV program.

poʻo hou *kik* Paragraph symbol (¶), in proofreading (preceded by *ke*). *Dic.*

poʻo kili·lau *kik* Shower head (preceded by *ke*). See *kililau*.

poʻo kula·nui *kik* Chancellor, as of a college or university (preceded by *ke*). *Lit.*, college director. Cf. *luna kulanui, pelekikena*.

poʻo kuni *kik* Letterhead (preceded by *ke*). *E ʻoluʻolu e pane mai ma ka pepa poʻo kuni.* Please reply on letterhead paper. *Lit.*, stamped heading. *Lau poʻo kuni.* Letterhead design.

poʻo·manaʻo *kik* Heading or subheading, as in a story. *Dic.*

poʻo pā·ʻā·lua *kik* Header information, file prefix, as codes at the beginning of each computer file (preceded by *ke*). *Lit.*, code heading.

poʻo·poʻo *kik* Inside corner. *Niʻihau.* Also *kūʻono*. Cf. *kihi*.

poʻo·poʻo *kik* Station, as for a computer network. *Dic., ext. mng. Poʻopoʻo pūnaewele.* Network station.

poroto·zoa *kik* Protozoa. *Eng.*

posa·pahate *kik* Phosphate. *Eng.*

poso·porusa *kik* Phosphorus. *Eng.*

potasi·uma *kik* Potassium. *Eng. Potasiuma kaianaside.* Potassium cyanide. *Potasiuma ʻiodiside.* Potassium iodide.

Potu·gala *iʻoa* Portugal. *Dic.* Also *Pokukala*.

pū *kik* Horn. *Dic.* See entries below.

pū Abb. for *pūkele* (bushel).

pua *kik* Post-larvae. *Dic., ext. mng.*

pū·ai *ʻa* To be suspended, as particles which are mixed but not dissolved in a fluid, solid or gas. *Sh. pūailewa.* See *pūaina*.

pū·aina *kik* Suspension, i.e. a mixture in which the particles are mixed but not dissolved in a fluid, solid or gas. *Comb. pūai + -na.* Cf. *māʻōʻā*. See *pūai, pūaina lahi*.

pū·aina lahi *kik* Colloid, i.e. a chemical mixture with particle size between that of solutions and suspensions. *Lit.*, delicate suspension. See *māʻōʻāna, pūaina*.

pua·hō·lani *kik* Tulip. *Lit.*, Dutch flower.

pua huika *kik* Straw. *Lit.*, wheat flower.

pua kalaunu See *pulelehua pua kalaunu*.

pua Kaliki·maka *kik* Poinsettia. *Lit.*, Christmas flower.

pua kaʻū·mana *kik* Azalea. *Lit.*, Kaʻūmana flower, so named because many azalea grow there.

pua kepela *kik* Zebrina, a kind of flower. *Lit.*, zebra flower. Also *kepela*.

pua·lā·paki *kik* Snapdragon. *Lit.*, rabbit flower.

pua·leo *heh* Timbre, in music. *Lit.*, voice emergence.

puale kai *kik* Sea vent. Comb. *puale* (Māori: *puare* [open]) + *kai*.

pua·lono *kik* Accent, in speech. *Sh. puana + hoʻolono. Pualono ʻē.* Foreign accent.

pū·alu See *maka pūalu*.

pua manu *kik* Bird of paradise, the flower. *Lit.*, bird flower. Cf. *manu palekaiko*.

puana *kik* Pronunciation. *Dic.*

puana hua·leo *kik* Allophone, in linguistics. *Lit.*, pronunciation (of) phoneme. See *hualeo*.

puana·leo *ham* Phone, in linguistics. *Lit.*, pronounce sound.

puana mā·mala *ham* To phrase, as in speaking or reading orally. *No ka puana māmala maikaʻi ma ka ʻōlelo Hawaiʻi, pono e maha ka leo ma hope wale nō o kekahi poke.* For good phrasing in Hawaiian, one must pause only after a poke. *Lit.*, (sentence) fragment pronunciation. Cf. *kūkulu māmala*.

puana·ʻī *kik/ham* Quotation; to quote (someone or something). Comb. *puana + ʻī*. See *kaha puanaʻī*.

pua·palani *kik* Iris, fleur-de-lis. *Lit.*, French flower.

pua pepa *kik* Bougainvillea. *Niʻihau*. Also *pukanawila*.

pua·puaʻi lā *kik* Solar prominences, i.e. puffs of gas which gently drift above the surface of the sun. *Lit.*, solar boiling. Cf. *kiko lā, lapa ahi lā, ʻale ahi lā*.

pua wī·kō·lia *kik* Rhododendron. *Lit.*, Victoria flower, named for the Victoria Gardens in Canada.

pua woela *kik* Vowel quality, in linguistics. *Lit.*, speak vowel. See *hoʻēmi woela* and entries under *woela*.

puaʻi manaʻo *heh* To brainstorm. *Lit.*, utter ideas.

puaʻi·wai *kik* Drinking fountain. *Dic.* Cf. *pūnāpuaʻi*.

pua ʻō·ʻili hau *kik* Crocus. *Lit.*, flower (that) appears (in) snow.

pueo kiwi hulu *kik* Great horned owl. *Lit.*, owl (with) feather horns.

pueo peke *kik* Elf owl.

puolo *kik* Music. Comb. *pū + olo*; also Māori *puoro. Kūkulu puolo.* Music arranger; to arrange music. *Mea puolo.* Musician (general term).

pū·hā·hā *heh* To spout, as a whale. *Dic., ext. def.*

Pū·hā·honu *iʻoa* Gardner Pinnacles. *Lit.*, surfacing of turtle for air.

pū·haʻu·haʻu See *palaoa pūhaʻu-haʻu*.

pū hele·uī *kik* Jack-o'-lantern. Also *palaʻai heleuī*. *Lit.* Halloween pumpkin.

puhi *ham* To fire, as clay or ceramics. *Dic., ext. mng.* See *maka puhi*.

puhi a piha *ham* To inflate, fill with air. *Niʻihau*. Also *hoʻopūhalalū*. See *ʻananuʻu*.

puhi·paka *Hōkū puhipaka.* Comet.

puhi wā·wahie See *uila puhi wāwahie*.

pū·hō·mona *kik* Steroid. *Hiki ke ʻike ʻia he mau hopena ʻano ʻē o ke kino ke hoʻohana ʻia ka pūhōmona me ka naʻaupō.* Some strange physical effects can result from taking steroids ignorantly. Sh. *pūhui + hōmona*.

pū hoʻo·kani *kik* Horn, i.e. a musical instrument.

pū·hui *kik* Compound, as in chemistry. Comb. *pū + hui.* See *kumumea, meakino, ʻakano. Pūhui kumumea lua.* Binary compound. *Pūhui naikokene kaʻawale.* Free nitrogen compound. *ʻAkika pūhui kalapona.* Carboxylic acid.

pū·hulu·hulu *ʻElepani pūhuluhulu.* Woolly mammoth. *Sila pūhuluhulu.* Fur seal.

pū·huna *kik* Crumb, i.e. clumps of mineral particles mixed into soil. Sh. *pū + pahunga* (Māori, crumb). See *māʻelenono*.

puk Abbreviation for *puna kī* (teaspoon).

puka *Helu puka.* Quotient. *Mea puka.* Winner, as in the consolation bracket of a sports tournament.

puka·ani·ani hoʻo·pono·pono *kik* Edit screen, in computer program. *Lit.*, edit window.

puka·ani·ani kolamu ʻike·pili *kik* List editor screen, in computer program. *Lit.*, data column window.

puka·ani·ani ʻō·lepe *kik* Jalousie. *Lit.*, blinds-style window. Also *puka-aniani ʻōlepelepe*.

puka ea *kik* Air vent. See *pōhaku puka ea*.

puka uai *kik* Sliding door. Also *ʻīpuka uai*.

puka uahi *kik* Chimney. *Dic.*

puka uila *kik* Electrical outlet. See *palaka.*

pū·kaha *kik* Defensive end, in football. Comb. *pū-* + *kaha.* *Pūkaha hema.* Left defensive end. *Pūkaha ʻākau.* Right defensive end.

puka·hanu *kik* Stomata. Comb. *puka* + *hanu.*

puka kahiko *kik* Anus, i.e. the posterior opening of the alimentary canal. *Dic.* Also *puka ʻamo.*

puka kani *kik* Sound hole, as on an ʻukulele or guitar.

puka·kī *kik* Key or keyhole, on basketball court. *Ua komo ke kī ʻana a ʻĀlapa mai ka uma mai o ka pukakī.* ʻĀlapa made the shot from the top of the key. *Lit.,* key hole. See *uma kī.*

puka kikī hou *kik* Sweat duct. *Lit.,* hole (through which) sweat flows.

pū kako·pone *kik* Saxophone. Comb. *pū* + Eng. Also *kakopone.*

puka lā *heh* To come out daily, as a newspaper.

puka ma kekahi ʻaoʻao (o) Through. *Ua kī ʻia kona lima a puka aku ma kekahi ʻaoʻao.* He was shot through the hand. *Lit.,* emerge on another side (of).

pukana·wila *kik* Bougainvillea. *Dic.* Also *pua pepa.*

puka·neʻe *heh* To emigrate. Comb. *puka* + *neʻe.* Cf. *komoneʻe.*

puka niho *kik* Cavity in a tooth, caries. *Dic.* Cf. *haka waha.*

puka·pakī *kik* Pore. *Dic.*

puka pihi *kik* Buttonhole. *Dic.*

puka·puka See *kapuahi pukapuka.*

puka ʻamo *kik* Anus, i.e. the posterior opening of the alimentary canal. *Mān.* Also *puka kahiko.* See *mākala ʻamo.*

pū·kaʻina *kik* Series. Comb. *pū* + *kaʻina.* See *ala pūkaʻina, ʻalakaine, ʻalakane, ʻalakene.* *Pūkaʻina hū pele.* Series of volcanic eruptions. *Pūkaʻina polokalamu kīwī.* TV series.

puke ala·kaʻi *kik* Teacher's guide, manual. *Lit.,* guiding book.

puke aʻo ana·lula *kik* Pattern book, as for teaching grammatical patterns in reading. *Lit.,* book (for) teaching patterns.

puke aʻo hou *kik* Reteaching book.

puke haʻa·wina *kik* Textbook. *Lit.,* lesson book.

puke helu·helu *kik* Reader, story book. *Lit.,* book (for) reading.

puke hoʻo·haliʻa maka·hiki *kik* Yearbook, annual. *Lit.,* book (to) evoke year's reminiscence.

puke hoʻo·make·ʻaka *kik* Humorous book, in literature. *Lit.,* amusing book.

puke hoʻo·maʻa·maʻa haʻa·wina *kik* Workbook, practice book. Usu. *puke hoʻomaʻamaʻa.* *Lit.,* book (for) practicing lessons.

puke hoʻo·nui ʻike *kik* Enrichment book, challenge book. *Lit.,* book (for) increasing knowledge.

puke huna·huna *kik* Scrapbook, as in computer program.

puke kā·koʻo *kik* Supplementary text or book; any book which supplements a primary text. *Lit.,* supporting book.

puke kumu·hana *kik* Information book. *Ua hele wau i ka hale waihona puke no ke kāinoa ʻana i kekahi mau puke kumuhana e pili ana i ke kai.* I went to the library to check out some information books about the sea. *Lit.,* book (on a) topic.

pū·kele *kik* Bushel, a unit of measurement. *Dic.* Abb. *pū.*

pū kele·awe *kik* Any brass instrument. *Lit.,* brass horn.

puke lina kui *kik* Ring binder. *Lit.,* ring book. Cf. *kālana kākau.*

puke mā·kau noʻo·noʻo *kik* Building thinking skills book. *Lit.,* book (for) thinking skills.

puke manaʻo lau·like *kik* Thesaurus. *Lit.,* book (of words with) similar meanings. See *manaʻo laulike, papa manaʻo laulike.*

puke moʻo·manaʻo *kik* Journal, diary. *Lit.,* book (of) series of thoughts.

puke noiʻi *kik* Reference or resource book, as an encyclopedia. *Lit.,* book (for) research. Cf. *kūmole*. *Puke noiʻi kūʻikena.* Encyclopedia.
puke noiʻi kū·ʻikena *kik* Encyclopedia. *Lit.,* fact reference book.
puke pane koho·koho *kik* Multiple-choice book.
puke ʻale·manaka *kik* Almanac. *Lit.,* almanac book. Cf. *ʻalemanaka puke.*
pū koa *kik* Bugle. *Lit.,* soldier horn. See *pū pihi.*
pū·kolo *kik* Team of draft animals. *Dic.*
pū·kowi *kik* Birch. *Czech.*
pula·pula *kik* Cutting, as of a plant. *Dic.*
pule *kik* Week. *Dic.* Abb. *pl.*
pule·lehua Kameha·meha *kik* Kamehameha butterfly.
pule·lehua pua kalauna *kik* Monarch butterfly. *Lit.,* crown flower butterfly.
pū·lima *kik/ham* Signature; to sign one's name. *Dic., ext. mng.* See *hua inoa.* *Pūlima hua.* To initial.
pulu *Poloka pulu.* Bullfrog.
puluka *kik* Flute. *Dic.* Also *ʻohekani puluka.*
Pulu·kalia *iʻoa* Bulgaria; Bulgarian. *Dic.* Also *Bulugaria.*
pulu kui *kik* Pin cushion. *Dic.*
pulu·pulu *kik* Cotton. *Dic. Lāʻau pulupulu.* Cotton swab, Q-tip. *Pulupulu uea.* Steel wool, wire gauze.
puna *kik* Cast, as for a broken arm. *Dic., ext. mng.* Also *kimeki iwi.*
pū·nae·wele *kik* Network. Comb./sh. *pūnāwelewele + nae.* See entry below. *ʻŌnaehana pūnaewele.* Network system.
pū·nae·wele mea·ʻai *kik* Food web. *Lit.,* Food network. Cf. *kuʻina meaʻai.*
pū·nao *kik* Metabolism. (Māori *pūngao.*) *Lōkuʻu hoʻokonukonu pūnao.* Thyroid gland.

puna·helu *kik* Mold. *Dic., ext. mng.*
puna kī *kik* Teaspoon, a unit of measurement (preceded by *ke*). Abb. *puk.*
puna kī·ʻo·e *kik* Ladle (preceded by *ke*). *Lit.,* ladle spoon. Also *puna ukuhi.*
pū·nana *kik* Nest. *Dic.* See *hoʻopūnana.*
puna pā·kau·kau *kik* Tablespoon, a unit of measurement (preceded by *ke*). Abb. *pup.*
puna Pā·lisa *kik* Plaster of Paris. *Lit.,* Paris plaster.
pū·nā·pua·ʻi *kik* Fountain, as for decoration. Sh. *pūnāwai + puaʻi.* Cf. *puaʻiwai.*
pū·nā·wai ʻau·ʻau *kik* Swimming pool. *Lit.,* spring (for) swimming.
puni *kik* Lap, complete circuit, revolution. *Ua ʻau ʻo ia ʻekolu puni o ka pūnāwai ʻauʻau.* He swam three laps in the pool. *Ua puni ʻekolu manawa iā ia.* He did three laps. *Trad.* Round, as in boxing. *Dic., ext. mng.* Hand, as a single round in a game of cards. *Dic., ext. mng. Puni o ka minuke (p/min).* Revolutions per minute (rpm).
puni ao kū·lohe·lohe *kik* Naturalist. *Lit.,* fond (of) nature. Also *kanaka puni ao kūlohelohe.*
pū·niu See *ʻukulele pūniu.*
puni uila *kik* Electric circuit. *ʻUʻoki puni uila.* Circuit breaker, i.e. a device which automatically interrupts electric current before wires in a circuit get too hot.
pū·nuku ea make *kik* Gas mask, as used during World War II. *Ua komo ka poʻe kinai ahi i kō lākou pūnuku ea make ma mua o ke komo ʻana i loko o ka hale e ʻā ana i ke ahi me ka puapua nui o ka uahi.* The firemen put on their gas masks before entering the burning house with all the smoke that was spewing out of it. *Trad.*
pup Abbreviation for *puna pākaukau* (tablespoon).

pupa *kik* Pupa; pupal. *Eng.* See *moeapupa.*

pupē *kik* Puffin. *Eng.* Also *manu pupē.*

pū pihi *kik* Trumpet. *Lit.*, horn (with) buttons. See *pū koa. Pū pihi poko.* Cornet.

pupū *'a* To be hung, as network system in computer program. *Ke pupū maila ka 'ōnaehana pūnaewele.* The network system is hung. *Dic., ext. mng.*

pū puhi uai *kik* Trombone. *Lit.*, sliding horn.

pū puhi Palani *kik* French horn.

pū·'ali ho'o·uka kaua *kik* Marine corps. *Lit.*, army (for) attacking.

pū·'ali kaua lewa *kik* Air force. *Lit.*, sky war army.

pū·'ali kaua moana *kik* Navy. *Lit.*, ocean war army. Also *'au moku kaua, 'oihana moku. Kahua pū'ali kaua moana.* Navy base.

pū·'ali kia'i mō·'ī *kik* King's guard. *Lit.*, soldiers (for) guarding kings.

pū·'ali koa *kik* Army; military service. *Mān. Kahua pū'ali koa.* Military base.

pū·'ali koa kū·ika·wā *kik* Militia. *Trad.*

pū·'ali nō·iki *kik* Alveolar duct, in anatomy. *Lit.*, alveolus isthmus.

pū·'ali pale kapa kai *kik* Coast guard. *Lit.*, coast guard army.

pū·'olo *kik* Bag; twelve-pack, as of drinks. *Ni'ihau.* Cf. *'ope.* See entries below and *pahu, 'eke, 'eke'eke. Pū'olo koloaka.* Twelve-pack of soda. *Pū'olo pia.* Twelve-pack of beer.

pū·'olo koho·koho *kik* Guessing bag.

pū·'olo pepa *kik* Paper bag. Cf. *'eke 'ea.*

pū·'o'a uahi *kik* Smokestack, as for a factory. *Lit.*, smoke tower.

pū 'o'ohe *kik* Any woodwind instrument. Comb. *pū* + redup. of *'ohe.*

pu'u *kik* Throat. *Dic.* See entries below.

pu'u *kik* Cone, a geological feature. *Dic. Pu'u ahupapa.* Composite cone. *Pu'u hakuhune.* Tuff cone. *Pu'u kuahene.* Shield cone. *Pu'u lehu.* Ash cone. *Pu'u 'ākeke.* Cinder cone.

pū·'uo *kik* Population, as in biology. Sh. *pū'ulu + 'uo. Ili pū'uo.* Population distribution, in geography. Also *ili pū'uo kanaka. Pa'apū pū'uo kanaka.* Population density, for humans only.

pū·'uo·'uo *kik/'a* Cohesion; cohesive. Comb. *pū + 'uo'uo.* Cf. *pīlekaleka.*

pu'u ha'a·pupū *kik* Speed bump, as on a road or in a parking lot. *Lit.*, bump (for) holding back.

pu'u·kani *kik* Singer. *Dic.*

pū·'ulu *kik* Group. *Dic.* See *ho'opū-'ulu, kūkā ma ka pū'ulu. Pū'ulu mea'ai.* Food group, i.e. one of the six food groups. *Pae pū'ulu mea'ai.* The food groups, i.e. the collective union of all six food groups (calcium/milk, vegetable, fruit, starch, meat and fat).

pu'u·naue *ham* Division; to divide, in math. *Dic.* See entries below. *Kaha pu'unaue.* Division sign. *Kumu pu'unaue.* Dividend.

pu'u·naue koena 'ole *ham* Divisible, in math. *Lit.*, division without remainder.

pu'u·naue lua *ham* Composite, in math. *Lit.*, double division. *Helu pu'unaue lua.* Composite number.

pu'u ne'ena hau *kik* Moraine. *Lit.*, hill (caused by) movement (of) ice.

pu'u pele *kik* Volcanic cone, in geology.

pu'u pō·hā·hā *kik* Spatter cone, in geology. *Lit.*, ejecta cone.

pu'u·pu'u *kik* Nodule, as on a leguminous plant. *Dic., ext. mng.* See entries below.

pu'u·pu'u *Hānai pu'upu'u.* To serve underhand, in volleyball. *Ku'i pu'upu'u.* To spike with closed fist.

pu'u·pu'u moa *kik* Chicken pox. *Ni'ihau.*

puʻu·wai pana ʻewa·ʻewa *kik* Cardiac arrythmia. *Lit.*, heart (with) irregular beat. See *hoʻoikaika puʻuwai, koʻe puʻuwai*.

Puruma *iʻoa* Burma; Burmese. *Eng.* Also *Buruma*.

pū·tē *heh* To scowl. *Ua pūtē maila ʻo Pāpā iaʻu i hoʻi lohi mai ai i ka hale.* Daddy scowled at me when I came home late. *Niʻihau.* Cf. *hoʻokuʻemaka*.

ph Abbreviation for *pāhaneli* (hecto-).

Ph Abbreviation for *Palanaheika* (Fahrenheit).

phk Abbreviation for *pihanahaka* (volume).

pk Abbreviation for *pākaukani* (kilo-).

PK Abbreviation for *ʻai pākaukani* (kilobyte).

pkl Abbreviation for *pākiliona* (tera-).

pl Abbreviation for *pule* (week).

PLH Abbreviation for *Papa Lawelawe Hoʻolaha* (Bulletin Board Service).

pll Abbreviation for *palela* (barrel).

pm Abbreviation for *pāmiliona* (mega-).

p.m. Post meridium, p.m. (pronounced *pīmū*). *Eng.* See *a.m.*

PM Abbreviation for *ʻai pāmiliona* (megabyte).

p/min Abbreviation for *puni o ka minuke* (revolutions per minute).

pp Abbreviation for *pāpiliona* (giga-).

PP Abbreviation for *ʻai pāpiliona* (gigabyte).

P·ĀH Abbreviation for *palena ʻāluna o ka hewa* (greatest possible error).

pʻm Abbreviation for *pāʻumi* (deka-).

W

wā *kik* Fret, as on an ʻukulele, guitar, etc. *Dic.* See *ʻukulele*.

wā *kik* Interval, i.e. the number of units between spaces on a graph's scale, in math. *Dic., ext. mng.*

wae·leʻa *ham* To distinguish. Comb. *wae + leʻa* (clearly, thoroughly).

wae moho *ham* Primary, primary election, i.e. a preliminary election to nominate candidates for office. *Ma ka wae moho, e koho kekahi ʻaoʻao kālaiʻāina i ka mea a lākou e kākoʻo ai i ka holo moho ʻana no kekahi kūlana koʻikoʻi o ke aupuni.* In the primary election, a political party chooses the person they will support in running for election for an important government position. Also *koho pāloka wae moho*. *Wae moho kūākea.* Open primary. *Wae moho kūloko.* Closed primary.

waena *Manamana waena.* Middle finger. *Niʻihau.* Also *manamana loa*.

waena alelo *kik* Central portion of tongue. *Lit.*, tongue center. See *kūʻau alelo, lau alelo, mole alelo, wēlau alelo*.

waena honua *Pōʻai waena honua.* Equator. Also *Kapikoowākea*.

waena moana Asea, at sea; midocean. *Aia nā moku a pau ōna i waena moana.* All his ships are at sea. *Trad. Kualapa waena moana.* Midocean ridge.

wae·waele *ham* To thin, as plants when gardening. Comb. *wae + waele*.

wae·ʻano *ham* To classify, categorize. *Lit.*, sort (by) types.

wae ʻano See *pēmāʻōʻā wae ʻano*.

wai *kik* Water. *Dic.* See entries below and *ana kaumaha wai, pena kuapapa wai, pena wai. Nele wai.* Anhydrous, i.e. without water. Cf. *ʻanahaidaraside*. *Papa kānāwai wai o ka mokuʻāina.* State water code. *ʻĀina kumu wai.* Watershed, i.e. an area from which water drains.

wai·apuni *kik* Hydrosphere. Comb. *wai + a + puni*.

wai·ehu *kik* File, the tool. *Dic.* Cf. *apuapu. Waiehu makaliʻi.* Fine-cut file.

waio·leka niho·ʻī·lio *kik* Dog's tooth violet, a kind of flower. Comb. Eng. *+ niho + ʻīlio*.

wai·olina *kik* Violin, fiddle. *Dic.*

Waio·mina *iʻoa* Wyoming; Wyomingite. *Dic.*

wai·ū *kik* Milk. *Dic.* See entries below and *pahu waiū, ʻōmole omo waiū.*

wai ua *kik* Rain water.

wai·ū ehu *kik* Powdered milk. *Niʻihau.* Also *waiū pauka.*

wai·ū·haku·haku *kik* Cottage cheese. *Dic.*

wai·ū heʻe *kik* Skim milk. See *heʻe.*

wai·ū luli·luli *kik* Milk shake. *Dic.*

wai·ū pauka *kik* Powdered milk. Also *waiū ehu.*

wai·ū·paʻa *kik* Cheese. *Dic. Waiūpaʻa keka.* Cheddar cheese. *Waiūpaʻa Kuikilani.* Swiss cheese.

wai·ū piha *kik* Whole milk. *Lit.,* complete milk.

wai·ū·tepe *kik* Yogurt. Comb. *waiū* + *tepe* (Māori, congealed).

wai hā·lana *kik* Flood. *Dic. Kāohi wai hālana.* Flood control. *Kūkala makaʻala wai hālana.* Flood watch. *Kūkala pōʻino wai hālana.* Flood warning.

wai hā·loʻa·loʻa *kik* Rapids, as in a river. *Lit.,* turbulent water.

waiho *ham* To file, as files in a file cabinet. *Dic., ext. mng.* Also *hoʻokomo.* See entries below.

waiho *ham* To leave as is, no change, as in computer program. *Dic., ext. mng. Kaha waiho.* A series of dots written under a word or words which have been lined out to show that no change should be made from the original, in proofreading; stet.

waiho *kik* Spread, as data on a graph, in math. *Dic., ext. mng. Ka waiho o ka ʻikepili.* Data spread.

wai·hona *kik* File, as in computer program. *Dic., ext. mng.* Cf. *wahī.* See *papa kuhi waihona, poʻo pāʻālua. Hulu waihona.* File format. *Loulou wai-hona.* File link. *Peleleu waihona.* File extension. *Waihona mahola.* Expanded file. *Waihona papaʻa.* Backup file.

wai·hona *kik* Account, as in a bank. *Lit.,* money repository. *Waihona kālā.* Bank account. *Waihona hoʻāhu kālā.* Savings account. *Waihona hoʻolilo.* Expense account. *Waihona kīkoʻo.* Checking account. *Waihona kāki.* Charge account, credit account.

wai·hona hoʻāhu *kik* Storage cabinet. Cf. *lumi hoʻāhu.*

wai·hona lā·ʻau lapa·ʻau *kik* Medicine cabinet. *Lit.,* cabinet (for) medicine.

wai·hona mea pā·ʻani *kik* Toy chest, toy box. Also *pahu mea pāʻani.*

wai·hona pāiki *kik* Locker. *Lit.,* satchel cabinet. Also *pahu laka.*

wai·hona pepa See *pahu waihona pepa.*

wai·hona wai·wai See *pahu waihona waiwai.*

wai·hona ʻike *kik* Memory, as in a computer program. *ʻEhia ka nui o ka waihona ʻike kaʻawale o kēia kamepiula?* How much available memory is there on this computer? *Lit.,* knowledge repository. *Waihona ʻike paʻaloko.* Built-in memory. *Waihona ʻike keu.* Extended memory. *Waihona ʻike māhuahua.* Expanded memory.

wai honua *kik* Groundwater. *Lit.,* earth water.

wai·hoʻo·luʻu hui kea *kik* Additive color, i.e. one of the primary colors (red, blue, green) which, when added together, produce white light. *Lit.,* color (which) combines white.

wai kai *kik* Salty water. *Dic.* See *wai paʻakai paʻapūhia. Hoʻomānalo wai kai.* To desalinate / desalinize salty water.

wai kahe See *uila wai kahe.*

wai kō·ī *kik* Cataract, i.e. steep rapids in a large river. *Lit.,* water flowing with force.

wai koko *kik* Plasma. *Lit.,* blood fluid. Also *palasema.*

wai kō·ʻie·ʻie *kik* Run, as in a stream. *Lit.,* rushing water.

wai·lele *Ki'o wai wailele.* Plunge pool, i.e. the pool at the base of a waterfall.

wai·lelele *kik* Cascade. Redup. of *wailele.*

wai lemi *kik* Lemonade. *Dic.*

wai·nola *kik* Vinyl. *Eng.*

wai paipu *kik* Tap water. *Lit.,* pipe water. *Wai wela paipu.* Hot tap water.

wai pa'a·kai pa'a·pū·hia *kik* Brine, a concentrated solution of salt or ocean water. *Lit.,* concentrated salt water. Also *wai pa'akai.* See *ho'omānalo wai kai.*

wai·pele·kī *kik* Geyser. Comb. *wai + pele + kī.*

wai pi'i·pi'i *kik* Mineral or sparkling water. *Dic., ext. mng.*

wai pua *kik* Nectar, i.e. sweet liquid secreted by nectaries of a plant. *Lit.,* flower liquid.

wai·wai *kik* Value. *Ua like ka waiwai o kēia 'ōkeni me ka 'elima kēneka.* The value of this coin is five cents. *Dic. Wai- wai kū'ai.* Market value. See *hokona, ho'omohala waiwai, kālaiho'okele waiwai. Mo'okūlana waiwai.* Balance sheet, i.e. a listing of assets, liabilities and owner's equity. *Waiwai kū'ike.* Face value. *Waiwai wānana.* Expected value. *Waiwai 'i'o.* Absolute value. *Waiwai*

wai wili·au *kik* Side pool, as in a stream. *Lit.,* pool (that) moves in eddies.

wai 'ili honua *kik* Surface water. *Lit.,* earth surface water. Also *wai 'ili.*

wai 'ula *Pani wai 'ula.* Tampon (preceded by *ke*).

wai 'ume·lau·oho *kik* Capillary water.

wao kua·hiwi *kik* Montane area. *Lit.,* mountain region. See *wao kumu kuahiwi. Wao kuahiwi ha'aha'a.* Lower montane area. *Wao kuahiwi ki'eki'e.* Upper montane area.

wao kumu kua·hiwi *kik* Vegetation area at base of mountain. *Lit.,* region (at) base (of) mountain. See *wao kuahiwi.*

wao la'a·lā·'au *kik* Alpine shrubland. *Lit.,* shrub region.

waha wali *kik* Smooth talk, smooth talker; to talk smooth; glib. *Ma muli o ka maika'i loa o kō kēlā kanaka kū'ai ka'a ma ka waha wali, nui ka po'e kū'ai ka'a maiā ia mai.* Because that car salesman is such a smooth talker, many people buy cars from him. *Ni'ihau.*

wahi *kik* Region, a specific area, in math. *Dic., ext. mng.*

wahī *kik* Folder, as in computer program. *Pono e hana kope 'ia kēlā waihona ma ka wahī 'ōnaehana.* That file needs to be copied to the system folder. *Dic., ext. mng.* Cf. *waihona.* See entries below. *Wahī o waho.* External folder.

wā·hia *'a'* Decomposed, i.e. broken down into component parts as through chemical reaction. *Dic., ext. mng.* Cf. *hāpopopo.*

wahī o waho *kik* External folder, in computer program. *Lit.,* outside folder.

wahi ho'o·malu *kik* Shelter. *Dic.*

wahine *Ho'okae wahine.* Misogyny, hatred of women. See *ho'okae.*

wahi noho *kik* Residence. *Dic.* Also *hale noho.*

wahī 'ano·'ano *kik* Seed pod. *Lit.,* seed case.

wahī 'ea *kik* Any plastic film for wrapping food, as Saran Wrap. *Lit.,* plastic wrapper.

wahī·'eha *kik* Band aid. *Dic., ext. mng.*

waho loa *Hōkūhele o waho loa.* Outer planet.

wā ho'o·hana *kik* Session, i.e. a period of time spent in an application of a computer program. *Lit.,* using time.

Wā·kea See *Ho'ohokuikalani.*

wā·kiuma *kik/ham* Vacuum; to vacuum. *Dic.*

Wakine·kona *i'oa* Washington; Washingtonian. *Dic.*

wale 'ili *kik* Cambium, i.e. the slippery layer under the bark of a plant which is the growing area of the stem. *Lit.,* bark slime.

wali *Waha wali.* Smooth talk, smooth talker; to talk smooth; glib.

walu *ham* To scratch with claws, as a cat. *Dic.* Cf. *waʻu.*

wā·nana *kik/ham* Prediction; to predict, as in a scientific experiment. *Dic., ext. mng.* See *waiwai wānana.*

wana·ʻā *kik* Laser. Comb. *wana* + *ʻā. Kukuna wanaʻā.* Laser beam.

waniki *kik* Lacquer. *Dic., ext. mng.*

wani·lina *kik* Vanilin, a crystalline solid used chiefly as a flavoring agent and in perfumery. *Eng.*

wā pā·ʻani *kik* Recess, as during school. *Lit.,* time (for) playing.

wā·wae *kik* Leg. *Dic. Wāwae noho.* Chair leg. *Wāwae pākaukau.* Table leg.

wā·wae *kik* Ray, as in geometry. *Legendre.* Also *ʻaoʻao.*

wā·wae·ʻala·lā *kik* Crow's feet, a kind of plant. Comb. *wāwae* + *ʻalalā.*

wā·wae·ʻami *kik* Arthropod. *Lit.,* jointed legs.

wā·wahi *ham* To break, change, as a twenty dollar bill. *Dic.*

wā·wahi *ham* To break apart, i.e. breaking a number into addends or factors, in math. *Dic., ext. mng.*

wā·wahie *kik* Fuel. Redup. of *wahie* / trad. See *uila puhi wāwahie. Wāwahie mōʻalihaku, wāwahie wīhaku.* Fossil fuel.

waʻa kai·aka *kik* Kayak. Comb. *waʻa* + Eng.

waʻa ʻIli·kini *kik* Canoe without ʻiako. *Lit.,* Indian canoe.

waʻu *ham* To scratch, as an itch. *Dic.* Also *waʻuwaʻu.* Cf. *walu.*

wā ʻukē *kik* Period of a pendulum. *Lit.,* time (of) pendulum swing.

wehe *ham* To open, remove. *Dic. Mea wehe kini.* Can opener. *Mea wehe ʻūmiʻi.* Staple remover.

wehe *ham* To open, as a file in computer program. *Dic., ext. mng.* See *pani. Wehe i ke kī wai.* To turn on the water. *Niʻihau.*

wehena papa·hana *kik* Opening ceremonies. *Lit.,* program opening.

wehe·wehe See *papa wehewehe ʻōlelo. Leka wehewehe.* Cover letter.

wehi *kik* Ornament. *Dic. Wehi lāʻau Kalikimaka.* Christmas tree ornament. *Pōpō wehi lāʻau Kalikimaka.* Christmas ball, the tree ornament.

weke·lia *kik* Wedelia, a ground cover. *Eng.*

wela *ʻaʻ* Temperature, when weather considered hot. *ʻEhia ka wela o kēia lā?* What's the temperature today? *Lit.,* hot. Cf. *anu, mahana, mehana.* See *kēkelē, wela lōpū.*

wē·lau *kik* Pole. *Dic. Wēlau ʻākau.* North pole. *Wēlau hema.* South pole.

wē·lau alelo *kik* Tip of tongue. *Lit.,* tongue tip. See *kūʻau alelo, lau alelo, mole alelo, waena alelo.*

wela lōpū *ʻaʻ* Medium heat.

wele *kik* Rarefaction, i.e. the least dense concentration of wave particles in a compressional wave. Sh. *wāele.* Cf. *ulu.* See *hawewe papamoe.*

Wele·moneka *iʻoa* Vermont; Vermonter. *Dic.* Also *Veremona, Veremoneta.*

weli *kik* Scion. *Dic.*

welo *kik* Hereditary trait. *Dic., ext. mng.* Cf. *ōewe.* See *kumu welo.*

welo·welo *Hōkū welowelo.* Shooting star.

welu ʻeha *kik* Gauze. *Lit.,* injury rag. Also *welu wahīʻeha* (Niʻihau), *ʻaʻamoʻo (dic.).*

Wene See *kiʻikuhi Wene.*

Wenuke *iʻoa* Venus, the name. *Eng.* Also *Wenuse.*

Wieka·nama *iʻoa* Vietnam; Vietnamese. *Eng.*

wī·haku *kik* Fossil. Sh. *iwi* + *pōhaku.* Also *mōʻalihaku.*

wika·mina *kik* Vitamin. *Eng.* Also *witamina.*

wiki See *pihi wiki.*

wiki·ō *kik* Video. *Eng. Lola wikiō.* Video cassette. *Pahu paʻi wikiō.* Camcorder, video camera.

wiki·ola *kik* Vitriol. *Eng.* Also *witiola.*

Wī·kini *kik* Viking. *Eng.*

wī·kō·lia *Pua wīkōlia.* Rhododendron.

Wikone·kina *iʻoa* Wisconsin; Wisconsinite. *Dic.* Also *Wikonesina.*

Wikone·sina *iʻoa* Wisconsin; Wisconsinite. *Dic.* Also *Wikonekina.*

wili *ham* To dial, as a telephone; to twirl, as a baton. *Dic.; dic., ext. mng.* See *pā wili, wili i hope, wili i mua, ʻaukaʻi wili.*

wili *ham* To turn, as a figure, in math. *Dic., ext. mng. Kikowaena wili.* Turn center, in math. *Kinona like wili hapahā.* Quarter-turn image. *ʻĀlikelike wili.* Rotational symmetry. See *ʻālikelike.*

wili·au *kik* Eddy. *Dic. Wai wiliau.* Side pool, as in a stream. *Wiliau hōkū.* Galaxy.

wili·aho *kik* Reel, as for fishing. Comb. *wili + aho/Mān. Wiliaho hāmama.* Open reel. *Wiliaho hekau maunu.* Bait-casting reel.

wili i hope *ham* To rewind, as film or audio tape. *Lit.,* wind back. See *wili i mua.*

wili i mua *ham* To fast forward, as film or audio tape. *Lit.,* wind forward. See *wili i hope.*

wili·ō See *manu wiliō.*

Wili·kinia *iʻoa* Virginia; Virginian. *Dic. Wilikinia Komohana.* West Virginia; West Virginian.

wili niho *ham* Dentist's drill. *Lit.,* tooth drill. See *ʻōhiki kauka niho.*

wili·pā *kik* Disc jockey. *Lit.,* "spin" records. Also *wilipāleo.*

wili·paipu *kik* Plumber. *Lit.,* turn pipe. Also *kanaka hoʻomoe paipu.* Cf. *wilikī* (dic.).

wili ʻaila *kik* Oil rig, for drilling oil on either land or sea. *Lit.,* oil drill.

wili·ʻō·kaʻi *kik* Chrysalis. *Dic.*

wini·kili·kini *kik* Vincristine, an alkaloid derived from the periwinkle. *Eng.*

wiʻu *ʻa* Pungent, sharp, as the smell of ammonia or vinegar. *Dic., new mng. Nalo wiʻu.* Midge fly.

woela *kik* Vowel, in linguistics. *Eng.* See entries below and *hoʻēmi woela, pua woela.*

woela emi *kik* Reduced vowel, in linguistics. See *hoʻēmi woela, pua woela.*

woela haʻa·haʻa *kik* Low vowel, in linguistics.

woela kau·hope *kik* Back vowel, in linguistics. Comb. *woela + kau + hope.*

woela kau·mua *kik* Front vowel, in linguistics. Comb. *woela + kau + mua.*

woela kau·waena *kik* Central vowel, in linguistics. Comb. *woela + kau + waena.*

woela kiʻe·kiʻe *kik* High vowel, in linguistics.

woela mā·lō *kik* Tense vowel, in linguistics. *Lit.,* taut vowel.

woela mō·kio *kik* Rounded vowel, in linguistics. *Lit.,* pucker vowel.

woela ʻalu *kik* Lax vowel, in linguistics. *Lit.,* slackened vowel.

ʻ

ʻā *ʻa* Active, as a volcano. *Dic., ext. mng. Lua pele ʻā.* Active volcano.

ʻae *ham* To lend (not to borrow). *E ʻoluʻolu e ʻae mai i kāu peni.* Please lend me your pen. (May I borrow your pen.) *Mān.*

ʻae omo·waho *kik* Solvent front, i.e. the leading edge of a moving solvent as in a developing chromatogram. *Lit.,* adsorbing edge; cf. *ʻae kai* (dic.).

ʻāeko poʻo hina *kik* Bald eagle. *Lit.,* white-haired eagle. Also *ʻāeto poʻo hina.*

ʻae·like See entry below. *Kūkaʻi ʻaelike ʻuniona.* Collective bargaining.

ʻae·like hoʻōki *kik* Cloture, i.e. a method of ending debate and causing an immediate vote to be taken. *Ke hāpai maila ka luna hoʻomalu o ka ʻaha kenekoa e komo i ka ʻaelike hoʻōki i hiki ke hoʻopau i ka paio kālaimanaʻo a hoʻoholo i ka pila.* The senate leader is proposing that the session enter into cloture so that the debate can end and the bill be decided. *Lit.,* agreement (to) terminate (debate).

ʻae·ʻae *ʻa* Fine, as sand. *Niʻihau/dic.* Cf. *mānoanoa*.

ʻai *kik* Point, as in a game or sporting event. *Dic.* See entries below and *heluʻai, kāpuka ʻai, lāʻau make ʻai, lilo ka ʻai iā Mea*.

ʻai *kik* Byte, in computer terminology. *Dic., ext. mng.* See *huna, ʻai pākaukani, ʻai pāmiliona, ʻai pāpiliona*.

ʻaia·ola *heh* To eat nutritious food. Comb. *ʻai + a + ola.* Cf. *paiola*. *Kūlana ʻaiaola*. Nutrition.

ʻAio·ā *iʻoa* Iowa; Iowan. *Eng.* Also *ʻIoa*.

ʻai hā·ʻawi wale *kik* Ace, in volleyball. *Niʻihau.* Also *ʻeki*.

ʻai hele wale *kik* Point from block, dink or spike, in volleyball. *Niʻihau*.

ʻai hemo *ham* To remove food from mouth and then eat it again, as gum. *Mān. (MMLH).*

ʻai hī·naʻi *kik* Basket, a score in basketball. *Lit.,* basket score. See *ʻai kolu*.

ʻai holo *kik* Touchdown, in football. *Lit.,* run score. Cf. *ʻai hopu, ʻai manuahi, ʻai peku*.

ʻai hopu *kik* Touchback, in football. *Lit.,* catch score. Cf. *ʻai holo, ʻai manuahi, ʻai peku*.

ʻai·hue *ham* To steal, in basketball. *ʻAihue akula ʻo Kevin Johnson i ke kinipōpō, a holo akula no ka ʻai.* Kevin Johnson stole the ball and went in for the goal. *Dic.*

ʻai·kalima *kik* Ice cream. *Dic. Kone ʻaikalima.* Ice cream cone. *ʻAikalima ʻau.* Popsicle. Cf. *kanakē ʻau*.

ʻai keu *kik* Extra credit, bonus. *Lit.,* extra point. Also *hoʻopiʻi kaha. Nīnau ʻai keu.* Extra credit question, bonus question.

ʻAi·kiopa *iʻoa* Ethiopia; Ethiopian. *Dic.*

ʻai kolu *kik* A successful three-point shot, in basketball. *Ua komo ka ʻai kolu a ke kī miomio ʻana a Piʻikea.* Piʻikea's expertly shot three-pointer went in. *Lit.,* three points. See *ʻai hīnaʻi. Kī ʻai kolu.* Three-point shot; to attempt such a shot.

ʻAiku·pika *iʻoa* Egypt; Egyptian. *Dic.* Also *ʻAikupita, ʻAigupita*.

ʻaila·hola *kik* Gasohol. Sh. *ʻaila + ʻalekohola*.

ʻaila hoʻo·hinu·hinu *kik* Wax, as for polishing a car. *Lit.,* oil (for) polishing.

ʻaila kā *kik* Petroleum. *Lit.,* tar oil. Also *ʻaila tā*.

ʻaila·kele *kik* Fat. Comb. *ʻaila + kele.* See entries below and *haʻakupu ʻailakele, ʻaʻaʻa hunaola ʻailakele. Meaʻai ʻailakele iki.* Low-fat food. Also *Meaʻai liʻiliʻi o ka ʻailakele. Meaʻai ʻailakele nui.* High-fat food. Also *meaʻai nui o ka ʻailakele*.

ʻaila·kele lau·paʻa·hapa *kik* Polyunsaturated fat. Comb. *ʻailakele + lau + paʻa + hapa.* Cf. *ʻailakele paʻahapa, ʻailakele paʻapū*.

ʻaila·kele paʻa·hapa *kik* Unsaturated fat. Comb. *ʻailakele + paʻa + hapa.* Cf. *ʻailakele laupaʻahapa, ʻailakele paʻapū*.

ʻaila·kele paʻa·pū *kik* Saturated fat. *Lit.,* dense fat. Cf. *ʻailakele laupaʻahapa, ʻailakele paʻahapa*.

ʻaila mea·kanu *kik* Vegetable oil. *Lit.,* plant oil. See *lauʻai*.

ʻaila pale lā *kik* Sunscreen, the lotion. *Lit.,* ointment (to) protect (against) sun. Cf. *ʻaila ʻōlala*.

ʻaila ʻaʻalo paʻa·hau *kik* Antifreeze. *Lit.,* oil (to) resist freezing.

ʻaila ʻō·lala *kik* Suntan lotion. *Lit.,* ointment (for) basking (in the sun). Cf. *ʻaila pale lā*.

'Ai·liki *i'oa* Irish. *Dic.* See *'Ilelani*.

'ai manu·ahi *kik* Point after touchdown, in football. *Lit.*, free point. See *'ai holo*, *'ai hopu*, *'ai peku*. *'Ai manuahi holo.* Point after by passing or running. *'Ai manuahi peku.* Point after by kicking.

'aina See *lumi 'aina*.

'āina *kik* Country. *Dic.* See entries below. *'Āina 'oi'enehana.* Developed or First World Country. *'Āina hō'oi'enehana.* Developing or Third World Country. *'āina Ho'ohana 'āina.* Land use, in geography. *Komikina Ho'ohana 'Āina o ka Moku'āina.* State Land Use Commission. *'Oihana Kumuwaiwai 'Āina.* Department of Land and Natural Resources (DLNR). *'Ōnaehana Ho'omalu 'Āina Kūlohelohe.* Natural Areas Reserves System (NARS).

'ai·nao·nao *kik* Anteater. Comb. *'ai + naonao*.

'āina ho'o·malu *kik* Reserve, i.e. a reservation or tract of land set apart. *Lit.*, land (to) protect. *'Āina ho'omalu ao kūlohelohe.* Nature reserve. *'Āina ho'omalu ululā'au.* Forest reserve.

'āina kumu wai *kik* Watershed, i.e. an area from which water drains. *Lit.*, water source land. *'Āina kumu wai kiwikā.* Municipal watershed.

'āina loli·loli *kik* Transition area, i.e. an area where natural topography changes from one land feature to another. *Lit.*, changing land.

'āina mau'u *kik* Grassland.

'āina muli pana·lā·'au *kik* Post-colonial country. *Lit.*, after colony land. Also *kaumoku'āina muli panalā'au*.

'āina no ka lehu·lehu *kik* Public land. *Ka'a nā 'āina no ka lehulehu ma lalo o ka ho'omalu 'ia 'ana o ke aupuni o ka Moku'āina.* Public lands fall under the administration of the State government. *Lit.*, land for the public. Cf. *'alokio*.

'Āina Pā·kē *i'oa* China. *Dic.* Also *Kina*. See *Pākē*.

'Āina Pili·pino *i'oa* Philippines. *Dic.* Also *'Āina Pinopino*.

'Āina Pino·pino *i'oa* Philippines. *Ni'ihau.* Also *'Āina Pilipino*.

'āina·puni·'ole *kik* Continent. *Dic.* Also *mokuhonua*. See *mokuhonua*.

'ai·nohu Kau·ō *kik* Laysan finch (telespiza cantanc). Comb. *'ai + nohu + Kauō.* See *hona, nuku 'ekue, 'ainohu Nīhoa.*

'ai·nohu Nī·hoa *kik* Nīhoa finch (telespiza ultima). Comb. *'ai + nohu + Nīhoa.* See *hona, nuku 'ekue, 'ainohu Kauō.*

'ai pā·kau·kani *kik* Kilobyte (K) in computer terminology. *Lit.*, thousandfold byte. Abb. *PK*. See *'ai*.

'ai pā·mili·ona *kik* Megabyte (Meg) in computer terminology. *Lit.*, millionfold byte. Abb. *PM*. See *'ai*.

'ai pā·pili·ona *kik* Gigabyte in computer terminology. *Lit.*, billionfold byte. Abb. *PP*. See *'ai*.

'ai peku *kik* Field goal, in football. *Lit.*, kick score. Cf. *'ai holo*, *'ai hopu*, *'ai manuahi*.

'ai puni *kik* Home run. *Lit.*, lap score.

'aiwi *kik* Ivy. *Eng.* Also *lau hihi pā*.

'ai·'ē *kik* Loan, i.e. money lent at interest; to have a loan. *Dic., ext. mng.* Also *lako 'ai'ē*. Cf. *ho'olako 'ai'ē*, *lawe 'ai'ē*.

'Aigu·pita *i'oa* Egypt; Egyptian. *Dic., sp. var.* Also *'Aikupika*, *'Aikupita*.

'ao Abbreviation for *'ao'ao* (page).

'ao·'ao *'Au 'ao'ao.* Side stroke, in swimming; to swim the side stroke. *Lit.*, swim (on the) side. See entries below and *kīloi 'ao'ao*.

'Ao·'ao *i'oa* Almak, a star. *Mān.* (HA).

'ao·'ao ho'ā·kāka *kik* Cover page. *Ua loa'a ka inoa a me ka helu wahi o ka mea kākau ma ka 'ao'ao ho'ākāka.* The author's name and address are found on the cover page. *Lit.*, explanation page. Also *'ao'ao inoa*.

'ao·'ao kau *kik* Base, as of a geometric triangle. *Lit.*, placing side. Abb. *'ak*.

'ao·'ao kū·pale *kik* Defense, in sports. *Lit.*, defending side. Also *'ao'ao pale*.

'ao·'ao launa *kik* Corresponding side, in math. *Lit.*, associating side.

'ao·'ao like 'ole *kik* Scalene, in math. *Lit.*, dissimilar sides. *Huinakolu 'ao'ao like 'ole*. Scalene triangle.

'ao·'ao pale *kik* Defense, in sports. *Lit.*, defense side. Also *'ao'ao kūpale*.

'ao·'ao 'elua *Aupuni 'ao'ao 'elua*. Two-party system of government.

'au *kik* Handle, as of a bureau drawer, faucet, frying pan, toilet, etc. (preceded by *ke*); neck, as of 'ukulele, guitar, etc. *Dic.*; Ni'ihau. Cf. *kākai*, *pōheo*. See *'au ho'oku'u wai o ka lua*, *'au kī wai*, *'au paikikala*, *'au pā palai*, *'au 'ume*; *'ukulele*.

'au·ae See *'umi'umi 'auae*.

'au·a'a *kik* Rhizome. *Lit.*, root stem.

'au·ina *kik* Band, gradient, as of colors. *Dic.*, *ext. mng*. *'Auina kala*. Color band, color gradient.

'au umauma *heh* Breast stroke; to swim the breast stroke. *Dic.*

'au·hau *kik* Tax. *Dic*. *Mea uku 'auhau*. Taxpayer. *Pākēneka 'auhau*. Tax rate. *'Auhau komo pū*. Tax included. *'Auhau kumukū'ai*. Sales tax.

'au·hō·kū *kik* Delphinium. Comb. *'au + hōkū*. Also *pua 'auhōkū*.

'au ho'o·ku'u wai o ka lua *kik* Toilet handle (preceded by *ke*). Also *'au ho'oku'u*.

'au·hua *kik* Corm, scientific usage. Comb. *'au + hua*. See *hua*.

'Auk. Abbreviation for *'Aukake* (August).

'auka *'a'* Out, in baseball. *Ua 'auka wau iā ia*. He put me out. *Dic*. Cf. *hō'auka*. See *hala akula i waho*.

'au·kā See entry below and *pakuhi 'aukā*, *pakuhi pa'a 'aukā*.

'au·kā holo·mua *kik* Fill bar, in computer program. *Lit.*, bar (showing) progress.

'Au·kake *i'oa* August. *Dic*. Abb. *'Auk*.

'au·ka'i *kik* Baton. Comb. *'au + ka'i*. See entries below.

'au·ka'i pāna *kik* Signal baton, as used by marching bandleader. *Lit.*, baton (for directing) bands.

'au·ka'i wili *kik* Baton for twirling. See *wili*.

'Au·keku·lia *i'oa* Austria; Austrian. *Dic*. Also *'Auseturia*.

'au kī wai *kik* Faucet handle (preceded by *ke*). See *kī wai*.

'au kolo *heh* Free style, crawl, in swimming; to swim using this syle. *Dic*.

'au kua *heh* Back stroke, in swimming; to swim the back stroke. *Lit.*, swim (on the) back.

'au·la'o *kik* Twig, small stick (preceded by *ke*). Sh. *'au + la'ol'ao*.

'au·lili'i *'a'* Precision; precise. Redup. of *'auli'i*.

'au mā·lolo *heh* Butterfly stroke, in swimming; to swim the butterfly stroke. *Lit.*, swim (like) mālolo fish.

'au·mana *kik* Tributary. *He 'aumana 'o Missouri no Mississippi*. The Missouri is a tributary of the Mississippi. Comb. *'au + mana*. *'Aumana kahawai*. Stream tributary. *'Aumana muliwai*. River tributary.

'Au·mani *i'oa* Alnitak, a star. *Mān*. (HA).

'au moku kaua *kik* Navy. *Trad*. Also *pū'ali kaua moana*, *'oihana moku*.

'au·neki *kik* Ounce. *Dic*. Abb. *'an*. *'Auneki wai*. Fluid ounce. Abb. *'an w*.

'au pai·kikala *kik* Handlebars on a bicycle (preceded by *ke*). Ni'ihau. Also *kalaiwa paikikala*.

'au pā palai *kik* Frying pan handle (preceded by *ke*).

'au·waha *kik* Geologic trench, as Aleutian Trench. *Dic.*, *ext. mng*. *Ka 'Auwaha 'Aleuta*. Aleutian Trench.

'au 'ao·'ao *heh* Side stroke, in swimming; to swim the side stroke. *Lit.,* swim (on the) side.

'au·'au kili·lau *heh* To take a shower, bathe by showering. See *kililau, lumi 'au'au.*

'au·'auna manu *kik* Birdbath. *Lit.,* bird bathing place.

'au·'au paipu hanu *heh* To snorkel. See *paipu hanu.*

'au 'ī·lio *heh* Dog paddle, in swimming; to dog paddle. *Lit.,* swim (like a) dog.

'au 'ume *kik* Drawer handle (preceded by *ke*). Cf. *pōheo 'ume.*

'Au·setu·ria *i'oa* Austria; Austrian. *Dic., sp. var.* Also *'Aukekulia.*

'aha *kik* Council. *Dic., ext. mng.* See entries below. *'Aha kalana.* County council.

'aha ho'o·kolo·kolo *Māhele 'aha ho'okolokolo.* Judicial branch (of a government).

'aha ho'o·lohe *kik* Hearing, i.e. a time for presenting official testimony or argument. *E mālama 'ia ana he 'aha ho'olohe e pili ana i nā kuleana wai o ka 'ao'ao Ko'olau o O'ahu i Kāne'ohe i kēia ahiahi.* A hearing will be held regarding water rights on the windward side of O'ahu in Kāne'ohe this evening. *Lit.,* gathering (for) listening. Also *hālāwai ho'olohe.*

'aha ho'o·nā 'āina *kik* Land court. *Lit.,* court (for) settling land claims.

'Aha·hui Maka·'ala Holo·holona *kik* Humane Society. *Lit.,* society (which) attends to animals.

'aha kuhina *kik* Cabinet, a council that advises a president, sovereign, etc. *Ua ho'okohu 'ia 'o Keoki Kahaele i ka 'aha kuhina no ka nui o kōna kāko'o a kōkua i ka pelekikena i kōna holo moho 'ana.* Keoki Kahaele was appointed to the cabinet for his great support and help to the president in his campaign efforts. *Dic.*

'aha kū·kā *kik* Conference. *Dic.* Cf. *hui.*

'aha pane ho'o·pi'i *kik* Arraignment, i.e. a court hearing in which a defendant is formally charged with a crime and enters a plea of guilty or not guilty. *Ho'opi'i pa'alula 'ia ke kanaka ma ka 'aha pane ho'opi'i, a pane akula 'o ia 'a'ohe ōna kū i ka hewa.* The man was formally charged in the arraignment wherein he entered a plea of not guilty. *Lit.,* court (for) answering accusation. See *ho'opi'i kū'ē.*

'aha·'aina *kik* Banquet. *Dic.* *'Aha'aina ho'okipa.* Welcome banquet. *'Aha'aina panina.* Closing banquet.

'ā·ha'i *kik* Halfback, in football. *Dic., new mng.*

'aha·'ō·lelo *Māhele 'aha'ōlelo.* Legislative branch (of a government).

'ā·hia *kik* Powdery tinder. *Dic.* Cf. *pulupulu* (dic.).

'ā·hiu *'a* Wild (general term); shy. *Dic.* Cf. *lapa.* See *lōhiu, lakauā.*

'ā·hina·hina 'ō·ma'o·ma'o *kik* Maui greensword. *Lit.,* green silversword.

'ā·holo *kik* Avalanche, landslide. *Dic., sp. var.* *'Āholo hau.* Snow avalanche.

'ahu honua *kik* Earth's mantle.

'ā·huli *kik/heh* Mutation; to mutate. *He 'āhuli ia o ke ōewe.* It's a mutation in the gene. Var. of *kāhuli.*

'ak Abbreviation for *'ao'ao kau* (base).

'Āk Abbreviation for *'ākau* (north).

'ā·kau *kik* North. *Dic.* Abb. *'Āk.* See *wēlau 'ākau. Kō'ai 'ākau.* Clockwise. *Poepoe hapa 'ākau.* Northern hemisphere.

'Akana·kā *i'oa* Arkansas; Arkansan. *Dic., sp. var.* Also *'Akanasā.*

'Akana·sā *i'oa* Arkansas; Arkansan. *Dic., sp. var.* Also *'Akanakā.*

'akano *kik* Substance. PPN *kakano* (body). See *kumumea, meakino, pūhui.* *'Akano laukua.* Amorphous substance.

'aka·'akai See *ilo 'aka'akai, lina, 'o'a.*

'ā·ka'a·ka'a *'a* To be peeling, as skin from sunburn. *Dic.*

'ā·kea *kik* Starboard hull of a double-hulled canoe or right side of a ship when looking forward. *Dic., ext. mng.* Cf. *ama, muku.*

'ā·keka *kik* Acetate, a salt/ester of ascetic acid. *Eng.* *'Ākeka 'eto.* Ethyl acetate.

'ā·keke *kik* Cinder. *Dic.* See *one 'ā.* *Pu'u 'ākeke.* Cinder cone.

'ake·kona *kik* Acetone. *Eng.*

'Ake·lanika *i'oa* Atlantic. *Dic.* Also *'Atelanika.*

'ā·ke'a *ham* To block out or screen, in basketball. *Ua ne'e akula 'o Kalama i mua o Mānai no ka 'āke'a 'ana i kā ia ala 'āpō 'ana mai.* Kalama moved in front of Mānai to block out is attempt to rebound. Comb. *'ā- + ke'a.* See entries below.

'ā·ke'a ne'e *ham* Illegal screen, in basketball. *'A'ole hiki ke 'āke'a ne'e i ke kūpale me ka holo pū 'ana.* Screening while moving along with the defender is not allowed. *Lit.*, moving screen. See *ku'ia 'āke'a.*

'ā·ke'a 'ū·niu *ham* Pick and roll, in basketball; to make such a play. *Pa'akikī ke kaupale 'ana i ke ka'ane'e 'āke'a 'ūniu.* Defending the pick and roll play is tough. *Lit.*, pivot screen.

'Ā·kia *i'oa* Asia; Asian, Asiatic. *Dic.* Also *'Āsia.*

'akiu *ham* To probe. *Dic.* *'Akiu lewa lipo.* Space probe.

'akika *kik* Acid. *Dic.* *Pepa ana 'akika.* Litmus paper, for measuring pH. *'Akika haidorokoloriku.* Hydrochloric acid. *'Akika kalapona.* Carbonic acid. *'Akika naikokene, 'akika nikiriku.* Nitric acid. *'Akika pūhui kalapona.* Carboxylic acid. *'Akika 'ūpalu kūlohelohe.* Naturally occurring weak acid. *'Akika forimiku.* Formic acid. *'Akika sulufuriku.* Sulfuric acid. *'Akika tanika.* Tannic acid. *'Anahaidaraside*

'akika kala·pona *kik* Carbonic acid. *Lit.*, carbon acid.

'ā·kili·kai *kik* Alkali; alkaline. Comb. *'ā- + kili + kai.* *Mekala 'ākilikai.* Alkali metal, i.e. one of the family of elements in Group 1 of the periodic table. *Mekala honua 'ākilikai.* Alkaline earth metal, i.e. one of the family of elements in Group 2 of the periodic table.

'ā·kili·lehu *kik* Lye. Sh. *'ākilikai + lehu.*

'Aki·mika *i'oa* Archimedes. *Eng.* *Ke kulehana a 'Akimika.* Archimedes' principle, i.e. the buoyant force on an object submerged in a fluid is equal to the weight of the fluid displaced by that object, in science.

'akino·ika *kik* Actinoid, i.e. one of the fourteen elements that follow actinium on the periodic table. *Eng.*

'ā·kō·lī See *kōkua huamele.*

'akomi *'a'* Automatic. *Eng.* *Hānai 'akomi.* To auto feed, continuous feed, as paper into computer printer.

'ā·kope *kik* Caffeine. Comb. *'ā- + kope.*

'ako·pie See *uinihapa 'akopie.*

'ā kua·lua *'a'* Secondary activity, of a volcano.

'aku·iki *kik* Chipmonk. (Ute *'akwiisi.*) Also *kiulela 'akuiki.*

'ā·kuli·kuli kula *kik* Portulaca. *Dic.*

'alā *Pōhaku 'alā.* Boulder, in Hawai'i, referring to poi pounder-size stones and larger. Cf. *nukahaku.*

'alaea *kik* Tribe, i.e. people in a district who have intermarried, specifically referring to Hawai'i. *Dic.* Cf. *hapū, nāki.*

'Ā·laka *i'oa* Alaska; Alaskan. *Dic.* Also *'Alaseka.*

'ala·kaine *kik* Alkyne. *Eng.* Cf. *'alakane, 'alakene.* *Pūka'ina 'alakaine.* Alkyne series, i.e. the group of unsaturated hydrocarbons with one triple bond.

'ala·kaloida *kik* Alkaloid. *Eng.*

'ala·kane *kik* Alkane. *Eng.* Cf. *'alakaine, 'alakene. Pūka'ina 'alakane.* Alkane series, i.e. saturated hydrocarbons where all the carbon atoms are joined by single covalent bonds.

'ala·keka *kik* Alligator. *Eng.*

'ala·kene *kik* Alkene. *Eng.* Cf. *'alakaine, 'alakane. Pūka'ina 'alakene.* Alkene series, i.e. the group of unsaturated hydrocarbons with one double bond.

'ala·meka *kik* Nutmeg. Sh. *hua'ala* + Eng.

'ala·neo *Lulu 'alaneo.* Rain shadow.

'ā·lani *Poloka kau lā'au 'ālani.* Orange tree frog.

'ala·nine *kik* Alanine, an amino acid. *Eng.*

'ā·lani pomelo *kik* Grapefruit. *Lit.*, pomelo orange. See *iāpona, pomelo.*

'ā·lapa *kik/'a'* Athlete; athletic. *Dic. Ha'awina kālā 'ālapa.* Athletic scholarship.

'ala·paina *'a'* Alpine, i.e. relating to the biogeographic zone above timberline. *Eng.* See *lalo 'alapaina, wao la'alā'au. Panoa 'alapaina.* Alpine desert.

'ā·lapa·kona- Prefix (Haw.); suffix (Eng.) -athalon. Comb. *'ālapa + kona.* See entries below.

'ā·lapa·kona·kolu *kik* Triathalon. Comb. *'ālapakona- + kolu.*

'ā·lapa·kona·lima *kik* Pentathalon. Comb. *'ālapakona- + lima.*

'ā·lapa·kona·'umi *kik* Decathalon. Comb. *'ālapakona- + 'umi.*

'Ala·pama *i'oa* Alabama; Alabaman, Alabamian. *Dic.* Also *'Alabama.*

'Ala·pia *'Alapia, 'Arabia. Saudi 'Alapia.* Saudi Arabia; Saudi. Also *Saudi 'Arabia.*

'Ala·bama *i'oa* Alabama; Alabaman, Alabamian. *Dic., sp. var.* Also *'Alapama.*

'Ala·bania *i'oa* Albania; Albanian. *Eng.* Also *'Alepania.*

'Ala·seka *i'oa* Alaska; Alaskan. *Dic., sp. var.* Also *'Ālaka.*

'ale *kik* Wave, as a swell in the open ocean. *Dic.* Cf. *nalu.* See *hokua, honua, ki'eki'ena, kōā.*

'ale ahi lā *kik* Solar granule, i.e. gigantic waves of gas which roll across the surface of the sun. *Lit.*, wave (of) solar fire. Cf. *kiko lā, lapa ahi lā, puapua'i lā.*

'Ale·uta *i'oa* Aleut; Aleutian. *Eng. Ka Pae'āina 'o 'Aleuta.* Aleutian Islands. *Ka 'Auwaha 'Aleuta.* Aleutian Trench.

'ale·kea *kik* Heron, general term. *Dic.* See *'aleku'u.*

'Ale·kelia *i'oa* Algeria; Algerian. *Dic.* Also *'Alegeria.*

'Ale·kina *i'oa* Argentina; Argentine, Argentinean. *Eng.*

'ale·kohola *kik* Alcohol. *Dic.*

'ale kua·kea *kik* Whitecap. *Dic.* See *niho.*

'ale·ku'u *kik* Egret, general term. *Papapū ka 'āina mahi kō i ka 'aleku'u kau pipi ma hope o ka puhi 'ana i ke kō i ke ahi.* The cane field is covered with cattle egrets after the cane is burned by fire. Sh. *'alekea + 'auku'u.* See *'alekea. 'Aleku'u kau pipi.* Cattle egret.

'ale·manaka *kik* Calendar. *Dic. 'Alemanaka puke.* Date book, appointment book. Cf. *puke 'alemanaka.*

'ā·lepa *kik* Alpha. *Dic., sp. var. Huna 'ālepa.* Alpha particle, i.e. a positively charged particle made up of two protons and two neutrons.

'Ale·pania *i'oa* Albania; Albanian. *Dic.* Also *'Alabania.*

'ale·'ale See *hawewe 'ale'ale.*

'Ale·geria *i'oa* Algeria; Algerian. *Dic., sp. var.* Also *'Alekelia.*

'ali *ham* To dig (the ball), in volleyball. *Dic., ext. mng.* See *'ali 'ūlau. Mea 'ali, 'ali.* Digger. *'Ali 'ūlau.* Pancake dig.

'ali·upa *ham* Alley-oop, a basketball play. *E kakali wale ana 'o Loa i ke kīloi 'ia mai i hiki ai iā ia ke 'aliupa.* Loa was just waiting to be passed the ball so that he could make the alley-oop play. *Eng.*

ʻalihi·kū·lele *kik* Quarterback, in football. Sh. *ʻalihikaua + kūlele.* Also *ʻalihi.*

ʻĀ·lika *iʻoa* Arctic. *Dic.*

ʻā·like *ʻa* Identical, matching. *Dic.* *Nā hapa ʻālike.* Identical parts.

ʻā·like·like *kik/ʻa* Symmetry; symmetric, symmetrical, in math. Redup. of *ʻalike. Kaha ʻālikelike.* Line of symmetry, a line on which a figure can be folded so the two parts fit exactly, in math. *Kinona ʻālikelike.* Symmetric figure. *ʻĀlikelike aka.* Reflection symmetry, in math. *ʻĀlikelike kau.* Translation symmetry. *ʻĀlikelike wili.* Rotational symmetry.

ʻali·koka *kik* Artichoke. *Eng.*

ʻAli·kona *iʻoa* Arizona; Arizonan, Arizionian. *Dic.* Also *ʻArizona.*

ʻā·lina *kik* Scar (preceded by *ke*). *Dic.* Also *ninanina.*

ʻali·dirina *kik* Aldrin, a kind of insecticide. *Eng.* Cf. *dielidirina.* See *lāʻau make.*

ʻalo·kio *kik* Private land. *Dic., ext. mng.* Also *ʻalodio.* Cf. *ʻāina no ka lehulehu.*

ʻalo·peke ʻĀ·lika *kik* Arctic fox. Also *ʻalopeka ʻĀlika.*

ʻaloʻa·hia *kik* Emotional stress. *Mān.* (MMLH).

ʻalo·dio *kik* Private land. *Dic., ext. mng., sp. var.* Also *ʻalokio.* Cf. *ʻāina no ka lehulehu.*

ʻalu *ʻa* Lax, as articulation in linguistics. *Dic., ext. mng.* Cf. *mālō. Woela ʻalu.* Lax vowel.

ʻā·lua·lua *Papa ʻālualua.* Multiplication tables. Comb. *papa + dic.* See *ʻālualua* (dic.).

ʻalumi·numa *kik* Aluminum. *Eng.*

ʻā·luna See *palena ʻāluna o ka hewa.*

ʻalu·ʻalu *kik* Bark, of a plant; skin. *Niʻihau.* Also *ʻili.*

ʻama·kila *kik* Armadillo. *Eng.*

ʻā·mana *Kuʻi ʻāmana.* To bump (the ball), in volleyball.

ʻā·mana koho *kik* Dichotomous key. *Lit.,* Y-shaped branch (for) choosing.

ʻā·mana·puʻu *kik* Bronchus, bronchiole; bronchial. Comb. *ʻāmana + puʻu. ʻĀmanapuʻu kuamua.* Primary bronchus. *ʻĀmanapuʻu kualua.* Secondary bronchus, lobar bronchus. *ʻĀmanapuʻu kuakolu.* Tertiary bronchus, segmental bronchus. *ʻĀmanapuʻu kuahope.* Terminal bronchiole.

ʻā·maʻa·mau *heh* In rapid succession. *Dic.*

ʻAma·sona *iʻoa* Amazon. *Eng. Ka muliwai ʻo ʻAmasona.* Amazon river.

ʻAme·lika *iʻoa* America; American. *Dic.* See entries below.

ʻAme·lika Hema *iʻoa* South America; South American. *Dic.*

ʻAme·lika Hui Pū ʻia *iʻoa* United States of America; American. *Dic., sp. var.*

ʻAme·lika Waena *iʻoa* Central America, Latin America; Central American, Latin American. *Dic.*

ʻAme·lika ʻĀ·kau *iʻoa* North America; North American. *Dic.*

ʻami *kik* Hinge. *Dic. ʻAmi puka.* Door hinge. Also *ʻami ʻīpuka.*

ʻamino *kik* Amino. *Eng. ʻAkika ʻamino.* Amino acid.

ʻamo *Mākala ʻamo.* Sphincter, i.e. an annular muscle surrounding and able to contract or close a bodily opening or channel. *Puka ʻamo.* Anus, i.e. the posterior opening of the alimentary canal. Also *puka kahiko.*

ʻamo·nia *kik* Ammonia. *Eng.*

ʻamoni·uma *kik* Ammonium. *Eng. ʻAmoniuma molaibadahate.* Ammonium molybdate.

ʻā·mui *kik* Assembly, i.e. a gathering of people for a specific purpose. *Tah.*

ʻan Abbreviation for *ʻauneki* (ounce).

ʻā·nai *ham* To rub, as one's eyes. *Niʻihau.* Cf. *ʻanaʻanai.*

'ana·hai·dara·side *kik* Anhydride, i.e. a compound formed from another by the removal of water. *Eng.* Cf. *nele wai.* '*Anahaidaraside kuapapa.* Basic anhydride, a metallic oxide that forms a base when added to water. '*Anahaidaraside 'akika.* Acidic anhydride.

'**Ana·heu·heu** *i'oa* Corona Borealis, a constellation. *Tah.*

'**ana·kio·pua** *kik* Angiosperm. Comb. *angio* (Gr.) + *pua.*

'**Ana·kolo·meka** *i'oa* Andromeda. *Eng. Ka wiliau hōkū 'o 'Anakolomeka.* Andromeda galaxy.

'**Ana·muli** *i'oa* Alderamin, a star. (Tah. '*Anamuri.*)

'**ana·naka** *kik* Jackfruit. (Ilocano *ananka.*)

'**ana·nu'u** *'a'* Deflated, as a balloon. *Dic., ext. mng.* Also *puhalu* (*dic.*), *emi* (Ni'ihau). Cf. *paki'i*. See *ho'opūhalalū*.

'**ana·pu'u** *kik* Lymph. *Mān. Lōku'u 'anapu'u.* Lymph gland, lymph node. *Ma'i 'a'ai 'anapu'u.* Lymphoma.

'**ana·'anai** *ham* To rub repeatedly, as one's eyes. *Ni'ihau.* Cf. *'ānai.*

'**Ana·gola** *i'oa* Angola; Angolan. *Eng.*

-'**āne** *Hua'āne.* Sperm. Cf. *hua'ine.*

'**āne** *'a'* Positive, as of electrical charge or north pole of a magnet. *Inv.* See *hohoki, 'ine, 'ūholo uila 'āne. Huna 'āne.* Proton.

'**ane hala·pohe** *'a'* Endangered. *Lit.,* almost extinct. Also *'ane make loa, 'ane nalowale loa. Kānāwai Lāhulu 'Ane Halapohe.* Endangered Species Act.

'**ane make loa** *'a'* Endangered. *Lit.,* almost extinct. Also *'ane halapohe, 'ane nalowale loa.*

'**ane nalo·wale loa** *'a'* Endangered. *Lit.,* almost extinct. Also *'ane halapohe, 'ane make loa.*

'**Ane·'ā·lika** *i'oa* Antarctica; Antarctic. *Dic., sp. var.*

'**anini** *kik* Eaves (preceded by *ke*). *Dic., ext. mng.*

'**anini lau·lā hawewe** *kik* Amplitude modulation. *Lit.,* amplitude variation. Also *AM* (pronounced *'āmū*). Cf. *FM.*

'**ano like** *'a'* Similar, in math. *Lit.,* somewhat alike. *Kinona 'ano like.* Similar figure.

'**ano·pili** *kik* Property, i.e. distinctive attribute, as of a number, in math (preceded by *ke*). *Dic., sp. var.* See entries below.

'**ano·pili o ka 'ē·ko'a** *kik* Opposites property, in math (preceded by *ke*). *Lit.,* property of the opposite.

'**ano·pili helu** *kik* Number property, in math (preceded by *ke*).

'**ano·pili ho'o·ili** *kik* Distributive property, in math (preceded by *ke*). *Lit.,* transferring property. Cf. *'anopili ka'ina ho'i hope.*

'**ano·pili ho'o·like** *kik* Associative property, in math (preceded by *ke*). *Lit.,* equalizing property.

'**ano·pili ho'o·pū·'ulu** *kik* Grouping property, in math (preceded by *ke*).

'**ano·pili kau·like** *kik* Equality property, in math (preceded by *ke*).

'**ano·pili ka'ina ho'i hope** *kik* Commutative property, in math (preceded by *ke*). *Lit.,* property (with) order reversed. Also *'anopili ho'i hope.* Cf. *'anopili ho'oili.*

'**ano·pili kemi·kala** *kik* Chemical property (preceded by *ke*).

'**ano·pili 'ekahi** *kik* One property, in multiplication (preceded by *ke*).

'**ano·pili 'ole** *kik* Zero property (preceded by *ke*). *'Anopili 'ole o ka ho'onui.* Zero property of multiplication.

'**ano·'ano** *kik* Seed. *Dic. Wahī 'ano'ano.* Seed pod.

'**anu'u** *kik* Stair, step. *Dic.* See *'anu'u hana. Papa 'anu'u lalo kai.* Underwater terrace.

'**anu'u hana** *kik* Step, as in problem solving. *Dic., ext. mng.* Also *'anu'u.*

'**an w** Abbreviation for *'auneki wai* (fluid ounce).

ʻAp. Abbreviation for ʻApelila (April).

ʻā·pahu·pahu ham To repel, as like charges in a magnet. Comb. ʻā- + pahupahu.

ʻā·pahu·pahu ʻa' Faded, as material which has been left in the sun. Niʻihau.

ʻā·pā lole kik Bolt of material. Dic. See ʻiālole.

ʻā·pana hapa·hā kik Quadrant. Lit., quarter piece. Cf. ʻāpana noiʻi.

ʻā·pana kaha kik Line segment, in math.

ʻā·pana noiʻi kik Quadrat, i.e. a rectangular plot used for ecological or population studies. Lit., research section. Cf. ʻāpana hapahā.

ʻā·pana·pana Moena ʻili ʻāpanapana. Floor tile. Also kile ʻiʻili, kile papahele.

ʻā·pana pā·ʻoi·hana kau·waena kik Central business district. Cf. kaona.

ʻā·papapa kik Reef. Niʻihau. Ula ʻāpapapa. Slipper lobster. Also ula pāpapa. See ʻōmā.

ʻā·pa·ʻa·kuma ʻa' Endemic. Dic., ext. mng. Cf. ʻōiwi. Meakanu ʻāpaʻakuma. Endemic plant.

ʻApe·kani·kana iʻoa Afghanistan; Afghan, Afghani. Dic. Also ʻAfekanisana.

ʻApe·lika iʻoa Africa; African. Dic. Also ʻAferika. Lepupalika ʻApelika Waena. Central African Republic. Līlia ʻApelika. Amaryllis. ʻApelika Hema. South Africa; South African.

ʻApe·lila iʻoa April. Dic. Abb. ʻAp.

ʻā·pika·pika Halo ~. Suction cup fin, as beneath the stomach of an ʻoʻopu.

ʻapo ham To catch, as a ball; to receive or reception, in football. Ua ʻapo kōna hoa kime i ke kinipōpō, a holo akula i ke kī pai. His teammate caught the ball and went in for a layup. Dic., ext. mng. See lawena, ʻapo lilo.

ʻā·pō ham To rebound, in basketball. He 45 ʻai a 8 ʻāpō a Karl Malone. Karl Malone has 45 points and 8 rebounds. Var. of ʻapo.

ʻā·poho ʻāina kik Geologic depression, as Death Valley. Comb. ʻāpoho (dic., ext. mng.) + ʻāina.

ʻā·pohu kik Fullback, in football. Comb. ʻā- + pohu [var. of pahu].

ʻapo kani kā·kau kik Phonics. Lit., catch written sounds.

ʻapo kele·pona kik Telephone receiver. Lit., telephone grasp.

ʻapo lilo ham To intercept (the ball), in football. Lit., take-possession catch.

ʻapo·manaʻo heh Comprehension; to comprehend. Lit., grasp meaning. Nīnau ʻapomanaʻo. Comprehension question.

ʻā·pona kik A take, i.e. a successful shot in a movie or video production. He ʻāpona! It's a take! Dic., ext. def. See paʻi.

ʻā·poʻe kik Camp, i.e. a gathering of people to learn or practice certain skills. Sh. ʻāpoʻepoʻe. See hoʻomoana. ʻĀpoʻe kamepiula. Computer camp. ʻĀpoʻe pōhīnaʻi. Basketball camp.

ʻā·poʻo poho pepa kik Paper tray slot, as for a computer printer. Lit., paper tray hole (Tah.). See poho pepa, poho pākuʻi.

ʻawa·hia ʻa' Toxic. Dic., ext. def.

ʻawa·keke kik Gingerbread. Sh. ʻawapuhi + malakeke.

ʻā·waʻa kik Safety, in football. Dic., new mng. See lala, muku. ʻĀwaʻa lala. Weak safety. ʻĀwaʻa muku. Strong safety.

ʻawe kik Backpack, knapsack. Dic. Also pāiki hāʻawe, pāisi hāʻawe.

ʻawe·hā kik Hemoglobin. Comb. ʻawe + hā; Māori kawehā.

ʻawe·like kik Average; mean, in math. Eng. ʻAwelike o ka ua. Average rainfall. ʻAwelike māmā holo. Average speed. ʻAwelike nuipaʻa ʻātoma. Average atomic mass.

ʻawe·ʻawe kik Tentacle. Dic.

ʻā·we·ʻa·we·ʻa ʻa' Trace, small amount. Dic. Kumumea ʻāweʻaweʻa. Trace element.

'a'ai *Ma'i 'a'ai 'anapu'u.* Lymphoma.

'a'aia·ani·lā *'a'* Weathered; weathering. *Lit.,* eroded by weather.

'a'aia·nalu *'a'* Eroded or cut by waves, as a cliff. *Lit.,* eroded by surf. *Pali 'a'aianalu.* Wave-cut cliff.

'a'aia·wā *heh/'a'* Erosion; to erode; eroded. *Lit.,* eroded (by) time.

'a'ahu *kik* Clothing. *Dic. Nā 'a'ahu hana keaka.* Wardrobe, as stage costumes for a play, movie or video production. Usu. *nā 'a'ahu.*

'a'a kā·nā·wai *ham* Civil disobedience, i.e. breaking a law because it goes against personal morals. *Ua kaulana 'o Martin Luther King no kōna a'o 'ana i ka 'a'a kānāwai 'ana me ka hakakā 'ole.* Martin Luther King was famous for his teaching of non-violent civil disobedience. *Lit.,* defy law.

'a'alo *ham* To resist, as water on corrosive things. *Dic., ext. mng. Uaki 'a'alo wai.* Water-resistant watch. Also *uāki 'a'alo wai. 'Aila 'a'alo pa'ahau.* Antifreeze. *'A'alo pili.* Teflon. *'A'alo wai.* Waterproof, water-resistant.

'a'a·nahoa *kik* Adventure, as stories or movies. Comb. *'a'a + nahoa.*

'a'ape·hihi *kik* Pothos. Redup. of *'ape + hihi. 'A'apehihi lau li'i.* Philodendron.

'ā·'apo *kik* Flanker, in football. Comb. *'ā- + 'apo.*

'a'a'a huna·ola *kik* Tissue, as structural material of a plant or animal. *Lit.,* cell tissue. *'A'a'a hunaola 'ailakele.* Adipose tissue, i.e. animal tissue in which fat is stored. See *ha'akupu 'ailakele, 'ailakele.*

'a'ehi *heh* To cross, as a street. Comb. *'A'e + -hi* (transitive ending). See *'a'ehina.*

'a'e·hina *kik* Crosswalk. Comb. *'a'ehi + -na.* See *'a'ehi. Kukui 'a'ehina.* Crosswalk light.

'a'e kā·nā·wai *ham* To break the law. *Dic.* Also *ha'iha'i kānāwai.* Cf. *pale kānāwai.*

'a'ena *kik* Violation, as in basketball. *'O ke kake iki akula nō ia o Niu, a ho'ōho maila ka 'uao i ka 'a'ena 'ekolu kekona.* Niu just shifted a little, and the official called him on the three-second violation. Comb. *'a'e + -na.* See entry below. *'A'ena laina kūwaena.* Backcourt violation. *'A'ena 'ekolu kekona.* Three-second violation. *'A'ena 'umi kekona.* Ten-second violation.

'a'ena *kik* Violation, as in volleyball. Comb. *'a'e + -na. 'A'ena hāpai.* Carrying violation. *'A'ena kukuna.* Antenna violation. *'A'ena pa'i ulele.* Service violation. *'A'ena pa'i lua.* Double-hit violation. *'A'ena 'ekolu mika.* Three-meter line violation. See *laina 'ekolu mika. 'A'ena 'umi kapua'i.* Ten-foot line violation. See *laina 'umi kapua'i. 'A'ena 'upena.* Net violation.

'a'e palena *ham* To go out of bounds, in sports. *Lit.,* trespass (a) boundary.

'ā·'ī *kik* Collar. *Mān.* Also *'ā'ī lole, 'ā'ī kala, kala. Mān. Ho'omālō 'ā'ī.* Neck stretches, i.e. a warm-up exercise for sports such as volleyball; also to do this exercise.

'ā·'iwa *kik* Defensive corner back, in football. Comb. *'ā- + 'iwa.*

'a'ohe launa *'a'* Inappropriate. *Ni'ihau.*

'a'ole i pau "Stay tuned," "to be continued," as during a TV program. *Lit.,* not finished.

'Afe·kani·sana *i'oa* Afghanistan; Afghan, Afghani. *Eng.* Also *'Apekanikana.*

'Afe·rika *i'oa* Africa; African. *Dic., sp. var.* Also *'Apelika. 'Aferika Hema.* South Africa; South African.

'Ara·bia *Saudi 'Arabia.* Saudi Arabia; Saudi. Also *Saudi 'Alapia.*

'ara·gona *kik* Argon, an element. *Eng.*

'Ari·zona *i'oa* Arizona; Arizonan, Arizonian. *Dic., sp. var.* Also *'Alikona.*

'asete·line *kik* Acetylene. *Eng.*

'Ā·sia *i'oa* Asia; Asian, Asiatic. *Dic., sp. var.* Also *'Ākia.*

'Ate·la·nika *i'oa* Atlantic. *Dic., sp. var.* Also *'Akelanika*.

'ā·toma *kik* Atom, atomic. *Eng.* Lou *'ātoma*. Bond between atoms or ions as a result of gaining, losing or sharing electrons.

'ea *kik* Melody, tune. *Eng.* (air). Also *leo*. See entries below and *mū hōlapu pale 'ea pau, 'ōnaehana pale 'ea, 'ukulele 'ea honu*.

'ea *kik* Plastic. *Ni'ihau. Kanaka 'ea.* Mannequin. *'Eke 'ea*. Plastic bag (preceded by *ke*). Cf. *pū'olo pepa*.

'ea kau lole *kik* Hanger (made of plastic). *Lit.*, plastic (for) placing clothes. See *uea kau lole, lā'au kau lole, mea kau lole*.

'ea kāki *kik* Charge card. *Lit.*, plastic (for) charging. Also *kāleka kāki*.

'ea paina·'ā·pala *kik* Polyethylene. *Lit.*, pineapple plastic (from the plastic used when planting pineapples). See *hāli'i 'ea*.

'ea 'eke·'eke *kik* Six-pack ring, i.e. the plastic ring which holds cans together. *Lit.*, six-pack plastic. *'Ea 'eke'eke koloaka*. Six-pack soda ring. *'Ea 'eke'eke pia*. Six-pack beer ring.

'eono 'ī·niha *kik* Six inches, i.e. a warm-up exercise for sports such as volleyball.

'Eu·lā·sia *i'oa* Eurasia; Eurasian. *Eng. Ka Una Honua 'Eulāsia*. Eurasian Plate.

'Eu·lopa *i'oa* Europe. *Dic.* See entry below. *'Eulopa Hikina*. Eastern Europe; Eastern European. *'Eulopa Komohana*. Western Europe; Western European.

'Eu·lopa *i'oa* Europa, a moon of Jupiter. *Eng.*

'ē·heu See *pihi wili 'ēheu*.

'ehia How, what, as in asking about any kind of measurement. *'Ehia ka lō'ihi o kēlā pākaukau?* How long is that table? *Ni'ihau*. Also *he aha*.

'ē·kaka'a *heh* To separate easily, as a nut from its shell. *Ke pūlehu kūpono 'oe i ka hua kukui, a i ke 'ano o kou kīkē 'ana i ka iwi, e 'ēkaka'a wale mai nō ka 'i'o mai ka iwi mai*. If you broil the kukui nut well, as you break open the shell, the meat will separate easily from the shell. *Mān. (LKK).*

'eke *kik* Bag (preceded by *ke*). See entries below and *pū'olo*.

'eke ukana *kik* Basket, as on a bicycle (preceded by *ke*). *Ni'ihau*. See *'ie*.

'eke keni·keni *kik* Coin purse (preceded by *ke*). *Lit.*, bag (for) loose change.

'eke mimi *kik* Bladder (preceded by *ke*). *Mān.*

'eke moe *kik* Sleeping bag (preceded by *ke*). Also *'eke hiamoe*.

'eke pela *kik* Mattress cover (preceded by *ke*). *Lit.*, mattress bag.

'eke 'ea *kik* Plastic bag (preceded by *ke*). Cf. *pū'olo pepa*.

'eke·'eke *kik* Six-pack, as of drinks. *Ni'ihau*. Cf. *'ope*. See *pahu, pū'olo*. *'Eke'eke koloaka*. Six-pack of soda. *'Eke'eke pia*. Six-pack of beer.

'eke·'eke See *'ea 'eke'eke*.

'eki *kik* Ace, in volleyball. *Dic., ext. mng.* Also *'ai hā'awi wale*.

'ekolu mika See *laina 'ekolu mika, 'a'ena 'ekolu mika*.

'ē·kona *kik* Acorn. *Eng.* Also *hua kumu 'oka*.

'ē·ko'a *'a* Opposite. *Sh. 'ē + 'oko'a*. *'Ēko'a me*. To be the opposite of. *Ua 'ēko'a ka 'ele'ele me ke ke'oke'o*. Black is the opposite of white.

'Ekua·kola *i'oa* Ecuador; Ecuadoran, Ecuadorean, Ecuadorian. *Dic.* Also *'Ekuadora*.

'Ekua·dora *i'oa* Ecuador; Ecuadoran, Ecuadorean, Ecuadorian. *Dic.* Also *'Ekuakola*.

'ekue *Nuku 'ekue*. King Kong finch (chloridops regiskongi). See *hona, 'ainohu Kauō, 'ainohu Nīhoa*.

'ē·lau *kik* Crown, as on a pineapple. *Dic., ext. mng.* *'Ēlau hala kahiki, 'ēlau paina'āpala.* Pineapple crown.

'elala *kik* Insect, bug. (Wallis Futuna, *ngarara.*) *Pine 'elala.* Insect mounting; to mount insects. *'Ōmole mālama 'elala.* Insect holding jar. *'Ōmole pepehi 'elala.* Insect killing jar. *'Upena 'elala.* Insect net. *'Upena 'elala ho'olewalewa.* Insect fixed net. *'Upena 'elala kā'e'e.* Insect sweep net. *'Upena 'elala 'eke.* Insect bag net.

'Ela Sala·vadora *i'oa* El Salvador; Salvadoran, Salvadorian. *Eng.*

'ele·ao *kik* Aphid, a kind of insect. *Dic. Meli 'eleao.* Honeydew, i.e. a sweet juice secreted by aphids.

'ele·hune *kik* Silt. Sh. *kelekele* (PPN *lepo*) + *hune*.

'ē·leka *kik* Moose. *Dic. (elk).*

'ele·kanu *kik* Planting medium. Sh. *kelekele (PPN lepo)* + *kanu.* Cf. *lepo kanu meakanu.*

'elele mana·koho *kik* Elector, as in the US Electoral College. *Lit.,* voter delegate.

'ele·lū kī·kē·kē *kik* American cockroach (Periplaneta americana). *Dic.*

'ele·lū la'a·loa *kik* German cockroach (Blattella germanica). Comb. *'elelū* + dic.

'ele·lū Nū·hō·lani *kik* Australian cockroach (Periplaneta australasiae).

'ele·makua *kik* Loam. Sh. *kelekele* (PPN *lepo*) + *onematua (Māori,* loam).

'ele·muku *Ko'e 'elemuku.* Nematode.

'ele·nahu *kik* Peat. Sh. *kelekele* (PPN *lepo*) + *nanahu*.

'ele·pani o ke kai *kik* Walrus. *Lit.,* elephant of the sea. Also *pala'o.*

'ele·pani pū·hulu·hulu *kik* Woolly mammoth. *Lit.,* hairy elephant.

'ele·peli *Pī'ai 'elepeli.* Elderberry.

'ele·popo *kik* Humus. Sh. *kelekele* (PPN *lepo*) + *popopo*.

'elima *Nā Hui Nui 'Elima.* The Big Five, i.e. the five corporations that controlled most of the sugar industry in Hawai'i.

'elua *Kūlana 'elua.* Runner-up, second place.

'elua hale *kik* Bicameral, as a legislature. *'Elua hale o ka 'aha'ōlelo.* The legislature is bicameral. *Lit.,* two houses. Cf. *aupuni 'ao'ao 'elua.*

'elua 'ao·ao like Isosceles. *Lit.,* two equal sides. *Huinakolu 'elua 'ao'ao like.* Isosceles triangle.

'eme·pela *Aupuni 'emepela.* Empire. *Pae Mauna Kai 'Emepela.* Emperor Seamounts. Also *Pae Mauna Kai 'o 'Emepela.*

'ena makani *kik* Gale, stormy wind; whole trees in motion and inconvenience felt in walking against the wind, in meteorology. *Dic., ext. mng.* See *makani.*

'ene·hana *kik* Technology. Sh. *'enekini + mea hana.* Cf. *'oi'enehana. Mea 'enehana.* Technician. *Luna 'enehana.* Production engineer, as for a movie or video production. *Hope luna 'enehana.* Assistant production engineer. *Manakia 'enehana.* Production manager. *Mea 'enehana kani.* Sound technician. *Mea 'enehana ki'i.* Graphics technician.

'Ene·kela·kuke *i'oa* Enceladus, a small moon of Saturn. *Eng.*

'ene·kini *Pani 'enekini.* Hood, as of a car or truck.

'ene·kinia *kik* Engineer. *Dic. 'Ene-kinia mīkini.* Mechanical engineer.

'ene·kini kī·kaha *kik* Maneuvering engine, as for a spacecraft. *Lit.,* maneuvering engine.

'Ene·lani *i'oa* England, English person; English (of England). *Dic.* Also *Pelekāne.* Cf. *Pelekānia.*

'enuhe hamu·i·a *kik* Carnivorous caterpillar (Eupithecia spp).

'enuhe hele pō *kik* Cutworm. *Lit.,* caterpillar (that) goes (at) night. Also *poko.*

'epa *ham* To fake out, in basketball. *'Epa aku nei 'o ia ma ka 'ākau, ka hema; kaha ihola 'o ia ma waena o nā kūpale 'elua.* He faked to the right, the left; he made the drive right through the two defenders. *Lit.,* deceive. See *pākī 'epa.*

'epaki *kik* Phase. *Mān.* (HKM)/Eng. *'Epaki mahina.* Phase of the moon (Western concept).

'epane *kik* Apron. *Dic.* Also *pale kuene.*

'epe·kema *kik* Science. (Gr. *epetema.*) Also *akeakamai. Kauhelu 'epekema.* Scientific notation. *Kanaka noi'i 'epekema.* Scientific researcher.

'epe·soma *kik* Epsom. *Eng. Pa'akai 'epesoma.* Epsom salt.

'ewa·'ewa *Pu'uwai pana 'ewa'ewa.* Cardiac arryhthmia.

'Ewe·leka *i'oa* Everest. *Eng. Mauna 'Eweleka.* Mount Everest.

'e'e *heh* To log on, log in, as of a network or other computer system. *Dic.,* new mng. Cf. *lele.*

'e'ele *'a'* Concave, i.e. hollowed or rounded inward as the inside of a bowl. Sh./redup. of *ka'ele.* Cf. *'e'emu. Aniani 'e'ele.* Concave mirror. *Aniani kaulona 'e'ele.* Concave lens.

'e'emu *'a'* Convex, i.e. curved or rounded as the exterior of a sphere or circle. Sh./redup. of *lemu.* Cf. *'e'ele. Aniani 'e'emu.* Convex mirror. *Aniani kaulona 'e'emu.* Convex lens.

'e'epa pau·'aka *kik* Goblin. *Lit.,* grotesque person with miraculous powers.

'eto *kik* Ethyl. *Eng. 'Ākeka 'eto.* Ethyl acetate.

'I Abbreviation for *'ili* (area).

'ī·ā *kik* Yard (unit of measurement). *Eng.* No abbreviation. *'Īā pa'a'iliono.* Cublic yard.

'ī·ā·lole *kik* Material, cloth. *Mān.* (MMLH, HHLH). See *'āpā lole.*

'ie *kik* Basket (preceded by *ke*). *Dic.* See *'eke ukana.*

'Ioa *i'oa* Iowa; Iowan. *Dic., sp. var.* Also *'Aioā.*

'io·kine *kik* Iodine. *Eng.* See *hō'iokine.*

'iole *kik* Mouse, as for a computer. *Dic., ext. mng.* Cf. *nahau 'iole.*

'iole *kik* Mouse, rat. *Dic.* See entries below. *'Iole kaupoku.* Roof rat. *'Iole kia.* Deer mouse. *'Iole wāwae kea.* White-footed mouse.

'iole kawia *kik* Guinea pig. Comb. *'iole + cavia* (Lat.).

'iole kepila *kik* Gerbil. Comb. *'iole +* Eng. Also *'iole kebira.*

'iole lā·piki *kik* Rabbit. *Ni'ihau.* Also *lāpiki, lāpaki.* See entries under *lāpaki.*

'iona *kik* Ion.

'io·'io *Pene 'io'io.* Brooder.

'iodi·side *kik* Iodide. *Eng. Potasiuma 'iodiside.* Potassium iodide.

'Ika·hō *i'oa* Idaho; Idahoan. *Dic.*

'Ī·kā·lia *i'oa* Italy; Italian. *Dic., sp. var.* Also *'Ītālia.*

'ikamu *kik* Entry, item, object. *E koho i kekahi o nā 'ikamu i hō'ike 'ia.* Choose one of the given objects. *Dic., ext. mng. Ma ka 'ikamu.* À la carte, as on a menu. Also *'oka pākahikahi.*

'ike *kik* Information. *Dic., ext. mng.* See entry below and *po'o pā'ālua.*

'ike *Laina 'ike.* Line of sight, sight line. Also *laina lena.*

'ike hā·nau See *lawena.*

'ike·pili *kik* Data. *Lit.,* associated information. See entry below and *ili, kāhuakomo, kāhuapuka, kākuhi, waiho. Hōkeo 'ikepili.* Data bank, database. *Laina 'ikepili.* Data stream, as in computer program. *Pukaaniani kolamu 'ikepili.* List editor screen, in computer program.

'ike·pili helu *kik* Statistics, i.e. numerical facts or data, in math. *Lit.,* number data.

'ī·koi honua *kik* Earth's core. *Dic., ext. mng.*

'ī·komo *kik* Filling, as for a sandwich. Comb. *'ī-* (Tah.) + *komo.* Cf. *'īpiha.*

'iku·ana *kik* Iguana. *Eng.*

'Ilaka *i'oa* Iraq; Iraqi. *Dic.* Also *'Iraka.*

'Ilana *i'oa* Iran; Iranian. *Dic.* Also *'Irana.*

'ileika *kik* Eraser. *Eng.* Also *mea holoi.*

'Ile·lani *i'oa* Ireland; Irish. *Dic.* Also *'Irelani.* See *'Ailiki.*

'ili *kik* Skin. *Dic.* See entries below and *moena 'ili 'āpanapana. 'Ili kūloko.* Subcutus, in biology. *'Ili kūwaena.* Dermis. *'Ili kūwaho.* Epidermis. *'Ōnaehana 'ili.* Integumentary system, in biology.

'ili *kik* Bark, of a plant. *Dic.* Also *'alu'alu. Wale 'ili.* Cambium, i.e. the slippery layer under the bark of a plant which is the growing area of the stem. *'Ili iho.* Inner bark. *'Ili o waho.* Outer bark.

'ili alo *kik* Surface area, in math. Comb. *'ili + alo.* Also *'ili.*

'ili iho *kik* Inner bark, as on a tree. *Lit.*, inner-layer bark.

'ī·lio *'Au 'īlio.* Dog paddle, in swimming; to dog paddle. *Lit.*, swim (like a) dog.

'ī·lio kē·lia *kik* Terrier. (Lat. *terrarius.*) Also *kēlia.*

'Ili·oki *i'oa* Pluto, the planet. *Inv.*

'ili ho'o·lohe pu'u·wai *kik* Stethoscope. *Lit.*, tube (for) listening (to the) heart. Also *kiupe ho'olohe.*

'ili·kai *kik* Sea level. *Dic., ext. mng.* Cf. *'iliwai.*

'ili kalapu wā·wae *kik* Jess, a leg strap for falcons. *Lit.*, leg strap.

'Ili·kini See *wa'a 'Ilikini, 'Īnia.*

'ili lau·lā *kik* Area (quantitative measurement). *'Ehia ka 'ili laulā o kēia huinakolu?* What is the area of this triangle? *Lit.*, surface width and breadth. Also *'ili.* Abb. *'I.*

'Ili·noe *i'oa* Illinois; Illinoisan. *Dic.*

'ili·wai *kik* Carpenter's level. *Dic.* Cf. *'ilikai.*

'ili·wehi *kik* Veneer. Comb. *'ili + wehi.*

'ili·'ili *kik* Cobble. *Dic., ext. mng.*

'ī·maka *kik* Lookout, scenic viewpoint. *Dic.*

'imi hā·'ina *ham* To solve a problem, look for a solution. *E 'imi 'oe i ka hā'ina o ka polopolema helu 'ekolu.* Solve problem three. Cf. *ho'oponopono pilikia, huli hā'ina.*

'īn Abbreviation for *'īniha* (inch).

'ī·nana See *lau 'īnana.*

-'ine *Hua'ine.* Ovum. Cf. *hua'āne.*

'ine *'a'* Negative, as of electrical charge or south pole of a magnet. *Inv.* See *hohoki, 'āne, 'ūholo uila 'ine. Huna 'ine.* Electron.

'Ī·nia *i'oa* India; Indian, i.e. referring to India and its peoples. *Dic.* Cf. *'Iniana.*

'Ini·ana *Moana 'Iniana.* Indian Ocean. *Dic.* Cf. *'Īnia.*

'Ī·nio- Indo-. Sh. *'Īnia + o.* See entry below.

'Ī·ni·o·nū·hō·lani *i'oa* Indo-Australian. Comb. *'Īnio- + Nūhōlani. Ka Una Honua 'Inionūhōlani.* Indo-Australian Plate.

'ī·niha *kik* Inch. *Dic.* Abb. *'īn.*

'Ini·kiana *i'oa* Indiana; Indianian. *Dic.* Also *'Inidiana.*

'inik·ō See *manu 'inikō.*

'ini·kua *kik* Insurance. *Dic. Uku 'inikua.* Insurance premium. *'Inikua olakino.* Medical insurance. *Helu 'inikua olakino.* Medical coverage number.

'Ini·diana *i'oa* Indiana; Indianian. *Dic., sp. var.* Also *'Inikiana.*

'Ini·done·sia *i'oa* Indonesia; Indonesian. *Eng.*

'Inu·ika *kik* Eskimo person, language or culture. *Usu. 'Inuita.* Inuit.

'ī·pale *kik* Insulation. Comb. *'ī- + pale.* See *hō'ipale.*

'ī·piha *kik* Filling, as of a tooth. Comb. *'ī-* (Tah.) + *piha.* Cf. *'īkomo.*

ʻĪ·piki *Manu ʻīpiki.* Ibis, a flightless bird in prehistoric Hawaiʻi.

ʻĪ·puka *kik* Alias or gateway, as in computer program. *Dic., ext. mng.*

ʻĪ·puka uai *kik* Sliding door. Also *puka uai.*

ʻĪ·puka pakele pahū *kik* Explosive escape hatch, as in a spaceship. *Lit.,* explosive escape door.

ʻIwa·keliʻi *iʻoa* Cassiopeia, a constellation. *Mān. (HA).*

ʻiwa·ʻiwa *kik* Maidenhair fern. *Dic.*

ʻiʻo See entry below and *helu ʻiʻo, helu ʻiʻo ʻole, helu piha, waiwai ʻiʻo.*

ʻiʻo wili·wili *kik* Meat meal. *Lit.,* ground meat. Cf. *iwi wiliwili.*

ʻIraka *iʻoa* Iraq; Iraqi. *Dic., sp. var.* Also *ʻIlaka.*

ʻIrana *iʻoa* Iran; Iranian. *Dic., sp. var.* Also *ʻIlana.*

ʻIre·lani *iʻoa* Ireland; Irish. *Dic., sp. var.* Also *ʻIlelani.* See *ʻAiliki*

ʻIse·raʻela *iʻoa* Israel; Israeli. *Dic., sp. var.*

ʻita *kik* Ether. *Eng.*

ʻĪ·tā·lia *iʻoa* Italy; Italian. *Dic., sp. var.* Also *ʻĪkālia.*

ʻo2 Abbreviation for *ʻoki hapalua* (bisect).

ʻoā *kik/heh* Crack or split, as in a sidewalk; to crack or split. *Dic.* Cf. *koā.* See *neʻe ʻoā.*

ʻoi *ʻa* Acute, in math. *Dic. Huina ʻoi.* Acute angle. *Huinakolu ʻoi.* Acute triangle.

ʻoi aku ka nui Greater than, in math. Also *nui aʻe.* See *ʻoi aku ke emi.*

ʻoi aku ke emi Less than, in math. Also *emi iho.* See *ʻoi aku ka nui.*

ʻoi·hana *kik* Business, career, occupation; professional, professionally. *Dic.* Cf. *kāloaʻa, pāʻoihana.* See entries below and *kākoʻo ʻoihana olakino. Mea hulahula ʻoihana.* Professional dancer. *Paʻi ʻoihana ʻia.* Professionally printed. *ʻOihana pōhili.* Baseball career.

ʻOi·hana Iʻa me ka Holo·holona Lō·hiu o ʻAme·lika *kik* US Fish and Wildlife Service. *Lit.,* fish and wildlife department of America.

ʻOi·hana o nā Pāka a me nā Hana Hoʻo·nanea *kik* Department of Parks and Recreation. *Dic.*

ʻoi·hana haʻi·lono *kik* Journalism. *Lit.,* occupation (to) tell the news.

ʻOi·hana Hoʻo·lā·lā a me ka Hoʻo·mohala Wai·wai o ka Moku·ʻāina ʻo Hawaiʻi *kik* Hawaiʻi State Department of Planning and Economic Development. *Lit.,* planning and economic development department of the state of Hawaiʻi.

ʻOi·hana Kā·lā o ka Moku·ʻāina ʻo Hawaiʻi *kik* Hawaiʻi State Department of Finance. *Lit.,* money department of the State of Hawaiʻi.

ʻoi·hana kā·pili *kik* Manufacturing industry. Sh. *ʻoihana + hana kāpili.* Also *ʻoiʻenehana kāpili.*

ʻOi·hana Kumu·wai·wai ʻĀina *kik* Department of Land and Natural Resources (DLNR). *Lit.,* land resources department.

ʻoi·hana lawe·lawe *kik* Service industry.

ʻOi·hana Mahi ʻAi o ka Moku·ʻāina *kik* State Department of Agriculture. *Lit.,* agricultural department of the state.

ʻoi·hana moku *kik* Navy. *Dic.* Also *pūʻali kaua moana, ʻau moku kaua.*

ʻOi·hana Pāka Au·puni *kik* National Park Service. *Lit.,* national park department.

ʻoi·hana ani·lā *kik* Weather service.

ʻō·iho·iho *ʻa* Waxy, as in texture. Comb. *ʻō- + ihoiho.*

ʻō·iwi *ʻa* Indigenous, native. *Dic., ext. mng.* Cf. *ʻāpaʻakuma. Lau nahele ʻōiwi.* Natural vegetation. *Manu ʻōiwi.* Native bird. *Meakanu ʻōiwi.* Indigenous plant.

'oi·'ene·hana *kik* Industry, especially that with a highly technological structure of production or service; industrialized; developed, as a First World Country. *He 'āina 'oi'enehana 'o Kelemānia; 'o ka hana ka'a kekahi o nā 'oi'enehana o laila.* Germany is an industrialized country; car manufacturing is one of its businesses. Sh. *hō'oi + 'enehana.* Cf. *hō'oi'enehana.* See entries below and *'enehana.* *'Āina 'oi'enehana.* Developed country; First World Country.

'oi·'ene·hana kā·pili *kik* Manufacturing industry. Sh. *'oi'enehana + hana kāpili.* Also *'oihana kāpili.*

'oi·'ene·hana kū·kulu *kik* Construction industry. *Inā emi ka nui o nā pāhana kūkulu, a laila, 'ike 'ia ka 'alu nui ma ka 'oi'enehana kūkulu.* If there are not many construction projects going on, the construction industry falls into a real slump.

'oi·'oi See *papa 'oi'oi.*

'ō·ula·ula *kik* Plankton. Redup. of *koura* (*Eastern Polynesian* [shrimp]).

'oulu *kik* Culture, as bacteria grown in a prepared nutrient. *Dic., ext. mng.* *'Oulu one.* Sand culture. *'Oulu māhuaola.* Nutrient culture.

'Ohaio *i'oa* Ohio; Ohioan. *Dic.*

'ohana See entry below and *lumi 'ohana.*

'ohana 'ā·lani *kik* Citrus. *Lit.,* orange family.

'ō·ha'i *kik* Ore. (Tah. *'ōfa'i* [stone].)

'ō hā·'ule hua *kik* Ovipositor. *Lit.,* piercing instrument (for) laying eggs.

'ohe See entries below and *mau'u 'ohe.*

'ohe ho'o·nui 'ike *kik* Microscope. *Lit.,* tube (for) enlarging sight. See *aniani kaupane'e, paepae aniani kaupane'e.*

'ohe·kani puluka *kik* Flute. *Dic. + dic.* Also *puluka.*

'ohe kī·wī *kik* Cathode-ray tube (CRT). *Lit.,* TV tube. See *'ūholo uila 'ine.*

'ohe·nā·nā *kik* Telescope. *Dic., sp. var.* Pa'a 'ohenānā. Binoculars.

'ohi *ham* To collect, as fingerprints at the scene of a crime. *Dic.* *'Ohi i ka meheu manamana lima (māka manamana lima, ki'i manamana lima).* To collect fingerprints. Cf. *kāpala.* See entry below and *hano 'ohi.*

'ohi kā·lā *Mīkini 'ohi kālā.* Cash register. *Lit.,* machine (for) collecting money. *Mea (kanaka, wahine) 'ohi kālā.* Cashier.

'ō·hiki kauka niho *kik* Dentist's pick, probe. See *wili niho.*

'ohina *kik* Fact family, as in math. *Lit.,* gathering selection.

'ō ho'o·kani *kik* Tuning fork (preceded by *ke*). *Lit.,* musical fork. Also *hao ho'okani.*

'ō·hua *kik* Extra, i.e. one hired for crowd scenes in movie or video production. *Dic., ext. mng.* See *pepeke 'ōhua.*

'ō·hui *kik* Batch, as of cookies or recruits. Comb. *'ō- + hui.*

'ō·huka *'a'* Feral but formerly domesticated, as feral goats. Comb. *'ō- + mahuka.* See *'āhiu.*

'Ok. Abbreviation for *'Okakopa* (October).

'oka See *palapala 'oka, palapala 'oka kū'ai, pepa papa 'oka, pila 'oka kālā, 'oka pākahikahi.*

'Oka·kopa *i'oa* October. *Dic.* Abb. *'Ok.*

'ō·kala *kik* Sea anemone. *Dic.* Also *'ōkole.*

'Okala·homa *i'oa* Oklahoma; Oklahoman. *Dic.*

'oka·mila *kik* Oatmeal. *Eng. Ulahi 'okamila.* Oatmeal flake.

'okana See *pānini 'okana.*

'oka pā·kahi·kahi *ham* À la carte, as on a menu. *Ni'ihau.* Also *ma ka 'ikamu.*

'oka·tene *kik* Octane. *Eng.*

'ō·keni *kik* Coin. *Dic., ext. mng.* See *pepa kālā.*

'okesa·side *kik* Oxide. *Eng.* *Kupuriku 'okesaside.* Cupric oxide. *Feriku 'okesaside.* Ferric oxide. *Ferousa 'okesaside.* Ferrous oxide. *Ferosoferiku 'okesaside.* Ferrosoferric oxide.

'oki *ham* To cut, mow. *Dic.* See entries below. *'Oki i ka mau'u.* To mow the lawn. Also *'oki i ka mahiki.*

'oki *ham* To stop or break, as an electric circuit. *Dic., ext. mng.* See *ho'oku'i.*

'oki *ham* To record, as on a cassette. *Ni'ihau.* Also *ho'opa'a.*

'okia *'a'* Cutaway. *Dic., ext. mng.* *'Ukulele 'okia.* Cutaway 'ukulele.

'oki hapa·lua *ham* To bisect, in math. *Lit.,* to cut in half. *Abb. 'o2.* See *kaha 'oki hapalua.*

'oki·kaha *ham* To slice off. *Comb. 'oki + kaha.*

'oki·kene *kik* Oxygen. *Dic.*

'oki·kene kolu *kik* Ozone. *Lit.,* triple oxygen. See *lole ana 'okikene kolu.*

'oki pā·hi'a *ham* To cut diagonally. *Dic.* Also *'oki ma ka pāhi'a.*

'oki pō·kole *kik/heh* Shortcut; to take a shortcut. *Calque from Eng. idiom.*

'ō·kole *kik* Sea anemone. *Dic.* Also *'ōkala.*

'oko·tio See *pānini 'okotio.*

'ō·kuene *kik* Layout, as of a computer keyboard. *Comb. 'ō- + kuene.* Cf. *ka'akuene.* *'Ōkuene papa pihi.* Keyboard layout.

'ō·kuhi *kik* Directions. *Sh. 'ōlelo + kuhikuhi.*

'ō·lala See *'aila 'ōlala.*

'ō·lali *kik* Glide, in linguistics. *Dic., ext. mng.*

'ō·lapa *heh* Lift-off, as of a rocket or missile; to blast off. *Dic., ext. mng.* Cf. *ho'ōlapa.*

'ō·lapa haole *kik* Aspen. *Lit.,* foreign *'ōlapa.*

'ō·lea *kik* Horn, as on a car or bicycle. *Ni'ihau.* Also *'ōlē. Mān.*

'ole Kele·wine Absolute zero, i.e. a hypothetical temperature characterized by complete absence of heat; 0 degrees K (Kelvin). *Lit.,* zero Kelvin.

'Ole·kona *i'oa* Oregon; Oregonian. *Dic.* Also *'Oregona.*

'ō·lelo *kik* Statement. *Dic.* See entries below. *'Ōlelo ala nu'ukia.* Mission statement. *'Ōlelo nu'ukia.* Vision statement.

'ō·lelo ha'i mua *kik* Foreword, preface, as in a book. *Dic.* Also *'ōlelo mua.* Cf. *'ōlelo ho'ākāka.*

'ō·lelo ho'ā·kāka *kik* Introduction, as in a book. *Lit.,* word (of) explanation. Cf. *'ōlelo ha'i mua, 'ōlelo mua.*

'ō·lelo hō·'ike *kik* Oral report. Also *hō'ike ha'i waha.*

'ō·lelo ho'o·hani *kik* Hint. *Comb. 'ōlelo + ho'ohani.* See *ho'ohani.*

'ō·lelo ho'ōho *ham* Exclamatory statement; to make such a statement. *Dic., ext. mng.*

'ō·lelo·kona *kik* Talkathon. *Comb. 'ōlelo + Eng.*

'ō·lelo kuhi lima *kik* Sign language. *Lit.,* hand-gesture language. See *kuhi lima.*

'ō·lelo mua *kik* Preamble. *Trad.* Foreword, preface, as in a book. *Dic.* Also *'ōlelo ha'i mua.* Cf. *'ōlelo ho'ākāka.*

'ō·lepe *kik* Impatiens. *Dic.* See *pukaaniani 'ōlepe.*

'ō·lepe·lepe See *pale pukaaniani 'ōlepe- lepe, pukaaniani 'ōlepe.*

'oli·ō See *manu 'oliō.*

'olili·'ula *kik* Aurora borealis, northern lights. *Lit.,* ghostly shimmering.

'olo *kik* Bob, as of a pendulum. *Dic., ext. mng.*

'olo·ka'a See *paukū 'oloka'a.*

'olo·kele *kik* Swamp. *Dic.* See *ālialia, nāele.*

'olo·ke'a *kik* Outline, as a summary using letters and numbers in headings to indicate topics and subtopics. NOTE: Only vowels with subscript numbers used as letters in outlining: A, E, I, O, U, A_1, E_1, I_1, O_1, U_1, A_2, E_2.... Pronounced: *'ā (ma'aka) kahi, 'ā (ma'aka) lua....* Dic., new mng. See *hō'oloke'a*. *'Oloke'a palapala.* Document outline, as in computer program.

'olo·ke'a koina papa *kik* Syllabus, as for a college course. *Lit.,* outline (of) class requirements. Cf. *mo'oha'awina.*

'olo·laha *kik* Oval. Ni'ihau. Also *pō'ai lō'ihi.* *'Ololaha analahi.* Ellipse.

'olume·pika *kik* Olympics; olympic. Eng. *Nā Pā'ani 'Olumepika Ho'oilo.* Winter Olympic Games.

'Olume·pika *i'oa* Olympus. Eng. *Mauna 'Olumepika.* Mount Olympus; Olympus Mons, a volcano on Mars.

'oma *Pā 'oma.* Baking pan (preceded by *ke*).

'ō·mā *kik* Maine lobster. (Fr. *homard.*)

'ō·maka hua kanu *kik* Bulb tip. *Lit.,* bulb budding. See *hua kanu.*

'ō maka kolu *kik* Trident (preceded by *ke*). *Lit.,* three- pointed spear.

'oma kō·'ala *kik* Broiler oven.

'Omana *i'oa* Oman; Omani. Eng.

'oma·wawe *kik* Microwave oven. *Lit.,* fast oven.

'ome *kik* Ohm, a unit of resistance in electricity. Eng. Cf. *anakahi uila. Ana 'ome.* Ohmmeter.

'omo·hau *kik* Icecap. *Lit.,* ice cover.

'ō·mole iho uila *kik* Battery jar, i.e. a large cylindrical container of heavy glass with an open top as used in laboratories. *Lit.,* electric battery jar.

'ō·mole omo wai·ū *kik* Baby bottle. *Lit.,* bottle (for) sucking milk. Also *'ōmole waiū.*

'ō·mole ho'o·kulu *kik* Dropping bottle, i.e. a bottle used much like an eyedropper. *Lit.,* bottle (used to) cause drops.

'ō·mole kā·lani *kik* Gallon jar, gallon jug.

'ō·mole·li'i *kik* Vial. *Lit.,* small bottle.

'ō·mole mā·lama 'elala *kik* Insect holding jar. *Lit.,* jar (for) keeping insects. Cf. *'ōmole pepehi 'elala.*

'ō·mole pepehi 'elala *kik* Insect killing jar. *Lit.,* jar (for) killing insects. Cf. *'ōmole mālama 'elala.*

'ō·mole 'apo huna·huna *kik* Dustfall jar, as for scientific experiments. *Lit.,* jar (for) catching particles.

'ō·mo'o noho *kik* Bleachers. *Lit.,* ridge (of) seats.

'ōnae·ao *kik* Universe, as a scientific term only. Sh. *'ōnaehana + ao.*

'ō·nae·hana *kik* System. Comb. *'ō- + nae + hana.* See entries below.

'ō·nae·hana ola·kino kaia·ulu *kik* Community-based health system. *Lit.,* community health system.

'ō·nae·hana hanu *kik* Respiratory system. *Lit.,* respiration system.

'ō·nae·hana hō·mona *kik* Endocrine system, in biology. *Lit.,* hormone system.

'ō·nae·hana ho'o·hehe'e mea·'ai *kik* Digestive system.

'ō·nae·hana ho'o·hua *kik* Reproductive system, in biology.

'ō·nae·hana ho'o·kau·apono *kik* Balancing mechanism, in biology. *Lit.,* system (for) compensating.

'Ō·nae·hana Ho'o·malu 'Āina Kū·lohe·ohe *kik* Natural Areas Reserves System (NARS). *Lit.,* system (for) protecting natural land. Cf. *'āina ho'omalu ao kūlohelohe.*

'ō·nae·hana ho'o·nā 'āina *kik* Land registration system. *Lit.,* system (for) settling land claims.

'ō·nae·hana kauka no ka lapa·'au like 'ana *kik* Coordinated physician referral system. *Lit.,* doctors' system for treating medicinally together.

'ō·nae·hana keki·mala *kik* Decimal system, in math. See *kekimala.*

'ō·nae·hana lō·kino *kik* Organ system, in biology.

'ō·nae·hana lolo·kū *kik* Nervous system.

'ō·nae·hana mā·kala *kik* Muscular system, in biology. *Lit.,* muscle system.

'ō·nae·hana māno·wai *kik* Circulatory system.

'ō·nae·hana mī·kā emi *kik* Low pressure system, in meteorology. *Pā ka 'ōnaehana mīkā emi ma ke komohana 'ākau o Hawai'i.* Low pressure systems develop northwest of Hawai'i. Cf. *'ōnaehana mīkā pi'i. Lit.,* waning pressure system.

'ō·nae·hana mī·kā pi'i *kik* High pressure system, in meteorology. *Lit.,* ascending pressure system. Cf. *'ōnaehana mīkā emi.*

'ō·nae·hana pale 'ea *kik* Immune system, as in mammals. *Lit.,* system (to) ward off infectious diseases.

'ō·nae·hana pū·nae·wele *kik* Network system, as in computer system.

'ō·nae·hana 'ili *kik* Integumentary system, in biology. *Lit.,* skin system.

'oneki *kik* Desktop, in computer program. *Dic., ext. mng.*

'oneki hana *kik* Payload bay, i.e. the part of a spacecraft where scientific instruments and passengers are carried. *Lit.,* work deck.

'oneki pai·laka *kik* Flight deck, as on a spaceship. *Lit.,* pilot deck.

'oni a ka moku "Rock the boat," a jump rope game of jumping and bouncing a ball at the same time. *Mān.* See *lu'u nalu po'i.*

'oni·lele *kik* Aerobics. *Lit.,* jumping movements. See *ho'oikaika pu'uwai.*

'onina *kik* Move, as in a sports play. *'Ike aku nei 'oe i kēlā 'onina? Hō ka ma'e!* Did you see that move? Wow, that was sweet! Comb. *'oni + -na.*

'oni·pā *'a* Thigmotactic. *Lit.,* move (when) touched.

'ono *A'alonoa 'ono.* Taste receptor.

'Ō·nohi 'Ula Kū·ā·hewa *i'oa* Giant Red Spot, a huge gaseous feature on Jupiter. *Lit.,* vast red eyeball.

'ō·pae Pā·kē *kik* Crayfish. *Mān.*

'ō·pae Pola·pola *kik* Tahitian prawn. *Lit.,* Tahitian shrimp.

'ō·pao *kik* Cellar. *Lit.,* somewhat cavernous. Comb. *'ō- + pao.*

'ō·paka *kik* Prism. *Dic. 'Ōpaka huinahā lō'ihi.* Rectangular prism.

'opa·kuma *kik* Opossum. *Eng. 'Opakuma 'Amelika 'Ākau.* North American opossum.

'ō·pa'a *kik* Set, in math; also as of golf clubs or silverware. Comb. *'ō- + pa'a.* Cf. *huikaina.*

'ō·pa'a hopena *kik* Sample space, i.e. the set of all possible outcomes of an experiment, in math. *Lit.,* outcome set.

'ō·pa'u *kik* Carbon (not in chemistry). Comb. *'ō- + pa'u.* Cf. *kalapona. Pepa 'ōpa'u.* Carbon paper.

'ope *kik* Pack, for items other than drinks such as gum, baseball cards or cigarettes. *Dic., ext. mng.* See *pahu, pū'olo, 'eke'eke. 'Ope hā.* Four-pack. *'Ope ono.* Six-pack.

'opi *kik* Crease, as on a pair of pants. *Dic.* Also *haki.* See entry below.

'opi *ham* To compress or collapse, as a file in computer program. *E 'opi i ka waihona i hiki ke loa'a ma ke pā malule.* Compress the file so that it can be put onto the floppy disk. *E 'opi i ka papa kuhikuhi a i ke kū'ono 'ākau o lalo.* Collapse the menu to the lower right hand corner. *Dic., ext. mng.* Cf. *ho'omahola.* See *'opihia.*

'opi·hia *'a'* Compressed or collapsed, as a file in computer program. *Pehea 'oe e wehe ai i ka waihona 'opihia?* How do you open a compressed file? Comb. *'opi + -hia.* See *'opi, ho'omahola. Waihona 'opihia.* Compressed file, collapsed file.

ʻō·piki·piki *kik/ʻa* Anxiety. *Nui ka ʻōpikipiki o kuʻu manaʻo i ka noʻonoʻo i ka holo ʻana i luna o ke kai a mamao loa.* My mind was filled with anxiety when thinking about the long trip over the sea. *Dic.*

ʻō·pili *heh* To close up tight, as a flower bud. *Dic.*

ʻō·pū *kik* Body, as of ʻukulele, guitar, etc. *Niʻihau.* See *ʻukulele. Mākala ʻōpū.* Abdominal muscle.

ʻō·pua *Ao ʻōpua.* Cumulus cloud. Comb. *ao* + dic.

ʻō·puʻu *kik* Geometric cone. *Dic.*

ʻō·puʻu *kik* Bulb. *Niʻihau.* Cf. *ōpuʻuahi, ʻōpuʻukukui. Ana kawaūea ʻōpuʻu pulu a maloʻo.* Wet-and-dry-bulb hygrometer.

ʻō·puʻu·ahi *kik* Spark plug. *Niʻihau.*

ʻō·puʻu·hame *kik* Clove, the spice. Comb. *ʻōpuʻu + hame.*

ʻō·puʻu·kukui *kik* Light bulb. *Niʻihau.*

ʻowaka·waka *kik* Reflector. *Dic., ext. mng.* Also *kukui ʻowakawaka.*

ʻō·wī *ham* To peer. *Niʻihau.* Also *kiʻei.*

ʻō·wili *kik* Roll, as of film. *Dic., ext. mng. ʻŌwili kiʻi.* Roll of film. *Niʻihau. ʻŌwili kiʻiaka.* Filmstrip.

ʻoʻa *kik* Green onion (purple bulb becoming white close to tip). *Mān.* (RNM). Cf. *lina.*

ʻō·ʻā *ʻa* Mixed, combined, in math and science. *Dic., ext. mng. Helu ʻōʻā.* Mixed number. *Kekimala ʻōʻā.* Mixed decimal. *Mekala ʻōʻā.* Alloy. Also *metala ʻōʻā. ʻŌʻā kemikala ʻia.* Chemically combined.

ʻō·ʻaki *kik* Geometrid moth. *Ua maopopo ʻia ka poʻiiʻa ʻana a ka piohē a ka ʻōʻaki i ka luapoʻi ola.* Larvae of the geometrid moth has been known to catch active prey. Comb. *ʻōkaʻi + ʻaki/* metathesis of *ʻōkaʻi.*

ʻoʻe *ham* To skim, as oil from top of stew. *Mān.* Also *kīʻoʻe.*

ʻō ʻeli *kik* Spading fork (preceded by *ke*). Lit., fork (for) digging.

ʻoʻeno *kik* Twill plaiting. *Dic.* Also *maka pūalu.*

ʻō·ʻili See *papa ʻōʻili.*

ʻoʻopu Pā·kē *kik* Catfish. *Mān.*

ʻō·ʻū *ham* To abort, as in computer program. *Ua ʻōʻū ʻia ka hoʻoneʻe waihona ʻana.* The file transfer was aborted. *Dic., ext. mng.*

ʻora·gano·poso·pahate *kik* Organophosphate. *Eng.*

ʻOre·gona *iʻoa* Oregon; Oregonian. *Eng.* Also *ʻOlekona.*

ʻota *kik* Otter. *Eng.*

ʻū- A prefix indicating the instrument or cause of a particular action. *Dic., ext. mng.* See entries below.

ʻuao *kik/ham* Referee, umpire; to referee. *Dic.* Also *ʻuao haʻuki.* See entry below and *kanaka makaʻala ʻupena.*

ʻuao *ham* To arbitrate. *Ma kekahi mau ʻano hihia o kekahi hui me nā poʻe limahana, na kekahi luna hoʻokolokolo e ʻuao.* In some disputes between a company and the employees, a judge will arbitrate. *Dic. Ka ʻuao ʻana.* Arbitration.

ʻuala kahiki See entries below. *Kipi uala kahiki.* Potato chip.

ʻuala kahiki koli·koli *kik* Hash-brown potatoes. *Lit.*, whittled potato. Also *ʻuala kolikoli.*

ʻuala kahiki pepei·ao *kik* Scalloped potatoes. *Lit.*, potatoes (like) scallops. Also *ʻuala pepeiao.*

ʻuiki uila *kik* Fuse. *Lit.*, electric fuse. *Pahu ʻuiki uila.* Fuse box.

ʻuiki ʻā *kik* Filament, as in a light bulb. *Lit.*, wick (for) lighting. *Kukui ʻuiki ʻā.* Incandescent light.

ʻui·ʻuiki See *nalo ʻuiʻuiki.*

ʻū·omo *kik* Sorbent, an absorbent material such as used in chromatography. Comb. *ʻū- + omo.* See *omo.*

ʻū·omo ikehu lā *kik* Solar panel. *Lit.*, instrument (for) sucking solar energy.

Māmaka Kaiao / 175

'ū·hā moa *kik* Chicken thigh. See *pālaumoa*.

'ū·hehe'e *kik* Solvent. Comb. *'ū-* + *hehe'e*. See *mea hehe'e*. *'Ūhehe'e wai*. Aqueous, i.e. having water as a solvent, in science. *Mā'ō'āna 'ūhehe'e wai*. Aqueous solution.

'ū·hili *kik* Bat, club, racket. Comb. *'ū-* + *hili*. *'Ūhili kolepa*. Golf club.

'ū·hini *kik* Grasshopper. *Dic*.

'ū·hini·hone *Pāpapa 'ūhinihone*. Honey locust bean.

'ū·hini nēnē *kik* Cricket. *Lit*., chirping cricket. *'Ūhini nēnē kahakai*. Beach cricket. *'Ūhini nēnē pele*. Lava cricket.

'ū·hini·pule *kik* Praying mantis. *Lit*., praying grasshopper.

'ū·holo uila *kik* Electrode. *Lit*., instrument (for) conducting electricity. *'Ūholo uila 'āne*. Anode, i.e. the positive electrode in an electrical circuit. *'Ūholo uila 'ine*. Cathode, i.e. the negative electrode in an electric circuit.

'ū·hō·lo·a *kik* Dispenser, i.e. a dispensing container of any kind. Comb. *'ū-* + *hōlo'a*. See entries below and *hōlo'a*. *'Ūhōlo'a kāwele pepa*. Paper towel dispenser. *'Ūhōlo'a kopa*. Soap dispenser.

'ū·hō·lo·a kaka·lina *kik* Carburetor, as in an internal-combustion engine. *Lit*., gasoline dispenser.

'ū·hō·lo·a mā·'ō·'āna *kik* Buret, i.e. a precision-made piece of glassware used to measure and deliver accurate volumes of solutions, in science. *Lit*., solution dispenser.

'ū·hū *kik* Enzyme. Comb. *'ū-* + *hū*.

'ū·kaomi hano kui *kik* Syringe plunger. Comb. *'ū-* + *kaomi* + *hano kui*. Also *'ūkaomi*, *'ūkōmi hano kui*, *'ūkōmi*. Cf. *pāuma*.

'ū·kake uila *kik* Commutator, i.e. a switch on a motor running on direct current that causes the current to reverse every half turn. *Lit*., instrument (for) slipping electricity back and forth.

'ukē *heh* To swing, as a pendulum. *Dic*. See *ule'o*. *Wā 'ukē*. Period of a pendulum.

'ū·kele *kik* Mud. *Dic*. Also *lepo pohō*.

'ū·kōmi See *'ūkaomi hano kui*.

'uku·lele *kik* 'Ukulele. *Dic*. See entries below. For parts, see *kaula, nī'au, nī'au li'ili'i, nī'au nui, papa kī, wā, 'au, 'ōpū*.

'uku·lele Ohta-san *kik* Ohta-san 'ukulele.

'uku·lele hā·'oi *kik* Baritone 'ukulele. See *hā'oi*.

'uku·lele leo 'ekahi *kik* Soprano 'ukulele. See *leo 'ekahi*.

'uku·lele leo 'ekolu *kik* Tenor 'ukulele. See *leo 'ekolu*.

'uku·lele Lili'u *kik* Lili'u 'ukulele.

'uku·lele pahu kī·kā *kik* Cigar-box 'ukulele. *Lit*., cigar-box 'ukulele.

'uku·lele pū·niu *kik* Coconut shell 'ukulele.

'uku·lele 'ea honu *kik* Turtle shell 'ukulele.

'uku·lele 'elua puka *kik* Double-hole 'ukulele. *Lit*., two holes 'ukulele.

'uku·lele 'ewalu kaula *kik* Eight-string 'ukulele.

'uku·lele 'okia *kik* Cutaway 'ukulele. See *'okia*.

'uku wai *kik* Daphnia. *Lit*., water flea.

'ū·lau *kik* Spatula, pancake turner. *Lit*., flat instrument. Comb. *'ū-* + *lau*. See *'ali 'ūlau*. *'Ūlau kahi*. Rubber spatula.

'ula·kai·ano *kik* Anthocyanin, i.e. a kind of pigment producing blue to red coloring in flowers and plants. Comb. *'ula* + *kyanos* [*Gr*., blue].

'ulā·li'i *kik* Measles. *Dic*.

'ula mā·ku'e 'a' Magenta. *Dic*., *ext. mng*.

'ula·'ula *Manu 'ula'ula*. Cardinal. *Dic*. Also *manu māka'i*.

'ulea *kik* Urea. *Eng*.

Māmaka Kaiao / 176

'ulī·keke *kik* Baby rattle. *Sh.* *'ulī'ulī +nakeke. Lina 'ulīkeke.* Tambourine.

'ū·lili *kik* Whistle, as a referee's. *Dic.*

'ū·lili *kik* Railing support, balluster. *Dic.* Also *hūlili.* Cf. *paehumu.*

'ū·lou *kik* Bonding instrument. Comb. *'ū- + lou.*

'ū·lū *ham* To pack, as a suitcase. *Wilcox:* u-lu.

'Ulu·kuae *i'oa* Uruguay; Uruguayan. *Eng.* Also *'Uruguae.*

'ū·mau·pa'a *kik* Component, constituent. Comb. *'ū- + maupa'a.*

'ume *kik* Drawer. *Dic., ext. mng.* See *pahu 'ume.*

'ume·kau·maha *kik* Gravity. *Dic. Mīkini ho'opau 'umekaumaha.* Antigravity machine. *Piko 'umekaumaha.* Center of gravity. *'Umekaumaha māiki.* Microgravity. *'Umekaumaha 'ole.* Zero gravity.

'ume·lau·oho *kik* Capillary. Comb. *'ume + lauoho.* See *paipuli'i 'umelauoho. Wai 'umelauoho.* Capillary water.

'ume mā·kē·neki *kik* Magnetism. *Lit.*, magnet attraction.

'ume niniu *ham* Centripetal, i.e. acting in a direction toward a center. *Lit.*, spinning attraction. Cf. *lele niniu. Manehu 'ume niniu.* Centripetal force.

'umi See entries below and *hapa 'umi.*

'umi *ham* To pressure, in basketball. *'Umi nui 'ia 'o Karl Malone e 'ekolu mea kūpale i nā minuke hope loa o ka ho'okūkū.* Karl Malone usually gets pressured by three defenders in the last few minutes of the game. *Dic., ext. mng.*

'umi·ā·pau *kik* Damping-off, i.e. a diseased condition of seedlings or cuttings caused by fungi and characterized by wilting or rotting. Comb. *'umi + ā + pau.*

'umi kapu·a'i See *laina 'umi kapua'i, 'a'ena 'umi kapua'i.*

'ū·mi'i *ham* To staple. *Ni'ihau.* See entries below and *kui 'ūmi'i pepa, mea 'ūmi'i pepa, mea wehe 'ūmi'i, papa 'ūmi'i, pihi 'ūmi'i.*

'ū·mi'i *ham* Clamp. *Dic. 'Ūmi'i hano ho'okolohua.* Test tube clamp. *'Ūmi'i ho'opa'a.* Utility clamp. Cf. *'ūpā ho'opa'a. 'Ūmi'i pani.* Pinch clamp.

'ū·mi'i kaula *kik* Capo, as used on a fretted instrument to raise the pitch of all strings. *Lit.*, string clamp.

'ū·mi'i·lau *kik* Planthopper (Oliarus tamehameha). Comb. *'ūmi'i + lau.* Cf. *'ūmi'ikō* (dic.).

'ū·mi'i lau·oho *ham* Bobby pin. *Ni'ihau.*

'ū·mi'i·nalo *kik* Venus flytrap. Comb. *'ūmi'i + nalo.*

'ū·mi'i 'ili·kuapo *ham* Belt buckle. Also *'ūmi'i.*

'umi·'umi See *pakuhi pahu me ka 'umi'umi.*

'umi·'umi lehe·lehe *kik* Moustache. *Lit.*, lip beard. Cf. *'umi'umi 'auae.*

'umi·'umi 'au·ae *kik* Beard, excluding the moustache. Usu. *'umi'umi.* *Lit.*, chin beard. Cf. *'umi'umi lehelehe.*

'ū·mō·'aui *kik* Reactant, reagent. Comb. *'ū- + mō'aui.* See *mō'aui.*

'ū·mō·'aui·wawe *kik* Catalyst, i.e. a substance which increases the rate of a chemical reaction without being permanently changed itself. Comb. *'ūmō'aui + wawe.* Also *hō'eleu mō'aui.*

'uni·ona *kik* Union. *Dic., sp. var. Kūka'i 'aelike 'uniona.* Collective bargaining.

'ū·niu *heh* To pivot. *Sh. 'ū- + 'ōniu.* See *kū 'ūniu.*

'ū·nina *kik* Gelatin. Var. of *'ūlina,* ext. def. Cf. *palaholo.*

'unu *'a* Sprained. *Mān.*

'ū·pā ho'o·pa'a *kik* Forceps. *Lit.*, instrument (for) holding fast. Cf. *'ūmi'i ho'opa'a.*

ʻū·pā kā·pō·ʻai *kik* Compass, an instrument for describing circles or transferring measurements, in math. Comb. ʻūpā + -kāpōʻai. Cf. *pānānā*.

ʻū·palu ʻa' Mild, as a solution. *E hoʻomākaukau i kekahi māʻōʻāna kopa ʻūpalu.* Prepare a mild solution of soap. *Dic.* See ʻakika ʻūpalu kūlohelohe.

ʻupena *kik* Net, as of a basket on basketball court or a volleyball net. *He ʻupena wale iho nō.* Nothing but net. *Dic.*, ext. mng. *Ua ʻupena ke kinopōpō.* Net ball, in volleyball. *Niʻihau.* Also *ua ʻupena. Kanaka makaʻala ʻupena.* Referee, in volleyball. See ʻuao. *ʻAʻena ʻupena.* Net violation. *ʻUpena pōpaʻipaʻi.* Volleyball net.

ʻupena ʻelala *kik* Insect net. See entries below.

ʻupena ʻelala hoʻo·lewa·lewa *kik* Insect fixed net, as hung in a wind corridor to catch insects. *Lit.*, hung insect net.

ʻupena ʻelala kā·ʻe·ʻe *kik* Insect sweep net. *Lit.*, kāʻeʻe-style net (for) insects.

ʻupena ʻelala ʻeke *kik* Insect bag net, as for collecting insects from a small bush. *Lit.*, bag insect net.

ʻū·pī·hu·ʻa *kik* Styrofoam. *Lit.*, foam sponge.

ʻū·piki *ham* Trap, in basketball; to make such a play. *Dic.*, ext. mng.

ʻū·piki lima *kik* Handcuffs. *Dic.*

ʻū·pī·lā·ʻau *kik* Cork, the material or the tree. *Lit.*, wooden sponge.

ʻū·pī·ʻū ʻa' Spongy, as leaves of the *pānini.* Comb. ʻūpī + ʻū-.

ʻū·poho *kik* Bagpipe. *Dic.* Also *pila ʻūpoho.*

ʻū·po·ʻi *ham* To dunk (the ball), in basketball. *Dic.*, ext. mng. Also *pakā.* Cf. *pakī.*

ʻū·ʻoki puni uila *kik* Circuit breaker, i.e. a device which automatically interrupts electric current before wires in a circuit get too hot. *Lit.*, instrument (which) breaks electric circuit.

ʻUgana *iʻoa* Uganda; Ugandan. *Eng.*

ʻUru·guae *iʻoa* Uruguay; Uruguayan. *Eng.* Also *ʻUlukuae.*

ʻŪ·tā *iʻoa* Utah; Utahan, Utahn. *Dic.*, sp. var. Also *Mauna Pōhaku.*

B

Bahama *iʻoa* Bahamas; Bahamian. *Dic.* Also *Pahama.*

bā·lē *kik* Ballet. *Eng.* Also *pālē, hulahula pālē.*

Bana·gala·desa *iʻoa* Bangladesh. *Eng.*

Bara·zila *iʻoa* Brazil; Brazilian. *Dic.* Also *Palakila.*

bari·uma *kik* Barium. *Eng.*

Bele·giuma *iʻoa* Belgium; Belgian. *Dic.* Also *Pelekiuma.*

Belize *iʻoa* Belize; Belizean. *Eng.*

bene·zene *kik* Benzene. *Eng.*

beta *kik* Beta. *Eng. Huna beta.* Beta particle, in chemistry.

bisula·fahate *kik* Bisulfate. *Eng. Sodiuma bisulafahate.* Sodium bisulfate.

Boli·via *iʻoa* Bolivia; Bolivian. *Eng.*

Botu·ana *iʻoa* Botswana. *Eng.*

Bulu·garia *iʻoa* Bulgaria; Bulgarian. *Dic.* Also *Pulukalia.*

Bura·kina Faso *iʻoa* Burkina Faso. *Eng.*

Buruma *iʻoa* Burma; Burmese. *Eng.* Also *Puruma.*

Butana *iʻoa* Bhutan; Bhutanese. *Eng.*

butane *kik* Butane. *Eng.*

C

CD *kik* CD, compact disk (pronounced *sēdē*). *Eng.* Also *sēdē; pā CD, pā sēdē* (preceded by *ke*).

D

Dakota Hema *iʻoa* South Dakota; South Dakotan. *Eng.* Also *Kakoka Hema.*

Dakota ʻĀ·kau *iʻoa* North Dakota; North Dakotan. *Eng.* Also *Kakoka ʻĀkau.*

Dek. Abbreviation for *Dekemapa* (December). See *Kekemapa*.

Deke·mapa *i'oa* Var. of *Kekemapa* (December). Abb. *Dek*.

Dela·uea *i'oa* Delaware; Delawarean. *Dic.*, *sp. var.* Also *Kelauea*.

Dene·maka *i'oa* Denmark; Dane; Danish. *Dic.* Also *Kenemaka*.

diazi·nona *kik* Diazinon. *Eng.*

dieli·dirina *kik* Dieldrin, a kind of insecticide. *Eng.* Cf. *'alidirina*. See *lā'au make*.

dio·kesa·side *kik* Dioxide. *Eng.* *Sulufura diokesaside*. Sulfur dioxide. *Naikokene diokesaside*. Nitrogen dioxide.

disuli·faside *kik* Disulfide. *Eng.* *Karabona disulifaside*. Carbon disulfide.

F

Faka·lana *Pae Moku Fakalana*. Falkland Islands, Falklands.

Farani *i'oa* France; French. *Dic.* Also *Palani*.

Faso *Burakina Faso*. Burkina Faso.

fea *kik* Fair. *Eng.* Also *hō'ike'ike*.

feriku 'okesa·side *kik* Ferric oxide.

fero·usa Ferrous. *Eng.* See entries below.

fero·usa kara·bona·hate *kik* Ferrous carbonate. *Eng.*

fero·usa 'okesa·side *kik* Ferrous oxide. *Eng.*

fero·usa sula·fahate *kik* Ferrous sulfate. *Eng.*

fero·usa sula·faside *kik* Ferrous sulfide. *Eng.*

fero·sofe·riku 'okesa·side *kik* Ferrosoferric oxide. *Eng.*

Fini·lana *i'oa* Finland; Finn; Finnish. *Dic.* Also *Finilani*.

Fini·lani *i'oa* Finland; Finn; Finnish. *Eng.* Also *Finilana*.

Folo·rida *i'oa* Florida; Floridan, Floridian. *Dic.* Also *Pololika*.

fori·miku Formic. *Eng.* *'Akika forimiku*. Formic acid.

FM *kik* FM, frequency modulation (pronounced *fāmū*). *Eng.* Cf. *AM*.

G

galai·sine *kik* Glycine. *Eng.*

Gāna *i'oa* Ghana; Ghanaian, Ghanian. *Eng.*

Gabona *i'oa* Gabon; Gabonese. *Eng.* Also *Kapona*.

Guama *i'oa* Guam; Guamanian. *Eng.*

R

Rea *i'oa* Rhea, the second largest moon of Saturn. *Eng.*

rese·pine *kik* Reserpine, an alkaloid used as a tranquilizer. *Eng.*

rī·taia *heh* To retire. *Eng.* Also *līkaia, ho'omaha loa*.

Romā·nia *i'oa* Romania; Romanian. *Eng.*

Rode 'Ai·lana *i'oa* Rhode Island; Rhode Islander. *Dic.* Also *Loke 'Ailana*.

Rua·nada *i'oa* Rwanda; Rwandan. *Eng.*

Rū·sia *i'oa* Russia; Russian. *Dic.*, *sp. var.* Also *Lūkia*.

S

Saudi 'Ala·pia *i'oa* Saudi Arabia; Saudi. Comb. *Eng.* + *'Alapia* (dic.). Also *Saudi 'Arabia*.

Saudi 'Ara·bia *i'oa* Saudi Arabia; Saudi. *Eng.* Also *Saudi 'Alapia*.

Sahara Komo·hana *i'oa* Western Sahara; Western Saharan. Comb. *Eng.* + *komohana*.

sala·mena *kik* Salamander. *Eng.* Also *kalamena*.

Sana Helena *Mauna Sana Helena*. Mount Saint Helens. Also *Mauna Kana Helena*.

sawana *kik* Savanna, i.e. a tropical or subtropical grassland containing scattered trees. *Eng.*

sasa·palasa *kik* Sassafras. *Eng.*

satano·usa kolori·side *kik* Stannous chloride. *Eng.*

Seko·tia *i'oa* Scotland; Scot, Scots, Scottish. *Dic.* Also *Kekokia*.

Sepa·nia *i'oa* Spain. *Dic.* Also *Kepania*.

sē·dē See CD.

sila *kik* Seal. *Mān. Sila Hawai'i.* Hawaiian monk seal. *Sila pūhuluhulu.* Fur seal.

silaka *kik* Silica. *Eng. Palaholo silaka g.* Silica gel g, a powder used as the sorbent layer in thin-layer chromatography (pronounced *palaholo silaka gā*).

sili·kone *kik* Silicon. *Eng.*

sī·wila *Kānāwai sīwila.* Civil law. Also *kānāwai kīwila.*

-side Suffix in chemical compounds and terms: -ide.

siri·ala *kik* Cereal. *Eng.* Also *kiliala.*

solono·kiuma *kik* Strontium. *Eng.*

Soma·lia *i'oa* Somalia; Somalian. *Eng.*

sodi·uma *kik* Sodium. *Eng. Sodiuma kitarahate.* Sodium citrate. *Sodiuma bisulafahate.* Sodium bisulfate.

sū·kini *kik* Zucchini. *Eng.*

sula·fahate *kik* Sulfate. *Eng. Kupuriku sulafahate.* Cupric sulfate.

sula·faside *kik* Sulfide. *Eng. Kupuriku sulafaside.* Cupric sulfide. *Ferousa sulafaside.* Ferrous sulfide.

sulu·fura dio·kesa·side *kik* Sulfur dioxide. *Eng.* Also *kūkaepele 'okikene lua.*

sulu·furiku Sulfuric. *Eng. 'Akika sulufuriku.* Sulfuric acid.

supero·posa·pahate *kik* Superphosphate. *Eng.*

Sudana *i'oa* Sudan; Sudanese. *Eng.*

Suria *i'oa* Syria; Syrian. *Trad.*

T

tā *kik* Tar. *Dic.* Also *kā.*

taea *kik* Tire. *Eng.* Also *kaea. Taea paikikala.* Bicycle tire.

Tai·uana *i'oa* Taiwan; Taiwanese. *Eng.*

taika *kik* Taiga. *Eng.*

tala·pia *kik* Tilapia. *Eng.*

Tana·zania *i'oa* Tanzania; Tanzanian. *Eng.*

tanika *'a'* Tannic. *Eng. 'Akika tanika.* Tannic acid.

Tekasa *i'oa* Texas; Texan. *Eng.* Also *Kekeka, Teseta.*

Tene·sī *i'oa* Tennessee; Tennessean. *Dic., sp. var.* Also *Kenekī*

Teseta *i'oa* Texas; Texan. *Dic.* Also *Kekeka, Tekasa.*

Tetisa *i'oa* Tethys, a moon of Saturn. *Eng.*

tō·fū *kik* Tofu, bean curd. *Japn.*

tō·tia *kik* Tortilla. *Sp.*

tū·kana *kik* Toucan. *Eng.*

tuko *kik* Glue. (*Eng. Duco.*) *Tuko ke'oke'o.* Paste. *Tuko laholio.* Rubber cement.

tuna *kik* Tuna. *Eng. Kini tuna.* Can of tuna.

Tuni·sia *i'oa* Tunisia; Tunisian. *Eng.*

Tureke *i'oa* Turkey; Turk; Turkish. *Dic.* Also *Kuleke.*

V

Vere·mona *i'oa* Vermont; Vermonter. *Eng.* Also *Welemoneka, Veremoneta.*

Vere·moneta *i'oa* Vermont; Vermonter. *Dic.* Also *Welemoneka, Veremona.*

Z

Zā·ire *i'oa* Zaire; Zairian. *Eng.*

Zami·bia *i'oa* Zambia; Zambian. *Eng.*

Zima·babue *i'oa* Zimbabwe; Zimbabwean. *Eng.*

Māhele ʻŌlelo Pelekānia

Māmaka Kaiao
Māhele ʻŌlelo Pelekānia

A

abacus Kunipona.
abalone Pāua.
abbreviation Hua hōʻailona. See *initial*.
abdominal muscle Mākala ʻōpū.
-able See Hawaiian entry pē-.
abort To ~, as in computer program. ʻŌʻū.
absolute location In geography. Kuhikuhina. See *relative location*.
absolute value In math. Waiwai ʻiʻo. See *value*.
absolute zero A hypothetical temperature characterized by complete absence of heat; also zero degrees K (Kelvin). ʻOle Kelewine.
absorb Omo. See *adsorb, sorbent*.
AC Alternating current. Au māʻaloʻalo. ~ *electricity*. Uila au māʻaloʻalo. See *DC*.
accelerate Hoʻopiʻi i ka māmā holo; piʻi ka māmā holo. See *acceleration, decelerate*.
acceleration Piʻi māmā holo. See *accelerate, deceleration*.
accent Or stress, in linguistics. Kālele. ~ *unit or measure*. Paukū kālele. *In speech*. Pualono. *Foreign* ~. Pualono ʻē.
access To ~, as in computer program. Komo (i loko o).
accessories Or peripherals, as for a computer. Lakolako.
accident Ulia. *Car* ~. Ulia kaʻa.
account As in a bank. Waihona kālā. *Charge or credit* ~. Waihona kāki. *Checking* ~. Waihona kīkoʻo. *Expense* ~. Waihona hoʻolilo. *Savings* ~. Waihona hoʻāhu kālā. *As in a computer program or any listing of charges*. Moʻokāki.

accounting Mālama moʻohelu kālā. See *budget*.
accumulate To lay away, store away. Hoʻāhu.
ace In volleyball. ʻAi hāʻawi wale, ʻeki.
acetate A salt/ester of ascetic acid. ʻĀkeka. *Ethyl* ~. ʻĀkeka ʻeto.
acetone ʻAkekona.
acetylene ʻAseteline.
Achernar A star. Hinalua.
achievement Certificate of ~. Palapala hoʻokō. See *record*.
acid ʻAkika. ~ *indicator*. Ana ʻakika. See *litmus paper*. *Amino* ~. ʻAkika ʻamino. *Carbonic* ~. ʻAkika kalapona. *Carboxylic* ~. ʻAkika pūhui kalapona. *Formic* ~. ʻAkika forimiku. *Hydrochloric* ~. ʻAkika haidorokoloriku. *Naturally occurring weak* ~. ʻAkika ʻūpalu kūlohelohe. *Nitric* ~. ʻAkika naikokene, ʻakika nikiriku. *Sulfuric* ~. ʻAkika sulufuriku. *Tannic* ~. ʻAkika tanika.
acidic anhydride ʻAnahaidaraside ʻakika. See *anhydride*.
acorn Hua kumu ʻoka, ʻēkona.
acoustics The science of ~. Kālaikani.
acquired immune deficiency syndrome AIDS. Maʻi pale ʻea pau, pale ʻea pau. See *HIV*.
across As in a crossword puzzle. Pololei aʻe. See *down*. *Pages* ~, *as in computer program*. ʻEhia ʻaoʻao haʻaʻeʻe?
acrylic Hūkaʻa ʻea.
act As a law, decree or edict, in government. Kānāwai. See Hawaiian entries under *kānāwai*. *Endangered Species* ~. Kānāwai Lāhulu ʻAne Halapohe.
act To ~, as in a play, movie or video production. Hana keaka. See *act out*.
actinoid One of the fourteen elements that follow actinium on the periodic table. ʻAkinoika.

action-reaction pair *Two forces having equal strength but opposite directions, in science.* Paʻa manehu kūʻēʻē.

active *As a volcano.* ʻĀ. See *activity*. ~ *volcano*. Lua pele ʻā.

activity *Chemical* ~. Mōʻaui kemikala. *Secondary* ~, *of a volcano*. ʻĀ kualua. See *active*.

actor Mea hana keaka. See *extra, role*.

act out *To* ~, *as a math problem*. Hana keaka.

acute *In math.* ʻOi. ~ *angle*. Huina ʻoi. ~ *triangle*. Huinakolu ʻoi.

adapt *To* ~, *as a written document by shortening or lengthening, or by changing the form or style.* Hakuloli. See *modernize*.

adapt Hoʻomaʻa. See *adaptive radiation*. *To become* ~*ed to*. Maʻa. *To* ~ *biologically*. Hoʻoliliuwelo. *To be biologically* ~*ed to*. Liliuwelo.

adaptive radiation *In biology*. Malele hoʻoliliuwelo.

add *In math.* Hoʻohui. See *addition, plus sign*.

addend *In math.* Helu hoʻohui.

addiction *Also addicted*. Hei.

addition *In math.* Hōʻuluʻulu. See *add, plus sign*.

additive color *One of the primary colors (red, blue, green) which, when added together, produce white light.* Waihoʻoluʻu hui kea.

adhesion *Also adhesive*. Pīlekaleka. See *cohesion*.

adipogenesis *The formation of fat or fatty tissue in a body; also adipogenetic.* Haʻakupu ʻailakele. See *adipose tissue*.

adipose tissue *Animal tissue in which fat is stored.* ʻAʻa hunaola ʻailakele.

administration *A team of executive branch officials appointed by the President, in government.* Papa luna hoʻokele. See *director*.

administrator *As a controller for computer network.* Kahu. *Network* ~. Kahu pūnaewele.

adobe ʻAkopie. ~ *block*. Uinihapa ʻakopie.

adopt *As a highway or other public area for environmental cleanup or maintenance.* Lawe mālama.

adsorb Omowaho. See *absorb, solvent front*.

advanced level Pae holomua.

advantage Keu pono.

adventure *As stories or movies.* ʻAʻanahoa.

aerate Hōʻeaea. See *aerobic*. Aerated. Eaea.

aerobic *Living, active, or occurring only in presence of oxygen.* Eaea. See entry below and *anaerobic decomposition*. ~ *decomposition or putrefaction*. Ka hoʻohāpopopo eaea ʻana.

aerobic Hoʻoikaika puʻuwai. See *aerobics*. ~ *activity*. Hana hoʻoikaika puʻuwai. ~ *point*. ʻAi hoʻoikaika puʻuwai.

aerobics ʻOnilele. See *aerobic*.

aerosol can Kini kīkī.

affinity *To have an* ~ *for something*. Hiaʻume.

affix Pākuʻina. See *prefix, infix, suffix*.

affricate *In linguistics*. Pōhahī.

Afghanistan *Also Afghan, Afghani.* ʻApekanikana, ʻAfekanisana.

Africa *Also African.* ʻApelika, ʻAferika. *Central African Republic*. Lepupalika ʻApelika Waena. *South* ~. ʻApelika Hema, ʻAferika Hema.

after- Muli. See *post-*. ~*school sports*. Haʻuki muli kula.

agapanthus Līlia ʻAikupika, līlia ʻAigupita.

age *To* ~, *as a person; aged*. Mākuakua. *Aging*. Ka mākuakua ʻana. *Ice* ~. Au paʻahau.

agenda *As for a meeting.* Papa kumumanaʻo.

aggregate *To bind together.* Hoʻopili pū.
aggression *As an attack by one country upon another.* Lele kaua. *As a threat of attack by one country upon another.* Lele hoʻonanā.
agriculture *College of ~.* Koleke mahiʻai. *State Department of ~.* ʻOihana Mahi ʻAi o ka Mokuʻāina.
aid *Hearing ~.* Pihi hoʻonui lohe *(preceded by* ke).
AIDS *Acquired immune deficiency syndrome.* Maʻi pale ʻea pau, pale ʻea pau. See *HIV*.
air conditioner Mīkini hōʻolu ea, hōʻolu ea.
aircraft *Military transport ~.* Mokulele hali koa.
air displacement Pohupani ea.
air force Pūʻali kaua lewa.
airmail *Also to send by airmail.* Halilele. *~ letter.* Leka halilele. *~ stamp.* Poʻoleka halilele *(preceded by* ke).
air mass *As in weather.* Ahu ea.
air mattress Pela hoʻolana.
air pollution Haumia ea.
air pressure *As in a tire.* Mīkā ea.
air resistance Āohiohi ea. See *resistance*.
air stone *The porous rock in an aquarium that creates tiny bubbles at the surface of the water to facilitate the exchange of gases.* Pōhaku puka ea.
airtight Paʻa ea. *An ~ container.* He hōkelo paʻa ea.
air valve *As on a tire.* Pihi pāumu ea *(preceded by* ke).
air vent Puka ea.
aisle *As in a supermarket.* Ala, alakaha.
ajar *Also unlocked, open for business.* Hemo. See *open wide*.
Alabama *Also Alabaman, Alabamian.* ʻAlapama, ʻAlabama.
à la carte *As on a menu.* Ma ka ʻikamu, ʻoka pākahikahi.
alanine *An amino acid.* ʻAlanine.

alarm *~ clock.* Uaki hoʻāla, uāki hoʻāla. *Smoke ~.* Oeoe uahi.
Alaska *Also Alaskan.* ʻĀlaka, ʻAlaseka.
Albania *Also Albanian.* ʻAlepania, ʻAlabania.
alcohol ʻAlekohola.
Alderamin *A star.* ʻAnamuli.
aldrin *A kind of insecticide.* ʻAlidirina. See *dieldrin, poison*.
Aleut See *Aleutian*.
Aleutian *Also Aleut.* ʻAleuta. *~ Islands.* Ka Paeʻāina ʻo ʻAleuta. *~ Trench.* Ka ʻAuwaha ʻAleuta.
alfalfa sprout Kawowo ʻalapapa.
algae *General term.* Līoho.
algebra Hōʻailona helu. *Algebraic expression.* Haʻi hōʻailona helu.
Algeria *Also Algerian.* ʻAlekelia, ʻAlegeria.
Algol *A star.* Pōʻā.
alias *Also gateway, in computer program.* ʻĪpuka.
alien *Illegal ~; to arrive as an illegal ~.* Pae malū. *Legal ~; to arrive as a legal ~.* Pae kānāwai. *Space ~, extraterrestrial.* Mea ao ʻē.
align *To ~, as type in computer program.* Hoʻolālani.
alkali *Also alkaline.* ʻĀkilikai. See *entries below*.
alkali metal *One of the family of elements in Group 1 of the periodic table.* Mekala ʻākilikai. See *alkaline earth metal*.
alkaline earth metal *One of the family of elements in Group 2 of the periodic table.* Mekala honua ʻākilikai. See *alkali metal*.
alkaloid ʻAlakaloida.
alkane ʻAlakane. See *alkene, alkyne*. *~ series, i.e. saturated hydrocarbons where all the carbon atoms are joined by single covalent bonds.* Pūkaʻina ʻalakane.
alkene ʻAlakene. See *alkane, alkyne*. *~ series, i.e. the group of unsaturated hydrocarbons with one double bond.* Pūkaʻina ʻalakene.

alkyne ʻAlakaine. See *alkane, alkene*. ~ series, *i.e. the group of unsaturated hydrocarbons with one triple bond.* Pūkaʻina ʻalakaine.

alley *Also alleyway.* Ala hānuku.

alley-oop *A basketball play.* ʻAliupa.

alliance *A group of nations that have agreed to help or protect each other; to form such an* ~. Hui kuʻikahi. See *consortium*.

allied health professional Kākoʻo ʻoihana olakino.

alligator ʻAlakeka.

allophone *In linguistics.* Puana hualeo. See *phoneme*.

allotrope *A different molecular form of an element, in science.* Kino lātoma.

alloy Mekala ʻōʻā, metala ʻōʻā.

allspice Pimeka.

all-terrain vehicle *ATV.* Mokohuilahā.

alluvial soil Lepo makaili.

Almak *A star.* ʻAoʻao.

almanac Puke ʻalemanaka. See *appointment book*.

Al Nair-Alpha Gruis *A star.* Lanihaʻi.

Alnilam *A star.* Kauano.

Alnitak *A star.* ʻAumani.

aloha ball *In volleyball.* Kinipōpō aloha.

aloha shirt Palaka aloha.

alphabet Pīʻāpā. See *alphabetize*.

alphabetical order Kaʻina pīʻāpā. See *alphabetize*.

alphabetize *To put in alphabetical order.* Hoʻokaʻina pīʻāpā.

alpha particle *A positively charged particle made up of two protons and two neutrons.* Huna ʻālepa. See *beta particle*.

Alphekka *A star in the constellation Corona Borealis.* Keaopō.

Alpheratz *A star.* Māpono.

alpine *Relating to the biogeographic zone above timberline.* ʻAlapaina. See *subalpine*. ~ desert. Panoa ʻalapaina. ~ shrubland. Wao laʻalāʻau.

Alpha Tuscanae *A star.* Kapoʻe.

alternate *To* ~, *as in computer program.* Hōʻalo. ~ key. Pihi hōʻalo (*preceded by* ke).

alternate player *First* ~ *or substitute, also called first off the bench or six man, in basketball.* Kūono.

alternating current AC. A u māʻaloʻalo. See *direct current*. ~ electricity. Uila au māʻaloʻalo.

altimeter Ana kiʻekiʻena. See *altitude*.

altitude Kiʻekiʻena.

aluminum ʻAluminuma. ~ foil. Pepa kini.

alveolar *In linguistics.* Lapa niho.

alveolus *An air sac of the lungs, in anatomy.* Nōiki. *Alveolar duct.* Pūʻali nōiki.

a.m. *Ante meridium.* A.m. (*pronounced* ʻāmū).

AM *Amplitude modulation.* AM (*pronounced* ʻāmū), ʻanini laulā hawewe. See *FM*.

amaryllis Līlia ʻApelika.

Amazon ʻAmasona. ~ river. Ka muliwai ʻo ʻAmasona.

ambassador Kanikela nui. See *consul*.

amend See *amendment*.

amendment *An addition or change to a bill, constitution, etc.; also to amend* Pakuʻi hoʻololi.

America *Also American.* ʻAmelika. See *entries below. Central* ~ *or Latin* ~. ʻAmelika Waena. *North* ~. ʻAmelika ʻĀkau. *South* ~. ʻAmelika Hema. *United States of* ~. ʻAmelika Hui Pū ʻia.

American Baseball League Kuʻikahi Pōhili ʻAmelika.

American cockroach *Periplaneta americana.* ʻElelū kīkēkē.

American Football Conference *AFC.* Hui Pōpeku ʻAmelika.

American Sāmoa *Also American Sāmoan.* Kāmoa ʻAmelika, Haʻamoa ʻAmelika.

amino ʻAmino. ~ acid. ʻAkika ʻamino.

ammeter *An instrument used to measure the amount of electric current in a circuit.* Ana au uila.
ammonia ʻAmonia.
ammonium ʻAmoniuma.
ammonium molybdate ʻAmoniuma molaibadahate.
amorphous *Having no regular crystalline form.* Laukua. *~ substance.* ʻAkano laukua.
amount Helu, heluna.
amphibian Pepeʻekua.
amphidromous *Migrating from fresh to salt water, or from salt to fresh water, at some stage of the life cycle other than the breeding period.* Pōʻaiwaiakai.
amplifier Pahu hoʻonui leo. See *speaker.*
amplify *To increase the amplitude of a wave.* Hoʻolaulā hawewe. See *amplitude.*
amplitude *The amount of energy in a sound wave.* Ikaika hawewe kani. See entry below and *sound wavelength.*
amplitude *The greatest distance the particles in a wave rise or fall from their rest position, in science.* Laulā hawewe. *~ modulation.* ʻAnini laulā hawewe. See entry above and *AM. As of a pendulum.* Palena piʻi.
amusement park Pāka kāniwala.
anaerobic decomposition *Also anaerobic putrefaction.* Ka hoʻohāpopo eaea ʻole ʻana. See *aerobic.*
anagram Huaneʻe.
analog *~ watch or clock, i.e. having hands.* Uaki lima kuhikuhi, uāki lima kuhikuhi. See *digital.*
analysis *Cost ~.* Huli kumukūʻai.
analyze Kālailai.
Andromeda ʻAnakolomeka. *~ galaxy.* Ka wiliau hōkū ʻo ʻAnakolomeka.
anemometer Ana māmā makani.
anemone *Sea ~.* ʻŌkala, ʻōkole.
aneroid barometer Ana mīkā ea kuhikuhi.
anesthetic Lāʻau hoʻomāʻeʻele.

anesthetize Hoʻomāʻeʻele.
angiosperm ʻAnakiopua.
angle *In math.* Huina. *See entries below. Acute ~.* Huina ʻoi. *Central ~, an angle that has its vertex at the center of a circle.* Huina kikowaena. *Complementary ~s, two angles whose measures have a sum of 90°.* Nā huina hoʻopiha kūpono. *Exterior ~, in math.* Huina kūwaho. *Obtuse ~.* Huina peleleu. *Right ~.* Huina kūpono. *Straight ~, an angle that has a measure of 180°.* Huina kaha. *Supplementary ~s, two angles whose measures have a sum of 180°.* Nā huina hoʻopiha kaha.
angle of incidence *The angle made between a wave striking a barrier and the normal to the surface.* Huina papā. See *angle of reflection.*
angle of reflection *The angle between a reflected wave and the normal to the barrier from which it is reflected.* Huina kūpī. See *angle of incidence.*
angle spike *In volleyball.* Hili ʻaoʻao. See *spike.*
Angola *Also Angolan.* ʻAnagola.
anhydride *A compound formed from another by the removal of water.* ʻAnahaidaraside. See *anhydrous. Acidic ~.* ʻAnahaidaraside ʻakika. *Basic ~, a metallic oxide that forms a base when added to water.* ʻAnahaidaraside kuapapa.
anhydrous *Without water.* Nele wai. See *anhydride.*
animal Holoholona. *Fish or any marine ~.* Iʻa, iʻa kai. See *fish. Vertebrate ~.* Holoholona iwikuamoʻo. *Invertebrate ~.* Holoholona iwikuamoʻo ʻole.
Ankaa *A star.* Kapela.
annex *To ~, in math, as in ~ing a zero to show both decimal parts as a hundreth.* Pākuʻi.
anniversary card Kāleka piha makahiki. See *birthday card.*

annual *Yearbook.* Puke hoʻohaliʻa makahiki.

anode *The positive electrode in an electrical circuit.* ʻŪholo uila ʻāne. *See* cathode, electrode.

answer *A solution to a problem.* Hāʻina.

Antarctica *Also Antarctic.* ʻAneʻālika.

anteater ʻAinaonao.

ante meridium *A.m.* A.m. *(pronounced* ʻāmū*).*

antenna *As of a lobster, insect, television, etc.* Kukuna. *Volleyball ~.* Kukuna pōpaʻipaʻi. *~ violation.* ʻAʻena kukuna.

Antennariv Commersonil *A kind of fish.* Hahili poloka.

anterior *In biology.* Laumua. *See* dorsal, posterior, ventral. *~ dorsal fin, of a fish.* Kualā laumua.

anthocyanin *A kind of pigment producing blue to red coloring in flowers and plants.* ʻUlakaiano.

anthropology Hulikanaka.

antibiotic Pale mūhune ʻino. *See* pathogen.

antifreeze ʻAila ʻaʻalo paʻahau.

antigravity machine Mīkini hoʻopau ʻumekaumaha. *See* gravity.

antiseptic Pale palahō.

antonym Huaʻōlelo manaʻo ʻēkoʻa. *See* homonym, synonym.

anus *The posterior opening of the alimentary canal.* Puka kahiko, puka ʻamo. *See* sphincter.

anxiety ʻŌpikipiki.

aphid *A kind of insect.* ʻEleao. *See* honeydew.

apocope *In linguistics.* Hua hope hāʻule.

apostrophe Koma luna.

apparatus *Device or mechanism, ordinarily including some mechanical part or parts.* Maomeka. *See* device, instrument, tool.

appeal *To ask a higher court to review a decision made by a lower court.* Hoʻopiʻi kūʻē. *See* appellate jurisdiction.

appearance *General ~ or impression.* Hiʻona. *See* feature.

appellate jurisdiction *A court's authority to hear an appeal of a decision made by another court.* Mana hoʻokolokolo. *See* appeal.

appendix *As in a book.* Pākuʻina.

appliance Mīkini. *Home ~.* Mīkini home. *Office ~.* Mīkini keʻena. *~ store.* Hale kūʻai mīkini home.

application *As in computer program; also program, as for computer.* Polokalamu.

appointment book *Also date book.* ʻAlemanaka puke. *See* almanac.

approach *Or strategy, as in solving a math problem.* Kaʻakālai.

approximate *Also approximation.* Kokekau.

April ʻApelila. *Abb.* ʻAp.

apron Pale kuene, ʻepane.

aquaculture Mahi iʻa.

aquarium Pahuwaiea.

aqueous *Having water as a solvent, in science.* ʻŪheheʻe wai. *~ solution.* Māʻōʻāna ʻūheheʻe wai.

Arabia *Also Arabian.* ʻAlapia, ʻArabia. *Saudi ~, Saudi.* Saudi ʻAlapia, Saudi ʻArabia.

arbitrate ʻUao. *Arbitration.* Ka ʻuao ʻana.

arborial Kau lāʻau. *See* orange tree frog, treehouse.

arc *In math.* Piʻo. *See* chord. *Island ~.* Pae moku hoaka. *Three-point ~, in basketball.* Hoaka kīkolu.

arch *As the Arch of Triumph in Paris.* Hoaka kū.

archaeology Hulikoehana. *Archaeological site.* Kahua hulikoehana. *Archaeologist.* Kanaka hulikoehana, mea hulikoehana.

Archimedes 'Akimika. *~' principle, i.e. the buoyant force on an object submerged in a fluid is equal to the weight of the fluid displaced by that object, in science.* Ke kulehana a 'Akimika.

archive *Or backup, as in computer program.* Papa'a. See *backup*.

Arctic 'Ālika. *~ fox.* 'Alopeka 'Ālika, 'alopeke 'Ālika. *~ ground squirrel.* Kiulela 'Ālika.

area *In math.* 'Ili. *Abb.* 'I. *Quantitative measurement.* 'Ili laulā, 'ili. *Surface ~.* 'Ili alo.

area *Transition ~, an ~ where natural topography changes from one land feature to another.* 'Āina loliloli.

Argentina *Also Argentine, Argentinean.* 'Alekina.

argon *An element.* 'Aragona.

Arizona *Also Arizonan, Arizonian.* 'Alikona, 'Arizona.

Arkansas *Also Arkansan.* 'Akanakā, 'Akanasā.

arm *Resistance ~, i.e. the distance from the fulcrum to the resistance force in a lever.* Lima āohiohi.

armadillo 'Amakila.

army *Also military service.* Pū'ali koa.

arraignment *A court hearing in which a defendant is formally charged with a crime and enters a plea of guilty or not guilty.* 'Aha pane ho'opi'i.

arrange music *Also music arranger.* Kūkulu puolo.

arrow *An indicator.* Nahau. *~ key, as on computer keyboard.* Pihi nahau *(preceded by ke). ~ key for moving right (left, up, down).* Pihi nahau holo 'ākau (hema, i luna, i lalo). *Mouse ~, pointer or cursor, as in computer program.* Nahau 'iole, nahau.

arrythmia *Cardiac ~.* Pu'uwai pana 'ewa'ewa.

art *Also artwork.* Pāheona. See *artistic, fine arts. ~ director, as for movie or video production.* Luna pāheona. *Performing ~.* Pāhiahia.

artemia *Brine shrimp.* Pokipoki ālia.

arteriolosclerosis *In medicine.* A'aha'apupū. See *arteriosclerosis*.

arteriosclerosis *Also atherosclerosis or hardening of the arteries, in medicine.* A'alā'au. See *arteriolosclerosis*.

artery A'a koko pu'uwai, a'a pu'uwai. See *arteriosclerosis, vein.*

arthropod Wāwae'ami.

artichoke 'Alikoka.

artifact Koehana. See *archaeology.*

artificial reef Umuko'a.

artisan *Also craftsman.* Mālalaioa.

artist *Storyboard ~, as in movie or video production.* Lima kaha mo'olelo. See *storyboard.*

artistic *Esthetically appealing or having ~ talent.* Heona. See *art. To make ~, decorate ~ally.* Ho'oheona.

arts and sciences *College of ~.* Koleke pāheona me ka 'epekema. See *dean.*

asbestos Awe pale ahi.

asea *At sea.* I waena moana. See *midocean.*

ash cone *In geology.* Pu'u lehu.

Asia *Also Asian, Asiatic.* 'Ākia, 'Āsia.

aspen 'Ōlapa haole.

asphalt Unukā. See *pave. ~ compound, a brown or black tar-like substance, a variety of distilled tar (bitumen) found in a natural state or obtained by evaporating petroleum; pitch.* Kēpau kā.

assemble *As when splicing film or video segments together for movie or video production.* Ho'oku'iku'i. *~ editor.* Luna ho'oku'iku'i.

assembly *A gathering of people for a specific purpose.* 'Āmui.

assign *To ~ a value or power, as in math problems.* Ho'āmana.

assimilate Ho'okemua. *Assimilated.* Kemua. See *assimilation.*

assimilation *In linguistics.* Kīlikelike.

assist *To feed or ~, as in basketball and most team sports except baseball.* Hānai.

associative *In math.* Hoʻolike. ~ **property.** ʻAnopili hoʻolike (*preceded by* ke).
assume *Also assumption.* Manaʻo kuhi.
asteroid Hōkūnaʻi. ~ *belt.* Kāʻei hōkūnaʻi.
astronaut Kelalani.
at bat *Also up (to bat), in baseball.* Manawa hili.
-ate *Suffix in chemical compounds and terms.* -hate.
-athalon *Suffix (Eng.); prefix (Haw.).* ʻĀlapakona-. See *decathalon, pentathalon, triathalon, -thon.*
atherosclerosis *Also arteriosclerosis or hardening of the arteries, in medicine.* Aʻalāʻau. See *arteriolosclerosis.*
athlete ʻĀlapa. See *athletic.*
athletic *Also athlete.* ʻĀlapa. ~ **scholarship.** Haʻawina kālā ʻālapa. ~ **club, fitness center.** Hale hoʻoikaika kino. See *gymnasium.*
Atlantic ʻAkelanika, ʻAtelanika.
ATM *Automated-teller machine.* Mīkini panakō.
atmosphere *Around planets.* Lewapuni. See *space.*
atoll Moku kuaʻau.
atomic *Also atom.* ʻĀtoma. See entries below and *bond, nucleus, particle.* ~ **radiation.** Pāhawewe ʻātoma.
atomic mass Nuipaʻa ʻātoma. ~ **unit.** Anakahi nuipaʻa ʻātoma. *Average* ~. ʻAwelike nuipaʻa ʻātoma.
atomic number Heluna huna ʻāne.
attack *Raid; also to attack or raid.* Hoʻouka. *Counter~; also to counter~.* Hoʻouka pānaʻi.
attempt See *vain attempt.*
attendant *Flight* ~. Kuene mokulele.
attic Lumi huna; lumi kaupaku, lumi kaupoku, lumi kaupuku.
attribute *Style, as italic or bold in printing or computer program.* Kaila hua. See *code style, font, property.*
ATV *All-terrain vehicle.* Mokohuilahā.

auditor Luna hōʻoia.
August ʻAukake. *Abb.* ʻAuk.
aurora borealis *Also northern lights.* ʻOililiʻula.
Australia *Also Australian.* Nūhōlani. See entry below and *Indo-Australian.*
Australian cockroach *Periplaneta australasiae.* ʻElelū Nūhōlani.
Austria *Also Austrian.* ʻAukekulia, ʻAuseturia.
auto- *Or self- (prefix).* Hika-.
autobiographical Hikapiliolana. See *biographical. Autobiography.* Moʻolelo hikapiliolana, hikapiliolana.
auto feed *To* ~, *as paper into computer printer.* Hānai ʻakomi.
autoharp Hāpa paʻa lima, pila hāpa.
automated-teller machine *ATM.* Mīkini panakō.
automatic ʻAkomi. See *auto feed.*
autumn *Fall.* Hāʻulelau. ~**al equinox.** Ka māuiili o ka hāʻulelau. See *equinox.*
avalanche *Also landslide.* ʻĀholo. *Snow* ~. ʻĀholo hau.
average ʻAwelike. ~ **atomic mass.** ʻAwelike nuipaʻa ʻātoma. ~ **rainfall.** ʻAwelike o ka ua. ~ **speed.** ʻAwelike māmā holo.
avian malaria Malaria manu.
Avior *A star.* Kīnaʻu.
avocado Pea Hawaiʻi, pea. See *pear.*
axe Koʻi, koʻi lipi.
axis *In math.* Iho. *Coordinate axes, i.e. two intersecting perpendicular number lines used for graphing ordered number pairs.* Iho kuhikuhina.
axle *A shaft on which a wheel turns.* Iho, paepae komo huila.
azalea Pua kaʻūmana.
azobacter *A type of bacteria containing nitrogen.* Koʻohune naikokene.

B

baby bottle ʻŌmole omo waiū, ʻōmole waiū.
baby carriage Kaʻapēpē. See *crib.*

baby rattle 'Ulīkeke. See *tambourine*.
back *Of seat.* Kua noho. *Of tongue.* Kū'au alelo. See *tongue*. ~ *vowel.* Woela kauhope. See *vowel*.
back *Defensive corner* ~, *in football.* 'Ā'iwa. *Running* ~, *general term.* Mea holo.
back-door pass *In basketball; to throw such a pass.* Kīloi palemo.
backboard *In basketball.* Papa hīna'i, papa hupa, papa.
backcourt violation *In basketball.* 'A'ena laina kūwaena. See *violation*.
background *As in a photo or movie/video scene, or on a computer screen.* Kā'ei kua. See *foreground*.
backpack *Knapsack.* Pāiki hā'awe, pāisi hā'awe, 'awe.
back set *To make a* ~, *in volleyball.* Hānai i hope, hānai kīkala.
backslash *In printing* (\). Kaha hiō iho. See *slash*.
backspace *To* ~, *as on an IBM computer.* Holoi i hope. See *delete*.
back stroke *Also to swim the* ~. 'Au kua. See *stroke*.
back up Pēki (i hope).
backup *Archive, as in computer program.* Papa'a. ~ *copy.* Kope papa'a. ~ *file.* Waihona papa'a. *To* ~, *as a file.* Ho'opapa'a.
backward *With palms facing* ~. Pohokua. See *chin-up, forward, hit*.
bacon Pekona.
bacteria Ko'ohune. See *azobacter*. *Mesophilic* ~. Ko'ohune ola mehana. *Thermophilic* ~. Ko'ohune ola wela.
badge *General term.* Pihi hō'ailona *(preceded by* ke). *Police* ~. Pihi māka'i.
badminton Kenika manu.
bag Pū'olo; 'eke *(preceded by* ke). See *insect bag net. Guessing* ~. Pū'olo kohokoho. *Paper* ~. Pū'olo pepa. *Plastic* ~. 'Eke 'ea. *Sleeping* ~. 'Eke moe, 'eke hiamoe.
bagpipe Pila 'ūpoho, 'ūpoho.

Bahamas *Also Bahamian.* Pahama, Bahama.
bail *Money a defendant gives a court as a promise to return for trial.* Pēla.
bait-casting reel *As for fishing.* Wiliaho hekau maunu. See *reel*.
baking pan Pā 'oma *(preceded by* ke).
baking powder Hū. See *baking soda*.
baking soda Pauka koka. See *baking powder*.
balance *To* ~ *something.* Ho'okaualewa. See entries below and *scales*.
balance beam Lā'au kaukahi. See *parallel bars*.
balanced '*a*' *As equal distribution of weight.* Kaualewa. *Also evenly* ~, *in science; fair, just, equitable.* Kaulike. ~ *chemical equation.* Ha'ihelu kemikala kaulike. ~ *force.* Manehu kaulike.
balances *Checks and* ~, *as in government.* Ho'oku'ia.
balance sheet *A listing of assets, liabilities and owner's equity.* Mo'okūlana waiwai.
balancing mechanism *In biology.* 'Ōnaehana ho'okauapono.
bald "*Balahead/bolohead*," *as a tire.* Nemonemo. See *tread*.
bald eagle 'Āeko po'o hina, 'āeto po'o hina.
ball Kinipōpō. See *glass ball; baseball, basketball, football, volleyball, etc. Aloha* ~, *in volleyball.* Kinipōpō aloha. *Christmas* ~, *the tree ornament.* Pōpō wehi lā'au Kalikimaka.
ballet Hulahula pālē, pālē, bālē.
balluster *Railing support.* 'Ūlili, hūlili. See *ballustrade*.
ballustrade *Railing.* Paehumu. See *balluster*.
balsa Haulāpa.
banana poka Poka mai'a.
band *Or gradient, as of colors.* 'Auina. *Color* ~. 'Auina kala.
band aid Wahī'eha.
bandmaster's baton Maile pana.

Bangladesh Banagaladesa.
banjo Panakiō.
banjolele Panakiōlele.
bank Panakō. See *ATM, account, check*. *~ check.* Pila kīkoʻo. *~ draft.* Pila kīkoʻo panakō. *Piggy ~.* Panakō hale.
banked curve *Also banked turn.* Uakeʻe hiō.
bank shot *In basketball; to make such a shot.* Kī papa.
banquet ʻAhaʻaina. *Welcome ~.* ʻAhaʻaina hoʻokipa. *Closing ~.* ʻAhaʻaina panina.
bar *See bars. ~ graph.* Pakuhi ʻaukā. *See histogram. Double ~ graph.* Pakuhi paʻa ʻaukā. *Fill ~, in computer program.* ʻAukā holomua. *Menu ~, on computer screen.* Papa koho. *Space ~, on typewriter or computer keyboard.* Pihi hoʻokōā, pihi kaʻahua (*preceded by* ke).
barbiturate Lāʻau hoʻomālū.
bare *As a tree without leaves.* Launea.
bargaining *Collective ~.* Kūkaʻi ʻaelike ʻuniona.
baritone Hāʻoi. *~ ʻukulele.* ʻUkulele hāʻoi.
barium Bariuma.
bark *Of a plant.* ʻIli, ʻaluʻalu. *Inner ~.* ʻIli iho. *Outer ~.* ʻIli o waho.
bark cloth *Tapa.* Paʻūpaʻū.
barometer Ana mīkā ea. *Aneroid ~.* Ana mīkā ea kuhikuhi.
barrel *A unit of measurement.* Palela. *Abb.* pll.
barrel cactus Pānini palala.
barrette *Hairclip.* Pine lauoho.
barrier *Sound ~.* Palena holo kani.
bars *Parallel ~.* Lāʻau kaulua. *Even parallel ~.* Lāʻau kaulua kaulike. *Uneven parallel ~.* Lāʻau kaulua kaulike ʻole. *See balance beam. Monkey ~, as playground equipment.* Haokeko. *See jungle gym.*
barter Hailawe. *~ system.* Ka hailawe ʻana.
-base Kuapapa. *Water-base paint.* Pena kuapapa wai.

base Kahua. *See entries below. Military ~.* Kahua pūʻali koa. *Navy ~.* Kahua pūʻali kaua moana. *Of a leaf, as hala.* Poʻo (*preceded by* ke).
base *As on a baseball diamond.* Pahu. *See home plate. First ~.* Pahu ʻekahi. *Second ~.* Pahu ʻelua. *Third ~.* Pahu ʻekolu.
base *In math.* Kumu hoʻohui. *See binary. ~ five.* Kumu hoʻohui ʻelima. *In exponential notation.* Kumu pāhoʻonui. *As of a geometric triangle.* ʻAoʻao kau. *Abb.* ʻak.
baseball *The sport.* Pōhili. *The ball.* Kinipōpō pōhili. *~ glove or mitt.* Mikilima pōhili. *~ field.* Kahua pōhili. *~ diamond, infield.* Kaimana pōhili. *~ inning.* Pale pōhili. *American ~ League.* Kuʻikahi Pōhili ʻAmelika. *National ~ League.* Kuʻikahi Pōhili Aupuni.
baseball pass *In basketball; to throw such a pass.* Nou.
base line *End line, as on basketball court.* Laina kumu. *See line (as on basketball court).*
basic *Simple, uncomplicated.* Nōhie. *See entries below and complex.*
basic anhydride *A metallic oxide that forms a base when added to water.* ʻAnahaidaraside kuapapa. *See anhydride.*
basic counting principle *In math.* Kulehana no ka helu ʻana.
basket ʻIe (*preceded by* ke). *As on a bicycle.* ʻEke ukana (*preceded by* ke).
basket *In basketball.* Hīnaʻi, hupa. *See backboard, rim, shoot, three-point shot. A score.* ʻAi hīnaʻi. *To make or sink a ~.* Hoʻokomo i ke kinipōpō. *Made a ~.* Komohia.
basketball *The sport.* Pōhīnaʻi. *The ball.* Kinipōpō pōhīnaʻi. *~ net.* Hīnaʻi. *~ court.* Kahua pōhīnaʻi, kahua. *~ camp.* ʻĀpoʻe pōhīnaʻi.
bass clef *In music.* Hōʻailona mele leo kāne, leo kāne. *See treble clef.*
bass viol *Also string bass.* Pila kū nui, pila nui.

bat *Also club, racket.* ʻŪhili. *At ~, up (to ~), in baseball.* Manawa hili.
batch *As of cookies or recruits.* ʻŌhui.
bathe *See* shower.
bathroom Lua, lumi hoʻopaupilikia, lumi ʻauʻau. *~ scales.* Anapaona home, *usu.* anapaona.
bathtub Kapu ʻauʻau.
baton Maile, ʻaukaʻi. *Bandmaster's ~.* Maile pana. *~ used in relay race.* Maile hoʻoili. *~ for twirling.* ʻAukaʻi wili. *Signal ~, as used by marching bandleader.* ʻAukaʻi pāna.
batter *As when making pancakes.* Kale palaoa.
battery Iho, pakalē. *See entries below. Button-shape ~.* Iho pihi. *For flashlight, radio, etc.* Iho poke. *Six-volt ~.* Iho ʻeono. *Twelve-volt ~.* Iho ʻumikūmālua.
battery jar *A large cylindrical container of heavy glass with an open top as used in laboratories.* ʻŌmole iho uila.
battery tester *A machine.* Mīkini hoʻāʻo iho. *Not a machine.* Hāmeʻa hoʻāʻo iho.
bay *Payload ~, the part of a spacecraft where scientific instruments and passengers are carried.* ʻOneki hana.
BBS *Bulletin Board Service, on computer programs.* PLH (Papa Lawelawe Hoʻolaha).
B-complex vitamin Kauwikamina B.
beach cricket ʻŪhini nēnē kahakai.
bead Olopī.
beaker Hano kānuku.
beam *Balance ~.* Lāʻau kaukahi. *See parallel bars. Laser ~.* Kukuna wanaʻā. *~ of a boat.* Kua uma.
beam reach (port) *Beam reach on the port side, i.e. sailing at a 90° angle from the direction of the wind, with the port side windward.* Kele ama kāmoe. *See beam reach (starboard), broad reach (port, starboard), close hauled (port, starboard), downwind.*
beam reach (starboard) *Beam reach on the starboard side, i.e. sailing at a 90° angle from the direction of the wind, with the starboard side windward.* Kele ʻākea kāmoe. *See beam reach (port), broad reach (port, starboard), close hauled (port, starboard), downwind.*
bean Pāpapa. Seeentries below and *pea. Bush ~.* Pāpapa haʻa. *Honey locust ~.* Pāpapa ʻūhinihone. *Jelly ~.* Pāpapa kele. *Lima ~.* Pāpapa laima. *Long ~.* Pāpapa loloa. *Mung ~.* Pāpapa munukō. *Soya ~.* Pāpapa koiū. *String ~.* Pāpapa hihi.
bean curd *Also tofu.* Tōfū.
bean sprout Kawowo pāpapa.
bear Pea. *Polar ~.* Pea ʻĀlika. *Teddy ~.* Pea kiʻi, pea pāʻani. *See panda.*
beard *Excluding the moustache.* ʻUmiʻumi ʻauae, *usu.* ʻumiʻumi. *See moustache.*
beat *As in music or linguistics.* Pana.
beaver Peawa. *Mountain ~.* Peawa kuahiwi.
bed *See entries below and* mattress, riverbed, streambed.
bedframe Hao pela. *See headboard.*
bedpan *Also urinal.* Ipu mimi. *See toilet bowl, urinal.*
bedpost Pou moe.
bedrock Kūpapakū.
bedroom Lumi moe. *Master ~.* Lumi moe haku. *Guest room.* Lumi moe malihini.
bedsheet Hāliʻi moe, hāliʻi pela.
bedside table *Also nightstand.* Pākaukau moe.
bedspread Uhimoe.
bedsprings Pilina moe.
beef *See corned beef.*
beep *As sound effect on computer.* Pīpa.
beer *Six-pack of ~.* ʻEkeʻeke pia. *Twelve-pack of ~.* Pūʻolo pia. *Case of ~.* Pahu pia.
beet Pike.
beetle Ponu. *Larder ~, dermestid.* Ponu ʻili.

Māmaka Kaiao / 191

beforehand *Early, as registration for a conference.* Hiki mua. See *early, late.*

begin *To start, as a computer program.* Hoʻomaka. See *quit.*

beginning level *Also introductory level.* Pae hoʻomaka.

begonia Pīkōnia.

behavior *As the way animals act.* Lawena. *Instinctive ~.* Lawena ʻike hānau. *Learned ~.* Lawena ʻapo.

behind-the-back pass *In basketball; to throw such a pass.* Kīloi kua.

Belgium *Also Belgian.* Pelekiuma, Belegiuma.

Belize *Also Belizean.* Belize.

bell Pele.

Bellatrix *A star.* Kaluakoke.

bellows nozzle Nuku ʻūpā makani.

belt *Asteroid ~.* Kāʻei hōkūnaʻi.

belt buckle ʻŪmiʻi ʻilikuapo, ʻūmiʻi.

bench See *first off the bench.*

benchmark *In math.* Kaha ana.

benzene Benezene.

benzoin *A resin used in perfume and cosmetics.* Penekui.

Bernoulli's principle *In science.* K e kulehana a Penuli.

berry Pīʻai. See *Hawaiian entries under pīʻai.*

best boy *An assistant gaffer.* Hope luna uila. See *gaffer.*

beta particle *A negatively charged electron moving at high speed.* Huna beta. See *alpha particle.*

Bhutan *Also Bhutanese.* Butana.

bias *Also biased.* Pāʻewaʻewa. *Systematic error in gathering data, in math.* Pāʻewa.

bicameral *As a legislature.* ʻElua hale.

bicycle Paikikala. See *basket, bike.* *~ chain.* Kaulahao paikikala. *~ chain cog.* Pānihoniho o ke kaulahao paikikala. *~ crossbar.* Kua hao paikikala. *~ handlebars.* Kalaiwa paikikala, ʻau paikikala (*preceded by* ke). *~ mud guard.* Pale lepo paikikala. *~ seat.* Noho paikikala. *~ tire.* Kaea paikikala, taea paikikala.

Big Dipper Nāhiku.

Big Five *The ~, the five corporations that controlled most of the sugar industry in Hawaiʻi.* Nā Hui Nui ʻElima.

bike *Dirt ~.* Mokokaikala holo lepo. *Mountain ~.* Paikikala holo kuahiwi. See *bicycle.*

bill *A draft of a law presented to a legislature.* Pila. *A piece of paper money.* Pepa kālā. See *coin. One dollar ~.* Pepa pākahi. *Five dollar ~.* Pepa pālima. *Ten dollar ~.* Pepa pāʻumi.

billion See *giga-, nano-.*

bill of rights Palapala pono kanaka.

binary *A base-two system of numeration, in math.* Kumu hoʻohui ʻelua. *~ compound.* Pūhui kumumea lua.

binary compound Pūhui kumumea lua.

binder *Ring ~.* Puke lina kui. See *notebook, ring.*

bingo *Name of Hawaiian language version.* Keola.

binoculars Paʻa ʻohenānā.

biochemistry Kemika meaola.

biodegradable Pēhāpopopo.

biographical *Also biography.* Piliolana. See *autobiographical.* *~ novel.* Nōwela piliolana.

biological *See entries below.* *~ community.* Kaiameaola. *Natural ~ community.* Kaiameaola kūlohelohe. *~ control.* Kāohi meaola. *~ family.* ʻOhana kālaimeaola. *To be ~ly adapted to.* Liliuwelo.

biologist Kanaka kālaimeaola, mea kālaimeaola.

biology Kālaimeaola. See *biological, cell, microbiology.*

biomass Kōpū meaola.

biome Kaiawao.

birch Pūkowi.

bird See *Hawaiian entries under* manu.

birdbath ʻAuʻauna manu. See *feeder.*

bird of paradise *The bird.* Manu palekaiko. *The flower.* Pua manu.

birthday card Kāleka lā hānau, kāleka piha makahiki. See *anniversary card*.

biscuit Palaoa pikeke, pikeke.

bisect *To* ~, *in math*. 'Oki hapalua. *Abb*. 'o2. See *bisector*.

bisector *In math*. Kaha 'oki hapalua. See *bisect*. *Perpendicular* ~. Kaha 'oki hapalua kūpono.

bisulfate Bisulafahate. *Sodium* ~. Sodiuma bisulafahate.

bit *A computer unit of information*. Huna. See *byte*.

bitmap *To* ~, *a style of printing a graphic image as on a computer printer*. Kākiko. *A* ~*ped graphic image*. Ki'i kiko. *Precision* ~*ping*. Kākiko miomio.

black widow *A kind of spider*. Nananana hese 'ele'ele.

bladder 'Eke mimi (*preceded by* ke).

blade *Of tongue*. Lau alelo. See *tongue*.

blanket Kapa, kapa moe. See *quilt, shawl*. *Electric* ~. Kapa uila. *Heavy or woolen* ~. Kapa huluhulu, huluhulu.

blank footage *As of video tape*. Līpine ma'ema'e. See *footage*.

blast off *To* ~, *as a rocket*. 'Ōlapa. *To cause to* ~. Ho'ōlapa.

Blattella germanica *German cockroach*. 'Elelū la'aloa.

bleachers 'Ōmo'o noho.

blind pass *Also no-look pass, in basketball; to throw such a pass*. Kīloi ho'opalai.

blinds *Venetian* ~. Pale pukaaniani 'ōlepelepe.

blizzard Pāhili hau, makani pāhili hau.

block *A child's toy*. Palaka. *Adobe* ~. Uinihapa 'akopie. *Pier* ~, *in construction*. Palaka kimeki. *Termite* ~. Palaka kimeki pale mū. *City* ~. Pōlaka.

block *To* ~ *or highlight text, as in computer program*. Kahiāuli. See *shade*.

block *To* ~ *(a shot), in basketball*. Paku. See *roof*. *To* ~ *out or screen*. 'Āke'a. *To* ~ *(the ball), in volleyball*. Paku, pālulu. *To pass through the* ~. Hala ka pālulu. ~*er*. Mea paku, paku. *Point from* ~. 'Ai hele wale.

block and tackle *An arrangement of pulleys and rope or cable used to lift or haul*. Hāme'a pokaka'a.

blocking foul *In basketball*. Ku'ia 'āke'a. See *foul*.

blood Koko. ~ *cell*. Hunaola koko. ~ *glucose*. Monakō koko. ~ *pressure*. Mīkā koko. ~*stream*. Kahena koko. ~ *type*. Hulu koko. *White* ~ *cell*. Hunaola koko ke'oke'o. *Red* ~ *cell*. Hunaola koko 'ula'ula. *Cold*-~*ed*. Koko hu'ihu'i. *Warm*-~*ed*. Koko mehana.

blouse Lakeke, palauki. See *jacket*.

blow *As the wind*. See *wind*. *To* ~ *one's nose*. Hūkē, ho'okē.

bluefish I'auli.

blue jay Manu kēuli, kēuli.

blueprint Ki'i kūkulu, ki'i kūkulu hale. *To draft or draw* ~*s; also draftsman or drafter*. Kaha ki'i kūkulu.

blush *Also rouge, as makeup*. Hehelo pāpālina.

boar's tusk Niho kepa.

board Papa. See *BBS, member, windsurf*. *Four-by-four* ~. Papa hā hā. *Two-by-four* ~. Papa lua hā. *Bulletin* ~. Papa hō'ike'ike. ~ *game, as checkers*. Kēmu. *Game* ~. Papa kēmu.

bob *As of a pendulum*. 'Olo.

bobby pin 'Ūmi'i lauoho.

body *As of a composition or text*. Kino. See *opening, closing*. *As of 'ukulele, guitar, etc*. 'Ōpū. See *'ukulele*.

bog *With no trees and soft ground*. Nāele. See *marsh, swamp*.

boil Paila. ~*ing point*. Kēkelē paila. See *freezing point, melting point*.

bold See *boldface*.

boldface *On computer or in typesetting; also bold*. Kā'ele. *To bold, i.e. set in* ~ *type*. Ho'okā'ele.

Bolivia *Also Bolivian*. Bolivia.

bolt *As in nuts and ~s.* Kui kolū. See *nut. Of material.* ʻĀpā lole.
bomb *Missile ~.* Kao lele pahū.
bond Lou. *Between atoms or ions as a result of gaining, losing or sharing electrons.* Lou ʻātoma. *~ing instrument.* ʻŪlou. *A certificate bought from a government or corporation which agrees to pay back the cost of the bond plus interest after a set period of time.* Pona.
bonemeal Iwi wiliwili. See *meat meal.*
bonus *Extra credit, as a class assignment or question on a quiz.* Hoʻopiʻi kaha, ʻai keu. *~ question.* Nīnau hoʻopiʻi kaha, nīnau ʻai keu.
book *Humorous ~.* Puke hoʻomakeʻaka. *Information ~.* Puke kumuhana. *Pattern ~.* Puke aʻo analula. *See other Hawaiian entries under* puke.
bookmark Lepe puke.
bookshelf Haka kau puke.
boom *To operate a ~, as for movie or video production.* Kīkoʻo ipuleo. *~ operator.* Mea kīkoʻo ipuleo.
booster *Solid rocket ~.* Kao wāwahie kinopaʻa, kao wāwahie paʻa.
boot *Rubber ~.* Lapa puki, laba puki, puki lapa. *Ski ~.* Kāmaʻa puki heʻe hau.
booth *As at a carnival, etc.* Kāmala.
borealis See *aurora borealis, Corona Borealis.*
borer *A kind of insect.* Huhupao.
borrow *To ~, take on credit.* Lawe ʻaiʻē. See *lend, loan. To ~ or check out something by signing for it, as a book.* Kāinoa. *To ~, as a word from another language; also to introduce, as plants and animals to a particular place.* Lawekahiki. See *introduce. A ~ed word.* He huaʻōlelo i lawekahiki ʻia.
botannical garden Māla hōʻikeʻike meakanu.
botany Kālailau nahele.
Botswana Botuana.

bottle *Baby ~.* ʻŌmole omo waiū, ʻōmole waiū. *Dropping ~, a bottle used much like an eyedropper.* ʻŌmole hoʻokulu.
bottom *Clothing.* Lole o lalo. See *top.*
bottom margin Lihi o lalo. See *margin.*
bougainvillea Pua pepa, pukanawila.
boulder *Generic term, particularly outside of Hawaiʻi.* Nukahaku. *In Hawaiʻi, referring to poi pounder-size stones and larger.* Pōhaku ʻalā.
bounce *As a check.* Leleneo; ua hoʻihoʻi ʻia (ka pila kīkoʻo) no ka lawa ʻole o ke kālā ma ka waihona panakō.
bounce pass *In basketball; to throw such a pass.* Kīloi papahele.
boundary *Convergent ~ in plate techtonics, in geology.* Palena kuʻi. *Divergent ~.* Palena neʻe ʻoā. *Transform ~.* Palena kākele.
bounds *To go out of ~, in sports.* ʻAʻe palena.
bow *As ribbon or string.* Hīpuʻu pewa. See *knot. ~ tie.* Lei ʻāʻī pewa.
bow *Of a boat.* Ihu.
bowl *Toilet ~.* Ipu hoʻopaupilikia. See *chamber pot, urinal.*
bowling Maika. *~ frame.* Kuea maika. *~ pin.* Pine maika.
box *Cardboard ~.* Pahu pepa. *Fuse ~.* Pahu ʻuiki uila. *Meter ~.* Pahu mika. *Toy ~.* Pahu mea pāʻani, waihona mea pāʻani.
box *Dialog ~, in computer program.* Pahu aʻo.
box and whiskers graph *In math.* Pakuhi pahu me ka ʻumiʻumi.
boxcar *As of a train.* Kaʻapahu.
boxing round Puni.
box turtle Honu pahu.
boycott *To abstain from buying from or dealing with (a company) as a means of coercion.* Nāʻiāʻumi.
Boyle Poila. *~'s law, i.e. decreasing the volume of a gas will increase the pressure the gas exerts if the temperature remains constant.* Ke kānāwai a Poila.

brace *As for body parts.* Kāliki. *Wrist ~.* Kāliki pūlima.
bracket *In punctuation.* Kahaapo kihikihi. See entry below and *parenthesis. Open ~.* Kahaapo kihikihi wehe. *Close ~.* Kahaapo kihikihi pani.
bracket *As in a sports tournament.* Māhele. *Consolation ~.* Māhele hāʻule. *Winner's ~.* Māhele lanakila.
brainstorm Puaʻi manaʻo.
brake Peleki. *~ cable, as on a bicycle.* Uea peleki. *~ disk.* Pā peleki *(preceded by* ke). *Disk ~.* Peleki pā. *~ pad.* Pale peleki.
bran Pelene. *~ muffin.* Māpina pelene.
branch *As of a government.* Māhele. *Executive ~.* Māhele mana hoʻokō. *Judicial ~.* Māhele ʻaha hoʻokolokolo. *Legislative ~.* Māhele ʻahaʻōlelo.
brand new Hou loa.
brass Keleawe. *~ instrument.* Pū keleawe.
Brazil *Also Brazilian.* Palakila, Barazila.
bread Palaoa. *See Hawaiian entries under* palaoa. *~ crumbs.* Hunahuna palaoa. *Brown ~, a layman's term for any bread made with dark flower.* Palaoa mākuʻe. *Wheat ~.* Palaoa huika. *Whole wheat ~.* Palaoa huika piha. *White ~.* Palaoa keʻokeʻo.
breadth *Also width, in math.* Ākea, ana ākea, laulā *(abb.* ll), ana laulā. *See height, length.*
break *To ~ the law.* Haʻihaʻi kānāwai, ʻaʻe kānāwai. *See outlaw.*
break *To ~ apart, in math, i.e. ~ing a number into addends or factors; also to ~ or change, as a twenty dollar bill.* Wāwahi.
break *To ~ or stop, as an electric circuit.* ʻOki. *See open. Circuit ~r, a device which automatically interrupts electric current before wires in a circuit get too hot.* ʻŪʻoki puni uila.
break *Page ~, as in computer program.* Hoʻokaʻawale ʻaoʻao.
break *Fast ~, in basketball; also to make a fast ~.* Ulele kikī. *See lead pass.*

breast *Chicken ~.* Umauma moa.
breast stroke *Also to swim the ~.* ʻAu umauma.
breathing equipment *As for use in space exploration.* Lako hanu.
breed *Also to impregnate.* Hoʻopiʻi. *To ~ animals or propagate plants.* Haʻakipu. *See crossbreed.*
breeze *Gentle ~; dust raised and small branches move, in meteorology.* Aheahe. *See wind. Leaves in constant motion.* Kolonahe.
breezeway *As an open area between buildings.* Holona makani.
bridge *As on an ʻukulele or guitar.* Nīʻau nui. *See ʻukulele.*
brim *Of a hat.* Kihikihi, pekekeu. *Of a floppy hat.* Laulau.
brine *A concentrated solution of salt or ocean water.* Wai paʻakai paʻapūhia, wai paʻakai.
brine shrimp *Artemia.* Pokipoki ālia.
bring back out *To ~, in basketball; also to slow down, as in a fast break.* Kuemi, kuemi iki.
Britain *Also British.* Pelekāne, Pelekānia. *See England, English.*
British *See Britain.*
brittle *As dry* hala *leaves.* Paʻapaʻaʻina. *See peanut brittle.*
broad reach (port) *Broad reach on the port side, i.e. sailing downwind at an angle between 90° and directly downwind, with the port side windward.* Kele ama kaʻakepa. *See broad reach (starboard), beam reach (port, starboard), close hauled (port, starboard), downwind.*
broad reach (starboard) *Broad reach on the starboard side, i.e. sailing downwind at an angle between 90° and directly downwind, with the starboard side windward.* Kele ʻākea kaʻakepa. *See broad reach (port), beam reach (port, starboard), close hauled (port, starboard), downwind.*
broccoli Palakalī.
broiler oven ʻOma kōʻala.

bromine Polomine. ~ *gas.* Kinoea polomine.
bronchial *Also bronchiole, bronchus.* ʻĀmanapuʻu. *See entries below.*
bronchiole *Also bronchial, bronchus.* ʻĀmanapuʻu. *Terminal ~.* ʻĀmanapuʻu kuahope.
bronchus *Also bronchiole, bronchial.* ʻĀmanapuʻu. *Primary ~.* ʻĀmanapuʻu kuamua. *Secondary or lobar ~.* ʻĀmanapuʻu kualua. *Tertiary or segmental ~.* ʻĀmanapuʻu kuakolu.
bronze Keleawekini.
brooder Pene ʻioʻio.
broom closet Keʻena pūlumi.
Brown *Also Brownian.* Palaunu. *See entries below. ~ian motion, in chemistry.* Lelekē Palaunu.
brown bread *A layman's term for any bread made with dark flour.* Palaoa mākuʻe. *See Hawaiian entries under* palaoa.
brownie *The dessert.* Meaʻono palauni, palauni.
brown rice Laiki mākuʻe, lāisi mākuʻe.
browser *An animal that eats twigs and leaves.* Hamulau lāʻau. *See* grazer.
brumby *A wild Australian horse.* Palami.
brush *A contact that supplies electric current to a commutator.* Awe uholo uila. *See* commutator, conductor. *For bathing.* Palaki ʻauʻau. *Paint ~.* Hulu pena.
bubble chamber *In chemistry.* Hōkelo huʻa.
bubble wand *For blowing bubbles.* Lina puhi huʻahuʻa.
buckle *Belt ~.* ʻŪmiʻi ʻilikuapo, ʻūmiʻi.
bud *Of a leaf.* Muʻo. *See* leaf.
budget *A listing of expenditures and receipts.* Moʻohelu kālā, moʻohelu. *See* accounting. *To make a ~.* Hoʻopaʻa moʻohelu kālā.
buffer Pale hoʻokaʻawale.
bug *See* insect, sow bug.
buggy *Dune ~.* Kaʻa holo one.

bugle Pū koa. *See* cornet, trumpet.
build *To put together, as a model.* Kāpili. *See* manufacture. *To ~ a model airplane.* Kāpili kūkohu mokulele.
build *To ~, in math.* Hoʻomahele. *See* undo. *To ~ a shield (volcano).* Hoʻāhua kuahene.
built-in Paʻaloko. *See* hard disk, hard drive. *~ memory, in a computer.* Waihona ʻike paʻaloko.
bulb ʻŌpuʻu. *Light ~.* ʻŌpuʻukukui. *As of a lily or tulip.* Hua kanu. *~ tip.* ʻŌmaka hua kanu. *Wet-and-dry-~ hygrometer.* Ana kawaūea ʻōpuʻu pulu a maloʻo.
Bulgaria *Also Bulgarian.* Pulukalia, Bulugaria.
bulk *Mass.* Nuipaʻa.
bulletin board Papa hōʻikeʻike.
Bulletin Board Service *On computer programs (BBS).* Papa Lawelawe Hoʻolaha. *Abb.* PLH.
bullfrog Poloka pulu.
bullsnake Nāhesa pulu.
bump *Speed ~, as on a road or in a parking lot.* Puʻu haʻapupū. *To bang into; to crash, as cars.* Hoʻokuʻi. *To ~ (the ball), in volleyball.* Kuʻi ʻāmana.
Bunsen burner Kapuahi ula kahi. *See* burner.
bunting *Indigo ~.* Manu ʻinikō.
buoyant force *The upward force of a fluid on an object in it.* Manehu hoʻolana.
bureau *Dresser.* Pahu ʻume.
bureaucracy *Also bureaucratic.* Pākulekele. *Bureaucrat.* Kanaka pākulekele.
buret *A precision-made piece of glassware used to measure and deliver accurate volumes of solutions, in science.* ʻŪhōloʻa māʻoʻāna.
Burkina Faso Burakina Faso.
Burma *Also Burmese.* Puruma, Buruma.
burn *Slash and ~, a method of land cultivation.* Kā makawela.

burner *As on a stove.* Pā kapuahi. *See* hot plate. *Bunsen ~.* Kapuahi ula kahi. *Fisher ~.* Kapuahi pukapuka. *Meeker ~.* Kapuahi Mika.

bush *Shrub.* Laʻalāʻau. *See* shrubland, twig.

bush bean Pāpapa haʻa.

bushel *A unit of measurement.* Pūkele. *Abb.* pū.

business *Career or occupation.* ʻOihana. *Purchase and sale of goods and services.* Kāloaʻa. *A person or company engaged in ~.* Pāʻoihana. *~ cycle, a repeated series of economic growth and recession.* Pōʻaiapuni kāloaʻa. *Central ~ district.* ʻĀpana pāʻoihana kauwaena. *See* downtown.

bus stop Kūna kaʻa ʻōhua.

butane Butane.

butcher Mea lole pipi, kanaka lole pipi. *~ paper.* Pepa lole pipi.

butter *Peanut ~.* Pīnekipaka.

butterfly *Kamehameha ~.* Pulelehua Kamehameha. *Monarch ~.* Pulelehua pua kalaunu. *~ stroke; also to swim the ~ stroke.* ʻAu malolo. *See* stroke.

button *Also to ~.* Pihi, pihi lole *(preceded by* ke*). Turbo ~, as in Nintendo games.* Pihi pīnaʻi. *See* warp zone.

buttonhole Puka pihi.

byte *In computer terminology.* ʻAi. *See* bit, kilobyte, megabyte, gigabyte.

C

cabbage *Skunk ~.* Kāpiki ponī.

cabinet *A council that advises a president, sovereign, etc.* ʻAha kuhina. *See entry below.*

cabinet *File ~.* Pahu waihona pepa. *Medicine ~.* Waihona lāʻau lapaʻau. *Storage ~.* Waihona hoʻāhu.

cable Kaula uea. *Also* uea. *Brake ~, as on a bicycle.* Uea peleki.

cache *As in a computer program.* Ahu hoʻokoe. *To ~, as in computer function.* Hoʻokoe. *To ~ disks.* Hoʻokoe pā.

cactus *General term; also prickly pear ~.* Pānini. *See* barrel cactus, cholla, ocotillo, organ pipe cactus, prickly pear cactus.

caffeine ʻĀkope.

cage Pene. *See* kennel.

caladium Kalo kalakoa.

calcareous Paʻapuna. *~ rock, calcium carbonate.* Pōhaku paʻapuna.

calcite Ōpuna.

calcium Kalipuna. *~ carbonate, calcareous rock.* Pōhaku paʻapuna.

calculate Huli a loaʻa, huli, hoʻomaulia.

calculator Mīkini helu. *~ display screen.* Papakaumaka mīkini helu. *Graphing ~.* Mīkini kākuhi.

caldera Lua kīlauea.

calendar ʻAlemanaka.

calibrate *Also* calibration. Kauanakahi.

California *Also* Californian. Kaleponi. *~ grass.* Mauʻu Kaleponi.

calligraphy Limahilu.

Callisto *A moon of Jupiter.* Kalito.

call number *As for a library book.* Helu kuhi puke. *See* card catalog, catalog card.

call sheet *A list of jobs for movie or video production.* Papa māhele hana. *See* jobs.

calm *As the wind; smoke rises vertically, and direction of wind shown by smoke drift rather than wind vanes, in meteorology.* Pohu. *See* wind. *Also cool-headed, even-tempered.* Māio.

calorie Ikehuʻā.

calorimeter *An instrument used to measure changes in thermal energy.* Ana ikehu kāʻokoʻa.

cambium *The slippery layer under the bark of a plant which is the growing area of the stem.* Wale ʻili.

Cambodia *Also* Cambodian. Kamabodia.

camcorder *Video camera.* Pahu paʻi wikiō.

Cameroon *Also* Cameroun, Cameroonian, Camerounian. Kameruna.

camouflaged Nalopeʻe. *To camouflage.* Hoʻonalopeʻe.
camp *Gathering of people to learn or practice certain skills.* ʻĀpoʻe. See *camper, campground. Computer ~.* ʻĀpoʻe kamepiula. *Basketball ~.* ʻĀpoʻe pōhīnaʻi. *To ~.* Hoʻomoana.
camper *Camping vehicle.* Kaʻa hoʻomoana.
campground Kahua hoʻomoana.
can *Aerosol ~.* Kini kīkī. *~ of corned beef.* Kini pipi. *~ of tuna.* Kini tuna. *~ opener.* Mea wehe kini. *Watering ~.* Kini hoʻopulu meakanu.
Canada *Also Canadian.* Kanakā.
Canary Isles Pae Moku Kenele.
cancel *To ~, as in computer function.* Hoʻōki. See *put away, undo.*
cancel *To ~, i.e. the compression of one wave at the same time as the rarefaction of another wave, in science.* Kuʻipē. *To be ~led (out), in science or argumentation; ~lation.* Kuʻipēhia.
candidate *As in politics.* Moho. See *primary election.*
candlenut Kukui, kuikui.
candy *~ cane.* Kanakē koʻokoʻo. *Caramel ~.* Kanakē kalamela. See *lollipop.*
canned fish Kini iʻa.
cannibal *Among animals, insects, etc.* Hamuhika. See *cannibal* (dic.).
canoe *Without* ʻiako. Waʻa ʻIlikini. *The portion of a ~ between forward and aft outrigger booms.* Ukuwai. See *port, starboard.*
canopy *~ layer of vegetation between understory and emergent layers.* Papa kaupoku. See *vegetation layer.*
cantaloupe Ipuʻala. See *melon.*
canteen Kini huewai.
canvass *To go door to door handing out political information and asking people which candidate they support.* Anamanaʻo pāloka.
canyon Awāwa kūhōhō. See *passageway. Grand ~.* Ke awāwa kūhōhō nui ʻo Hakaʻama, Hakaʻama.

cap *Dunce ~.* Pāpale kone. *Shower ~.* Pāpale kililau. *Ski ~, stocking ~.* Pāpale kapuhau. *Swim ~.* Pāpale ʻau.
cap *As for toothpaste tube; lid, as for jar.* Pani (preceded by ke). See *manhole cover. Pen ~.* Poʻi peni (preceded by ke).
capacity Pihanaʻū. *Abb.* piʻū. See *volume. Field ~, for holding water.* Palena ū wai.
capillary ʻUmelauoho. *Capillarity.* Pēʻumelauoho. *~ pipette.* Paipuliʻi ʻumelauoho. *~ water.* Wai ʻumelauoho. *One of the minute blood vessels between the arteries and the veins.* Oho.
capital *Upper case.* Maʻaka. See entry below and *capitalize, letter. ~ letter.* Hua maʻaka.
capital *Anything produced in an economy that is accumulated or used to produce other goods and services.* Ahu kāloaʻa. See *capitalism.*
capitalism Paikāloaʻa, paihoʻāhu kāloaʻa.
capitalize *To ~ (a letter of the alphabet).* Hoʻomaʻaka. See *lower case. Three lines drawn under a letter to indicate that the letter is to be ~d, in proofreading.* Kaha hoʻomaʻaka. *A line drawn diagonally through a capital letter to indicate the letter is not to be ~d.* Kaha hoʻonaʻinaʻi.
capo *As used on a fretted instrument to raise the pitch of all strings.* ʻŪmiʻi kaula.
capping *As the last stage of volcano formation.* Pani poʻo (preceded by ke).
caprock *In geology.* Pōhaku hoʻopaʻa wai.
caps *Key ~, on computer program.* Hōʻike hua pihi. *~ lock, as on computer or typewriter keyboard.* Laka maʻaka. *~ lock key.* Pihi laka maʻaka, pihi laka (preceded by ke).
capsule *Space ~.* Kelena moku ahikao.
caption *Also to ~.* Lepe kiʻi. See *subtitle.*
caramel Kalamela. *~ candy.* Kanakē kalamela.

carbohydrate Kōpia.
carbon *Not in chemistry.* 'Ōpa'u. *See entries below.* *~ paper.* Pepa 'ōpa'u.
carbon Karabona, kalapona. *See entries below.*
carbonate Karabonahate. *See calcareous. Calcium ~, calcareous rock.* Pōhaku pa'apuna. *Cupric ~.* Kupuriku karabonahate. *Ferrous ~.* Ferousa karabonahate.
carbon dating *Also radiocarbon date.* Helu makahiki kalapona.
carbon dioxide Karabona diokesaside, kalapona 'okikene lua. *Oxygen-~ cycle.* Pō'aiapuni 'okikene kalapona 'okikene lua.
carbon disulfide Karabona disulifaside.
carbonic acid 'Akika kalapona.
carbon monoxide Karabona monokesaside.
carboxylic acid 'Akika pūhui kalapona.
carburetor *As in an internal-combustion engine.* 'Ūhōlo'a kakalina.
card Kāleka. *See entry below and postcard. Birthday ~.* Kāleka lā hānau. *Birthday or anniversary ~.* Kāleka piha makahiki. *Graduation ~.* Kāleka puka kula, kāleka hemo kula. *Greeting ~.* Kāleka aloha.
card *Charge ~.* Kāleka kāki, 'ea kāki. *Fitness ~, as for sports or physical education.* Kāleka olakino. *Flash ~.* Kāleka a'o. *Index ~.* Kāleka pahu.
cardboard *Corrugated paper.* Pepa pahu. *~ box.* Pahu pepa.
card catalog *As in a library.* Pahu kāleka kuhi puke. *See call number, catalog card.*
cardiac arrythmia Pu'uwai pana 'ewa'ewa.
cardinal *The bird.* Manu māka'i, manu 'ula'ula.
cardinal number Helu heluna. *See ordinal number.*
cardinal points *The four ~, or four primary directions of the compass, in geography.* Nā kūkulu 'ehā.

career *Occupation.* 'Oihana. *See business. Baseball ~.* 'Oihana pōhili.
caret *An editing mark (^) used to show where something is to be inserted, in proofreading.* Kaha ho'okomo. *See insert.*
Caribbean Kalepiana, Karebiana.
caries *Cavity in a tooth.* Puka niho. *See oral cavity.*
Carina *The star in the center of the constellation ~.* Mākoi. *Another star in this constellation.* Makawela.
carnival *See amusement park.*
carnivore *Also carnivorous.* Hamui'a.
carnivorous caterpillar *Eupithecia spp.* 'Enuhe hamui'a.
Carolina *Also Carolinian.* Kalolaina. *See Caroline Isles. North ~.* Kalolaina 'Ākau. *South ~.* Kalolaina Hema.
Caroline Isles Pae Moku Kalolaina, Pae Moku Karolaina.
carpenter's level 'Iliwai.
carpet Moena weleweka. *See rug.*
carriage *Baby ~.* Ka'apēpē.
carry *To palm or ~ (the ball), in basketball.* Poholuna.
carrying violation *In volleyball.* 'A'ena hāpai. *See lift.*
cart *Shopping ~.* Ka'a mākeke. *Push~.* Ka'a pahu.
cartilage Iwi kamumu.
carton *Milk ~.* Pahu waiū.
cartoon Kātuna, kākuna, kākuni. *See comic book.*
cartridge *As for a computer printer.* Pāpahu. *Font ~.* Pāpahu kinona hua.
cascade Wailelele.
case *Cassette ~, usually made of plastic.* Poho lola. *Tape ~, cassette holder.* Pāiki lola.
case Pahu. *See pack, six-pack, twelve-pack. Of beer.* Pahu pia. *Of soda.* Pahu koloaka.
case sensitive *As in computer program.* Maka'ala ma'aka.
cash Kālā kū'ike. *Petty ~.* Kālā kini.
cashbox Kini kālā.

Māmaka Kaiao / 199

cashier Mea ʻohi kālā, kanaka ʻohi kālā, wahine ʻohi kālā. See *cash register*.

cashier's check Pila kīkoʻo panakō.

cash register Mīkini ʻohi kālā. See *cashier*.

cassette *As for music tapes.* Lola. *See entry below.* ~ *recorder/player.* Mīkini lola. ~ *player.* Mīkini hoʻokani lola. ~ *recorder.* Mīkini hoʻopaʻa lola. See *recorder*. ~ *case, usually made of plastic.* Poho lola. ~ *holder or tape case.* Pāiki lola. *Video* ~. Lola wikiō.

cassette *Paper* ~, *as for a computer printer.* Poho pepa.

Cassiopeia *A constellation.* ʻIwakeliʻi.

cast *As for a broken arm.* Kimeki iwi, puna.

catalog card *As in a library.* Kāleka helu kuhi puke. See *call number, card catalog*.

catalyst *A substance which increases the rate of a chemical reaction without being permanently changed itself.* ʻŪmōʻauiwawe, hōʻeleu mōʻaui.

catamaran Moku kaulua.

cataract *Steep rapids in a large river.* Wai kōī.

catbird Manu pōpoki.

catch *To* ~, *as a ball.* ʻApo. See *receive*.

categorize *Also to classify.* Waeʻano.

caterpillar *Carnivorous* ~ *(Eupithecia spp).* ʻEnuhe hamuiʻa.

catfish ʻOʻopu Pākē.

cathode *The negative electrode in an electrical circuit.* ʻŪholo uila ʻine. See *anode, electrode.* ~*-ray tube (CRT).* ʻOhe kīwī.

Catskills *A mountain range.* Katakila.

cattail Huelopōpoki.

cattle egret ʻAlekuʻu kau pipi.

caucus *A meeting of political party leaders to determine policy, choose candidates, etc.* Haiamui.

cauliflower Kalipalaoa.

cause Kumu. See *effect*. *A prefix indicating the instrument or* ~ *of a particular action.* ʻū-.

cavity *In a tooth, caries.* Puka niho. *Nasal* ~, *in linguistics.* Haka ihu. *Oral* ~. Haka waha.

CD *Also compact disc.* CD (*pronounced* sēdē), sēdē; *also* pā CD, pā sēdē (*preceded by* ke).

ceiling Kilina, huna.

celestial equator Pōʻai waena lani.

cell *As in databases or tables.* Kūʻono.

cell *Biological* ~. Hunaola. See *blood, tissue*.

cellar ʻŌpao.

cellulose Kelulose.

Celsius Kelekia. *Abb.* Klk.

cement *Rubber* ~. Tuko laholio. See *glue, paste*.

census *A periodic official enumeration of a population and its characteristics.* Helu kanaka.

cent Kēneka. ~ *sign.* Kaha kēneka.

center *Of a circle.* Kikowaena. See entries below and *learning center, shopping center*. *Of tongue.* Waena alelo. *Turn* ~, *in math.* Kikowaena wili.

center *To* ~, *as type on printed page.* Kauwaena. *To* ~ *justify.* Hoʻokauwaena.

center *Also five man, in basketball.* Kūlima. *In football.* Huki pōpō. See *hike*.

center circle *On basketball court.* Pōʻai waena.

center feed *To* ~, *as paper into a printer or copy machine.* Hānai waena.

center of gravity Piko ʻumekaumaha. See *gravity*.

centi- *A prefix meaning one hundredth (c).* Hapa haneli. *Abb.* hhn. *Also* keni-. See entries below and *deci-, milli-, micro-, nano-, pico-*.

centigram Kenikalame. *Abb.* kkal.

centiliter Kenilika. *Abb.* kl.

centimeter Kenimika. *Abb.* knm.

Central African Republic Lepupalika ʻApelika Waena.

Central America *Also Central American, Latin America, Latin American.* ʻAmelika Waena.

central angle *An angle that has its vertex at the center of a circle, in math.* Huina kikowaena.

central business district 'Āpana pā'oihana kauwaena. *See downtown.*

central vowel *In linguistics.* Woela kauwaena. *See vowel.*

centrifugal *Acting in a direction away from a center.* Lele niniu. *See centripetal.* ~ *force.* Manehu lele niniu.

centripetal *Acting in a direction toward a center.* 'Ume niniu. *See centrifugal.* ~ *force.* Manehu 'ume niniu.

ceramic Lāmeka. ~ *tile.* Kile lāmeka.

cereal Kiliala, siriala.

ceremonies *Opening* ~. Wehena papahana. *See closing banquet.*

certificate *Of achievement.* Palapala ho'okō. *Gift* ~. Palapala makana.

certified check Pila kīko'o panakō.

Chad *Also Chadian.* Kada.

chain Kaulahao; ku'ina; pae. *See food net, range, series. Bicycle* ~. Kaulahao paikikala. ~ *of craters.* Pae lua pele. *Food* ~. Ku'ina mea'ai.

chair leg Wāwae noho.

chalk Poho (*preceded by* ke). ~ *dust.* Ehu poho. ~ *tray.* Paepae poho. *Colored* ~. Poho kala.

challenge ~ *or enrichment book.* Puke ho'onui 'ike.

chamber *Bubble* ~, *in chemistry.* Hōkelo hu'a. *Cloud* ~, *a scientific device which detects nuclear particles through the formation of cloud tracks.* Hōkelo ao. *Magma* ~. Nupa pelemaka.

champion *Also champions.* Moho. *See championship.*

championship *In sports.* Ho'okūkū kahului. *See scrimmage, tournament.*

chance *Possibility of an indicated outcome, in math.* Papaha. *See outcome, probability.* ~ *space, as on a game board such as Monopoly.* Kuea huki pepa.

chancellor *As of a college or university.* Po'o kulanui. *See president, provost.*

change *As from a purchase.* Koena. *Loose* ~. Kālā helele'i, kenikeni. *To* ~ *or break, as a twenty dollar bill.* Wāwahi.

change *To* ~ *or replace, as in a search-and-replace feature in computer program.* Kuapo. *To find and* ~, *search and replace.* Huli a kuapo. *To not make any* ~, *leave as is, as in computer program.* Waiho.

change *Chemical* ~. Loli kemikala. *Geologic* ~. Loli honua. *To* ~ *something into different form.* Ho'olilo.

channel *Also station, as on radio or television.* Kānela.

character *As in a story, play, movie, etc.* Hāme'e.

character *As of type in computer program.* Hua pa'i, hua.

character operator Mea ulele hua. *See set type.*

charcoal Nānahu. *See coal.*

charge Kāki. *See entry below and account, cost, price.* ~ *card.* Kāleka kāki, 'ea kāki. ~ *or credit account, as in a bank.* Waihona kāki.

charge *Electric* ~. Ikehu uila. *Neutral* ~. Ikehu uila hohoki, ikehu hohoki. *See positive, negative. To* ~, *as a battery.* Ho'oikehu.

Charles Kale. ~' *law, in science, i.e. the volume of a gas increases as its temperature increases if the pressure remains constant.* Ke kānāwai a Kale.

Charon *A moon of Pluto.* Kālona.

chart *Also graph, plot.* Pakuhi. *See Hawaiian entries under* pakuhi *and* graph, plot. *Conversion* ~. Pakuhi ho'ololi. *Metric conversion* ~. Pakuhi ho'ololi mekalika. *Flow* ~. Pakuhi ka'ina. *To* ~, *make a* ~ *or graph.* Kākuhi. *To make a flow* ~. Kākuhi ka'ina.

charter *A document defining the organization of a city, colony, or corporate body.* Palapala ho'okumu.

cheat Kikiki.

check ~ *mark.* Kahamakau. *To verify or give proof, as for a math problem.* Hōʻoia. *Spell-~er; to spell check.* Loipela.
check *Bank ~.* Pila kīkoʻo. See *money order. Cashier's or certified ~; also bank draft.* Pila kīkoʻo panakō. *Traveler's ~.* Pila kīkoʻo huakaʻi.
checkers Mū. See *chess. Chinese ~.* Mū Pākē.
check in *To ~ or register, as at a conference or hotel.* Kāinoa komo, kāinoa. See *check out, registration.*
checking account *As in a bank.* Waihona kīkoʻo. See *account.*
check out *To ~, as of a hotel.* Kāinoa puka. See *check in, registration. To ~ or borrow something by signing for it.* Kāinoa.
checkpoint *Also review.* Nāʻana.
check register Moʻo pila kīkoʻo.
checks and balances *As in government.* Hoʻokuʻia.
cheddar Keka. *~ cheese.* Waiūpaʻa keka.
cheese Waiūpaʻa. *Cheddar ~.* Waiūpaʻa keka. *Cottage ~.* Waiūhakuhaku. *Parmesan ~.* Waiūpaʻa pamesana. *Process(ed) ~.* Waiūpaʻa i haʻaliu ʻia. *Swiss ~.* Waiūpaʻa Kuikilani.
cheetah Leopaki kikī.
chemical Kemikala. See *coefficient. ~ activity.* Mōʻaui kemikala. *~ change.* Loli kemikala. *~ equation.* Haʻihelu kemikala. *Balanced ~ equation.* Haʻihelu kemikala kaulike. *~ formula.* Haʻilula kemikala. *~ property.* ʻAnopili kemikala (*preceded by* ke). *~ solution.* Māʻōʻāna kemikala. *~ly combined.* ʻŌʻā kemikala ʻia. *To treat ~ly, as sewage.* Kāemikala.
chemistry Kemika.
cherry Keli.
chess Mū kākela. See *checkers.*
chest *Toy ~.* Pahu mea pāʻani, waihona mea pāʻani. *Treasure ~.* Pahu waihona waiwai.
chest pass *In basketball; to throw such a pass.* Kīloi umauma.

chick *Young ~; also sound to call chickens by imitating a young ~.* Piopio.
chickadee Manu kikakī.
chicken *Drumstick.* Pālaumoa. *~ breast.* Umauma moa. *~ thigh.* ʻŪhā moa.
chicken pox Puʻupuʻu moa.
Chile *Also Chilean.* Kile, Kili.
chili Kili.
chimney Puka uahi.
China Kina, ʻĀina Pākē. See *Chinese.*
chinchilla rabbit Lāpaki kinikila, lāpiki kinikila, ʻiole lāpiki kinikila.
Chinese Pākē. See *China.*
Chinese checkers Mū Pākē.
chin-up Hukialewa, hukialewa pohokua. See *pull-up.*
chip *As used in checkers, counting, pocker, etc.* Hiu. *As potato chip.* Kipi. *Potato ~.* Kipi ʻuala kahiki. *Taro ~.* Kipi kalo.
chipmonk ʻAkuiki, kiulela ʻakuiki.
chiropractic *Also to practice ~.* Pālomi. *Chiropractor.* Kauka pālomi.
chisel Kila pao.
chloride Koloriside. *Cobalt ~.* Kobalata koloriside. *Stannous ~.* Satanousa koloriside.
chloridops *~ kona, grosbeak finch.* Hona. *~ regiskongi, King Kong finch.* Nuku ʻekue.
chlorine Kolorine.
chlorodane Kolorodane.
chlorofluorocarbon Kolorofolorokalapona.
chloroform Kolopoma.
chlorophyll Kolopila. See *plastid.*
chloroplast Kolopalake.
chlorosis *A condition in plants as a result of deficient nitrogen.* Makenaikokene.
choice *As in computer program.* Koho.
cholesterol Naʻokoko.
cholla *A kind of cactus.* Pānini kioia.
choose *To ~, as in computer program.* Koho.

chopstick Lāʻau ʻai.
chord *Of an arc, in math.* Kaula hōʻike piʻo.
choreographer *Also to choreograph.* Kūkulu hulahula.
Christmas ball *The tree ornament.* Pōpō wehi lāʻau Kalikimaka. See *ornament*.
chromatography Hōʻauikala. See *silica gel g*. *Paper* ~. Hōʻauikala pepa. *Thin-layer* ~. Hōʻauikala papa lahilahi. *Chromatograph.* Kiʻi hōʻauikala. *Chromatographic paper.* Pepa hōʻauikala.
chromosome Awe ōewe.
chrysalis Wiliʻōkaʻi.
cigar-box ʻukulele ʻUkulele pahu kīkā.
cilium *Also cilia.* Huluheu.
cinder ʻĀkeke. ~ *cone.* Puʻu ʻākeke. *Volcanic* ~. One ʻā.
cinnamon Kinamona.
circle *Circular shape; as in preschool programs; to sit in a* ~. Lina poepoe. *The geometric shape.* Pōʻai. ~ *graph.* Pakuhi pōʻai. *Center of a* ~. Kikowaena. *Radius of a* ~. Kahahānai. *Concentric* ~s. Nā pōʻai kikowaena kahi. *Semi*~. Pōʻai hapalua. *Center* ~, *on basketball court.* Pōʻai waena. *To* ~, *i.e. draw a* ~ *around something.* Kahalina. *A* ~ *around a period, colon, or semicolon to show that it has been inserted, in proofreading.* Lina hoʻokomo.
circuit *Complete* ~, *lap.* Puni. *Electric* ~. Puni uila. ~ *breaker, a device which automatically interrupts electric current before wires in a circuit get too hot.* ʻŪʻoki puni uila.
circulatory system ʻŌnaehana mānowai.
circumference Anapuni.
circumstances *Extenuating* ~. Kumu kūikawā.
circus Keleku.
cirrus cloud Ao lālahilewa. See *cloud*.
citizen Kupa, makaʻāinana. *Dual* ~. Kupa kaumokuʻāina pālua, makaʻāinana kaumokuʻāina pālua.

citrate Kitarahate. *Sodium* ~. Sodiuma kitarahate.
citrus ʻOhana ʻālani.
city *General term; town.* Kūlanakauhale. ~ *block.* Pōlaka. *Downtown.* Kaona. *Urban area.* Kiwikā.
civil disobedience *Breaking a law because it goes against personal morals.* ʻAʻa kānāwai.
civil law Kānāwai kīwila, kānāwai sīwila.
civil unrest Haunaele kūloko.
claim ~ *for damages, as to an insurance company.* Koi pohō. *To make a* ~ *for damages.* Hoʻopiʻi i ke koi pohō. *To settle, as a* ~. Hoʻonā. See *land court, land registration system*.
clamp ʻŪmiʻi. See *forceps*. *Pinch* ~. ʻŪmiʻi pani. *Test tube* ~. ʻŪmiʻi hano hoʻokolohua. *Utility* ~. ʻŪmiʻi hoʻopaʻa.
clan *Also subtribe.* Hapū. See *tribe*.
ClarisWorks *A nickname for the computer program.* Kaleiwahana.
classify *Also to categorize.* Waeʻano.
clause *Or grammatical sentence.* Pepeke. *Dependent* ~. Pepeke ʻōhua. *Main* ~. Pepeke haku.
claw Maiʻuʻu.
clay *Modeling* ~. Kalē. See *Play-Doh*. *As for ceramics;* ~ *dirt.* Pālolo.
cleaner wrasse *Labroides Phthirophegus, a kind of fish.* Hīnālea nāʻuke.
clear *To* ~, *as data in a computer program.* Holoi.
clearing *In pasture or range land.* Pāhuʻa.
clef *In music.* Hōʻailona mele. *Bass* ~. Hōʻailona mele leo kāne, leo kāne. *Treble* ~. Hōʻailona mele leo wahine, leo wahine.
click *As the sound produced when* ~*ing a computer mouse.* Paʻina. *To press or depress, as in computer program.* Kōmi, kaomi.
cliff *Wave-cut* ~. Pali ʻaʻaianalu. See *weathered*. *Small* ~s. Kīpāpali.
climate Aniau. See *climatology, microclimate, weather*.

climatology Kālaianiau.
Climatologist. Kanaka kālaianiau, mea kālaianiau.
climax community *In biology.* Kaiaulu ʻahaʻi.
clip *Also to ~ together.* Pine. *See dink.* *Paper ~.* Pine pepa.
clipboard *As in computer program.* Papa ʻūmiʻi. *To show ~.* Hōʻike papa ʻūmiʻi.
clipper *A kind of ship.* Mokupeʻa holo māmā.
clock *Also watch.* Uaki, uāki. *Alarm ~.* Uaki hoʻāla, uāki hoʻāla. *Analog ~.* Uaki lima kuhikuhi, uāki lima kuhikuhi. *Digital ~.* Uaki kikohoʻe, uāki kikohoʻe.
clockwise Kōʻai ʻākau. *See counter-clockwise.*
close *Near.* Kokoke. *See entries below and close-up.*
close *To ~, as in computer program.* Pani. *See closed, bracket, parenthesis. To ~ up tight, as a flower bud.* ʻŌpili.
closed *As a frame in a computer program.* Paʻa. *See open.* *~ frame.* Mōlina paʻa. *As a primary election.* Kūloko. *~ primary.* Wae moho kūloko.
close hauled (port) *Close hauled on the port side, i.e. sailing into the wind at the closest angle possible, generally 67°, with the port side windward.* Kele ama kūnihi. *See beam reach (port, starboard), broad reach (port, starboard), close hauled (starboard), downwind.*
close hauled (starboard) *Close hauled on the starboard side, i.e. sailing into the wind at the closest angle possible, generally 67°, with the starboard side windward.* Kele ʻākea kūnihi. *See beam reach (port, starboard), broad reach (port, starboard), close hauled (port), downwind.*
closet *Broom ~.* Keʻena pūlumi.

close-up *As of a photograph or in movie or video production.* Paʻi kokoke *(preceded by ke). See medium shot, wide shot. To take a ~.* Paʻi a kokoke. *Extreme ~.* Paʻi kokoke loa. *To take an extreme ~.* Paʻi a kokoke loa.
closing *As of a composition or story.* Ka pau ʻana. *See opening, body.*
closing banquet ʻAhaʻaina panina.
cloth *Material.* ʻĪlole. *See bolt.*
cloth duct tape *Electrician's tape.* Leki uea.
clothes *~ hook.* Lou kau lole. *~ rack, as on wheels in a clothing store.* Hao kau lole, haka lole.
clothesline Kaula kaulaʻi lole.
clothing ʻAʻahu. *See wardrobe.*
cloture *A method of ending debate and causing an immediate vote to be taken.* Hoʻōki.
cloud Ao. *Cirrus ~.* Ao lālahilewa. *Cumulus ~.* Ao ʻōpua. *Stratus ~.* Ao loa.
cloud chamber *A scientific device which detects nuclear particles through the formation of cloud tracks.* Hōkelo ao.
clove *The spice.* ʻŌpuʻuhame.
clown Kalaona. *~ hat.* Pāpale kone.
club *Also bat, racket.* ʻŪhili. *Golf ~.* ʻŪhili kolepa.
clue *Also to give a ~ about.* Ahuoi.
cluster *A prefix which indicates a ~ing together.* Kaia-. *See Hawaiian entries under kaia-.*
cluster *To find addends or factors that are nearly alike, in math.* Hoʻokokoke.
coach *Also to ~ or train (someone) for sports, etc.* Kaʻi. *~ for sports or physical education.* Kaʻi ʻālapa. *Drama ~.* Kaʻi hana keaka. *Sports trainer.* Kaʻi haʻuki. *Vocal ~.* Kaʻi puʻukani.
coal Lānahu. *See charcoal.* *~ gasification, i.e. the process in which steam and hot coal produce hydrocarbons.* Kākinoea lānahu.
coarse *As sand.* Mānoanoa. *See fine.*
coast *Ivory ~; Ivorian.* Kapa Kai Palaoa.
coast guard Pūʻali pale kapa kai.

cobalt Kobalata, kopalaka. ~ *chloride.* Kobalata koloriside.
cobble ʻIliʻili.
cocaine Kōkeina.
cochlea *Inner ear cavity.* Haka moʻoni.
cockroach *American ~ (Periplaneta americana).* ʻElelū kīkēkē. *Australian ~ (Periplaneta australasiae).* ʻElelū Nūhōlani. *German ~ (Blattella germanica).* ʻElelū laʻaloa.
coconut *Sponge-like material in sprouting ~.* Haku. *Sprouting ~ or one with eye emerging.* Niu haku.
coconut shell ʻukulele ʻUkulele pūniu.
Cocos Kokosa. *~ Plate.* Ka Una Honua Kokosa.
coda *Of a syllable, in linguistics.* Muli.
code Pāʻālua. See entry below and *color code.* *~ style, as in computer program.* Haka pāʻālua. *Key ~, as for the order to press keys on a calculator to find an answer.* Pāʻālua kaʻina hana.
code *A systematic collection of existing laws.* Papa kānāwai. *State water ~.* Papa kānāwai wai o ka mokuʻāina.
coefficient *A number placed in front of a chemical symbol or formula in order to balance the chemical equation.* Helu hoʻonui kemikala.
cog Pānihoniho. *Bicycle chain ~.* Pānihoniho o ke kaulahao paikikala.
coherent light *Light in which all the waves vibrate in a single plane, with the crests and troughs all aligned.* Mālamalama aukahi.
cohesion *Also cohesive.* Pūʻuoʻuo. See *adhesion.*
coin ʻŌkeni. See *bill, heads, tails.* *~ purse.* ʻEke kenikeni *(preceded by ke).* *~ toss.*
cold-blooded *As an animal.* Koko huʻihuʻi. See *warm-blooded.*
cold front *As of weather.* Kuʻina huʻihuʻi. See *front.*
cold war *Intense rivalry between nations but without miliary combat.* Kaua koʻekoʻe.

cole slaw Kāpiki meoneki.
coleus Lau noʻe. See *croton.*
collapse See *compress.*
collar ʻĀʻī, ʻāʻī lole, ʻāʻī kala, kala.
collate Kakekaʻi.
collect Hōʻiliʻili. See *collection.* *As fingerprints.* ʻOhi. See *fingerprint.* *To ~ fingerprints.* ʻOhi i ka meheu manamana lima (māka manamana lima, kiʻi manamana lima).
collection Hōʻiliʻilina. *Stamp ~.* Hōʻiliʻilina poʻoleka.
collection tube *A test tube used to collect gas generated in an experiment.* Hano ʻohi.
collective bargaining Kūkaʻi ʻaelike ʻuniona.
college *As a division or department within a university.* Koleke. *~ of agriculture.* Koleke mahiʻai. *~ of arts and sciences.* Koleke pāheona me ka ʻepekema. *Community ~.* Kulanui kaiaulu.
colloid *A chemical mixture with particle size between that of solutions and suspensions.* Pūaina lahi. See *solution, suspension.*
Colombia *Also Colombian.* Kolomepia, Kolomebia.
colon *In punctuation.* Kolona. See *semicolon.*
colonial See *postcolonial.*
colonize *To ~, as a land by either people, animals or plants.* Hoʻopanalāʻau. *To ~, particularly from the perspective of a people who have been ~d by a dominant culture or political entity.* Hoʻokolonaio. *Colonized.* Kolonaio.
colony *As a territory ruled by a more powerful nation.* Panalāʻau.
color *Additive ~, one of the primary colors (red, blue, green) which, when added together, produce white light.* Waihoʻoluʻu hui kea. *See entries below.*

Māmaka Kaiao / 205

Colorado *Also Coloradan.* Kololako, Kolorado. See *Grand Canyon.* ~ *River.* Ka muliwai ʻo Kololako, ka muliwai ʻo Hakaʻama.
color code *Also to* ~ *something.* Kalakuhi.
colored pencil Penikala kala.
color gradient *Also color band.* ʻAuina kala.
coloring *Food* ~. Kala meaʻai.
column Kolamu. *To place in* ~s. Hoʻokolamu.
combination *Also mixture.* Huihuina. *As for a lock.* Helu laka. ~ *lock.* Laka helu.
combined *Also mixed.* ʻŌʻā. *Chemically* ~. ʻŌʻā kemikala ʻia.
comet Hōkū puhipaka. See *shooting star.* *Halley's* ~. Ka hōkū puhipaka ʻo Hēli.
comic book Puke kātuna.
comma Kiko koma, kiko hoʻomaha.
commercial *Relating to business or commerce.* Pāʻoihana. ~ *growers.* Pāʻoihana hoʻoulu meakanu.
commission Komikina. *State Land Use Commission.* Komikina Hoʻohana ʻĀina o ka Mokuʻāina. *Water* ~. Komikina wai. *A fee paid to an agent for transacting business or performing a service.* Uku ʻēkena, uku ʻākena.
common *As in math terms.* Like. ~ *factor.* Helu hoʻonui like. *Greatest* ~ *factor.* Helu hoʻonui like kiʻekiʻe loa. ~ *multiple.* Helu māhua like. *Least* ~ *multiple.* Māhua haʻahaʻa loa. *Least* ~ *denominator.* Kinopiha haʻahaʻa loa.
common law Kānāwai kumu.
communicate Hoʻokaʻaʻike. See *communication.*
communication Kaʻaʻike. See *telecommunication.* *Oral* ~. Kaʻaʻike haʻi waha, kaʻaʻike waha. *Two-way* ~, *inter*~. Kaʻaʻike pānaʻi.

community Kaiaulu. ~ *college.* Kulanui kaiaulu. ~-*based health system.* ʻŌnaehana olakino kaiaulu. *Biological* ~, *as in science.* Kaiameaola. *Natural biological* ~. Kaiameaola kūlohelohe. *Climax* ~, *as in biology.* Kaiaulu ʻāhaʻi.
commutative property *In math.* ʻAnopili kaʻina hoʻi hope, ʻanopili hoʻi hope (*preceded by* ke).
commutator *A switch on a motor running on direct current that causes the current to reverse every half turn.* ʻŪkake uila. See *brush.*
compact disc See *CD.*
compare Hoʻokūkū.
compass *An instrument for describing circles or transferring measurements, in math.* ʻŪpā kāpōʻai. See *directions. As for navigation.* Pānānā (*preceded by* ke). *Pocket* ~. Pānānā paʻa lima (*preceded by* ke).
compatible *As of computer programs.* Launa. See *incompatible.* ~ *file format.* Hulu waihona launa. *As numbers in math.* Makalauna. ~ *number.* Helu makalauna.
compensation Kauapono. *To compensate.* Hoʻokauapono.
complement *To* ~, *as angles, in math.* Hoʻopiha kūpono. See *complementary angles, supplement.*
complementary angles *Two angles whose measures have a sum of 90°, in math.* Nā huina hoʻopiha kūpono. See *supplementary angles.*
complete *To* ~, *as a geometric figure, in math.* Kaha kinona.
complete *Also to open, as an electric circuit.* Hoʻokuʻi. See *break.*
complete fertilizer *Fertilizer which contains the six necessary elements for plant growth.* Mea hoʻomomona lepo kāʻokoʻa.
complex Nōhihi. See *simple. A prefix referring to vitamins.* Kau-. *B-*~ *vitamin.* Kauwikamina B.

component *Also constituent.* ʻŪmaupaʻa.
composed *To be ~ of, consist of, be made up of.* Maupaʻa.
composer *Also to compose songs or chants.* Haku mele.
composite Huihuina. *~ sample.* Hāpana huihuina. *As volcanic cone.* Ahupapa. *~ cone.* Puʻu ahupapa. *In math.* Puʻunaue lua. *~ number.* Helu puʻunaue lua.
compost *Also to ~.* Kīpulu. *See fertilize. To make ~.* Hana kīpulu.
compound *As in chemistry.* Pūhui. *See element, matter, substance. Binary ~.* Pūhui kumumea lua. *Free nitrogen ~.* Pūhui naikokene kaʻawale. *~ machine.* Kaumīkini.
comprehend *See comprehension.*
comprehension *Also to comprehend.* ʻApomanaʻo. *~ question.* Nīnau ʻapomanaʻo.
compress *To ~ or collapse, as a file in computer program.* ʻOpi. *See expand. ~ed or collapsed.* ʻOpihia. *~ed file.* Waihona ʻopihia.
compression *The most dense concentration of wave particles in a ~al wave.* Ulu. *See compressional wave, rarefaction.*
compressional wave *A wave in which matter vibrates in the same direction as the wave moves.* Hawewe papamoe. *See compression, transverse wave.*
compromise Kuʻikoli.
computer Kamepiula, lolouila, mīkini hoʻonohonoho ʻikena. *~ camp.* ʻApoʻe kamepiula. *~ keyboard.* Papa pihi kamepiula. *~ monitor.* Pahu papakaumaka kamepiula. *See screen. Laptop ~.* Kamepiula lawelima, lolouila lawelima.
concave *Hollowed or rounded inward as the inside of a bowl.* ʻEʻele. *See convex. ~ lens.* Aniani kaulona ʻeʻele. *~ mirror.* Aniani ʻeʻele.

concentrate *To make less dilute.* Hoʻopaʻapūhia. *See dilute. Concentrated.* Paʻapūhia.
concentric Kikowaena kahi. *~ circles.* Nā pōʻai kikowaena kahi.
concept Manaʻo.
concert *Indoor ~.* ʻAha mele maluhale. *Outdoor ~.* ʻAha mele kaupokulani.
conclusion Hopena. *To draw a ~.* Hoʻoholo i hopena.
condensation *Also to condense, as gas to liquid.* Kōkaha.
condense *To ~, as text in a computer document.* Hoʻohāiki. *See condensation, extend.*
conditioner *Air ~.* Mīkini hōʻolu ʻea, hōʻolu ʻea.
condom *For men.* Pāpalekimo.
conduct *To ~ a drive, as for cans or clean-up.* Alu. *See drive.*
conductor *Of electricity.* Mea uholo uila.
cone *Geometric ~.* ʻŌpuʻu. *Ice cream ~.* Kone ʻaikalima. *~ used as traffic marker.* Kone alanui.
cone *A geological feature.* Puʻu. *Ash ~.* Puʻu lehu. *Cinder ~.* Puʻu ʻākeke. *Composite ~.* Puʻu ahupapa. *Shield ~.* Puʻu kuahene. *Spatter ~.* Puʻu pōhāhā. *Tuff ~.* Puʻu hakuhune. *Volcanic ~.* Puʻu pele.
confer Kūkā. *See conference.*
conference *To ~, as part of the writing process.* Kūkā ma ka pūʻulu. *See entry below and prewrite.*
conference ʻAha kūkā. *In sports.* Hui. *See league. American Football ~ (AFC).* Hui Pōpeku ʻAmelika. *National Football ~ (NFC).* Hui Pōpeku Aupuni.
Congo *Also Congolese.* Konokō. *Democratic Republic of the ~.* Lepupalika Kemokalaka ʻo Konokō.
congruent *In math.* Komolike. *~ figure.* Kinona komolike. *~ triangle.* Huinakolu komolike.

Māmaka Kaiao / 207

conifer *Pine or any tree which resembles a pine.* Paina, paina lau kukuna, paina tidara. See *cypress, ironwood.*
connect *To ~, as in computer program.* Hoʻokuʻi. See *connection, disconnect. As dots, etc.* Hoʻohui.
Connecticut Konekikuka, Konetikuta.
connection *kik As in computer program.* Kuʻina. See *connect.*
conscience Lunaʻikehala. *To have a guilty ~.* Noho ka hewa i ka lunaʻikehala.
consecutive *In sequence.* Moekahi.
consist *To ~ of, be composed of, be made up of.* Maupaʻa.
consolation bracket *As in a sports tournament.* Māhele hāʻule. See *bracket.*
consonant Koneka.
consortium Kuʻikahi. See *alliance.*
constant *In math.* Helu hoʻohana.
constant *Solar ~.* Kāʻei kau lā.
constellation Huihui hōkū.
constituent *Also component.* ʻŪmaupaʻa.
construct *In geometry, to ~, as in making a surveying figure with the use of only a compass and a straightedge; construction.* Kāpiʻokaha.
construction industry ʻOiʻenehana kūkulu.
construction paper Pepaānue.
consul Kanikela. See *ambassador.*
contact *A person to whom certain information is communicated.* Mea kaʻa launa.
contact poison Lāʻau make pā ʻili.
container *General term.* Hōkelo. *An airtight ~.* He hōkelo paʻa ea. *Toothbrush ~, usually made of plastic.* Poho palaki niho.
contents *Table of ~.* Papa kuhikuhi. See *index.*
context Pōʻaiapili.
contiguous Pili lihi.

continental *Also continent.* Mokuhonua, ʻāinapuniʻole. *~ crust.* Pāpaʻa mokuhonua. *~ shelf.* Holopapa mokuhonua. *~ slope.* Hene mokuhonua.
continued *"To be ~," "stay tuned," as during a TV program.* ʻAʻole i pau.
continuous feed See *auto feed.*
contour *As the elevations of a particular place.* Hiʻona ʻāina.
contract labor Kepa.
control Kāohi. See entries below. *Biological ~.* Kāohi meaola. *Flood ~.* Kāohi wai hālana.
control *Also control group, as in an experiment.* Kumu hoʻohālikelike.
control *As in computer program.* Hoʻoholo. *General ~s.* Hoʻoholo laulā. *~ key.* Pihi hoʻoholo (*preceded by* ke). *~ panel.* Papa hoʻoholo.
controller *As an administrator for computer network.* Kahu. *Network ~.* Kahu pūnaewele. *As in Nintendo games.* Pahu hoʻokele.
controls *Light ~, as for stage productions.* Une kukui.
convectional *To circulate, as air or liquid, between a lower and higher stratum due to variations in density, heat and gravity; also convection, convective.* Paialewa.
convergent *Meeting in plate techtonics, in geology.* Kuʻi. See *divergent, intertropical convergent zone, transform. ~ boundary.* Palena kuʻi.
conversion chart Pakuhi hoʻololi. *Metric ~.* Pakuhi hoʻololi mekalika.
conversion scale Papa pālākiō.
convertible Kaʻa kaupaku pelu, kaʻa kaupoku pelu, kaʻa kaupuku pelu.
convex *Curved or rounded as the exterior of a sphere or circle.* ʻEʻemu. See *concave. ~ lens.* Aniani kaulona ʻeʻemu. *~ mirror.* Aniani ʻeʻemu.
convulsion Maʻi huki. *Schizophrenic ~.* Maʻi huki huohuoi. See *schizophrenia.*

Cook pine Kumu paina Kuke, paina Kuke.
cool-headed Also even-tempered, calm. Māio.
coordinate To put in order. Hoʻolaukaʻi. See entries below. Coordinated. Laukaʻi. ~d physician referral system. ʻŌnaehana kauka no ka lapaʻau like ʻana.
coordinate Also reference, in math. Kuhikuhina. ~s; ordered pair, i.e. two numbers used to give location of a point on a graph. Paʻa helu kuhikuhina. ~ axes, i.e. two intersecting perpendicular number lines used for graphing ordered number pairs. Iho kuhikuhina. ~ plane. Papa kuhikuhina. Geographical ~s. Nā kuhikuhina hōʻike honua.
coordinated Having physical dexterity. Lehilehia.
coordinator See Hawaiian entries under luna.
copper Keleaweʻula.
co-processor unit As for a computer (CPU). Mīkini heluhelu pā. Abb. MHP.
copy As of a document. Kope. Original or master ~. Kope kumu. To make a ~. Hana kope. Backup ~. Kope papaʻa. See backup.
cord A unit for measuring firewood. Koka.
core Earth's ~. ʻĪkoi honua. See crust, mantle.
cork The material or the tree. ʻŪpīlāʻau.
corm As of taro. Hua. Scientific usage. ʻAuhua.
corned beef Fresh ~ (as opposed to canned). Pipi Kelemānia. Canned ~. Kini pipi, pipi kini. Can of ~. Kini pipi.
corner Particularly an outside ~. Kihi. Inside ~. Kūʻono, poʻopoʻo.
corner back Defensive ~, in football. ʻĀʻiwa.
cornet Pū pihi poko. See bugle, trumpet.
corn smut Kalina paʻu kūlina.
Corona Borealis A constellation. ʻAnaheuheu.

corps Marine ~. Pūʻali hoʻouka kaua.
corral Pāʻeke.
correspondence Written ~; also to correspond by letter. Kūkaʻi leka. ~ course. Papa kūkaʻi leka.
corresponding side In math. ʻAoʻao launa.
corridor Flight ~. Ala lele mokulele.
corrugated paper Cardboard. Pepa pahu.
cortisone A hormone used in the treatment of arthritis. Kokikone. See hydrocortisone.
cosmic ray Kukuna lewa lipo.
cosmos A kind of flower. Komosa.
cost ~ analysis. Huli kumukūʻai. Estimated ~ or charge, as for services. Kāki koho.
Costa Rica Also Costa Rican. Koka Rika.
cottage cheese Waiūhakuhaku.
cotton Pulupulu. ~ swab, Q-tip. Lāʻau pulupulu.
cottontail rabbit Lāpaki huelo pulupulu, lāpiki huelo pulupulu, ʻiole lāpiki huelo pulupulu.
cotyledon Lau ʻīnana. Mono~. Lau ʻīnana kahi. Di~. Lau ʻīnana lua.
council ʻAha. County ~. ʻAha kalana.
count To skip ~, in math. Helu lele.
countdown Also to count down, as in launching a rocket. Helu ʻōlapa.
counter As in a kitchen. Papakau. As beans or bottle caps to help with math problem. Mea kōkua helu.
counterattack Hoʻouka pānaʻi.
counterclockwise Kōʻai hema. See clockwise.
Countercurrent Equatorial ~, in oceanography. Hiapo. See current.
counterexample Laʻana hōʻole.
counterpunch Kuʻi pānaʻi.
counting on A strategy used in mental math. Helu kūana. See unit of counting.
counting principle Basic ~, in math. Kulehana no ka helu ʻana.

country *Developed or First World* ~. ʻĀina ʻoiʻenehana. *Developing or Third World* ~. ʻĀina hōʻoiʻenehana. *Nation-state.* Kaumokuʻāina. *Postcolonial* ~. Kaumokuʻāina muli panalāʻau, ʻāina muli panalāʻau.

county Kalana. ~ *council.* ʻAha kalana. ~ *fair.* Hōʻikeʻike kalana. See *fair.* ~ *Planning Department.* Keʻena Hoʻolālā o ke Kalana.

coupon Kūpona.

course *Slalom* ~. Ala heihei kīkeʻekeʻe.

court *As for basketball.* Kahua. See entry below and *field.* *Basketball* ~. Kahua pōhīnaʻi, kahua. *Volleyball* ~. Kahua pōpaʻipaʻi, pahu.

court *Land* ~. ʻAha hoʻonā ʻāina. See *land registration system, settle.*

courtyard Pāmalae.

cover *To* ~ *or shield, as one's mouth.* Pale. ~ *page.* ʻAoʻao hoʻākāka. *Ground* ~. Kapauli. *Manhole* ~, *as for a sewer.* Pani paipu lawe ʻino. See *cap.* *Mattress* ~. ʻEke pela (*preceded by* ke).

coverage *Medical* ~ *number.* Helu ʻinikua olakino.

coveralls *Overalls.* Lole wāwae kāʻawe, lole wāwae ʻepane.

cover letter Leka wehewehe.

CPU *Co-processor unit, as for a computer.* MHP (mīkini heluhelu pā).

crack *As space between fence boards.* Kōā. *As in a sidewalk; also to* ~. ʻOā.

craftsman *Also artisan.* Mālalaioa.

crane *Space* ~, *remote manipulator arm.* Lima kia pihi.

crash *To* ~, *as cars; to bump or bang into.* Hoʻokuʻi.

crater *Chain of* ~s. Pae lua pele. See *volcano.*

cravat Kalawake. See *necktie.*

crawl *Free style in swimming; also to swim using this style.* ʻAu kolo. See *stroke.*

crayfish ʻŌpae Pākē.

crayon Kala, peni kala.

crease *As on a pair of pants.* Haki, ʻopi.

creation *Also origin of the world.* Kumu honua. ~ *literature.* Moʻokalaleo kumu honua.

creative writing Kākau makakū.

credit *As at a bank or store.* Kumu hōʻaiʻē. *As the name of a person who has contributed to a performance.* Pailaha.

credit account *Also charge account, as in a bank.* Waihona kāki. See *bank account.*

crepuscular *Appearing or flying in the twilight.* Ala mōlehu. See *diurnal, nocturnal*

crest *Of a wave.* Hokua, hokua o ka nalu, hokua o ka ʻale. See *trough, wave.*

Crete *Also Cretan.* Keleke, Kerete.

crew *Member of a work* ~. Limahana. *Video production* ~. Nā limahana paʻi wikiō.

crib *As for babies.* Moe pēpē.

cricket ʻŪhini nēnē. *Beach* ~. ʻŪhini nēnē kahakai. *Lava* ~. ʻŪhini nēnē pele.

crime See *criminalistics, criminology.*

criminalistics *The scientific study of physical evidence in the commission of crimes.* Kālaimeheu kalaima. See *criminology.* *Criminalist.* Kanaka kālaimeheu kalaima, mea kālaimeheu kalaima.

criminology *The study of crime and criminals.* Kālaikalaima. See *criminalistics.* *Criminologist.* Kanaka kālaikalaima, mea kālaikalaima.

crisp *Or brittle, as dry* hala *leaves.* Paʻapaʻaʻina.

critical thinking Noʻonoʻo loi.

crocus Pua ʻōʻili hau.

crop *Or planting, i.e. the number of plantings of a particular plant.* Kanu. *A plant that is grown and harvested, usually for profit.* Meaulu.

cross *To* ~, *as a street.* ʻAʻehi. See entries below and *crosswalk.*

crossbar *On a bicycle.* Kua hao paikikala.

crossbreed Hoʻopiʻi kaʻakepa. See *breed, cross-pollinate.*

cross-country ski He'e hau pe'a 'āina.
cross out Kahape'a.
cross-pollinate Ho'ēhu pua ka'akepa. See *crossbreed, pollinate.*
cross product *In math.* Hualoa'a kaupe'a.
cross section Hi'ona kaha.
crosswalk 'A'ehina. See *cross.* ~ *light.* Kukui 'a'ehina.
crossword puzzle Nane hua'ōlelo.
croton Lau kalakoa. See *coleus.*
crow's feet *A kind of plant.* Wāwae'alalā.
crown *As on a pineapple.* 'Ēlau. *Pineapple* ~. 'Ēlau hala kahiki, 'ēlau paina'āpala.
CRT *Cathode-ray tube.* 'Ohe kīwī. See *cathode.*
crumb *Bread* ~s. Hunahuna palaoa. *Clumps of mineral particles mixed into soil.* Pūhuna. See *tilth.*
crumbled Nāhāhā.
crunchy *General term, but especially for* loli, 'opihi, *etc.* Kamumu. *As fresh potato chips.* Kakani, nakeke. *As an apple.* Nakekeke.
crust *In geology.* Pāpa'a. See *core, mantle. Continental* ~. Pāpa'a mokuhonua. *Earth's* ~. Pāpa'a honua. *Ocean* ~. Pāpa'a moana.
crustacean Pāpaka. *Land* ~. Pāpaka 'āina.
crystal Pōaka.
Cuba *Also Cuban.* Kupa, Kuba.
cubby hole Kapi.
cube *In math.* Pa'a'iliono analahi, pa'a'iliono. See *cubic, hexahedron. Snap* ~. Palaka kepa.
cubed *As in exponential counting, in math.* Pāho'onui kolu. See *square.*
cubic Pa'a'iliono. See *cube.* ~ *yard.* 'Iā pa'a'iliono.
cubit *An ancient unit of measurement used in Bible times.* Kūpita.
cue *As in the game of pool.* Kiu. *Pool* ~. Kiu pahupahu.

cultivation *Shifting* ~, *in geography.* Mahi 'ai mahakea.
cultivator *Also to cultivate.* Kīko'u. See *rotary tiller. Hand* ~. Kīko'u pa'a lima.
culture *Also cultural.* Mo'omeheu. See entry below and *custom.*
culture *As bacteria grown in a prepared nutrient.* 'Oulu. *Nutrient* ~. 'Oulu māhuaola. *Sand* ~. 'Oulu one.
cumulus cloud Ao 'ōpua. See *cloud.*
cup *As for measurement.* Kī'aha. *Abb.* kh. *Measuring* ~. Kī'aha ana.
cupric ~ *carbonate.* Kupuriku karabonahate. ~ *oxide.* Kupuriku 'okesaside. ~ *sulfate.* Kupuriku sulafahate. ~ *sulfide.* Kupuriku sulafaside.
curare *A poison for South American Indians' arrows; also a muscle relaxant in modern medicine.* Kulali.
curd *Bean* ~, *tofu.* Tōfū.
cure *To prepare by chemical or physical processing for keeping or use.* Ho'ohāo'o. *Cured.* Hāo'o.
curious Nīele, pena.
currency *Money.* Kālā.
current Au. *Dic. Electric* ~. Au uila. *Alternating* ~ *(AC) electricity.* Uila au mā'alo'alo. *Direct* ~ *(DC) electricity.* Uila aukahi. *Drift* ~, *in oceanography.* Au 'ae'a. *Equatorial* ~. Au kā'ei pō'ai waena honua. *Northern Equatorial* ~. Kūkahikahi. *Southern Equatorial* ~. Kalekale. *Stream* ~. Au kikī.
curriculum Papa ha'awina. *A catalog listing or sequence of lessons of a* ~. Mo'oha'awina.
curriculum vitae *Also résumé, vita.* Mo'omō'ali.
cursor *Also I-bar or insertion point in computer program.* Kaha'imo. *Also mouse arrow or pointer.* Nahau 'iole, nahau.
curtain *Shower* ~. Pale kililau. *Window* ~. Pale pukaaniani.

curve *Or turn, as in a road or on a trail.* Uakeʻe. *Banked ~.* Uakeʻe hiō. *Geometric ~, or as on a graph.* Uma. *Parabolic ~.* Uma palapola.
cushion *Pin ~.* Pulu kui.
custom *A learned cultural value or behavior.* Mēheuheu. See entry below and *culture*.
custom *Or ~-made, i.e. made to individual specifications.* Pilikino. *~ format, as for computer program.* Hoʻonohonohona pilikino.
cut *A command to stop the filming of a movie or video scene.* Ua oki *(pronounced* uoki*)! See entry below.*
cut *To ~ diagonally.* ʻOki pāhiʻa, ʻoki ma ka pāhiʻa.
cutaway ʻukulele ʻUkulele ʻokia.
cutting *As of a plant.* Pulapula.
cuttlebone Mūheʻe iwi.
cuttlefish *As per local definition; squid, as per Haole definition.* Mūheʻe.
cutworm Poko, ʻenuhe hele pō.
cyanide Kaianaside. *Potassium ~.* Potasiuma kaianaside.
cycle Pōʻaiapuni. See *oxygen, recycle*. *Business ~, a repeated series of economic growth and recession.* Pōʻaiapuni kāloaʻa. *Life ~.* Pōʻaiapuni ola.
cylinder *The shape.* Paukū ʻolokaʻa. *The container.* Hano. *Graduated ~.* Hano ana. See *test tube*.
cypress *Portuguese ~.* Paina Pukikī, paina tireza.
Cyprus *Also Cypriot.* Kupelo, Kupero.
Czechoslovakia *Also Czech.* Kekosolowakia.

D

daffodil Kuikina haole. See *narcissus*.
daikon Kaikona.
daily *To come out ~, as a newspaper.* Puka lā. See *Percent Daily Value*.
dairy product Meaʻai waiū.
daisy *Marguerite.* Makalike.

Dakota Kakoka, Dakota. *North ~.* Kakoka ʻĀkau, Dakota ʻĀkau. *South ~.* Kakoka Hema, Dakota Hema.
damages See *claim for damages*.
damp *~ or moist with fog or dew, wet from cold.* Kawaū.
damping-off *A diseased condition of seedlings or cuttings caused by fungi and characterized by wilting or rotting.* ʻUmiāpau.
damselfly *Megalagrion spp.* Pinapinao. *Larva of ~ and other dragonflies.* Lohaloha, lohelohe.
dance-a-thon Hulahulakona.
Dane See *Denmark*.
Danish See *Denmark*.
daphnia ʻUku wai.
dart *As for dart game.* Pāhiʻu.
dash *In punctuation.* Kaha maha. See *hyphen*.
dash *Also to sprint.* Holo kikī.
data ʻIkepili. See *database*. *To distribute ~, as on a graph, in math.* Kākuhi, kākuhi i ka ʻikepili. *~ distribution.* Ka ili o ka ʻikepili. *~ spread.* Ka waiho o ka ʻikepili. *To input ~, as into a computer.* Kāhuakomo ʻikepili. *To output ~.* Kāhuapuka. *~ link.* Loulou ʻikepili. See *file link*. *~ stream.* Laina ʻikepili.
data bank See *database*.
database *As in computer program; also data bank, i.e. an organized collection of information, in math.* Hōkeo ʻikepili. See *data*. *~ program.* Polokalamu hōkeo ʻikepili.
date Lā. *Format for ~ in Hawaiian:* June 10, 1998. 10 Iune 1998. 6/10/98. 10/VI/98.
date book *Also appointment book.* ʻAlemanaka puke. See *almanac*.
date line *International ~.* Laina helu lā.
dating *Carbon ~, radiocarbon date.* Helu makahiki kalapona.
day Lā. *No abbreviation.* See *date*.
daydream Lauele.
DC *Direct current.* Aukahi. See *AC*. *~ electricity.* Uila aukahi.

deadfall *A kind of animal trap.* Hā'uleāpa'a.

deadline Palena pau. *~ hour.* Hola palena pau. *~ day.* Lā palena pau. *To set a ~.* Kaupalena.

deal *To ~, as cards; to distribute or pass out, as papers in a class; to dole out.* Kāka'ahi. See *shuffle*.

dean *As in a college or university.* Luna. See *provost*. *~ of the college of arts and sciences.* Luna koleke pāheona me ka 'epekema.

debate Paio kālaimana'o. *~ club.* Hui paio kālaimana'o.

deca- *A prefix meaning ten (da).* Pā'umi. *Abb.* p'm. *Also* keka-. See entries below and *hecto-, kilo-, mega-, giga-, tera-*.

decade Kekeke.

decagon *A ten-sided polygon.* Huina 'umi.

decagram Kekakalame. *Abb.* kekal.

decaliter Kekalika. *Abb.* kel.

decameter Kekamika. *Abb.* kek.

decathalon 'Ālapakona'umi. See *triathalon, pentathalon*.

decelerate Ho'ēmi i ka māmā holo, emi ka māmā holo. See *accelerate, deceleration*. *Decelerated.* Emi ka māmā holo.

deceleration Emi māmā holo. See *acceleration, decelerate*.

December Kekemapa. *Abb.* Kek. *Also* Dekemapa. *Abb.* Dek.

deci- *A prefix meaning one tenth (d).* Hapa'umi *Abb.* h'm. *Also* keki-. See entries below and *centi-, milli-, micro-, nano-, pico-*.

decibel Ikakani.

decigram Kekikalame. *Abb.* kkkal.

deciliter Kekilika. *Abb.* kkl.

decimal Kekimala. *~ place.* Kūana kekimala. *~ point.* Kiko kekimala. *~ system.* 'Ōnaehana kekimala. *Mixed ~.* Kekimala 'ō'ā. *Repeating ~.* Kekimala pīna'i. *Terminating ~.* Kekimala pani.

decimeter Kekimika. *Abb.* kkm.

deck *Flight ~, as on a spaceship.* 'Oneki pailaka.

decoded Mākalakala. *To decode.* Ho'omākalakala.

decomposed *Also putrefied.* Hāpopopo. See *decomposition*. *To decompose or putrefy something.* Ho'ohāpopopo. *Broken down into component parts as through chemical reaction.* Wāhia.

decomposition *Aerobic ~ or putrefaction.* Ka ho'ohāpopopo eaea 'ana. *Anaerobic ~ or putrefaction.* Ka ho'ohāpopopo eaea 'ole 'ana. See *decomposed*.

decorate *To make artistic.* Ho'oheona. *To ~ sets, as for a movie or video production.* Ho'oponopono kahua. *Set decorator.* Mea ho'oponopono kahua.

decrease *Greatest ~, in math.* Emi ha'aha'a loa. See *increase*.

deep-fry Palai ho'olu'u.

deer *~ mouse.* 'Iole kia. *Roe ~.* Kia lō.

default *As in computer program.* Pa'amau.

defend *To ~, in sports.* Pale. See *defense*. *As your basket in basketball.* Kūpale. *To ~ against, as an opponent.* Kaupale.

defense *In sports.* Pale; 'ao'ao pale, 'ao'ao kūpale. See entries below and *defend, offense*. *Man-to-man ~, as in basketball.* Pale alo. *Press ~.* Pale lulumi. *Zone ~.* Pale kā'ei.

defensive corner back *In football.* 'Ā'iwa.

defensive encroachment *In football.* Lele 'ē na ke kūpale.

defensive end *In football.* Pūkaha. *Left ~.* Pūkaha hema. *Right ~.* Pūkaha 'ākau.

defensive line *In football.* Laina kūpale, laina pale.

defensive linebacker *In football.* Mahikua.

defensive middle guard *Also nose guard, nose tackle, in football.* Haunaku.

defensive slide *To execute a ~, in basketball.* Pāpaʻi.
defensive stance *As in basketball.* Kūlana pale.
deflated *As a balloon.* ʻAnanuʻu, emi, puhalu. See *flat.*
deforestation *Also to deforest.* Hoʻoneo ʻāina ululāʻau.
degree Kēkelē. See *boiling point, freezing point, melting point, temperature.* *~ Celsius.* Kēkelē Kelekia. *~ Fahrenheit.* Kēkelē Palanaheika.
dehydrate *To ~ something.* Hoʻopīkaʻo. *~d.* Pīkaʻo.
Deimos *A moon of Mars.* Keimoka.
deka- See *deca-.*
Delaware *Also Delawarean.* Kelauea, Delauea.
delay *As in computer program.* Kaʻukaʻu.
delete *To ~, as in computer program.* Holoi. *To ~ with ~ key on a Macintosh computer.* Holoi i hope. See *backspace.* *A line used to indicate that something is to be ~d, in proofreading.* Kaha kāpae. *To strike through or line out, also used to indicate that the letters or words lined out are to be ~d and replaced by those written above.* Kahawaena.
deliberately *To foul ~, in team sports such as basketball.* Hoʻokuʻia. See *foul.*
delirium *Maniacal ~.* Maʻi hehena.
delphinium ʻAuhōkū, pua ʻauhōkū.
delta *Of a river.* Kaha nuku muliwai.
deluxe Linohau. See *standard.* *~ room, as in a hotel.* Lumi linohau.
Democratic Republic of the Congo Lepupalika Kemokalaka ʻo Konokō.
demonstrate *To show, as how a math problem is solved.* Kuhikuhi.
denier *A unit of fineness for nylon, etc.* Māʻumi.
Denmark *Also Dane, Danish.* Kenemaka, Denemaka.
denomination *Monetary ~.* Kūana kālā.

denominator *In math.* Kinopiha. See *numerator.* *Least common ~.* Kinopiha haʻahaʻa loa.
density *As of a computer disk.* Paʻapū. *High ~.* Paʻapū ʻoi. *Low ~.* Paʻapū emi.
density *Population ~, for humans only.* Paʻapū pūʻuo kanaka.
dental *In linguistics.* Niho.
dental floss *Also to floss (one's teeth).* Lopi niho.
dentist See *drill, orthodontist, pick.*
deodorant Lūkini pōʻaeʻae.
Dep *Hair gel.* Palaholo lauoho.
department *See entries below.* *County Planning ~.* Keʻena Hoʻolālā o ke Kalana. *Hawaiʻi State ~ of Finance.* ʻOihana Kālā o ka Mokuʻāina ʻo Hawaiʻi. *Hawaiʻi State ~ of Planning and Economic Development.* ʻOihana Hoʻolālā a me ka Hoʻomohala Waiwai o ka Mokuʻāina ʻo Hawaiʻi. *State ~ of Agriculture.* ʻOihana Mahi ʻAi o ka Mokuʻāina.
Department of Agriculture *State ~.* ʻOihana Mahi ʻAi o ka Mokuʻāina.
Department of Land and Natural Resources *DLNR.* ʻOihana Kumuwaiwai ʻĀina.
Department of Parks and Recreation ʻOihana o nā Pāka a me nā Hana Hoʻonanea.
dependent clause *In grammar.* Pepeke ʻōhua.
dependent variable Kumuloli kaukaʻi. See *independent variable.*
depress *To click or press, as in computer program.* Kōmi, kaomi.
depressant Lāʻau hoʻoloha. See *stimulant.*
depression *Geologic ~, as Death Valley.* ʻĀpoho ʻāina.
depth *Or height, in math.* Hohonu. See *length, width.* *To measure ~, as in the ocean.* Hoʻopapā hohonu.
derivation *Root, source or origin, as the etymology of a word.* Molekumu.
dermestid *Larder beetle.* Ponu ʻili.

dermis *In biology.* ʻIli kūwaena. See *epidermis.*

desalinate *Also to desalinize salty water.* Hoʻomānalo wai kai.

desalinize *Also to desalinate salty water.* Hoʻomānalo wai kai.

desert Panoa. *Alpine ~.* Panoa ʻalapaina.

desertification *The processes by which an area becomes a desert, in geography.* Hoʻopanoa.

design *Letterhead ~.* Lau poʻo kuni. *To make drawings or plans.* Hakulau. *To ~ sets, as for movie or video production.* Hakulau kahua. *Set ~er.* Mea hakulau kahua.

desktop *In computer program.* ʻOneki.

dessert Monamona.

detail Mea kikoʻī, mea liʻiliʻi, mea liʻiliʻi kikoʻī. See *detailed.*

detailed *As a design.* Lāliʻi. See *detail.*

develop *To ~ land, as the work of a developer.* Kūkulu hale, kūkulu hale ma luna o ka ʻāina. *See entries below.*

developed *As a First World Country.* ʻOiʻenehana. See *developing.* *~ country.* ʻĀina ʻoiʻenehana.

developing *As a Third World Country.* Hōʻoiʻenehana. See *developed.* *~ country.* ʻĀina hōʻoiʻenehana.

development *Economic ~.* Hoʻomohala waiwai. *Hawaiʻi State Department of Planning and Economic ~.* ʻOihana Hoʻolālā a me ka Hoʻomohala Waiwai o ka Mokuʻāina ʻo Hawaiʻi. *Housing ~, subdivision.* Kaiahale.

deviation *In math.* Haiahū. See *normal. Standard ~.* Haiahū kūmau.

device *Something made or used for a particular purpose; doohickey, gadget, gizmo, thingamajig.* Hāmeʻa. See *instrument, tool. Input ~, as on a computer.* Hāmeʻa huakomo. *Output ~.* Hāmeʻa huapuka. *Ordinarily including some mechanical part or parts.* Maomeka.

diabetes Maʻi kōpaʻa, mimi kō.

diachronic *In linguistics.* Kōāwā. See *synchronic. ~ rule.* Lula kōāwā.

diagonal *In math.* Lala. See *horizontal, vertical. A segment other than a side connecting two vertices of a polygon.* Kaha lala. *~ly.* Papalala. *To cut ~ly.* ʻOki pāhiʻa, ʻoki ma ka pāhiʻa.

diagram *Schematic drawing.* Kiʻikuhi. *Tree ~, in math.* Kiʻi kuhi pahiki. *Venn ~, a ~ using overlapping circles to show relationship of data.* Kiʻikuhi Wene.

dial Pā wili (preceded by ke). *~ tone.* Kani ʻā. *To ~, as a telephone.* Wili.

dialog box *In computer program.* Pahu aʻo. See *dialogue.*

dialogue *As in a play, movie or video production.* Pāpāʻōlelo.

diameter *In math.* Anawaena. *Abb.* anw.

diamond *Baseball ~, infield.* Kaimana pōhili. See *baseball field.*

diaphragm Houpo.

diary *Also journal.* Puke moʻomanaʻo.

diazinon Diazinona.

dichotomous key ʻĀmana koho.

dicotyledon Lau ʻīnana lua. See *cotyledon.*

dictionary *As in computer program.* Papa huaʻōlelo. See *glossary. Main ~.* Papa huaʻōlelo kūmau. *User ~.* Papa huaʻōlelo pākuʻi.

die *To ~ a bad death, as in punishment for evil deeds.* Make hopena.

dieldrin *A kind of insecticide.* Dielidirina. See *aldrin, poison.*

diet *The food that is eaten.* Papaʻai. *To reduce.* Hoʻēmi kino.

difference *Remainder, in math.* Koena. *Abb.* K.

difficulty *Also problem, as in the plot of a story.* Hihia. See *resolution.*

diffusion *Also to be diffused.* Maholahune.

dig *To ~ (the ball), in volleyball.* ʻAli. See *pancake dig. Digger.* Mea ʻali, ʻali.

digest *To ~ food.* Hoʻohehe'e mea'ai, hoʻowali 'ai, hoʻonapele.

digestive system 'Ōnaehana hoʻohehe'e mea'ai.

digit *In math.* Kikoho'e. *Front end ~.* Kikoho'e hapa mua.

digital *~ clock or watch.* Uaki kikohoʻe, uāki kikohoʻe. See *analog.*

dike *Geological formation.* Huku 'ou pele.

dilute Hoʻokaiaka. *Diluted.* Kaiaka. *To ~ or mix, as a drink.* Pa'ipa'i.

dime *Also loose change.* Kenikeni.

dimension *In math.* Ana, nui.

dimensional See *two-dimensional, three-dimensional.*

dining room Lumi 'aina.

dink *To mishit or clip (the ball), in volleyball.* Hoʻokulu, pa'i lihi. *Point from ~.* 'Ai hele wale.

dinosaur Nalala.

Dione *A moon of Saturn.* Kione.

dioxide Diokesaside. *Nitrogen ~.* Naikokene diokesaside, naikokene 'okikene lua. *Sulfur ~.* Sulufura diokesaside.

diphthong Huēwoela.

diploma *Professional ~ for teaching.* Palapala 'oihana a'o.

Dipper *Big ~.* Nāhiku.

Diptha *A star.* Kapanui.

direct *To ~, as a movie or video production.* Kuhikuhi. See *director.*

direct current *DC.* Aukahi. See *alternating current. ~ electricity.* Uila aukahi.

direction Huli. *The four primary ~s, or four cardinal points of the compass, in geography.* Nā kūkulu 'ehā. *Intermediate ~s.* Nā kūkulu o waena.

directions 'Ōkuhi. *To follow ~.* Hahai 'ōkuhi.

director *One who serves as a leader in conducting any kind of business.* Luna hoʻokele. See *administration. As for a movie or video production.* Luna kuhikuhi. *Assistant ~.* Hope luna kuhikuhi. *Executive ~.* Poʻo kuhikuhi. *Art ~.* Luna pāheona. *Lighting ~.* Luna hoʻomālamalama.

directory *Of computer files.* Papa kuhi waihona.

directrix *In math.* Kaha kau.

dirt bike Mokokaikala holo lepo.

disc jockey Wilipā, wilipāleo.

disconnect *To ~, as in computer program.* Hoʻohemo. See *connect.*

discount *Also to ~, as a price for merchandise.* Hoʻēmi.

discover Kaunānā. *~ed.* Hi'ohia.

discrepancy Kāwā.

discus Pāhelene. *To throw a ~.* Kīloi pāhelene.

disease *To be susceptible or vulnerable to ~.* Pāma'i.

dish Pā (*preceded by* ke). *~ rack.* Haka kaula'i pā. *Petri ~.* Pā piki. *Soap ~.* Pā kopa. *Water ~.* Pā wai.

disk Pā (*preceded by* ke). See entries below. *Computer ~.* Pā kamepiula. *Blank ~.* Pā ma'ema'e. *Floppy ~.* Pā malule. *Program ~.* Pā polokalamu. *Startup ~.* Pā hoʻomaka. *Hard ~.* Pā pa'aloko. *Removable hard ~.* Pā pa'aloko wehe. *~ partitioning.* Māhele pā. *~ space.* Hakahaka pā. *To cache ~s.* Hoʻokoe pā.

disk brake Peleki pā. See *brake disk.*

disk drive *As on a computer.* Kakena. *Hard drive.* Kakena pa'aloko. *Internal drive.* Kakena kūloko. *External drive.* Kakena kūwaho.

disobedience *Civil ~, i.e. breaking a law because it goes against personal morals.* 'A'a kānāwai.

dispense *To provide in measured quantities.* Hōlo'a. See *dispenser.*

dispenser *A dispensing container of any kind.* 'Ūhōlo'a. See *dispense*. *Paper towel ~.* 'Ūhōlo'a kāwele pepa. *Soap ~.* 'Ūhōlo'a kopa. *Water ~, as in a bird cage.* Kāhāinu. See *feeder*.

displacement *Also to displace.* Pohupani. *Air ~.* Pohupani ea. *Water ~.* Pohupani wai.

display *As on computer screen.* Hō'ike.

display screen *As on a calculator.* Papakaumaka. *Calculator ~.* Papakaumaka mīkini helu.

dissimilation *In linguistics.* Kī'ōko'ako'a.

dissolve *To ~ something.* Ho'ohehe'e.

distinction Hanohano. See *honors*. *With ~, as when graduating from a college or university.* Me ka hanohano.

distinguish Waele'a.

distribute *To ~, as in delivering or making publications available to the public.* Ho'omalele. *To ~ or pass out, as papers in a class.* Kāka'ahi. *To ~ data, as on a graph, in math.* Kākuhi, kākuhi i ka 'ikepili. See *distribution*.

distribution *Also to be distributed, as data on a graph, in math.* Ili. See *distribute*. *Data ~.* Ka ili o ka 'ikepili. *Population ~.* Ili pū'uo, ili pū'uo kanaka. *Rain ~.* Ka ili o ka ua.

distributive property *In math.* 'Anopili ho'oili (*preceded by* ke).

district *Central business ~.* 'Āpana pā'oihana kauwaena. See *downtown*.

diurnal *Active during the daytime.* Ala ao. See *crepuscular, nocturnal*.

dive *To ~, in volleyball.* Lele 'ōpū, lu'u, moe pālahalaha. *To sky ~.* Lu'u lewa. *Sky ~r.* Mea lu'u lewa. *Diving goggles or mask.* Makaaniani lu'u kai, makaaniani lu'u. See *scuba*.

divergent *Spreading in plate techtonics, in geology.* Ne'e 'oā. See *convergent, transform*. *~ boundary.* Palena ne'e 'oā.

divide See *division*.

dividend *In math.* Kumu pu'unaue.

divisible *In math.* Pu'unaue koena 'ole.

division *Also to divide, in math.* Pu'unaue. See *composite*. *~ sign.* Kaha pu'unaue.

divisor *In math.* Helu komo.

DLNR *Department of Land and Natural Resources.* 'Oihana Kumuwaiwai 'Āina.

do *The first note on the musical scale.* Pā.

Doctor *For use as a title before a person's name.* Kauka. *Abb.* Kk.

document *As in computer program.* Palapala. See *draft, subsummary*. *Text of a ~.* Kikokikona. *~ outline.* 'Oloke'a palapala. *~ specific.* Pili ho'okahi palapala. *~ summary.* Hō'ulu'ulu palapala.

dodecahedron *A space figure with twelve faces, in math.* Pa'a'ili 'umikūmālua.

dog's tooth violet *A kind of flower.* Waioleka niho'īlio.

doghouse Hale 'īlio.

dog paddle *Also to ~, in swimming.* 'Au 'īlio. See *stroke*.

dole out See *deal*.

doll *A child's plaything.* Pēpē ki'i.

dollar Kālā. See *bill, half dollar, quarter*. *~ sign.* Kaha kālā. *Silver ~.* Kālā ke'oke'o.

domesticated *As a pet or for work.* Lakauā. See *feral*.

Domincan Kominika. *~ Republic.* Lepupalika Kominika.

domino Iwi pā'ani. *To play ~es.* Pā'ani iwi.

doohickey *Device, gadget, gizmo, thingamajig.* Hāme'a. See *apparatus, instrument, tool*.

door *As opposed to doorway.* Pani puka (*preceded by* ke). See *molding*. *~frame.* Kikihi. *~ hinge.* 'Ami puka, 'ami 'īpuka. *~ threshold.* Paepae puka. *Screen ~.* Pani puka uea makika, pani puka maka'aha. *Sliding ~.* Puka uai, 'īpuka uai.

doorknob Pōheo puka, pōheoheo puka.

doorstop Koʻo puka, koʻo ʻīpuka.
dormant Kaʻoko.
dormitory Hale moe, hale noho haumāna.
dorsal *In biology.* Laukua. See *anterior, posterior, ventral.* ~ *fin, of a fish, nonscientific term.* Kualā. *Scientific term.* Kualā laukua. *Anterior* ~. Kualā laumua. *Posterior* ~. Kualā lauhope.
dot *On a grid.* Kiko huina. See entry below and *intersection.*
dots *A series of* ~ *written under a word or words which have been lined out to show that no change should be made from the original, in proofreading; stet.* Kaha waiho.
double *In math.* Kaulua. See entries below. *As when throwing dice.* Māhoe. ~ *number.* Helu māhoe.
double bar graph *In math.* Pakuhi paʻa ʻaukā. See *bar graph.*
double dribble *In basketball.* Pākimokimo pālua, pāloiloi pālua, paʻipaʻi pālua.
double extra large XXL, *as shirt size.* Nui keu pālua. See *large.*
double hit *To lift or make a* ~, *in volleyball.* Hāpai. See *carrying violation.* ~ *violation.* ʻAʻena paʻi lua.
double-hole ʻukulele ʻUkulele ʻelua puka.
double space See *spacing.*
dough Paʻipalaoa.
dowel Poke kaola.
down *Pages* ~, *as in computer program.* ʻEhia ʻaoʻao haʻalalo? See *across.*
download *To* ~, *as in computer program.* Hoʻoili. See *install, load.*
downtown Kaona. See *central business district, city.*
downward Haʻalalo. See *round off.*
downwind *To sail directly* ~. Kele kaʻalalo. See *beam reach, broad reach, close hauled.*

draft *A preliminary version; also to prepare a* ~. Kāmua. See entries below. *First* ~. Kāmua ʻekahi. *Second* ~. Kāmua ʻelua.
draft *To draw blueprints.* Kaha kiʻi kūkulu. See *draftsman. To draw up documents.* Kāpalapala. *A person who* ~*s documents.* Kanaka kāpalapala.
draft *Bank* ~. Pila kīkoʻo panakō.
draft animals *A team of* ~. Pūkolo.
drafter See *draftsman.*
draftsman *One who draws blueprints.* Kaha kiʻi kūkulu. See *draft.*
drag *To* ~, *as in computer program.* Alakō, kiʻi a alakō. *To* ~ *onto.* Alakō ma luna o, alakō a kau ma luna o.
dragon *As in fairy tales.* Kalekona, kelekona. See *skeleton.*
dragonfly See *damselfly.*
drain Paipu omo wai.
drainage *Also to have good drainage.* Nōkahea.
drama *Also dramatic.* Paiwa. ~ *coach.* Kaʻi hana keaka. ~*tic play.* Hana keaka paiwa.
draw *To* ~ *a conclusion.* Hoʻoholo i hopena. *To* ~ *or withdraw money from the bank.* Kīkoʻo.
drawer ʻUme. See *bureau.* ~ *handle.* ʻAu ʻume (*preceded by* ke). ~ *knob.* Pōheo ʻume.
drawing *Scale* ~, *in math.* Kiʻi pālākiō.
dresser *Bureau.* Pahu ʻume.
dribble *To* ~, *as a basketball.* Pākimokimo, pāloiloi, paʻipaʻi. *Double* ~. Pākimokimo pālua, pāloiloi pālua, paʻipaʻi pālua. *To* ~, *as with kicks in soccer.* Pekupeku.
dried See *freeze dried.*
drift current *In oceanography.* Au ʻaeʻa.
drill *Dentist's* ~. Wili niho.
drinking fountain Puaʻiwai.
drive *Disk* ~, *as on a computer.* Kakena. *Hard* ~. Kakena paʻaloko. *Internal* ~. Kakena kūloko. *External* ~. Kakena kūwaho.

Māmaka Kaiao / 218

drive *To ~, in basketball.* Kaha.
drive *As for cans; to conduct a ~.* Alu. *Newspaper ~.* Alu hōʻiliʻili nūpepa. *School clean-up ~.* Alu hoʻomaʻemaʻe pā kula.
drive-through *As at a restaurant or bank.* Holona kaʻa.
driveway Alakalaiwa.
dropper Omo hoʻokulu.
dropping bottle *A bottle used much like an eyedropper.* ʻŌmole hoʻokulu.
Drosophilidae *Genus ~, pomace fly.* Pōnalo.
drug *Also medication.* Lāʻau. *Prescription ~.* Lāʻau kuhikuhi. *Prescription for ~ or medication.* Kuhikuhi lāʻau. *Over-the-counter ~.* Lāʻau kūʻai wale. *Narcotic ~.* Lāʻau ʻona. *To overdose on ~s.* Pākela ʻai lāʻau.
drumstick *As of a chicken.* Pālaumoa.
dual citizen Kupa kaumokuʻāina pālua, makaʻāinana kaumokuʻāina pālua.
duct *Alveolar ~, in anatomy.* Pūʻali nōiki. *Sweat ~.* Puka kikī hou.
dull *Not shiny.* Hāpaʻupaʻu.
dumb *See ignorance.*
dump Hoʻohanini. *~ truck.* Kalaka hoʻohanini. *To ~, in volleyball.* Hōʻanuʻu.
dumplings Palaoa mokumoku, palaoa pakūpakū, palaoa keko.
dunce cap Pāpale kone.
dune buggy Kaʻa holo one.
dunk *To ~ (the ball), in basketball.* Pākā, ʻūpoʻi. *To slam ~.* Pākī.
duplicate *As in computer program.* Lua like.
duration *In music.* Kō huamele.
dusk *Twilight.* Mōlehulehu, hola mōlehulehu.
dust Ehu lepo, ehu. *Chalk ~.* Ehu poho. *To brush or apply lightly a thin coat, such as sulphur to a plant.* Kāehuehu. *To ~ with a cloth.* Kāwele. *To ~ with a dry cloth.* Kāwele maloʻo. *To ~ with a damp cloth.* Kāwele maʻū. *To ~ with a duster.* Kāhilihili. *See duster.*
duster Mea kāhilihili.
dustfall jar *As for scientific experiments.* ʻŌmole ʻapo hunahuna.
dustpan Pā ehu lepo (*preceded by* ke).

E

eagle *Bald ~.* ʻĀeko poʻo hina, ʻāeto poʻo hina.
ear *~ lobe.* Lepepepeiao. *Inner ~ cavity, cochlea.* Haka moʻoni.
early Ma mua o ka manawa, ma mua o ka hola. *Beforehand, pre-.* Hiki mua. *~ registration.* Kāinoa hiki mua.
earphone Pihi lohe (*preceded by* ke). *See headphone.*
Earth *The planet.* Honua (*cap.*). *See core, crust, globe, mantle.*
earth metal *Alkaline ~, one of the family of elements in Group 2 of the periodic table.* Mekala honua ʻākilikai. *See alkali metal.*
earthquake Ōlaʻi. *Epicenter.* Kiko ōlaʻi.
earthworm Koʻe honua.
easel Kū pena kiʻi.
east Hikina. *Abb.* Hk. *See entries below.*
Eastern Europe *Also Eastern European.* ʻEulopa Hikina.
eastern hemisphere Poepoe hapa hikina. *See hemisphere.*
eaves ʻAnini (*preceded by* ke).
eccentric Lalaʻē.
ecology Kālaikaiaola. *See ecosystem.*
economic development Hoʻomohala waiwai. *Hawaiʻi State Department of Planning and ~.* ʻOihana Hoʻolālā a me ka Hoʻomohala Waiwai o ka Mokuʻāina ʻo Hawaiʻi.
economics Kālaihoʻokele waiwai.
ecosystem Kaiaola. *See ecology.*
Ecuador *Also Ecuadoran, Ecuadorean, Ecuadorian.* ʻEkuakola, ʻEkuadora.
eddy Wiliau. *See galaxy.*
edge *As of a three-dimensional geometric figure.* Kaʻe. *See straightedge.*
edge feed *To ~, as paper into a printer or copy machine.* Hānai kaʻe.

edit *To ~, as on a computer.* Hoʻololi. *See entries below. ~ screen, in computer program.* Pukaaniani hoʻoponopono. *List editor or screen.* Pukaaniani kolamu ʻikepili.

edit *To ~, as movies or movie productions.* Hoʻoponopono kiʻiʻoniʻoni. *See editing facility, editor. To ~, as videos or video productions.* Hoʻoponopono wikiō. *To ~ sound, as for a movie or video production.* Hoʻoponopono kani.

editing facility *For movies.* Hale hoʻoponopono kiʻiʻoniʻoni. *For videos.* Hale hoʻoponopono wikiō.

editor *Also coordinator, manager, etc., as in producing a movie or video.* Luna. *Assemble ~.* Luna hoʻokuʻikuʻi. *Sound ~.* Luna hoʻoponopono kani.

education support staff Kākoʻo hoʻonaʻauao.

effect Hopena *See cause.*

effects Hiʻohiʻona. *See sound. Printer ~, as on a computer printer.* Hiʻohiʻona paʻi. *Special ~.* Hiʻohiʻona naʻiau. *To add special ~.* Hoʻonaʻiau (i ka hiʻohiʻona). *To have special ~.* Naʻiau.

egg *White or yolk.* Kauō. *~ white.* Kauō keʻokeʻo. *~ yolk.* Kauō melemele.

egret *General term.* ʻAlekuʻu. *See heron. Cattle ~.* ʻAlekuʻu kau pipi.

Egypt *Also Egyptian.* ʻAikupika, ʻAikupita, ʻAigupita.

eight-string ʻukulele ʻUkulele ʻewalu kaula.

EIS *Environmental Impact Statement.* Palapala Hōʻike Hopena Kaiapuni.

eject *To ~, as disk from computer or video cassette from a VCR.* Kīpeku.

ejecta *Volcanic ~.* Pōhāhā. *See spatter cone.*

elapsed Kaʻahope. *~ time.* Hola kaʻahope.

elderberry Pīʻai ʻelepeli.

election *Primary ~.* Koho pāloka wae moho, wae moho. *Closed ~ election.* Wae moho kūloko. *Open ~ election.* Wae moho kūākea.

elector *As in the US Electoral College.* ʻElele manakoho.

electric *~ blanket.* Kapa uila. *~ circuit.* Puni uila. *~ current.* Au uila. *~ charge.* Ikehu uila. *Neutral charge.* Ikehu uila hohoki, ikehu uila. *See brush, charge, electricity, conductor, fan.*

electrical *~ force field.* Kāʻei manehu uila. *See force. ~ outlet.* Puka uila. *See plug.*

electrician Kanaka hana uila.

electrician's tape *Cloth duct tape.* Leki uea.

electricity Uila. *Geothermal ~.* Uila māhu pele. *Hydro~.* Uila wai kahe. *Wind-generated ~.* Uila huila makani. *See thermoelectricity.*

electrode ʻŪholo uila. *See anode, cathode.*

electrolysis *Also to be affected by ~.* Pā uila. *To utilize the process of ~.* Hoʻopā uila.

electron Huna ʻine. *See neutron, proton.*

electronic mail *See E-mail.*

elegant *Fancy.* Hoʻohiluhilu.

element Kumumea. *Traditional ~s of Hawaiian poetry, story telling, oratory and narration.* Meiwi.

element *Trace ~.* Kumumea ʻāweʻaweʻa.

elevated train *As Japan monorail.* Kaʻaahi kau lewa.

elevation Kiʻekiʻena. *~ pole, as for surveying.* Lāʻau ana kiʻekiʻena. *See range pole, sighter.*

elf owl Pueo peke.

ellipse Pōʻai lōʻihi analahi, ʻololaha analahi. *See oval.*

ellipsis *In punctuation.* Kiko kolu.

El Salvador *Also Salvadoran, Salvadorian.* ʻEla Salavadora.

E-mail *Electronic mail, as in telecommunication.* Leka uila.

emergency Pōulia. *~ room or facility.* Keʻena mālama pōulia.

emergent ~ *layer of vegetation, as trees sticking out at top.* Papa ʻoiʻoi. See *vegetation layer.*

emigrate Pukaneʻe. See *immigrate.*

emotional stress ʻAloʻahia.

Emperor Seamounts Pae Mauna Kai ʻEmepela, Pae Mauna Kai ʻo ʻEmepela.

empire Aupuni ʻemepela.

empty *As a bowl.* Hakahaka, kaʻele.

empty trash *To* ~, *as in computer program.* Kīloi.

emulation *As in a computer printer.* Hoa māhuʻi.

enamel Pena paʻa mania.

Enceladus *A small moon of Saturn.* ʻEnekelakuke.

encourage *A prefix meaning to* ~, *laud; -ism, a suffix in English meaning devotion or adherence to something.* Pai-. See *capitalism.*

encroachment *In football.* Lele ʻē. See *offsides. Defensive* ~. Lele ʻē na ke kūpale.

encyclopedia Puke noiʻi kūʻikena.

end *Of a sporting field or court.* Poʻo (*preceded by* ke), kumu. See *line, side.* ~ *line or base line, as on basketball court.* Laina hīnaʻi, laina hupa, laina kumu, laina poʻo. ~ *zone, on football field.* Pahu ʻai holo.

end *Defensive* ~, *in football.* Pūkaha. See *safety. Left defensive* ~. Pūkaha hema. *Right defensive* ~. Pūkaha ʻākau. *Split* ~. Lala. *Tight* ~. Muku.

endangered ʻAne halapohe, ʻane make loa, ʻane nalowale loa. See entry below and *extinct.*

Endangered Species Act Kānāwai Lāhulu ʻAne Halapohe.

endemic ʻĀpaʻakuma. ~ *plant.* Meakanu ʻāpaʻakuma.

endnote *As in a book or research paper.* Kuhia o hope. See *note, footnote.*

endocrine gland Lōkuʻu kuʻuloko. See entry below and *exocrine gland.*

endocrine system *In biology.* ʻŌnaehana hōmona.

endoskeleton Iwi kūloko. See *exoskeleton.*

endothermic Omo wela. See *exothermic.*

end user *As of computer programs.* Mea hoʻohana.

energy Ikehu. ~ *pyramid.* Pelamika ikehu. *Nuclear* ~. Ikehu nukelea. *Thermal* ~, *i.e. the total* ~ *of all the particles in an object.* Ikehu kāʻokoʻa. See *calorimeter.*

engine *Maneuvering* ~, *as for a spacecraft.* ʻEnekini kīkaha.

engineer ʻEnekinia. *Mechanical* ~. ʻEnekinia mīkini. *Production* ~, *as for a movie or video production.* Luna ʻenehana. *Assistant production* ~. Hope luna ʻenehana. *To* ~ *genetically.* Hoʻoliliuewe. *Genetic* ~*ing.* Ka hoʻoliliuewe ʻana.

England *Also Britain, British, English (of England), English person.* Pelekāne, ʻEnelani. See *British, English.*

English *Also British, Britain.* Pelekānia. See *British, England. Of England.* Pelekāne, ʻEnelani. ~ *language.* ʻŌlelo Pelekānia.

enhanced *To be* ~, *have special effects.* Naʻiau. See *effects.*

enhanced *Or expanded, as a computer keyboard.* Keu. ~ *keyboard.* Papa pihi keu.

Enif *A star.* Mākaʻi.

enrich *To improve the nutritive value of something.* Hoʻopaiola. *Enriched.* Hoʻopaiola ʻia. *To increase knowledge.* Hoʻonui ʻike. ~*ment book, challenge book.* Puke hoʻonui ʻike.

enter *To* ~ *or input, as typing data into a computer database or calculator.* Kāhuakomo. *To send or* ~ *data into a computer database or calculator after it has been typed.* Hoʻouna. *To use the* ~ *or return key on a computer or typewriter keyboard in order to return the cursor or carriage to the left margin on a new line;* ~ *or return, as the key just above the shift key on a computer keyboard.* Kāhoʻi.

entertain *To ~, as in a speech.* Mikolololehua. See *speech*. *A speech to ~, expressive speech.* Ha'i'ōlelo mikolololehua.

entry *Also item, object.* 'Ikamu. See *thesaurus entry*.

environment Kaiapuni. See *medium. Learning ~.* Kaiapuni a'o. *Total healing ~.* Kaiapuni ho'ōla piha.

Environmental Impact Statement EIS. Palapala Hō'ike Hopena Kaiapuni.

enzyme 'Ūhū. See *papain*.

epenthetic sound *In linguistics.* Hua komo.

epicenter Kiko ōla'i.

epidermis *In biology.* 'Ili kūwaho. See *dermis*.

epiglottis Pani paipu hanu (*preceded by* ke). See *larynx, trachea*.

Epsom 'Epesoma. *~ salt.* Pa'akai 'epesoma.

equal *Or equality, as a mathematical relation of being exactly the same.* Like. *~ sign.* Kaha like. *~ ratio.* Lākiō like. *~ly likely outcomes.* Like ka papaha o nā mea e loa'a ana.

equality See *equal*. *~ property, in math.* 'Anopili kaulike (*preceded by* ke).

equation *In math and science.* Ha'ihelu. See *problem. Chemical ~.* Ha'ihelu kemikala. *Balanced chemical ~.* Ha'ihelu kemikala kaulike. *Linear ~.* Ha'ihelu lālani.

equator Kapikoowākea, pō'ai waena honua. *Celestial ~.* Pō'ai waena lani.

Equatorial Countercurrent *In oceanography.* Hiapo. See *current*.

equatorial current *In oceanography.* Au kā'ei pō'ai waena honua. See *current, Equatorial Countercurrent*.

equilateral triangle Huinakolu like.

equilibrium Anakonu. See *isostasy*.

equinox Māuiili. See *solstice. Autumnal ~.* Ka māuiili o ka hā'ulelau. *Vernal ~.* Ka māuiili o ke kupulau.

equipment Lako, pono. See *props. Breathing ~, as for use in space exploration.* Lako hanu. *Video ~.* Pono hana wikiō.

equitable *Fair, just, balanced.* Kaulike.

equivalent expression *In math.* Ha'i heluna like.

equivalent fraction *In math.* Hakina heluna like.

eraser Mea holoi, 'ileika.

erode *Also eroded, erosion.* 'A'aiawā. See *weathered. ~d smooth.* Koea a mania. *~d or cut by waves, as a cliff.* 'A'aianalu. *Wave-cut cliff.* Pali 'a'aianalu.

errand Hana.

error *As in computer program.* Ku'ia. See *entry below*.

error *Greatest possible ~, in math.* Palena 'āluna o ka hewa. *Abb.* P'ĀH. *Overflow ~, as on a calculator display.* Hū. *Logic ~, as message on calculator display that shows an operation is not logical.* Hewa kūpili.

eruption *Series of volcanic ~s.* Pūka'ina hū pele.

escape *To ~, as in computer program.* Pēki. *~ key.* Pihi pēki (*preceded by* ke).

escape hatch *Explosive ~, as in a spaceship.* 'Īpuka pakele pahū.

Eskimo *~ person, language or culture.* 'Inuika, *usu.* 'Inuita.

esophagus Paipu moni. See *trachea*.

estimate *Also estimated, estimation.* Koho. *~d price, as for goods.* Kumuku'ai koho. *~d cost or charge, as for services.* Kāki koho. *To over~.* Koho'oi. *To under~.* Kohoemi. *Front end estimation.* Koho hapa mua.

estuary Nuku muliwai.

etch Kaha koe. *Etching.* Ki'i kaha koe.

ether 'Ita.

Ethiopia *Also Ethiopian.* 'Aikiopa.

ethnomusicology Kālaipuolo lāhui. See *musicology*.

ethyl 'Eto. *~ acetate.* 'Ākeka 'eto.

etymology *Root, source, derivation or origin of a word.* Molekumu.
Eupithecia spp *Carnivorous caterpillar.* ʻEnuhe hamuiʻa.
Eurasian *Also Eurasia.* ʻEulāsia. *~ Plate.* Ka Una Honua ʻEulāsia.
Europa *A moon of Jupiter.* ʻEulopa.
Europe ʻEulopa. *Eastern ~.* ʻEulopa Hikina *Western ~.* ʻEulopa Komohana.
evacuate *To ~, as a building.* Haʻalele. *To ~, as people from a building.* Hoʻohaʻalele.
evaluate *To find the number that an algebraic expression names, in math.* Huli.
evaporate Omoāea.
evapotranspiration Piʻikomoāea.
even *See parallel bars.*
even number Helu kaulike.
event *As in math; also as a happening in a story.* Hanana.
even-tempered *Also calm, cool.* Māio.
Everest ʻEweleka. *Mount ~.* Mauna ʻEweleka.
evidence *As in the commission of a crime.* Meheu kalaima.
evolution Ka liliuewe ʻana. *See evolve, genetic engineering.*
evolve Liliuewe. *See evolution, genetic engineering.*
example Laʻana. *Model, as of behavior.* Kumu hoʻohālike.
exception *~ to a rule.* Kūʻē lula.
exclaim Hoʻōho. *See exclamatory statement.*
exclamation point Kiko pūʻiwa.
exclamatory statement *Also to make an ~.* ʻŌlelo hoʻōho.
excursion *Field trip.* Huakaʻi makahiʻo, huakaʻi. *See explore.*
executive branch *As of a government.* Māhele mana hoʻokō. *See branch.*
exhaust pipe *As on a car.* Paipu ahi. *See muffler.*
exocrine gland Lōkuʻu kuʻuwaho. *See endocrine gland.*

exoskeleton Iwi kūwaho. *See endoskeleton.*
exothermic Kuʻu wela. *See endothermic.*
expand *To ~ or explode, as a file in computer program.* Hoʻomahola. *See compress, expanded.*
expanded *Also exploded, as a file in computer program.* Mahola. *See expand, extended. ~d file.* Waihona mahola. *As of computer memory.* Māhuahua. *~ memory.* Waihona ʻike māhuahua. *Also enhanced, as a computer keyboard.* Keu. *~ keyboard.* Papa pihi keu.
expanded *~ form, in math; also to expand.* Unuhi kūana. *~ numeral.* Helu unuhi kūana.
expected value *In math.* Waiwai wānana. *See value.*
expense account Waihona hoʻolilo. *See account.*
experiment *Also to ~, as in a laboratory.* Hoʻokolohua. *To ~ on.* Hoʻokolohua no. *To ~ with.* Hoʻokolohua me. *~al probability.* Pahiki hoʻokolohua.
expert *Wildlife ~.* Loea holoholona lōhiu.
explode *See expand, expanded.*
explore Makahiʻo. *See excursion.*
explosive escape hatch *As in a spaceship.* ʻĪpuka pakele pahū.
exponent *Also power, i.e. a product in which each factor is the same, in math.* Pāhoʻonui. *See square. ~ial notation.* Kauhelu pāhoʻonui.
export Kāpuka. *See import.*
expression *In math.* Haʻi. *Algebraic ~.* Haʻi hōʻailona helu. *Equivalent ~.* Haʻi heluna like.
expression *In grammar, a term of more than one word which has one meaning.* Māpuna ʻōlelo.
expressive speech *Also speech to entertain.* Haʻiʻōlelo mikolololehua. *See speech.*

extend *To ~, as text in computer word processing.* Hoʻākea. See *condense*. *As a math problem which can be ~ed into other similar problems or situations.* Hoʻomahola.

extended *As of computer memory.* Keu. See *expanded*. *~ memory.* Waihona ʻike keu.

extension *As of a computer file.* Peleleu. *File ~.* Peleleu waihona.

extenuating circumstances Kumu kūikawā.

exterior angle *In math.* Huina kūwaho.

external Kūwaho. See *internal*. *~ drive, as on a computer.* Kakena kūwaho. *~ folder, in computer program.* Wahī o waho.

external fuel tank *As on a spaceship.* Pahu wāwahie kūwaho.

extinct Halapohe, make loa, nalowale loa. See *endangered*.

extinguisher *Fire ~.* Kini hoʻopio ahi, kini kinai ahi.

extra *Beyond the usual size, extent or degree.* Keu, loa. See *large*. *~ large, XL (as shirt size).* Nui keu. *Extra lean (as meat).* Pākā loa.

extra *One hired for crowd scenes in movie or video production.* ʻŌhua.

extra credit *As a class assignment or question on a quiz.* Hoʻopiʻi kaha, ʻai keu. *~ question.* Nīnau hoʻopiʻi kaha, nīnau ʻai keu.

extract Kāwina. *Vanilla ~.* Kāwina wanila. *To ~.* Kāwī.

extraterrestrial *Also space alien.* Mea ao ʻē.

eyebrow pencil Pena kuʻemaka. *To "put on" or "do" one's eyebrows.* Hana i ka pena kuʻemaka.

eyedropper Omo hoʻokulu.

eyelashes *False ~.* Lihilihi maka kuʻi. *To put on false ~.* Kau i ka lihilihi maka kuʻi, komo i ka lihilihi maka kuʻi.

eye liner Mahaka maka.

eye shadow Pauka maka. *To put on ~.* Hana i ka pauka maka.

F

fa *The fourth note on the musical scale.* Hā.

fabric *Gas fading control ~, as in meteorology.* Lole ana kinoea. *Ozone-sensitive ~.* Lole ana ʻokikene kolu.

face *As one side of a space figure, in math.* Alo. *~ value.* Waiwai kūʻike. See *value*.

face powder Pauka helehelena. *To put on ~.* Hana i ka pauka helehelena, kau i ka pauka helehelena.

facility *Something that is built, installed or established to serve a particular purpose.* Pono lako.

fact Kūʻikena.

factor *In math.* Helu hoʻonui. See entries below. *Common ~.* Helu hoʻonui like. *Greatest common ~.* Helu hoʻonui like kiʻekiʻe loa. *~ tree.* Papa helu hoʻonui kumu.

factorial *In math.* Hoʻonui pāʻanuʻu.

factorization *Prime ~.* Huli helu hoʻonui kumu.

faded *As material which has been left in the sun.* ʻĀpahupahu.

Fahrenheit Palanaheika. *Abb.* Ph. *Degrees ~.* Kēkelē Palanaheika.

fair Hōʻikeʻike, fea. *Science ~.* Hōʻikeʻike ʻepekema. *County ~.* Hōʻikeʻike kalana. *State ~.* Hōʻikeʻike mokuʻāina.

fair *Just, equitable, balanced.* Kaulike. *~ game, as one in which each player has the same chance of winning.* Pāʻani kaulike.

fake *To ~ or hit, in volleyball.* Hana kolohe, mīʻoi wale. *To make a ~ spike, an off-speed shot.* Pākī ʻepa. *To ~ out, in basketball.* ʻEpa.

falcon *Peregrine ~.* Palekona kāluʻu. See *jess*.

Falkland Islands *Also Falklands.* Pae Moku Fakalana.

fall *Autumn.* Hāʻulelau.

false eyelashes Lihilihi maka kuʻi. *To put on false ~.* Kau i ka lihilihi maka kuʻi, komo i ka lihilihi maka kuʻi.
family *Of facts, as in math.* ʻOhina. *Biological ~.* ʻOhana kālaimeaola.
family room Lumi ʻohana.
fan *Electric ~.* Pelamakani.
fancy *Elegant.* Hoʻohiluhilu.
fantasy Moemoeā.
farm Pāumu.
Faso *Burkina ~.* Burakina Faso.
fast break *In basketball; also to make a ~.* Ulele kikī. See *lead pass, slow down.*
fastener *Snap.* Pihi ʻūmiʻi (*preceded by* ke), ʻūmiʻi. See *Velcro.*
fast food Meaʻai hikiwawe. *Fast-food restaurant.* Hale ʻaina meaʻai hikiwawe.
fast forward *To ~, as film or audio tape.* Wili i mua. See *rewind.*
fat ʻAilakele. *Low-~ food.* Meaʻai ʻailakele iki, meaʻai liʻiliʻi o ka ʻailakele. *High-~ food.* Meaʻai ʻailkele nui, meaʻai nui o ka ʻailakele. *Saturated ~.* ʻAilakele paʻapū. *Unsaturated ~.* ʻAilakele paʻahapa. *Polyunsaturated ~.* ʻAilakele laupaʻahapa.
fatal Pāmake.
faucet Kī wai. *~ handle.* ʻAu kī wai (*preceded by* ke).
fault *Geologic ~, as San Andreas Fault.* Hakinaheʻe.
favor *Party ~.* Alelomoʻo.
fax *Also to ~.* Kelepaʻi. *~ machine.* Mīkini kelepaʻi.
feature *General appearance, impression.* Hiʻona. *Land ~, as mountains, valleys, etc.* Hiʻona ʻāina. See *landscape. Water ~ or form.* Hiʻona wai. *Man-made topographical ~.* Hiʻona na ke kanaka.
February Pepeluali. *Abb.* Pep.
federal Pekelala. See *national. ~ organization.* ʻAhahui pekelala.
feed *To ~ or assist, as in basketball and most team sports except baseball.* Hānai.

feed *To ~, as paper into a printer or copy machine.* Hānai. *To center ~.* Hānai waena. *To edge ~.* Hānai kaʻe. *To auto ~.* Hānai ʻakomi.
feeder *As for birds.* Kāhānai. See *water dispenser. Sheet ~, as for a computer printer.* Poho pepa. *Additional sheet ~.* Poho pākuʻi.
feign *To ~ ignorance.* Hoʻohūpō, hoʻopalō.
felt *A type of fabric.* Peleka.
felt pen Peni kuni.
feral *Formerly domesticated.* ʻŌhuka. See *domesticated, wild.*
fern *Maidenhair ~.* ʻIwaʻiwa.
ferric oxide Feriku ʻokesaside.
ferrosoferric oxide Ferosoferiku ʻokesaside.
ferrous Ferousa. *~ carbonate.* Ferousa karabonahate. *~ oxide.* Ferousa ʻokesaside. *~ sulfate.* Ferousa sulafahate. *~ sulfide.* Ferousa sulafaside.
fertilize *To ~, as an egg.* Hoʻolūmaua. *Fertilized.* Lūmaua.
fertilizer Mea hoʻomomona lepo. See *compost. Complete ~, i.e. ~ which contains the six necessary elements for plant growth.* Mea hoʻomomona lepo kāʻokoʻa. *To fertilize.* Hoʻomomona.
few *Also sparse.* Kākaʻikahi.
fiber *As referring to diet.* Hāʻaʻa ʻai.
fiberglass Aniani awe. See *plexiglass.*
fiction *Also fictitious.* Hakupuni. See *nonfiction. ~ book.* Puke hakupuni. *Historical ~.* Hakupuni mōʻaukala. *Realistic ~.* Hakupuni kohu ʻoiaʻiʻo. *Science ~.* Mōhihiʻo.
fiddle *Also violin.* Waiolina.
field *As in a database.* Kahua. See entry below and *subfield.*
field *As for football.* Kahua. See *baseball, court, meadow. Football ~.* Kahua pōpeku, kahua.
field capacity *For holding water.* Palena ū wai.
field goal *In football.* ʻAi peku.

Māmaka Kaiao / 225

field map *To ~ a site.* Kaha palapala 'āina.

field station *As used when mapping a certain area.* Kikowaena pānānā.

field trip *Excursion.* Huaka'i makahi'o, huaka'i. See *explore*.

figure *Number (the character), numeral.* Huahelu. *Also geometric ~.* Kinona. *Congruent ~.* Kinona komoloko. *Plane ~.* Kinona papa. *Similar ~.* Kinona 'ano like. *Solid ~.* Kinona pa'a. *Space ~.* Kinona pihanahaka. *Symmetric ~.* Kinona 'ālikelike. *As illustration in a textbook.* Ki'i.

filament *As in a light bulb.* 'Uiki 'ā. *~ tape, strapping tape.* Leki a'a.

file *The tool.* Waiehu. *Fine-cut ~.* Waiehu makali'i.

file *~ cabinet.* Pahu waihona pepa. *To ~, as ~s in a ~ cabinet.* Ho'okomo, waiho.

file *As in computer program.* Waihona. See entries below and *backup, directory, folder*. *Backup ~.* Waihona papa'a. *Compressed ~.* Waihona 'opihia. *Expanded ~.* Waihona mahola.

file extension *As in computer program.* Peleleu waihona.

file format *As in computer program.* Hulu waihona. *Compatible ~.* Hulu waihona launa. *Incompatible ~.* Hulu waihona launa 'ole.

file link *As in computer program.* Loulou waihona. See *data link*.

file prefix *Also header information, as codes at the beginning of each computer file.* Po'o pā'ālua (preceded by ke).

Filipino Pilipino, Pinopino. See *Philippines*.

fill bar *In computer program.* 'Aukā holomua.

filling *As for a sandwich.* 'Īkomo. *As of a tooth.* 'Īpiha.

film *As for a movie or video.* Līpine. See *shoot*. *~ movement, as in a movie or video camera.* Holo lola. *Roll of ~.* 'Ōwili ki'i.

filmstrip 'Ōwili ki'iaka.

fin *As of a fish, general term.* Lā. See *dorsal fin, ray*. *The ~s of a fish.* Nā lā o ka i'a. *Suction cup ~, as beneath the stomach of an 'o'opu.* Halo 'āpikapika.

final *Terminal, as last in time, order or importance.* Kuahope. See *primary, secondary, tertiary*.

finals *As in sporting events.* Ho'okūkū moho.

finance *Hawai'i State Department of ~.* 'Oihana Kālā o ka Moku'āina 'o Hawai'i.

finch *General term.* Ōpuhe. *Woodpecker ~.* Ōpuhe pao lā'au. *Grosbeak ~.* Hona. *King Kong ~.* Nuku 'ekue. *Laysan ~.* 'Ainohu Kauō. *Nīhoa ~.* 'Ainohu Nīhoa.

find *As an archeological ~.* Mea hi'ohia.

find *To calculate, in math.* Huli a loa'a, huli. See *calculate*.

find *To search for, as in computer program.* Huli. *To ~ and change, search and replace.* Huli a kuapo.

fine *As sand.* 'Ae'ae. See *coarse*.

fine arts Pāheona.

fine-cut file Waiehu makali'i.

fine point *Also fine line, as of a pen point.* Makakui. *~ pen.* Peni makakui.

finger Manamana lima, manamana. *Thumb.* Manamana nui. *Index ~.* Manamana miki, manamana kuhikuhi. *Middle ~.* Manamana loa, manamana waena. *Ring ~.* Manamana pili, manamana komo. *Little ~.* Manamana iki, manamana li'ili'i.

fingerprint Meheu manamana lima, māka manamana lima, ki'i manamana lima. *Groove on finger.* Māioio manamana lima. *To collect ~s.* 'Ohi i ka meheu manamana lima (māka manamana lima, ki'i manamana lima). *To take the ~s of (someone).* Kāpala, kāpala i ka meheu manamana lima (māka manamana lima, ki'i manamana lima).

fingertips See *jab*.

finish *~ point, as in a race.* Pahuhope. See *starting*. *~ line.* Laina pahuhope.

Finland *Also Finn, Finnish.* Finilana, Finilani.

Finn *Also Finland, Finnish.* Finilana, Finilani.

fire *To ~, as clay or ceramics.* Puhi. See *ring of fire.*

firecracker Pahūpahū (preceded by ke). See *fireworks. String of ~s.* Kālī pahūpahū.

fire extinguisher Kini hoʻopio ahi, kini kinai ahi.

firefly Nalo ʻuiʻuiki.

fire hydrant Paipu kinai ahi, piula wai.

fireplace Kapuahi hoʻopumehana.

fireworks Ahihoʻoleʻaleʻa. See *firecracker, pop-pops, Roman candle.*

first aid kit Kini lapaʻau, poho lāʻau pōulia.

first base *In baseball.* Pahu ʻekahi. See *base.*

first draft Kāmua ʻekahi. See *draft.*

first off the bench *Also six man, i.e. first alternate or substitute player in basketball.* Kūono.

first pass *Also to receive a serve, in volleyball.* Kiʻi.

First World Country ʻĀina ʻoiʻenehana. See *developed, Third World Country.*

fish *Also any marine animal.* Iʻa. See entries below and *aquaculture. Canned ~.* Kini iʻa. *~ cake, kamaboko.* Kamapoko. *~ flake.* Ulahi iʻa. *~ food flake.* Ulahi meaʻai iʻa. *Guppy.* Iʻa kapi. *Molly.* Iʻa moli. *Mosquito ~, medaka.* Iʻa makika. *Large school of ~ such as akule or aku.* Kumu iʻa. *Small school of reef ~ such as manini.* Naho iʻa, naha iʻa.

fish and game management *Also to manage fish and game.* Hoʻomalu lawaiʻa a me ka hahai holoholona.

Fish and Wildlife Service *US ~.* ʻOihana Iʻa me ka Holoholona Lōhiu o ʻAmelika.

Fisher burner Kapuahi pukapuka. See *burner.*

fishing float See *glass ball.*

fitness card *As for sports or physical education.* Kāleka olakino.

fitness center *Athletic club.* Hale hoʻoikaika kino. See *gymnasium.*

five man *Also center, in basketball.* Kūlima.

fixed net See *insect fixed net.*

fixed swing *As with two or more ropes or chains.* Paiō. See *free swing.*

flagrant *To commit a ~ foul, in team sports such as basketball.* Hoʻokuʻia kīpaku. See *foul.*

flake Ulahi. *Fish ~.* Ulahi iʻa. *Fish food ~.* Ulahi meaʻai iʻa. *Oatmeal ~.* Ulahi ʻokamila. *Snowflake.* Ulahi hau.

flame retardant Pale ahi.

flamingo Manu palamiko, palamiko.

flammable *Also flammability.* Pēʻāhia. See *inflammable.*

flanker *In football.* ʻĀʻapo.

flare *Solar ~.* Lapa ahi lā. See *solar, sunspot.*

flash *As for a camera.* Kukui ʻoaka, ʻoaka.

flash card Kāleka aʻo.

flat *As a tire.* Pakiʻi. See *deflated.*

flatbed trailer Pākihuila.

flatworm Koʻe pālahalaha.

flavor Maʻono. *To ~ or make tasty.* Hōʻonoʻono. *~ing.* Mea hōʻonoʻono.

fleur-de-lis *Also iris.* Puapalani.

flexed-arm hang Paʻaalewa.

flight *~ attendant.* Kuene mokulele. *~ corridor.* Ala lele mokulele. *~ deck, as on a spaceship.* ʻOneki pailaka. *Manned space ~.* Lele lewa lipo kanaka.

flightless rail Moho lele ʻole.

flip *To turn a figure to its reverse side, in math.* Hoʻohuli. See *slide. To ~, as a coin.* Pana hoʻolei.

flood Wai hālana. *~ control.* Kāohi wai hālana. *~ warning.* Kūkala pōʻino wai hālana. *~ watch, as in weather report.* Kūkala makaʻala wai hālana.

floor *Story, as in a building.* Papahele. *~ tile.* Kile papahele, kile ʻili, moena ʻili ʻāpanapana. See *linoleum.*

floppy *As computer disk.* Malule. *~ disk.* Pā malule (preceded by ke).

Florida *Also Floridan, Floridian.* Pololika, Folorida.

floss *Dental ~; also to ~ (one's teeth).* Lopi niho.

flour Palaoa maka. *See Hawaiian entries under* palaoa. *Whole wheat ~.* Palaoa maka huika piha.

flow chart Pakuhi kaʻina. *To make a ~.* Kākuhi kaʻina.

flower *~ pot.* Poho meakanu. *~ vase.* Pika pua. *~ing plant.* Meakanu pua.

fluctuate *To ~, as the tide.* Hanuʻu.

fluid ounce ʻAuneki wai. *Abb.* ʻan w.

fluke Koʻelau. *Liver ~.* Koʻelau ake.

fluorescent *As colors.* Hālino. *~ pink.* ʻĀkala hālino. *As light; also phosphorescent.* Hāweo. *~ light.* Kukui hāweo.

flush *To ~ a toilet.* Hoʻokuʻu i ka wai o ka lua, hoʻoholo i ka wai.

flute ʻOhekani puluka, puluka.

fly *Fishhook with feathers.* Makaunalo. *Fruit ~.* Pōnalo huaʻai. *Midge ~.* Nalo wiʻu. *Pomace ~.* Pōnalo.

flyer *Pamphlet.* Pepelu.

flying saucer Pālele.

flytrap *Venus ~.* ʻŪmiʻinalo.

FM *Frequency modulation.* FM (*pronounced* fāmū). *See AM.*

focus point Kiko kau.

foil *Aluminum ~.* Pepa kini.

folder *As in computer program.* Wahī. *See file. External ~.* Wahī o waho.

folktale *A traditional tale, especially one relating to a particular culture.* Kaʻao, moʻokaʻao. *See Hawaiian entries under* kaʻao.

Fomalhaut *A star.* Ahiwela.

font *Typeface, as in printing or computer program.* Kinona hua. *See style. ~ cartridge.* Pāpahu kinona hua.

food Meaʻai. *See entries below and* nutritious, remove, serving. *~ coloring.* Kala meaʻai. *~ chain.* Kuʻina meaʻai. *~ web.* Pūnaewele meaʻai. *Health ~.* Meaʻai hāʻehuola. *High-fat ~.* Meaʻai nui o ka ʻailakele. *Low-fat ~.* Meaʻai liʻiliʻi o ka ʻailakele.

food group *As one of the six ~s.* Pūʻulu meaʻai. *The ~s, i.e. the collective union of all six ~s (calcium/milk, vegetable, fruit, starch, meat and fat).* Pae pūʻulu meaʻai.

food label *As for giving product information on a package of food.* Lepili māhuaola.

foot *Unit of measurement.* Kapuaʻi. *Abb.* kp. *See square foot. ~ or head of trail.* Nuku. *See pass.*

footage *As of video tape.* Līpine. *Blank ~.* Līpine maʻemaʻe. *Raw ~.* Līpine paʻi maka. *As the number of minutes of video tape shot.* Minuke līpine.

football *The sport.* Pōpeku. *The ball.* Kinipōpō pōpeku. *~ field.* Kahua pōpeku, kahua. *American ~ Conference (AFC).* Hui Pōpeku ʻAmelika. *National ~ Conference (NFC).* Hui Pōpeku Aupuni. *National ~ League (NFC).* Kuʻikahi Pōpeku Aupuni.

footer *As in computer documents.* Kau lalo. *See header.*

footnote *As in a book or research paper.* Kuhia o lalo. *See endnote, note.*

force *Power to affect physical relations or conditions.* Manehu. *Balanced ~.* Manehu kaulike. *Buoyant ~, i.e. the upward force of a fluid on an object in it.* Manehu hoʻolana. *Centrifugal ~.* Manehu lele niniu. *Centripetal ~.* Manehu ʻume niniu. *Electrical ~ field.* Kāʻei manehu uila. *Natural ~.* Manehu kūlohelohe. *Resistance ~.* Manehu āohiohi.

forceps ʻŪpā hoʻopaʻa. *See utility clamp.*

foreground *As in a photo or movie/video scene.* Kāʻei alo. *See background.*

foreign accent Pualona 'ē.
forest Ululā'au, nahele. See *ranger watchtower*. *~ reserve*. 'Āina ho'omalu ululā'au. *Rain ~*. Nahele ma'ukele. *Subalpine ~*. Ululā'au lalo 'alapaina. *Temperate ~*. Nahele kemepale.
foreword *Also preface, as in a book*. 'Ōlelo ha'i mua, 'ōlelo mua. See *introduction*.
fork *Spading ~*. 'Ō 'eli *(preceded by ke)*. *Tuning ~*. Hao ho'okani, 'ō ho'okani *(preceded by ke)*.
form *Order ~*. Palapala 'oka. *Registration ~*. Palapala kāinoa.
form *Standard ~, as for numbers*. Kino huahelu. *Expanded ~*. Unuhi kūana.
formalin Pomalina.
format *As of a computer file*. Hulu. See *compatible, disk. File ~*. Hulu waihona. *To ~*. Ho'onohonoho. *As of a document in computer program*. Ho'onohonohona. *Custom ~*. Ho'onohonohona pilikino. *To ~ or initialize, as a computer disk*. Ho'āla.
formic Forimiku. *~ acid*. 'Akika forimiku.
formula *In math and science*. Ha'ilula. *Chemical ~*. Ha'ilula kemikala.
forward *With palms facing ~*. Pohoalo. See *backward, hit, pull-up, fast forward. Power ~ or four man, in basketball*. Kūhā. *Shooting ~, swing man, or three man*. Kūkolu.
fossil Mō'alihaku, wīhaku. *~ fuel*. Wāwahie mō'alihaku, wāwahie wīhaku.
foul *In team sports such as basketball*. Ku'ia. *Blocking ~ (in basketball)*. Ku'ia 'āke'a. *Offensive ~*. Ku'ia kūlele. *Personal ~*. Ku'ia pilikino. *Team ~*. Ku'ia kime. *Technical ~*. Ku'ia kūhelu. *To deliberately ~*. Ho'oku'ia. *To commit an intentional ~*. Ho'oku'ia ahuwale. *To commit a flagrant ~*. Ho'oku'ia kīpaku.
foundation *For makeup*. Palaina helehelena.
fountain *Drinking ~*. Pua'iwai. *For decoration*. Pūnāpua'i.

fountain pen Peni pāuma.
four-by-four Hā hā. *~ board or lumber*. Papa hā hā.
four man *Also power forward, in basketball*. Kūhā.
four-pack See *pack*.
fox *Arctic ~*. 'Alopeka 'Ālika, 'alopeke 'Ālika.
fraction *In math*. Hakina. *Equivalent ~*. Hakina heluna like. *Improper ~*. Hakina lapa. *Terms of a ~*. Palena. See *terms*.
fractional part Māhele hapa. *One-half (part)*. Māhele hapalua.
fragile *Easily broken*. Haki wale. *As glass*. Nahā wale. *Susceptible to change*. Pāloli.
frame *As in bowling*. Kuea. See entries below and *molding. Bowling ~*. Kuea maika. *Bed~*. Hao pela. *Door~*. Kikihi. *Picture ~*. Mōlina ki'i. *Window ~*. Mōlina pukaaniani.
frame *As in computer program*. Mōlina. *Open ~*. Mōlina ka'aka'a. *Closed ~*. Mōlina pa'a.
frame *A single ~ of a movie or video film; also to ~ or arrange the content of a photograph, movie or video picture within certain borders*. Mōlina.
France *Also French*. Palani, Farani.
free *Exempt from external restrictions*. Kūnoa. *Independent*. Kū'oko'a. *No charge*. Manuahi. *Not in use*. Ka'awale. See entries below and *freedom, toll free*.
freedom *Also liberty*. Kūnoa, kūkā'oko'a. See *free*.
freely *To go ~, i.e. to have freedom to go wherever one pleases, to "have the run of the place."* Hele lanakila.
free nitrogen compound Pūhui naikokene ka'awale.
free style *Crawl, in swimming; also to swim using this style*. 'Au kolo. See *stroke*.
free swing *As a single rope hanging from a tree branch*. Lele koali. See *fixed swing*.

free throw *In basketball; to make such a shot.* Kī noa. *Single ~.* Kī noa pākahi. *One-and-one ~.* Kī noa kī hou. *Two-shot ~.* Kī noa pālua. *~ line.* Laina kī noa.

freeze *To ~ something.* Hoʻopaʻahau. *See entries below. Frozen.* Paʻahau. *To ~ dry something.* Hoʻokaʻohau. *~ dried.* Kaʻohau. *~r.* Pahu paʻahau.

freezer tape *Masking ~.* Leki pahu.

freezing point Kēkelē paʻahau. *See boiling point, melting point.*

French Frigate Shoals Mokupāpapa.

French horn Pū puhi Palani.

frequency *In math.* Alapine.

frequency modulation FM. FM (*pronounced* fāmū). *See AM.*

fresh-water marsh Ālialia wai maoli.

fret *As on an ʻukulele, guitar, etc.* Wā. *See ʻukulele.*

fricative *In linguistics.* Hahī.

friction *As when one thing rubs against another.* Manehu ʻānai.

Friday Poʻalima. *Abb.* P5.

friendly *See user friendly.*

frieze Kāʻei kiʻi kālai.

frog Poloka. *Tree ~.* Poloka kau lāʻau. *Orange tree ~.* Poloka kau lāʻau ʻālani. *Wrinkled ~.* Poloka mimino.

front *As of weather.* Kuʻina. *See solvent front. Cold ~.* Kuʻina huʻihuʻi. *Warm ~.* Kuʻina mehana. *Stationary ~.* Kuʻina paʻa.

front-end *In math.* Hapa mua. *~ digit.* Kikohoʻe hapa mua. *~ estimation.* Koho hapa mua.

front vowel *In linguistics.* Woela kaumua. *See vowel.*

frown Hoʻokuʻemaka. *See scowl.*

frozen yogurt Hauwaiūtepe. *See freeze.*

fructose Huakō. *See glucose.*

fruit fly Pōnalo huaʻai.

fry *See deep-fry.*

frying pan Pā palai (*preceded by* ke). *~ handle.* ʻAu pā palai (*preceded by* ke).

fudge Kokoleka pāhoehoe.

fuel Wāwahie. *External ~ tank, as on a spaceship.* Pahu wāwahie kūwaho. *Fossil ~.* Wāwahie mōʻalihaku, wāwahie wīhaku.

fulcrum Lona hulei.

fullback *In football.* ʻĀpohu.

full-court press *In basketball.* Lulumi piha. *See press.*

full justified *As type in printing.* Kaulihi like. *See justify.*

fume Ea puka, ea.

fumigant Lāʻau make hanu. *See poison.*

function *As on a calculator or computer keyboard.* Hana. *~ key.* Pihi hana (*preceded by* ke). *As on a calculator.* Lawelawe hana. *In math.* Hahaina. *Linear ~.* Hahaina lālani. *~ rule.* Lula hahaina.

fungus *General term.* Kalina.

funnel Kānuku.

fur seal Sila pūhuluhulu.

fuse ʻUiki uila. *~ box.* Pahu ʻuiki uila.

fusion *Nuclear ~.* Kuʻi nukeliu.

G

Gabon *Also Gabonese.* Kapona, Gabona.

gadget *Device, doohickey, gizmo, thingamajig.* Hāmeʻa. *See apparatus, instrument, tool.*

gaffer *As for movie or video production.* Luna uila. *See best boy.*

galaxy Wiliau hōkū. *Andromeda ~.* Ka wiliau hōkū ʻo ʻAnakolomeka.

gale Kelawini, makani kelawini. *See wind. Stormy wind; whole trees in motion and inconvenience felt in walking against the wind, in meteorology.* ʻEna makani.

Galileo *Also Galilean.* Kalileo. *Galilean moons.* Nā mahina ʻo Kalileo.

gallon Kālani. *Abb.* kln. *Half ~.* Hapalua kālani. *~ jar or jug.* ʻŌmole kālani.

game *Board ~, as checkers.* Kēmu. *~ board.* Papa kēmu. *Fair ~, as one in which each player has the same chance of winning.* Pā'ani kaulike. *Fish and ~ management; also to manage fish and ~.* Ho'omalu lawai'a a me ka hahai holoholona.
Ganymede *A moon of Jupiter.* Kanimeki.
garden *To ~; ~ing.* Mahi māla. *Botannical ~.* Māla hō'ike'ike meakanu. *~ing book.* Puke mahi māla. *~ rake.* Hao kope. *~ store, ~ing store.* Hale kū'ai mahi māla. *~ trowel.* Kopalā lima.
Gardner Pinnacles Pūhāhonu.
gas *Also gaseous, as opposed to solid or liquid.* Kinoea. *See entries below and Charles' law. Bromine ~.* Kinoea polomine. *~ generator, a device used for producing gases in a chemistry lab.* Hāme'a hana kinoea. *~ mask, as used during World War II.* Pūnuku ea make.
gas fading control fabric *As in meteorology.* Lole ana kinoea.
gasification *Also to gasify, i.e. convert into gas.* Kākinoea. *Coal ~, i.e. the process in which steam and hot coal produce hydrocarbons.* Kākinoea lānahu.
gasify *See gasification.*
gasohol 'Ailahola.
gateway *Also alias, as in computer program.* 'Īpuka.
gauge *A measuring instrument.* Mea ana.
gauze Welu 'eha, welu wahī'eha, 'a'amo'o. *Wire ~, steel wool.* Pulupulu uea.
gear *As in machinery.* Kia.
gel Palaholo. *Hair ~, Dep.* Palaholo lauoho. *Silica ~ g.* Palaholo silaka g (*pronounced* palaholo silaka gā).
gelatin 'Ūnina.
gene *Also genetic.* Ōewe. *See genetics. Genetic engineering.* Kūkulu ōewe.
genealogy Mo'okū'auhau. *Genealogical story.* Mo'olelo mo'okū'auhau.

general controls *As in computer program.* Ho'oholo laulā.
generalize Ho'olaulā.
generator *See gas generator.*
genetic engineering Ka ho'oliliuewe 'ana.
genetics Kālaiōewe. *See gene.*
gentle breeze *Dust raised and small branches move, in meteorology.* Aheahe. *See wind. Leaves in constant motion.* Kolonahe.
geoboard *In math.* Papakui anahonua.
geographical coordinates Nā kuhikuhina hō'ike honua.
geography Hō'ike honua. *See geographical coordinates. Geographic region.* Māhele 'āina.
geologic *See geology. ~ change.* Loli honua. *~ depression, as Death Valley.* 'Āpoho 'āina. *~ fault, as San Andreas Fault.* Hakinahe'e. *~ trench, as Aleutian Trench.* 'Auwaha. *~al site.* Kahua hulihonua.
geologist Kanaka hulihonua.
geology Hulihonua. *See geologic.*
geometric *~ cone.* 'Ōpa'a. *~ curve.* Uma. *~ figure.* Kinona. *~ solid.* Pa'a. *See plane figure, space figure.*
geometrid moth 'Ō'aki.
geometry Anahonua, moleanahonua.
geophysics Kālaihonua. *See geology.*
Georgia *Also Georgian.* Keokia.
geothermal electricity Uila māhu pele. *See electricity.*
geranium Laniuma.
gerbil 'Iole kepila, 'iole kebira.
germ Mūhune. *See pathogen.*
German cockroach *Blattella germanica.* 'Elelū la'aloa.
Germany *Also German.* Kelemānia.
germinate *To sprout.* Ilo. *To cause to ~ or sprout.* Ho'oilo.
gesture *Hand ~; also to ~ with the hands, to use sign language.* Kuhi lima. *See sign language.*
geyser Waipelekī.
Ghana *Also Ghanaian, Ghanian.* Gāna.

Giant Red Spot *A huge gaseous feature on Jupiter.* 'Ōnohi 'Ula Kūāhewa.
giant sloth Melalemu pilikua.
gift certificate Palapala makana.
giga- *A prefix meaning billion (G).* Pāpiliona. *Abb.* pp. *See entries below and* deca-, hecto-, kilo-, mega-, tera-.
gigabyte 'Ai pāpiliona. *Abb.* PP. *See* byte.
gigajoule *A unit of energy.* Kule pāpiliona. *See* joule.
gills *Of a fish.* Pihapiha.
gingerbread 'Awakeke.
gingham Kinamu.
give and go *To ~, in basketball.* Hā'awiaholo.
given *As in a math problem.* Hō'ike 'ia.
gizmo *Device, doohickey, gadget, thingamajig.* Hāme'a. *See* apparatus, instrument, tool.
glaciation Ka haunene'e 'ana.
glacier Haunene'e.
Glacier National Park Pāka Aupuni 'o Haunene'e.
gland Lōku'u. *Endocrine ~.* Lōku'u ku'uloko. *Exocrine ~.* Lōku'u ku'uwaho. *Lymph ~.* Lōku'u 'anapu'u. *Salivary ~.* Lōku'u hā'ae. *Thyroid ~.* Lōku'u ho'okonukonu pūnao.
glass ball *A Japanese fishing float.* Pōpō aniani.
glasses *Safety ~.* Makaaniani kaupale. *Sun ~.* Makaaniani kala, makaaniani lā.
glass wool Hulu aniani.
glaucoma Kaukoma.
glib *Also smooth talk, smooth talker.* Waha wali.
glide *In linguistics.* 'Ōlali.
glider *Hang ~.* Lupekau.
glitter Hune hulili.
global warming *Greenhouse effect.* Ho'omehana Honua.
globe *Also sphere.* Poepeo. *~ of Earth.* Poepeo Honua.
glossary Papa wehewehe 'ōlelo. *See* dictionary.

glove *Baseball ~ or mitt.* Mikilima pōhili.
glowing *As in the dark; fluorescent, phosphorescent.* Hāweo.
glucose Monakō. *See* fructose. *Blood ~.* Monakō koko.
glue Tuko. *See* paste, rubber cement.
glycine Galaisine.
goal Pahuhopu, pahuhopu laulā. *See* objective. *Field ~, in football.* 'Ai peku.
goblin 'E'epa pau'aka.
go freely *To ~, i.e. to have freedom to go wherever one pleases, to "have the run of the place."* Hele lanakila.
goggles *Diving ~ or mask.* Makaaniani lu'u kai, makaaniani lu'u. *Protective ~.* Makaaniani kaupale.
golden rectangle *A rectangle in which the ratio of the width to the length is the same as that of the length to the sum of the width plus the length.* Huinahā lō'ihi kula.
golf Kolepa. *~ club.* 'Ūhili kolepa. *Municipal ~ course.* Kahua pā'ani kolepa kiwikā.
good night *Sleep well.* E hiamoe pono 'oe, e hiamoe maika'i 'oe, a hui hou i kakahiaka.
goto *As in computer program.* E lele i.
government Aupuni. *Two-party system of ~.* Aupuni 'ao'ao 'elua.
gradient *Or band, as of colors.* 'Auina. *Color ~.* 'Auina kala.
graduated cylinder Hano ana.
graduation card Kāleka puka kula, kāleka hemo kula.
graffiti Kahakaha kolohe.
graft Pāku'i. *~ing wax.* Pīlali pāku'i. *To grow by ~ing.* Ho'oulu pāku'i.
grain Napoe. *Pigment ~, in biology.* Huna kaukala.
gram Kalame. *Abb.* kal.
grammar Pilina'ōlelo. *See* pattern. *~ lesson, a lesson related to sentence structure.* Ha'awina pilina'ōlelo. *~ or sentence structure skill.* Mākau pilina'ōlelo.

Māmaka Kaiao / 232

grammatical sentence *Or clause.* Pepeke. See *clause, sentence.*

Grand Canyon Haka'ama, ke awāwa kūhōhō nui 'o Haka'ama. See *Colorado River.*

grand total Huinanui pau loa. See *subtotal.*

granule *Solar ~, gigantic waves of gas which roll across the surface of the sun.* 'Ale ahi lā. See *solar, sunspot.*

grapefruit 'Ālani pomelo. See *pomelo.*

grapevine Kumu waina.

graph *Also chart, in math.* Pakuhi. *Bar ~.* Pakuhi 'aukā. *Double bar ~.* Pakuhi pa'a 'aukā. *Box and whiskers ~.* Pakuhi pahu me ka 'umi'umi. *Circle ~.* Pakuhi pō'ai. *Line ~.* Pakuhi lākiō. *~ origin.* Piko pakuhi. *~ paper.* Pepa maka'aha. *To ~ or chart.* Kākuhi. *To ~ the point.* Kākuhi i ke kiko.

graphics Ki'i. See *bitmap.* *~ technician, as for movie or video production.* Mea 'enehana ki'i.

graphing calculator Mīkini kākuhi.

graphite Kalapaike.

grass *General term.* Mau'u, mahiki. *California ~.* Mau'u Kaleponi. *Nut~.* Mau'u pīneki.

grasshopper 'Ūhini.

grassland 'Āina mau'u.

gravel Haku'ili.

gravity 'Umekaumaha. See *microgravity.* *Anti~ machine.* Mīkini ho'opau 'umekaumaha. *Center of ~.* Piko 'umekaumaha. *Specific or relative ~.* Lākiō pa'apū wai. *Zero ~.* 'Umekaumaha 'ole.

grazer *An animal that eats grass.* Hamulau mau'u. See *browser.*

grease *As used in machines or for tools with moving parts.* Hinukele.

greater than *In math.* Nui a'e, 'oi aku ka nui. See *less than.*

greatest *~ decrease, in math.* Emi ha'aha'a loa. *~ increase.* Pi'i ki'eki'e loa.

greatest possible error *In math.* Palena 'āluna o ka hewa. *Abb.* P'ĀH.

great horned owl Pueo kiwi hulu.

Greece *Also Greek, Grecian.* Helene.

greenhouse Hale ho'oulu meakanu. *~ effect, global warming.* Ho'omehana Honua.

green onion *Purple bulb becoming white close to tip.* 'O'a. *White bulb with purple inside.* Lina.

greensword *Maui ~.* 'Āhinahina 'ōma'oma'o.

greeting card Kāleka aloha.

grid Maka'aha. See *graph paper, spreadsheet.*

grind *To ~ one's teeth.* Nau kuai i ka niho.

grip *Stagehand, as for movie or video production.* Mea kūkulu kahua. *Key ~, stage manager.* Luna kūkulu kahua.

groove *On finger as appears in fingerprint.* Māioio manamana lima. See *fingerprint.*

grosbeak finch *Chloridops kona.* Hona. See *finch.*

ground cover Kapauli.

groundhog *Also marmot.* Māmota.

ground layer *Of vegetation.* Papa kū honua. See *vegetation layers.*

groundnut *Also peanut or any edible nut.* Pīneki, pineki, pīnaki.

groundwater Wai honua.

ground zero *As in field mapping.* Papahonua.

group Pū'ulu. See *food group.* *To form or break into ~s; also to ~, in math.* Ho'opū'ulu. *~ing property.* 'Anopili ho'opū'ulu (*preceded by* ke).

grow See entry below and *hydroponics.* *To ~ by grafting.* Ho'oulu pāku'i. *To ~ wild, as weeds.* Ulu wale. *To ~ wild and lush.* Uluāhewa.

grow *To ~, as in a computer program.* Ulu. *To ~ vertically.* Ulu papakū. *To ~ horizontally.* Ulu papamoe. *~ limit.* Palena ulu.

Guam *Also Guamanian.* Guama.

Māmaka Kaiao / 233

guarantee *An assurance of quality or length of use with promise of reimbursement.* Palapala hoʻohiki. *See* warranty.

guard *See entry below and* mud guard. *Coast* ~. Pūʻali pale kapa kai. *King's* ~. Pūʻali kiaʻi mōʻī. *Security* ~. Kiaʻi, kiaʻi pō, mākaʻi kiaʻi (pō).

guard *In football.* Kūkahi. *Left* ~. Kūkahi hema. *Right* ~. Kūkahi ʻākau. *Defensive middle* ~, *nose* ~, *or nose tackle.* Haunaku. *Point* ~ *or one man, in basketball.* Kūkahi. *Shooting* ~ *or two man.* Kūlua.

Guatemala *Also Guatemalan.* Kuakemala.

guava Kūawa.

guess *Also estimate; to* ~, *estimate.* Koho. *See* estimate. ~*ing bag.* Pūʻolo kohokoho.

guest room Lumi moe malihini.

guide *Page* ~, *as in a computer document or dictionary.* Kuhi lihi. *Teacher's* ~ *or manual.* Puke alakaʻi.

guided imagery *To utilize* ~. Hoʻohele moeā.

Guinea *See* Papua New Guinea.

guinea pig ʻIole kawia.

guitar Kīkā. *For parts, see* ʻukulele.

guppy Iʻa kapi.

guyot Mauna kai pālahalaha. *See* seamount.

gym *Jungle* ~, *as playground equipment.* Hao pīnana. *See* gymnasium, monkey bars.

gymnasium Hale haʻuki. *See* athletic club.

gymnastics *Also gymnast.* Kaʻalehia.

H

habitat Kaianoho.

hair *To style* ~, *as for a play, movie or video production.* Hoʻoponopono lauoho. ~ *stylist.* Mea hoʻoponopono lauoho.

hairband Apo poʻo.

hairclip *Barrette.* Pine lauoho. *Folding* ~ *with teeth.* Kahi ʻūmiʻi lauoho.

hair gel *Also Dep.* Palaholo lauoho.

hairs *See* root hairs.

Haiti *Also Haitian.* Heiti.

half Hapalua. ~ *dollar.* Hapalua kālā, hapalua. ~ *gallon.* Hapalua kālani. *One-~ part.* Māhele hapalua.

halfback *In football.* ʻĀhaʻi.

half-court line *On a basketball court.* Laina kūwaena. *See* line (as on basketball court).

half-court press *In basketball.* Lulumi hapa. *See* press.

half-rectangle principle Kulehana huinahā lōʻihi hapalua.

halftime *In sports or games.* Hoʻomaha hapalua.

half-turn image *In math.* Kinona like wili hapalua. *See* turn image.

hall *Residence* ~, *as at a school.* Hale noho haumāna. *See* hallway.

Halley Hēli. ~'s *comet.* Ka hōkū puhipaka ʻo Hēli.

Halloween Heleuī, lā hoʻomākaʻukaʻu.

hallucination *To cause* ~. Hōʻolalau manaʻo. *See* hallucinogen.

hallucinogen Lāʻau hōʻolalau manaʻo.

hallway Holoē, holo.

Hampshire *See* New Hampshire.

hand *As opposed to arm.* Peʻahi lima. *See* gesture, hand-held. *As of an analog clock or watch.* Lima kuhikuhi. *Minute* ~. Lima kuhikuhi minuke. *Hour* ~. Lima kuhikuhi hola.

hand *As a single round in a game of cards.* Puni. *See* lap, round.

handcuffs ʻŪpiki lima.

hand cultivator Kīkoʻu paʻa lima.

hand-held Paʻa lima. *See* hand mirror, pocket compass.

handkerchief Hainakā, hinakā.

handle *For lifting, as of bucket or suitcase.* Kākai. *Knob-style* ~. Pōheo, pōheoheo. *As of bureau drawer, faucet, frying pan, toilet, etc.* ʻAu (*preceded by* ke).

Māmaka Kaiao / 234

handlebars *On a bicycle.* 'Au paikikala (*preceded by* ke), kalaiwa paikikala.
hand lens *Magnifying glass.* Aniani hoʻonui ʻike.
hand mirror Aniani paʻa lima.
hand off *To ~ (the ball), in football.* Hoʻoili.
handstand *Also to do a ~.* Kū lima. See *headstand*.
hang *Flexed-arm ~.* Paʻaalewa. See *hung*.
hanger Uea kau lole, lāʻau kau lole, mea kau lole, ʻea kau lole.
hang glider Lupekau.
happy face spider Nananana makakiʻi, nanana makakiʻi.
harassment *Sexual ~; also to subject to sexual ~.* Kekohala.
hard disk *As in a computer.* Pā paʻaloko (*prededed by* ke). *Removable ~.* Pā paʻaloko wehe.
hard drive *On a computer.* Kakena paʻaloko.
hardening of the arteries *Also arteriosclerosis or artherosclerosis, in medicine.* Aʻalāʻau. See *arteriolosclerosis*.
hardware *As for a computer.* Lako paʻa. See *software*. *As tools made of metal.* Lako hao. *~ store.* Hale kūʻai lako hao.
harmonica Pila puhipuhi.
harmonize Hoʻokūlauna. See *harmony*.
harmony *In music.* Kūlauna. See *harmonize*. *To sing in ~.* Hīmeni kūlauna like.
harp *The musical instrument.* Hāpa. See *autoharp, Jew's harp*.
hash-brown potatoes ʻUala kahiki kolikoli, ʻuala kolikoli.
hatch *To incubate eggs.* Hoʻomoe.
hatch *Explosive escape ~, as in a spaceship.* ʻĪpuka pakele pahū.
hatred *Of males, misandry.* Hoʻokae kāne. *Of mankind, misanthropy.* Hoʻokae kanaka. *Of women, misogyny.* Hoʻokae wahine.

hauled See *close hauled*.
haunted Lapu. *~ house (not Halloween variety).* Hale lapu.
Hawaiʻi *Also Hawaiian.* Hawaiʻi. See entries below. *~ State Department of Finance.* ʻOihana Kālā o ka Mokuʻāina ʻo Hawaiʻi. *~ State Department of Planning and Economic Development.* ʻOihana Hoʻolālā a me ka Hoʻomohala Waiwai o ka Mokuʻāina ʻo Hawaiʻi.
Hawaiʻi Volcanoes National Park Pāka Aupuni ʻo Kīlauea.
Hawaiian medium Kaiapuni Hawaiʻi. *~ class.* Papa kaiapuni Hawaiʻi. *~ school.* Kula kaiapuni Hawaiʻi.
Hawaiian monk seal Sila Hawaiʻi.
hawthorne Haukona. *~ berry.* Pīʻai haukona.
head *~ or foot of trail.* Nuku. See *pass, shower head*. *As of an ʻukulele or guitar.* Papa kī. *~ nut.* Nīʻau liʻiliʻi. See *ʻukulele*.
headboard *Of bed.* Kūmoe. See *bedframe*.
header *As in computer documents.* Kau luna. See *footer*. *~ information or file prefix, as codes at the beginning of each computer file.* Poʻo pāʻālua (*preceded by* ke).
heading *Also subheading, as in a story.* Poʻomanaʻo.
headlight Kukuipoʻo, kukuipoʻo o mua.
headphone *Headset.* Apo lohe. See *earphone*.
heads *As in coin toss.* Poʻo (*preceded by* ke), ʻaoʻao poʻo. See *tails*.
headset *Headphone.* Apo lohe. See *earphone*.
headstand *Also to do a handstand.* Kū poʻo. See *handstand*.
healing *Total ~ environment.* Kaiapuni hoʻōla piha.
health Olakino. See *healthy*. *~ food.* Meaʻai hāʻehuola. *~ status.* Kūlana olakino. *Allied ~ professional.* Kākoʻo ʻoihana olakino. *Community-based ~ system.* ʻŌnaehana olakino kaiaulu.

healthy *Also healthful, wholesome, i.e. promoting physical health.* Hāʻehuola. *See health, vigor.*

hearing *Sense of ~.* Lonoa pepeiao. *A time for presenting official testimony or argument.* Hālāwai hoʻolohe, ʻaha hoʻolohe.

hearing aid Pihi hoʻonui lohe (*preceded by* ke).

heart *Shape.* Haka. *~ rate, pulse rate.* Helu pana puʻuwai. *Transplanted ~.* Puʻuwai ili. *To transplant a ~.* Hoʻoili puʻuwai.

heartworm Koʻe puʻuwai.

heat *Medium ~.* Wela lōpū. *Specific ~, in physics.* Ana piʻi wela.

heater *Water ~.* Kula hoʻowela wai, pahu hoʻowela wai.

heating lamp Kukui hoʻomehana.

hectare *A metric unit of land measurement.* Hekekale, heketare. *Abb.* ht.

hecto- *A prefix meaning hundred (h).* Pāhaneli. *Abb.* ph. *Also* heko-. *See entries below and* deca-, kilo-, mega-, giga-, tera-.

hectogram Hekokalame. *Abb.* hkkal.

hectoliter Hekolika. *Abb.* hkl.

hectometer Hekomika. *Abb.* hkm.

height Kiʻekiʻe, ana kiʻekiʻe. *Abb.* kiʻe. *See length, width. ~ or depth, in math.* Hohonu. *~ of a wave.* Kiʻekiʻena, kiʻekiʻena nalu, kiʻekiʻena ʻale. *See wavelength.*

helicopter Helekopa. *Also* mokulele helekopa.

helium Hiliuma.

helmet Paleupoʻo.

hem *As of a dress.* Pelu. *Of a net.* Pelu ʻupena.

hemisphere Poepoe hapa. *See sphere.* *Northern ~.* Poepoe hapa ʻākau.

hemisphere *Eastern ~.* Poepoe hapa hikina. *Northern ~.* Poepoe hapa ʻākau. *Southern ~.* Poepoe hapa hema. *Western ~.* Poepoe hapa komohana.

hemlock Hemalaka.

hemoglobin ʻAwehā.

heptagon *A seven-sided polygon.* Huinahiku.

herb *As basil, thyme, etc.* Lauʻala.

herbicide Lāʻau make nāhelehele.

herbivore *Also herbivorous.* Hamulau. *See browser, grazer.*

heredity Kumu welo. *See gene. Hereditary trait.* Welo.

Hermes *Pearl and ~ reef.* Holoikauaua.

heroin Heroina.

heron *General term.* ʻAlekea. *See egret.*

herringbone weave Maka puhi, iwipuhi.

hexagon Huinaono.

hexahedron *A space figure with six faces, in math.* Paʻaʻiliono. *See cube.*

hex nut Pihi wili ono.

hibernate *Also hibernation.* Moekau.

hibernation *See hibernate.*

hieroglyph *Also hieroglyphics.* Lalinoka.

high-fat food Meaʻai ʻailakele nui, meaʻai nui o ka ʻailakele. *See low-fat food.*

high jump Lele kiʻekiʻe.

highlight *To block text, as in computer program.* Kahiāuli. *See shade.*

high post *In basketball.* Kūliu waho. *See low post.*

high pressure system *In meteorology.* ʻŌnaehana mīkā piʻi. *See low pressure system.*

highrise *As a building.* Nuʻuoʻa. *See lowrise, skyscraper.*

high vowel *In linguistics.* Woela kiʻekiʻe. *See vowel.*

hike *Also to go on a ~.* Hekehi. *See entry below and stroll. Hiker.* Mea hekehi. *Hiking shoe.* Kāmaʻa hekehi. *Hiking trail.* Ala hekehi.

hike *To ~ (the ball), in football.* Huki pōpō, huki i ka pōpō, huki i ke kinipōpō. *See center.*

hilly *Also small cliffs.* Kīpāpali.

Māmaka Kaiao / 236

hinge ʻAmi. *Door ~.* ʻAmi puka, ʻami ʻīpuka.

hint ʻŌlelo hoʻohani. *To ~ at, give a ~.* Hoʻohani.

hippopotamus Hipopōkamu.

histogram *A bar graph showing frequencies, in math.* Pakuhi ʻaukā alapine.

historical fiction Hakupuni mōʻaukala.

history Mōʻaukala.

hit *To ~ with a racket.* Kīpehi. *To ~ forehand.* Kīpehi pohoalo. *To ~ backhand.* Kīpehi pohokua. *To ~ or fake, in volleyball.* Hana kolohe, mīʻoi wale. *Hitter.* Mea pākī, pākī. *See spike.*

HIV *Human immunodeficiency virus.* Mū hōlapu pale ʻea pau. *See AIDS.*

hockey Hōkē. *Street ~.* Hōkē alanui.

hoe Koʻi kālai, hō, ʻōʻō kālai. *To ~.* Kālai, hō.

holder *Cassette ~, tape case.* Pāiki lola. *Toothbrush ~.* Kauna palaki niho.

holding *Insect ~ jar.* ʻŌmole mālama ʻelala.

hole *Sound ~, as on an ʻukulele or guitar.* Puka kani.

hole punch *For paper.* Pāniki pepa.

hollow tile Paomeki.

home appliance Mīkini home. *See appliance store.*

homemade Hana ʻia ma kauhale.

home plate *In baseball.* Pahu eo.

home run *In baseball.* ʻAi puni.

home screen *In computer program.* Kahua paʻa.

homonym Huaʻōlelo puana like. *See synonym, antonym.*

Honduras *Also Honduran.* Honodurasa.

honeycreeper *General term.* Manu mūkīkī.

honeydew *A sweet juice secreted by aphids.* Meli ʻeleao.

honey locust bean Pāpapa ʻūhinihone.

honors *With ~, as when graduating from a college or university.* Me ka hoʻomaikaʻi. *With high ~.* Me ka hoʻomaikaʻi nui. *See distinction.*

hood *As of a car or truck.* Pani ʻenekini (*preceded by ke*). *As an exhaust ~ above a stove.* Kaupokupoku omo, kaupokupoku.

hoof Maiʻao.

Hoʻohokuikalani *Daughter of Wākea and Papa.* Hoʻohokuikalani.

hook *As for hanging things.* Lou. *Clothes ~.* Lou kau lole.

hook pass *In basketball; to throw such a pass.* Kīloi ʻaoʻao. *See hook shot.*

hook shot *In basketball; to make such a shot.* Kī piʻo. *See hook pass, lob pass.*

hopper Kānuku. *~ car, as on a train.* Kaʻa kānuku.

horizontal Papamoe. *See grow, vertical. To grow ~ly, as in a computer program.* Ulu papamoe.

horizontal line *~s written above and below a word or words to indicate that they should be written or printed straight, in proofreading.* Kaha hoʻolālani.

hormone Hōmona. *See endocrine system. Rooting ~.* Hōmona hoʻāʻa.

horn *A musical instrument.* Pū hoʻokani. *As on a car or bicycle.* ʻŌlea, ʻōlē. *See Hawaiian entries under pū and great horned owl.*

horror Hoʻokauweli. *~ movie.* Kiʻiʻoniʻoni hoʻokauweli. *~ story.* Moʻolelo hoʻokauweli.

horse *Rocking ~.* Lio paipai. *See brumby.*

horticulture Kālaikanu. *Horticulturist.* Mea kālaikanu.

host *As of a parasite.* Kauomolia. *See parasite.*

hot dog Naʻaukake ʻAmelika.

hot key *As on computer keyboard.* Pihi wiki (*preceded by ke*). *~s.* Nā pihi wiki.

hot plate Kapuahi papakau. *See burner.*

hot spot *In geology.* Piko pele.

hour Hola. *Abb.* hl. ~ *hand.* Lima kuhikuhi hola.
household product *Any of a variety of products used for cleaning floors, sinks, etc.* Lāʻau hoʻomaʻemaʻe hale.
housing development *Also subdivision.* Kaiahale.
how *Also what, as in asking about any kind of measurement.* ʻEhia, he aha. ~ *many to each, to a group.* Pāhia.
Hubble Hāpela. ~ *space telescope.* Ka ʻohenānā lewa lipo ʻo Hāpela.
hull See *port, starboard.*
hum *To ~ a tune.* Nūnū.
Humane Society ʻAhahui Makaʻala Holoholona.
human immunodeficiency virus HIV. Mū hōlapu pale ʻea pau. See *AIDS.*
humidity Kawaūea. See *hygrometer.* Relative ~. Pā kawaūea.
hummingbird Manu hū.
humorous Hoʻomakeʻaka. ~ *book.* Puke hoʻomakeʻaka.
humpback whale Koholā kuapiʻo.
humus ʻElepopo.
hundred Haneli. See entries below and *centi-, hecto-.*
hundreds *Place value, in math.* Kūana haneli.
hundreths Hapa haneli.
hung *To be ~, as network system in computer program.* Pupū.
Hungary *Also Hungarian.* Hunakalia, Hunagaria.
hunting spider *No-eyed big-eyed ~.* Nananana maka ʻole, nanana maka ʻole.
hurricane Makani pāhili. ~ *watch.* Kūkala makaʻala makani pāhili. ~ *warning.* Kūkala pōʻino makani pāhili.
hydrant See *fire hydrant.*
hydrochloric Haidorokoloriku. ~ *acid.* ʻAkika haidorokoloriku.
hydrocortisone Kokikone wai. See *cortisone.*

hydroelectric *Also hydroelectricity.* Uila wai kahe. See *electricity.* ~ *power.* Ikehu uila wai kahe.
hydrogen Haikokene. ~ *peroxide* (H_2O_2). Haikokene lua ʻokikene lua. See *peroxide.*
hydrology Kālaiwai. *Hydrologist.* Kanaka kālaiwai, mea kālaiwai.
hydrolysis Ka hoʻokāwaihia ʻana.
hydrolyze Hoʻokāwaihia. See *hydrolysis.*
hydrometer Ana kaumaha wai. See *hygrometer.*
hydroponics *The growing of plants in a nutrient solution.* Kāmāhuaola. *Hydroponic solution.* Māʻōʻāna kāmāhuaola. *To grow hydroponically in water.* Hoʻoulu kāmāhuaola wai. *In sand.* Hoʻoulu kāmāhuaola one. *In vermiculite.* Hoʻoulu kāmāhuaola hunehune ʻūpī.
hydrosphere Waiapuni.
hygrometer Ana kawaūea. See *hydro- meter, psychrometer. Wet-and-dry bulb ~.* Ana kawaūea ʻōpuʻu pulu a maloʻo.
hygroscopic Kīpuni. ~ *water.* Wai kīpuni.
Hyperion *A moon of Saturn.* Haipeliona.
hypertension *Abnormally high arterial blood pressure.* Pākela koko piʻi.
hyphen *Also to hyphenate.* Kaha moe. See *dash.*
hypodermic needle Kui mōpina.
hypotenuse Lala kūpono.
hypothesis Kuhiakau.

I

Iapetus *A moon of Saturn.* Iapetusa.
I-bar *Also cursor or insertion point in computer program.* Kahaʻimo. See *mouse arrow.*
ibis *A flightless bird in prehistoric Hawaiʻi.* Manu ʻīpiki.
-ic *Suffix in chemical compounds and terms.* -iku.

Māmaka Kaiao / 238

ice age Au paʻahau.
iceberg Mokuhaulana.
icecap ʻOmohau.
ice cream ʻAikalima. ~ *cone.* Kone ʻaikalima. ~ *topping.* Pāhina.
ice skate Kāmaʻa holo hau. *To skate with ~s.* Holo hau.
icicle Kuluna hau, kulu hau paʻa.
icon *As in computer program.* Kiʻiona.
icosahedron *A space figure with twenty faces, in math.* Paʻaʻili iwakālua.
Idaho *Also Idahoan.* ʻIkahō.
-ide *Suffix in chemical compounds and terms.* -side.
idea *Main ~ or thought, as of a paragraph or story.* Manaʻo nui. *Supporting ~, as in a composition.* Manaʻo kākoʻo. *To sequence ~s, as in a composition.* Hoʻokaʻina manaʻo.
identical ʻĀlike. ~ *parts.* Nā hapa ʻālike.
igneous rock *Rock formed by the solidification of molten magma.* Pōhaku pelemaka.
ignorance *To feign ~.* Hoʻohūpō, hoʻopalō.
iguana ʻIkuana.
illegal *To outlaw, make something ~.* Pāpā kānāwai. *See entries below.*
illegal alien *Also to arrive as an ~.* Pae malū. *See legal alien.*
illegal screen *In basketball.* ʻĀkeʻa neʻe. *See blocking foul.*
Illinois *Also Illinoisan.* ʻIlinoe.
illusion *Magic trick, sleight of hand.* Pāhaʻohuna. *Optical ~.* Kuhi hewa o ka maka.
image *In math.* Kinona like. *Turn ~.* Kinona like wili. *Half-turn ~.* Kinona like wili hapalua. *Quarter-turn ~.* Kinona like wili hapahā. *Reflection ~.* Kinona aka like o kekahi ʻaoʻao. *Rotation ~.* Kinona like o kekahi ʻaoʻao. *Translation ~.* Kinona like kau.
imagery *See guided imagery.*
imaginary Moeā. *See imagine.* ~ *line.* Laina moeā.

imagination *Creative ~; also to use one's ~.* Makakū. *See imagine.*
imagine *To ~ oneself to be something or someone.* Moeā. *To ~ deliberately.* Hoʻomoeā. *See imaginary.*
imitation Hoʻopilipili. ~ *milk.* Waiū hoʻopilipili.
immersion *See medium.*
immigrate Komoneʻe. *See emigrate.*
immune system *As in mammals.* ʻŌnaehana pale ʻea. *See AIDS, HIV.*
impact *Environmental ~ Statement (EIS).* Palapala Hōʻike Hopena Kaiapuni.
impatiens ʻŌlepe.
impeach *To formally accuse (a public official) of misconduct in office.* Hoʻāhewa.
imply Hoʻohuʻu. *See infer.*
import *To ~, also as in a computer program.* Kākomo. *See export.*
impregnate *Also to breed.* Hoʻopiʻi.
impression *General appearance or ~.* Hiʻona. *See feature.*
improper *In math.* Lapa. ~ *fraction.* Hakina lapa.
improve Holomua. *Suggested ~ments.* He mau manaʻo e holomua ai ka hana.
imu *To set an ~.* Kuʻi i ka imu. *To open an ~.* Huaʻi i ka imu.
inappropriate ʻAʻohe launa. *See incompatible.*
inbound pass *In basketball; to throw such a pass.* Kīloi ulele.
incandescent light Kukui ʻuiki ʻā. *See filament.*
inch ʻIniha. *Abb.* ʻīn.
incidence *Angle of ~, i.e. the angle made between a wave striking a barrier and the normal to the surface.* Huina papā. *See angle of reflection.*
included Komo pū. *Tax ~.* ʻAuhau komo pū.
incompatible *As of computer programs.* Launa ʻole. *See compatible, inappropriate.*

increase *Greatest ~, in math.* Piʻi kiʻekiʻe loa. See *decrease*.

incubate *To hatch (eggs).* Hoʻomoe.

incubator *For eggs.* Mīkini hoʻomoe hua.

indent *To ~, as the first line of a paragraph on a typewriter or computer.* Kīpoʻo. See *tab*.

independent variable Kumuloli kūʻokoʻa. See *dependent variable*.

index Papa kuhikuhi kikoʻī. See *table of contents*. *~ card.* Kāleka pahu. *~ finger.* Manamana kuhikuhi, manamana miki.

India *Also Indian, i.e. referring to India and its peoples.* ʻInia. See entry below.

Indiana *Also Indianian.* ʻInikiana, ʻInidiana.

Indian Ocean Moana ʻIniana. See *India*.

indicator *Also to indicate.* Kuhikuhi. *Ninhydrin ~.* Ninahaidirina kuhikuhi.

indigenous *Native.* ʻŌiwi. *~ plant.* Meakanu ʻōiwi.

indigo bunting Manu ʻinikō.

Indo- ʻInio-. See entry below.

Indo-Australian ʻInionūhōlani. *~-Plate.* Ka Una Honua ʻInionūhōlani.

Indonesia *Also Indonesian.* ʻInidonesia.

indoor Maluhale. *~ concert.* ʻAha mele maluhale. *~ market.* Mākeke maluhale. *~ sport.* Haʻuki maluhale.

inductive reasoning *Generalizing from examples, as in math.* Hoʻoholo pili laʻana.

industrialize Hōʻoiʻenehana.

industry *Especially that with a highly technological structure of production or service; industrialized.* ʻOiʻenehana. See *technology*. *Construction ~.* ʻOiʻenehana kūkulu. *Manufacturing ~.* ʻOihana kāpili, ʻoiʻenehana kāpili. *Service ~.* ʻOihana lawelawe.

inequality *In math.* Kaulike ʻole. *~ statement.* ʻŌlelo no ke kaulike ʻole.

inertia Ehuō.

infection *Also infected.* Palahēhē.

infer Huʻu. See *imply*.

infield *Baseball diamond.* Kahua kaimana pōhili. See *baseball field*.

infiltrate *To pass through by filtering or permeating, in science.* Kānono.

infinity *In math.* Pau ʻole.

infix Pākuʻina kau loko. See *affix*.

inflammable *Also inflammability.* Pēʻāhia. See *flammable*.

inflate *To fill with air.* Hoʻopūhalalū, puhi a piha.

informal Pōnolu.

information ʻIke. See *header information*. *~ book.* Puke kumuhana.

initial Hua inoa. See *abbreviation, signature*. *To ~.* Pūlima hua.

initialize *To format, as a computer disk.* Hoʻāla. See *disk*.

initiate Hoʻokomo pae. See *initiation*.

initiation *Passage, as into a group.* Komo pae. See *initiate*. *Rite of passage.* Hana komo pae.

inning Pale. *Baseball ~.* Pale pōhili.

input *As in computer program.* Huakomo. See *output*. *~ device.* Hāmeʻa huakomo. *To ~.* Kāhuakomo. *To ~ data.* Kāhuakomo ʻikepili.

insect *Also bug.* ʻElala. *~ mounting; also to mount ~s.* Pine ʻelala. *~ net.* ʻUpena ʻelala. *~ bag net.* ʻUpena ʻelala ʻeke. *~ fixed net.* ʻUpena ʻelala hoʻolewalewa. *~ sweep net.* ʻUpena ʻelala kāʻeʻe. *~ holding jar.* ʻŌmole mālama ʻelala. *~ killing jar.* ʻŌmole pepehi ʻelala. *~ sucker.* Mea omo ʻelala.

insecticide See *aldrin, dieldrin, systemic insecticide*.

insectivore *Also insectivorous.* Hamu ʻelala.

insert *To put in, as disk into computer.* Hoʻokomo.

insert *Caret (^), an editing mark used to show where something is to be ~ed, in proofreading.* Kaha hoʻokomo. *A circle around a period, colon, or semicolon to show that it has been ~ed.* Lina hoʻokomo. See *pound sign*.

insertion point *Also cursor or I-bar in computer program.* Kahaʻimo. See *mouse arrow.*

inside out Lolea. See *upside down.*

install *To ~, as computer software; also to load, as a program onto a computer.* Hoʻouka. See *download.*

instinctive behavior Lawena ʻike hānau. See *learned behavior.*

instrument *As a specialized tool for a particular occupation.* Mauhaʻa. See entry below and *apparatus, device, tool. Any musical ~, but esp. string ~s.* Pila. *Brass ~.* Pū keleawe. *Woodwind ~.* Pū ʻoʻohe.

instrument *A prefix indicating the ~ or cause of a particular action.* ʻŪ-. *Bonding ~.* ʻŪlou. See *bond.*

insulate Hōʻīpale. See *insulation.*

insulation ʻĪpale. See *insulate.*

insurance ʻInikua. *~ premium.* Uku ʻinikua. *Medical ~.* ʻInikua olakino. See *medical coverage number.*

integer *Whole number, in math.* Helu piha. *Positive ~.* Helu piha ʻiʻo. *Negative ~.* Helu piha ʻiʻo ʻole.

integrate *To incorporate (parts) into a whole.* Hoʻononiakahi. *Integrated.* Noniakahi.

integumentary system *In biology.* ʻŌnaehana ʻili.

intentional *To commit an ~ foul, in team sports such as basketball.* Hoʻokuʻia ahuwale. See *foul.*

interactive *As computer programs.* Kūkaʻipā.

intercept *To ~ (the ball), in football.* ʻApo lilo. See *receive.*

intercommunication *Also two-way communication.* Kaʻaʻike pānaʻi.

interdependence *Also interdependent.* Kūkaukaʻi.

interest *On principal, as a charge for borrowing money.* Uku paneʻe. See *principal. Rate of ~.* Pākēneka uku paneʻe.

integrated *As computer software.* Huikuʻi.

interim release *Also maintenance release, as of a computer program.* Hoʻopuka hoʻoponopono ʻia. See *update.*

intermediate directions *On a compass, in geography.* Nā kūkulu o waena. See *primary directions.*

intermediate level Pae waena.

intermission Hoʻomaha. See *halftime.*

internal Kūloko. See *external. ~ drive, as on a computer.* Kakena kūloko. *~ memorandum, as in telecommunication.* Memo kūloko.

international Kauʻāina. *~ date line.* Laina helu lā.

interrogate Ninaninau. See *interview, questionnaire.*

intersect *As lines on a grid, in math.* Hui. See *intersection. The intersection of two or more lines, all of which go through the intersection point; to ~ thus.* Hui kaupeʻa. *The intersection of two lines wherin one or both lines do not continue beyond the point of intersection; to ~ thus.* Hui poʻo. *~ing lines.* Nā kaha huina.

intersection *An ~ of two lines on a grid, in math.* Huina keʻa, huina. See *dot.*

intertropical convergent zone *ITCZ.* Kāʻei kuʻina kopikala. *Abb.* KKK.

interval *The number of units between spaces on a graph's scale, in math.* Wā.

interview Nīnauele. See *interrogate.*

intonation Kiʻina leo.

intricate Lāliʻi.

introduce *To ~, as plants and animals to a particular place.* Lawekahiki. See *borrow. Introduced.* Lawekahiki ʻia, malihini.

introduction *As in a book.* ʻŌlelo hoʻākāka. See *foreword, preamble.*

introductory level *Also beginning level.* Pae hoʻomaka.

invent Hoʻohakuhia. *~ed.* Hakuhia.

inventory Moʻolako.

inverse *In math.* Huli hope. *~ operation.* Hana hoʻomākalakala huli hope.
invertebrate Iwikuamoʻo ʻole. See *vertebrate.* *~ animal.* Holoholona iwikuamoʻo ʻole.
invest Hoʻopukapuka. *~ment.* Mea hoʻopukapuka kālā, hoʻopukapuka.
investigation *Also to investigate, in math.* Noiʻi.
invisible Kūnalohia. See *visible.*
inward Haʻaloko.
iodide ʻIodiside. *Potassium ~.* Potasiuma ʻiodiside.
iodine ʻIokine.
iodize Hōʻiokine.
ion ʻIona.
Iowa *Also Iowan.* ʻAioā, ʻIoa.
Iran *Also Iranian.* ʻIlana, ʻIrana.
Iraq *Also Iraqi.* ʻIlaka, ʻIraka.
Ireland *Also Irish.* ʻIlelani, ʻIrelani. See *Irish.*
iris *Also fleur-de-lis.* Puapalani.
Irish ʻAiliki. See *Ireland.*
iron *The element.* Meki.
ironwood Paina luhe, paina.
irrational number *In math.* Helu puʻunaue koena. See *rational number.*
irregular *As in shape.* Laukua. See *regular.* *~ shape.* Kinona laukua.
irrigate Hoʻokahe wai.
island *Aleutian ~s.* Ka Paeʻāina ʻo ʻAleuta. *Kure ~.* Kānemilohaʻi. *Laysan ~.* Kauō. *Lisianski ~.* Papaʻāpoho. *Midway ~.* Pihemanu. *Necker ~.* Mokumanamana. *Palmyra ~.* Honuaiākea.
island arc Pae moku hoaka.
-ism *A suffix meaning devotion or adherence to something; in Hawaiian, a prefix meaning to laud, encourage.* Paʻi-. See *capitalism.*
isosceles *In math.* ʻElua ʻaoʻao like. *~ triangle.* Huinakolu ʻelua ʻaoʻao like.
isostacy *The equilibrium of the earth's crust, in geology.* Mīkā anakonu. See *equilibrium.*
Israel *Also Israeli.* ʻIseraʻela.

italic Hiō, hua hiō.
italicize Hoʻohiō.
Italy *Also Italian.* ʻĪkālia, ʻĪtālia.
ITCZ *Intertropical convergent zone.* Kāʻei kuʻina kopikala. *Abb.* KKK.
-ite *Suffix in chemical compounds and terms.* -hite.
item *Also entry, object.* ʻIkamu.
Ivory Coast *Also Ivorian.* Kapa Kai Palaoa.
ivy Lau hihi pā, ʻaiwi.

J

jab *To ~ with fingertips, in volleyball.* Koʻu.
jabong *A type of citrus.* Iāpona. See *pomelo.*
jacket Lākeke. See *blouse.*
jackfruit ʻAnanaka.
jack-in-the-box Keakapahu.
jack-in-the-pulpit *A kind of flower.* Keakaikaʻāwai.
jack-oʻ-lantern Palaʻai heleuī, pū heleuī.
jacks *The game.* Kimo. *A jack.* Hōkūkimo.
jade *Also jadeite.* Pounamu. *~ plant.* Nukukikiwi.
jalousie Pukaaniani ʻōlepe, pukaaniani ʻōlepelepe.
jam Kele pahē.
Jamaica *Also Jamaican.* Iāmaika, Iāmeka.
January Ianuali. *Abb.* Ian.
jar ʻŌmole. *Battery ~.* ʻŌmole iho uila. *Dustfall ~, as for scientific experiments.* ʻŌmole ʻapo hunahuna. *Gallon ~ or jug.* ʻŌmole kālani. *Insect holding ~.* ʻŌmole mālama ʻelala. *Insect killing ~.* ʻŌmole pepehi ʻelala.
jay See *blue jay.*
jelly bean Pāpapa kele.
jellyfish Pololia.
Jersey See *New Jersey.*
jess *A leg strap for falcons.* ʻIli kalapu wāwae.

jet Hēkī. ~ *airplane.* Mokulele hēkī. ~ *stream.* Au makani kikī.
Jew's harp Nī'aukani.
jewelry Lako kāhiko, lako hoʻonani.
jigsaw puzzle Nane ʻāpana.
jobs *As for movie or video production.* Nā māhele hana. See *call sheet.*
jog *Also jogging.* Holo peki.
join *A curved line (or lines) linking two letters or words to indicate that the letters or words should be ~ed, in proofreading.* Kaha hoʻokuʻi.
Jordan *Also Jordanian.* Ioredāne.
joule *A unit of energy.* Kule *Giga~.* Kule pāpiliona.
journal *Also diary.* Puke moʻomanaʻo.
journalism ʻOihana haʻilono.
Jovian *In astronomy.* Iowiana. ~ *planet.* Hōkūhele Iowiana.
judicial branch *As of a government.* Māhele ʻaha hoʻokolokolo. See *branch.*
judo Kulo. See *sidewinder serve.*
jug See *gallon jar.*
juggle Hoʻoleialewa.
July Iulai. *Abb.* Iul.
jumble *To mix up the order.* Hoʻokake kaʻina.
jump *Vertical ~.* Lele haʻaluna. ~ *rope.* Kaula lele. *To ~ rope.* Lele kaula. *Running under the rope.* Luʻu nalu poʻi. See *high jump, long jump, rock the boat.*
jump ball *In basketball.* Lele paʻi.
jump shot *In basketball; to make such a shot.* Kī lele.
junco *A kind of bird.* Kunuko, manu kunuko.
June Iune. *Abb.* Iun.
jungle gym *A kind of playground equipment.* Hao pīnana. See *monkey bars.*
juniper Iunipela.
Jupiter *The planet.* Kaʻāwela.
jurisdiction *Appellate ~, a court's authority to hear an appeal of a decision made by another court.* Mana hoʻokolokolo. See *appeal.*

just *Fair, equitable, balanced.* Kaulike.
justified *As type in printing.* Kaulihi. See *justify. Left ~.* Kaulihi hema. *Right ~.* Kaulihi ʻākau. *Full ~.* Kaulihi like. *Two vertical lines written to the left of lines of print to indicate that the left margin should be ~, in proofreading.* Kaha hoʻokaulihi.
justify *To ~, as type in printing.* Hoʻokaulihi. See *center, justified. To center ~.* Hoʻokauwaena. *To full ~.* Hoʻokaulihi like. *To left ~.* Hoʻokaulihi hema. *To right ~.* Hoʻokaulihi ʻākau.

K

K *Kilobyte, in computer terminology.* PK (ʻai pākaukani).
kamaboko *Fish cake.* Kamapoko.
Kamehameha butterfly Pulelehua Kamehameha.
Kansas *Also Kansan.* Kanesasa.
kayak Waʻa kaiaka.
Kelvin Kelewine. *Zero degrees K (Kelvin); absolute zero, a hypothetical temperature characterized by complete absence of heat.* ʻOle Kelewine.
kennel *A crate for transporting animals.* Pene halihali. *A shelter for a dog.* Pene ʻīlio. *An establishment for boarding or breeding dogs.* Hale mālama ʻīlio.
Kentucky *Also Kentuckian.* Kenekuke, Kenetuke.
Kenya *Also Kenyan.* Kenia.
key *In music.* Kī. See entries below and *note, pitch.*
key *Dichotomous ~.* ʻĀmana koho.
key *Also keyhole, as on a basketball court.* Pukakī. *Side line of the ~.* Laina iwi kī. *Top of the ~.* Uma kī, uma, pōheo.

Māmaka Kaiao

key *As on typewriter or computer keyboard.* Pihi *(preceded by* ke*). See Hawaiian entries under* pihi *and* escape, memory, option, tab, space bar, *etc. Name of* ~. Inoa o ke pihi. *Arrow* ~. Pihi nahau. *Caps lock* ~. Pihi laka maʻaka, pihi laka, laka maʻaka. *Control* ~. Pihi hoʻoholo. *Hot* ~s. Nā pihi wiki. *Return* ~. Pihi kāhoʻi. *Shift* ~. Pihi kake.
keyboard *As on a typewriter or computer.* Papa pihi. *Computer* ~. Papa pihi kamepiula. ~ *layout.* ʻŌkuene papa pihi. ~ *mapping.* Kaʻakuene papa pihi.
key caps *On computer program.* Hōʻike hua pihi.
key code *The order to press keys on a calculator to find an answer.* Pāʻalua kaʻina hana.
keyhole *Also key, as on a basketball court.* Pukakī.
kidney Hakuʻala.
kill *In volleyball.* Kinipōpō hele wale.
killing *Insect* ~ *jar.* ʻŌmole pepehi ʻelala.
kilo- *A prefix meaning thousand (k).* Pākaukani. *Abb.* pk. *See entries below and* deca-, hecto-, mega-, giga-, tera-.
kilo Kilo. *Abb.* kl.
kilobyte *K, in computer terminology.* ʻAi pākaukani. *Abb.* PK. *See* byte.
kilocalorie Ikehuʻā pākaukani. *Abb.* ikpk
kilogram Kilokalame. *Abb.* klkal.
kiloliter Kilolika. *Abb.* kll.
kilometer Kilomika. *Abb.* klm.
kilowatt Kilouate. *Abb.* klt. *See* watt.
king's guard Pūʻali kiaʻi mōʻī.
kingdom *In Egyptology.* Au Palaʻo. *Old* ~ *(2780-2080 BC).* Au Palaʻo Kūkahiko. *Middle* ~ *(2133-1780 BC).* Au Palaʻo Kūwaena. *New* ~ *(1574-1085 BC).* Au Palaʻo Kūhou.
kingfisher Pakūkaʻā.
King Kong finch *Chloridops regiskongi.* Nuku ʻekue.
Kingman Reef Koʻanakoʻa.

kit *First aid* ~. Kini lapaʻau, poho lāʻau pōulia. *Repair* ~ *for tires.* Kini poho ea.
kit *As of equipment needed for a particular activity.* Hōkeo. *Standard soil-testing* ~. Hōkeo kūmau hoʻāʻo lepo.
kitchen Lumi kuke.
kiwi fruit Huaʻai kiwi, lahomāpū.
knapsack *Backpack.* Pāiki hāʻawe, pāisi hāʻawe, ʻawe.
knife *See* putty knife.
knit Kā pāaniani. *See* yarn.
knob Pōheo, pōheoheo. *Door*~. Pōheo puka, pōheoheo puka. *Drawer* ~. Pōheo ʻume.
knot Hīpuʻu. *See* bow.
Komephoros *A star.* Lukuʻāina.
Korea *Also Korean.* Kōlea, Kōrea. *North* ~. Kōlea ʻĀkau, Kōrea ʻĀkau. *South* ~. Kōlea Hema, Kōrea Hema.
kumquat Kamakūaka.
Kure island Kānemilohaʻi.
Kuwait *Also Kuwaiti.* Kuete.
kw *Kilowatt.* Klt (kilouate). *See* watt.

L

la *The sixth note on the musical scale.* Lā.
label *Tag; also to* ~. Lepili. *Food* ~, *as for giving product information on a package of food.* Lepili māhuaola.
labial *In linguistics.* Lehelehe.
labor *To contract* ~. Kepa.
laboratory Keʻena hoʻokolohua.
labroides Phthirophegus *Cleaner wrasse, a kind of fish.* Hīnālea nāʻuke.
lacquer Waniki.
ladle Puna kīʻoʻe, puna ukuhi. *To* ~, *scoop.* Kīʻoʻe, ʻoʻe. *See* skim.
ladybug Ponumomi.
lake *Also large pond.* Māluawai.
laminate Lamineka.
lamp *Standing* ~. Kukui kū, kukui kū hale. *Table* ~. Kukui kū pākaukau. ~*shade.* Pale kukui.
lamp *Heating* ~. Kukui hoʻomehana.
land *To* ~, *as an airplane or bird.* Kuʻu.

land *Private ~.* 'Alokio, 'alodio. *Public ~.* 'Āina no ka lehulehu. *Department of ~ and Natural Resources (DLNR).* 'Oihana Kumuwaiwai 'Āina.
land court 'Aha ho'onā 'āina. See *land registration system, settle.*
land feature *As mountains, valleys, etc., in geography.* Hi'ona 'āina. See *water feature.*
landing *Staircase ~.* Paepae alapi'i.
land registration system 'Ōnaehana ho'onā 'āina. See *land court, settle.*
landscape Hi'onaina. See *feature.* *To ~, as a yard.* Kāhi'onaina.
landscape orientation *As of page in computer program.* Kuana moe. See *portrait orientation.*
landslide *Also avalanche.* 'Āholo.
land use See *State Land Use Commission.*
land use *In geography.* Ho'ohana 'āina. *State ~ Commission.* Komikina Ho'ohana 'Āina o ka Moku'āina.
lane *As on a highway or in a bowling alley.* Ala.
language See *sign language.*
language arts Mākau 'ōlelo.
lantern *Hanging ~, as Japanese type.* Kukui lākene.
Laos *Also Laotian.* Laosa.
lap *Complete circuit.* Puni. *To run or take a ~.* Holo puni.
La Pérouse Rock Kuamanō.
laptop computer Kamepiula lawelima, lolouila lawelima.
larder beetle *Dermestid.* Ponu 'ili.
large *As shirt or drink size.* Nui. See *small, medium.* *~ soda.* Koloaka nui. *Extra ~ (XL), as shirt size.* Nui keu. *Double-extra ~ (XXL).* Nui keu pālua. *Triple-extra ~ (XXXL).* Nui keu pākolu.
lark Manu lāke.
larva Piohē. *Of damselfly and other dragonflies.* Lohaloha, lohelohe.
larvae See *post-larvae.*

laryngopharynx *The lower part of the pharynx adjacent to the larynx, in anatomy.* Haka moni o lalo. See *pharynx.*
larynx Kani'ā'ī, paipu hanu o luna. See *epiglottis, trachea.*
laser Wana'ā. *~ beam.* Kukuna wana'ā.
latch *Sliding ~.* Laka uai.
late *As registration for a conference.* Hiki hope. *~ registration.* Kāinoa hiki hope.
lateral *In linguistics.* Lālelo.
lateral line *A linear series of sensory pores and tubes along the side of a fish, in biology.* Kahana lonoa.
latex Lekesa.
Latin America *Also Latin American, Central America, Central American.* 'Amelika Waena.
latitude Lakikū, latitū. See *longitude, parallel.*
laud *A prefix meaning to ~, encourage; -ism, a suffix in English meaning devotion or adherence to something.* Pai-. See *capitalism.*
launch *Also to cause to blast off.* Ho'ōlapa. See *lift off.* *~ pad.* Kahua ho'ōlapa.
lava cricket 'Ūhini nēnē pele.
lava lizard Mo'o pōhaku pele.
lava tube Ana kahe pele.
lavender *Both flower and plant.* Poni'ala.
law Kānāwai. *To break the ~.* Ha'iha'i kānāwai, a'e kānāwai. See *outlaw.* *Boyle's ~, i.e. decreasing the volume of a gas will increase the pressure the gas exerts if the temperature remains constant.* Ke kānāwai a Poila. *Charles' ~, i.e. the volume of a gas increases as its temperature increases if the pressure remains constant.* Ke kānāwai a Kale. *Civil ~.* Kānāwai kīwila, kānāwai sīwila. *Common ~.* Kānāwai kumu.
lawn *To mow the ~.* 'Oki i ka mau'u, 'oki i ka mahiki. See *grass.*
lax *As articulation in linguistics.* 'Alu. *~ vowel.* Woela 'alu. See *tense, vowel.*

lay away *To accumulate, store away.* Hoʻāhu.
layer *As of skin or tissue beneath the skin.* Papa. See *vegetation layer*.
layout *As of a computer keyboard.* ʻŌkuene. *Keyboard ~.* ʻŌkuene papa pihi. See *keyboard mapping*.
Laysan finch *Telespiza cantanc.* ʻAinohu Kauō.
Laysan island Kauō.
lay-up *In basketball; to make such a shot.* Kī kīkoʻo, kī pai.
LDEF *Long Duration Exposure Facility, a kind of experimentation satellite placed in orbit by a space shuttle.* Poelele hoʻokolohua wā loa.
leach *To ~, the action of liquid percolating through layers of soil thus removing nutrients from the soil.* Heʻeaholo. *To ~, subject to the action of percolating liquid.* Hoʻoheʻeaholo.
lead *Also leaden.* Kēpau.
leading question Nīnau pākākā.
lead pass *In basketball; to throw such a pass.* Kīloi ulele kikī, kīloi kaha. See *fast break*.
leaf Lau. *Newly opened ~.* Liko. *Bud of a ~.* Muʻo. *Node, where a ~ is connected to the stem.* Piko. *Base of a ~, as* hala. Poʻo (*preceded by* ke).
leaf miner Mū pao lau.
league *In sports.* Kuʻikahi. See *conference. American Baseball ~.* Kuʻikahi Pōhili ʻAmelika. *National Baseball ~.* Kuʻikahi Pōhili Aupuni. *National Football ~ (NFL).* Kuʻikahi Pōpeku Aupuni.
lean *As meat.* Pākā. *Extra ~.* Pākā loa.
lean-to shelter Hale kāpiʻo.
learned behavior Lawena ʻapo. See *instinctive behavior*.
learning center Kaunoʻo.
learning environment See *environment*.
leash Kaula kaʻi.
least common denominator *In math.* Kinopiha haʻahaʻa loa.

leave as is *To make no change, as in computer program.* Waiho.
Lebanon *Also Lebanese.* Lepanona, Lebanona.
left guard *In football.* Kūkahi hema.
left justified *As type in printing.* Kaulihi hema.
left margin Lihi hema. See *justify, margin*.
left tackle *In football.* Kūlua hema. See *tackle*.
leg *Chair ~.* Wāwae noho. *Table ~.* Wāwae pākaukau.
legal Kū kānāwai. See *entries below*.
legal alien *Also to arrive as a ~.* Pae kānāwai. See *illegal alien*.
legal-size paper Pepa loio. See *letter-size paper, tabloid paper*.
legislative *~ branch, as of a government.* Māhele ʻahaʻōlelo. See *branch. ~ powers.* Mana kau kānāwai.
legislative powers Mana kau kānāwai.
legume Lekeuma.
lemonade Wai lemi.
lemur Lāmia.
lend *Not to borrow.* ʻAe. See *sample sentence under Hawaiian entry* ʻae *and borrow, loan. To ~, as money lent at interest.* Hoʻolako ʻaiʻē.
length *In math.* Lōʻihi. *Abb.* lō. *Also* ana lōʻihi; loa (*no abb.*), ana loa. See *lengthwise, height, width*.
length *Of a wave, wave~.* Kōā, kōā nalu, kōā ʻale. See *height, wave*.
lengthwise Lau loa.
lens *As for a camera or microscope.* Aniani kaulona. *Concave ~.* Aniani kaulona ʻeʻele. *Convex ~.* Aniani kaulona ʻeʻemu. *Water ~, in geology.* Papa wai kau luna.
lentil Lenekila.
leptospirosis Lepopiloki.
lesson *A catalog listing or sequence of lessons of a curriculum.* Moʻohaʻawina.
less than *In math.* Emi iho, ʻoi aku ke emi. See *greater than*.

let *To assign a value or power, as in math problems.* Hoʻāmana.
letter *Of the alphabet.* Huapalapala. *See case sensitive, correspondence. Lower case (small) ~.* Hua naʻinaʻi. *Upper case (capital) ~.* Hua maʻaka. *Cover ~.* Leka wehewehe.
letterhead Poʻo kuni *(preceded by* ke*). ~ design.* Lau poʻo kuni.
letter-size paper Pepa leka. *See legal-size paper, tabloid paper.*
leukemia Lūkīmia.
level *Of difficulty; also stage of development.* Pae. *See sea level. Novice ~.* Pae ʻakahi akahi. *Beginning or introductory ~.* Pae hoʻomaka. *Intermediate ~.* Pae waena. *Advanced ~.* Pae holomua.
level *Carpenter's ~.* ʻIliwai.
Liberia *Also Liberian.* Lipelia, Liberia.
liberty *Also freedom.* Kūnoa, kūkāʻokoʻa. *Statue of ~.* Kūkāʻokoʻa Kiahoʻomanaʻo, ke kiahoʻomanaʻo ʻo Kūkāʻokoʻa, Kūkāʻokoʻa.
Libra *A constellation.* Iloano.
Libya *Also Libyan.* Libia.
lichen *General term.* Nahi.
lid *As for jar; also cap, as for toothpaste tube.* Pani *(preceded by* ke*).*
life cycle Pōʻaiapuni ola.
lifesaving skills Mākau hoʻopakele ola.
life span Kāwā ola.
lift *To ~ or make a double hit, in volleyball.* Hāpai. *See carrying violation. As a ski ~.* Noho piʻi mauna.
lift-off *As of a rocket or missile; also blast off.* ʻŌlapa. *See launch.*
lift weights Amo hao, hāpai hao.
light Kukui, kuikui. *~ bulb.* ʻŌpuʻukukui. *~ switch.* Kuiki kukui, pana kukui. *Filament in ~ bulb.* ʻUiki ʻā. *Incandescent ~.* Kukui ʻuiki ʻā. *Fluorescent ~.* Kukui hāweo. *~ controls, as for stage productions.* Une kukui. *Traffic ~.* Kukui hoʻokū.

light *To ~, as a set for a movie or video production.* Hoʻomālamalama. *~ing director.* Luna hoʻomālamalama.
light *Speed of ~.* Māmā kukuna lā, māmā holo o ke kukuna lā. *~ year.* Makahiki holo kukuna lā.
light *Coherent ~, i.e. light in which all the waves vibrate in a single plane, with the crests and troughs all aligned.* Mālamalama aukahi.
Liliʻu ʻukulele ʻUkulele Liliʻu.
lima bean Pāpapa laima.
lime Laimi.
limit *Grow ~, as in a computer program.* Palena ulu. *See grow.*
limousine Kaʻa limo.
line *In math.* Kaha, kaha laina, laina. *See entries below. Imaginary ~.* Laina moeā. *~ segment.* ʻĀpana kaha. *Number ~.* Laina helu. *Intersecting ~s.* Nā kaha huina. *Parallel ~s.* Nā kaha pilipā. *Perpendicular ~s.* Nā kaha kūpono. *Sight ~.* Laina ʻike. *Skew ~.* Laina pāweo. *~ graph.* Pakuhi lākiō. *~ of symmetry.* Kaha ʻālikelike.
line *As on basketball court or in sports.* Laina. *Base or end ~.* Laina hīnaʻi, laina hupa, laina kumu, laina poʻo. *Half-court ~.* Laina kūwaena. *Side ~.* Laina iwi, laina ʻaoʻao. *Free throw ~.* Laina kī noa. *Defensive ~, in football.* Laina kūpale, laina pale. *Offensive ~.* Laina kūlele. *Scrimmage ~.* Laina hoʻouka. *Over the ~, in volleyball.* Kaʻahi hewa, keʻehi hewa. *Three-meter ~.* Laina ʻekolu mika. *Ten-foot ~.* Laina ʻumi kapuaʻi. *Starting ~, as in a race.* Laina pahukū. *Finish ~.* Laina pahuhope.
line *Lateral ~, a linear series of sensory pores and tubes along the side of a fish, in biology.* Kahana lonoa. *Safety ~, as in a spacecraft.* Kaula piko.
linear equation Haʻihelu lālani.
linear function *In math.* Hahaina lālani.
linear scale *In geography.* Pālākiō lālani.

linebacker *Defensive ~, in football.* Mahikua.
line note *In music.* Huamele laina. See *musical note.*
line of sight *Also sight line.* Laina lena, laina ʻike.
line out *To strike through, as on a typewriter or computer; also used to indicate that the letters or words lined out are to be deleted and replaced by those written above, in proofreading.* Kahawaena. *A series of dots written under a word or words which have been lined out to show that no change should be made from the original; stet.* Kaha waiho.
liner *Eye ~.* Mahaka maka.
line spike *In volleyball.* Hili laina. See *spike.*
line up *To ~ vertically.* Hoʻokolamu.
linguistics Kālaiʻōlelo.
link *To ~, as in computer program.* Loulou. *File ~.* Loulou waihona. *Data ~.* Loulou ʻikepili. *A curved line (or lines) ~ing two letters or words to indicate that the letters or words should be joined, in proofreading.* Kaha hoʻokuʻi.
linoleum *Also linoleum flooring.* Linoleuma, moena ʻili. See *floor tile.*
lion *Sea ~.* Liona kai.
lipliner Peni pena waha, peni pena lehelehe. See *lipstick.*
lipstick Pena waha, pena lehelehe. See *lipliner. To put on ~.* Hana i ka pena waha.
liquid Kinowai.
Lisianski island Papaʻāpoho.
list Papa. *~ of computer commands.* Papa kauoha kamepiula. *Mailing ~.* Papa helu wahi.
list editor screen *In computer program.* Pukaaniani kolamu ʻikepili.
litchi *Also lychee.* Laikī.
liter Lika. *Abb.* l.

literature *General term.* Moʻokalaleo. See *tale. Creation ~.* Moʻokalaleo kumu honua. *Oral ~.* Moʻokalaleo haʻi waha. *Traditional ~.* Moʻokalaleo kuʻuna. *Written ~.* Moʻokalaleo palapala.
lithified Paʻa pōhaku.
lithium Likiuma.
lithograph Kiʻi māio.
litmus paper *For measuring pH.* Pepa ana ʻakika.
little finger Manamana iki, manamana liʻiliʻi.
liver fluke Koʻelau ake.
living room Lumi hoʻokipa.
lizard *Lava ~.* Moʻo pōhaku pele.
load *To install, as programs onto a computer.* Hoʻouka. See *download.*
loafer *Slip-on style shoe.* Kāmaʻa pohopū.
loam ʻElemakua.
loan *As money lent at interest; also to have a ~.* Lako ʻaiʻē, ʻaiʻē. See *lend, borrow.*
lobar bronchus *Also secondary bronchus, in anatomy.* ʻĀmanapuʻu kualua.
lobe *Ear ~.* Lepepepeiao.
lob pass *In basketball; to throw such a pass.* Kīloi piʻo. See *hook shot.*
lobster *Maine ~.* ʻŌmā. *Slipper ~.* Ula pāpapa, ula ʻāpapapa.
location *Absolute ~, in geography.* Kuhikuhina. *Relative ~.* Pilina henua.
lock *Also to ~.* Laka. *See entries below. Combination ~.* Laka helu. *Combination, as for a ~.* Helu laka.
lock *Caps ~, as on typewriter or computer keyboard.* Laka maʻaka. *Caps ~ key.* Pihi maʻaka, pihi laka (*preceded by* ke).
locker Waihona pāiki, pahu laka.
locket Pihipoho (*preceded by* ke).
locust *Honey ~ bean.* Pāpapa ʻūhinihone.

logic *Also logical.* Kūpili. *~ error, as message on calculator display that shows an operation is not logical.* Hewa kūpili. *~al thinking.* Noʻonoʻo kūpili.

log in See *log on.*

logo Lōkō.

log off *Or to log out, as of a network or other computer system.* Lele. See *log on.*

log on *Or to log in, as of a network or other computer system.* ʻEʻe. See *log off.*

log out See *log off.*

lollipop *Also sucker.* Kanakē ʻau, kō omōmo.

long Loa. See *length.*

long bean *A common Filipino dish.* Pāpapa loloa.

Long Duration Exposure Facility *LDEF, a kind of experimentation satellite placed in orbit by a space shuttle.* Poelele hoʻokolohua wā loa.

longitude Lonikū, lonitū. See *latitude.*

long jump *Standing ~.* Lele loloa. *Running ~.* Holo a lele loloa.

long-range *Also long-term.* Hikiāloa. See *short-range, medium-range. ~ plan.* Papa hoʻolālā hikiāloa.

long-term See *long-range.*

lookout *Scenic viewpoint.* ʻImaka.

lose Eo, hāʻule. See *Hawaiian entries.*

loss Kumulilo. See *profit.*

lottery Pili helu laki.

lotus Kalo Pākē, līkao.

Louisiana *Also Louisianan, Louisianian.* Luikiana, Luisiana.

lousewort Pekikulali.

lower case *Small.* Naʻinaʻi. See *letter. To change (a letter of the alphabet) from capital to ~.* Hoʻonaʻinaʻi. See *capitalize. A line drawn diagonally through a capital letter to indicate that the letter is to be written in ~, in proofreading.* Kaha hoʻonaʻinaʻi.

lowest *~ terms of a fraction, in math.* Palena haʻahaʻa loa. *~-terms fraction.* Hakina palena haʻahaʻa loa.

low-fat food Meaʻai ʻailakele iki, meaʻai liʻiliʻi o ka ʻailakele. See *high-fat food.*

low post *In basketball.* Kūliu loko. See *high post.*

low pressure system *In meteorology.* ʻŌnaehana mīkā emi. See *high pressure system.*

lowrise *As a building.* Nuʻuhaʻa. See *highrise.*

low vowel *In linguistics.* Woela haʻahaʻa. See *vowel.*

lumber Papa. *Four-by-four ~.* Papa hā hā. *Two-by-four ~.* Papa lua hā.

lunar rover Kaʻa holo mahina.

lunch pail Kini ʻaiō, kini ʻai.

lychee *Also litchi.* Laikī.

lye ʻĀkililehu.

lymph ʻAnapuʻu. See *lymphoma. ~ gland or node.* Lōkuʻu ʻanapuʻu.

lymphoma Maʻi ʻaʻai ʻanapuʻu.

Lyra *A constellation.* Kehoʻoea.

M

macaroni Makaloni.

machine See *Hawaiian entries under* mīkini. *Compound ~.* Kaumīkini.

macro- Mānui. See entries below.

macro *As in computer program.* Kōmi ʻōkuhi.

macronutrient Māhuaola mānui. See *micronutrient.*

Madagascar *Also Madagascan.* Madagaseka.

magazine Makakina, makasina.

magenta ʻUla mākuʻe.

maggot Ilo. *Onion ~.* Ilo ʻakaʻakai.

magic *As supernatural or enchanted.* Hoʻokalakupua. *~ trick, illusion, sleight of hand.* Pāhaʻohuna.

magma Pelemaka. *~ chamber.* Nupa pelemaka.

magnesium Makanekiuma.

magnet Mākēneki.

magnetism 'Ume mākēneki.
magnifying glass *Hand lens.* Aniani ho'onui 'ike.
mahogany *The wood.* Mahakonia.
maidenhair fern 'Iwa'iwa.
mail See entries below and *air mail, E-mail.*
mailing list Papa helu wahi.
mail merge *As in computer program.* Ho'oku'i helu wahi.
main clause *In grammar.* Pepeke haku.
main dictionary *As in computer program.* Papa hua'ōlelo kūmau. See *user dictionary.*
Maine Maine, Meine. ~ *lobster.* 'Ōmā.
main idea *Also main thought, as of a paragraph or story.* Mana'o nui.
main menu *As in computer program.* Papa kuhikuhi kahua pa'a.
maintenance release *Also interim release, as of a computer program.* Ho'opuka ho'oponopono 'ia. See *update.*
major *As an academic field of specialization.* Mēkia. See *minor.*
makeup Pena maka. *To put on* ~. Ho'ou'iu'i, ho'onaninani, pena maka. ~ *artist, as for a play, movie or video production.* Mea pena maka.
malaria Malaria. *Avian* ~. Malaria manu.
malathion Malationa.
Malawi *Also Malawian.* Malaui.
Malaysia *Also Malaysian.* Malaisia.
males *Hatred of* ~; *misandry.* Ho'okae kāne. See *misanthropy, misogyny.*
Mali *Also Malian.* Māli.
mall *Shopping center.* Kikowaena kū'ai.
mallee bird *Of Australia.* Mālī, manu mālī.
mammal Holoholona 'ai waiū, māmela.
mammoth *Woolly* ~. 'Elepani pūhuluhulu.

management *Fish and game* ~; *also to manage fish and game.* Ho'omalu lawai'a a me ka hahai holoholona.
manager Manakia. *Product* ~. Luna huahana. *Production* ~, *as for a movie or video production.* Manakia 'enehana.
maneuvering engine *As for a spacecraft.* 'Enekini kīkaha.
Maneuvering Unit *Manned* ~, *as for a space flight.* Ahikao hā'awe.
manganese Manakanika.
mangrove Kukunaokalā.
manhole cover *As for a sewer.* Pani paipu lawe 'ino. See *sewer pipe.*
maniacal delirium Ma'i hehena.
manipulator arm *Remote* ~, *space crane.* Lima kia pihi.
mankind *Hatred of* ~; *misanthropy.* Ho'okae kanaka. See *misandry, misogyny.*
man-made topographical feature Hi'ona na ke kanaka. *See Hawaiian entries* hi'ona wai, hi'ona 'āina.
Manned Maneuvering Unit *As for a space flight.* Ahikao hā'awe.
manned space flight Lele lewa lipo kanaka.
mannequin Kanaka 'ea.
man offense *Offense for attacking face defense, in basketball.* Kūlele alo.
mantis *Praying* ~. 'Ūhinipule.
mantle *Earth's* ~. 'Ahu honua. See *core, crust.*
man-to-man defense *As in basketball; to execute such a play.* Pale alo.
manual *Teacher's* ~ *or guide.* Puke alaka'i.
manufacture Hana kāpili. See entry below and *build. manufacturer.* Hui hana kāpili, kanaka hana kāpili.
manufacturing industry 'Oihana kāpili, 'oi'enehana kāpili.
many See *how many, multi-.*

map *Rainfall ~.* Palapala ʻāina ua. *Site ~.* Palapala ʻāina kahua. *To field ~ a site.* Kaha palapala ʻāina. *Space ~.* Palapala lewa lipo. *Thematic ~.* Palapala ʻāina kumuhana. *Topographic ~.* Palapala hiʻona ʻāina.

map *To ~, as a computer keyboard.* Kaʻakuene. *Keyboard ~ping.* Kaʻakuene papa pihi.

maple Mēpala.

marathon Malakona.

March Malaki. *Abb.* Mal.

margarine *Also oleomargarine.* Makalina.

margin *As on printed page.* Lihi. *Left ~.* Lihi hema. *Right ~.* Lihi ʻākau. *Top ~.* Lihi o luna. *Bottom ~.* Lihi o lalo. *To set the ~s.* Hoʻopaʻa i nā lihi. *Two vertical lines written to the left of lines of print to indicate that the left ~ should be justified, in proofreading.* Kaha hoʻokaulihi.

marguerite *Daisy.* Makalike.

maria *A crater-free plain on the surface of the moon.* Maria.

marine Kai. *Fish or any ~ animal.* Iʻa, iʻa kai. See *fish.* *~ sediment.* Koʻana kai.

marine corps Pūʻali hoʻouka kaua.

Marineris Malineli. *Valles ~, a valley on Mars.* Ke awāwa ʻo Malineli.

marionette Pāpeka kaula, pāpeta kaula.

market *Indoor ~.* Mākeke maluhale. *Outdoor ~.* Mākeke kaupokulani. *To ~ something, i.e. to make available and promote the sale of a product.* Hokona. *~ value.* Waiwai kūʻai.

markup *As in the price of an article.* Pākēneka hoʻopiʻi.

marmot *Also groundhog.* Māmota.

Maro Reef Nalukākala.

marquisette *A kind of curtain.* Pākū makaliʻi.

Mars *The planet.* Hōkūʻulapīnaʻau, Hōkūʻula.

marsh *With salt or brackish water and no trees.* Ālialia. See *bog, swamp.* *Fresh-water ~.* Ālialia wai maoli.

Marshall Islands *Also Marshallese.* Mākala, Mākala ʻAilana, Pae Moku Mākala.

marshmallow Mahamelo, masamelo.

marsh pen Peni kuni.

marshy Nenelu.

Maryland *Also Marylander.* Melelana, Merelana.

mascara Pena lihilihi maka. *To put on ~.* Hana i ka pena lihilihi maka.

mask *Diving goggles.* Makaaniani luʻu kai, makaaniani luʻu. *Gas ~, as used during World War II.* Pūnuku ea make.

masking tape *Freezer tape.* Leki pahu.

mass *Bulk.* Nuipaʻa. *Air ~.* Ahu ea. *Atomic ~.* Nuipaʻa ʻātoma. See *atomic mass.*

Massachusetts Makakukeka, Masakuseta.

master See *props master.*

master bedroom Lumi moe haku.

master copy *Also original, a master used for making additional copies.* Kope kumu.

match *To ~, as in game of concentration.* Hoʻolikelike. *As one thing to its counterpart by drawing a line.* Hoʻopili.

matching *Identical.* ʻĀlike.

material *Cloth. See entry below.* ʻIālole. *Bolt of ~.* ʻĀpā lole.

material *A general term but not relating to cloth.* Makelia, memea. *Raw ~.* Makelia kūlohelohe, memea kūlohelohe.

math sentence *Also number sentence.* Hopunahelu. See *mental math.*

matter *Physical substance.* Meakino.

mattress *Also bed.* Pela, pela moe. *Air ~.* Pela hoʻolana. *~ cover.* ʻEke pela (*preceded by* ke).

Maui *Name of the island.* Maui. See entries below.

Māui *Name of the demigod.* Māui. See *Maui.*

Maui greensword ʻĀhinahina ʻōmaʻomaʻo.

Maui parrotbill *Pseudonestor xanthophrys.* Kīkēkoa.
Mauritania *Also Mauritanian.* Mauritania.
maximum Palena nui. See *minimum. The ~ weight.* Ka palena nui o ke kaumaha.
May Mei. *No abbreviation.*
mayonnaise Meoneki.
maytansine *A chemical compound once investigated for therapeutic uses but later found to be too toxic for human use.* Maikeni.
meadow *Also grassy field.* Kula mauʻu.
mealworm Ane koʻe.
mealy bug Ane ʻuku.
mean *In math.* ʻAwelike.
measles ʻUlāliʻi.
measure *To ~ depth, as in the ocean.* Hoʻopapā hohonu. See entries below and *accent unit.*
measurement *Also used when referring to dimensions.* Ana. See *height, length, width; how, what, measure. Unit of ~.* Anakahi. *Metric unit of ~.* Anakahi mekalika. *US standard or customary unit of ~.* Anakahi ʻAmelika.
measuring cup Kīʻaha ana. See *cup.*
meat meal ʻIʻo wiliwili. See *bonemeal.*
mechanical *Also mechanics.* Kūmikini. *~ engineer.* ʻEnekinia mīkini.
mechanism *Apparatus or device, ordinarily including some mechanical part or parts.* Maomeka. See *device, instrument, tool. Balancing ~, in biology.* ʻŌnaehana hoʻokauapono.
medaka *Mosquito fish.* Iʻa makika.
media *As radio, TV, etc.* Pāpaho.
median Kūwaena. *~ number, in math.* Helu kūwaena.
medical *~ insurance.* ʻInikua olakino. *~ coverage number.* Helu ʻinikua olakino.

medication *Also drug.* Lāʻau. *Prescription ~.* Lāʻau kuhikuhi. *Prescription for ~ or drug.* Kuhikuhi lāʻau. *Over-the-counter ~.* Lāʻau kūʻai wale.
medicine *Also medication, medicinal drug.* Lāʻau. *~ cabinet.* Waihona lāʻau lapaʻau.
medium *A means of affecting or conveying something.* Kaiapuni. See entries below. *Hawaiian ~ class.* Papa kaiapuni Hawaiʻi. *Hawaiian ~ school.* Kula kaiapuni Hawaiʻi.
medium *As drink size.* Lōpū. *Abb.* lō. See *small, large, medium shot. ~ heat.* Wela lōpū. *~ soda.* Koloaka lōpū.
medium heat Wela lōpū.
medium-range *Also medium-term.* Hikiālōpū. See *short-range, long-range. ~ plan.* Papa hoʻolālā hikiālōpū.
medium rare *As meat.* Hapa moʻa, moʻa hapa.
medium shot *As of a photograph or in movie or video production.* Paʻi lōpū (*preceded by* ke). See *close-up, wide shot. To take a ~.* Paʻi a lōpū.
medium-term See *medium-range.*
Meeker burner Kapuahi Mika. See *burner.*
meeting See *convergent.*
Meg *Megabyte, in computer terminology.* PM (ʻai pāmiliona).
mega- *A prefix meaning million (M).* Pāmiliona. *Abb.* pm. See entry below and *deca-, hecto-, kilo-, giga-, tera-.*
megabyte *In computer terminology.* ʻAi pāmiliona. *Abb.* PM. See *byte.*
Megalagrion spp See *damselfly.*
mejiro Manu peleita.
melodeon Melokiana.
melody *Also tune.* Leo, ʻea. *One who sings the ~ of a song.* Leo alakaʻi.
melon Meleni, ipu. See *cantaloupe.*
melt Heheʻe. See *melting point.*
melting point Kēkelē heheʻe. See *boiling point, freezing point.*

member *As of an organization.* Lālā. *Board ~s.* Nā lālā o ka papa.
membrane Niniki.
memo *Or note for conveying a message to someone; message.* Memo. See *memorandum, note.*
memorandum *Also memo.* Memo. *Internal ~, as in telecommunication.* Memo kūloko.
memory *As in a computer program.* Waihona ʻike. *Built-in ~.* Waihona ʻike paʻaloko. *Expanded ~.* Waihona ʻike māhuahua. *Extended ~.* Waihona ʻike keu. *Virtual ~.* Hope waihona ʻike. *~ key, as on calculator keyboard.* Pihi hoʻomanaʻo (*preceded by* ke).
mental math Helu naʻau, makemakika naʻau.
menu *As in computer program.* Papa kuhikuhi. *Main ~.* Papa kuhikuhi kahua paʻa. *Pop-up ~.* Papa ʻōʻili. *~ bar.* Papa koho.
merchandise Mea kūʻai.
mercury *The metallic element in chemistry.* Melekulia. *The planet.* Ukalialiʻi.
merge *To ~, as in computer program.* Hoʻokuʻi pū. *Mail ~.* Hoʻokuʻi helu wahi.
meridian *Prime ~, in geography.* Kumu lonikū, kumu lonitū.
mesophilic *Midtemperature-loving.* Ola mehana. See *thermophilic.* *~ bacteria.* Koʻohune ola mehana.
message *A memo or note for conveying a ~ to someone.* Memo. See *note.*
metabolism Pūnao.
metal Mekala, metala. See *alkali metal, alkaline earth metal, alloy.*
metamorphosis Kūaloli. *Morphological ~.* Kūaloli kino.
metathesis *Transposition of letters, syllables or sounds in a word.* Panoko.
meteor Koli.
meteorology Kālaianilā. See *wind.*

meter *The unit of measurement.* Mika. *Abb.* m. See *metric. In music.* Lauana wā.
meter *An instrument that automatically measures and registers quantity.* Mīka. *~ box.* Pahu mīka. *Parking ~.* Mīka kāki. *~ed parking or any parking for which there is a charge.* Kū kāki.
methane Mēkene, mētene.
methanol Metanola.
method *Also technique.* Kiʻina hana, kiʻina. *Sampling ~s.* Nā kiʻina ʻohi hāpana.
methyl Meto.
metric Mekalika. *~ unit of measure.* Anakahi mekalika. *~ system.* ʻŌnaehana mekalika. *~ conversion chart.* Pakuhi hoʻololi makalika.
Mexico *Also Mexican.* Mekiko. *New ~.* Nūmekiko.
mi *The third note on the musical scale.* Lī.
Miaplacidus *A star in the constellation Carina.* Makawela.
Michigan *Also Michigander, Michiganite.* Mikikana.
micro- *A prefix meaning one millionth (u).* Hapa miliona. *Abb.* hml. See entries below and *deci-, centi-, milli-, nano-, pico-.*
microbiology Kālaimeaolahune. See *biology.*
microclimate Aniau hāiki.
microgram Māikikalame.
microgravity ʻUmekaumaha māiki. See *gravity.*
micron *0.0001 centimeter.* Maikolona.
micronutrient Māhuaola māiki. See *macronutrient.*
microorganism Meaola māiki.
microphone Ipuleo, mea hoʻolele leo.
microscope ʻOhe hoʻonui ʻike. *~ slide.* Aniani kaupaneʻe, *usu.* aniani. *~ stage.* Paepae aniani kaupaneʻe.
microscopic Māiki.

microsecond *In math.* Hapa miliona kekona.
microwave oven ʻOmawawe.
middle *Used only in special terminology.* Kūwaena. See entries below and *dermis, new, old.* ~ *Kingdom, in Egyptology.* Au Palaʻo Kūwaena.
Middle East *Also Middle Eastern.* Hikina Waena.
middle finger Manamana loa, manamana waena.
midge fly Nalo wiʻu.
midocean Waena moana. ~ *ridge.* Kualapa waena moana.
midpoint *In math.* Kiko kauwaena.
Midway island Pihemanu.
migrate *Also migration, migratory.* Neʻekau.
mild *As a solution.* ʻŪpalu.
mile Mile. *Abb.* mil. ~*s per hour.* Mile o ka hola. *Abb.* mil/hl.
military base Kahua pūʻali koa.
military service *Also army.* Pūʻali koa.
military transport aircraft Mokulele hali koa.
militia Pūʻali koa kūikawā.
milk Waiū. See *dairy product. Imitation* ~. Waiū hoʻopilipili. *Skim* ~. Waiū heʻe. *Whole* ~. Waiū piha. ~ *carton.* Pahu waiū. ~ *shake.* Waiū luliluli. *Residue of* ~ *after beating.* Kale ʻai.
milk *Powdered* ~. Waiū ehu, waiū pauka.
milli- *A prefix meaning one thousandth (m).* Hapa kaukani. *Abb.* hkk. *Also* mili-. See entries below and *deci-, centi-, micro-, nano-, pico-.*
milligram Milikalame. *Abb.* mkal.
milliliter Mililika. *Abb.* ml.
millimeter Milimika. *Abb.* mm.
million See *mega-, micro-.*
millisecond *In math.* Hapa kaukani kekona.
Mimas *A moon very near to Saturn.* Mima.

mineral Minelala, minerala.
mineral water *Also sparkling water.* Wai piʻipiʻi.
minimum Palena iki. See *maximum.* *The* ~ *weight.* Ka palena iki o ke kaumaha.
Minnesota *Also Minnesotan.* Minekoka.
minor *As a* ~ *academic field of study.* Māina. See *major.*
Mintaka *A star.* Kaʻawili.
minus Lawe. ~ *sign.* Kaha hoʻolawe.
minute *Time.* Minuke. *Abb.* min. *Revolutions per* ~ *(rpm).* Puni o ka minuke. *Abb.* p/min. ~ *hand.* Lima kuhikuhi minuke.
Mira *A star.* Lanihou.
Mirach *A star.* Kōkoʻolua.
Mirphack *A star.* Hānaipono.
mirror Aniani, aniani nānā, aniani kilohi, aniani kilo. *Bicycle* ~. Aniani kilohi paikikala, aniani kilo paikikala, aniani paikikala. *Concave* ~. Aniani ʻeʻele. *Convex* ~. Aniani ʻeʻemu. *Full-length* ~. Aniani kū. *Hand* ~. Aniani paʻa lima, aniani lima. *Rear-view* ~ *for car.* Aniani kilohi kaʻa, aniani kaʻa. *Small* ~ *to keep in purse.* Aniani pāiki, aniani liʻiliʻi.
misandry *Hatred of males.* Hoʻokae kāne. See *misanthropy, misogyny.*
misanthropy *Hatred of mankind.* Hoʻokae kanaka. See *misandry, misogyny.*
misogyny *Hatred of women.* Hoʻokae wahine. See *misandry, misanthropy.*
missile Kao lele. ~ *bomb.* Kao lele pahū.
mission *As in the* ~ *statement of an organization.* Ala nuʻukia. See *vision.* ~ *statement.* ʻŌlelo ala nuʻukia.
Mississippi *Also Mississippian.* Mikikipi, Misisipi.
Missouri *Also Missourian.* Mikouli, Misouri.

misspelled word *A circle around a ~ with the letters* ph *(pela hewa) written above the word, in proofreading.* Kaha pela hewa.
mitogen *Any substance or agent that stimulates mitotic cell division.* Mikokene.
mitt *Baseball glove.* Mikilima pōhili.
mix *To ~ or dilute, as a drink.* Pa'ipa'i. See *dilute.*
mixed *Also combined, in math and science.* 'Ō'ā. See *alloy, whole number. Chemically combined.* 'Ō'ā kemikala 'ia. *~ decimal.* Kekimala 'ō'ā. *~ number.* Helu 'ō'ā.
mixture *Also combination.* Huihuina.
mix up *To jumble the order.* Ho'okake ka'ina.
mobility *In geography.* Pēne'e.
mochi Mōchī. *~ rice.* Laiki mōchī, lāisi mōchī.
mode *As the number(s) that occur most often in a set, in math.* Lauika. *As in computer program.* Pē'ano. *~ of transportation.* Alakau.
model *Example, as of behavior.* Kumu ho'ohālike. *Usually miniature.* Kūkohu. *~ boat.* Kūkohu moku. *To ~, i.e. to mold or shape, as clay.* Hō'omo'omo. See *clay.*
modem Mōkema.
moderator *As of a panel.* Luna ho'omalu.
modern Kaila hou.
modernize *To ~ a written document using modern spelling and punctuation standards.* Hō'ano hou. See *adapt.*
modulation See *amplitude modulation, frequency modulation.*
moist *Damp or ~ with fog or dew, wet from cold.* Kawaū.
mold Punahelu. *To ~, i.e. model or shape as clay.* Hō'omo'omo.
molding *As around windows or doors.* Mōlina. See *frame.*
mole *The animal.* Mio'awi.
molecule Lātoma. See *structure.*

mollusk Hakuika.
molly I'a moli.
molt *To ~, as a crab its shell.* Ho'omalule. *As a snake its skin.* Māunu.
molybdate Molaibadahate. *Ammonium ~.* 'Amoniuma molaibadahate.
molybdenum Molaibedenuma.
monarch butterfly Pulelehua pua kalaunu.
Monday Po'akahi. *Abb.* P1.
monetary denomination Kūana kālā.
money Kālā. *~ order.* Pila 'oka kālā. *To draw ~ from the bank.* Kīko'o.
Mongolia *Also Mongolian.* Monokolia, Monogolia.
monitor *As for a computer or in movie or video production.* Pahu papakaumaka. See *screen. Computer ~.* Pahu papakaumaka kamepiula. *TV ~.* Pahu papakaumaka kīwī.
monkey *Owl ~.* Keko pueo. *Rhesus ~.* Keko lekuka.
monkey bars *A kind of playground equipment.* Hao keko. See *jungle gym.*
monkfish Mōnekakai.
monk seal *Hawaiian ~.* Sila Hawai'i.
monocotyledon Lau 'īnana kahi. See *cotyledon.*
monofilament Aho 'ea.
monolith Pōhakukūkahi.
monotheism *Also monotheistic.* Akua kahi. See *polytheism.*
monoxide Monokesaside. *Carbon ~.* Karabona monokesaside.
monstera Lā'ape.
Montana *Also Montanan.* Monakana, Monekana.
montane area Wao kuahiwi. *Lower ~.* Wao kuahiwi ha'aha'a. *Upper ~.* Wao kuahiwi ki'eki'e. *Vegetation area at base of mountain.* Wao kumu kuahiwi.
month Mahina, māhina. *Abb.* mhn.
monument Kiaho'omana'o. *National ~.* Pāka kiaho'omana'o aupuni.
mood *As in music.* Au.
moose 'Ēleka.

Māmaka Kaiao / 255

mop *Also to ~.* Māpa. *~ head.* Hulu māpa.
moraine Puʻu neʻena hau.
Morocco *Also Moroccan.* Moloko, Moroko.
morphine Mōpine.
morphological metamorphosis Kūaloli kino.
mosquito fish *Medaka.* Iʻa makika.
mosquito netting Pākū makika.
moss *General term.* Mākōpiʻi. *See sphagnum. Peat ~.* Mākōpiʻi ʻelenahu.
moth *Geometrid ~.* ʻŌʻaki.
mothball Pōpō pale mū.
motion *Brownian ~, in chemistry.* Lelekē Palaunu.
mount *To ~ insects; also insect ~ing.* Pine ʻelala.
mount *Slide ~.* Mōlina kiʻiaka. *See entries below.*
mountain *~ range.* Pae kuahiwi. *~ pass.* Nuku. *Volcanic ~.* Kuapele. *See montane, passageway, seamount.*
mountain beaver Peawa kuahiwi.
mountain bike Paikikala holo kuahiwi.
Mount Everest Mauna ʻEweleka.
Mount Olympus Mauna ʻOlumepika.
Mount Saint Helens Mauna Kana Helena, Mauna Sana Helena.
mouse ʻIole. *Deer ~.* ʻIole kia. *White-footed ~.* ʻIole wāwae kea.
mouse *As for a computer.* ʻIole. *~ arrow; also pointer or cursor.* Nahau ʻiole, nahau.
moustache ʻUmiʻumi lehelehe. *See beard.*
mouth *River ~.* *See estuary.*
move *A circle around a word or words with an arrow going from the words to the place where they are to be ~d, in proofreading.* Kaha hoʻoneʻe. *As in a sports play.* ʻOnina. *To ~, as files in computer program.* Hoʻoneʻe.
movement Neʻena. *Video camera ~.* Neʻena pahu paʻi wikiō. *Film ~, as in a movie or video camera.* Holo lola.

movements *As in dancing.* Kiʻina. *Hand ~.* Kiʻina lima. *Foot ~.* Kiʻina wāwae.
movie Kiʻiʻoniʻoni. *See entry below and movie studio. ~ projector.* Mīkini hoʻolele kiʻiʻoniʻoni, mīkini kiʻiʻoniʻoni. *~ screen.* Pākū hoʻolele kiʻi. *To shoot a ~ film.* Paʻi kiʻiʻoniʻoni *(preceded by* ke*).*
movie studio *The building where movies are made.* Hale hana kiʻiʻoniʻoni. *The company responsible for making movies.* Keʻena hana kiʻiʻoniʻoni.
mow *To ~ the lawn.* ʻOki i ka mauʻu, ʻoki i ka mahiki.
Mozambique *Also Mozambican.* Mozamabika.
mud ʻŪkele, lepo pohō. *Pond ~.* Pohō. *~ guard.* Pale lepo. *Bicycle ~ guard.* Pale lepo paikikala.
muffin Māpina. *Bran ~.* Māpina pelene.
muffler *As on a car.* Kini paipu ahi. *See exhaust pipe.*
multi- *Also many.* Lau-. *~engined spaceships.* Nā moku ahikao lauʻenekini.
multiple *In math.* Helu māhua, māhua. *Common ~.* Helu māhua like, māhua like. *Least common ~.* Helu māhua haʻahaʻa loa, māhua haʻahaʻa loa.
multiple-choice Kohokoho, pane kohokoho. *~ question.* Nīnau kohokoho. *~ book.* Puke pane kohokoho.
multiplication *In math.* Hoʻonui. *~ sign.* Kaha hoʻonui. *~ tables.* Papa ʻālualua. *Zero property of ~.* ʻAnopili ʻole o ka hoʻonui.
multiply Hoʻonui.
mumps Pēheu.
mung bean Pāpapa munukō.
municipal *Note that in Hawaiʻi most things are county rather than municipal.* Kiwikā. *~ golf course.* Kahua pāʻani kolepa kiwikā. *~ watershed.* ʻĀina kumu wai kiwikā.
muscle Mākala. *Abdominal ~s.* Mākala ʻōpū.
muscular system *In biology.* ʻŌnaehana mākala.

mush *Hawaiian-style ~, made of flour and water.* Palaoa lūlū.
mushroom Melehune, kūkaelio. *Puffball, a kind of ~.* Melehune pōpōehu.
mushy *As rice cooked with too much water.* Palahē.
music Puolo. *See entries below.* *~ box.* Pohokuikilani. *To arrange ~; also ~ arranger.* Kūkulu puolo.
musical note Huamele. See *line note.*
musical scale Alapiʻi mele, pākōlī. *See Hawaiian entries.*
musical staff Kōkua huamele, koʻokoʻo, kumu ʻākōlī.
musician *General term.* Mea puolo. *Particularly one who plays Hawaiian music.* Mea hoʻokani pila.
musicology Kālaipuolo. *Ethno~.* Kālaipuolo lāhui. *Musicologist.* Mea kālaipuolo, kanaka kālaipuolo.
musk-ox Pipi ʻĀlika.
mustang Makekana, masetana.
mustard Masakeke.
musubi *Rice ball.* Musubī, pōpō laiki, pōpō lāisi.
mutate See *mutation.*
mutation *Also to mutate.* ʻĀhuli.
mystery *As stories or movies.* Pōliu. *~ novel.* Nōwela pōliu.

N

name *As of file in computer program.* Inoa. See *document.* *~ of key.* Inoa o ke pihi.
Namibia *Also Namibian.* Namibia.
nano- *A prefix meaning one billionth (n).* Hapa piliona. *Abb.* hpl. See *deci-, centi-, milli-, micro-, pico-.*
narcissus Kuikina. See *daffodil.*
narcotic drug Lāʻau ʻona.
narrate *To ~ orally, as in a speech.* Kūhahaʻi. See *narrative speech.*
narration *As in movie or video production.* Moʻolelo haʻi waha. *Traditional elements of Hawaiian poetry, story telling, oratory and ~.* Meiwi.

narrative speech Haʻiʻōlelo kūhahaʻi. See *speech.*
NARS *Natural Areas Reserves System.* ʻŌnaehana Hoʻomalu ʻĀina Kūlohelohe.
nasal *In linguistics.* Manā. *~ cavity.* Haka ihu.
nasopharynx *The portion of the pharynx behind the nasal cavity and above the soft palate, in anatomy.* Haka moni o luna. See *pharynx.*
nation *Also country.* Kaumokuʻāina.
national Aupuni, kaumokuʻāina. See entries below and *federal.* *~ organization.* ʻAhahui kaumokuʻāina. *~ monument.* Pāka kiahoʻomanaʻo aupuni.
National Baseball League Kuʻikahi Pōhili Aupuni.
National Football Conference *NFC.* Hui Pōpeku Aupuni.
National Football League *NFL.* Kuʻikahi Pōpeku Aupuni.
national park Pāka aupuni. *See entry below. Glacier National Park.* Pāka Aupuni ʻo Hauneneʻe. *Hawaiʻi Volcanoes ~.* Pāka Aupuni ʻo Kīlauea. *Yosemite National Park.* Pāka Aupuni ʻo ʻIosemite.
National Park Service ʻOihana Pāka Aupuni.
native *Indigenous.* ʻŌiwi. *~ bird.* Manu ʻōiwi.
natural *Lacking human intervention or contamination.* Kūlohelohe. See entries below and *nature, raw.* *~ biological community.* Kaiameaola kūlohelohe. *~ food.* Meaʻai kūlohelohe. *~ force.* Manehu kūlohelohe. *~ resource.* Kumuwaiwai kūlohelohe.
Natural Areas Reserves System *NARS.* ʻŌnaehana Hoʻomalu ʻĀina Kūlohelohe.
naturalist Puni ao kūlohelohe, kanaka puni ao kūlohelohe.
naturally occurring *~ weak acid.* ʻAkika ʻūpalu kūlohelohe.

natural resources *Department of Land and ~ (DLNR).* ʻOihana Kumuwaiwai ʻĀina.
natural vegetation Lau nahele ʻōiwi.
nature Ao kūlohelohe. See *natural.* *~ reserve.* ʻĀina hoʻomalu ao kūlohelohe.
Navaho *Also Navajo.* Nawahō.
navy Pūʻali kaua moana, ʻau moku kaua, ʻoihana moku. *~ base.* Kahua pūʻali kaua moana.
Nazca Naseka. *~ Plate.* Ka Una Honua Naseka.
near *Close.* Kokoke.
Nebraska *Also Nebraskan.* Nepalaka, Nebaraka.
neck *As of ʻukulele, guitar, etc.* ʻAu. See *ʻukulele.*
Necker Island Mokumanamana.
neck stretches *A warm-up exercise for sports such as volleyball; also to do this exercise.* Hoʻomālō ʻāʻī.
necktie Lei ʻāʻī, lei ʻāʻī kalawake, lei kalawake. See *bow tie, cravat.*
nectar *Sweet liquid secreted by nectaries of a plant.* Wai pua.
needle *Hypodermic ~.* Kui mōpina.
negative *Photo ~.* Akakiʻi.
negative *As of electrical charge or south pole of a magnet.* ʻIne. See *electron, neutral, positive.* *~ number, in math.* Helu ʻiʻo ʻole. *~ integer.* Helu piha ʻiʻo ʻole.
neighbor *Not necessarily next door.* Hoa kaiahome. See *neighborhood.*
neighborhood Kaiahome.
nematode Koʻe ʻelemuku.
neon Nīane.
Nepal *Also Nepalese.* Nepala.
Neptune Nepekune.
nerve Aʻalolo.
nervous system ʻŌnaehana lolokū.
nest Pūnana. *To ~.* Hoʻopūnana. *~ing season.* Kau hoʻopūnana.

net ʻUpena. *See entry below.* *Hem of ~.* Pelu ʻupena. *Insect ~.* ʻUpena ʻelala. *Insect bag ~.* ʻUpena ʻelala ʻeke. *Insect fixed ~.* ʻUpena ʻelala hoʻolewalewa. *Insect sweep ~.* ʻUpena ʻelala kāʻeʻe.
net *As of a basket on basketball court, or a volleyball ~.* ʻUpena. *Basketball ~.* Hīnaʻi. *Into the ~, in volleyball.* Kala. *~ ball.* Ua ʻupena ke kinipōpō. *~ violation.* ʻAʻena ʻupena. *Volleyball ~.* ʻUpena pōpaʻipaʻi.
Netherlands *The ~; also Netherlander, Netherlandian.* Nekelana.
netting *Mosquito ~.* Pākū makika.
network Pūnaewele. *~ controller or administrator, as for computers.* Kahu pūnaewele. *~ server, as for computer ~.* Kikowaena pūnaewele. *~ station.* Poʻopoʻo pūnaewele. *~ system.* ʻŌnaehana pūnaewele.
neutral *As particles in an atom.* Hohoki. See *charge, positive, negative, neutron.* *~ electric charge.* Ikehu uila hohoki, ikehu hohoki. *As neither base nor acid on a pH scale.* Kūpapa.
neutron Huna hohoki. See *proton, electron.*
Nevada *Also Nevadan.* Newaka, Newada.
new *Brand ~.* Hou loa. *Used only in special terminology.* Kūhou. See *middle, old.* *~ Kingdom, in Egyptology.* Au Palaʻo Kūhou.
New Guinea *Also New Guinean.* Nūkini. See *Papua New Guinea.*
New Hampshire *Also New Hampshirite, New Hampshireman.* Nūhamekia, Nūhamesia.
New Jersey *Also New Jerseyite.* Nūierese, Nūkelese.
New Mexico *Also New Mexican.* Nūmikiko.
New York *Also New Yorker.* Nūioka.
New Zealand Aotearoa. *Also New Zealander.* Nukilani.
Nicaragua *Also Nicaraguan.* Nikalakua, Nikarakua.

nichrome Nikoroma. ~ *wire*. Uea nikoroma.
nickel *Five cents*. Hapaʻumi. *The metallic element*. Nikala.
nicotine Nikotina.
Niger *Also Nigerien*. Naigera.
Nigeria *Also Nigerian*. Naigeria.
nightgown *Pajamas*. Lole moe pō.
nightstand *Bedside table*. Pākaukau moe.
Nīhoa *The island*. Nīhoa. ~ *finch (Telespiza ultima)*. ʻAinohu Nīhoa.
ninhydrin indicator Ninahaidirina kuhikuhi.
nitrate Nitarahate.
nitric Nikiriku. ~ *acid*. ʻAkika nikiriku, ʻakika naikokene.
nitrite Nitarahite.
nitrogen *Also nitric*. Naikokene. See *azobacter, nitric acid*. *Free* ~ *compound*. Pūhui naikokene kaʻawale. ~ *dioxide*. Naikokene diokesaside, naikokene ʻokikene lua. ~ *cycle*. Pōʻaiapuni naikokene.
nocturnal Ala pō. See *crepuscular, diurnal*.
node *Where a leaf is connected to the stem*. Piko. *Lymph* ~. Lōkuʻu ʻanapuʻu.
nodule *As on a leguminous plant*. Puʻupuʻu.
no-eyed big-eyed hunting spider Nananana maka ʻole, nanana maka ʻole.
no-look pass *Also blind pass, in basketball; to throw such a pass*. Kīloi hoʻopalai.
nomad Kīhoe.
nonagon *A nine-sided polygon*. Huinaiwa.
nonfiction Hakuleʻi. See *fiction*. ~ *book*. Puke hakuleʻi.
non-point source pollution Kumu hoʻohaumia ʻike ʻole ʻia. See *point source pollution*.
nonstandard *As in units of measurement*. Kūhelu ʻole.
noodle Nulu. See *pasta*.
nook *Inside corner*. Kūʻono, poʻopoʻo.

normal *In math*. Haiakonu. See *deviation*.
Norse See *Norway*.
north ʻĀkau. *Abb*. ʻĀk. See entries below and *opossum*. ~ *pole*. Wēlau ʻākau.
North America *Also North American*. ʻAmelika ʻĀkau.
North Carolina *Also North Carolinean*. Kalolaina ʻĀkau.
North Dakota *Also North Dakotan*. Kakoka ʻĀkau, Dakota ʻĀkau.
Northern Equatorial Current *In oceanography*. Kūkahikahi. See *Southern Equatorial Current, Equatorial Countercurrent*.
northern hemisphere Poepoe hapa ʻākau. See *hemisphere*.
northern lights *Also aurora borealis*. ʻOliliʻula.
North Korea *Also North Korean*. Kōlea ʻĀkau, Kōrea ʻĀkau.
North Yemen *Also North Yemenite, North Yemeni*. Iemene ʻĀkau. See *South Yemen*.
Norway *Also Norwegian, Norse*. Nolewai.
nose guard *In football; also defensive middle guard, nose tackle*. Haunaku.
nose tackle See *nose guard*.
notation *In math*. Kauhelu. *Exponential* ~. Kauhelu pāhoʻonui. *Scientific* ~. Kauhelu ʻepekema.
note *Or memo for conveying a message to someone; message*. Memo. See *notes*. *As in a book or research paper*. Kuhia. See *endnote, footnote*.
note *On music staff, musical* ~. Huamele. See *key*. *Line* ~. Huamele laina.
notebook *Tablet*. Kālana kākau. See *binder*.
notes *As taken during a lecture, etc.; to take such* ~. Kakaha. See *memo*.
novel *As a work of literature*. Nōwela. *Biographical* ~. Nōwela piliolana. *Mystery* ~. Nōwela pōliu. ~*ette*. Nōwela pōkole.

November Nowemapa. *Abb.* Now.
novice level Pae 'akahi akahi.
nozzle Nuku. *Bellows ~.* Nuku 'ūpā makani.
nuclear Nukelea. See *nucleus.* *~ energy.* Ikehu nukelea. *~ fusion.* Ku'i nukeliu. *~ radiation.* Pāhawewe nukelea.
nucleus *As in an atom.* Nukeliu. *Of a syllable in linguistics.* Iho.
number *In math.* Helu. See entries below and *integer, numeral. See also atomic number. Figure (the character) or numeral.* Huahelu. *Even ~.* Helu kaulike. *Odd ~.* Helu kau'ewa. *Cardinal ~.* Helu heluna. *Ordinal ~.* Helu ka'ina. *Whole ~.* Helu piha. *Mixed ~.* Helu 'ō'ā. *Double ~.* Helu māhoe. *Real ~.* Helu maoli.
number *Positive ~.* Helu 'i'o. *Negative ~.* Helu 'i'o 'ole. *Rational ~.* Helu pu'unaue koena 'ole. *Irrational ~.* Helu pu'unaue koena. *Composite ~.* Helu pu'unaue lua. *~ line.* Laina helu. *~ pair.* Pa'a helu. *~ pattern.* Lauana helu. *~ property.* 'Anopili helu *(preceded by* ke).
number *Prime ~.* Helu kumu. *Relatively prime ~s, i.e. numbers which share one factor between them, and that factor is 1.* Hoa helu ho'onui like kahi. *Twin primes.* Helu kumu kūlua. *~ or math sentence.* Hopunahelu. *~ puzzle.* Nane huahelu.
numeral *The character.* Huahelu. *Expanded ~.* Helu unuhi kūana. *Roman ~.* Helu Loma.
numerator *In math.* Kinohapa. See *denominator.*
numerical problem Ha'ihelu.
nut *As on an 'ukulele or guitar.* Nī'au. See *'ukulele. Head ~.* Nī'au li'ili'i. *As in ~s and bolts.* Pihi, pihi wili. See *bolt. Hex ~.* Pihi wili ono. *Wing ~.* Pihi wili 'ēheu.
nut *Pea~ or any edible ~.* Pīneki, pineki, pīnaki.
nutgrass Mau'u pīneki.

nuthatch *A kind of bird.* Manu nūhata.
nutmeg 'Alameka.
nutrient Māhuaola. *~ culture.* 'Oulu māhuaola. *~ salts, the deposits that remain after a liquid has been removed.* Pa'amāhuaola.
nutrition Kūlana 'aiaola. See *nutritious.*
nutritious Paiola. *To eat ~ food.* 'Aiaola.
nutritive value Waiwai 'aiaola.
nylon Naelona.

O

oaktag *A strong cardboard used for posters; also called tagboard.* Pepa papa 'oka.
oatmeal 'Okamila. *~ flake.* Ulahi 'okamila.
object *Also entry, item.* 'Ikamu. *Reference ~, as in science.* Kiko kuhia. See *referent.*
objective Pahuhopu hāiki. See *goal.*
observatory Hale kilo hōkū. See *planetarium.*
obsidian Mākā.
obtuse *In math.* Peleleu. *~ angle.* Huina peleleu. *~ triangle.* Huinakolu peleleu.
occupation *Also career.* 'Oihana. See *business.*
ocean *Also oceanic.* Moana. *~ crust.* Pāpa'a moana. *Pacific ~.* Moana Pākīpika.
ocotillo *A kind of cactus.* Pānini 'okotio.
octagon Huinawalu.
octahedron *A space figure with eight faces, in math.* Pa'a'iliwalu.
octane 'Okatene.
October 'Okakopa. *Abb.* 'Ok.
octopus *Haole definition; squid (local definition).* He'e. See *cuttlefish.*
odd number Helu kau'ewa.

offense *As in sporting events; to play ~.* Kūlele. *See entries below. Man ~, i.e. ~ for attacking face defense, in basketball.* Kūlele alo. *Zone ~.* Kūlele kāʻei.

offensive foul *In team sports such as basketball.* Kuʻia kūlele. *See foul.*

offensive line *In football.* Laina kūlele.

office appliance Mīkini keʻena.

Office of Instructional Services *OIS.* Keʻena Hoʻonohonoho Haʻawina.

official *As an ~ representative or language.* Kūhelu. *See unofficial.*

off-line *Describing the state of an electronic device not ready to receive data, or not connected to a computer or computer network.* Pahemo. *See on-line. To take ~, as a computer system.* Hoʻopahemo.

offsides *In football.* Mīʻoi. *See encroachment. ~ on the offense.* Mīʻoi na ke kūlele.

Ohio *Also Ohioan.* ʻOhaio.

ohm *A unit of resistance in electricity.* ʻOme. *See ohmmeter, volt.*

ohmmeter Ana ʻome. *See ohm.*

Ohta-san ʻukulele ʻUkulele Ohta-san.

oil *Vegetable ~.* ʻAila meakanu.

oil rig *For drilling oil on either land or sea.* Wili ʻaila.

OIS *Office of Instructional Services.* Keʻena Hoʻonohonoho Haʻawina.

ʻokina *Printer's symbol for single open quote.* Kaha puanaʻī pākahi wehe.

Oklahoma *Also Oklahoman.* ʻOkalahoma.

old *Also olden, used only in special terminology. See middle, new. ~ Kingdom, in Egyptology.* Au Palaʻo Kūkahiko.

olden *See old.*

oleomargarine *Also margarine.* Makalina.

Oliarus tamehameha *Planthopper.* ʻŪmiʻilau.

-ology *Scientific study of something with no specific intent to influence change.* Huli-. *Scientific study of something with intent to influence change.* Kālai-.

olympic *Also Olympics.* ʻOlumepika. *See Olympus. ~ Winter Games.* Nā Pāʻani ʻOlumepika Hoʻoilo.

Olympus ʻOlumepika. *See olympic. Mount ~; ~ Mons, a volcano on Mars.* Mauna ʻOlumepika.

Oman *Also Omani.* ʻOmana.

omnivore *Also omnivorous.* Hamuʻakoʻa.

one-and-one free throw *In basketball.* Kī noa kī hou.

one and one-half space *As on a typed document.* Koana pākahi me ka hapalua.

one man *Also point guard, in basketball.* Kūkahi. *See guard.*

one property *In multiplication.* ʻAnopili ʻekahi *(preceded by* ke*).*

ones *Place value, in math.* Kūana ʻekahi.

one way *As a street or trip.* Holokahi. *See round trip.*

onion *Green ~ with purple bulb becoming white close to tip.* ʻOʻa. *With white bulb with purple inside.* Lina.

onion maggot Ilo ʻakaʻakai.

on-line *Describing the state of an electronic device ready to receive data, connected to a computer network, or accessible by means of a computer or computer network.* Paʻeʻe. *See off-line. To bring ~, as a computer system.* Hoʻopaʻeʻe.

onset *Of a syllable, in linguistics.* Kaʻi.

on time (I ka) hola kūpono.

opaque Aʻiaʻi hauʻoki. *See transparent.*

open *As for business; unlocked; ajar.* Hemo. *See entries below and bracket, imu, leaf, parenthesis. Wide ~.* Hāmama. *~ reel, as for fishing.* Wiliaho hāmama. *To ~ an imu.* Huaʻi i ka imu.

open *As a primary election.* Kūākea. See *closed.* ~ *primary.* Wae moho kūākea.

open *To complete, as an electric circuit.* Hoʻokuʻi. See *break.*

open *As a frame in a computer program.* Kaʻakaʻa. See *close, closed.* ~ *frame.* Mōlina kaʻakaʻa. *To ~, as a file.* Wehe.

open *To be ~, as for a play in basketball.* Hemo. *To get oneself ~.* Hoʻohemo.

opener *Can ~.* Mea wehe kini.

opening *As of a story.* Hoʻomaka. See *body, closing, topic sentence.* ~ *ceremonies.* Wehena papahana.

operating system *As for computer program.* Pae ʻōnaehana.

operation *In math.* Hana hoʻomākalakala. *Order of ~s in math problems.* Kaʻina hoʻomākalakala. *Inverse ~.* Hana hoʻomākalakala huli hope.

opinion survey Anamanaʻo.

opossum ʻOpakuma. *North American ~.* ʻOpakuma ʻAmelika ʻĀkau.

opponent *As in a sporting event.* Hoa paio.

opposite ʻĒkoʻa. *To be the ~ of.* ʻĒkoʻa me.

opposites property *In math.* ʻAnopili o ka ʻēkoʻa (*preceded by* ke).

optical disk CD, sēdē.

optical illusion Kuhi hewa o ka maka.

option *As on computer keyboard.* Koho. ~ *key.* Pihi koho (*preceded by* ke).

oral Haʻi waha. See *paraphrase, written.* ~ *communication.* Kaʻaʻike haʻi waha, kaʻaʻike waha. ~ *literature.* Moʻokalaleo haʻi waha. ~ *report.* Hōʻike haʻi waha, ʻōlelo hōʻike. ~ *report, presented as a speech.* Haʻiʻōlelo hōʻike.

oral cavity *In linguistics.* Haka waha.

orange tree frog Poloka kau lāʻau ʻālani.

oratory *Traditional elements of Hawaiian poetry, story telling, ~ and narration.* Meiwi.

orbit Ala pōʻai. *To ~.* Pōʻai.

order *Money ~.* Pila ʻoka kālā. ~ *form.* Palapala ʻoka. *Purchase ~ (PO).* Palapala ʻoka kūʻai.

order *Also sequence.* Kaʻina. *Alphabetical ~.* Kaʻina pīʻāpā. ~ *of operations in math problems.* Kaʻina hoʻomākalakala. *To put in ~ or sequence.* Hoʻokaʻina. *To coordinate or put in ~.* Hoʻolaukaʻi.

ordered pair *Two numbers used to give location of a point on a graph, in math.* Paʻa helu kuhikuhina.

ordinal number Helu kaʻina. See *cardinal number.*

ore ʻŌhaʻi.

Oregon *Also Oregonian.* ʻOlekona, ʻOregona.

organ *As of an animal.* Lōkino. ~ *system.* ʻŌnaehana lōkino.

organic *Relating to the branch of chemistry concerning the carbon compounds of living things.* Paʻupopo.

organism Meaola. *Micro~.* Meaola māiki.

organophosphate ʻOraganoposopahate.

organ pipe cactus Pānini ʻokana.

orientation *As of page in computer program.* Kuana pepa. *Landscape ~.* Kuana moe. *Portrait ~.* Kuana kū.

origin *Of the world; creation.* Kumu honua. See *creation. Of a graph.* Piko pakuhi, piko. *Root, source or derivation, as the etymology of a word.* Molekumu.

original *Also master copy, a master used for making additional copies.* Kope kumu.

oriole Manu ʻoliō.

ornament Wehi. *Christmas tree ~.* Wehi lāʻau Kalikimaka. See *Christmas ball.*

orographic *Dealing with mountains.* Pili pali. ~ *rainfall.* Ua pili pali.

oropharynx *The lower part of the pharynx contiguous to the mouth, in anatomy.* Haka moni o waena. See *pharynx.*

orthodontist Kauka hoʻopololei niho.
osteopathy *Also to practice osteopathy.* Haʻihaʻi iwi. *Osteopath.* Kauka haʻihaʻi iwi.
otter ʻOta.
ounce ʻAuneki. *Abb.* ʻan. *Fluid ~.* ʻAuneki wai. *Abb.* ʻan w.
out *In baseball.* ʻAuka. *To tag or strike ~.* Hōʻauka. *In volleyball.* Hala akula i waho. *Side ~.* Hāʻawi i ke kinipōpō i kekahi ʻaoʻao. *Time ~, in team sports such as volleyball.* Manawa hoʻomaha.
outcome *A possible result in a probability experiment, in math.* Hopena. *Equally likely ~s.* Like ka papaha o nā mea e loaʻa ana.
outdoor Kaupokulani. See *indoor.* *~ concert.* ʻAha mele kaupokulani. *~ market.* Mākeke kaupokulani. *~ sport.* Haʻuki kaupokulani.
outer planet Hōkūhele o waho loa.
outlaw Mea pale kānāwai. *To break laws, act as an ~.* Pale Kānāwai. *To make something illegal.* Pāpā kānāwai.
outlet *Electrical ~.* Puka uila. See *plug.*
outline *A summary using letters and numbers in headings to indicate topics and subtopics.* ʻOlokeʻa. See Hawaiian entry ʻolokeʻa. *Document ~, as in computer program.* ʻOlokeʻa palapala. *To ~.* Hōʻolokeʻa.
outline *As a line marking the outer limits of an object or figure.* Mahaka. *To ~, as type on computer or in typesetting.* Hoʻomeheu. *Outlined.* Meheu.
output *As in computer program.* Huapuka. See *input. To ~.* Kāhuapuka. *To ~ data.* Kāhuapuka ʻikepili. *~ device.* Hāmeʻa huapuka.
outside set *To make an ~, in volleyball.* Hānai lōʻihi.
outward Haʻawaho.
oval Pōʻai lōʻihi, ʻololaha. See *ellipse.*
ovary Lōkino huaʻine. See *ovulate, ovum.*

oven *Broiler ~.* ʻOma kōʻala. *Microwave ~.* ʻOmawawe.
overalls *Coveralls.* Lole wāwae kāʻawe, lole wāwae ʻepane.
overdose *To ~ on drugs.* Pākela ʻai lāʻau.
overestimate Kohoʻoi. See *underestimate.*
overflow error *As on a calculator display.* Hū.
override *To ~, as in computer program.* Mauʻaʻe.
over-the-counter Kūʻai wale. See *prescription.* *~ drug or medication.* Lāʻau kūʻai wale.
over the line *In volleyball.* Kaʻahi hewa, keʻehi hewa.
overtime Kaulele. *~ pay.* Uku kaulele. *~ hours.* Hola kaulele. *~ work.* Hana kaulele.
ovipositor ʻŌ hāʻule hua.
ovoid Paʻaʻololaha.
ovulate Hoʻokuʻu huaʻine. See *ovary, ovum.*
ovum *In biology.* Huaʻine. See *ovary, ovulate, sperm.*
owl *Elf ~.* Pueo peke. *Great horned ~.* Pueo kiwi hulu. *~ monkey.* Keko pueo.
Oxford *Saddle shoe.* Kāmaʻa ʻili helei.
oxide ʻOkesaside. *Cupric ~.* Kupuriku ʻokesaside. *Ferric ~.* Feriku ʻokesaside. *Ferrosoferric ~.* Ferosoferiku ʻokesaside. *Ferrous ~.* Ferousa ʻokesaside.
oxidize *Also oxidized.* Kāʻokikene.
oxygen ʻOkikene. *~ tank.* Kini ʻokikene. *~--carbon dioxide cycle.* Pōʻaiapuni ʻokikene kalapona ʻokikene lua.
oyster *Edible ~.* Kupekio. *Pearl ~.* Pipi.
ozone ʻOkikene kolu. *~--sensitive fabric.* Lole ana ʻokikene kolu.

P

Pacific Ocean Moana Pākīpika.
pack *To ~, as a suitcase.* ʻŪlū.

pack *For items other than drinks, as gum, baseball cards or cigarettes.* 'Ope. See *case, six-pack, twelve-pack.* *Four-~.* 'Ope hā. *Six-~.* 'Ope ono.

pack saddle Noho 'āmana.

pad *Brake ~.* Pale peleki. See *launch pad.*

page 'Ao'ao. *Abb.* 'ao. *Cover ~, as in a computer document.* 'Ao'ao ho'ākāka. *~ break.* Ho'oka'awale 'ao'ao. *~ guide.* Kuhi lihi. *~ setup.* Ho'okuene 'ao'ao.

pail Pākeke li'ili'i. *Lunch ~.* Kini 'aiō, kini 'ai.

paint *Also the area within the key below the free throw line on a basketball court.* Pena. See *spray paint.* *~ brush.* Hulu pena. *~ roller.* Lola pena. *To ~ with a roller.* Pena lola. *Tempera ~.* Pena pelaha. *Water-base ~.* Pena kuapapa wai.

pair *Number ~, in math.* Pa'a helu. See *action-reaction pair.* *Ordered ~.* Pa'a helu kuhikuhina. *To ~ off.* Ho'okūlua.

pajamas *Nightgown.* Lole moe pō.

Pakistan *Also Pakistani.* Pakitana.

pala'ai Pumpkin. See *squash.*

palate *In linguistics.* Palaku. *Hard ~.* Palaku iwi. *Soft ~.* Palaku kīleo.

paleontology Hulimō'alihaku. *Paleontologist.* Kanaka hulimō'alihaku, mea hulimō'alihaku.

palette *As in computer program.* Papa pena.

palindrome Huaaka.

palm *To carry or ~ (the ball), in basketball.* Poholuna.

Palmyra island Honuaiākea.

pamphlet *Also flyer.* Pepelu.

pan *Baking ~.* Pā 'oma *(preceded by* ke*).* *Frying ~.* Pā palai *(preceded by* ke*).* *Sauce ~.* Ipuhao hana kai. See *handle.*

pan *To ~, as with a movie or video camera.* Pa'i kāhela *(preceded by* ke*).*

Panama *Also Panamanian.* Panamā.

pancake *Unleavened ~.* Palaoa linalina. *~ turner, spatula.* 'Ūlau.

pancake dig *In volleyball.* 'Ali 'ūlau.

panda Pea Kina. See *teddy bear.*

panel Pānela. See *paneling.* *Control ~, on computer.* Papa ho'oholo. *Solar ~.* 'Ūomo ikehu lā.

paneling Papa pānela. *Wood ~.* Papa pānela lā'au.

pant *To ~, as a dog.* Haha.

papain *An enzyme found in papayas and used as a meat tenderizer.* Papaina.

paper Pepa. See entries below and *posterboard.* *Butcher ~.* Pepa lole pipi. *Carbon ~.* Pepa 'ōpa'u. *Construction ~.* Pepaānue. *Corrugated ~.* Pepa pahu. *~ bag.* Pū'olo pepa. *~ clip.* Pine pepa. *~ tape.* Leki pepa. *~ towel dispenser.* 'Ūhōlo'a kāwele pepa.

paper *Graph ~.* Pepa maka'aha. *Litmus ~, for measuring pH.* Pepa ana 'akika. See *chromatography.*

paper Pepa. *Legal-size ~.* Pepa loio. *Letter-size ~.* Pepa leka. *Tabloid ~.* Pepa 11" X 17" *(pronounced* pepa 'umikūmā-kahi 'īniha i ka 'umikūmāhiku 'īniha*).* *~ tray or cassette in a computer printer.* Poho pepa. *~ tray slot.* 'Āpo'o poho pepa.

papier mâché Pepa paluhē.

Papua New Guinea *Also Papua New Guinean.* Pāpua Nūkini.

papyrus Kaluhā.

parabola *Also parabolic.* Palapola. *Parabolic curve.* Uma palapola.

parachute Ha'upoho.

paradise *Bird of ~, the bird.* Manu palekaiko. *The flower.* Pua manu.

paraffin Uepa ihoiho.

paragraph Paukū. See *phrase.* *~ symbol* (¶). Po'o hou *(preceded by* ke*).* *A line written from the end of one ~ to the beginning of the next ~ to indicate that the two ~s should be combined, in proofreading.* Kaha hopu. *To ~, as in written compositions.* Paukūkū.

Paraguay *Also Paraguayan.* Palakuae, Paraguae.

parakeet Pāloke'i'i.

parallel Pilipā. See entries below and balance beam. ~ lines. Nā kaha pilipā. ~ bars. Lāʻau kaulua. Even ~ bars. Lāʻau kaulua kaulike. Uneven ~ bars. Lāʻau kaulua kaulike ʻole.

parallel An imaginary circle on the earth's surface parallel to the equator and designated in degrees of latitude. Laina lakikū, laina latitū.

parallel As of a computer port. Ala pilipā. ~ port. Awa ala pilipā.

parallelogram Huinahā pilipā.

paraphrase To ~ orally. Haʻi hou ma kekahi ʻano. In writing. Kākau hou ma kekahi ʻano.

parasite Also to live as a parasite. Omoola. See host.

parasitic worm General term. Koʻe omoola. See heartworm, nematode, roundworm, tapeworm, etc.

parenthesis Kahaapo. See bracket. Open ~. Kahaapo wehe. Close ~. Kahaapo pani.

parent rock Rocks in upper surface of the earth which break down to form rocks, sand, dirt, etc. Pōhaku makua.

park Amusement ~. Pāka kāniwala. Department of ~s and Recreation. ʻOihana o nā Pāka a me nā Hana Hoʻonanea. National ~. Pāka aupuni. National ~ Service. ʻOihana Pāka Aupuni. Glacier National ~. Pāka Aupuni ʻo Hauneneʻe. Hawaiʻi Volcanoes National ~. Pāka Aupuni ʻo Kīlauea. Yosemite National ~. Pāka Aupuni ʻo ʻIosemite. State ~. Pāka mokuʻāina. ~ keeper. Kahu pāka.

parking meter Mīka kāki. Metered parking or any parking for which there is a charge. Kū kāki.

Parmesan Pamesana. ~ cheese. Waiūpaʻa pamesana.

parrot Pāloke, manu pāloke.

parrotbill Maui ~, pseudonestor xanthophrys. Kīkēkoa.

parsley Pakalī.

part Fractional ~. Māhele hapa. One-half ~. Māhele hapalua.

particle As in an atom. Huna. See proton, electron, neutron. Alpha ~, a positively charged particle made up of two protons and two neutrons. Huna ʻālepa. Beta ~, a negatively charged electron moving at high speed. Huna beta. Visible airborne ~s, as from a spray can. Ehu kīkina. See substance.

partitioning Disk ~, in computer hard drive. Māhele pā.

party Two-~ system of government. Aupuni ʻaoʻao ʻelua.

party favor Alelomoʻo.

pass In mountains. Nuku. See entries below and passageway, trail.

pass To ~, in basketball. Kīloi. Back-door ~. Kīloi palemo. Behind-the-back ~. Kīloi kua. Blind ~, no-look ~. Kīloi hoʻopalai. Bounce ~. Kīloi papahele. Chest ~. Kīloi umauma. Hook ~. Kīloi ʻaoʻao. Inbound ~. Kīloi ulele. Lead ~. Kīloi ulele kikī, kīloi kaha. Lob ~. Kīloi piʻo. Tip ~. Kīloi papaʻi. Touch ~. Hoʻopāhiʻa. See baseball pass. First ~, in volleyball; also to receive a serve. Kiʻi. ~ through the block. Hala ka pālulu.

passage Initiation, as into a group. Komo pae. See initiate. Rite of ~. Hana komo pae.

passageway Narrow ~, as in a canyon. Hānuku.

pass out See deal.

passport Palapala holo ʻāina ʻē.

pasta Nulu ʻĪkālia. See noodle.

paste Tuko keʻokeʻo. See glue, rubber cement.

pathogen A disease-producing agent. Mūhune ʻino. See antibiotic.

pattern Repeating series. Lauana. Number ~. Lauana helu. As a word or sentence ~ in Hawaiian grammar. Analula. ~ book, as for teaching grammatical ~s in reading. Puke aʻo analula. Settlement ~, in geography. Lauana hoʻokahua.

pave To ~ with asphalt. Hoʻūnukā. See asphalt.

payload bay *The part of a spacecraft where scientific instruments and passengers are carried.* ʻOneki hana.

pea Pāpapa poepoe.

peanut *Also groundnut or any edible nut.* Pīneki, pineki, pīnaki. *~ brittle.* Pakē pīneki. *~ butter.* Pīnekipaka.

pear *Usually Bartlett ~.* Pea pakeleke. See *avocado*.

Pearl and Hermes Reef Holoikauaua.

pearl oyster Pipi. See *oyster (edible)*.

peat ʻElenahu.

peck *A unit of measurement.* Peka.

pedal Mea hehi wāwae.

pedicab Kalaikikala lawe ʻōhua.

pedometer Ana hele wāwae.

peel *To ~, as an orange or taro.* Ihi. *As a banana; to strip.* Uhole. *Easy to ~, as small corms of cooked taro.* Pohole.

peeling *To be ~ing, as skin from sunburn.* ʻĀkaʻakaʻa.

peer Kiʻei, ʻōwī.

peewee *Wood ~, a kind of bird.* Manu pīuīlāʻau.

peg *As for tuning stringed instruments.* Kī. *Wooden ~.* Kui lāʻau.

pen Peni, peni ʻīnika. *Fine point ~.* Peni makakui. *Fountain ~.* Peni pāuma. *Marsh or felt ~.* Peni kuni. *~ cap.* Poʻi peni (*preceded by* ke).

pencil See *eyebrow pencil*. *Colored ~.* Penikala kala.

pendulum Uleʻo. See *amplitude, bob, swing*. *Period of a ~.* Wā ʻukē.

Pennsylvania *Also Pennsylvanian.* Penekelewinia, Peneselevinia.

pennyroyal *A kind of flower.* Penialiʻi.

pension Uku hoʻomau. *To draw or take a ~.* Lawe i ka uku hoʻomau.

pentagon Huinalima.

pentathalon ʻĀlapakonalima. See *decathalon, triathalon*.

pentomino *In math.* Penatomino.

pepperoni Pepaloni.

percent *Also percentage.* Pākēneka. See entry below and *markup, rate*.

Percent Daily Value *Formerly known as percentage of US Recommended Daily Allowances (USRDA).* Pākēneka o ka papaʻai.

percolate *To ~, as water passing through a porous substance.* Manono.

Peregrine falcon Palekona kāluʻu.

performing art Pāhiahia.

perimeter *In math.* Anapuni. *Abb.* anp.

period *In punctuation.* Kiko pau. *As each set of three numerals, in math.* Poke. *Of a pendulum.* Wā ʻukē.

peripherals *Or accessories, as for a computer.* Lakolako.

Periplaneta *~ americana, American cockroach.* ʻElelū kīkēkē. *~ australasiae, Australian cockroach.* ʻElelū Nūhōlani.

permeable *Also permeability.* Nono.

permutation *A selection of objects from a set in a particular order, in math; also to permute.* Kake kaʻina.

peroxide Perokesaside. *Hydrogen ~ (H_2O_2).* Haikokene lua ʻokikene lua.

perpendicular *In math.* Kūpono. *~ bisector.* Kaha ʻoki hapalua kūpono. *~ lines.* Nā kaha kūpono.

Perseus *A constellation.* Ānui.

personal foul *In team sports such as basketball.* Kuʻia pilikino. See *foul*.

perspective Kuanaʻike.

persuade *To induce change of opinion.* Hoʻohuli manaʻo. See *persuasive speech*.

persuasive speech Haʻiʻōlelo hoʻohuli manaʻo. See *speech*.

Peru *Also Peruvian.* Pelū, Perū.

pest *Any plant or animal detrimental to humans or their interests.* Haipilikia. See *pesticide*.

pesticide Lāʻau make haipilikia, lāʻau haipilikia.

pet Hānaiahuhu. *~ shop.* Hale kūʻai hānaiahuhu.

petri dish Pā piki (*preceded by* ke).

petrolatum *Vaseline.* Kele hoʻopaheʻe.

petroleum ʻAila kā, ʻaila tā.
petting zoo Kahua hamohamo holoholona.
petty cash Kālā kini.
petunia Pekunia.
Pharaoh Palaʻo. See *kingdom*.
pharynx *In anatomy.* Haka moni. *Laryngo~, i.e. the lower part of the ~ adjacent to the larynx.* Haka moni o lalo. *Naso~, i.e. the portion of the ~ behind the nasal cavity and above the soft palate.* Haka moni o luna. *Oro~, i.e. the lower part of the ~ contiguous to the mouth.* Haka moni o waena.
phase ʻEpaki. *~ of the moon (Western concept).* ʻEpaki mahina.
Philippines ʻĀina Pilipino, ʻĀina Pinopino. See *Filipino*.
philodendron ʻAʻapehihi lau liʻi. See *pothos*.
philosophy Kālaimanaʻo.
phloem Kikiʻuʻai. See *xylem*.
Phobos *A moon of Mars.* Popoka.
Phoebe *The most distant moon of Saturn.* Poepe.
phone *In linguistics.* Puanaleo.
phoneme *In linguistics.* Hualeo.
phonics ʻApo kani kākau.
phonology *In linguistics.* Kālaileo.
phosphate Posapahate.
phosphorescent *Also fluorescent.* Hāweo.
phosphorus Posoporusa.
photograph Kiʻi paʻi. *Negative of a ~.* Akakiʻi. *To take, shoot or snap a picture, either still or motion.* Paʻi kiʻi. *~er.* Mea paʻi kiʻi.
photolysis Kāʻamawāhiwai. See *photosynthesis*.
photosynthesis Kāʻamaʻai.
phrase *In grammar.* Lālā. See *paragraph. In literary or general use.* Māmalaʻōlelo. *To ~, as in speaking or reading orally.* Puana māmala. *As in written compositions.* Kūkulu māmala.

physical *As a scientific term relating to ~ matter.* Paku. *~ properties.* Nā ʻanopili paku. *~ science.* Kālaiaopaku
physical education Mākau kino.
physical therapy *To provide ~.* Pākōlea. *Physical therapist.* Mea pākōlea, kanaka pākōlea.
physician *Coordinated ~ referral system.* ʻŌnaehana kauka no ka lapaʻau like ʻana.
physics Kālaikūlohea.
pi π, *in math.* Pai.
piccolo Pikolō.
pick *Dentist's probe.* ʻŌhiki kauka niho. *To ~, as an ʻukulele or guitar.* Hiku, panapana.
pick and roll *In basketball; to make such a play.* ʻĀkeʻa ʻūniu.
pico- *A prefix meaning one trillionth (p).* Hapa kiliona. *Abb.* hkl. See *deci-, centi-, milli-, micro-, nano-*.
pictograph Pakuhi kiʻi.
picture frame Mōlina kiʻi.
pie *Pot ~.* Kinipai.
pier block *In construction.* Palaka kimeki. See *termite block*.
piggy bank Panakō hale.
pigment Kaukala. *~ grain, in biology.* Huna kaukala.
pillow Uluna. *~case.* Pale uluna.
pin *Bowling ~.* Pine maika. *Safety ~.* Pine kaiapa.
piñata Piniaka, piniata.
pinch clamp ʻŪmiʻi pani.
pin cushion Pulu kui.
pine *Conifer or any tree which resembles a ~.* Paina, paina lau kukuna, paina tidara. See *cypress, ironwood*. *Cook ~.* Kumu paina Kuke, paina Kuke.
pineapple Hala kahiki, painaʻāpala. See *polyethylene. ~ crown.* ʻĒlau hala kahiki, ʻēlau painaʻāpala.
ping-pong *Table tennis.* Kenika pākaukau.
Pinnacles *Gardner ~.* Pūhāhonu.
pint Paina. *Abb.* pin.
pinwheel *A toy.* Pelahū.

Māmaka Kaiao / 267

pipe *See Hawaiian entries under* paipu *and plumber, tap water.*

pipette Paipuli'i. *Capillary* ~. Paipuli'i 'umelauoho.

pitch Kēpau kā. *See entries below and asphalt compound.*

pitch *To make a* ~, *as a sales* ~, *or to "sell" an idea.* Paialou.

pitch *In linguistics and music.* Ki'eleo. *See capo. High* ~. Ki'eleo ki'eki'e. *Low* ~. Ki'eleo ha'aha'a.

pivot *As a position in basketball; also* ~ *point.* Kū 'ūniu. *To* ~. 'Ūniu.

pizza Pai pika, pika.

place ~ *value, usually in compound terms.* Kūana. ~ *value of a number.* Kūana helu. *Ones.* Kūana 'ekahi. *Tens.* Kūana 'umi. *Hundreds.* Kūana haneli. *Decimal* ~. Kūana kekimala.

plain *Expanse of flat land.* Kula laulaha, 'āina kula laulaha. *See plateau.*

plaiting *Twill* ~. Maka pūalu, 'o'eno.

plan *Particularly one which involves thought and decision-making.* Papa ho'olālā. *See short-range, medium-range, long-range. Informal* ~. Papa hana.

planaria Ko'e pāki'i.

plane *Coordinate* ~, *in math.* Papa kuhikuhina.

plane figure *A figure that lies on a flat surface, in math.* Kinona papa. *See geometric figure, space figure.*

planet Hōkūhele. *Jovian* ~. Hōkūhele Iowiana. *Outer* ~. Hōkūhele o waho loa.

planetarium Hale a'o kilo hōkū. *See observatory.*

plankton 'Ōulaula

planning *County* ~ *Department.* Ke'ena Ho'olālā o ke Kalana. *Hawai'i State Department of* ~ *and Economic Development.* 'Oihana Ho'olālā a me ka Ho'omohala Waiwai o ka Moku'āina 'o Hawai'i.

plant Meakanu. *See crop. Flowering* ~. Meakanu pua.

plant Meakanu.

planter *As for growing plants.* Pahu ho'oulu meakanu.

planthopper *Oliarus tamehameha.* 'Ūmi'ilau.

planting medium 'Elekanu. *See potting soil.*

plasma Palasema, wai koko.

plaster of Paris Puna Pālisa.

plastic 'Ea. ~ *bag.* 'Eke 'ea (*preceded by* ke). *Any* ~ *film for wrapping food, as Saran Wrap.* Wahī 'ea. ~ *sheeting, general term.* Hāli'i 'ea. *See polyethyline.*

plastid *Tiny structures inside plant cells that contain pigment as well as chlorophyll.* Palasika.

plate *Geologic* ~. Una honua. *See base (in baseball). Cocos* ~. Ka Una Honua Kokosa. *Eurasian* ~. Ka Una Honua 'Eulāsia. *Indo-Australian* ~. Ka Una Honua 'Inionūhōlani. *Nazca* ~. Ka Una Honua Naseka.

plateau *High level land.* Nu'u laulaha. *See plain.*

platelet Pāhune (*preceded by* ke).

plate techtonics *In geology.* Ku'ina una honua. *See boundary, convergent, divergent, transform.*

platform *As DOS, UNIX, Macintosh, etc., for computer program.* Pae. *See operating system.*

platinum Palakiniuma.

play *As a particular maneuver in a sporting event; to execute a* ~. Ka'ane'e.

play *Dramatic* ~. Hana keaka paiwa.

Play-Doh Palēkō. *See clay.*

player *Record* ~. Mīkini ho'okani pāleo, mīkini pāleo. *See recorder. Cassette* ~. Mīkini ho'okani lola, mīkini lola. *Reel-to-reel tape* ~. Mīkini ho'okani pōka'a, mīkini pōka'a leo.

playoff *As in sporting events.* Ho'okūkū moho.

plexiglass Aniani 'ea. *See fiberglass.*

pliers Palaea, palaea huki.

plot *Chart or graph, in math.* Pakuhi. *See Hawaiian entries under* pakuhi *and* chart, graph. *To ~ or chart.* Kākuhi. *Stem and leaf ~.* Pakuhi ʻau me ka lau.
plug Palaka. *See outlet, prong, spark plug. Electrical ~.* Palaka uila. *Two-pronged ~.* Palaka niho lua. *Three-pronged ~.* Palaka niho kolu.
plumber Kanaka hoʻomoe paipu, wilipaipu.
plunge pool Kiʻo wai wailele.
plunger *As for cleaning clogged drains.* Pāuma lua. *Syringe ~.* ʻŪkaomi hano kui, ʻūkaomi, ʻūkōmi hano kui, ʻūkōmi.
plus sign Kaha hui.
Pluto *The planet.* ʻIlioki.
p.m. *Post meridium.* P.m. *(pronounced* pīmū*).*
pneumonia Nūmōnia.
PO *Purchase order.* Palapala ʻoka kūʻai.
pocket compass Pānānā paʻa lima.
pod *Seed ~.* Wahī ʻanoʻano.
podium Pākau, pākau haʻiʻōlelo.
poem *Also poetry, general term.* Mele *(preceded by* ke*)*.
poetry *Also poem.* Mele *(preceded by* ke*). Traditional elements of Hawaiian ~, story telling, oratory and narration.* Meiwi.
pogo stick Aeʻolele.
poi *Residue of ~ after pounding.* Kale ʻai. *To take up ~ with the fingers.* Miki.
poinsettia Pua Kalikimaka.
point *As in a game or sporting event.* ʻAi. *See entries below and* basket, pivot, score, touchback, touchdown. *~ for Mea.* Lilo ka ʻai iā Mea. *~ after touchdown, in football.* ʻAi manuahi. *~ after by passing or running.* ʻAi manuahi holo. *~ after by kicking.* ʻAi manuahi peku. *~ from block, dink or spike, in volleyball.* ʻAi hele wale.
point *In math; also a unit of measurement for type size.* Kiko. *See* decimal, referent. *To graph the ~.* Kākuhi i ke kiko. *Reference ~.* Kiko kuhia.

point *Boiling ~.* Kēkelē paila. *Freezing ~.* Kēkelē paʻahau. *Melting ~.* Kēkelē heheʻe. *Fine ~, fine line, as of a pen ~.* Makakui. *To ~, as a mouse arrow in computer program.* Kuhikuhi. *See* pointer.
pointer *Also mouse arrow or cursor, as in computer program.* Nahau ʻiole, nahau. *As used in a classroom.* Lāʻau kuhikuhi.
point guard *Also one man, in basketball.* Kūkahi. *See* guard.
points *The four cardinal ~, or four primary directions of the compass, in geography.* Nā kūkulu ʻehā.
point source pollution Kumu hoʻohaumia ʻike ʻia. *Non-~.* Kumu hoʻohaumia ʻike ʻole ʻia.
poison Lāʻau make. *See* aldrin, curare, dieldrin, fumigant, systemic insecticide. *Contact ~.* Lāʻau make pā ʻili. *Stomach ~.* Lāʻau make ʻai.
poka *Banana ~.* Poka maiʻa.
pokeweed Pīʻai poku.
Poland *Also Pole, Polish.* Pōlani.
polar bear Pea ʻĀlika.
pole Wēlau. *North ~.* Wēlau ʻākau. *South ~.* Wēlau hema. *Elevation ~, as for surveying.* Lāʻau ana kiʻekiʻena. *See* sighter. *Range ~, surveying rod.* Lāʻau ana ʻāina.
pole vault Koʻo lele. *To ~.* Lele koʻo.
police badge Pihi mākaʻi *(preceded by* ke*)*.
policy Kulekele.
polio Poliō.
polish *See* wax.
poll *Also to take a poll.* Anamanaʻo.
pollen Ehu. *See* pollinate. *Flower ~.* Ehu pua.
pollinate Hoʻēhu pua. *See* pollen. *Cross-~.* Hoʻēhu pua kaʻakepa.
polliwog *Tadpole.* Polewao.
pollution Haumia. *Air ~.* Haumia ea. *Source ~.* Kumu hoʻohaumia. *Point source ~.* Kumu hoʻohaumia ʻike ʻia. *Non-point source ~.* Kumu hoʻohaumia ʻike ʻole ʻia.

poly- *A prefix for chemical terms.* Polai-. *See entries below.*

polychaete worm *A kind of worm found underneath stream rocks.* Moeʻalā, koʻe moeʻalā.

polyethylene ʻEa painaʻāpala. *See plastic sheeting.*

polygon Huinalehulehu. *Regular ~.* Huinalehulehu analahi.

polyhedron *A space figure with many faces, in math.* Paʻaʻili lehulehu, paʻaʻili.

polyphosphate Polaiposapahate.

polytheism *Also polytheistic.* Akua lehulehu. *See monotheism.*

polyunsaturated fat ʻAilakele laupaʻahapa. *See fat.*

pomace fly *Genus Drosophilidae.* Pōnalo.

pomelo Pomelo. *See grapefruit, jabong.*

pompom Pōpō kīlepalepa, kīlepelepa.

pond *Large ~, lake.* Māluawai. *~ mud.* Pohō.

pony Lio pone.

pool *Of water, as in a stream.* Kiʻo wai. *Plunge ~.* Kiʻo wai wailele. *Side ~, as in a stream.* Wai wiliau. *Swimming ~.* Pūnāwai ʻauʻau.

pool cue Kiu pahupahu.

popover Palaoa pūhaʻuhaʻu.

pop-pops *Fireworks that explode on impact.* Lūpahū.

poppy *California ~.* Papi. *~ flower.* Pua papi.

popsicle ʻAikalima ʻau.

population *As in biology.* Pūʻuo. *~ density, for humans only.* Paʻapū pūʻuo kanaka. *~ distribution, in geography.* Ili pūʻuo, ili pūʻuo kanaka.

pop-up menu *As in computer program.* Papa ʻōʻili.

porcupine Kīpoka.

pore Pukapakī.

port *As in a computer.* Awa. *Parallel ~.* Awa ala pilipā. *Serial ~.* Awa ala pūkaʻina.

port *Left or ~ side of a double-hulled canoe or a ship when looking forward.* Ama. *See starboard.*

portable Lawelima. *See laptop computer.*

portrait orientation *As of page in computer program.* Kuana kū. *See landscape orientation.*

Portugal Pokukala, Potugala.

Portuguese cypress Paina Pukikī, paina tireza.

portulaca ʻĀkulikuli kula.

positive *As of electrical charge or north pole of a magnet.* ʻĀne. *See negative, neutral.* *~ number, in math.* Helu ʻiʻo. *~ integer.* Helu piha ʻiʻo.

possibility *See chance.*

possum *See opossum.*

post- *After-.* Muli. *See after, postcolonial, posttest.*

post *High ~, in basketball.* Kūliu waho. *Low ~.* Kūliu loko.

postage Uku leka.

postcard Kāleka poʻoleka.

postcolonial Muli panalāʻau. *~ country.* Kaumokuʻāina muli panalāʻau, ʻāina muli panalāʻau.

poster Pelaha.

posterboard Pepa mānoanoa.

posterior *In biology.* Lauhope. *See anterior, dorsal, ventral.* *~ dorsal fin, of a fish.* Kualā lauhope.

post-larvae Pua.

post meridium *P.m.* P.m. *(pronounced* pīmū*).*

posttest Hōʻike muli aʻo. *See pretest.*

pot *See flower pot.*

potash *Potassium carbonate or potassium insoluble compounds.* Pokala.

potassium Potasiuma. *~ cyanide.* Potasiuma kaianaside. *~ iodide.* Potasiuma ʻiodiside.

potato chip Kipi ʻuala kahiki.

potatoes *Hash-brown ~.* ʻUala kahiki kolikoli, ʻuala kolikoli. *Scalloped ~.* ʻUala kahiki pepeiao, ʻuala pepeiao.

potential Palena papaha.

pothos ʻAʻapehihi. See *philodendron*.
pot pie Kinipai.
potting soil Lepo kanu meakanu. See *planting medium*.
Poughkeepsie Pakipi.
pound *Unit of weight.* Paona. *Abb.* pon.
pound sign *A sign (#) used in proofreading to indicate that a space should be inserted; a superscript number written next to the symbol indicates the number of spaces if more than one (#²).* Kaha kaʻahua.
powder *Face ~.* Pauka helehelena. *To put on face ~.* Hana i ka pauka helehelena, kau i ka pauka helehelena.
powdered milk Waiū ehu, waiū pauka.
power Ikehu. See entries below and *energy*. *Hydroelectric ~.* Ikehu uila wai kahe. *Solar ~.* Manehu lā. *Thermoelectric ~.* Ikehu uila puhi wāwahie.
power *A product in which each factor is the same, in math.* Pāhoʻonui. See *exponent*.
power forward *Also four man, in basketball.* Kūhā.
powers *Legislative ~.* Mana kau kānāwai.
pox *Chicken ~.* Puʻupuʻu moa.
practical life skill Mākau ola.
practice Hoʻomaʻamaʻa. *~ book.* Puke hoʻomaʻamaʻa haʻawina, puke hoʻomaʻamaʻa.
prairie dog Kokeiʻa.
praise Hoʻomaikaʻi. See *honors*.
prank *Trick; to play a ~, usually with malicious intent.* Kēpuka. See *trick*.
prawn *Tahitian ~.* ʻŌpae Polapola.
praying mantis ʻŪhinipule.
pre- *Early, beforehand.* Hiki mua. See entries below and *late*. *~registration.* Kāinoa hiki mua.
preamble ʻŌlelo mua, ʻōlelo haʻi mua. See *introduction, preface*.

precipitate *A substance separated from a solution or suspension by chemical or physical change.* Koʻakoʻana.
precipitation Kimu.
precision *Also precise.* ʻAuliliʻi. *In math.* Pololei. *As high-quality print resolution on a computer printer.* Miomio. *~ bitmapping.* Kākiko miomio.
predator *Also predatory, to prey.* Poʻiiʻa. *Victim of a ~.* Luapoʻi.
predictable *As the ending of a story.* Hopena ahuwale. *~ story.* Moʻolelo hopena ahuwale.
prediction *Also to predict, as in a scientific experiment.* Wānana.
preface *Also foreword, as in a book.* ʻŌlelo haʻi mua, ʻōlelo mua. See *introduction, preamble*.
preference Makemake. *~s, as in computer program.* Nā makemake.
prefix Pākuʻina kau mua. See *affix*. *A ~ indicating a process.* Kā-. *A ~ meaning one one-hundredth (1/100).* Keni-. *File ~ or header information, as codes at the beginning of each computer file.* Poʻo pāʻālua (*preceded by* ke).
prehistoric Kuamanawa.
premium *Insurance ~.* Uku ʻinikua.
preschool Kula kamaliʻi.
prescription *For drug or medication; also to prescribe.* Kuhikuhi lāʻau. See *over-the-counter*. *~ drug or medication.* Lāʻau kuhikuhi.
president *As of a college or university.* Pelekikena. See *chancellor, provost*.
press *To click or depress, as in computer program.* Kōmi, kaomi.
press *To ~, in basketball.* Lulumi. See *press defense*. *Half-court ~.* Lulumi hapa. *Three-quarter-court ~.* Lulumi ʻekolu hapahā. *Full-court ~.* Lulumi piha.
press defense *As in basketball; to execute such a play.* Pale lulumi.

pressure Mīkā. *Air ~, as in a tire.* Mīkā ea. *Blood ~.* Mīkā koko. *High ~ system, in meteorology.* 'Ōnaehana mīkā pi'i. *Low ~ system.* 'Ōnaehana mīkā emi. *~ receptor.* A'alonoa mīkā. See *receptor*.
pressure *To ~, in basketball.* 'Umi.
pressurize Ho'omīkā. *Pressurized.* Ho'omīkā 'ia.
pretest Hō'ike mua a'o. See *posttest*.
pretzel Pelena pe'a.
preview Nāmua. See *view*. *Print ~, as in computer program.* Nāmua pa'i.
prewrite *To ~, as part of the writing process, i.e. introducing the topic through brainstorming, discussion, presentations, etc.* Hō'ike mana'o. See *conference*.
prey *To ~; also predator, predatory.* Po'ii'a. *Victim of a predator.* Luapo'i.
price Kumukū'ai, kāki. *Estimated ~.* Kumukū'ai koho. *Reasonable ~.* Kumukū'ai kūpono. *Retail ~.* Kumukū'ai hale kū'ai. *Sale ~.* Kāki kū'aiemi. *Unit ~.* Kumukū'ai anakahi. *Wholesale ~.* Kumukū'ai kālepa.
prickly pear cactus Pānini, pānini maoli, pāpipi. See *cactus*.
primary *As first in time, order or importance.* Kuamua. See entries below and *secondary, tertiary, terminal*. *~ bronchus, in anatomy.* 'Āmanapu'u kuamua. *~ shield volcano.* Lua pele kuahene kuamua. *~ volcanic activity.* Hū pele kuamua.
primary *Also ~ election, a preliminary election to nominate candidates for office.* Koho pāloka wae moho, wae moho. *Closed ~.* Wae moho kūloko. *Open ~.* Wae moho kūākea.
primary directions *The four ~, or four cardinal points of the compass, in geography.* Nā kūkulu 'ehā. See *intermediate directions*.
primate *An order of animals including man, apes and monkeys.* Māpūnaka.

prime *~ number, in math.* Helu kumu. *Relatively ~ numbers, i.e. numbers which share one factor between them, and that factor is 1.* Hoa helu ho'onui like kahi. *~ factorization.* Huli helu ho'onui kumu. *Twin ~s.* Helu kumu kūlua.
prime meridian *In geography.* Kumu lonikū, kumu lonitū.
primitive Makakumu.
principal *Money loaned, usually at a given interest rate and for a specified time.* Kumupa'a, kālā kumupa'a. See *interest*.
principle *As an accepted rule of action.* Kulehana, kahua hana. *Archimedes' ~, i.e. the buoyant force on an object submerged in a fluid is equal to the weight of the fluid displaced by that object, in science.* Ke kulehana a 'Akimika. *Bernoulli's ~.* Ke kulehana a Penuli. *Basic counting ~, in math.* Kulehana no ka helu 'ana. *Half-rectangle ~.* Kulehana huinahā lō'ihi hapalua.
print *As in handwriting.* Limahakahaka. *Also to ~.* Kākau pākahikahi. See entry below and *resolution, script*. *To~, as on a computer.* Pa'i (preceded by ke). *~ style or attribute, as italic or bold.* Kaila hua. *~ preview.* Nāmua pa'i.
print *To impress or stamp something in or on something else.* Kāpala. *As something impressed or stamped with a ~.* Lau kāpala.
printer *As for a computer.* Mīkini pa'i. *~ effects.* Hi'ohi'ona pa'i.
prioritize *To ~, set priorities.* Ho'oka'ina makakoho. See *priority*.
priority Makakoho. See *prioritize*. *To make something a ~.* Ho'omakakoho.
prism 'Ōpaka. *Rectangular ~.* 'Ōpaka huinahā lō'ihi.
private land 'Alokio, 'alodio. See *public land*.
privilege *Or rights, as in a computer network.* Kuleana.

Mamaka Kaiao / 272

probability Pahiki. See *chance*. *High ~.* Pahiki nui. *Low ~.* Pahiki liʻiliʻi. *Experimental ~.* Pahiki hoʻokolohua. *Mathematical ~.* Pahiki makemakika.

probe *Dentist's pick.* ʻŌhiki kauka niho. *To ~.* ʻAkiu. *Space ~.* ʻAkiu lewa lipo.

problem *In math.* Polopolema. See *equation, solve*. *Numerical ~.* Haʻihelu.

problem *Also difficulty, as in the plot of a story.* Hihia. See *resolution*.

proboscis *As of a butterfly.* Nūkihu.

procedure *Process to follow.* Kaʻina hana.

process Haʻaliu. *~(ed) cheese.* Waiūpaʻa i haʻaliu ʻia. *A prefix indicating a ~.* Kā-.

processor *Word ~, as a computer program.* Polokalamu kikokiko palapala.

produce *To ~, as a movie or video production.* Hoʻopuka. See entry below and *production*. *~r.* Luna hoʻopuka. *Project ~r.* Luna hoʻopuka papahana.

producer *An organism that can make its own food, such as green plants.* Kāpuka ʻai.

product *Something that has been produced or manufactured.* Huahana. See *household product, input*. *~ manager.* Luna huahana. *Dairy ~.* Meaʻai waiū.

product *In multiplication.* Hualoaʻa. *Cross ~.* Hualoaʻa kaupeʻa.

production *~ manager, as for a movie or video ~.* Manakia ʻenehana. See *produce*. *~ engineer.* Luna ʻenehana. *Assistant ~ engineer.* Hope luna ʻenehana. *Video ~ crew.* Nā limahana paʻi wikiō.

professional *Also professionally.* ʻOihana. *Allied health ~.* Kākoʻo ʻoihana olakino. *~ dancer.* Mea hulahula ʻoihana. *~ly printed.* Paʻi ʻoihana ʻia.

professional diploma *For teaching.* Palapala ʻoihana aʻo.

profit Kumuloaʻa. See *loss*.

program *As for computer; also application, as in computer program; also as on TV.* Polokalamu. See *spreadsheet*. *Database ~.* Polokalamu hōkeo ʻikepili. *~ disk.* Pā polokalamu (*preceded by* ke). *~ title, as for a TV ~.* Poʻo inoa polokalamu (*preceded by* ke). *Space ~.* Polokalamu lewa lipo.

project *As for a class.* Pāhana.

projector *Slide ~.* Mīkini hoʻolele kiʻiaka, mīkini kiʻiaka. See *transparency*. *Movie ~.* Mīkini hoʻolele kiʻiʻoniʻoni, mīkini kiʻiʻoniʻoni.

prominences *Solar ~, puffs of gas which gently drift above the surface of the sun.* Puapuaʻi lā.

prompt *On time.* (I ka) hola kūpono.

prong *Of electrical plug.* Niho palaka. *Two-~ed plug.* Palaka niho lua. *Three-~ed plug.* Palaka niho kolu.

pronunciation Puana.

proof See *verify*.

proofread Loihape. See *Hawaiian entries under* kaha *for proofreading symbols*.

propaganda Kalapepelo.

propagate *To ~ plants or breed animals.* Haʻakipu.

propane Pōpene.

property *Distinctive attribute, as of a number, in math.* ʻAnopili (*preceded by* ke). *Associative ~.* ʻAnopili hoʻolike. *Chemical ~.* ʻAnopili kemikala. *Commutative ~.* ʻAnopili kaʻina hoʻi hope. *Distributive ~.* ʻAnopili hoʻoili. *Equality ~.* ʻAnopili kaulike. *Grouping ~.* ʻAnopili hoʻopūʻulu. *Number ~.* ʻAnopili helu. *One ~.* ʻAnopili ʻekahi. *Opposites ~.* ʻAnopili o ka ʻēkoʻa. *Zero ~.* ʻAnopili ʻole. *Zero ~ of multiplication.* ʻAnopili ʻole o ka hoʻonui.

proportion *In math.* Lākiō like.

props *As for a play, movie or video production.* Pono kahua. *~ master.* Luna pono kahua. *~ needed.* Nā pono kahua e pono ai.

protected *Write ~, as a computer file or disk.* Hoʻopale kākau ʻia.

protective ~ *glasses or goggles.* Makaaniani kaupale.
protein Kumuʻiʻo, polokina.
pro tem *Also pro tempore.* No ka manawa. *President* ~. Pelekikena no ka manawa.
proton Huna ʻāne. See *electron, neutron.*
protozoa Porotozoa.
protractor Ana huina. *Right angle* ~. Ana huina kūpono.
prove *To check, verify.* Hōʻoia.
provost *As of a college or university.* Luna kulanui. See *chancellor, president.*
pseudonestor xanthophrys *Maui parrotbill.* Kīkēkoa.
psychrometer Ana kawaūea kūlua. See *hygrometer. Sling* ~. Maʻa ana kawaūea kūlua.
publicist Mea hoʻolaulaha. See *publicize.*
publicize Hoʻolaulaha.
public land ʻĀina no ka lehulehu. See *private land.*
publish Hoʻopuka. See *release, update.*
puddle Hālokoloko.
Puerto Rico *Also Puerto Rican.* Pokoliko.
puffball *A kind of mushroom.* Melehune pōpōehu.
puffin Pupē, manu pupē.
pull-up Hukialewa, hukialewa pohoalo. See *chin-up.*
pulse Pana. See *beat.* ~ *rate, heart rate.* Helu pana puʻuwai.
pump *Also to* ~, *as air or water.* Pāuma. See *valve. Air* ~, *as for tires.* Pāuma ea, pāuma paikikala.
punch *Hole* ~, *as for paper.* Pāniki pepa.
punctuate *Also punctuation mark.* Kaha kiko.
pungent *Also sharp, as the smell of ammonia or vinegar.* Wiʻu.
pupa *Also pupal.* Pupa. *To pupate.* Moeapupa.

puppet Pāpeka, pāpeta, kiʻi lima. See *marionette.*
purchase order *PO.* Palapala ʻoka kūʻai.
purse *Also suitcase.* Pāiki, pāisi. *Coin* ~. ʻEke kenikeni (*preceded by* ke).
push Pahu, pohu. ~*cart.* Kaʻa pahu.
pushup *Also to do pushups.* Koʻo lima.
put away *To* ~, *as in computer program.* Hoʻokaʻawale. See *cancel, undo.*
put in *To insert, as disk into computer.* Hoʻokomo. *To* ~ *order or sequence.* Hoʻokaʻina. See *alphabetize.*
put on *To* ~ *makeup.* Hoʻouʻiuʻi, hoʻonaninani.
putrefaction *Aerobic* ~ *or decomposition.* Ka hoʻohāpopopo eaea ʻana. See *putrefied. Anaerobic* ~ *or decomposition.* Ka koʻohāpopopo eaea ʻole ʻana.
putrefied *Decomposed.* Hāpopopo. See *putrefaction. To decompose or putrefy something.* Hoʻohāpopopo.
put together *To* ~, *as a model.* Kāpili. See *manufacture. To* ~ *a model airplane.* Kāpili kūkohu mokulele.
putty Pake. ~ *knife.* Pahi pake.
puzzle Nane. *Crossword* ~. Nane huaʻōlelo. *Jigsaw* ~. Nane ʻāpana. *Number* ~. Nane huahelu.
pyramid ~ *shape.* Pelamika. *As in Egypt.* Puʻu pelamika. *Energy* ~. Pelamika ikehu.
Pyrex Paileki. ~ *test tube.* Hano hoʻokolohua paileki.
pyrogallol Pairogalola.
Pythagorean *Also Pythagoras.* Paekakoleo. ~ *theorum, in math.* Manaʻohaʻi o Paekakoleo.

Q

Q-tip *Cotton swab.* Lāʻau pulupulu.
quadrant ʻĀpana hapahā.
quadrat *A rectangular plot used for ecological or population studies.* ʻĀpana noiʻi.

quadrilateral Huinahā. *See Hawaiian entries under* huinahā.
quality *See resolution, service, vowel.*
quarantine Hoʻomalu maʻi. *~ station.* Hale hoʻomalu maʻi.
quart Kuaka. *Abb.* kk.
quarter *The coin.* Hapahā. *To ~, as an animal.* Pākā hapahā. *See skin.*
quarterback *In football.* ʻAlihikūlele, ʻalihi.
quarter-turn image *In math.* Kinona like wili hapahā, kinona like wili 1/4.
question *Bonus or extra credit ~.* Nīnau hoʻopiʻi kaha, nīnau ʻai keu. *Leading ~.* Nīnau pākākā. *Multiple-choice ~.* Nīnau kohokoho. *~ mark.* Kiko nīnau.
questionnaire Palapala ninaninau. *See interrogate.*
quilt Kapa kuiki.
quinine Kinikona.
quit *To ~, as a computer program.* Haʻalele.
quota Kuanaki.
quotation *Also to quote.* Puanaʻī. *~ mark.* Kaha puanaʻī. *Single open quote; printer's symbol for* ʻokina. Kaha puanaʻī pākahi wehe. *Double close quote.* Kaha puanaʻī pālua pani.
quote Puanaʻī. *See quotation. A stated price, as for merchandise.* Kumukūʻai.
quotient Helu puka.

R

rabbit Lāpaki, lāpiki, ʻiole lāpiki. *Cottontail ~.* Lāpaki huelo pulupulu, lāpiki huelo pulupulu, ʻiole lāpiki huelo pulupulu. *Chinchilla ~.* Lāpaki kinikila, lāpiki kinikila, ʻiole lāpiki kinikila.
raccoon Lakuna.
race *Relay ~.* Heihei hoʻoili, kūkini hoʻoili. *See baton.*
rack *For clothes, as on wheels in a clothing store.* Hao kau lole, haka lole. *For drying dishes.* Haka kaulaʻi pā. *Towel ~.* Kaola kāwele.
racket *Also bat, club.* ʻŪhili. *See hit.*

radiate *See radiation.*
radiation *Also to radiate.* Malele. *Adaptive ~, in biology.* Malele hoʻoliliuwelo. *Also to radiate, as in the form of waves.* Pāhawewe. *Atomic ~.* Pāhawewe ʻātoma. *Nuclear ~.* Pāhawewe nukelea. *Solar ~.* Pāhawewe lā.
radio Lēkiō, pahu hoʻolele leo.
radioactivity Pāhawewe ikehu.
radiocarbon date *Also carbon dating.* Helu makahiki kalapona.
radish Lakika.
radius *Of a circle.* Kahahānai. *Abb.* khh.
raffia *The fiber of the ~ palm of Madagascar.* Pāʻā pāma.
raft Lāpa. *Rubber ~.* Lāpa laholio. *Wooden ~.* Lāpa lāʻau.
raid *Also attack.* Hoʻouka. *See counterattack.*
rail *Flightless ~.* Moho lele ʻole.
railing *Ballustrade.* Paehumu. *~ support, balluster.* ʻŪlili, hūlili.
rain *In small area while sun is shining, sometimes considered an omen of misfortune.* Kualā, ua kualā. *~ distribution.* Ka ili o ka ua. *~fall.* Ua. *Orographic ~ distribution.* Ua pili pali. *~ forest.* Nahele maʻukele. *~ map.* Palapala ʻāina ua. *~ shadow.* Lulu ʻaleneo. *~ water.* Wai ua. *Rainy side, as of a mountain.* Alo ua.
raisin Hua waina maloʻo.
rake *As for leaves.* Kope ʻōpala. *Garden ~.* Hao kope. *To ~.* Kope, kopekope, pūlumi.
ramp Alahiō. *As for skateboarding.* Heʻena. *Skateboard ~.* Heʻena papa huila.
random Pono koho. *~ sample.* Hāpana pono koho.
range *As a series of mountains.* Pae. *See chain, series. Mountain ~.* Pae kuahiwi. *The difference between the largest and smallest number or value.* Laulā, laulā loa.
range pole *Also surveying rod.* Lāʻau ana ʻāina. *See elevation pole, sighter.*

ranger Lanakia. ~ *watchtower, esp. for watching for forest fires.* Hale kiaʻi ululāʻau.
rank *As position or social standing.* Kūlana. *As in an orderly arrangement.* Pae. *To ~, as from small to large.* Hoʻokaʻina pae.
rap ~ *music; also to ~.* Pāleoleo.
rapid *In ~ succession.* ʻAmaʻamau.
rapids *As in a river.* Wai hāloʻaloʻa.
rare *As meat.* Koko, kokoko. *Medium ~.* Hapa moʻa, moʻa hapa.
rarefaction *The least dense concentration of wave particles in a compressional wave.* Wele. *See* compression.
Rasalhague *A star.* Hopuhopu.
rasp *The tool.* Apuapu.
rat ʻIole. *Roof ~.* ʻIole kaupoku.
rate *Also percent, percentage rate.* Pākēneka. *See* ratio, repeat rate. *Tax ~.* Pākēneka ʻauhau. ~ *of interest.* Pākēneka uku paneʻe. *A ratio that compares different kinds of units; quantity, amount or degree of something measured per unit of something else, as of time.* Lākiō. *Rating response.* Pane pālākiō. *To ~, as on a scale.* Loipālākiō.
ratio Lākiō. *See* proportion, rate. *Equal ~.* Lākiō like.
rational number *In math.* Helu puʻunaue koena ʻole. *See* irrational number.
rattan Pāma hihi.
rattle *Baby ~.* ʻUlīkeke. *See* tambourine.
raw *Unprocessed, as raw materials.* Kūlohelohe. *See entries below and* natural. ~ *material.* Makelia kūlohelohe, memea kūlohelohe.
raw footage *As of video tape.* Līpine paʻi maka. *See* footage.
raw sewage Kaekene maka. *See* treat (chemically).

ray *As in geometry.* Wāwae, ʻaoʻao. *Cathode-~ tube (CRT).* ʻOhe kīwī. *Cosmic ~.* Kukuna lewa lipo. *Ultraviolet ~.* Kukuna kuawehi. *One of the bony spines supporting the membrane of a fish's fin.* Nīʻau lā.
re *The second note on the musical scale.* Kō.
reach *See* beam reach, broad reach.
react *Also reaction, as chemical compounds.* Mōʻaui. *See* reactant, reactor.
reactant *Also reagent.* ʻŪmōʻaui. *See* reaction, reactor.
reaction *Also to react, as chemical compounds.* Mōʻaui. *See* action-reaction pair, reactant, reactor.
reactor Mea mōʻaui. *See* reactant, reaction.
read *Speed ~.* Heluwawe. *See* skim read, speed write. *Speed ~ing.* Ka heluwawe ʻana.
read *See* skim read.
reader *Story book.* Puke heluhelu.
reagent *Also reactant.* ʻŪmōʻaui. *See* reaction, reactor.
realistic Kohu ʻoiaʻiʻo. ~ *fiction.* Hakupuni kohu ʻoiaʻiʻo.
real number *In math.* Helu maoli.
real time *As in computer program.* Manawa ʻānō.
reasonable Kūpono. ~ *price.* Kumukūʻai kūpono.
reasoning *Inductive ~, i.e. generalizing from examples, as in math.* Hoʻoholo pili laʻana.
rebound *To ~, in basketball.* ʻĀpō.
receive *To ~, in football; reception.* ʻApo. *See* intercept. *Receiver.* Mea ʻapo. *To ~ a serve, in volleyball; also first pass.* Kiʻi.
receiver *Telephone ~.* ʻApo kelepona.
reception *See* receive.
receptor *As of nerve endings in the body, in biology.* Aʻalonoa. *Pressure ~.* Aʻalonoa mīka. *Taste ~.* Aʻalonoa ʻono.
recess *As during school.* Wā pāʻani.

recipe Lekapī.
reciprocal *In math.* Pālike.
Recommended Daily Allowances *USRDA; now known as Percent Daily Value.* Pākēneka o ka papaʻai.
record *A quantity of facts treated as a unit.* Moʻokūʻikena. *As a list of facts about achievements or tasks accomplished; also résumé, vita, curriculum vitae.* Moʻomōʻali. *Greatest achievement or performance to date.* Kūhoʻe. *To set the ~.* Mākia i ke kūhoʻe.
record *As for a record player.* Pāleo, pāʻōlelo. *~ player.* Mīkini hoʻokani pāleo, mīkini pāleo. *To ~, as on a cassette.* Hoʻopaʻa, ʻoki. *~ing tape.* Līpine.
recorder *Tape ~.* Mīkini hoʻopaʻa leo. *See player. Cassette ~.* Mīkini hoʻopaʻa lola, mīkini lola. *Reel-to-reel tape ~.* Mīkini hoʻopaʻa pōkaʻa, mīkini pōkaʻa leo.
recreation *Department of Parks and ~.* ʻOihana o nā Pāka a me nā Hana Hoʻonanea.
rectangle Huinahā lōʻihi. *See half-rectangle principle. Golden ~, a rectangle in which the ratio of the width to the length is the same as that of the length to the sum of the width plus the length.* Huinahā lōʻihi kula. *Rectangular prism.* ʻŌpaka huinahā lōʻihi.
rectangular *See rectangle.*
recycle Hoʻopōʻaiapuni. *See cycle.*
red blood cell Hunaola koko ʻulaʻula.
red-eyed vireo *A kind of bird.* Manu wiliō mākole.
Red Spot *Giant ~, a huge gaseous feature on Jupiter.* ʻŌnohi ʻUla Kūāhewa.
reduce *To diet.* Hoʻēmi kino.
reduction *Vowel ~, in linguistics.* Hoʻēmi woela. *See vowel. Reduced vowel.* Woela emi.
reed Mauʻu ʻohe.

reef ʻĀpapapa. *See slipper lobster. Artificial ~.* Umukoʻa. *Kingman ~.* Koʻanakoʻa. *Maro ~.* Nalukākala. *Pearl and Hermes ~.* Holoikauaua.
reel *For recording tape.* Pōkaʻa līpine. *See player, recorder, tape. ~-to-~ tape.* Līpine pōkaʻa.
reel *As for fishing.* Wiliaho. *Open ~.* Wiliaho hāmama. *Bait-casting ~.* Wiliaho hekau maunu.
referee *Also umpire; also to ~.* ʻUao, ʻuao haʻuki. *In volleyball.* Kanaka makaʻala ʻupena.
reference *Source, as a dictionary or other ~ material.* Kūmole. *See resource.*
reference *Also coordinate, in math.* Kuhikuhina. *See coordinate, ordered pair, referent. ~ object.* Kuhia. *~ point.* Kiko kuhia.
referent *In math.* Kuhia (O-class).
referral *Coordinated physician ~ system.* ʻŌnaehana kauka no ka lapaʻau like ʻana.
reflect *To ~, as light, heat or sound.* Kūpī, hoʻokūpī.
reflection *In math.* Aka aniani. *See angle of incidence. Angle of ~, i.e. the angle between a reflected wave and the normal to the barrier from which it is reflected.* Huina kūpī. *~ image.* Kinona aka like o kekahi ʻaoʻao. *~ symmetry.* ʻĀlikelike aka.
reflector ʻOwakawaka, kukui ʻowakawaka.
reformat *To ~, as a computer disk.* Hoʻāla hou. *See format.*
region *A specific area, in math.* Wahi. *Geographic ~; also regional.* Māhele ʻāina.
register *Cash ~.* Mīkini ʻohi kālā. *See cashier. Check ~.* Moʻo pila kīkoʻo. *To ~ or check in, as at a conference or hotel.* Kāinoa komo, kāinoa. *See check out, registration.*

registration Kāinoa. See *check out, register. Early ~, pre~.* Kāinoa hiki mua. *Late ~.* Kāinoa hiki hope. *~ form.* Palapala kāinoa.

registration system *Of land.* 'Ōnaehana ho'onā 'āina. See *land court, settle.*

regular *As in shape.* Analahi. See *irregular. ~ polygon.* Huinalehulehu analahi. *~ shape.* Kinona analahi.

regulate *To fix the time, amount, degree or rate of something by making adjustments.* Ho'okonukonu.

related species *In biology.* Pili lāhulu.

relative gravity *Also specific gravity.* Lākiō pa'apū wai.

relative humidity Pā kawaūea.

relative location *In geography.* Pilina henua. See *absolute location.*

relatively prime numbers *Numbers which share one factor between them, and that factor is 1, in math.* Hoa helu ho'onui like kahi.

relay race Heihei ho'oili, kūkini ho'oili. See *baton, shuttle run.*

release *Interim or maintenance ~, as of a computer program.* Ho'opuka ho'oponopono 'ia. See *update.*

remainder *Difference, in math.* Koena. Abb. K.

remote control *Also to control by ~.* Kia pihi. See *remote manipulator arm.*

remote manipulator arm *Also space crane.* Lima kia pihi.

removable hard disk *As in a computer.* Pā pa'aloko wehe *(preceded by ke).*

remove Wehe. *Staple ~r.* Mea wehe 'ūmi'i. *To ~, as an 'opihi from its shell.* Kua'i, poke, po'e. *To ~ food from mouth and eat it again, as gum.* 'Ai hemo.

rename *To ~, in math.* Ho'onoho kūana helu.

repair kit *For tires.* Kini poho ea.

repeat *To ~, as the action of a computer key when held down.* Pīna'i. See *turbo button. ~ rate.* Māmā pīna'i.

repeating decimal Kekimala pīna'i.

repel *To ~, as like charges in a magnet.* 'Āpahupahu.

replace *To change or ~, as in search-and-~ feature in computer program.* Kuapo. *To find and change, search and ~.* Huli a kuapo.

report Hō'ike. *Oral ~.* Hō'ike ha'i waha, 'ōlelo hō'ike. *Oral ~, presented as a speech.* Ha'i'ōlelo hō'ike. *Written ~.* Hō'ike palapala.

reproductive system *In biology.* 'Ōnaehana ho'ohua.

reptile Mo'ohana.

republic *Central African ~.* Lepupalika 'Apelika Waena. *Democratic ~ of the Congo.* Lepupalika Kemokalaka 'o Konokō. *Dominican ~.* Lepupalika Kominika.

requirement Koina.

research Noi'i. *~er.* Kanaka noi'i. *Scientific ~er.* Kanaka noi'i 'epekema.

reserpine *An alkaloid used as a tranquilizer.* Resepine.

reservation See *reserve.*

reserve *A reservation or tract of land set apart.* 'Āina ho'omalu. *Forest ~.* 'Āina ho'omalu ululā'au. *Nature ~.* 'Āina ho'omalu ao kūlohelohe. *Natural Areas ~s System (NARS).* 'Ōnaehana Ho'omalu 'Āina Kūlohelohe.

residence Hale noho, wahi noho. *~ hall or dormitory, as at a school.* Hale noho haumāna.

residue *Of poi after pounding, or of milk after beating.* Kale 'ai.

resin *For musical instrument strings.* Hūka'a.

resist *To ~, as water on corrosive things.* 'A'alo. See *Teflon, waterproof.*

resistance *Opposition to the flow of electricity, or any opposition that slows down or prevents movement of electrons through a conductor.* Āohiohi. *Air ~.* Āohiohi ea. *~ arm, i.e. the distance from the fulcrum to the resistance force in a lever.* Lima āohiohi. *~ force.* Manehu āohiohi.

resolution *Low-quality print ~, as on a computer printer.* Kalakala. *Precision or high-quality print ~.* Miomio.
resolution *Also solution, as of a problem in a story.* Hopena holo. See *problem.*
resource *Or reference book, as an encyclopedia.* Puke noiʻi. See *reference.*
resource *A source of supply.* Kumuwaiwai. *Natural ~.* Kumuwaiwai kūlohelohe.
respiration *Also respiratory.* Hanu. See *respiratory system. Also to respire.* Kōpiaʻā.
respiratory system ʻŌnaehana hanu.
response *As to a stimulus.* Hāpane.
response rating *In math.* Pane pālākiō.
restaurant Hale ʻaina. *Fast-food ~.* Hale ʻaina meaʻai hikiwawe.
résumé *Also vita, curriculum vitae.* Moʻomōʻali.
retail price Kumukūʻai hale kūʻai. See *wholesale price.*
retardant *Flame ~.* Pale ahi.
reteaching book Puke aʻo hou.
retire Līkaia, rītaia, hoʻomaha loa.
return *To use the enter or ~ key on a computer or typewriter keyboard in order to return the cursor or carriage to the left margin on a new line; enter or ~, as the key just above the shift key on a computer keyboard.* Kāhoʻi. See *enter. ~ key.* Pihi kāhoʻi (*preceded by* ke).
reverse *A curved line written over a word or letter and then under the adjoining word or letter to indicate that the order of the words or letters should be ~d, in proofreading.* Kaha kuapo.
revert *To ~, as in computer program.* Hoʻi. *To ~ to previous save.* Hoʻi i ka mālama. See *save.*
review *Checkpoint.* Nāʻana.
revolution Puni. *~s per minute (rpm).* Puni o ka minuke. *Abb.* p/min.
revolution *As against a government.* Hoʻokahuli aupuni. *~ary war.* Kaua hoʻokahuli aupuni.

rewind *To ~, as film or audio tape.* Wili i hope. See *fast forward.*
Rhea *The second largest moon of Saturn.* Rea.
rhesus monkey Keko lekuka.
rhizome ʻAuaʻa.
Rhode Island *Also Rhode Islander.* Loke ʻAilana, Rode ʻAilana.
rhododendron Pua wīkōlia.
rhombus Huinahā hiō like.
rhythm *In linguistics.* Aupana. *In music.* Papana.
rice Laiki, lāisi. *Brown ~.* Laiki mākuʻe, lāisi mākuʻe. *White ~.* Laiki keʻokeʻo, lāisi keʻokeʻo. *Mōchī ~.* Laiki mōchī, lāisi mōchī. *~ ball, musubi.* Pōpō laiki, pōpō lāisi, musubī.
Richter scale Pālākiō ikehu ōlaʻi.
ride *As at a carnival or amusement park.* Hololeʻa.
ridge *Midocean ~.* Kualapa waena moana.
riffle *As in a stream.* Kahena hulili.
rift Māwae. *~ valley.* Awāwa māwae. *Series of ~ valleys.* Pae awāwa māwae. *~ zone.* Kāʻei māwae.
rig *Oil ~, for drilling oil on either land or sea.* Wili ʻaila.
right angle *In math.* Huina kūpono. *~ protractor.* Ana huina kūpono.
right guard *In football.* Kūkahi ʻākau.
right justified *As type in printing.* Kaulihi ʻākau.
right margin Lihi ʻākau. See *justify, margin.*
rights *Or privilege, as in a computer network.* Kuleana. *Bill of ~.* Palapala pono kanaka.
right tackle *In football.* Kūlua ʻākau. See *tackle.*
rim *Of basket, in basketball.* Hao, kuku. See *basket. Of a wheel.* Kuapo hao.
rimless *Also swish, i.e. to make a basket without touching the rim, in basketball.* Kuhō. See *shot.*

ring Komo. ~ *finger*. Manamana komo, manamana pili. *As in a ~ binder.* Lina kui. *~ binder.* Puke lina kui. *Six-pack ~, i.e. the plastic ~ which holds cans together.* ʻEa ʻekeʻeke. *Six-pack beer ~.* ʻEa ʻekeʻeke pia. *Six-pack soda ~.* ʻEa ʻekeʻeke koloaka.
ring of fire *In geology.* Lei o Pele.
ring stand *As for a test tube.* Kū hano hoʻokolohua.
rite of passage *Also initiation.* Hana komo pae.
river See *delta, estuary. ~ tributary.* ʻAumana muliwai.
riverbed Papakū, papakū muliwai.
robot Lopako.
rock *Black, porous, light ~ used to scrape gourds.* Kūnānahu. See *calcarious rock, igneous rock. Parent ~, i.e. rocks in upper surface of the earth which break down to form rocks, sand, dirt, etc.* Pōhaku makua.
Rock *La Pérouse ~.* Kuamanō.
rock See *calcareous rock, igneous rock.*
rocket *As space or fireworks.* Ahikao. See *Manned Maneuvering Unit. ~ ship.* Moku ahikao. *Solid ~ booster.* Kao wāwahie kinopaʻa, kao wāwahie paʻa.
rocking horse Lio paipai.
rock the boat *A jump rope game of jumping and bouncing a ball at the same time.* ʻOni a ka moku. See *jump rope.*
rod *Surveying ~.* Lāʻau ana ʻāina. See *elevation pole, sighter.*
rodeo Hoʻokūkū hana paniolo.
roe deer Kia lō.
role *As in a play or movie.* Hāmeʻe.
roll *As of film.* ʻŌwili. See entries below and *pick and roll. ~ of film.* ʻŌwili kiʻi.
roller *Paint ~.* Lola pena. *To paint with a ~.* Pena lola. *Also steam~.* Kimalola.
rollerblade Kāmaʻa lapa huila. *To skate with ~s.* Holo lapa huila.
roller coaster Kaʻa lola.

roller skate Kāmaʻa huila. *To skate with ~s.* Holo kāmaʻa huila.
rolling pin Lola palaoa.
Roman candle Ihoihokī.
Romania *Also Romanian.* Romānia.
Roman numeral Helu Loma.
roof *To ~ (a shot), in basketball.* Paku ʻino. See *block. ~ rat.* ʻIole kaupoku.
room See Hawaiian entries under lumi. *~ temperature.* Mehana ea, mehana lumi.
root *Source, derivation or origin, as the etymology of a word.* Molekumu. See *square root. Of tongue.* Mole alelo.
root *To enable to develop ~s.* Hoʻāʻa, hoʻoaʻa. *~ing hormone.* Hōmona hoʻāʻa, hōmona hoʻoaʻa. *~ hairs.* Huluhulu aʻa.
rope See *jump rope.*
rose *Wood ~.* Loke lāʻau.
rosette Pākaʻapohe.
rotary tiller *Also rotary cultivator, Rototiller.* Mīkini kipikipi lepo. See *cultivator.*
rotate *To ~, in volleyball; also to switch sides.* Kuapo.
rotational symmetry *In math.* ʻĀlikelike wili.
rotation image *In math.* Kinona like o kekahi ʻaoʻao.
rotenone *A chemical compound.* Lokeni.
Rototiller See *rotary tiller.*
rouge *Also blush, as makeup.* Hehelo pāpālina.
round *To ~ off, in math.* Kolikoli. *To ~ down.* Kolikoli haʻalalo. *To ~ up.* Kolikoli haʻaluna.
round *As in boxing.* Puni. See *hand, lap.*
rounded *In linguistics.* Mōkio. See *vowel. ~ vowel.* Woela mōkio.
round trip Holopuni. See *one way.*
roundworm Koʻe poepoe.
routine Moʻokiʻina.
rover *Lunar ~.* Kaʻa holo mahina.
rpm See *revolutions per minute.*

Māmaka Kaiao / 280

rub *To ~, as one's eyes.* ʻĀnai. *To ~ repeatedly.* ʻAnaʻanai.
rubber *~ band.* Apo laholio. *~ boot.* Lapa puki, laba puki, puki lapa. *~ cement.* Tuko laholio. See *glue, paste.*
rubbing *To make a ~, as of petroglyphs.* Kāmahaka.
rug *For any large room.* Hāliʻi papahele, moena. See *carpet. Small ~, as in bathroom or beside bed.* Pale papahele, pale wāwae.
rule *Function ~, in math.* Lula hahaina. *Exception to a ~.* Kūʻē lula.
ruler *Measuring device.* Lula. See *tape measure. Wooden ~.* Lula lāʻau.
run Holo. See *lap, long jump, shuttle run. Three-hundred yard run.* Holo ʻekolu haneli ʻīā. *As in a stream.* Wai kōʻieʻie.
runner-up *Also second place.* Kūlana ʻelua.
running back *General term, in football.* Mea holo.
runoff *As water running from the land into the sea.* Holo kele wai.
runway Ala kuʻu mokulele.
Russia *Also Russian.* Lūkia, Rūsia.
rustle *To ~, as leaves or the sea.* Nehe.
Rwanda *Also Rwandan.* Ruanada.

S

saddle *Pack ~.* Noho ʻāmana.
saddle shoe *Oxford.* Kāmaʻa ʻili helei.
Sadr *A star.* Hikiwawe.
safety *In football.* ʻĀwaʻa. *Strong ~.* ʻĀwaʻa muku. *Weak ~.* Āwaʻa lala.
safety glasses *Also protective glasses.* Makaaniani kaupale.
safety line *As in a spacecraft.* Kaula piko.
safety pin Pine kaiapa.
Sahara *Western ~, Western Saharan.* Sahara Komohana.
sail *To ~ directly downwind.* Kele kaʻalalo. See *beam reach, broad reach, close hauled.*
saimin Kaimine.

Saint Helens *Mount ~.* Mauna Kana Helena, Mauna Sana Helena.
salamander Kalamena, salamena. *Red-backed ~.* Kalamena kuaʻula.
sale *Also to be or put on sale.* Kūʻaiemi. *~ price.* Kāki kūʻaiemi.
sales pitch *To make a pitch, as a ~, or to "sell" an idea.* Paialou.
sales tax ʻAuhau kumukūʻai.
saliva *Also salivary.* Hāʻae. See *salivary gland.*
salivary gland Lōkuʻu hāʻae.
salt *Epsom ~.* Paʻakai ʻepesoma. *Nutrient ~s, the deposits that remain after a liquid has been removed.* Paʻamāhuaola.
salty water Wai kai. *To desalinate/desalinize ~.* Hoʻomānalo wai kai.
Salvador *El ~, Salvadoran, Salvadorian.* ʻEla Salavadora.
Sāmoa *Also Sāmoan.* Kāmoa. *Also* Haʻamoa. *American Sāmoa, American Sāmoan.* Kāmoa ʻAmelika. *Also* Haʻamoa ʻAmelika.
sample *As a small part of a larger whole.* Hāpana. *Composite ~.* Hāpana huihuina. *Random ~.* Hāpana pono koho. *Sampling methods.* Nā kiʻina ʻohi hāpana.
sample space *The set of all possible outcomes of an experiment, in math.* ʻŌpaʻa hopena.
sand culture ʻOulu one.
sandstone Pōhāone.
sandwich Kanauika. See *filling.*
sanitary pad *Niʻihau usage.* Palemaʻi. See *underpants.*
sap Kohu.
sapling Kumulāʻau ʻōpiopio.
Saran Wrap *Any plastic film for wrapping food.* Wahī ʻea.
sassafras Sasapalasa.
satellite Ukali, poelele. See *Long Duration Exposure Facility. ~ star.* Hōkū ukali.
saturated fat ʻAilakele paʻapū. See *fat.*

Saturday Poʻaono. *Abb.* P6.
Saturn *The planet.* Makulu.
sauce pan Ipuhao hana kai.
saucer See *flying saucer.*
Saudi Arabia *Also Saudi.* Saudi ʻAlapia, Saudi ʻArabia.
savanna *A tropical or subtropical grassland containing scattered trees.* Sawana.
save *To ~, in basketball.* Kiʻilou. *In volleyball.* Hoʻihoʻi, lou.
save *To ~, as in computer program.* Mālama. *To ~ as.* Mālama ma ka inoa ʻo. *To revert to previous ~.* Hoʻi i ka mālama.
savings *As money saved on a sale item.* Kālā mālama. *~ account, as in a bank.* Waihona hoʻāhu kālā. See *account.*
sawdust Oka lāʻau.
saxophone Kakopone, pū kakopone.
scale *In math.* Pālākiō. See entries below and *scale selection. Conversion ~.* Papa pālākiō. *~ drawing.* Kiʻi pālākiō. *To rate, as on a ~.* Loipālākiō.
scale *Linear ~, in geography.* Pālākiō lālani. *Richter ~.* Pālākiō ikehu ōlaʻi.
scale *Musical ~.* Alapiʻi mele, pākōlī. See *Hawaiian entries.*
scalene *In math.* ʻAoʻao like ʻole. *~ triangle.* Huinakolu ʻaoʻao like ʻole.
scales *For weighing something.* Anapaona. *Bathroom~.* Anapaona home, *usu.* anapaona. *Balance ~.* Anapaona kaulike. *Spring ~.* Anapaona pilina. *Balancing tray for ~.* Pā ana *(preceded by* ke). *Weight for ~.* Koihā.
scale selection *As in computer program.* Koho pālākiō.
scalloped potatoes ʻUala kahiki pepeiao, ʻuala pepeiao.
scan *To ~ or scroll, as in a computer program.* Lolelole. *To ~ forward.* Lolelole i mua. *To ~ backward.* Lolelole i hope. *To ~ search, as with audio or video equipment.* Huli lolelole.
Scandanavia *Also Scandanavian.* Kanakawia.

scanner *As for computer program.* Mīkini hoʻoili kiʻi.
scar Ninanina, ʻālina *(preceded by* ke).
scarecrow Kiʻi hoʻomakaʻu manu.
scarf Kāʻei ʻāʻī.
scattergram *In math.* Pakuhi kikokiko.
scattergraph *In math.* Pakuhi lū.
scavenger *Also to scavenge.* Hamupela.
scene *Also scenery, as for a stage production.* Nānaina. *Forest ~.* Nānaina ululāʻau.
scenery See *scene.*
scenic viewpoint *Lookout.* ʻĪmaka.
Scheat *A star.* Mākahi.
schematic drawing *Also diagram.* Kiʻikuhi.
schizophrenia Maʻi huohuoi. *Schizophrenic convulsion.* Maʻi huki huohuoi.
scholarship Haʻawina kālā hele kula, haʻawina kālā. *Athletic ~.* Haʻawina kālā ʻālapa.
school *Large ~ of fish such as* akule *or* aku. Kumu iʻa. *Small ~ of reef fish such as* manini. Naho iʻa, naha iʻa.
schoolbox Pahu pono haʻawina. See *school supplies.*
school supplies Pono haʻawina. See *schoolbox.*
science ʻEpekema, akeakamai. *Physical ~.* Kālaiaopaku. *~ fair.* Hōʻikeʻike ʻepekema.
science fiction Mōhihiʻo. *~ movie.* Kiʻiʻoniʻoni mōhihiʻo.
scientific *~ notation.* Kauhelu ʻepekema. *~ researcher.* Kanaka noiʻi ʻepekema.
scientist Kanaka ʻepekema, kanaka akeakamai.
scion Weli.
scoop *To ladle, skim.* Kīʻoʻe, ʻoʻe. See *ladle.*
scooter *Child's ~.* Peke, kaʻa peke.
score *In sports or games.* Heluʻai. See *point.*
scoreboard *As for sports.* Papa heluʻai.

Māmaka Kaiao / 282

scorpion Kopiana. *See other entries in dictionary.*

Scotch tape *Also transparent tape.* Leki 'ea.

Scotland *Also Scot, Scots, Scottish.* Kekokia, Sekotia.

scowl Pūtē. See *frown.*

scrapbook *As in computer program.* Puke hunahuna.

scratch *To ~, as an itch.* Wa'u, wa'uwa'u. *To ~ with claws, as a cat.* Walu.

screen *As for windows.* Uea makika, maka'aha. *~ door.* Pani puka uea makika, pani puka maka'aha *(preceded by ke). For projecting slides or movies.* Pākū ho'olele ki'i.

screen *As on a TV or computer monitor.* Papakaumaka. See *monitor. Calculator display ~.* Papakaumaka mīkini helu. *Computer monitor ~.* Papakaumaka kamepiula. *Edit ~, in computer program.* Pukaaniani ho'oponopono. *Home ~.* Kahua pa'a. *TV ~.* Papakaumaka kīwī. *List editor ~.* Pukaaniani kolamu 'ikepili.

screen *Also to block out, in basketball.* 'Āke'a. See *blocking foul. Illegal ~.* 'Āke'a ne'e.

screenplay Mo'olelo ki'i'oni'oni. See *screenwriter. To write a ~.* Kākau mo'olelo ki'ioni'oni, kākau mo'olelo.

screenwriter Mea kākau mo'olelo ki'i'oni'oni, mea kākau ki'i'oni'oni. See *screenplay.*

screw Kui nao.

screwdriver Kolūkalaiwa.

scribe *Also secretary.* Kākau 'ōlelo.

scrimmage *As for sports.* Ho'okūkū kio. See *championship, tournament. ~ line, in football.* Laina ho'ouka.

script *As in handwriting.* Limahiō. *Also to write in ~.* Kākau maoli. See entry below and *print.*

script *As for a play or movie.* Mo'olelo hana keaka, mo'olelo. See *screenplay. ~writer.* Mea kakau mo'olelo. *~ supervisor.* Luna kākau mo'olelo.

scroll *To ~ or scan, as in a computer program.* Lolelole. *To ~ forward.* Lolelole i mua. *To ~ backward.* Lolelole i hope.

scroll *Oriental-style ~, usually decorative.* Kiuna.

scrutinize *To look over critically.* Loi. See *critical thinking.*

scuba *To ~ dive; ~ diving.* Lu'u kini ea. *~ diver.* Kanaka lu'u kai. *~ tank.* Kini ea lu'u kai, kini ea.

sculpture Ki'i ku'ikepa.

sea *At ~,* asea. I waena moana. See *midocean.*

sea anemone 'Ōkala, 'ōkole.

seagull Kalapuna.

sea horse Mo'olio.

seal Sila. *Fur ~.* Sila pūhuluhulu. *Hawaiian monk ~.* Sila Hawai'i.

sea level 'Ilikai.

sea lion Liona kai.

seal-of-Solomon *A kind of flower.* Kilaokolomona.

seamount Mauna kai. See *guyot.*

seamount *Emperor ~s.* Pae Mauna Kai 'Emepela, Pae Mauna Kai 'o 'Emepela.

search *To find or ~ (for), as in computer program.* Huli. See *scan search. To find and change, ~ and replace.* Huli a kuapo.

season Kau. *Nesting ~.* Kau ho'opūnana.

seasonal Kū kau, kū i ke kau.

seat *Bicycle ~.* Noho paikikala. *Toilet ~.* Noho lua. *~ back.* Kua noho.

sea vent Puale kai.

secant *A line which intersects a circle at two points, in math.* Kaha 'oki pō'ai. See *tangent.*

second *Unit of time.* Kekona. *Abb.* kkn.

secondary *As second in time, order or importance.* Kualua. See *primary, tertiary, terminal. ~ activity, of a volcano.* 'Ā kualua. *~ or lobar bronchus, in anatomy.* 'Āmanapu'u kualua.

Māmaka Kaiao / 283

second base *In baseball.* Pahu ʻelua. See *base.*

second-hand *Used.* Pāmia. ~ *car.* Kaʻa pāmia.

second place *Also runner-up.* Kūlana ʻelua.

secretary *Also scribe.* Kākau ʻōlelo.

section *Cross* ~, *in math.* Hiʻona kaha.

security guard Kiaʻi, kiaʻi pō, mākaʻi kiaʻi (pō).

sediment *Marine* ~. Koʻana kai. *Stream* ~. Koʻana kahawai.

seed ʻAnoʻano. ~ *pod.* Wahī ʻanoʻano.

seedling *As of* ʻilima *plants.* Hehu. See *shoot.*

seesaw Papa hulei. *To* ~. Hulehulei.

Segin *A star.* Laniholoʻokoʻa.

segment *Line* ~, *in math.* ʻĀpana kaha. *Sound* ~, *in linguistics.* Hua.

segmental bronchus *Also tertiary bronchus, in anatomy.* ʻĀmanapuʻu kuakolu.

seismograph Mīkini ana ōlaʻi, ana ōlaʻi.

selection *Scale* ~, *as in computer program.* Koho pālākiō.

selective solubility Pēmāʻōʻā wae ʻano.

self- *Or auto-(prefix).* Hika-.

semicircle Pōʻai hapalua.

semicolon Hapa kolona. See *colon.*

sense Lonoa. ~ *of hearing.* Lonoa pepeiao. ~ *of sight.* Lonoa maka. ~ *of smell.* Lonoa ihu. ~ *of taste.* Lonoa alelo. ~ *of touch.* Lonoa ʻili.

sensitive *Case* ~, *as in computer program.* Makaʻala maʻaka.

sentence *A grammatical unit.* Hopunaʻōlelo, pepeke. See *clause.* *Math or number* ~. Hopunahelu. *Topic* ~, *as of a paragraph.* Hopunaʻōlelo wehe kumuhana.

separate Hoʻokaʻawale. See *buffer.* *To* ~ *easily, as a nut from its shell.* ʻĒkakaʻa.

separated *A "straight" Z-shaped line written to indicate where two words written as one should be* ~, *in proofreading.* Kaha hoʻokōā, kaha hoʻokaʻahua.

September Kepakemapa. *Abb.* Kep.

sequence Kaʻina. See *alphabetize.* *In math.* Laukaʻina. *In* ~, *consecutive.* Moekahi. *To put in order.* Hoʻokaʻina. *To* ~ *ideas, as in a compositon.* Hoʻokaʻina manaʻo.

serial *As of a computer port.* Ala pūkaʻina. ~ *port.* Awa ala pūkaʻina.

series Pūkaʻina. See *alkane, alkene, alkyne, chain, range.* ~ *of volcanic eruptions.* Pūkaʻina hū pele. *TV* ~. Pūkaʻina polokalamu kīwī. ~ *of geological features.* Pae. ~ *of valleys.* Pae awāwa.

serious *To act or "get* ~.*"* Hoʻokūoʻo.

serve *To* ~, *in volleyball.* Hānai, paʻi ulele. See *service, set.* *To* ~ *underhand.* Hānai puʻupuʻu. *To make a sidewinder* ~. Paʻi kulo. *To receive a* ~; *also first pass.* Kiʻi.

server *Network* ~, *as for computer network.* Kikowaena pūnaewele. See *network station.*

service Lawelawe. See entry below and *Bulletin Board Service, weather service.* *High-quality* ~. Lawelawe poʻokela. ~ *industry.* ʻOihana lawelawe. *Military* ~; *also army.* Pūʻali koa. *National Park* ~. ʻOihana Pāka Aupuni. *US Fish and Wildlife* ~. ʻOihana Iʻa me ka Holoholona Lōhiu o ʻAmelika.

service *In volleyball; also to serve (the ball).* Paʻi ulele. See *serve, side out.* ~ *violation.* ʻAʻena paʻi ulele.

serving *Of food.* Haʻawina ʻai.

session *A period of time spent in an application of a computer program.* Wā hoʻohana.

set *A collection of like items or elements.* Huikaina. *See entries below. As of golf clubs or silverware.* ʻŌpaʻa. *To ~, as a record.* Mākia. *To ~, as the sun.* Napoʻo, anapoʻo. *To ~ an imu.* Kuʻi i ka imu. *To ~ a deadline.* Kaupalena. *See deadline.*

set *To ~, as margins or tabs on computer file or typewriter.* Hoʻopaʻa. *See margin, set up, setup, spacing, tab. To ~ the margins.* Hoʻopaʻa i nā lihi. *To ~ the tabs.* Hoʻopaʻa i nā kāwāholo. *To ~ spacing.* Hoʻokoana.

set *As for movie or video production.* Kahua. *To decorate ~s.* Hoʻoponopono kahua. *~ decorator.* Mea hoʻoponopono kahua. *To design ~s.* Hakulau kahua. *~ designer.* Mea hakulau kahua.

set *To ~ or ~ up (the ball), in volleyball.* Hānai, hāʻawi. *To make a back ~.* Hānai i hope, hānai kīkala. *To make an outside ~.* Hānai lōʻihi. *To make a short ~.* Hānai pōkole. *~ter.* Mea hānai, hānai.

set shot *In basketball; to make such a shot.* Kī kū.

settle *To ~, as a claim.* Hoʻonā. *See land court, land registration system.*

settlement pattern *In geography.* Lauana hoʻokahua.

set type *To ~, as for video captions.* Ulele hua. *See character operator.*

set up *To ~, as printer specifications for computer.* Hoʻonoho.

setup *As in computer program.* Hoʻokuene. *Page ~.* Hoʻokuene ʻaoʻao.

sewage *~ sludge.* Kaekene. *Raw ~.* Kaekene maka. *Treated ~.* Ke kaekene i kāemikala ʻia.

sewer pipe Paipu lawe ʻino. *See manhole cover.*

sexism Hoʻokae keka.

sextant Ana kilo lani.

sexual harassment *Also to subject to ~.* Kekohala.

shade *For a lamp.* Pale kukui. *To ~, as with a pencil.* Kahiāuli. *See highlight.*

shadow *As on a computer or in typesetting.* Hoʻāka. *See eye shadow. ~ed.* Aka. *Rain ~.* Lulu ʻalaneo.

shake *Milk ~.* Waiū luliluli.

shallow *As a dish.* Pānainai.

shampoo Kopa lauoho. *See soap.*

shape *Geometric figure, in math.* Kinona. *Regular ~.* Kinona analahi.

shape *To model or mold, as clay.* Hōʻomoʻomo.

sharp *Pungent, as the smell of ammonia or vinegar.* Wiʻu.

shave ice *Snow cone.* Haukōhi.

shavings *Wood ~.* Hānā.

shaving soap Kopa kahi ʻumiʻumi, *usu.* kopa ʻumiʻumi.

shawl *Also light blanket.* Kīhei, kīhei pili.

sheet *As of stamps.* Laulahi. *~ of stamps.* Laulahi poʻoleka. *See bedsheet, call sheet.*

sheet feeder *As for a computer printer.* Poho pepa. *Additional ~.* Poho pākuʻi.

sheeting *Plastic ~, general term.* Hāliʻi ʻea. *See polyethyline.*

shelf Haka kau. *Book~.* Haka kau puke. *See continental shelf.*

shelter Wahi hoʻomalu. *Lean-to ~.* Hale kāpiʻo.

shield *As for battle.* Pale kaua. *As in volcanoes.* Kuahene. *~ building; to build a shield (volcano).* Hoʻāhua kuahene. *~ cone.* Puʻu kuahene. *~ volcano.* Lua pele kuahene. *Primary ~ volcano.* Lua pele kuahene kuamua. *To ~ or cover, as one's mouth.* Pale.

shift *To ~, as on computer or typewriter keyboard.* Kake. *~ key.* Pihi kake (*preceded by* ke).

shifting cultivation *In geography.* Mahi ʻai mahakea.

shirt *With short or long sleeves.* Palaka, pālule. *Aloha ~.* Palaka aloha. *T-~.* Palaʻili, paleʻili. *Any pullover style shirt.* Palaʻili.

Shoals *French Frigate ~.* Mokupāpapa.

shock therapy Lapaʻau hoʻomiki uila.
shoe *Hiking ~.* Kāmaʻa hekehi. See *hike*. *Saddle ~*, *Oxford*. Kāmaʻa ʻili helei. *Snow ~.* Kāmaʻa hele hau.
shoot *To ~, as a photograph.* Paʻi *(preceded by* ke*)*. See *shot, take. To ~ a movie film.* Paʻi kiʻiʻoniʻoni. *To ~ a video.* Paʻi wikiō.
shoot *From root of a plant.* Kauwowo, kawowo, kā, ʻelia, ilo. See *seedling*.
shooting forward *Also swing man or three man, in basketball.* Kūkolu.
shooting guard *Also two man, in basketball.* Kūlua.
shooting star Hōkū welowelo. See *comet*.
shopping cart Kaʻa mākeke.
shopping center Kikowaena kūʻai.
shortcut *Also to take a ~.* ʻOki pōkole.
short-range *Also short-term.* Hikiāpoko. See *medium-range, long-range*. *~ plan.* Papa hoʻolālā hikiāpoko.
short set *To make a ~, in volleyball.* Hānai pōkole.
short-term See *short-range*.
shot *Photograph.* Kiʻi paʻi. See *close-up, medium shot, wide shot*. *As of a photograph or in movie or video production.* Paʻi *(preceded by* ke*)*. *Types of ~s.* Nā ʻano paʻi.
shot *Also to shoot, as in basketball.* Kī. See *basket*. *Bank ~.* Kī papa. *Hook ~.* Kī papaʻi. *Jump ~.* Kī lele. *Lay-up.* Kī kīkoʻo, kī pai. *Set ~.* Kī kū. *Slam dunk.* Pākī. *Swish, rimless ~.* Kuhō. *Three-point ~.* Kī ʻai kolu. *Tip-in.* Kī papaʻi.
shovel Kopalā. See *trowel, spade*. *Steam ~.* Kewe kopalā.
show *To demonstrate, as how a math problem is solved.* Kuhikuhi.
show and tell *As in a preschool or elementary school class.* Hōʻikeʻike.

shower *For bathing.* Kililau. *To take a ~, bathe by ~ing.* ʻAuʻau kililau. *Hand-held ~.* Kililau lima. *~ cap.* Pāpale kililau. *~ curtain.* Pale kililau. *~ stall.* Keʻena kililau. *~ head.* Poʻo kililau *(preceded by* ke*)*.
shoyu *Soy sauce.* Koiū. See *soybean*.
shrimp *Brine ~.* Pokipoki ālia.
shrub *Bush.* Laʻalāʻau. *Alpine ~land.* Wao laʻalāʻau.
shuffle *To ~, as cards.* Kakekake. See *deal*.
shuttle Kaʻa halihali. *Space ~.* Mokuhali lewa lipo.
shuttle run *In track.* Holo hoʻoili.
shy *Also wild (general term).* ʻĀhiu. See *wild*.
side *Of a sporting field or court.* Iwi, ʻaoʻao. See entries below and *end, line (as on basketball court)*. *~ line.* Laina iwi, laina ʻaoʻao. *~ line of the key on a basketball court.* Laina iwi kī.
side *Corresponding ~, in math.* ʻAoʻao launa.
side out *In volleyball.* Hāʻawi i ke kinipōpō i kekahi ʻaoʻao; kaʻa paʻi ulele, kaʻa. See *service*.
side pool *As in a stream.* Wai wiliau.
side stroke *Also to swim the ~.* ʻAu ʻaoʻao. See *stroke*.
sidewalk Alapīpā.
sideward Haʻaaʻe.
sidewinder serve *To make a ~, in volleyball.* Paʻi kulo.
sight *Sense of ~.* Lonoa maka. *~ line.* Laina ʻike.
sighter *As for surveying.* Lena māka. See *elevation pole, surveying rod*. *~ arm.* Lima lena māka.
sight line *Also line of sight.* Laina lena, laina ʻike.
sign *As political or business, etc.* Papa hoʻolaha, hōʻailona. See Hawaiian entries under *kaha* and *signature, symbol*. *Cent ~.* Kaha kēneka. *Dollar ~.* Kaha kālā.
signal baton *As used by marching bandleader.* ʻAukaʻi pāna.

Māmaka Kaiao / 286

signature *Also to sign one's name.* Pūlima. See *initial.*

sign language ʻŌlelo kuhi lima. *To use ~.* Kuhi lima. *American ~ (ASL).* ʻŌlelo Kuhi Lima ʻAmelika.

silence *A command for ~ on the set of a film, play or video production.* Hāmau, e hāmau kō ke kahua.

silica Silaka. *~ gel g, a powder used as the sorbent layer in thin-layer chromatography.* Palaholo silaka g (*pronounced* palaholo silaka gā).

silicon Silikone.

sill *Window ~.* Paepae pukaaniani.

silt ʻElehune.

silver dollar Kālā keʻokeʻo.

similar *In math.* ʻAno like. *~ figure.* Kinona ʻano like.

simple *Basic, uncomplicated.* Nōhie. See *complex.*

simplify *As in a math problem.* Hoʻomaʻalahi.

simulate Hoʻokūkohukohu. See *simulation.*

simulation *In math.* Hoʻomeamea.

sing *To ~ in harmony.* Hīmeni kūlauna like.

singer Pūʻukani.

single space See *spacing.*

sink *As in bathroom or kitchen.* Kinika.

sink *To make a basket, in basketball.* Hoʻokomo i ke kinipōpō.

site Kahua. *Archaeological ~.* Kahua hulikoehana. *Geological ~.* Kahua hulihonua. *~ map.* Palapala ʻāina kahua.

situp *Also to do situps.* Pelu ʻōpū.

six inches *A warm-up exercise for sports such as volleyball.* ʻEono ʻīniha.

six man *Also first off the bench, i.e. first alternate or substitute player in basketball.* Kūono.

six-pack *As of drinks.* ʻEkeʻeke. See *case, pack, twelve-pack. ~ of soda.* ʻEkeʻeke koloaka. *~ of beer.* ʻEkeʻeke pia. *~ ring, the plastic ring which holds cans together.* ʻEa ʻekeʻeke. *Six-pack beer ring.* ʻEa ʻekeʻeke pia. *Six-pack soda ring.* ʻEa ʻekeʻeke koloaka.

size *As of clothes.* Helu. *Small, as of clothes or drinks.* Liʻiliʻi. *Abb.* liʻi. *Medium.* Lōpū. *Abb.* lō. *Large.* Nui. See *extra large.*

skate *Ice ~.* Kāmaʻa holo hau. *To ~ with ice ~s.* Holo hau. *Roller ~.* Kāmaʻa huila. *To ~ with roller ~s.* Holo kāmaʻa huila. *Rollerblade.* Kāmaʻa lapa huila. *To ~ with rollerblades.* Holo lapa huila.

skateboard Papa huila. *~ ramp.* Heʻena papa huila.

skeleton Kinanahiwi. *As for Halloween.* Kanaka iwi, kelekona. See *dragon.*

skew *To ~, as a deviation from a straight line, in math.* Pāweo. *~ line.* Laina pāweo.

ski *To ~, in snow.* Heʻe hau. See *lift. To cross-country ~.* Heʻe hau peʻa ʻāina. *To water ~.* Heʻe wai. *~ boot.* Kāmaʻa puki heʻe hau. *~ cap, stocking cap.* Pāpale kapuhau.

skid *To ~, as a car; to slip.* Pakika.

skill Mākau. See *language arts, physical education. Grammar or sentence structure ~.* Mākau pilinaʻōlelo. *Life-saving ~.* Mākau hoʻopakele ola. *Practical life ~.* Mākau ola. *Thinking ~.* Mākau noʻonoʻo. *Building thinking ~s book.* Puke mākau noʻonoʻo. *Word ~.* Mākau huaʻōlelo.

skim *To ~, as milk.* Heʻe. See *ladle. ~ milk.* Waiū heʻe. *To ~, as oil from top of stew.* Kīʻoʻe, ʻoʻe.

skim read Heluhelu pākākā. *~ing.* Ka heluhelu pākākā ʻana.

skin ʻIli, ʻaluʻalu. See *dermis, epidermis, subcutus. To ~, as a pig or sheep.* Pākā. See *quarter.*

skip count *In math.* Helu lele.

skunk Ponī. *~ cabbage.* Kāpiki ponī.

sky dive Luʻu lewa. *Sky diver.* Mea luʻu lewa.
skyscraper Kiʻenaoʻa. See *highrise*.
slalom course Ala heihei kīkeʻekeʻe.
slam dunk *In basketball.* Pākī. See *shoot*.
slang Palaualea.
slash *In printing (/).* Kaha hiō, kaha hiō piʻi. *Back~ (\).* Kaha hiō iho.
slash and burn *A method of land cultivation.* Kā makawela.
slat Leka.
slaw See *cole slaw*.
sled *For snow.* Hōlua hau.
sleek *Also streamlined.* Mio. See *sports car*.
sleep *~ing bag.* ʻEke moe, ʻeke hiamoe (*preceded by* ke). *To be ~ing or snoring, as a response when asked where someone is.* Kulaʻi hāpuʻu. *~ well.* Hiamoe pono, hiamoe maikaʻi. See *good night*.
sleight of hand *Magic trick, illusion.* Pāhaʻohuna.
slice *To ~ off.* ʻOkikaha.
slide *Photographic transparency.* Kiʻiaka. See entries below. *~ mount.* Mōlina kiʻiaka. *~ projector.* Mīkini hoʻolele kiʻiaka, mīkini kiʻiaka. *Movie or ~ screen.* Pākū hoʻolele kiʻi.
slide *As for a microscope.* Aniani kaupaneʻe, *usu.* aniani. See *microscope stage*.
slide *To move a geometric figure without flipping or turning, in math.* Hoʻoneʻe. See *flip*.
slide *To ~, as a door.* Uai. *Sliding door.* Puka uai, ʻīpuka uai. *Sliding latch.* Laka uai.
slide *To execute a defensive ~, in basketball.* Pāpaʻi.
slide *Water ~, as Slip 'n' Slide; to go on a water ~.* Paheʻe wai. *~ slide mat.* Moena paheʻe wai.
sliding See *transform*.
sling psychrometer Maʻa ana kawaūea kūlua. See *hygrometer, psychrometer*.

slip *To ~, as on a wet sidewalk; to skid.* Pakika.
Slip 'n' Slide See *water slide*.
slipper lobster Ula pāpapa, ula ʻāpapapa.
sliver *Also splinter.* Māmalamala.
slope *Continental ~.* Hene mokuhonua. See *continental shelf*.
slot *Paper tray ~, as for a computer printer.* ʻĀpoʻo poho pepa.
sloth *The animal.* Melalemu. *Giant ~.* Melalemu pilikua.
slow down *To ~, as in a fast break in basketball; also to bring back out.* Kuemi, kuemi iki.
sludge *Sewage ~.* Kaekene.
slug *A gastropod closely related to land snails.* Kamaloli.
slurry *A viscous solution of liquid and a solid.* Kaluli.
small *As drink size.* Liʻiliʻi. See *medium, large.* Abb. liʻi. *~ soda.* Koloaka liʻiliʻi.
small *Lower case.* Naʻinaʻi. See *letter. ~ letter.* Hua naʻinaʻi.
smell *Sense of ~.* Lonoa ihu.
smoke *To ~, as meat or fish.* Hoʻouahi.
smoke alarm Oeoe uahi.
smokestack *As for a factory.* Pūʻoʻa uahi.
smooth *To ~, as in computer program.* Hoʻolaumania. See *unsmooth*.
smooth talk *Also smooth talker, to talk smooth; glib.* Waha wali.
smut *A kind of plant disease or the fungus which causes it.* Kalina paʻu. *Corn ~.* Kalina paʻu kūlina.
snail *Land ~.* Homeka.
snakeweed Nāhelehesa.
snap *Fastener.* Pihi ʻūmiʻi (*preceded by* ke), ʻūmiʻi. *~ cube.* Palaka kepa.
snap *To ~, as a photograph.* Paʻi (*preceded by* ke). See *take*.
snapdragon Pualāpaki.
sneaker *Tennis shoe.* Kāmaʻa lole.

snoring *To be ~ or sleeping, as a response when asked where someone is.* Kūlaʻi hāpuʻu.
snorkel Paipu hanu. *To ~.* ʻAuʻau paipu hanu.
snow *~ avalanche.* ʻĀholo hau. *See entries below. ~ cone, shave ice.* Haukōhi. *~ shoe.* Kāmaʻa hele hau.
snowflake Ulahi hau.
snowman Kanaka hau.
snowmobile Kaʻa hau.
so *The fifth note on the musical scale.* Nō.
soap Kopa. See *shampoo. Shaving ~.* Kopa kahi ʻumiʻumi, *usu.* kopa ʻumiʻumi. *~ dish.* Pā kopa (*preceded by* ke). *~ dispenser.* ʻŪhōloʻa kopa.
soccer Pōwāwae. *~ ball.* Kinipōpō pōwāwae.
social services Lawelawe kōkua.
social studies Pilikanaka.
society *An enduring social group.* Kaiapili. *Humane ~.* ʻAhahui Makaʻala Holoholona.
sociology Kālailauna kanaka.
soda Koloaka. See *baking soda. Six-pack of ~.* ʻEkeʻeke koloaka. *Twelve-pack of ~.* Pūʻolo koloaka. *Case of ~.* Pahu koloaka. *~ can tab.* Une kini koloaka.
sodium Sodiuma. *~ bisulfate.* Sodiuma bisulafahate. *~ citrate.* Sodiuma kitarahate.
software *As for a computer.* Lako polokalamu. See *hardware.*
soil Lepo. See *planting medium. Alluvial ~.* Lepo makaili. *Potting ~.* Lepo kanu meakanu. *Standard ~ testing kit.* Hōkeo kūmau hoʻāʻo lepo.
solar Lā. See *sunspot. ~ constant.* Kāʻei kau lā. *~ flare.* Lapa ahi lā. *~ granule, gigantic waves of gas which roll across the surface of the sun.* ʻAle ahi lā. *~ prominences, i.e. puffs of gas which gently drift above the surface of the sun.* Puapuaʻi lā. *~ panel.* ʻŪomo ikehu lā. *~ power.* Manehu lā. *~ radiation.* Pāhawewe lā. *~ system.* Poe lā.

solid *As opposed to liquid or gas.* Kinopaʻa, paʻa. See *solid rocket booster. Geometric ~.* Paʻa. *~ figure.* Kinona paʻa.
solid rocket booster Kao wāwahie kinopaʻa, kao wāwahie paʻa.
solstice Māuikiʻikiʻi. See *equinox. Summer ~.* Ka māuikiʻikiʻi o ke kauwela. *Winter ~.* Ka māuikiʻikiʻi o ka hoʻoilo.
solubility *Also soluble.* Pēmāʻōʻā. See *solution. Selective ~.* Pēmāʻōʻā wae ʻano.
solute Mea heheʻe. See *solvent.*
solution *To a problem.* Hāʻina. See entry below and *problem, solve. Also resolution, as of a problem in a story.* Hopena holo.
solution *A homogeneous mixture.* Māʻōʻāna. See *solubility, suspension. Aqueous ~.* Māʻōʻāna ʻūheheʻe wai. *Chemical ~.* Māʻōʻāna kemikala. *Hydroponic ~.* Māʻōʻāna kāmāhuaola. See *hydroponics. To be in ~.* Māʻōʻā.
solve Hana a loaʻa ka hāʻina. *To resolve difficulties.* Hoʻoponopono pilikia. *To look for a solution.* Huli hāʻina, huli i ka hāʻina, ʻimi hāʻina. *To ~ a problem.* Hoʻomākalakala i ka polopolema. *Decoded, ~d.* Mākalakala.
solvent ʻŪheheʻe. See *solute. ~ front, i.e. the leading edge of a moving ~ as in a developing chromatogram.* ʻAe omowaho.
Somalia *Also Somalian.* Somalia.
soprano Leo ʻekahi. *~ ʻukulele.* ʻUkulele leo ʻekahi.
sorbent *An absorbent material such as used in chromatography.* ʻŪomo. See *absorb.*
sound *Speed of ~.* Māmā kani, māmā holo o ke kani. *~ barrier.* Palena holo kani. See *entries below.*
sound *Also sound effects, as on a computer.* Kani. See *beep. ~ effects, as for a play, movie or video production.* Kani keaka. *~ editor.* Luna hoʻoponopono kani. *~ effects coordinator.* Luna kani keaka. *~ technician.* Mea ʻenehana kani.

sound ~ *segment, in linguistics.* Hua. *Epenthetic* ~. Hua komo.
sound hole *As on an ʻukulele or guitar.* Puka kani.
sound wavelength Kōā hawewe kani. See *amplitude, sound waves.*
sound waves *As used in measuring ocean depths.* Hawewe kani. See *sound wavelength.*
source *Reference material, as a dictionary.* Kūmole. See entry below and *resource. Root, derivation or origin, as the etymology of a word.* Molekumu.
source pollution Kumu hoʻohaumia. *Point* ~. Kumu hoʻohaumia ʻike ʻia. *Non-point* ~. Kumu hoʻohaumia ʻike ʻole ʻia.
south Hema. *Abb.* Hm. *See entries below.* ~ *pole.* Wēlau hema.
South Africa *Also South African.* ʻApelika Hema, ʻAferika Hema.
South America *Also South American.* ʻAmelika Hema.
South Carolina *Also South Carolinean.* Kalolaina Hema.
South Dakota *Also South Dakotan.* Kakoka Hema, Dakota Hema.
Southern Equatorial Current *In oceanography.* Kalekale. See *Northern Equatorial Current, Equatorial Countercurrent.*
southern hemisphere Poepoe hapa hema. See *hemisphere.*
South Korea *Also South Korean.* Kōlea Hema, Kōrea Hema.
South Yemen *Also South Yemenite, South Yemeni.* Iemene Hema. See *North Yemen.*
sow bug Pokipoki.
soybean *Also soya bean.* Pāpapa koiū.
soy sauce Shoyu. Koiū.
space *As a crack between fence boards.* Kōā. See entries below and *crack. As on a game board such as Monopoly.* Kuea. *Chance* ~. Kuea huki pepa.

space *As between words when typing on computer or typewriter.* Kaʻahua. See *tab, spacing.* ~ *bar.* Pihi hoʻokōā, pihi kaʻahua (preceded by ke). *As in tab settings on computer or typewriter.* Kāwā. *Disk* ~, *as on computer hard drive or floppy disk.* Hakahaka pā.
space *A pound sign (#) used in proofreading to indicate that a* ~ *should be inserted, in proofreading; a superscript number written next to the symbol indicates the number of* ~*s if more than one* ($\#^2$). Kaha kaʻahua.
space Lewa. See entries below and *atmosphere. Outer* ~. Lewa lipo. ~ *alien, extraterrestrial.* Mea ao ʻē. ~ *map.* Palapala lewa lipo. ~ *walk.* Hele lewa lipo. ~ *capsule.* Kelena moku ahikao.
spacecraft *Also spaceship.* Moku ahikao.
space crane *Also remote manipulator arm.* Lima kia pihi.
space figure *In math.* Kinona pihanahaka. See *geometric figure, plane figure.*
space flight Lele lewa lipo. *Manned* ~. Lele lewa lipo kanaka.
space probe ʻAkiu lewa lipo.
space program Polokalamu lewa lipo.
spaceship *Also spacecraft.* Moku ahikao.
space shuttle Mokuhali lewa lipo.
space station Oʻioʻina lewa lipo.
space suit Paʻalole hele lewa.
spacing *As lines in a printed document.* Koana. See *space. Single space, single- line* ~. Koana pākahi. *One and one-half space, one and one-half line* ~. Koana pākahi hapalua. *Double space, double-line* ~. Koana pālua. *To set* ~. Hoʻokoana.
spade *Small* ~, *as a garden tool.* Kopalā liʻiliʻi.
spading fork ʻŌ ʻeli (preceded by ke).
spaghetti Pakeki.
Spain Kepania, Sepania.
span *Life* ~. Kāwā ola.
sparkler *Fireworks.* Hōkūpaʻalima.

sparkling water *Also mineral water.* Wai piʻipiʻi.

spark plug ʻŌpuʻuahi.

sparrow Manu kālā.

sparse *Also few.* Kākaʻikahi.

spatter cone *In geology.* Puʻu pōhāhā. See *ejecta.*

spatula *Also pancake turner.* ʻŪlau. *Rubber ~.* ʻŪlau kahi.

speaker *As for a stereo.* Pahu leo. See *amplifier.*

special effects Hiʻohiʻona naʻiau. *To have ~.* Naʻiau. *To add ~.* Hoʻonaʻiau (i ka hiʻohiʻona). *~ coordinator, as for movie or video production.* Luna hiʻohiʻona naʻiau.

specialist Laekahi.

species *In biology.* Lāhulu, lāhui. *Endangered ~ Act.* Kānāwai Lāhulu ʻAne Halapohe. *Related ~.* Pili lāhulu.

specific Kikoʻī. See entries below and *document specific.*

specifications *Also specs, to specify.* Kuhiʻī.

specific gravity *Also relative gravity.* Lākiō paʻapū wai.

specific heat *In physics.* Ana piʻi wela.

specify See *specifications.*

specimen Laʻana.

speech Haʻiʻōlelo. See *oral report. Expressive ~; ~ to entertain.* Haʻiʻōlelo mikololoʻlehua. *Narrative ~.* Haʻiʻōlelo kūhahaʻi. *Persuasive ~.* Haʻiʻōlelo hoʻohuli manaʻo.

speed Māmā holo. See entries below and *accelerate, decelerate. Average ~.* ʻAwelike māmā holo. *~ of light.* Māmā kukuna lā, māmā holo o ke kukuna lā. *~ of sound.* Māmā kani, māmā holo o ke kani.

speed bump *As on a road or in a parking lot.* Puʻu haʻapupū.

speed read *To ~.* Heluwawe. *~ing.* Ka heluwawe ʻana. See *speed write*

speed write *To ~; also any document which has been written using speed writing.* Kāwawe. See *speed read.*

spell See *misspelled word.*

spell checker *As of a computer document; also to spell check.* Loipela. See *proofread.*

sperm *Spermatozoon.* Huaʻāne. See *ovum.*

sphagnum Hulupōʻēʻē, mākōpiʻi hulupōʻēʻē. See *moss.*

sphere Poepoe. *See globe, hemisphere. In math.* Paʻapoepoe.

sphincter *An annular muscle surrounding and able to contract or close a bodily opening or channel.* Mākala ʻamo.

spider Nananana, nanana. See *tarantula. Black widow ~.* Nananana hese ʻeleʻele, nanana hese ʻeleʻele. *Happy face ~.* Nananana makakiʻi, nanana makakiʻi. *No-eyed big-eyed hunting spider.* Nananana maka ʻole, nanana maka ʻole.

spike *To ~ (the ball), in volleyball.* Hili, pākī. See *hitter. To ~ with closed fist.* Kuʻi puʻupuʻu. *To ~ with open hand.* Paʻi pālahalaha. *To make a fake ~, an off-speed shot.* Pākī ʻepa. *Angle ~.* Hili ʻaoʻao. *Line ~.* Hili laina. *Point from ~.* ʻAi hele wale.

spinach Lūʻau Haole.

spinner *As in board games.* Pāniniu *(preceded by* ke).

splice *To ~, as film or video segments for movie or video production.* Hoʻokuʻikuʻi. See *assemble editor.*

splinter *Also sliver.* Māmalamala.

split *As in a sidewalk; also to ~.* ʻOā. See *crack.*

split end *In football.* Lala. See *tight end, safety.*

spoke *As on a bicycle wheel.* Kukuna. *Bicycle ~.* Kukuna huila paikikala.

sponge *The aquatic animal.* Huʻakai.

spongy *As leaves of the pānini.* ʻŪpīʻū. See *coconut.*

sport Haʻuki. *Indoor ~.* Haʻuki maluhale. *Outdoor ~.* Haʻuki kaupokulani. *Coach for ~s.* Kaʻi ʻālapa. *~s trainer.* Kaʻi haʻuki.

sports car Ka'a mio.
spout *To ~, as a whale.* Pūhāhā.
sprained 'Unu.
spray Kīkī. See *substance*. *~ paint.* Pena kīkina.
spread *As data on a graph, in math.* Waiho. *Data ~.* Ka waiho o ka 'ikepili.
spreading See *divergent*.
spreadsheet *As in computer program.* Pakuhi maka'aha. *~ program.* Polokalamu pakuhi maka'aha.
spring Kupulau. See *vernal equinox*.
spring beauty *A kind of flower.* Nanikupulau.
sprint *Dash.* Holo kikī.
sprout Kawowo. See *coconut*. *Alfalfa ~.* Kawowo 'alapapa. *Bean ~.* Kawowo pāpapa. *To germinate.* Ilo. *To cause to ~.* Ho'oilo.
spur *Also to ~; to gore with a tusk.* Kepa, kēpā. See *boar's tusk*.
square *In math.* Pāho'onui lua. See entries below and *cubed*. *The ~ of the number.* Ka pāho'onui lua o ka helu. *Geometric shape.* Huinahā like.
square foot *In math.* Kapua'i pāho'onui lua. *Abb.* kp ph^2. *Lay term.* Kapua'i kuea.
square root *In math.* Kumu pāho'onui lua.
squash *General term.* Ipu. See *pumpkin*. *An edible variety.* Pipinola.
squid *As per Haole definition; cuttlefish as per local definition.* Mūhe'e. *As per local definition; octopus as per Haole definition.* He'e.
squirrel Kiulela. See *chipmonk*. *Arctic ground ~.* Kiulela 'Ālika.
stable Hale lio.
stack *To ~, as windows in computer program.* Ho'okūpa'i. *To ~ windows.* Ho'okūpa'i pukaaniani.
staff *Musical ~.* Kōkua huamele, ko'oko'o, kumu 'ākōlī.

stage *As of a microscope.* Paepae aniani kaupane'e. See *slide (microscope)*. *As level of development or difficulty.* Pae. See *level*.
stagehand *Or grip, as for movie or video production.* Mea kūkulu kahua. See *stage manager*.
stage manager *Or key grip, as for movie or video production.* Luna kūkulu kahua. See *stagehand*.
stair 'Anu'u. See *step*.
staircase landing Paepae alapi'i.
stake *Tent ~.* Pine halepe'a.
stalactite Kuluna.
stalagmite Kulalo.
stall *Shower ~.* Ke'ena kililau.
stamp *Airmail ~.* Po'oleka halilele. *Sheet of ~s.* Laulahi po'oleka.
stance *Defensive ~, as in basketball.* Kūlana pale.
stand Kū. See *tripod, easel*. *Ring ~, as for a test tube.* Kū hano ho'okolohua.
standard Ma'amau, kūmau. See entries below and *deluxe*. *~ room, as in a hotel.* Lumi ma'amau. *~ soil- testing kit.* Hōkeo kūmau ho'ā'o lepo. *An established model or example.* Ana ho'ohālike. *To set the ~.* Ho'opa'a i ke ana ho'ohālike.
standard *US or customary unit of measurement.* Anakahi 'Amelika. *~ form, as for numbers.* Kino huahelu.
standard *As in deviation, in math.* Kūmau. See *normal*. *~ deviation.* Haiahū kūmau.
stand for *To ~, as in a math problem.* Kūhō'ailona.
stand-in *As for an actor in a movie or video production.* Pani hakahaka, pani.
standing long jump Lele loloa.
stannous chloride Satanousa koloriside.
staple *For paper.* Kui 'ūmi'i pepa. *To ~.* 'Ūmi'i. *Stapler.* Mea 'ūmi'i pepa. *~ remover.* Mea wehe 'ūmi'i.
star *Shooting ~.* Hōkū welowelo. *The ~ in the center of the constellation Carina.* Mākoi.

starboard *Right or ~ side of a single-hulled canoe when looking forward.* Muku. *See* port. *~ hull of a double-hulled canoe or right side of a ship when looking forward.* ʻĀkea.

starch *A white, tasteless, solid carbohydrate found in plants.* Piaʻai.

starfish Hōkū kai.

starfruit Hua hōkū.

start *To ~, as a computer program.* Hoʻomaka. *See* quit. *To ~, as a machine; also to play, as a film or tape.* Hoʻoholo.

starting *~ point, as in a race.* Pahukū. *~ line.* Laina pahukū. *See* finish.

startup disk *As in computer program.* Pā hoʻomaka (*preceded by* ke).

state *As one of the United States.* Mokuʻāina. *See entries below. ~ fair.* Hōʻikeʻike mokuʻāina. *~ park.* Pāka mokuʻāina.

State Department of Agriculture ʻOihana Mahi ʻAi o ka Mokuʻāina.

State Land Use Commission Komikina Hoʻohana ʻĀina o ka Mokuʻāina.

statement ʻŌlelo. *Exclamatory ~; also to make such a statement.* ʻŌlelo hoʻōho. *Inequality ~, in math.* ʻŌlelo no ke kaulike ʻole. *Mission ~.* ʻŌlelo ala nuʻukia. *Vision ~.* ʻŌlelo nuʻukia.

station *As for a computer network.* Poʻopoʻo. *See* network server. *Network ~.* Poʻopoʻo pūnaewele. *Also channel, as on radio or television.* Kānela.

station *Field ~, as used when mapping a certain area.* Kikowaena pānānā. *See* subway. *Quarantine ~.* Hale hoʻomalu maʻi.

stationary front *As of weather.* Kuʻina paʻa. *See* front.

statistics *Numerical facts or data, as in math.* ʻIkepili helu. *See* table.

Statue of Liberty Kūkāʻokoʻa Kiahoʻomanaʻo, ke kiahoʻomanaʻo ʻo Kūkāʻokoʻa, Kūkāʻokoʻa.

status Kūlana. *Health ~.* Kūlana olakino.

stay tuned *"To be continued," as during a TV program.* ʻAʻole i pau.

steal *To ~, in basketball.* ʻAihue.

steamroller Kimalola.

steam shovel Kewe kopalā.

steel wool *Wire gauze.* Pulupulu uea.

stem and leaf plot *In math.* Pakuhi ʻau me ka lau. *See* chart.

stencil Anakuhi mahaka.

step *Also stair.* ʻAnuʻu. *As in problem solving.* ʻAnuʻu hana, ʻanuʻu.

steps *As in a dance or routine.* Kaʻina wāwae.

stereo *See* record player.

steroid Pūhōmona.

stet *A series of dots written under a word or words which have been lined out to show that no change should be made from the original, in proofreading.* Kaha waiho.

stethoscope ʻIli hoʻolohe puʻuwai, kiupe hoʻolohe.

steward(ess) *Flight attendant.* Kuene mokulele.

stick *Small ~, twig.* ʻAulaʻo (*preceded by* ke).

sticker Pepili.

stilt *Bird or toy.* Kūkuluaeʻo.

stimulant Lāʻau haʻinole. *See* depressant.

stimulate *Also stimulus.* Kūlale. *See* response, stimulant. *To ~, as with a drug.* Haʻinole.

stock *As in the ~ market.* Kea hoʻopukapuka, kea. *See* invest.

stocking cap Pāpale kapuhau.

stomach poison Lāʻau make ʻai.

stomata Pukahanu.

stone *Air ~, the porous rock in an aquarium that creates tiny bubbles at the surface of the water to facilitate the exchange of gases.* Pōhaku puka ea.

stool *Without a back.* Noho kū.

stop *In linguistics.* Pohā. *To ~ or break, as an electric circuit.* ʻOki. *See* open.

stoplight Kukui hoʻokū.

stop sign Hōʻailona hoʻokū.
stopwatch Uaki helu manawa, uāki helu manawa.
storage cabinet Waihona hoʻāhu. See *storeroom*.
store Hale kūʻai. Garden ~, gardening ~. Hale kūʻai mahi māla.
store away *Also to accumulate, lay away*. Hoʻāhu.
storeroom Lumi hoʻāhu. See *storage cabinet*.
storm See *gale*.
story Floor, as in a building. Papahele. See entries below and *tale*. *Predictable ~, in literature*. Moʻolelo hopena ahuwale.
storyboard *As in movie or video production*. Moʻolelo kaha. *~ artist*. Lima kaha moʻolelo. *~ terms*. Huaʻōlelo kaha moʻolelo.
story book *Reader*. Puke heluhelu.
story telling *Traditional elements of Hawaiian poetry, ~, oratory and narration*. Meiwi.
straight *Horizontal lines written above and below a word or words to indicate that they should be written or printed ~, in proofreading*. Kaha hoʻolālani.
straight angle *An angle that has a measure of 180°, in math*. Huina kaha.
straightedge Kaʻe pololei.
strap Kāʻawe. See *coveralls, tank top*. *Slipper ~*. Kāʻawe kalipa.
strapping tape *Also filament tape*. Leki aʻa.
strategy *Or approach, as in solving a math problem*. Kaʻakālai.
stratus cloud Ao loa. See *cloud*.
straw *Drinking ~*. Meaomōmo. *Grain stalk*. Pua huika.
stream Kahawai. See *data stream*. *~ current, in oceanography*. Au kikī. *Jet ~*. Au makani kikī. *~ sediment*. Koʻana kahawai.
streambed Papakū, papakū kahawai, kahena wai.

stream current *In oceanography*. Au kikī.
streamlined *Also sleek*. Mio. See *sports car*.
stream tributary ʻAumana kahawai.
stress *Emotional ~*. ʻAloʻahia. *Or accent, in linguistics*. Kālele.
stretch *To ~, as for warming up before exercise*. Hoʻomālō. See *neck stretches*.
stride Kaʻi wāwae.
strike *To tag or ~ out, in baseball*. Hōʻauka. *To ~, as a match*. Koe.
strike through *To line out, as on a typewriter or computer; also used to indicate that the letters or words lined out are to be replaced by those written above, in proofreading*. Kahawaena.
string *As on an ʻukulele or guitar*. Kaula. See *ʻukulele*. *Names of ~s on an ʻukulele*: ke kaula o luna loa (G), ke kaula ʻelua (C), ke kaula ʻekolu (E), ke kaula ʻehā (A). *Eight-~ ʻukulele*. ʻUkulele ʻewalu kaula.
string bass *Also bass viol*. Pila kū nui, pila nui.
string bean Pāpapa hihi.
string instrument Pila.
string of firecrackers Kālī pahūpahū.
stroke *Breast ~; to swim the breast ~*. ʻAu umauma. *Back ~; to swim the back ~*. ʻAu kua. *Side ~; to swim the side ~*. ʻAu ʻaoʻao. *Butterfly ~; to swim the butterfly ~*. ʻAu mālolo. See *crawl, dog paddle*.
stroll *Also to go for a ~*. Holoholo wāwae. See *hike*.
strong *As wind; large branches in motion and whistling heard in wires between utility poles, in meteorology*. Ulūlu. See *wind*.
strong safety *In football*. ʻĀwaʻa muku. See *weak safety*.
strontium Solonokiuma.
structure *As of a molecule*. Hakakino.
strum *To ~, as an ʻukulele or guitar*. Koekoe.

studio *The building where movies are made.* Hale hana kiʻiʻoniʻoni. *The company responsible for making movies.* Keʻena hana kiʻiʻoniʻoni. *~ teacher.* Kumu keʻena hana kiʻiʻoniʻoni.

study *To examine, observe something.* Kilo. *Scientific ~: With no specific intent to influence change.* Huli-. *With potential intent to influence change.* Kālai-.

stunt *A feat which requires unusual daring or skill, as in a movie or video production; to do or perform a ~.* Pāhaʻoweli. *~person.* Kanaka pāhaʻoweli. *~ coordinator.* Luna pāhaʻoweli.

style *Also attribute, as italic or bold in printing or computer program.* Kaila hua. See *code style, font.*

style *To ~ hair, as for a play, movie or video production.* Hoʻoponopono lauoho. *Hair stylist.* Mea hoʻoponopono lauoho.

styrofoam ʻŪpīhuʻa.

sub- *Also under-.* Lalo. See entries below and *under-*.

subalpine Lalo ʻalapaina. See *alpine*. *~ forest.* Ululāʻau lalo ʻalapaina.

subconference *In telecommunications.* Hālāwai malū.

subcutus *In biology.* ʻIli kūloko.

subdivision *Also housing development.* Kaiahale.

subfield *As in computer program.* Hope kahua. See *field*.

subheading *Also heading, as in a story.* Poʻomanaʻo.

subject *General ~ or topic, as in literature.* Kumuhana.

submarine *Also submerged, undersea.* Lalo kai. See *submerged*.

submerged *Also submarine, undersea.* Lalo kai. *~ volcano.* Lua pele lalo kai.

subsand Lalo one.

subscript *As in computer program or printing.* Kauhaʻa. See *superscript*.

subsoil Lalo lepo. See *topsoil*.

substance ʻAkano. See *compound, element, matter, particles, spray paint*. *Amorphous ~.* ʻAkano laukua. *As sprayed from an aerosol can.* Kīkina.

substitute *As in sports; also to ~.* Pani, pani hakahaka (*preceded by* ke). *First ~ player or alternate, in basketball; also called first off the bench or six man.* Kūono.

substrate *As in a stream.* Papa o lalo.

subsummary *As in computer program.* Hope hōʻuluʻulu palapala. See *summary*.

subtitle Lepe unuhi. See *caption*.

subtotal Huinanui hapa. See *grand total*.

subtract *Also subtraction.* Hoʻolawe.

subtribe *Also clan.* Hapū. See *tribe*.

subtropical Lalo kopikala.

suburb Kaona ukali.

subway *~ train.* Kaʻakōnelo. *~ tunnel.* Ala kaʻakōnelo. *~ station.* Kahua kaʻakōnelo.

subzone Kāʻei iki.

succession Moʻona. *In rapid ~.* ʻĀmaʻamau.

sucker *Also lollipop.* Kanakē ʻau, kō omōmo.

sucker *Insect ~, an instrument for drawing an insect into a tube by suction.* Mea omo ʻelala.

suction cup fin *As beneath the stomach of an ʻoʻopu.* Halo ʻāpikapika.

Sudan *Also Sudanese.* Sudana.

suffix Pākuʻina kau hope. See *affix*.

suffocate *To experience a suffocating sensation.* Kenakena.

suit *Space ~.* Paʻalole hele lewa. See *warm-up suit*.

suit *As in a deck of playing cards.* Paʻa likelike.

suitcase *Also purse.* Pāiki, pāisi.

sulfate Sulafahate. *Cupric ~.* Kupuriku sulafahate. *Ferrous ~.* Ferousa sulafahate.

sulfide Sulafaside. *Cupric ~.* Kupuriku sulafaside. *Ferrous ~.* Ferousa sulafaside.

sulfur dioxide Sulufura diokesaside, kūkaepele ʻokikene lua.
sulfuric Sulufuriku. ~ *acid.* ʻAkika sulufuriku.
sum *Total.* Huinanui.
summary *Also to summarize.* Hōʻuluʻulu manaʻo. See *subsummary. Document ~, as in computer program.* Hōʻuluʻulu palapala.
summer Kauwela. ~ *solstice.* Ka māuikiʻikiʻi o ke kauwela.
Sunday Lāpule. *Abb.* Lp.
sun glasses Makaaniani kala, makaaniani lā.
sunscreen *The lotion.* ʻAila pale lā. See *suntan lotion.*
sunspot Kiko lā. See *solar flare, solar granule, solar prominences.*
suntan lotion ʻAila ʻōlala. See *sunscreen.*
superphosphate Superoposapahate.
superscript *As in computer program or printing.* Kaupiʻi. See *subscript.*
supervisor *Script ~, as in movie or video production.* Luna kākau moʻolelo.
supplement *To ~, as angles, in math.* Hoʻopiha kaha. See *complement, supplementary angles.*
supplementary ~ *book or text; also any book which supplements a primary text.* Puke kākoʻo.
supplementary angles *Two angles whose measures have a sum of 180°, in math.* Nā huina hoʻopiha kaha. See *complementary angles.*
support *Education ~ staff.* Kākoʻo hoʻonaʻauao. See *allied health professional.*
supporting idea *As in a composition.* Manaʻo kākoʻo.
surface area *In math.* ʻIli alo.
surface water Wai ʻili honua, wai ʻili.
surf break *Where a wave breaks.* Poʻina nalu (*preceded by* ke).
survey *Opinion ~; also to conduct an opinion ~.* Anamanaʻo.

surveying rod *Also range pole.* Lāʻau ana ʻāina. See *elevation pole, sighter.*
susceptible *Also vulnerable.* Pā wale. *Fragile, ~ to change.* Pāloli. *To be ~ or vulnerable to disease.* Pāmaʻi.
suspension *A mixture in which the particles are mixed but not dissolved in fluid, solid or gas.* Pūaina. See *solution. To be suspended.* Pūai.
sustained Paʻa mau. ~ *yield, as in crop production.* Loaʻa paʻa mau.
swab *Cotton ~, Q-tip.* Lāʻau pulupulu.
swamp ʻOlokele. See *bog, marsh.*
sweat duct Puka kikī hou.
sweatshirt Kueka haʻuki. See *warm-up suit.*
Sweden *Also Swede, Swedish.* Kuekene.
sweep net See *insect sweep net.*
swim ~ *cap.* Pāpale ʻau. ~ *styles.* See *stroke.*
swimming ~ *pool.* Pūnāwai ʻauʻau. ~ *tube.* Lina hoʻolana.
swing *Free ~, as a single rope hanging from a tree branch.* Lele koali. *Fixed ~, as with two or more ropes or chains.* Paiō. *To ~, as a pendulum.* ʻUkē. See *pendulum.*
swing man *Also shooting forward or three man, in basketball.* Kūkolu.
swish *Also rimless, i.e. to make a basket without touching the rim, in basketball.* Kuhō. See *shot.*
Swiss cheese Waiūpaʻa Kuikilani.
switch *Light ~.* Kuiki kukui, pana kukui. *As on radio, TV set, etc.* Pihi (*preceded by* ke).
switch sides *To ~, in volleyball; also to rotate.* Kuapo.
Switzerland *Also Swiss.* Kuikilani, Kuikilana.
syllabary *In linguistics.* Hakalama. ~ *symbol.* Huahakalama.
syllable Kāpana. *Nucleus of a ~, in linguistics.* Iho. *Onset of a ~.* Kaʻi. *Coda of a ~.* Muli.

syllabus *As for a college course.* ʻOlokeʻa koina papa.
symbol *Also to symbolize, stand for.* Hōʻailona.
symmetry *Also symmetric, symmetrical, in math.* ʻĀlikelike. *Line of ~, a line on which a figure can be folded so the two parts fit exactly.* Kaha ʻālikelike. *Reflection ~.* ʻĀlikelike aka. *Rotational ~.* ʻĀlikelike wili. *Symmetric figure.* Kinona ʻālikelike. *Translation ~.* ʻĀlikelike kau.
synchronic *In linguistics.* Kikowā. See *diachronic.* *~ rule.* Lula kikowā.
synonym Huaʻōlelo manaʻo like. See *antonym, homonym.*
synthesize *To ~, as compounds; also synthetic.* Hakuahua. *~d compounds.* Nā pūhui i hakuahua ʻia.
Syria *Also Syrian.* Suria.
syringe Hano kui. *~ plunger.* ʻŪkōmi hano kui, ʻūkōmi, ʻūkaomi hano kui, ʻūkaomi.
syrup Hone, malakeke.
system ʻŌnaehana. See entries below. *Community-based health ~.* ʻŌnaehana olakino kaiaulu. *Coordinated physician referral ~.* ʻŌnaehana kauka no ka lapaʻau like ʻana. *Land registration ~.* ʻŌnaehana hoʻonā ʻāina. See *land court, settle.* *Natural Areas Reserves ~ (NARS).* ʻŌnaehana Hoʻomalu ʻĀina Kūlohelohe. *Two-party ~ of government.* Aupuni ʻaoʻao ʻelua.
system *Decimal ~.* ʻŌnaehana kekimala. *Metric ~.* ʻŌnaehana mekalika. *Solar ~.* Poe lā. *High pressure ~, in meteorology.* ʻŌnaehana mīkā piʻi. *Low pressure ~.* ʻŌnaehana mīkā emi.
system *In biology: Circulatory ~.* ʻŌnaehana mānowai. *Digestive ~.* ʻŌnaehana hoʻoheheʻe meaʻai. *Endocrine ~.* ʻŌnaehana hōmona. *Immune ~, as in mammals.* ʻŌnaehana pale ʻea. *Integumentary ~.* ʻŌnaehana ʻili. *Muscular ~.* ʻŌnaehana mākala. *Nervous ~.* ʻŌnaehana lolokū. *Organ ~.* ʻŌnaehana lōkino. *Reproductive ~.* ʻŌnaehana hoʻohua. *Respiratory ~.* ʻŌnaehana hanu.
system *Network ~, as for computer program.* ʻŌnaehana pūnaewele. *Operating ~.* Pae ʻōnaehana.
systemic insecticide Lāʻau make laoa. See *poison.*

T

tab *As on an audio cassette which can be removed to prevent erasing of what has been recorded, or an index ~ on a notebook divider page.* Lepe. See entry below. *As on soda cans.* Une kini. *Soda can ~.* Une kini koloaka.
tab *As on computer or typewriter.* Kāwāholo. See *indent, space, shift.* *~ key.* Pihi kāwāholo (*preceded by* ke). *To set ~s.* Hoʻopaʻa i nā kāwāholo. *To ~.* Hoʻokāwāholo.
table *Bedside ~, nightstand.* Pākaukau moe (*also preceded by* ke). See *water table.* *~ leg.* Wāwae pākaukau. *~ lamp.* Kukui kū pākaukau.
table *As of statistics, etc.* Pakuhi papa. See *multiplication tables.*
table of contents Papa kuhikuhi. See *index.*
tablespoon *A unit of measurement.* Puna pākaukau (*preceded by* ke). Abb. pup.
tablet *Notebook.* Kālana kākau. See *binder.*
table tennis *Ping-pong.* Kenika pākaukau.
tabloid paper Pepa 11" X 17" (*pronounced* pepa ʻumikūmākahi ʻīniha i ka ʻumikūmāhiku ʻīniha). See *paper.*
tackle *The act of seizing and throwing down an opposing player with the ball, in football; to ~ (someone).* Kulaʻi, hoʻohina. See *block and tackle, nose tackle.* *Either an offensive or defensive player.* Kūlua. *Left ~.* Kūlua hema. *Right ~.* Kūlua ʻākau.
tadpole *Polliwog.* Polewao.

tag *Label; to label.* Lepili. *To ~ or strike out, in baseball.* Hōʻauka.
tagboard *A strong cardboard used for posters; also called oaktag.* Pepa papa ʻoka.
Tahitian prawn ʻŌpae Polapola.
taiga Taika.
tails *As in coin toss.* Hiʻu, ʻaoʻao hiʻu. See *heads*.
Taiwan *Also Taiwanese.* Taiuana.
take *To ~, as a photograph.* Paʻi *(preceded by* ke*).* See *close-up, shoot*. *To photograph or ~ a picture, either still or motion.* Paʻi kiʻi. *A ~, i.e. a successful shot in a movie or video production.* He ʻāpona!
take off *To ~, as a bird or plane taking flight.* Ulele.
take turns Māhele manawa.
takuwan Kakuana.
tale *A folk~ or traditional ~, especially one relating to a particular culture.* Kaʻao, moʻokaʻao. See *Hawaiian entries under* kaʻao.
talk *To ~ smooth; also smooth talker; glib.* Waha wali.
talkathon ʻŌlelokona.
tally Helu kaha.
tambourine Lina ʻulīkeke. See *baby rattle*.
tampon Pani wai ʻula *(preceded by* ke*)*.
tangent *A line which touches a circle at one point, in math.* Kaha pā lihi. See *secant*.
tank *Oxygen ~.* Kini ʻokikene. *Scuba ~.* Kini ea luʻu kai.
tank top Palaʻili kāʻawe, paleʻili kāʻawe. See *T-shirt*.
tannic Tanika. *~ acid.* ʻAkika tanika.
Tanzania *Also Tanzanian.* Tanazania.
tapa *Bark cloth.* Paʻūpaʻū.
tape Leki. *See entries below. Electrician's ~.* Leki uea. *Masking ~.* Leki pahu. *Paper ~.* Leki pepa. *Strapping ~.* Leki aʻa. *Transparent ~.* Leki ʻea.

tape *Recording ~.* Līpine. See *cassette, player, recorder*. *Reel-to-reel ~.* Līpine pōkaʻa. *~ case, cassette holder.* Paiki lola.
tape measure *As tailor's or for track events, etc.* Līpine ana. See *ruler*. *Carpenter's ~.* Lula poho.
tap water Wai paipu. *Hot ~.* Wai wela paipu.
tar Kā, tā.
tarantula Kalanakula, nananana kalanakula, nanana kalanakula. See *spider*.
target Māka.
taro See *corm*. *~ chip.* Kipi kalo.
taste *Sense of ~.* Lonoa alelo. *~ receptor.* Aʻalonoa ʻono. See *receptor*.
tasty *To flavor, make ~.* Hōʻonoʻono. See *flavoring*.
tax ʻAuhau. *Sales ~.* ʻAuhau kumukūʻai. *~ included.* ʻAuhau komo pū. *~ rate.* Pākēneka ʻauhau. *~payer.* Mea uku ʻauhau.
taxonomy *The science of classifying plants and animals.* Kālaikapa inoa.
teaberry Pīʻai kī.
teacher's guide *Also teacher's manual.* Puke alakaʻi.
teaching certificate Palapala ʻoihana aʻo.
teak *A kind of wood.* Kiaka.
team *Of draft animals.* Pūkolo.
team foul *In team sports such as basketball.* Kuʻia kime. See *foul*.
teaspoon *A unit of measurement.* Puna kī *(preceded by* ke*).* Abb. puk.
technical foul *In team sports such as basketball.* Kuʻia kūhelu. See *foul*.
technician Mea ʻenehana. *Graphics ~.* Mea ʻenehana kiʻi. *Sound ~.* Mea ʻenehana kani.
technique Kiʻina hana. See *method*.
technology ʻEnehana. See *industry*.
techtonics *Plate ~, in geology.* Kuʻina una honua. See *boundary, convergent, divergent, transform*.
teddy bear Pea kiʻi, pea pāʻani. See *panda*.

teetertotter Papa hulei. *To ~.* Hulehulei.
Teflon ʻAʻalo pili. See *resist, waterproof.*
telecommunication Kelekaʻaʻike.
telephone receiver ʻApo kelepona.
telescope ʻOhenānā.
telespiza *~ cantanc, Laysan finch.* ʻAinohu Kauō. *~ ultima, Nīhoa finch.* ʻAinohu Nīhoa.
telethon Kīwīkona.
television Kelewikiona. *TV.* Kīwī, kelewī.
tell time Helu uaki, helu uāki. See *time.*
tempera paint Pena pelaha.
temperate Kemepale. See *tropical. ~ forest.* Nahele kemepale.
temperature *When weather considered cold.* Anu. *When weather considered warm.* Mahana, mehana. *When weather considered hot.* Wela. *See Hawaiian entries. Room ~.* Mehana ea, mehana lumi. *To take the ~ of.* Ana wela.
template Anakuhi.
tempo *In music.* Māmā.
ten See *deci-, deca-.*
ten-foot line *In volleyball.* Laina ʻumi kapuaʻi. See *three-meter line. ~ violation.* ʻAʻena ʻumi kapuaʻi.
tenderizer See *papain.*
Tennessee *Also Tennessean.* Kenekī, Tenesī.
tennis shoe *Sneaker.* Kāmaʻa lole.
tenor Leo ʻekolu. *~ ʻukulele.* ʻUkulele leo ʻekolu.
tens *Place value, in math.* Kūana ʻumi.
tense *As articulation in linguistics.* Mālō. See *lax, vowel. ~ vowel.* Woela mālō.
ten-second violation *In basketball.* ʻAʻena ʻumi kekona. See *violation.*
tent Halepeʻa. *~ stake.* Pine halepeʻa.
tentacle ʻAweʻawe.
tenths Hapa ʻumi.

tera- *A prefix meaning trillion (T).* Pākiliona. *Abb.* pkl. See *deca-, hecto-, kilo-, mega-, giga-.*
terminal *Final, as last in time, order or importance.* Kuahope. See *primary, secondary, tertiary. ~ bronchiole, in anatomy.* ʻĀmanapuʻu kuahope.
terminating decimal Kekimala pani.
termite block *In construction.* Palaka kimeki pale mū. See *pier block.*
terms *~ of a fraction, in math.* Palena. *Lowest ~.* Palena haʻahaʻa loa.
terrace *Underwater ~.* Papa ʻanuʻu lalo kai.
terrarium Pahuhonuaea.
terrier Kēlia, ʻīlio kēlia.
tertiary *As third in time, order or importance.* Kuakolu. See *primary, secondary, terminal. ~ or segmental bronchus, in anatomy.* ʻĀmanapuʻu kuakolu.
tesselation *In math.* Makalau.
test *To ~ for something, as in a scientific experiment.* Hoʻāʻo. See *trial.*
tester *As a battery ~, when the ~ is a machine.* Mīkini hoʻāʻo. *Battery ~ (a machine).* Mīkini hoʻāʻo iho. *Battery ~ (not a machine).* Hāmeʻe hoʻāʻo iho.
testimony See *hearing.*
test tube Hano hoʻokolohua. See *collection tube, cylinder, ring stand. Pyrex ~.* Hano hoʻokolohua paileki. *~ clamp.* ʻŪmiʻi hano hoʻokolohua.
Tethys *A moon of Saturn.* Tetisa.
tetrahedron *A space figure with four faces, in math.* Paʻaʻilihā.
Texas *Also Texan.* Kekeka, Tekasa, Teseta.
text *Of a document, as in computer program.* Kikokikona.
textbook Puke haʻawina. See *supplementary text.*
texture Hiʻonapāʻili.
thematic map Palapala ʻāina kumuhana.
theorum *In math.* Manaʻohaʻi. *Pythagorean ~.* Manaʻohaʻi o Paekakoleo.

Māmaka Kaiao / 299

therapy *To provide physical ~.* Pākōlea. *Physical therapist.* Kanaka pākōlea, mea pākōlea. *Shock ~.* Lapaʻau hoʻomiki uila.

thermal energy *The total energy of all the particles in an object.* Ikehu kāʻokoʻa. See *calorimeter.*

thermoelectric *Also thermoelectricity.* Uila puhi wāwahie. See *electricity.* *~ power.* Ikehu uila puhi wāwahie.

thermometer Ana wela. See *temperature.*

thermophilic *Heat-loving.* Ola wela. *~ bacteria.* Koʻohune ola wela.

thermos Hano.

thesaurus Puke manaʻo laulike. *As in computer program.* Papa manaʻo laulike. *~ entry.* Manaʻo laulike.

thick Mānoanoa, mānoʻanoʻa.

thigh *Chicken ~.* ʻŪhā moa. See *drumstick.*

thigmotactic ʻOnipā.

thin *To ~, as plants when gardening.* Waewaele.

thingamajig *Device, doohickey, gadget, gizmo.* Hāmeʻa. See *apparatus, instrument, tool.*

thinking *Critical ~.* Noʻonoʻo loi. *Logical ~.* Noʻonoʻo kūpili. *~ skills.* Mākau noʻonoʻo. *Building ~ skills book.* Puke mākau noʻonoʻo.

third base *In baseball.* Pahu ʻekolu. See *base.*

Third World Country ʻĀina hōʻoiʻenehana. See *developing, First World Country.*

-thon *Suffix.* -kona. See *-athalon, dance-a-thon, marathon, walkathon,* etc.

thorax Paukū kino, paukū.

thousand See *kilo-, milli-.*

thrasher *A bird related to the thrush.* Manu kelaka.

threat See *triple-threat position.*

threatened *As rare plants or animals.* Hopo halapohe, hopo make loa, hopo nalowale loa. See *endangered, extinct.*

three-dimensional *In math.* Paʻa. See *two-dimensional.* *~ figure.* Kinona paʻa.

three man *Also swing man or shooting forward, in basketball.* Kūkolu.

three-meter line *In volleyball.* Laina ʻekolu mika. See *ten-foot line.* *~ violation.* ʻAʻena ʻekolu mika.

three-point arc *In basketball.* Hoaka kīkolu.

three-point shot *In basketball; to attempt such a shot.* Kī ʻai kolu. *A successful ~.* ʻAi kolu.

three-quarter-court press *In basketball.* Lulumi ʻekolu hapahā. See *press.*

three-second violation *In basketball.* ʻAʻena ʻekolu kekona. See *violation.*

threshold *Of a door.* Paepae puka.

thrips *A kind of insect.* Pīnalonalo.

throat Puʻu.

through Puka ma kekahi ʻaoʻao (o).

throw *To ~ overhand.* Nou. *To ~ underhand.* Kiola. See *discus.*

throw away *To ~ (the ball), in basketball.* Kīloi paʻewa.

thrush Keluka, manu keluka. *Wood ~.* Manu keluka ululāʻau.

thumb Manamana nui. See *finger, scroll. To ~ through, as a magazine.* Lolelole.

thumbtack Kui pahu.

thunderbird Manu hekili.

Thursday Poʻahā. *Abb.* P4.

thyroid gland Lōkuʻu hoʻokonukonu pūnao.

ti *The seventh note on the musical scale.* Mī.

tick *To ~, as a clock.* Kani koʻele.

tickle Hoʻomāneʻoneʻo.

tic-tac-toe Kesaʻō.

tide Hoehoena o ke kai. See *fluctuate.*

tie *Bow ~.* Lei ʻāʻī pewa.

tight end *In football.* Muku. See *split end, safety.*

tilapia Talapia.

tile Kile. *Ceramic ~.* Kile lāmeka. *Floor ~.* Kile papahele, kile ʻili, moena ʻili ʻāpanapana. *Hollow ~.* Paomeki.

tile windows *As in computer program.* Kīpapa pukaaniani.

tiller See *rotary tiller.*

tilt *To ~ or tip, as a glass containing water.* Hoʻohiō.

tilt *To cause to ~, as the camera when filming a movie or video production.* Hoʻokīkiʻi.

tilth *The nature of soil with porous texture and well-aggregated crumb structure.* Māʻelenono. See *crumb.*

timbre *In music.* Pualeo.

time Manawa. See *on time, time zone.* *Real ~, as in computer program.* Manawa ʻānō. *Recorded duration.* Helu manawa. *To ~, as speed, duration, etc.* Helu manawa; uaki, uāki. *To tell ~.* Helu uaki, helu uāki.

time line Laina manawa.

time out *In team sports such as volleyball.* Manawa hoʻomaha.

time zone *As Pacific or Rocky Mountain ~.* Kāʻei hola.

tinder *Powdery ~.* ʻĀhia.

tin foil Pepa kini.

tip *To ~ or tilt, as a glass containing water.* Hoʻohiō.

tip *Of leaf.* Hiʻu, welelau. *Bulb ~.* ʻŌmaka hua kanu.

tip *Of tongue.* Wēlau alelo.

tip-in *As a basket in basketball; to make such a shot.* Kī papaʻi. See *tip pass.*

tiple *A musical instrument with ten strings.* Kipola.

tip pass *In basketball; to throw such a pass.* Kīloi papaʻi. See *tip-in.*

tire Kaea, taea. *Bicycle ~.* Kaea paikikala.

tissue *As structural material of a plant or animal.* ʻAʻa hunaola. See *cell.* *Adipose ~, i.e. animal ~ in which fat is stored.* ʻAʻa hunaola ʻailakele.

Titan *A moon of Saturn.* Kaikana.

title *As of a book or story.* Inoa; poʻo inoa (*preceded by* ke). *As at the beginning of a movie or video production.* Poʻo inoa. *Program ~, as for a TV program.* Poʻo inoa polokalamu.

tofu *Also bean curd.* Tōfū.

toilet Lua. *~ bowl.* Ipu lua. *~ handle.* ʻAu hoʻokuʻu wai o ka lua, ʻau hoʻokuʻu (*preceded by* ke). *~ seat.* Noho lua. *To flush the ~.* Hoʻokuʻu i ka wai o ka lua, hoʻoholo i ka wai.

toll free Kāki ʻole. *~ number.* Helu kelepona kāki ʻole.

ton Kana. *Abb.* k.

tone *In music.* Huakani. *In linguistics, as relating to Chinese or Navaho languages.* Nioe. *As of a literary work.* Au manaʻo.

toner *As for a computer printer.* Pauka ʻīnika.

tongue Alelo. *Back of ~.* Kūʻau alelo. *Blade of ~.* Lau alelo. *Central portion of ~.* Waena alelo. *Root of ~.* Mole alelo. *Tip of ~.* Wēlau alelo.

tool *As a shovel, crowbar, etc.* Mea hana. See *apparatus, device, instrument.* *As a specialized instrument for a particular occupation.* Mauhaʻa.

tooth Niho. See *drill, filling, grind, orthodontist, pick.*

toothbrush *~ container, usually made of plastic.* Poho palaka niho. *~ holder.* Kauna palaki niho.

toothpaste Pauka niho. See *cap.* *~ tube.* Poho pauka niho.

top *Clothing.* Lole o luna. See *bottom, tank top.*

topic *General ~ or subject, as in literature.* Kumuhana. *~ sentence, as of a paragraph.* Hopunaʻōlelo wehe kumuhana.

top margin Lihi o luna. See *margin.*

top of the key *On a basketball court.* Uma kī, uma, pōheo.

topographic *Also topography.* Hiʻona ʻāina. *See Hawaiian entries* hiʻona wai, hiʻona ʻāina. *~ map.* Palapala hiʻona ʻāina. *Man-made ~al feature.* Hiʻona na ke kanaka.
topping *As for ice cream.* Pāhina.
topsoil Lepo uhi. *See subsoil.*
tornado Makani kaʻawiliwili.
tortilla Tōtia.
total *Sum.* Huinanui. *Grand ~.* Huinanui pau loa. *Sub~.* Huinanui hapa.
totem pole Pou ʻaumakua ʻIlikini.
toucan Tūkana.
touch *Sense of ~.* Lonoa ʻili.
touchback *In football.* ʻAi hopu. *See point.*
touchdown *In football.* ʻAi holo. *See point.*
touch pass *In basketball; to make such a pass.* Hoʻopāhiʻa.
tournament *In sports.* Hoʻokūkū, hoʻokūkū moho. *See championship, scrimmage. Volleyball ~.* Hoʻokūkū pōpaʻipaʻi.
tow Kauō. *~ truck.* Kalaka kauō.
towel rack Kaola kāwele. *See paper towel dispenser.*
town Kūlanakauhale. *See city. Down~.* Kaona.
toxic ʻAwahia.
toy box *Also toy chest.* Pahu mea pāʻani, waihona mea pāʻani.
trace *A small amount.* ʻĀweʻaweʻa. *~ element.* Kumumea ʻāweʻaweʻa. *To ~, as a picture, etc.* Hoʻomahaka.
trachea *Also windpipe, in anatomy.* Paipi hanu. *See epiglottis, esophagus, larynx.*
track and field Haʻuki Helene. *~ events.* Nā haʻuki Helene. *Course for running events in ~.* Lina poepoe holo wāwae.
tractor Kaʻa huki palau, kaʻa palau.
trade *To ~, in math.* Kuapo.
trademark Kunikia.

traditional Kuʻuna. *~ literature.* Moʻokalaleo kuʻuna. *~ tale, i.e. a folktale, especially one relating to a particular culture.* Kaʻao, moʻokaʻao. *See Hawaiian entries under kaʻao.*
traffic *Especially the movement of ~.* Kaheaholo. *Highway ~.* Kaheaholo kaʻa. *Air ~.* Kaheaholo mokulele. *~ light.* Kukui hoʻokū. *~ sign.* Hōʻailona. *See stop sign, yield sign.*
trail *Head or foot of ~.* Nuku. *Hiking ~.* Ala hekehi. *See hike.*
trailer Kaleila. *Flatbed ~.* Pākihuila.
train *Elevated ~, as Japan monorail.* Kaʻaahi kau lewa.
train *To ~ (someone), as for sports.* Kaʻi. *Sports ~er.* Kaʻi haʻuki.
trait *Hereditary ~.* Welo. *See gene.*
trampoline Keʻelelena.
transcription Palapala leo. *To transcribe.* Palapala.
transect *A sample area, as of vegetation, usually in the form of a long strip.* Laina kālailai.
transfer *As funds in a bank account.* Hoʻoili.
transform *Sliding in plate techtonics, in geology.* Kākele. *See convergent, divergent. ~ boundary.* Palena kākele.
transition area *An area where natural topography changes from one land feature to another.* ʻĀina loliloli.
translation image *In math.* Kinona like kau.
translation symmetry *In math.* ʻĀlikelike kau.
transparency *As for an overhead projector.* Māliko.
transparent Aʻiaʻi. *See opaque.*
transparent tape *Scotch tape.* Leki ʻea.
transpiration *Also to transpire.* Piʻikū. *See evapotranspiration.*
transplant Hoʻoili. *To ~ a heart.* Hoʻoili puʻuwai. *~ed.* Ili. *~ed heart.* Puʻuwai ili.
transport *Military ~ aircraft.* Mokulele hali koa.

Māmaka Kaiao / 302

transportation *Mode of ~.* Alakau.
transversal *A line that intersects two given lines, in math.* Kaha ʻokiʻoki.
transverse wave *A wave in which matter vibrates at right angles to the direction in which the wave moves.* Hawewe ʻaleʻale. *See compressional wave.*
trap *In basketball; to make such a play.* ʻŪpiki. *Deadfall, a kind of animal ~.* Hāʻuleāpaʻa.
trapeze Koali lelepinao. *To use a ~.* Lelepinao.
trapezoid Huinahā paʻa pilipā.
trash *To empty ~, as in computer program.* Kīloi.
travel *To ~, in basketball; also ~ing.* Holoholo.
traveler's check Pila kīkoʻo huakaʻi.
tray Pā halihali *(preceded by* ke*). See entry below. Balancing ~ for scales.* Pā ana. *Chalk ~.* Paepae poho.
tray *Paper ~, as for a computer printer.* Poho pepa. *Paper ~ slot.* ʻĀpoʻo poho pepa.
tread *As on a tire.* Nihoniho. *See bald.*
treasure chest Pahu waihona waiwai.
treat *To ~ chemically, as sewage.* Kāemikala. *~ed sewage.* Ke kaekene i kāemikala ʻia.
treble clef *In music.* Hōʻailona mele leo wahine, leo wahine. *See bass clef.*
tree diagram *In math.* Kiʻikuhi pahiki.
tree frog Poloka kau lāʻau. *Orange ~.* Poloka kau lāʻau ʻālani.
treehouse Hale kau lāʻau.
treetop *Top of a tree or plant.* Ēulu.
tremor *As of an earthquake; to ~.* Manunu.
trench *Geologic ~.* ʻAuwaha. *Aleutian ~.* Ka ʻAuwaha ʻAleuta.
trend Kū i ke au, mea kū i ke au.
trial *A test as in a probability experiment, in math.* Hoʻāʻoamaka. *See test.*

triangle Huinakolu. *Acute~.* Huinakolu ʻoi. *Congruent ~.* Huinakolu komolike. *Equilateral ~.* Huinakolu like. *Isosceles ~.* Huinakolu ʻelua ʻaoʻao like. *Obtuse ~.* Huinakolu peleleu. *Scalene ~.* Huinakolu ʻaoʻao like ʻole. *Base of a ~.* ʻAoʻao kau.
triathalon ʻĀlapakonakolu. *See decathalon, pentathalon.*
tribe *People in a district who have intermarried, specifically referring to Hawaiʻi.* ʻAlaea. *See clan. Of people outside of Hawaiʻi.* Nāki.
tributary ʻAumana. *River ~.* ʻAumana muliwai. *Stream ~.* ʻAumana kahawai.
trick *As a dog's ~.* Nalea. *Magic ~ or illusion, sleight of hand.* Pāhaʻohuna. *Prank; to play a ~, usually with malicious intent.* Kēpuka.
trick or treat Kiliki o lapu.
tricycle Kalaikikala.
trident ʻŌ maka kolu *(preceded by* ke*).*
trillion *See pico-, tera-.*
triple-extra large *XXXL, as shirt size.* Nui keu pākolu. *See large.*
triple-threat position *In basketball; also to execute such a position.* Kūliukolu.
tripod Kū koʻokolu.
Triton *A moon of Neptune.* Kalaikona.
trivia Hunahuna ʻike.
trombone Pū puhi uai.
tropical *Also tropic.* Kopikala. *See temperate. ~ storm.* ʻIno kopikala. *The tropics.* Kāʻei kopikala.
troposphere Lewalanihaʻa.
trough *Of a wave.* Honua, honua o ka nalu, honua o ka ʻale. *See crest, wave.*
trout Iʻa punakea.
trowel *As used for digging.* Hāpale. *Garden ~.* Kopalā lima.
trumpet Pū pihi. *See bugle, cornet.*
T-shirt Palaʻili, paleʻili. *See tank-top. Any pullover-style shirt.* Palaʻili.

tube Kiupe. See *cap, cathode-ray tube, collection tube, lava tube, toothpaste*. Swimming ~. Lina hoʻolana. Toothpaste ~. Poho pauka niho.

tuber Huaaʻa.

tubifex Koʻe ʻula.

Tuesday Poʻalua. *Abb.* P2.

tuff *A rock composed of finer kinds of detritus, usually more or less stratified and in various states of consolidation, in geology.* Hakuhune. ~ *cone.* Puʻu hakuhune.

tulip Puahōlani.

tuna Tuna. *Can of* ~. Kini tuna.

tundra Nakilinaka.

tune *Also melody.* Leo, ʻea. *To* ~, *as a stringed instrument; to* ~ *up, as an engine.* Kī.

tuning fork Hao hoʻokani, ʻō hoʻokani (*preceded by* ke).

Tunisia *Also Tunisian.* Tunisia.

tunnel Kōnelo. See *subway*.

turbo button *As in Nintendo games.* Pihi pīnaʻi (*preceded by* ke). See *warp zone*.

Turkey *Also Turk, Turkish.* Kuleke, Tureke.

turn *Or curve, as in a road or on a trail.* Uakeʻe. *Banked* ~. Uakeʻe hiō. *To* ~, *as a figure in math.* Wili. ~ *center.* Kikowaena wili. ~ *image.* Kinona like wili. *Half-*~ *image.* Kinona like wili hapalua.

turn off *To* ~, *as a light, radio, TV, etc.* Hoʻopio. *To* ~ *the water.* Hoʻopaʻa i ke kī wai. See *faucet*.

turn on *To* ~, *as a light, radio, TV, etc.* Hoʻā. *To* ~ *the water.* Wehe i ke kī wai.

turnover *In basketball.* Lilo.

turns *To take* ~. Māhele manawa.

turquoise *The mineral.* Hakukuleke.

turtle *Box* ~. Honu pahu.

turtle shell ʻukulele ʻUkulele ʻea honu.

tusk *Boar's* ~. Niho kepa.

TV Kīwī, kelewī. See *television*. ~ *screen.* Papakaumaka kīwī. ~ *monitor.* Pahu papakaumaka kīwī. ~ *series.* Pūkaʻina polokalamu kīwī.

twelve-pack *As of drinks.* Pūʻolo. See *six-pack, case, pack*. ~ *of soda.* Pūʻolo koloaka. ~ *of beer.* Pūʻolo pia.

twig *Small stick.* ʻAulaʻo (*preceded by* ke).

twill plaiting Maka pūalu, ʻoʻeno.

twin *In math.* Kūlua. See *double number, prime number*. ~ *primes.* Helu kumu kūlua.

twirl *To* ~, *as a baton.* Wili.

twist tie *As used with plastic bags.* Uea nākiʻi.

two-by-four Lua hā. ~ *board or lumber.* Papa lua hā.

two-dimensional *In math.* Papa. ~ *figure.* Kinona papa. See *three-dimensional*.

two man *Also shooting guard, in basketball.* Kūlua.

two-party system *Of government.* Aupuni ʻaoʻao ʻelua.

type *Blood* ~. Hulu koko. See entry below.

type *To* ~, *as on a typewriter.* Kikokiko, paʻi hakahaka. ~ *style or attribute, as italic or bold.* Kaila hua. ~*face or font.* Kinona hua. See *font, style*. *To set* ~, *as for video captions.* Ulele hua. See *character operator*.

U

ʻukulele ʻUkulele. For kinds, see *baritone, cigar-box, coconut shell, cutaway, double-hole, eight-string, Liliʻu, Ohta-san, soprano, tenor, turtle shell*. For parts, see *body, bridge, fret, head, neck, nut, string*.

ultraviolet Kuawehi. ~ *ray.* Kukuna kuawehi.

umpire *Also referee.* ʻUao haʻuki, ʻuao.

uncomplicated *Basic, simple.* Nōhie. See *complex*.

under- *Also sub-.* Lalo. See entries below and *sub-*.

Māmaka Kaiao / 304

underestimate Kohoemi. See *overestimate*.
underground   Lalo honua.
underhand *To serve ~, in volleyball.* Hānai puʻupuʻu. See *spike*.
underline Kahalalo.
underpants Palemaʻi, lole wāwae palaʻili. See *sanitary pad*.
undersea *Also submarine, submerged.* Lalo kai.
understory *~ layer of vegetation, as low trees and shrubs.* Papa hapamalu. See *vegetation layers*.
underwater *Referring only to sea water.* Lalo kai. *~ terrace.* Papa ʻanuʻu lalo kai.
undo *To ~, in math.* Hoʻomakala. See *build*. *To ~, as in computer program.* Hoʻihoʻi mai. See *cancel, put away*.
uneven See *parallel bars*.
union ʻUniona. See *collective bargaining*. *As of states or countries into one political entity.* Hui ʻāina.
unit *Of measurement.* Anakahi. See *accent unit, CPU, place value*. *Metric ~ of measure.* Anakahi mekalika. *US standard or customary ~ of measure.* Anakahi ʻAmelika. *Of counting.* Kūana helu. *~ fraction.* Hakina anakahi. *~ price.* Kumukūʻai anakahi.
United States of America *Also American.* ʻAmelika Hui Pū ʻia. See *America*.
unitize *To ~, in math.* Hoʻānakahi.
universe *As a scientific term only.* ʻŌnaeao.
unleavened pancake Palaoa linalina.
unlocked *Also open, as for business; ajar.* Hemo.
unofficial *Also nonstandard, as in units of measurement.* Kūhelu ʻole. See *official*.
unprocessed *As raw materials.* Kūlohelohe. See *raw*.
unrest *Civil ~.* Haunaele kūloko.
unsaturated fat ʻAilakele paʻahapa. See *fat*.

unsmooth *To ~, as in computer program.* Hoʻokalakala. See *smooth*.
update *An ~.* Hoʻopuka hou loa. See *release*. *To ~, as a computer program.* Hōʻano hou.
upper case *Capital.* Maʻaka. See *letter*.
upside down Hulihia. See *inside out*.
up to bat *Also up, at bat, in baseball.* Manawa hili.
upward Haʻaluna. See *round off*.
Uranus Heleʻekela.
urban *~ area.* Kiwikā. See *city*. *To ~ize.* Hoʻokiwikā.
urea ʻUlea.
urinal Ipu mimi, mīana. See *bedpan, toilet bowl*.
Uruguay *Also Uruguayan.* ʻUlukuae, ʻUruguae.
use *Land ~.* Hoʻohana ʻāina. *State Land ~ Commission.* Komikina Hoʻohana ʻĀina o ka Mokuʻāina.
used *Second-hand.* Pāmia. *~ car.* Kaʻa pāmia.
useful Makehana.
user *End ~, as of computer programs.* Mea hoʻohana. *~ dictionary.* Papa huaʻōlelo pākuʻi. See *main dictionary*. *~ friendly.* Hana maʻalahi.
US Fish and Wildlife Service ʻOihana Iʻa me ka Holoholona Lōhiu o ʻAmelika.
u-shaped valley Awāwa uma.
USRDA *Percentage of US Recommended Daily Allowances; now known as Percent Daily Value.* Pākēneka o ka papaʻai.
Utah *Also Utahan, Utahn.* ʻŪtā, Mauna Pōhaku.
utilities *As electricity, gas, etc.* Mikaō.
utility clamp ʻŪmiʻi hoʻopaʻa. See *forceps*.

V

vaccine Lāʻau koʻokoʻo.
vacuum *Also to ~.* Wākiuma.
vain attempt "Missed out." Pohō.

Valles Marineris *A valley on Mars.* Ke awāwa ʻo Malineli.
valley *Rift ~.* Awāwa māwae. *Series of ~s.* Pae awāwa. *U-shaped ~.* Awāwa uma.
value Waiwai. See *nutritive value, Percent Daily Value, place value. Absolute ~.* Waiwai ʻiʻo. *Expected ~.* Waiwai wānana. *Face ~.* Waiwai kūʻike. *Market ~.* Waiwai kūʻai.
valve *Air ~, as on a tire.* Pihi pāuma ea (*preceded by* ke).
vamp *To ~, as in hula or singing.* Kiʻipā.
vane *Weather or wind ~.* Kuhimakani.
vanilin *A crystalline solid used chiefly as a flavoring agent and in perfumery.* Wanilina.
vapor Māhuea.
variable *As in a scientific experiment.* Kumuloli. *Dependent ~.* Kumuloli kaukaʻi. *Independent ~.* Kumuloli kūʻokoʻa. *A symbol that can stand for any quantitative value, in math.* Hualau. *~ width, as in computer program.* Laulā loli.
vase *Flower ~.* Pika pua.
vaseline *Petrolatum.* Kele hoʻopaheʻe.
vault *Pole ~.* Koʻo lele. *To pole ~.* Lele koʻo.
vegetable Lauʻai. *~ oil.* ʻAila meakanu.
vegetation *Natural ~.* Lau nahele ʻōiwi. *~ layer.* Papa meakanu. *~ area at base of mountain.* Wao kumu kuahiwi. See *montane* and separate layers: *ground, understory, canopy, emergent. ~ zonation sheet.* Palapala kāʻei meakanu.
vehicle *Ground ~ with wheels or runners.* Kaʻa.
vein Aʻa koko kino, aʻa kino. See *artery.*
Velcro Loupili. *~ fastener.* Mea hoʻopaʻa loupili.
veneer ʻIliwehi.
Venetian blinds Pale pukaaniani ʻōlepelepe.

Venn diagram *A diagram using overlapping circles to show relationship of data, in math.* Kiʻikuhi Wene.
vent *Air ~.* Puka ea. *Sea ~.* Puale kai.
ventral *In biology.* Laualo. See *anterior, dorsal, posterior.*
Venus *The planet.* Hōkūloa. *The name.* Wenuke, Wenuse.
Venus flytrap ʻŪmiʻinalo.
verify *To check, give proof, as for a math problem.* Hōʻoia.
vermiculite Hunehune ʻūpī. See *hydroponics.*
Vermont *Also Vermonter.* Welemoneka, Veremona, Veremoneta.
vernal equinox Ka māuiili o ke kupulau. See *equinox.*
version *As of computer program, network, etc.* Mana.
vertebrate Iwikuamoʻo. See *invertebrate. ~ animal.* Holoholona iwikuamoʻo.
vertex *In math.* Kihiʻaki.
vertical Papakū. See entry below and *grow, horizontal. To make ~.* Hoʻopapakū. *To grow ~, as in a computer program.* Ulu papakū. *~ jump.* Lele haʻaluna. *To line up ~ly, place in columns.* Hoʻokolamu.
vertical line *Two ~s written to the left of lines of print to indicate that the left margin should be justified, in proofreading.* Kaha hoʻokaulihi.
vial ʻŌmoleliʻi.
vibrate Kuekueni.
vice versa Kaʻina ʻēkoʻa, kaʻina ʻokoʻa.
victim *Of a predator.* Luapoʻi. See *predator.*
video Wikiō. *~ cassette.* Lola wikiō. *~ camera, camcorder.* Pahu paʻi wikiō. *~ camera movement.* Neʻena pahu paʻi wikiō. *~ equipment.* Pono hana wikiō. *To shoot a ~.* Paʻi wikiō (*preceded by* ke). *~ production crew.* Nā limahana paʻi wikiō.
Vietnam *Also Vietnamese.* Weikanama.

view *As in computer program.* Nānaina. See *preview.*
viewpoint *Scenic ~, lookout.* ʻĪmaka.
vigor Ehuola. See *healthy.*
Viking Wīkini.
vincristine *An alkaloid derived from the periwinkle.* Winikilikini.
vinyl Wainola.
viol *Bass ~, string bass.* Pila kū nui, pila nui.
violation *As in basketball.* ʻAʻena. See entry below. *Backcourt ~.* ʻAʻena laina kūwaena. *Ten-second ~.* ʻAʻena ʻumi kekona. *Three-second ~.* ʻAʻena ʻekolu kekona.
violation *As in volleyball.* ʻAʻena. See entry above. *Antenna ~.* ʻAʻena kukuna. *Carrying ~.* ʻAʻena hāpai. *Double-hit ~.* ʻAʻena paʻi lua. *Net ~.* ʻAʻena ʻupena. *Service ~.* ʻAʻena paʻi ulele. *Ten-foot line ~.* ʻAʻena ʻumi kapuaʻi. *Three-meter line ~.* ʻAʻena ʻekolu mika.
violet *Dog's tooth ~, a kind of flower.* Waioleka nihoʻīlio.
violin *Also fiddle.* Waiolina.
vireo *A kind of bird.* Manu wiliō. *Red-eyed ~.* Manu wiliō mākole.
Virginia *Also Virginian.* Wilikinia. *West ~, West ~n.* Wilikinia Komohana.
virtual memory *As in computer program.* Hope waihona ʻike.
virus *As in computer program.* Mū hōlapu.
visible Kūmaka. See *invisible.*
vision *As in the ~ statement of an organization.* Nuʻukia. See *mission.* *~ statement.* ʻŌlelo nuʻukia.
vita *Also curriculum vitae, résumé.* Moʻomōʻali.
vitamin Wikamina, witamina. *B-complex ~.* Kauwikamina B.
vitriol Wikiola, witiola.
vivarium Pahumeaolaea.
vocal coach Kaʻi puʻukani.
vog Polalauahi.
voice *As in linguistics.* Leo.

volcanic Pele. See *cinder, volcano.* *~ cone.* Puʻu pele. *~ ejecta.* Pōhāhā. *~ mountain.* Kuapele. *Primary ~ activity.* Hū pele kuamua. *Series of ~ eruptions.* Pūkaʻina hū pele.
volcano Luapele, pele. See *caldera, hot spot, spatter cone, volcanic. Active ~.* Lua pele ʻā. *Hawaiʻi ~es National Park.* Pāka Aupuni ʻo Kīlauea. *Shield ~.* Lua pele kuahene. *Primary shield ~.* Lua pele kuahene kuamua. *Submerged ~.* Lua pele lalo kai.
volley *To keep the ball in play, in volleyball.* Paʻi manamana, pohu. *To ~, as a volleyball.* Lelekīkē.
volleyball *The sport.* Pōpaʻipaʻi. *The ball.* Kinipōpō pōpaʻipaʻi. *~ antenna.* Kukuna pōpaʻipaʻi. See *antenna.* *~ court.* Kahua pōpaʻipaʻi, pahu. *~ net.* ʻUpena pōpaʻipaʻi. *~ tournament.* Hoʻokūkū pōpaʻipaʻi.
volt *In electricity.* Anakahi uila. See *ohm.*
volume Pihanahaka. *Abb.* phk. See *capacity, space figure.*
vowel *In linguistics.* Woela. *Back ~.* Woela kauhope. *Central ~.* Woela kauwaena. *Front ~.* Woela kaumua. *High ~.* Woela kiʻekiʻe. *Low ~.* Woela haʻahaʻa. *Rounded ~.* Woela mōkio. *Tense ~.* Woela mālō. *Lax ~.* Woela ʻalu. *Reduced ~.* Woela emi. *~ quality.* Pua woela. *~ reduction.* Hoʻēmi woela.
vulnerable *Also susceptible.* Pā wale. *To be susceptible or ~ to disease.* Pāmaʻi.

W

waffle Palaoa kīpoʻopoʻo.
wagon *Child's ~.* Kaʻaʻauhuki
waiting room Lumi hoʻolulu.
Wake Island Uēki ʻAilana.
walkathon Helekona.
walkie-talkie Pahu kāhea.
wallpaper Pepa paia.
walrus Palaʻo, ʻelepani o ke kai.
wand *Bubble ~ for blowing bubbles.* Lina puhi huʻahuʻa.

war Cold ~, i.e. intense rivalry between nations but without military combat. Kaua koʻekoʻe. *Revolutionary* ~. Kaua hoʻokahuli aupuni.

warbler *A kind of bird.* Manu kūolokū.

wardrobe *As stage costumes for a play, movie or video production.* Nā ʻaʻahu hana keaka, nā ʻaʻahu.

warm Mahana, mehana. See entries below and *temperature*.

warm-blooded *As an animal.* Koko mehana. See *cold-blooded*.

warm front *As of weather.* Kuʻina mehana. See *front*.

warming *Global* ~, *greenhouse effect.* Hoʻomehana Honua.

warm-up suit *As for sports.* Lole kueka haʻuki. See *sweatshirt*.

warning *As in weather report.* Kūkala pōʻino. See *watch*. *Flood* ~. Kūkala pōʻino wai hālana. *Hurricane* ~. Kūkala pōʻino makani pāhili.

warp *As in Nintendo games (not as wood).* Kaʻakepa. See *turbo button*. ~ *zone*. Kāʻei kaʻakepa.

warranty *A written guarantee of integrity of a product with promise to repair or replace.* Palapala hoʻokō. See *guarantee*.

washer *As used in plumbing.* Hoʻopiha; pihi hoʻopiha, pihipihi (*preceded by* ke).

Washington *Also Wahingtonian.* Wakinekona.

waste *As of plants and animals.* Moka.

watch *As in weather report.* Kūkala makaʻala. See *warning, clock*. *Flood* ~. Kūkala makaʻala wai hālana. *Hurricane* ~. Kūkala makaʻala makani pāhili.

watchtower *Ranger station, esp. for watching for forest fires.* Hale kiaʻi ululāʻau. See *ranger*.

water wai. *See entries below. To turn on the* ~. Wehe i ke kī wai. *To turn off the* ~. Hoʻopaʻa i ke kī wai. *Tap* ~. Wai paipu. *Hot tap* ~. Wai wela paipu.

water ~*ing can.* Kini hoʻopulu meakanu. ~ *dish.* Pā wai (*preceded by* ke). ~ *heater.* Kula hoʻowela wai, pahu hoʻowela wai. ~ *table, as used in preschools.* Pākaukau wai (*also preceded by* ke).

water *Body of* ~. See *water feature*. *Ground*~. Wai honua. *Mineral or sparkling* ~. Wai piʻipiʻi. *Rain* ~. Wai ua. *Surface* ~. Wai ʻili honua, wai ʻili. ~ *displacement.* Pohupani wai. ~ *lens, in geology.* Papa wai kau luna. ~ *table, in geology.* Papa wai.

water-base Kuapapa wai. ~ *paint.* Pena kuapapa wai.

water code *State* ~. Papa kānāwai wai o ka mokuʻāina.

watercolor Pena wai.

water commission Komikina wai.

water dispenser *As in a bird cage.* Kāhāinu. See *feeder*.

water feature *Also water form, as a lake, pond, river, etc., in geography.* Hiʻona wai. See *land feature*.

waterproof See *water-resistant*.

water-resistant *Also waterproof.* ʻAʻalo wai. See *resist*. ~ *watch.* Uaki ʻaʻalo wai, uāki ʻaʻalo wai.

watershed *An area from which water drains.* ʻĀina kumu wai. *Municipal* ~. ʻĀina kumu wai kiwikā.

water ski Heʻe wai. See *ski*.

water slide *Slip ʻnʻ Slide; also to go on a* ~. Paheʻe wai. ~ *mat.* Moena paheʻe wai.

watt Uate. *Abb.* uat. See *kilowatt*.

wave *As surf near the land.* Nalu. *As a swell in the open ocean.* ʻAle. *Height of a* ~. Kiʻekiʻena, kiʻekiʻena nalu, kiʻekiʻena ʻale. *Length of a* ~, ~*length*. Kōā, kōā nalu, kōā ʻale. *Crest of a* ~. Hokua, hokua o ka nalu, hokua o ka ʻale. *Trough of a* ~. Honua, honua o ka nalu, honua o ka ʻale. *Where a* ~ *breaks, surfbreak.* Poʻina nalu (*preceded by* ke). *Sound* ~, *as used in measuring ocean depths.* Hawewe kani. ~-*cut cliff.* Pali ʻaʻaianalu. See *erode, weathered*.

Māmaka Kaiao / 308

wave *To ~ something.* Hoʻāni.
wave *Scientific usage.* Hawewe. See *amplify, amplitude, compressional wave, sound wave, transverse wave, wavelength.*
wavelength *Sound ~.* Kōā hawewe kani.
wax Uepa, pīlali. See *paraffin. ~ paper.* Pepa pīlali, pepa ʻaila. *As for polishing a car.* ʻAila hoʻohinuhinu. *Grafting ~.* Pīlali pākuʻi. *Waxy, as in texture.* ʻŌihoiho.
wayfinding *Also to wayfind.* Hoʻokele waʻa, kele moana.
weak acid *Naturally occurring ~.* ʻAkika ʻūpalu kūlohelohe.
weak safety *In football.* ʻĀwaʻa lala. See *strong safety.*
weather Anilā. See *climate, erode, temperature. ~ service.* ʻOihana anilā. *~ station.* Kikowaena kilo anilā. *~ vane, wind vane.* Kuhimakani. *~ed.* ʻAʻaianilā.
weave *To ~, as on a loom.* Kālino. *Herringbone ~.* Maka puhi, iwipuhi.
web *Food ~.* Pūnaewele meaʻai.
webbed *As a duck's feet.* Pepewa.
wedelia *A ground cover.* Wekelia.
Wednesday Poʻakolu. *Abb.* P3.
weed Nāhelehele, nāʻeleʻele.
week Pule. *Abb.* pl.
weight *In math.* Kaumaha. *For scales.* Koihā.
weightless *As when in outer space.* Lewalana. See *zero gravity.*
weight lifting *Also to lift weights.* Amo hao, hāpai hao.
welcome banquet ʻAhaʻaina hoʻokipa.
weld Kuʻihao.
welfare *Public financial assistance for needy persons.* Kōkua nele.
well done *As meat.* Moʻa loa.
west Komohana. *Abb.* Km. See entries below.
Western Europe *Also Western European.* ʻEulopa Komohana.

western hemisphere Poepoe hapa komohana. See *hemisphere.*
Western Sahara *Also Western Saharan.* Sahara Komohana.
West Virginia *Also West Virginian.* Wilikinia Komohana.
wet *~ from cold, damp or moist with fog or dew.* Kawaū.
whale *Humpback ~.* Koholā kuapiʻo.
what *As in asking about any kind of measurement; also how.* ʻEhia, he aha.
wheat Huika. See *straw* and Hawaiian entries under *palaoa. ~ bread.* Palaoa huika. *Whole ~.* Huika piha. *Whole ~ bread.* Palaoa huika piha. *Whole ~ flour.* Palaoa maka huika piha.
wheat bread Palaoa huika. See Hawaiian entries under *palaoa. Whole ~.* Palaoa huika piha.
wheel Huila. *Bicycle ~.* Huila paikikala. *~ rim.* Kuapo hao.
whippoorwill Uipouila, manu uipouila.
whistle *As a referee's ~.* ʻŪlili.
white *Egg ~.* Kauō keʻokeʻo, kauō. See entries below and *yolk.*
white blood cell Hunaola koko keʻokeʻo.
white bread Palaoa keʻokeʻo.
whitecap ʻAle kuakea. *To have ~s.* Niho.
whitefish Iʻakea.
white-footed mouse ʻIole wāwae kea.
white rice Laiki keʻokeʻo, lāisi keʻokeʻo.
whole milk Waiū piha.
whole number *In math.* Helu piha. See *integer, mixed number.*
wholesale price Kumukūʻai kālepa. See *retail price.*
wholesome *Also healthful, healthy, i.e. promoting physical health.* Hāʻehuola. See *health food.*
whole wheat Huika piha. *~ bread.* Palaoa huika piha. *~ flour.* Palaoa maka huika piha.
wide open Hāmama. See *open.*

wide shot *As of a photograph or in movie or video production.* Paʻi laulā (preceded by ke). See *close-up, medium shot.* *To take a ~.* Paʻi a laulā. *Extreme ~.* Paʻi laulā loa. *To take an extreme ~.* Paʻi a laulā loa.

width *Also breadth, in math.* Ākea, ana ākea, laulā (abb. ll), ana laulā. See *height, length.* *Variable ~, as in computer program.* Laulā loli.

wild *General term; also shy.* ʻĀhiu. See *wildlife.* *Naturally wild, as tiger,* ʻiʻiwi, ʻaʻaliʻi, *etc.* Lōhiu. *Overactive, as an unruly child.* Lapa. *To grow ~ and lush.* Ulu wale, uluāhewa.

wildcat Pōpoki lōhiu.

wildlife Holoholona lōhiu.

wildlife Holoholona lōhiu. *~ expert.* Loea holoholona lōhiu. *US Fish and ~ Service.* ʻOihana Iʻa me ka Holoholona Lōhiu o ʻAmelika.

win See *Hawaiian entry* eo.

wind See *Hawaiian entries* pohu, kolonahe, aheahe, hoʻoholunape, ulūlu, ʻena makani.

wind-generated electricity Uila huila makani. See *electricity.*

windmill Huila makani.

window Pukaaniani. See *jalousie.* *~ curtain.* Pale pukaaniani. *~ frame or molding.* Mōlina pukaaniani. *~ sill.* Paepae pukaaniani.

windows See *stack, tile windows.*

windpipe *Also trachea, in anatomy.* Paipi hanu. See *epiglottis, esophagus, larynx.*

windsurf Holo papa peʻa. *Board for ~ing.* Papa peʻa.

wind vane *Also weather vane.* Kuhimakani.

wing nut Pihi wili ʻēheu.

wingspan Anana ʻēheu.

winner *As in the consolation bracket of a sports tournament.* Mea puka. *~ʻs bracket.* Māhele lanakila.

winter Hoʻoilo. See *equinox.* *~ solstice.* Ka māuikiʻikiʻi o ka hoʻoilo.

winterberry Pīʻai hoʻoilo.

wintergreen Pailola.

wipe See *dust.*

wire *Nichrome ~.* Uea nikoroma.

wire gauze *Steel wool.* Pulupulu uea.

Wisconsin *Also Wisconsinite.* Wikonekina, Wikonesina.

witch Hese. See *black widow.*

withdraw *To ~ money from the bank.* Kīkoʻo.

women *Hatred of ~; misogyny.* Hoʻokae wahine. See *misandry, misanthropy.*

wood Lāʻau. See entries below and *peg.* *~ paneling.* Papa pānela lāʻau.

woodpecker Manu pao lāʻau.

woodpecker finch Ōpuhe pao lāʻau.

wood peewee *A kind of bird.* Manu pīuīlāʻau.

wood rose Loke lāʻau.

wood shavings Hānā.

wood thrush Manu keluka ululāʻau.

woodwind instrument Pū ʻoʻohe.

wool Hulu. See *blanket.* *Glass ~.* Hulu aniani. *Steel ~.* Pulupulu uea.

woolly mammoth ʻElepani pūhuluhulu.

word Huaʻōlelo. *~ skill.* Mākau huaʻōlelo.

word processor *As a computer program.* Polokalamu kikokiko palapala.

workbook Puke hoʻomaʻamaʻa haʻawina, puke hoʻomaʻamaʻa.

workshop Hālāwai hoʻonaʻauao.

worm See *Hawaiian entries under* koʻe. *Polychaete ~, a kind of ~ found underneath stream rocks.* Moeʻalā.

wraparound *As a window or eyeglasses.* Kewe. *~ window.* Pukaaniani kewe.

wrasse *Cleaner ~,* labroides Phthirophegus, *a kind of fish.* Hīnālea nāʻuke.

wrinkled frog Poloka mimino.

wrist brace Kāliki pūlima.

write See *speed write.*

write protect *To ~, as a computer file or disk.* Hoʻopale kākau. *~ed.* Hoʻopale kākau ʻia.
writing *Creative ~.* Kākau makakū.
written Palapala. *~ literature.* Moʻokalaleo palapala. *~ report.* Hōʻike palapala.
Wyoming *Also Wyomingite.* Waiomina.

X

XL *Extra large, as shirt size.* Nui keu.
XXL *Double-extra large.* Nui keu pālua.
XXXL *Triple-extra large.* Nui keu pākolu.
xylem Kikiʻuwai. *See phloem.*

Y

yard *Unit of measurement.* ʻĪā. *No abbreviation. Cubic ~.* ʻĪā paʻaʻiliono.
yarn Pāaniani. *See knit.*
year Makahiki. *Abb.* MH. *Light ~.* Makahiki holo kukuna lā.
yearbook Puke hoʻohaliʻa makahiki.
yeast Hū.
Yemen *South ~; also South ~ite, South Yemeni.* Iemene Hema. *North ~; also North ~ite, North Yemeni.* Iemene ʻĀkau.
yield *To ~, as in traffic.* Hōʻae. *~ sign.* Hōʻailona hōʻae.
yield *Sustained ~, as in crop production.* Loaʻa paʻa mau.
yogurt Waiūtepe. *Frozen ~.* Hauwaiūtepe.
yolk *Egg ~.* Kauō melemele, kauō. *See white.*
York *See New York.*
Yosemite Iosemite. *See national park. ~ National Park.* Pāka Aupuni ʻo Iosemite.
yoyo Ioio.
Yugoslavia *Also Yugoslavian.* Iugosolawia.

Z

Zaire *Also Zairian.* Zāire.
Zambia *Also Zambian.* Zamibia.
Zealand *See New Zealand.*
zebrina *A kind of flower.* Pua kepela, kepela.
zero *Ground ~, as in field mapping.* Papahonua. *~ degrees K (Kelvin); absolute zero, a hypothetical temperature characterized by complete absence of heat.* ʻOle Kelewine.
zero gravity ʻUmekaumaha ʻole.
zero property *In math.* ʻAnopili ʻole *(preceded by* ke*). ~ of multiplication.* ʻAnopili ʻole o ka hoʻonui.
Zimbabwe *Also Zimbabwean.* Zimababue.
zinc Kiniki.
zip code Helu kuhi.
zipper Huka.
zonation sheet *Vegetation ~.* Palapala kāʻei meakanu.
zone Kāʻei. *See entry below and intertropical convergent zone, tropics. Rift ~.* Kāʻei māwae. *Time ~, as Pacific or Rocky Mountain.* Kāʻei hola. *Warp ~, as in Nintendo games.* Kāʻei kaʻakepa.
zone *End ~, on football field.* Pahu ʻai holo. *~ defense, as in basketball; to execute such a play.* Pale kāʻei. *~ offense.* Kūlele kāʻei.
zoo *Petting ~.* Kahua hamohamo holoholona.
zoom *To ~ in, as with a movie or video camera.* Hoʻokokoke. *To ~ out.* Hoʻolaulā.
Z-shaped line *A "straight" ~ written to indicate where two words written as one should be separated, in proofreading.* Kaha hoʻokaʻahua, kaha hoʻokōā.
Zuben Elgenubi *A star.* Hauhoa.
Zuben Elschamali *A star.* Nākiʻikiʻi.
zucchini Sūkini.

Māmaka Kaiao / 311